W0081159

Supply Chain Management

CONCEPTS, PRACTICES, AND IMPLEMENTATION

SUNIL SHARMA

Professor
Faculty of Management Studies (FMS)
University of Delhi

OXFORD

UNIVERSITY PRESS

OXFORD
UNIVERSITY PRESS

YMCA Library Building, Jai Singh Road, New Delhi 110001

Oxford University Press is a department of the University of Oxford.
It furthers the University's objective of excellence in research, scholarship,
and education by publishing worldwide in

Oxford   New York
Auckland   Cape Town   Dar es Salaam   Hong Kong   Karachi
Kuala Lumpur   Madrid   Melbourne   Mexico City   Nairobi
New Delhi   Shanghai   Taipei   Toronto

With offices in
Argentina   Austria   Brazil   Chile   Czech Republic   France   Greece
Guatemala   Hungary   Italy   Japan   Poland   Portugal   Singapore
South Korea   Switzerland   Thailand   Turkey   Ukraine   Vietnam

Oxford is a registered trade mark of Oxford University Press
in the UK and in certain other countries.

Published in India
by Oxford University Press

© Oxford University Press 2010

The moral rights of the authors have been asserted.

Database right Oxford University Press (maker)

First published 2010

All rights reserved. No part of this publication may be reproduced,
stored in a retrieval system, or transmitted, in any form or by any means,
without the prior permission in writing of Oxford University Press,
or as expressly permitted by law, or under terms agreed with the appropriate
reprographics rights organization. Enquiries concerning reproduction
outside the scope of the above should be sent to the Rights Department,
Oxford University Press, at the address above.

You must not circulate this book in any other binding or cover
and you must impose this same condition on any acquirer.

ISBN-13: 978-0-19-568913-6
ISBN-10: 0-19-568913-5

Typeset in Baskerville
by Innovative Processors, New Delhi 110002

and published by Oxford University Press
YMCA Library Building, Jai Singh Road, New Delhi 110001

Auckland
Kuala Lump
N

Dedicated to
the memory of my father
Dr Ram Murti Sharma
a great Sanskrit scholar

Preface

The paramount goal of supply chain management (SCM) is to deliver the best customer services through coordinated management of materials, finances, and information which flow across a network of suppliers as well as internal and external customers. SCM does it by following a systems approach to logistical procedures involved in the flows including the reverse ones, if any. Over the last 150 years, it has evolved from the conventional materials management to physical distribution management to logistics and integrated logistics management to what it is today. SCM requires mapping, re-engineering, and integration of processes, both within and outside the organization. These processes range from sourcing and manufacturing to transportation and distribution of products and services.

Today's business world is characterized by proliferation of product variety, uncertain product volume requirements, product design changes, increasing customer expectations, and shortening of product and technology life cycles. Of late, SCM has assumed a strategic perspective as it effects the bottom line, thus the return on investment (ROI) of companies, and in turn, the business performance by meeting the needs of the customer through appropriate design of supply chain.

The key feature of the current supply chain systems is their IT-enablement, which extends to customers and suppliers at all levels. Also, the use of information and communication technology (ICT), blanket purchasing and supply contracts incorporating electronic data interchange (EDI) together with the use of third- and fourth-party logistic (3PL/4PL) providers have all radically transformed the way procurement and distribution is being done today in India and the rest of the world. Most of the SCM implementations are being facilitated by the use of enterprise level resources planning and integration systems, along with the latest technology in transportation, distribution, replenishment, tracing and tracking. Focus is also being laid on building long-term collaborative partnerships with both suppliers and customers.

About the Book

This book is intended for those who are interested in SCM in its broadest sense and its corporate level implementation in real terms. The contents aim to provide an in-depth discussion of supply chain issues from strategic, practical, and managerial perspectives. The book significantly deals with cross-functional aspects of SCM with special reference to consumer goods and services. The book also aims to integrate some of the latest academic theory and research as reported in leading journals with the practice. Specifically, the book is intended for

(i) students of business management doing a foundation course in SCM or who want to specialize in SCM or even manufacturing/operations strategy;

(ii) students specializing in sales and distribution management/logistics management/supply chain management in the second year of their masters in management studies;

(iii) academic candidates of post graduation in business economics/operations research, carrying out live projects-based research in SCM;

(iv) professional managers active in managing logistics and supply chain in their organization, who want to improve the performance and efficiency of supply chain in their companies; and

(v) participants in management development programmes in the area of purchasing and SCM.

Framework

The text has been developed keeping the following in mind:

(i) *Cross-functional management perspective* In this book, focus has been laid on how SCM decisions are taken and how they are affected by and coordinated with sales, marketing, and distribution management, e.g., total order management from order entry to fulfilment and delivery, and initiatives such as efficient customer response (ECR). The interactions with information technology (IT) in terms of ERP packages and the modules thereof, and the CRM system elements and their interface with IT in SCM practice have been highlighted. Interaction of SCM with production systems, such as lean processing, has also been explained.

(ii) *Application orientation* The book focuses on practical orientation. For this, an extensive checklist for implementation of SCM has been suggested as an outcome of a research project in Chapter 7, and also a large number of industrial snapshots have been provided in Chapter 8. Each chapter has a global case study and an Indian case study to illustrate the SCM implementation in detail. The book does not aim to transform the reader into a modelling-based decision-maker. The intention is to focus on the basic concepts, cross-functional relationships, and world-class practices.

(iii) *Corporate performance improvement through SCM* Emphasis has been laid on corporate performance improvement through SCM, particularly its metrics-based benchmarking. Wherever possible, various issues are supplemented with research results from national and international studies.

(iv) *Focus on best practices*   Best practices in SCM have been discussed in detail, as the focus throughout is on responsiveness, effectiveness, and efficiency of supply chains by integrating best practices in an appropriate manner.

Pedagogical Features

Each chapter of the book has the following structural elements:

- An opening introduction to give a bird's eye view of the concepts and issues discussed in the chapter
- Main text explaining core concepts and techniques interspersed with examples, tables, and figures
- Exhibits and case studies to illustrate application of the key concepts in the chapter
- Recapitulatory remarks, summarizing as well as analysing the key concepts and issues discussed in the chapter
- Concept review questions to enable the readers to grasp the conceptual framework
- Critical thinking questions to stimulate the readers to think loud and extrapolate them with the allied practices and implementation
- Project assignments for the readers to gain deeper insights into the implementation issues
- A global case study to present SCM implementation from the point of view of best practices and benchmarking
- An Indian case study to develop insights into how Indian companies have arrived at solutions in real terms while implementing SCM
- Chapter-end references that list books, journals, and extensive Internet resources for further reading

Coverage and Structure

The book consists of nine chapters. The main contents and the focus of each chapter are discussed below.

Chapter 1 starts with the introduction of SCM, its evolutionary patterns, objectives, and the size and potential of SCM market in India. The chapter also provides the framework for supply chain planning and decision-making. The strategic aspects and managing the uncertainty in SCM are also dealt upon.

Chapter 2 focuses on the dynamics of SCM, particularly the alignment processes involved and various elements of customer order management. It also covers the supply chain integration through push and pull mechanisms and the demand inflating bullwhip effect.

Chapter 3 covers various information and communication technology (ICT) tools, software, and descriptions of their modules. Trends in ERP application in India and the future of IT in SCM are also outlined.

Chapter 4 is a treatise on the world-class best practices in SCM, such as supplier tierization, reverse logistics, vendor-managed inventory, milk round system, hub and spoke, third- and fourth-party logistic (3PL & 4PL) provisions, cross-docking, drop-shipping, and radio frequency identification (RFID). It also discusses lean operations, techniques, and corporate experiences.

Chapter 5 focuses on procurement and outsourcing strategies, and operational decisions and trends. Topics like strategic outsourcing and partnerships, bidding and negotiation processes, vendor rating and development, and e-procurement and purchasing in a lean environment have been focused. Continuous improvement of suppliers, together with waste elimination actions, value analysis/value engineering (VA/VE), and integrated supplier quality assurance (SQA) system are also discussed.

Chapter 6 addresses the concept of customer relationship management (CRM) and its linkage with SCM. Strategies oriented towards achieving superior customer value accomplished through SCM have been elaborated. The marketing implications, such as value added services, new product development, and strategic pricing, are duly addressed.

Chapter 7 unravels a comprehensive implementation plan of SCM in an organization. The other section of this chapter discusses the supply chain operating reference (SCOR) model followed by performance benchmarking in SCM, the metrics used, and how the corporate goals are linked to SCM performance. It also has an appendix on a checklist for SCM implementation, generated out of a real-life project that would serve as a ready reference for professionals.

Chapter 8 uniquely presents a miscellany of a number of industrial snapshots of SCM implementation in some of the best-known Indian and global companies. These snapshots provide an inside out view of the dynamics of SCM implementation and the solutions achieved.

Chapter 9 addresses various issues and challenges in SCM implementation and maps out a scenario particularly in the Indian industry.

A glossary of the key concepts used in SCM, appended at the end of the book, would act as a ready reckoner to the nomenclature used in SCM.

Acknowledgements

I would like to express my due acknowledgement to the Economic Times Intelligence Group (ETIG), Mumbai, for their permission to use some information about the companies contained on www.etig.com as also their studies on their publication, *Supply Chain & Logistics*, published in 2002, 2005, and 2007. I am also thankful to Selection and Awards Bureau of the University Grants Commission (UGC) for giving me research award and fellowship to carry out the research work that forms the backbone of this book.

I would like to express my gratitude to Prof. Deepak Pental, Vice Chancellor, University of Delhi, for the encouragement and resources he has provided from time to time in my academic pursuits. I would like to thank Prof. A.S. Narag, Professor and ex-Dean, Faculty of Management Studies (FMS), University of Delhi, for his encouragement in developing the book. Prof. K. Mamkoottam, Dean, FMS provided me a lot of support and facilitation. Prof. J.K. Mitra, ex-Dean, enabled me to devote time for refining the manuscript. I would also like to thank Prof. Pankaj Chandra, Director, IIM Bangalore, who very kindly allowed me to use his case on Amul. I would also like to thank Dr B. Bowonder at the Tata Management Training Centre, Pune, for allowing me to use his article on the use of ICT in Amul. My special thanks go to Ms Elana Veron, Executive Editor, CIO, USA, who allowed me to use the articles on Levi's in Wal-Mart and Nike.

I would also like to thank Prof. N. Ravichandran, Director, IIM Indore, Prof. Devanath Tirupati and Prof. Tathagat Bhattacharya of IIM Ahmedabad, Prof. Janat Shah of IIM Bangalore, Prof. Kampan Mukherjee of ISM Dhanbad, Prof. B.V.N. Sachendra of ASCI, Hyderabad, Prof. Sushil K. Gupta of Florida International University, Prof. A.S. Loomba of San Hose State University, Prof. Jatinder N.D. Gupta of University of Alabama in Huntsville, and Prof. T.S. Dhaker of Southern New Hampshire University for sharing their ideas related to the book.

All the companies and their concerned executives who shared the information, which has been included in the text in the form of exhibits or case studies, deserve a special mention here. Especially, the executives of Bharat Petroleum Corporation, Hindustan Petroleum, Camlin, SAIL, Nestle, Maruti Udyog Ltd, Ranbaxy, Ariba Cosultants, and CSD of Indian Army are to be thanked. In this regard, Praveen Gupta of HPCL, Wing Cmdr Muthukrishnan of IAF, Pravas Paikaray of Ariba, and

Anindya Munshi of Ranbaxy are to be specially thanked. I am also grateful to the sources of any proprietary information/data used in this book including those which would have been inadvertently omitted in referencing or attribution.

My former PhD scholars, Ashutosh Mohan teaching at the Faculty of Management Studies (FMS), BHU, and Anuradha Rajkonwar at Ramjas College, deserve special thanks for providing inputs to the text and compilation of references and glossary, respectively.

On the family front, I would like to express my gratitude to my mother, Mrs Chetan Sharma, whose blessings filled the void in my life created by the loss of my father, Dr Ram Murti Sharma, during the last phase of this book. I dedicate this book to him. I express my thanks to my wife, Kalpana, who extended the much needed support that facilitated me to work on this book and my daughter, Adya, who displayed forbearance while I was writing the book. I also thank my nieces, Shivi and Medha, and nephew Mahim, for being patient during my book writing phases.

I am thankful to the editorial and production staff of Oxford University Press, New Delhi, who have been working tirelessly for the book to reach your hands. The editors have been of immense help and support in bringing out the best from me.

Any suggestions to improve the book are welcome at ssharma@fms.edu.

Sunil Sharma

Contents

9. Issues, Challenges, and Opportunities in Implementation of SCM   520

1 Introduction to Supply Chain Management

L et us first analyse the term and concept of a 'supply chain', as put forward by various scholars. Mentzer (2001) categorized and defined a supply chain as follows:

- A 'basic supply chain' consists of a company, an immediate supplier, and an immediate customer directly linked by one or more of the upstream and downstream flows of products, services, finances, and information.
- An 'extended supply chain' includes suppliers of the immediate supplier and customers of the immediate customer, all linked by one or more of the upstream and downstream flows of products, services, finances, and information.
- An 'ultimate supply chain' includes all the companies involved in all the upstream and downstream flows of products, services, finances, and information from the initial supplier to the ultimate customer.

These supply chains are outlined in Fig. 1.1.

Lambert, Stock, and Ellram (1998) define a supply chain as the alignment of firms that brings products or services to a market. Christopher (1992) defines a supply chain as the network of organizations that are involved, through the upstream and downstream linkage in different processes and activities that produce value in the form of products and services in the hands of the ultimate customer.

Ayers (2001) defines supply chain as life cycle processes comprising physical, information, financial, and knowledge flows where the purpose is to satisfy end-user requirements with products and services from multiple linked suppliers. It may be noted that these processes range from sourcing and manufacturing to transportation and distribution of products and services. Also, the supply chain is not limited in terms of flow direction, i.e., backward flows such as product returns, rebates, incentive payments, etc. could be as important as forward flow of products and services. The other features are as follows:

1. Supply chain is made up of processes that cover a broad range, such as sourcing, manufacturing, transporting, and distributing products and services.

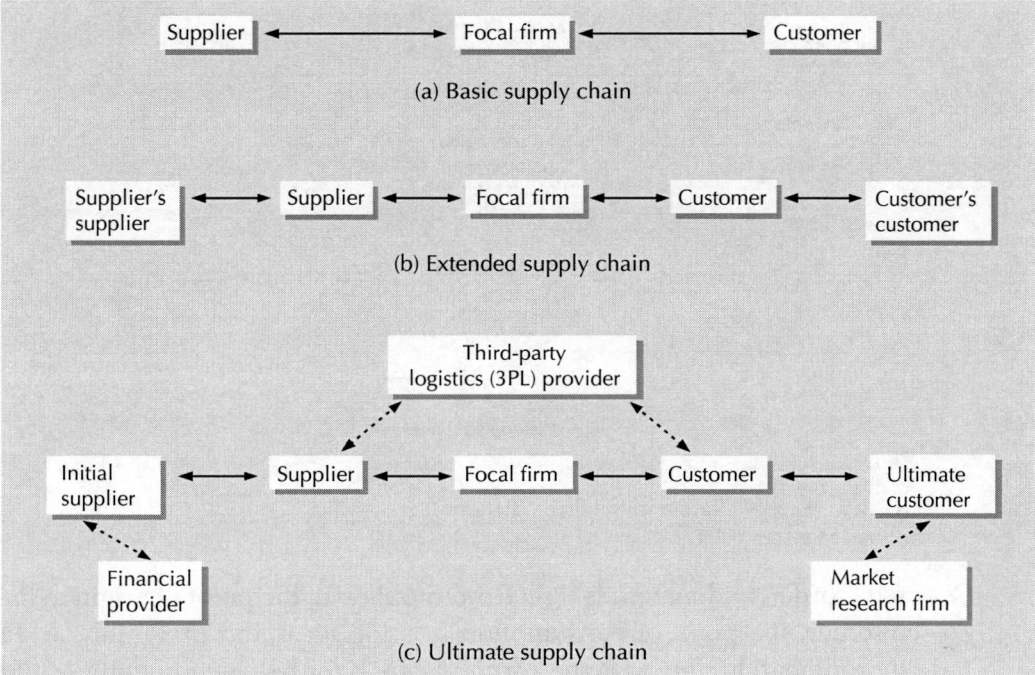

FIG. 1.1 Types of supply chain
Source: Mentzer 2001

2. Information and financial flow components are as important as physical flow in supply chain over the life cycle of product and services, i.e., market life cycle and usage life cycle.
3. The supply chain should support the satisfaction of end-user requirements.

Fawcett and Magnan (2001) refer to supply chain management as the collaborative effort of multiple channel members to design, implement, and manage seamless value added processes to meet the real needs of the end customer. The development and integration of people and technological resources as well as the coordinated management of materials, information, and financial flows underlie successful supply chain integration.

A typical supply chain in terms of various types of flows and their directions is described in Fig. 1.2. Needless to mention that coordination of these flows across various business partners right through supplier to customer requires a lot of information processing in an integrated manner, thus inevitably needing facilitation by the information technology (IT) systems and practices.

Supply chain management (SCM) thus refers to the PODSCORB (planning, organizing, directing, staffing, controlling, reporting, and budgeting) decisions as related to the coordination of flows (including reverse ones) of information, cash,

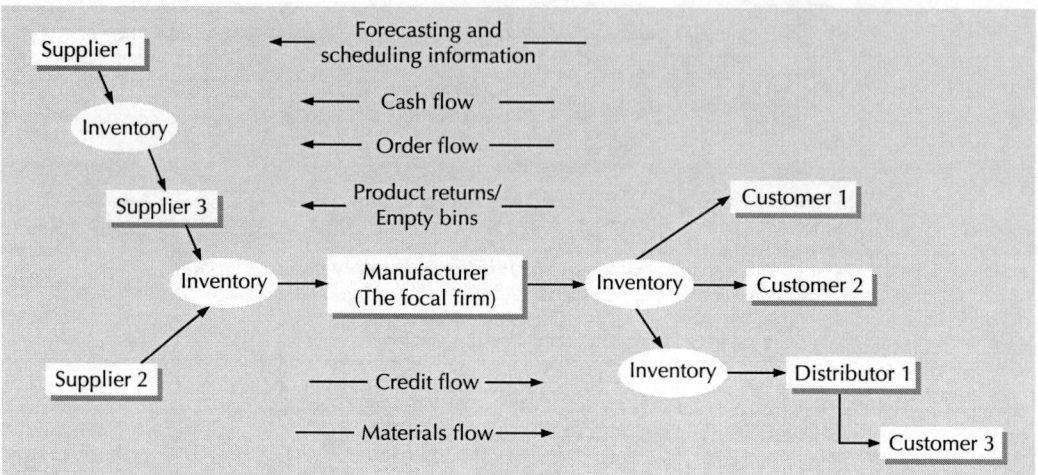

FIG. 1.2 Supply chain and the flows therein
Source: Mentzer 2001

credit, order, and materials right from supplier(s), the point of origin to the ultimate customer, the point of consumption in a logistical and preferably an IT-enabled environment, in tune with the corporate goals for being competitive in the market-place. The flows of information may pertain to sales, pricing, forecasted demands/orders, scheduling of operations, and deliveries, downstream and upstream, as the case may be.

Let us take for example a manufacturing company such as Maruti Udyog Ltd (MUL), where all kinds of flows—tangible and intangible—are envisaged. To start with, the company's production department makes a schedule based on aggregate forecasts of components and sub-assemblies based on the sales/demand patterns in the market for various variants. The information related to these forecasts and schedules is passed on to tier 1 suppliers who in turn pass it on to tier 2 and onwards, if any. The materials then flow from supplier(s) to the company with the credit offered by them. The focal firm, i.e., MUL will then assemble the final automobile product which will be supplied to warehouses and dealers based on orders received from them, on the basis of orders flowing from customers. After the deliveries are realized, cash starts flowing from customer to dealer, and then to the company, who would make or would have made payments to the supplier, in a way, converting some part of cash received from customers in making payment to suppliers. The time elapsed between the two activities of receiving the payment from customers and making payment to vendors is referred to as cash-to-cash cycle time, which is an index of efficient cash flow in the supply chain. Finally, there could be reverse flows, i.e., reverse logistics where there could be product call backs or returns from customers to dealers, and then to the company and the company may have reverse flows of empty bins/containers to suppliers in order to have deliveries on the (just-in-time (JIT) basis. So, all these flows have to be coordinated for the supply chain to function and deliver.

LOGISTICS VS SCM

The terms 'logistics' and 'supply chain' are many-a-times used interchangeably without much regard to the marked difference between the two. Logistics is that part of the supply chain that plans, implements, and controls the efficient, effective, forward and reverse flow, and storage of goods, services, and related information between the point of origin and the point of consumption in order to meet customers' requirements.[1] The Institute of Supply Management (ISM), which was founded way back in 1915 and has currently over 49,000 members, refers to logistics as an entire process of materials and products *moving into, through and out of firm* (Kauffman 2002). While logistics has conventionally focused its attention on coordinating the product, information management, and flow of activities of an individual firm, SCM is concerned with coordinating product, information, cash movement, and flow activities in a *logistical channel environment.*

Logistics is a part of the bigger supply chain, or SCM is an expanded version of the logistics process. While supply chain involves strateg(ies), tactics, and operations, logistics concentrates on the actual ways and means to fulfil the overall supply chain strategy. Both are incomplete without each other. Supply chains exist in both service and manufacturing organizations, although the complexity of the chain may vary greatly from industry to industry and from firm to firm.

PURCHASING VS SCM

Purchasing refers to any major function of an organization that is responsible for acquisition of required materials, services, and equipment. This comprises processes of buying, recognition and ascertainment of need, determination and description of quality and quantity, locating and selecting supplier, negotiating price and arriving at other contractual terms and conditions, and following it all up to delivery. While, another similar term, procurement, is referred to by ISM as a broader term that includes purchasing, stores, traffic, receiving, incoming inspection, and salvage.

There are four views on purchasing vs SCM (Larson 2000). The *traditional view* conceives SCM as a strategic aspect of purchasing, with emphasis on supplier development and partnerships with tiers 1 and 2 suppliers. The *relabellers* simply change the name of purchasing to SCM which narrows the scope of the latter. In the same manner, logistics and channel management could also be rechristened, which

---

[1] Adapted from a definition given by the Council of Logistics Management, USA.

is not so. However, purchasing managers could be relabelled 'supply managers' with no change in their job description. The *unionists* view purchasing as a part of SCM that completely subsumes purchasing including logistics, marketing, operations management, purchasing, etc. Here, the supply chain managers have greater decision-making authority. The *intersectionists'* view is that SCM is not the union of logistics, operation, and purchasing. Rather, it includes elements from all these disciplines, bringing about coordination of cross-functional efforts across multiple firms. SCM is thus considered a broader strategy cutting across business processes, both within the firm and through the channels.

In a way, logistics, which comprises inbound (from supplier) and outbound (to ultimate customer), together with purchasing would be referred to as SCM, while only inbound logistics together with purchasing would refer to supply management.

EVOLUTION OF SCM

SCM has evolved from the typical materials management function possibly in the following manner:

Materials management → Physical distribution management → Logistics management → Integrated logistics management → Supply chain management

The concept of SCM has evolved over a period of time with change in business environment and ever changing requirements of customers. The stages are represented in Fig. 1.3. The evolution starts from the stage of materials management and ends with that of integrated SCM.

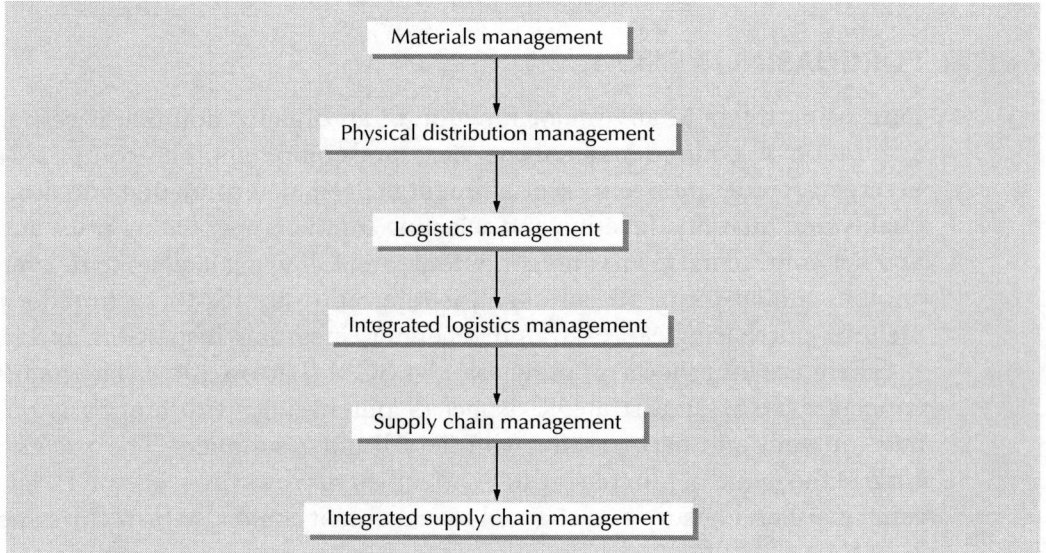

FIG. 1.3 Evolution of SCM

Phase One—The Origin of Materials Management

The early years of materials management and purchasing history can be traced back to the beginning of 1850. However, the purchasing of materials had received attention even before this period. The book of Charles Babbage—*On the Economy of Machinery and Manufacturers*—published in 1832, mentioned the importance of materials purchasing function. This function developed after 1850 with the introduction and development of railroads. Materials purchasing gained importance during World War I because of its role in receiving war supplies. So traditionally, materials management was responsible for various aspects related to material flow within an organization. This included the services of transportation, inventory management, acquisition of materials, the storage of materials acquired, and handling of those materials during manufacturing processes.

The ISM refers to materials management as a coordinating function concerned with inbound movement and storage of raw materials. It is one department responsible for flow of materials from supplier through production to consumer. It is responsible for planning and coordinating materials flow, with objectives of maximizing the firm's resources and provide the required level of customer service.

Phase Two—Development of Physical Distribution Management

This period witnessed that physical distribution was playing a key role in maintaining certain inventory levels and transporting them to the market, ultimately maintaining the market share of the company. An effective physical distribution involved addressing the issue of inventory (raw material as well as finished goods inventory at the point-of-sale), all outbound transportation, warehousing, storage, and communication from the focal firm. The difference between materials management and physical distribution was that under the latter, the importance of outbound transportation as well as storage, packaging, and warehousing increased significantly so that the finished goods could be delivered to customer(s) without any damage in transit. It can be said that physical distribution was total outbound logistics minus the non-physical part of customer order management.

Phase Three—Emergence of Logistics Management

Prior to World War II, business firms were small with limited market coverage. At the same time, easy availability of required materials for continuing the operations of firms made it easy for them to handle and solve different materials and logistics problems through their personal experience and gut feeling. However, during World War II, problems involving the movement of huge quantities of supply made the operations of logistics a distinct technical field for smooth functioning of the firm. Post World War II, rising interest rates and oil crisis made business firms think about the cost aspect also. Rapid recovery and industrialization activities around the world gave rise to severe competition within every industry. These developments made it tough for any firm to get the required materials or items easily and sell the finished products after adding profit margin over the actual cost incurred without concern towards the cost. It was recognised that with a fairly large number of players, organizations could not maintain huge inventories just to ensure uninterrupted flow of materials as it reduced their flexibility to respond to the changing customer demands. In a nutshell, organizations could not enjoy the smooth flow of resources with their physical distribution system and it forced them to adopt cost saving practices with full utilization of resources for meeting well-defined goals, particularly in terms of deliveries with respect to *time* and *place*. These developments gave rise to logistics management, which made the organizations' span of activities in managing the flows of raw materials, components, manufactured parts, and packaged products, through and out of the firm, wider.

Phase Four—Development of Integrated Logistics Management

In the previous phase, it was evident that inclusion of raw materials, components, manufactured parts, and packaged materials within the overall flow of materials expanded the responsibilities of management into a broader logistical concept. This broader view of management emphasized on strategic decision-making. As organizations expanded their wings for reaching a wider market base, it resulted in more complex requirements in terms of (inbound) sourced materials from different suppliers, their transportation, handling work-in-process (WIP) inventory, finished goods (FG) inventory as well as the outgoing traffic and transportation requirements together with the flows of information at respective points and levels. At times it included reverse flows of materials, products, empty bins, information, credit, cash, etc., reverse logistics, such as product returns, recalls, claims, refunds, discounts, and rebates. All different flow activities and their associated costs got interrelated. The logistics thus got implicated in every major function of management from purchase through production, warehousing, and dispatch to customer order management, which ultimately gave rise to the concept of integrated logistics management— integrating inbound, outbound, and the reverse one. Therefore, the integration of logistics function as a single unified system to optimize and control the entire process of materials, products, and information moving *into, through, and out of the firm*, i.e., inbound and outbound, is the essence of integrated logistics management.

Phase Five—Introduction of SCM

This phase started from the mid 1980s. Logistics has traditionally focused its attention on coordinating the physical flows of products and information across various departments within and outside a firm, whereas SCM is concerned with coordinating the flows of product, information, cash, credit, order, and materials in a *logistics channel environment* i.e. SCM is an expanded version of the logistics process (Coyle et al. 2000). All materials, finished goods with complete information, and all transactions flow through the supply chain loop as one continuous process. Introduction of supply chain became a necessity with the opening and widening of the economy all over the world. Rapid spread of information with IT-enabled services (ITES) and communication technology gave rise to the concept of the unified world as a global business village. Under these circumstances, organizations could not encash the opportunities existing throughout the world just by its own efforts. They needed business partners to pool the efforts and expertise of others to derive benefits of the same. This attitude within organizations changed the way of its operations. Prior to this stage, organizations were somewhat 'stand-alone' in nature, in terms of the inward thinking process related to improvements within themselves. However, under the changed scenario, organizations had to broaden the horizon of their (strategic) thinking process to achieve synergy within and outside the organization. SCM was an organizing and operating concept that started with customer service and resulted from the cumulative efforts of the entire channel partners (Sautter et al. 1999). Mentzer (2001) defines SCM as 'the systemic, strategic coordination of the traditional business functions within a particular company and across businesses within the supply chain, for improving the long-term performance of the individual companies and the supply chain as a whole.' The various elements which came to be clubbed under SCM can be listed broadly as the following:

1. An integrated systems approach with an outward strategic thinking
2. Long-term partnerships with vendors to focus on vendor development in all areas
3. Close cooperation and coordination throughout the supply chain
4. Free flow of information amongst different members of the chain
5. Mutual sharing of channel rewards and risks by all the members
6. Integrated objectives and goals with the single goal of best customer care
7. Integration of processes within and outside the organization under joint planning of operations especially with suppliers
8. Maintaining a long-term relationship with customers as well as supply chain partners, such as sources, subcontractors, third-party logistics (3PL), distribution centres, retailers, and even the customers
9. A self-regulating and control mechanism at every level of the supply chain to take care of the quality and delivery aspects of products/services

Phase Six—Convergence into Integrated SCM

This phase started in the mid 1990s. The basic idea behind the integrated SCM is that at each level the use of materials facilities, people, finance, and system must be coordinated and harmonized as the part of a single integrated system. The development of an integrated supply chain requires the management of material and information flows to be viewed from three perspectives: strategic, tactical, and operational (Mohanty and Deshmukh 2001). While the impetus for the development of the strategy may be a top-down approach, its success is likely to be achieved by a bottom-up approach. However, the realization of the full potential of inter-relationships among the components and partners of the supply chain is possible by designing an integrated system to manage and ensure customer product and service expectations, while taking care of cost, quality, delivery flexibility, and service factors without fail. Moreover, since the extent of outsourcing has increased especially in non-core competent activities by more and more companies for long-term cost reduction and with developed suppliers of critical activities for cost savings, the need for integration of purchasing with both inbound and outbound logistics in the supply chain across the extended enterprise has also increased. Also, the concept of integrating supply chain invariably involves channel alignment that is required to create a right balance between material order quantity, capacity requirements, prices, ownership of materials, transportation, and information processing requirements across all the channel partners. The purpose is to deliver the best value to the customer or the end-user.

OBJECTIVES OF SUPPLY CHAIN

The objectives of a supply chain are manifold but most of them are derived from the primary objective. The primary objective comprises creating a superior mutual value for the customer in terms of the product and service delivered at a time and place in response to customer needs and demand. By value, it is meant that the worth of the product and service delivered to the customer must far exceed the efforts and expenses put in by the company in fulfilling the customer's order, which gets paid in the form of price by the customer.

The derived or secondary objectives are given as follows.

Profitability

There must be supply chain profitability all over the chain, not only at individual stages or to individual partners. The revenue must exceed the expenses or the costs of the supply chain. In a competitive market, this implies decreasing the costs and not increasing the price to ensure supply chain profitability.

Reliability
A supply chain aims to provide time and place specific delivery with a superior service level in fulfilling the order, practically with negligible stock-out rates. However, stock-out rates of 2.5% are still common.

Flexibility/Agility
A good supply chain must be flexible to absorb fluctuations in demand without any extra costs. It refers to the upside production flexibility that can absorb extra demand. A flexibility to absorb 20 per cent extra demand is quite desirable.

Responsiveness
It refers to how much time it takes to meet the customer's needs, particularly when the design and volume needs to undergo a change.

Turnover Rate
It is important that a high turnover rate of assets used in the supply chain, whether financial, space, inventory, or machine resources, is set as only a fast turnover would not block capital, reduce the risk of obsolescence, increase productivity, and thus profitability or the return on investment used in these resources or assets.

Communication and Coordination
A supply chain objective is to provide good communication, coordination, and information sharing ability and competence across all the channel partners, right from suppliers to the distributors/retailers, the 3PLs and finally the customers.

SUPPLY CHAIN PLANNING FRAMEWORK

Fleischmann and Meyr (2003) provide the framework that encompasses the operational, tactical, and strategic analysis for decision-making at short-term, mid-term, and long-term levels respectively, consisting of different components as outlined in Fig. 1.4.

The model is supported by the following pillars.

Supplier Collaboration
It refers to collaboration with suppliers by sharing information and resources to ensure efficient delivery schedules from them. It also involves collaboration with them in terms of new product/design development, initiatives for long-term relationship, and commitment.

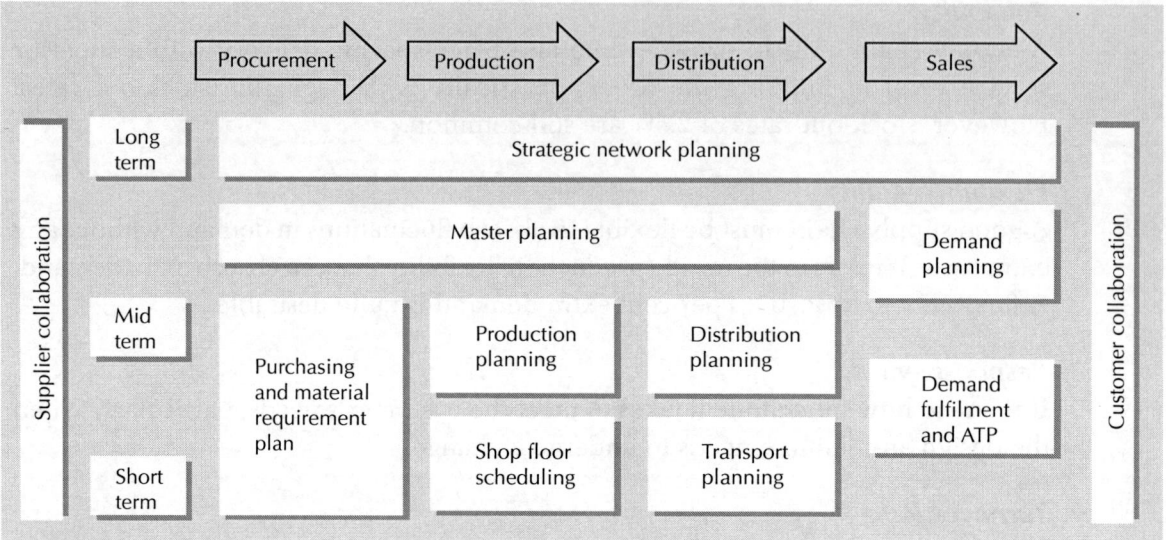

FIG. 1.4 Modules in supply chain planning framework
Source: Fleischmann and Meyr 2003

Customer Collaboration

This is in terms of demand planning, having regular feedback from customers, managing relationships, rendering services to customers, and meeting contractual obligations in a collaborative manner so as to make the order fulfilment process a satisfying one.

The activities at the three levels can be described as the following.

Strategic/Long-term level   This involves designing the supply chain network for all partners, namely suppliers and their suppliers, customers and their customers, and the 3PLs. Supply planning on the supplier side and demand planning on the customer side in a collaborative manner are also dealt with at this level.

Tactical/Mid-term level   This refers to sales and operations planning that involves allocation of resources and stipulating the order requirements/service level agreements (SLAs). The material requirement planning (MRP), capacity resources planning (CRP), master production scheduling (MPS), distribution planning and mid-term sales planning also occur at this level.

Operational/Short-term level   This level comprises planning and scheduling of materials, and production on the supplier side and transport, warehousing replenishment, and short-term sales on the customer side.

A similar supply chain planning framework was suggested by Accenture India, as given in Fig. 1.5.

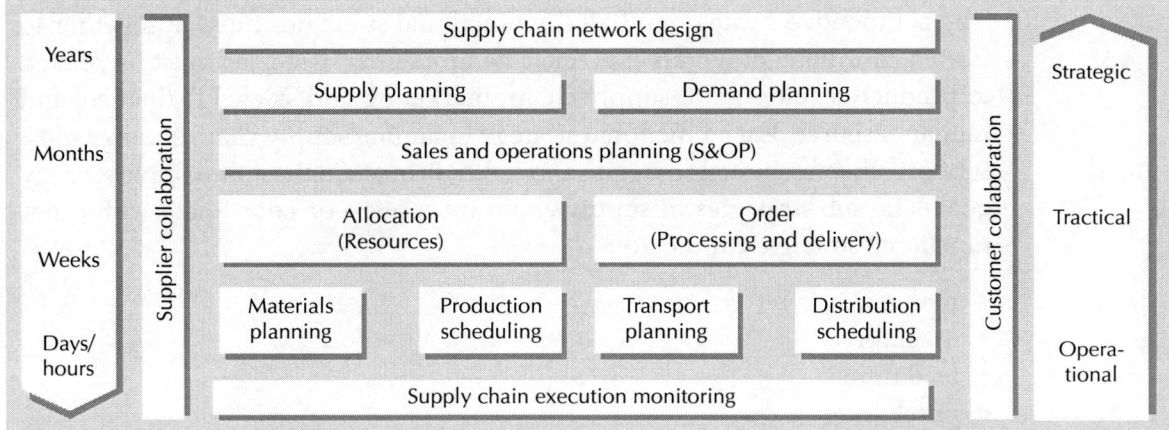

FIG. 1.5 Supply chain planning framework
Source: Accenture India

From both the supply chain planning frameworks, it emerges that the supply chain network design and planning is at the strategic or long-term level, while all the master planning for supply and demand is a tactical or mid-term level planning activity. The sales and operations planning (S&OP) is an aggregate planning activity in the mid-term range with planning horizon of about 6–18 months. This is the most important planning activity and horizon, particularly from production point of view. At the operational level, in terms of weeks/days, the supply chain comprises four activities, namely

- material planning
- production scheduling
- distribution scheduling
- transport and warehouse planning

This is followed by a transaction-based execution and monitoring of supply chain, say on an hourly basis, and doing follow-up and expediting of job and shop orders on real-time basis. As stated earlier, all these planning activities are supported by supplier collaboration on one side and customer collaboration on the other, particularly in the form of information sharing.

THE STRATEGIC FIT MODEL FOR SUPPLY CHAIN

The strategic fit means that both the competitive and supply chain strategies have the same goal. As is known, corporate success in a given environment is linked to the following considerations.

(i) The competitive strategy and all the functional strategies must fit together to form a coordinated overall strategy. The functional strategies must be related to product development, supply chain, marketing and sales, IT, finance, and human resource. Each functional strategy including supply chain strategy must support other functional strategies and help a firm attain the competitive strategy goal. The sub-strategies in supply chain must align or coordinate with other functional strategies in the area of

- manufacturing
- inventory
- lead time
- purchasing
- transportation

(ii) A company must appropriately structure the processes and resources to be able to execute these strategies successfully. Since processes and resources are structured to support functional goals, a conflict in functional goals would lead to conflicts during execution. For instance, if the marketing and sales department of a company publicizes the company's ability to provide a large variety of products very quickly in a *responsive* manner at a desired point-of-sale (PoS), it is possible that the distribution department of the same company may like to batch orders in order to get better transportation economies (*efficiency*). Both might be conflicting to each other. The issue is always to have a balance between the degree of flexibility and *responsiveness* (ability to supply different products quickly) versus the degree of *efficiency* (ability to supply with cost efficiency). It actually implies that flexibility and responsiveness comes at a price.

To attain the strategic fit, the company must ensure that the supply chain capabilities support the ability to satisfy the targeted customer segments. The various stages in attaining the strategic fit are as follows:

(a) The company must understand the customer and supply chain uncertainty.
(b) The company must ascertain the customer's needs for each targeted segment and the *implied supply uncertainty* the company would face to meet that uncertainty. The needs may be laid down in terms of the desired cost and service requirements. The company must be able to identify the extent of supply disruptions and the degree of its impact, severity, and tolerance by the company at a certain cost.

On the other hand, the company must be able to estimate the supply chain capabilities and strengths. If a mismatch occurs between the supply chain capabilities and the needs of the customer, the company would need to restructure the supply chain to support the existing competitive strategy or alter its strategy. Generally speaking, as Chopra and Meindl (2004) also put it, the customer needs from different segments may vary along several attributes, namely the following:

- Lot size of the delivery required
- Response time that customers are willing to have
- Variant of the product needed
- Service level required
- Pricing of the product
- Rate of innovation

Understanding Customer Needs

Each customer need can be translated into the metric of implied demand uncertainty that exists due to the portion of demand that the supply chain is required to meet.

Compared to demand uncertainty, which refers to uncertainty of customer demand for a product, the implied demand uncertainty is the resulting uncertainty from the specific customer desires for only that portion of demand which the supply chain must be able to handle. Various customer needs in terms of quantity, lead time, quality/variety, number of channels, rate of innovation, and required service levels increase the implied demand uncertainty.

Fischer (1997) pointed out that the correlation between the implied demand uncertainty and the other attributes is as following.

1. Products with uncertain demand are often found to be less mature in their product life cycle (PLC) stage and have less direct competition thereby resulting into high margins as well.
2. Forecasting errors tend to be lesser when demand is more certain.
3. An increase in the implied demand uncertainty leads to higher stock-out rate (10–40%), while low implied demand uncertainty leads to a lower stock-out rate of 1–2% per unit.
4. Mark-ups are kept high for products with high implied demand uncertainty which results into over-supply.

According to Lee (2002), requirements of specific capabilities would increase the supply uncertainty. The negative characteristics or weaknesses in capabilities would cause the supply uncertainty to increase. These weaknesses could be in terms of frequent breakdowns, low process yields, poor quality, limited fixed capacity to supply, and an evolving product/process technology.

As the product technology matures and process yields improve, companies are able to follow a fixed delivery schedule resulting in better service levels and resulting in low supply uncertainty.

Trade-off between Efficiency and Responsiveness

Supply chain efficiency mainly refers to the cost of making and delivering a product to the customer. For any strategic choice to increase responsiveness, there are additional costs which would ultimately lower efficiency.

On the other hand, a company would like to have a level of supply chain responsiveness that would refer to the supply chain's ability for the following.

- Respond to a wide range of quantities required
- Meet requirements of a short lead time
- Respond to requirements of a large variety
- Design, develop, and quickly deliver/market new innovative products
- Meet a high service level
- Handle stock-outs

In order to meet the aforesaid requirements, the company may have to invest in developing the capabilities and augmenting the capacities for manufacturing and distribution which would form the costs of responsiveness.

Getting the Right Fit

This last stage is to ensure that all the supply chain actions are consistent with the customer's needs and the supply chain uncertainties. To attain this, a mapping is done of supply chain responsiveness with the implied uncertainty. There is a positive correlation between the two. The greater the implied uncertainty, the more responsive the supply chain would be. The relationship is shown by a *zone of strategic fit*. As Chopra and Meindl put it, for a high level of performance, companies should move their competitive strategy (and thus the implied uncertainty) and supply chain strategy (and the resulting responsiveness) towards the zone of strategic fit. All the functional strategies within the value chain, as outlined earlier, must support the supply chain's level of responsiveness.

As it is acknowledged that at the maturity phase of the product life cycle, the demand becomes more certain, supply becomes predictable (low supply uncertainty), and margins are low because of increase in competition. Also, the price becomes a significant factor in customer buying. However, delivery schedules and distribution points are pre-established and standardized, which can make the supply chain less responsive. The opposite is true in the case of a product/variant in introduction or growth case. So, finally it can be inferred that in order to get that right strategic fit, the supply chain strategy must be adjusted over the PLC with the changing competitive scenario.

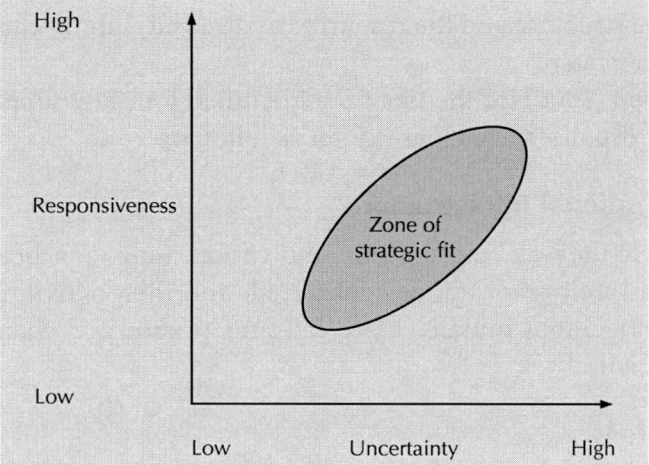

FIG. 1.6 Zone of strategic fit

However, getting the right fit might be rendered difficult because of

- increasing variety of products and services on offer by competitors to meet a broader market segment particularly in lean times
- decreasing PLCs
- disintegration of ownership

The last reason is reflective of the latest trend where many companies are shedding their vertical integration and relegating non-core competent functions to suppliers or third-party providers. The problem now is that each partner at each stage is prone to making decisions that meet business objectives at his level rather than the whole chain, which may adversely affect the overall supply chain profitability. Figure 1.6 illustrates the zone of strategic fit between a continuum of responsiveness and uncertainty in demand.

SUPPLY CHAIN DECISION-MAKING FRAMEWORK— THE SUPPLY CHAIN ENABLERS

As is assimilated by now, the companies begin with a competitive strategy and then decide about supply chain strategy like the other functional strategies. The strategy would be decided depending upon the extent of responsiveness and efficiency required keeping in view the customer needs, resources available, and foremost, the certainty in demand. The supply chain strategy in turn translates into a decision-making framework that would dictate a certain performance level, for which a supply chain uses certain *enablers* or *drivers*. However, the reverse is also true when depending upon the structure and the resources at disposal, supply chain strategy may have to be re-orientated.

Marien (2000) for the first time identified four key supply chain enablers based on 200 responses, which are given as follows.

Organizational Infrastructure

It refers to the way business units and various functions including SCM and its sub-functions are organized, de-centralized, and their activities coordinated and how the management initiatives are led and steered for change within the existing infrastructure.

Technology

It includes not only information technology (IT) but also 'materials design, processing/manufacturing and handling' technologies.

Strategic Alliances

This refers to developing long-term partnerships with all supply chain partners for collaboration.

Human Resource Management

It refers to the manner in which supply chain job descriptions are designed, positions filled, and people's work is recognized and compensated.

Chopra and Meindl (2004) and the company Flextronics identified four key drivers of supply chain structure that would provide a decision-making framework to SCM.[2] These four drivers are

- facilities or physical network
- inventory
- transportation management
- information systems and other technologies

Later on, Chopra and Meindl (2007) added two more drivers, namely sourcing and pricing. While the first three were grouped as *logistical drivers*, the rest three were grouped as cross-functional drivers (Fig. 1.7). The author feels that the list is not complete and keeping in view the importance of SCM as a profit-centre and the kind of staffing, management commitment, and leadership required for this approach, it is inevitable that one more cross-functional enabler/driver be added. Advocated by Marien (2000), the new enabler would be 'organisation structure and human

---

[2] www.flextronics.com/en/markets/logistics/performancedrivers

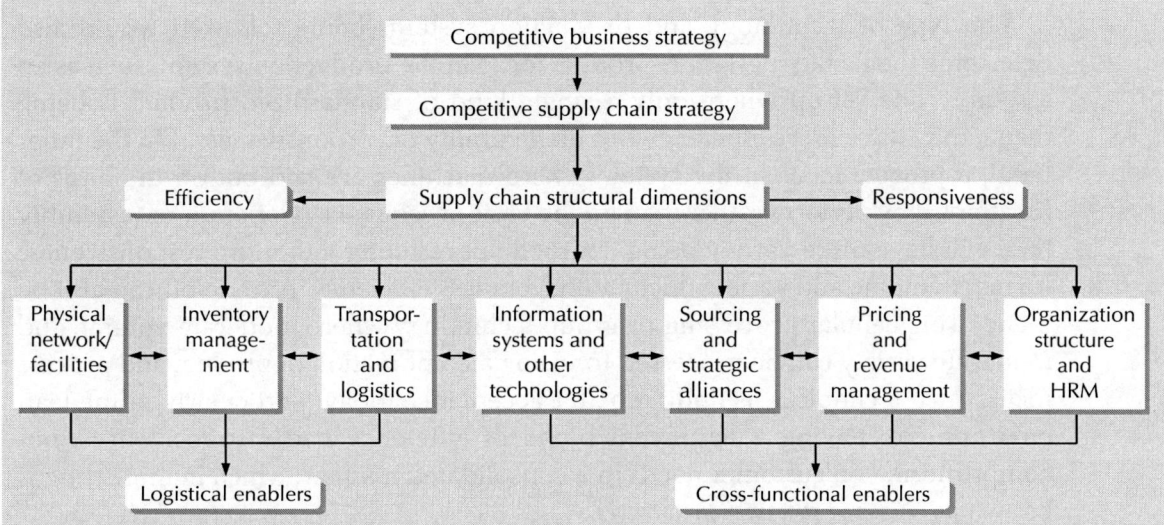

FIG. 1.7 Supply chain structural dimensions and enablers
Source: Partially based on Chopra and Meindl 2007

resource management'. The total list of SCM drivers/enablers now reaches seven. It is also recommended that strategic alliance be added to sourcing in that context, while the term 'physical network' be preferred over facilities, and revenue management be integrated with pricing, as also discussed by Chopra and Meindl (2007).

Together these enablers or drivers determine supply chain structure and thus a certain level of responsiveness and efficiency in it. Let us briefly discuss these.

Physical Network/Facilities

The facilities serve as nodes in the physical network of the company used for material design, supplies, processing, warehousing, order distribution, and fulfilment services, connected with each other in a spatially co-related manner. The facilities location aims to establish manufacturing, assembly, distribution centres (being closest to customers), near to the location of suppliers so as to yield minimum shipment costs. However, subjective factors, such as macroeconomic factors, quality of work-life, infrastructure, tax benefits and governmental guidelines, and legislations may also impact decision-making.

The design, planning, and operation of capacity of the facility is also an important factor. Although excess capacity is at the cost of efficiency yet it allows the facility to be flexible and responsive to demand variation. A limited capacity may be economical to operate but it results in difficulty in responding to demand fluctuations. A capacity higher than 20 per cent may result in efficiency as well as significant responsiveness.

The type of technology and production systems being followed would also determine the facility design. A product focus in the production system, such as an assembly line set up where only a single kind of standardized product is being made, may have more efficiency but no flexibility or responsiveness. On the other hand, a process focus in the system where machines are laid out on the basis of functions they perform rather than on the basis of sequence of operations (assembly line) will have more variety being churned out resulting into more responsiveness (to meet volume and variety fluctuations) but less efficiency. A trade-off can also be made using cellular processing or group technology where moderate volume and moderate variety can be processed for using a combination of product and process focus. Such technology is finding better acceptance today, particularly in the lean environment, having a significant blend of efficiency and responsiveness, not compromising on customer needs in a consolidated manner, which in marketing is known as *clustered customer preferences*.

The other factor which affects facilities' design and planning is the kind of warehousing and storage being required. The storage can be stock-keeping unit (SKU) based where one type of product is stocked together, which proves to be quite an efficient, particularly spacewise, way of storage.

The storage could also be job-orderwise where all the materials required for a job/order or customer are stored together. It might require more space but it facilitates more efficient picking and packing or technically speaking, positioning, lifting, and transferring (PLT) functions related to the same job.

However, things are quite different when no warehousing/storage is required as such, but what is required is a transit point where trucks from suppliers, each carrying a different product, deliver goods to a facility where orders are broken/sorted/re-sorted/re-packaged into smaller lots to be quickly loaded onto store bound trucks. This is especially true in retail industry where suppliers supply the finished goods and some accessorization or final assembly is done at the cross-docking point. Such facilities are better outsourced than being managed by the core firm itself.

Some facilities planned for distribution may also cater to light manufacturing/product customization or differentiation as a part of the postponement strategy, i.e., postponing the final product structure till the customer's end depending on the order. These may even cater to small product repairs in addition to other reverse logistics (reverse flow of products from retailers and customers).

Inventory Management

The location and quantity of inventory can be very instrumental in determining the cost and responsiveness of the supply chain. The company must exploit its capabilities and services to attain a mix of cost efficiency and responsiveness by maintaining optimal inventory levels. The best option is to manage the inventory at the vendor's end, preferably through hubs or cross-docking centres. The strategic procurement and outsourcing and collaborative planning, forecasting, and replenishment (CPFR) with the vendors helps in facilitating vendor-managed inventory (VMI) or facilitating online delivery of parts. As pointed out, the accessorization at customer's end also minimizes the inventory. The storage and warehousing policies, such as the re-order point (ROP) and lot-sizing for different materials, are key drivers of supply chain for attaining the desired mix of efficiency and responsiveness in it.

Transportation and Logistics Management

Choosing the right modes and routes can determine the effectiveness and efficiency of distributing the product to the customer's end. It could entail mode, route, and network selection, carrier selection, providing merge-in-transit services, cross-docking and tracking, and tracing services. It covers the inbound and outbound logistics. The use of material handling principles, such as load unitization, use of gravity and techniques such as automated storage and retrieval systems (ASRS), and palletization for multi-modal transport would also affect the output from logistics systems. Reverse logistics or a milk run to and from a cluster of proximal vendors would facilitate on-line delivery of parts and synchronization of delivery schedules with the production schedules. Thus, efficiency and responsiveness of transportation and logistics is going to be a very important factor for supply chain structure designed for performance.

Information Systems and Other Technologies

In today's environment, all the supply chain processes are IT-enabled and need information exchange across all the supply chain partners right from suppliers to customers. Further, the Web enablement of SCM has become important for 24×7 online order placement by customers and its capturing by the company, better order management, particularly in terms of build-to-order capabilities, tracking and tracing of order by customer herself, and integration with other e-commerce solutions. Systems like enterprise resource planning (ERP) have come a long way in enabling the supply chains to adopt information systems. Such systems provide end-to-end operational services and seamless integration right from purchasing and sourcing function to manufacturing to supply chain and logistics and distribution to customer's end. Technologies like electronic data interchange (EDI) and radio-frequency identification (RFID) have also been useful in this respect. Needless to mention, installation of information systems must be preceded by business process reengineering (BPR) of all the supply chain processes.

The technologies related to material design, processing/manufacturing, and handling also form an important part of the supply chain structure, particularly with regard to its efficiency in performance. So, these should also be included together with IT, as strongly put forward by Marien (2000).

Sourcing and Strategic Alliance

Decisions related to sourcing are very critical to supply chain structure in terms of efficiency and responsiveness, particularly through purchasing and distribution. In fact, the first decision is whether to insource/make or outsource/buy. The efficiency and responsiveness requirements would dictate such decisions. The next decision is whether to follow single or limited sources or multiple sources. The decision that follows next is to identify the criteria that would be used to select vendors on the basis of a set of subjective and objective factors. Selected vendors can also be undertaken for vendor development to meet specific needs. Based on their technical and subsequently commercial qualification at a bidding stage, negotiations might be entered into for arriving at (mutually) suitable terms and conditions of the contract. The structure of the contract is re-looked to improve the supply chain performance on a combination of both efficiency and responsiveness as per organizational requirements.

After the contracts with the suppliers are finalized, what follows is the procurement process by virtue of which supplier would ship the materials as per the delivery schedule—quantity and time-wise. Nowadays, more and more of procurement is done electronically and depending upon the degree of strategic importance of the material, organizations are going in for e-procurement aided by the Web and dedicated portals on it. They are organizing reverse-auctions on their specially designated portals to get the lowest price, facilitating decisions within a short time in a transparent manner thus bringing in transparency, effectiveness as well as efficiency in the procurement function of supply chains.

Organizations would make or insource materials and services if they have the core capabilities which they would like to retain. Activities in which the company is non-core competent would preferably be bought or outsourced for attaining efficiency and/or responsiveness. For instance, logistics could be outsourced to a third party if the core firm is non-competent in the same. However, all the sourcing decisions need to be frequently reviewed keeping in view the supply chain requirements.

Strategic alliances with select vendors are entered into for collaboration in terms of product design, cost reduction, and developing compatible information and processing/manufacturing systems and technologies. However, it should be done on a selective basis depending upon the nature of material to be purchased, specific requirements, if any, and the resources available for investment in vendors and their development.

Pricing and Revenue Management

The price of a product affects not only the buying behaviour of the relevant customer class but also its expectations. This in turn affects the demand profile that the supply chain would attempt to meet. Interestingly, pricing is also used as a *lever* that can be used to match supply and demand. For instance, short-term discounts can be used to decrease supply surpluses or flatten the spikes of peak seasonal demands. Also, some food chains such as McDonald's and Pizza Hut would offer *Happy Hours* discounts to average out demands, capacity use and planning. Same strategy is also followed by the hospitality chains.

Pricing is one sharp tool through which a firm can execute its supply chain strategy under the overall competitive strategy. Some customers do not mind low pricing for a late delivery while on the other hand, some others do not mind paying a higher price for delivery at a short notice or for responsiveness. For instance, the *Tatkal* service of Indian Railways provides responsiveness at a higher price, while *Apex* fares in airlines need a firm booking, no refunds are allowed, and fares vary depending upon how advance it is being booked—to facilitate the efficiency of the supply chain and bring about a better capacity plan and use. Another commonly cited case is that of Amazon.com, which provides a *menu pricing* based on what the customer can tolerate in terms of the shipping days on offer at a price (greater the shipping period, lesser is the price with certain limits on lower and upper sides).

So it has become important for a firm to structure its supply chain through menu pricing so as to meet the two divergent needs of customers in terms of efficiency and responsiveness and thus target a broader customer segment. Alternatively, some stores like Wal-Mart in the US and Big Bazaar in India offer everyday low pricing (based on their own efficient pricing from their vendors, bulk discounts, and efficient operations and logistics such as employing cross-docking) meeting the efficiency needs of their customers as well as keeping the demand stable over a period of time. On the other hand, some stores, such as Marks & Spencers in UK or Westside or Spencer's in India provide high-low pricing. This results in peak demand during discount weeks, say around Christmas and other festivals or off-season, followed by a drop in demand during other periods when merchandise is offered at high (normal) prices.

Revenue management through pricing is significant as supply chain management is seen as a profit-centre. So, in addition to reducing costs, it can yield more sales if price levels are properly manoeuvred. It would specially refer to the use of differential pricing over time or customer segments to maximize sales revenue, hence the profits from a select set of supply chain assets, particularly the level of finished goods (FG) stock. So, supply chain managers must have good information about the assets or stock availability, customer demand over a select frame of time/season, and customer buying patterns when customers are exposed to different levels of pricing. This is a cross-functional driver as it needs close coordination and working with the marketing department.

Organization Structure and Human Resource Management

Organization structure refers to the way business units and functional areas like SCM and its sub-functions are organized, how they are aligned towards the same goal, and their activities are co-coordinated within the existing structure. It is possible that the organization structure may have to be re-orientated in terms of providing a suitable context (such as climate) for implementation of SCM. It is also important that the new management initiatives and programmes are led and steered towards continuous improvement in supply chain processes. It is especially important to understand the way management interprets and aligns SCM goals with organizational goals in a given period. The organization structure should always facilitate cross-functional SCM project implementation, the sharing of information, and supporting a spirit of collaboration and group decision-making among the staff, irrespective of their functions and levels.

Human resource management (HRM) in the context of SCM would refer to the manner in which the job descriptions of SCM staff are designed, responsibilities fixed, and positions with specific skill requirements are filled. It is significant that the work of SCM staff, particularly those working in cross-functional projects is recognized, appraised, and compensated for. The importance of the way the management directs and motivates them to achieve a high level of performance and achieve professional goals and objectives in SCM cannot be undermined. The management may also choose to assign certain change agents or team leaders to manage SCM initiatives or implementations.

Interestingly, Ayers and Odegaard (2007) have suggested the following six SCM drivers exclusively for the retail industry.

- Innovation cycle from internal to external services
- Extended product design
- Globalization
- Flexibility imperative
- Process-centred management
- Collaboration

Detailed discussion about these is beyond the scope of this book. Readers can refer to the book *Retail Supply Chain Management* by Ayers and Odegaard.

MANAGING UNCERTAINTY IN SUPPLY CHAIN

Supply chains usually operate in uncertain and unpredictable environments. Some of the factors contributing to the uncertainty in supply chains are mentioned below.

Gap between Supply and Demand

In reality, a long time before the demand is finalized due to the supplying, manufacturing, and administrative lead times involved, advance commitments are executed at the production and in-turn at the supply level. It involves investments in workforce, inventory, and machines. Because of the unexpected gap, particularly when supply far exceeds demand in a competitive market, it involves lot of financial and supply risks. In a lean and recessionary environment that is in vogue today across the globe, particularly in developing countries, investments in supply chain have significant associated financial risks.

Accurate Demand Forecast—A Distant Dream

In reality, estimation of precise levels of demand, particularly geographically disaggregated ones, is not possible because no forecasting technique can yield the accurate forecast when a lot of environmental variables are involved. The only tool that works is monitoring the point-of-sale (PoS) data and supplies triggered by demand from retailers on a pull basis only.

Variations in Inventory, Back-order Levels, and Dynamic Priorities

More often than not, companies may have to face fluctuations in inventory levels and the order status, especially back-order ones, depending upon the real-time problems and priorities. A case in point is that of the bullwhip effect, dealt in the section that follows, in which there is wider fluctuation in demand at the distributor and onward level than at the retailer level.

Miscellaneous Unforeseen Factors

This holds true for India, where we may not have service levels of more than 95 per cent on an average, particularly when it comes to meeting the infrastructural requirements of supply chain and logistics. It can be attributed to poor transportation systems, power availability, and Net connectivity, delivery lead times, administrative lead times, poor manufacturing yields, difficult availability of critical components and even strikes or natural or man-made disasters in this part of the world.

While it may not be possible to eliminate the uncertainty in supply chains, the effect of these can surely be minimized by proper planning and designing the supply chains that are agile such chains have been discussed in a later chapter.

BENEFITS OF SCM

Key benefits accrued by implementation of SCM, mainly using an SCM decision-making framework with enablers approach would include the following.

- Reduction in working capital deployment (inventories, warehousing, and financial costs
- Re-engineering, simplification, and optimization of processes across different components and stages at different levels
- Optimization of workforce across various orders/clients at different levels and locations
- Reduction in time to market through disintermediation and better logistics
- Reduction in processing and administrative lead times at all stages
- Capturing and tracking of feedback from all supply chain partners at each stage and better collaboration based on the feedback
- Bringing about accurate inventory forecasting and planning
- Streamlining incoming material flow and synchronizing it with production at the plant level, particularly in a lean environment
- Ensuring a certain in-process/work-in-process (WIP) material and finished goods flow
- Tracing and tracking of order information, its fulfilment status, and maintaining a certain promised service delivery level
- Improved satisfaction levels of internal and external customers

SCM MARKET IN INDIA

India had a Purchasing Power Parity (PPP) equivalent to US$1.5 trillion in 2008 and thus she constitutes one of the fastest growing markets of the world.[3] The Growth Competitiveness Index survey conducted by the Geneva-based World Economic Forum (WEF) for 2006–07 puts India at the 43rd position among 125 countries in the Global Competitiveness Report and 27th in the Business Competitive Index.[4] These factors, together with shortening of PLC, proliferation of product variety, low reliability of supply chain networks in India have forced companies to adopt SCM and associated systems and practices. However, lack of proper logistics framework, poor infrastructural support together with poorly designed supply chains with low efficiency leads are the major obstacles to reap full advantages through large scale implementation of SCM. This is also cited in the UPS Asia Business Monitor

---

[3] economywatch.com as accessed on 27 September 2008

[4] weforum.org/en/initiatives/gcp as accessed on 27 September 2008

Survey, 2004.[5] Although latest figures are not available, figures estimated by Economic Times Intelligence Group (ETIG) in 2002 indicate the Indian market value for supply chain/logistics at 13 per cent GDP, i.e., around Rs 2,35,000 crore (approx. US$50 billion), a large share of which (35% + 9% = 44%) is accounted for transportation, handling, and warehousing, as shown in Fig. 1.8. As compared to 13 per cent of GDP spent in India, the spend is 15 per cent in China, 10 per cent of GDP in US, 10.6 per cent in UK, 11.6 per cent in France, and up to 12 per cent of GDP in rest of the world (ETIG, 2002). According to a working paper by Raghuram and Shah (2004), the logistics cost estimates as per cent of GDP are 8.5 per cent in USA, 8.7 per cent in Japan, 16.5 per cent in Korea, and 12.3 per cent in India.

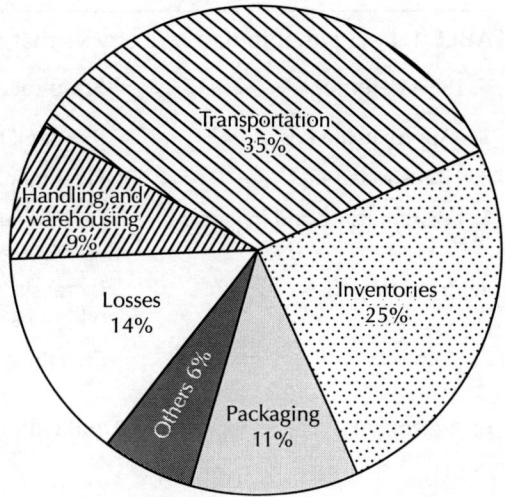

FIG. 1.8 Logistics cost estimates in India
Source: Centre for Monitoring Indian Economy (CMIE), as reported by ETIG, 2002

Though supply chain and logistics business in India is still at its infancy, there is tremendous potential ahead. The reason for the late start of supply chain and logistics business in India is that it took sometime for Indian industry to stream-line and reorganize their business processes and restructure their supply chain. According to an ETIG study, the state of the Indian industry in various SCM elements as compared with the state in the West and the relevant focus is highlighted in Table 1.1.

In most industries, such as automobiles, fast moving consumer goods (FMCG), consumer durables, foods, pharma, garments, paints, cement, and steel, SCM has been in the process of implementation or already been implemented or supply chains are being restructured and integrated, while in some other industries, the concept of SCM is yet to find takers. So, there is a lot of variability in terms of the extent of implementation of SCM in different industries in India.

As per the Centre for Monitoring Indian Economy (CMIE) data available in 2006 and given in Table 1.2, the industries have been reported to spend a total of 4.1 per cent (1.4% for inbound and 2.7% for outbound/distribution) of their net sales on logistics. However, these figures may not include losses, transaction, administration, and personnel costs together with costs of reverse logistics and marketing costs related to supply chain. Also, the costs of IT hardware and software

---

[5] eintelligence.com as accessed on 27 September 2008

TABLE 1.1   State of Indian industry vs that in the West with respect to various SCM elements

	SCM element	State in West	State in India
1.	Approximate costs	9% of GDP	13% of GDP
2.	Transportation	Fleet management concept	Tracking concept
3.	Warehousing and inventory	Collaborative/Vendor-managed inventories (VMI)	Minimal disruption of line, stocking at various stages of the chain
4.	Inventory costs	Increasing far slower than rise in other costs	Rising
5.	Information	Free flow, real time	In islands of knowledge, reluctance to share
6.	Personnel	Trained logistics managers	Personnel move from distribution stores and sales, few professional managers
7.	Organization structure	Logistics function is separate (stand-alone) with its own defined objectives, roles, and targets	Only leading companies are giving logistics a full functional status
8.	Infrastructure	Supports and enables sophisticated and efficient logistics solutions	Poor quality, spread, and facilities

Source: Adapted from Economic Times Intelligence Group (ETIG)

TABLE 1.2   SCM spend in major Indian manufacturing industries

SCM spend indicators	2000–02	2002–03	2003–04	2004–05
Inbound transportation costs as percentage of net sales	1.5%	1.4%	1.3%	1.4%
Inventory related costs as percentage of net sales	13.3%	13.9%	13.1%	13.1%
Distribution expenses as percentage of net sales	3.0%	2.8%	2.8%	2.7%
Total SCM spend as percentage of net sales	17.8%	18.1%	17.2%	17.2%

Source: CMIE, 2006

can only be collated using data as supplied by the companies and there are no reports on any such expenditure in Indian databases. Estimates, however, range from 3 to 5 per cent of sales for industries which have implemented SCM or are in the process of doing so. Overall, these kind of industries spend up to 9–10 per cent of total revenues on logistics. Variation in implementation of SCM is also attributed to the type of industry and the level of professionalism and adoption of new technology in a particular sector.

With more than half the goods being moved by road, the transportation costs in India accounts for almost 40 per cent of the cost of production. Trucking accounts for nearly 70 per cent of transportation and accounts for 60 per cent of all logistics costs. 67 per cent of truck ownership is in the hands of small unorganized players. Road is followed by rail and finally by coastal shipping. The freight movement of Indian railways rose to 492.31 metric tonnes in 2007–08. The railways have 222,147 freight wagons and freight operations information systems (FOIS) at 235 locations, equipped with the Rake Management System (RMS).[6] The total national highways length is 66,590 kilometres.[7] Though numerous maritime routes are available, poor government vision and policies and total lack of participation from the private sector, water—probably the cheapest mode of transport—is barely used and riverways are hardly developed. Air as a mode, on the other hand, is limited to a small percentage of courier shipments. Various SCM spend indicators, such as inbound transportation costs, inventory related costs, and distribution expenses as percentage of net sales vary from industry to industry. However, as per CMIE, these are coming down over a period of years. The aggregate of the same for nine major manufacturing industries for four years have been shown in Table 1.2. These industries spent nearly 17–18 per cent of their net sales on various supply chain activities, including distribution, warehousing, and inventory. Global averages are around 9–12 per cent. So, there is ample scope to reduce spend on logistics. This in turn allows companies to protect operating margins during downturns and make above-normal profits during upturns.

The focus on costs and information and communication technology (ICT) enabled services is leading to electronic (e-) procurement, which cuts time and costs (including transaction costs) and brings in transparency and speed. The enterprise resource planning (ERP) industry in India is worth US$300 million and is growing at over 15 per cent a year. Fifty two per cent of the respondents in the Economic Times Intelligence Group (ETIG) SCM 2004 survey have implemented ERP and three-fourths of these find ERP to be extremely effective in business. Forty four per cent of the companies surveyed had already implemented data warehousing and mining applications, and another 26 per cent had plans to do so. Almost every firm found this practice to yield good results in revealing sales and ordering patterns, potential segments, and integrate various functional areas in a seamless manner.

For supply chain tracking, the most preferred method is the truck driver reporting his location. Another method is use of short messaging service (SMS), where time lags can be pre-determined. Depending on the number of times the SMS signal is polled and sent to the base station, the location of the vehicle can be accurately

---

[6] http://www/indianrail.gov.in as accessed on 27 September 2008

[7] http://www.nhai.org as accessed on 27 September 2008

determined. With global positioning systems (GPS), determination of the location of the vehicle has become automatic. However, the use of GPS for SCM in India is relatively low. Service providers like Transport Corporation of India (TCI) have poured in US$0.34 million for installation of GPS in their trucks. Firms like Bajaj, Maruti Udyog Limited, TVS Motors and Bharat Shell are already using TCI's GPS systems.

CHANGES THAT LED TO MODERN SCM

(i) Until the late 1980s, most companies viewed logistics as comprising trucking, inventory, and warehousing activities only. However, many companies started appreciating the need for competition for their supply chains and associated networks also and not just for their products, by the fag end of the 80s.

(ii) From 1990s, the start of rapid improvement in telecom networks and a burgeoning IT industry together with increasing globalization of Indian business brought buyers and sellers closer, exploring new dimensions of buyers and supplier relationship.

(iii) In late 1990s, BPR came into vogue whereby companies streamlined their processes, making integration with customers and vendors at different ends. Suppliers came to be recognised as partners and by the turn of the century, they were recognised as business partners and had a role in cost reduction.

(iv) By virtue of emergence of ERP in late 1990s, companies further streamlined and mapped their processes, removed duplication, and carried out integration of different functions within the company as well as outside the company to suppliers and customers. A number of middle and small scale companies joined the race. Today, the ERP market in India is valued at around Rs 1200 crore.

(v) Advent and penetration of Internet in corporate buying and after-sales servicing has led to intensification of B2B commerce and reaching out to suppliers and customers. This has resulted in time and cost efficiency in order fulfilment and servicing, purchasing, procurement, and replenishments at the retailers level, ultimately leading to lower stock-outs, better service levels, and delivering better value to customers for a given price. The time to market a new product reduces as well. All these efficiencies result in a higher return on investment (ROI), more loyal customers, and higher market share. This also motivates the employees or internal customers of the company and so has a transforming impact on the organization culture in terms of communication, information sharing, developing a team spirit, striving for continuous improvement, focusing on customer satisfaction, and always considering supply chain partners as true business partners sharing risks and rewards on a pool basis rather than on individual basis.

It may be noted that while ERP integrates the corporate functional departments into a seamless organization, supply chain attempts to integrate the external factors into internal processes. Today, the extended enterprise concept of supply chain not only includes the core manufacturing company, customers, and vendors but also includes parties such as the following.

- Transporters
- Carrying and forwarding (C&F) agents
- Third-party logistics (3PL) providers
- Logistics consultants
- Consolidators
- Fleet operators
- Warehousing companies
- Software solution providers
- Telecom and hardware providers

CORPORATE SUCCESS THROUGH SCM

It is clear that SCM is at different developmental stages in different industries in India. While the apparel industry treats SCM as a fragmented entity constrained by various factors, automobile, consumer durables, and FMCG industries see SCM as a very tight, controlled, and integrated entity for their business. This can be gauged from the fact that there is a great amount of outsourcing in the automobile and consumer durables industry. While in automobiles and food industry, the critical SCM component is inbound logistics, in FMCG, pharma, apparel, cement, and paint industry, it is outbound logistics. However, there could be common cost, delivery, and cycle time measures at different stages of the supply chain. Post SCM

TABLE 1.3 Operational and business improvements in Indian FMCG industry post SCM implementation

(i)	Reduction in procurement cost	5–10%
(ii)	Reduction in processing cost	5–10%
(iii)	Reduction in inventory carrying cost	10–15%
(iv)	Reduction in distribution cost	10–15%
(v)	Reduction in procurement and manufacturing cycle times	15–20%
(vi)	Increase in online delivery	15–20%
(vii)	Increase in available to promise (ATP) performance	10–15%
(viii)	Reduction in time to market	10–15%
(ix)	Increase in sales turnover	15–20%
(x)	Increase in profits	10–15%

implementation, these would bring about marked improvements in business and operations, as is clear from Table 1.3.[8]

It is obvious that SCM results into better selection, streamlining of supply chain partners, fine-tuning of various SCM flows and their alignment because of

- value addition at all stages of supply chain processes
- cost efficiency
- volume flexibility
- variety flexibility
- delivery dependability
- delivery speed
- lesser product development times
- faster inventory replenishment

Reduction of cycle times, particularly by implementation of lean processing or single-piece flow, results in faster turnover of inventory and capital resources. It does not result in any blocked capital in the form of inventory or warehousing cost; the rejects and wastages are fewer; the obsolescence risks get reduced; and because of faster replenishments and virtually no stock-outs, customer service levels are higher. This ultimately results in better profitability by virtue of cost reduction or increase in net profit/ROI, thereby providing better products in lesser time at the retailer's end and then to the customer. Obviously, it will lead to increase in market share by virtue of being competitive in terms of time, cost, price, and better positioning of products in the marketplace. The focus on cost, time, delivery, and flexibility must percolate down from upstream supply chain members such as primary and secondary sources to distributors, retailers, and customers. Although it is targeted to shorten the supply chain by eliminating certain levels, ironically, while we can possibly eliminate some distribution channel members, we cannot eliminate their activities such as distribution, retailing, etc.

On slightly intangible fronts, SCM results in better customer reach, higher product availability, and better responsiveness to customers. It also invariably interacts with better adoption of customer relationship management (CRM) practices and fine-tuning of supply chain networks and flows for better transparency and faster processing at each stage. A case in point is that of value added tax (VAT). By introduction of VAT regime, facilities network and flows for SCM had to be redesigned by most companies, which resulted in savings in terms of reduction in number of warehouses, rationalization of transportation routes, and consolidation of fleet. Adoption of IT with VAT and outsourcing of non-core competence activities

---

[8] Unpublished PhD thesis by Ashutosh Mohan, completed under the supervision of the author, Faculty of Management Studies, University of Delhi, 2005

also augmented the concept of *hub and spoke*[9] in the logistics part of SCM. SCM results in better order fulfilment and management at the customer's end as 'time to market and distribute' decreases significantly by better management of supply chain, including redesign of supply chain and their networks and flows and their alignment and integration. Also it results in better customer retention and increased customer loyalty. For supply chain integration, the basic premises on which companies should act are given as the following.

  (i) Collaborative planning and forecasting for better demand management (both volume and varietywise) and sharing the information with appropriate supply chain partners
 (ii) Supply chain structure including facilities network design, taking into consideration the realistic transportation and logistics requirements including redesign and relocation of facilities (including fleet) and their capacities
(iii) Collaboration and partnership with various stakeholders like product developers, sources, channel partners, and endusers including 3PLs
 (iv) Adoption of information and communication technology (ICT) to facilitate all of the above

All these four activities executed for supply chain integration would facilitate better demand and supply planning, order tracking and fulfilment, better procurement, and replenishment patterns. It may even help in marketing new product designs faster and provide better service levels to customers—both internal and external.

Many companies in the Indian FMCG market have reported operational and business benefits, after implementation of SCM as indicated in Table 1.3.

Although these estimates may not be 'breakthrough' achievements, the values vary in the range depending upon the nature of the industry, the level in implementation of SCM, and other functionally related systems and practices such as ERP and CRM. These figures are just reflective of how much potential lies in the implementation of SCM by various industries, particularly in view of its benefits after implementation as reported by some global giants, cited at a later stage in this book.

RECAPITULATION

The opening chapter of this book starts by defining SCM as an alignment of firms or network of organizations that comprise various kinds of flows, which delivers value to the customer through upstream and downstream linkages of different processes and activities. The noteworthy aspect is that a basic supply chain, comprising a supplier, the focal firm, and the customer, could assume different levels of complexity based on its extension to customers and suppliers and the type

---

[9] A *hub* is an IT-enabled consolidation centre that receives small frequent lot deliveries from a network of supplier networks (*spokes*), normally managed by a 3PL. See Chapter 4 for detail

and levels of networks and service providers involved. Also the flows are not only of material goods but could also comprise information, finance, knowledge, credit, cash or order flows. There could be even reverse flows in terms of product returns, empty bins/containers, rebates, incentive payments, etc. (*reverse logistics*). The chapter then focuses on the evolution of SCM from the conventional materials management to physical distribution and logistics management to integrated logistics management, ultimately leading to integrated SCM. The important characteristics of the new evolved SCM that emerged are given as the following.

(i) It is a holistic system approach and has strategic focus.

(ii) It involves long-term partnerships with vendors and customers.

(iii) It is facilitated by the flow of information across all the supply chain partners who mutually share the reward and rights to deliver the best value to the customer.

(iv) The SCM system should have a self-check and control mechanism at every link in the chain to maintain the quality of products delivered.

(v) SCM needs joint working and collaboration with all partners, particularly the suppliers. Also, the role of logistics in SCM, particularly the third-party logistics (3PL) providers cannot be undermined when it is required to develop an integrated SCM framework and plan.

The key and primary objective of supply chain at the focal firm is to create a mutually superior value for the customer in terms of the product and service delivered at a time and place in response to the customer needs and demand. The secondary objectives derived from this are to possess certain degree of profitability, flexibility or agility, responsiveness, asset turnover and to provide for communication, coordination, and information sharing ability across all the supply chain partners and not just one partner.

The planning framework for supply chain is supported by collaboration with suppliers as well as with customers. There are four operational fronts in this model, namely material planning, production scheduling, distribution scheduling, and transport planning.

It is necessary that the supply chain strategy is aligned with the competitive business strategy in terms of the goals, i.e., it must have a 'strategic fit'. This may require the supply chain a set of coordinated actions with other functional strategies in the area of manufacturing, inventory, purchasing, and transportation. In order to attain the strategic fit, the company must understand the customer needs and the implied supply chain uncertainty. Compared to demand uncertainty, which is uncertainty of customer demand for a product, the implied demand uncertainty is the resulting uncertainty for only the portion of demand that the supply chain must handle and the specific customer desire. The greater the implied uncertainty, the more responsive the supply chain should be. For a high level of performance, companies should move their competitive strategy (and thus implied uncertainty) and supply chain strategy (and the resulting responsiveness) towards an intersecting area, and is so called the 'zone of strategic fit'. The 'strategic fit' however, is restricted by the increasingly demanding customers, decreasing product life cycles (PLCs), and disintegration of supply chain ownership focusing only on the individual goals than the whole chain. The structure of the supply chain is determined in terms of two dimensions, namely 'efficiency' and 'responsiveness'. While efficiency refers to the cost of making and delivering the product to the customer, responsiveness refers to the supply chain's ability to respond to a range of fluctuations in the demand of a product variant with significantly high service level. Since one comes at the cost of another, these are to be traded off. A supply chain decision-making framework is described by a set of enablers or drivers which influence the structure of the supply chain in terms of 'efficiency' and 'responsiveness'. Initially labelled as the facilities, inventory, transportation and information, the list of enablers or drivers can now be expanded to include sourcing and strategic alliances, pricing and revenue management, and organization structure and HRM. While the first three are logistical enablers, the latter four are cross-functional in nature. All these form elements of the supply chain decision-making framework.

There are multifaceted benefits of implementing a good SCM in terms of reducing working capital requirements, optimizing various processes, reducing time to market, reducing lead times across various levels, streamlining, and improving flow of inventory at in-process, work-in-progress, and finished goods stages. The pre-requisite is obviously better forecasting and planning through information sharing with supply chain partners.

The supply chain market in India is promising. As per recent studies, supply chain costs normally stand at 12.3 per cent of GDP compared to the US where the figure is 8.5 per cent. A large share of the supply chain costs, roughly 44 per cent of it, is accounted for transportation, handling, and warehousing. According to another study by CMIE in 2006, companies spent 17.2 per cent of their net sales on logistics and supply chains (global average being 9–12%) out of which 1.4 per cent was spent on inbound logistics, 2.7 per cent for outbound logistics, and 13.1 per cent on inventory. The ERP market is also promising with around 15 per cent growth rate. Indian industries have reported significant operational and business improvements post SCM implementation.

CONCEPT REVIEW QUESTIONS

1. What are the types of supply chain and what are the kinds of flows involved in a typical supply chain? When do you see the possibility of reverse flows (reverse logistics)?
2. Why is supply chain different from logistics management? How do the two terms differ? Outline the relationship amongst purchasing, logistics, and SCM.
3. Trace the evolution of the conventional materials management function to the modern day SCM, particularly in the Indian context.
4. What are the objectives of a supply chain? How can these objectives can be linked to corporate goals?
5. What are the different levels and elements of a supply chain planning framework? What purpose can be served by such a framework?
6. What is meant by the 'strategic fit' of a supply chain strategy? How can this fit be attained and what can be its limitations?
7. What are the enablers or drivers that support the supply chain decision-making framework? How can these help in determining the efficiency and responsiveness of the supply chain?
8. What is the state of business and its potential in SCM and ERP market in India? What are the trends in West vs India?

CRITICAL THINKING QUESTIONS

1. Why is modern SCM not only about forward physical flow of goods from suppliers to customers? How do the other types of flows emerge?

2. What are the challenges for management of logistics in the Indian context? How do you suggest these challenges to be tackled? What initiatives can be taken by the government in this regard?
3. What are the reasons of uncertainty in supply chain even when the demand is fairly stable?

Cite a few reasons particularly with reference to the Indian context.
4. How does SCM affect the business performance and results in a competitive corporate world? Indicate some broad metrics of business performance and how these can be impacted by better SCM operations?

PROJECT ASSIGNMENTS

1. Interview a sales and distribution/logistics/supply chain manager of a company and find out how SCM has evolved from a conventional material procurement and storage system to an integrated supply chain management system.
2. Visit different sites on the Internet, e.g., economywatch.com, cmie.org, or eintelligence.com and sketch out a scenario about business growth in logistics and supply chain market in India.
3. Analyse in detail the reasons for the present stage of SCM in India (The reasons could pertain to economy, market, technology, and competitiveness).
4. Analyse how developments in Information and Communication Technology (ICT) have contributed to the pace of progress in SCM.

CASE STUDY

GLOBAL CASE STUDY

HEWLETT-PACKARD (HP)[10]

Supply Chain Management Approach

HP is a major player in three highly competitive, price-sensitive businesses: printer and imaging solutions, personal computers, and technical solutions. The last one includes services as well as enterprise systems for mission critical applications. This broad product line positions HP against a large number of competitors. Other imperatives include a widely dispersed global operation that extends across 178 countries and a rapidly flowing new product pipeline, which launches hundreds of new products each year.

HP's supply chain effort is overseen by its *Supply Chain Council*, which includes a Senior VP in charge of supply chain and the supply chain leaders from each of the company's three business groups. Each year, the council updates its three-year plan and then translates it into a 12-month schedule. To monitor progress and ensure that the objectives are met, the Supply Chain Council meets every month. HP serves four customer segments: consumer, small/medium business, public sector, and enterprises.

The Supply Chain Network at HP

Just a few years ago, customers received product or services from HP via one of the 35 different

---

[10] *Source:* Partially adapted from www.hp.com/hpinfo/globalcitizenship as accessed on 2 April 2008; www.managingautomation.com/maonline/magazine/read/view/supply-chain-mastery-HP-2588698 as accessed on 22 September 2008

supply chains. Now, the company has consolidated its business into five supply chains—no-touch, low-touch, configure-to-order, high-volume, and solutions and services. Says Dick Conrad, Senior VP, Supply Chain, Global Operations, 'One size does not fit all. Relying on just one supply chain limits the company's ability to grow and effectively serve different customer requirements and different market needs. Right now, five is the right number but it is possible, one or two could be added.' The Director of Supply Chain Strategy at HP, Gianpaolo Callioni says, 'We are always putting customer first.' To meet this objective, the company has built a powerful supply chain network that provides the flexibility it needs to deliver products to customers the way they want to receive them. There are four routes to market which the company has designed—value direct, volume direct, partner assisted value indirect, and partner assisted volume indirect. This flexibility in channels and routes allows HP to address complex customer needs. It also helps HP to optimize its supply chain costs as products move through their life cycle by emphasizing on velocity and focusing on cost management.

Sourcing Policies and Programmes at HP

HP operates the IT industry's largest and most complex supply chain (Fig. 1.9). HP purchases approximately $53 billion of products and materials, components and manufacturing, transport and other services from approximately 7000 suppliers globally, out of which about 400 are contracted manufacturing suppliers. Also, 600 suppliers account for 95 per cent of the HP's expenditure on product materials, components, and manu-facturing (Fig. 1.10).

HP has a global policy and programme to offer under-represented businesses equal opportunities to become HP suppliers and resellers. In the US, these businesses include small, minority-owned, women-owned, veteran-owned, service-disabled

owned businesses. In other countries, they include aboriginal, ethnic minority, and immigrant-owned businesses. HP has in place a *corporate supplier diversity programme* for more than thirty years. HP's *Global Citizenship Policy* sets expectations for HP's human rights, labour practices, ethics, occupational health and safety, environmental impacts, and collaborations with non-governmental organizations (NGOs). HP's commitment to corporate social and environmental responsibility (SER) extends through their SER policy established in 2002 to their global supply base and aligning SCM with their global citizenship commitment minimizes supply chain risks while forging a clear connection to the corporate values. It is also committed to building SER capabilities at its suppliers' end by protecting workers' rights, suppliers' working conditions, health, and safety.

To offset some of the potential disadvantages of this concentrated sourcing approach, HP has maintained a *Corporate Multicultural Procurement Programme* for more than 30 years, a practice that continued to expand beyond the US into other markets like Europe, Canada, and South Africa. These efforts helped them to meet the expectations of the public sector and corporate customers while the consumers gained access to diverse ideas and contributed to the economic strength of the communities in which HP operates. Purchases from minority and women-owned businesses comprised 22.1 per cent of HP's total qualified procurement spending in the US during 2004. These exceeded all of HP's targets for awards in 2004, in particular to women-owned small businesses. It utilized these firms to provide logistics services, software development, and computer and electronic manufacturing services. These firms are involved in the repair, replacement, and warehousing of HP products and for providing temporary personnel. HP increased its goals for 2005, even though its qualified procurement spending still remained constant.

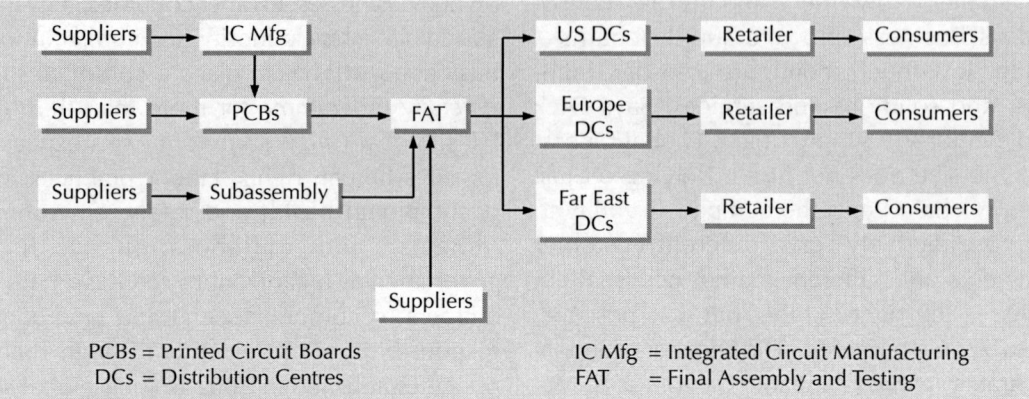

PCBs = Printed Circuit Boards
DCs = Distribution Centres

IC Mfg = Integrated Circuit Manufacturing
FAT = Final Assembly and Testing

FIG. 1.9 The network of supply chain at HP

In addition to their procurement efforts, HP promotes supplier and reseller diversity in a number of ways. HP's minority reseller programme provides an opportunity to strengthen HP's relationships with minority resellers and customers and to exchange information and ideas on how they can work together to meet customer needs. HP's Micro Enterprise Development Programme focuses largely on stimulating economic growth in low-income US communities. Similarly, the work in microfinance and e-inclusion provides support to small, minority-owned, and women-owned businesses across the world. Finally, HP actively mentor their suppliers and host events with local business councils that introduce diverse suppliers to potential customers. The company also led the development of electronic industry code of conduct (EICC).

HP Connect

The company launched its unique HP Connect Supplier Diversity Summit in August 2007. These events are held twice in a year on HP campuses. These events facilitate in identification of potential suppliers, informing them about the opportunities available to do business with HP. It also facilitates face-to-face interaction with HP buyers. In 2007, 120 pre-screened minority and women business owners were selected for 15 minute one-to-one 'match making' sessions with HP commodity managers and tier I suppliers. In 2008, the figure was 70. Through HP PartnerONE diversity network, HP provided marketing and sales support to more than 350 direct resellers in 2007 and 300 in 2008.

Supply Chain Mastery at HP

Everyday, HP delivers 1.3 million inkjet cartridges, 1,10,000 printers, 75,000 personal computer (PC) systems, and 3500 servers. As per Global Competitive Report (GCR) 2008, HP ship more than 1 million printers per week and more than 4.8 million PC units annually. It has 600 contracted materials and manufacturing suppliers located at more than 1200 locations worldwide. It has 3,40,000 workers at audited sites that produce HP products. Most of these products are produced by contract manufacturers or original design manufacturers. The company spends about $50 billion, or about 64 per cent of its revenue, on supply chain activities. At this spending and complexity, supply chain mastery is an imperative discipline to control costs and foster collaborative relationships with suppliers. According to Derek Conrad, Senior Vice-President, Supply Chain Global Operations at HP, as quoted in *Managing Automation*, an online magazine, 'Supply chain optimization has a direct impact on customer satisfaction, stock price and profitability.' As a result, HP management assigns supply chain optimization a high priority. They are continuously focused on supply chain improvement. The journey will never be done until they can do it for free or at a negative cost. They have to be vigilant to ensure that the supply chain is flexible and changes to meet ever increasing demands.

Benefits and Rewards

The supply chain organization and practices outlined above have reaped the company many benefits, such as saving HP over $1 billion since 2001, and earning HP the Managing Automation Progressive Manufacturer Supply Chain Mastery Award in 2005. With an increasing number of orders received directly from consumers using the HP website or working through an enterprise business partner, there's been considerable growth in the customer-centric, demand-driven, configure-to-order supply chain. 'We do more and more configure-to-order, especially on our mid to lower range of offerings,' said Randy Burdick, the then

Vice-President and Group Information Officer, Adaptive Infrastructure and Supply Chain IT at HP. Combining SKUs and options just before shipping eliminates the need for custom builds and reduces inventory requirements. However, this direct-to-consumer business also necessitates different support functions such as call centers for customer service and website design for easy use. The company's e-visibility system has connected HP to its 3PLs to generate proof of delivery in 48 hours on 92 per cent of shipments, thereby significantly quickening the invoice/payment process and improving cash flow.

By integrating social and environmental requirements into its sourcing operations through its SER programme, HP particularly focused on suppliers of product materials, components, and manufacturing and distribution services, such as contract manufacturers, original design and original equipment manufacturers, product design support, transportation, and product repair services, representing 90 per cent of HP's expenditure and brought about significant efficiencies, decrease costs, and strengthened partnerships (Fig. 1.11). As per GCR, 2008, HP employed a risk-

Geographic distribution of supplies at HP		
North, Central, and South America Region	**Europe, Middle East, and Africa (EMEA)**	**Asia Pacific Region**
Countries: Canada, Mexico, United States, Costa Rica, Brazil	**Countries:** Austria, France, Germany, Italy, Netherlands, Scotland, Switzerland, UK, Czech Republic, Hungary, Romania, Middle East and African countries	**Countries:** China, India, Indonesia, Japan, Korea, Malaysia, Phillippines, Singapore, Taiwan, Thailand
Business: Contract design and manufacturing, software, semi-conductors, storage, interconnect, power supplies, packaging materials	**Business:** Contract design and manufacturing, semi-conductors, media, packaging materials	**Business:** Contract design and manufacturing, semiconductors, displays, storage, interconnect, power supplies, media, packaging materials
Per cent spend: 20% of total spend	**Per cent spend:** 5% of total spend	**Per cent spend:** 75% of total spend

FIG. 1.10 Major regions of HP's product materials, components, and service suppliers
Source: Based on www.hp.com/hpinfo/globalcitizenship/gcreport/supplychain/auditresult as accessed on 19 February 2010

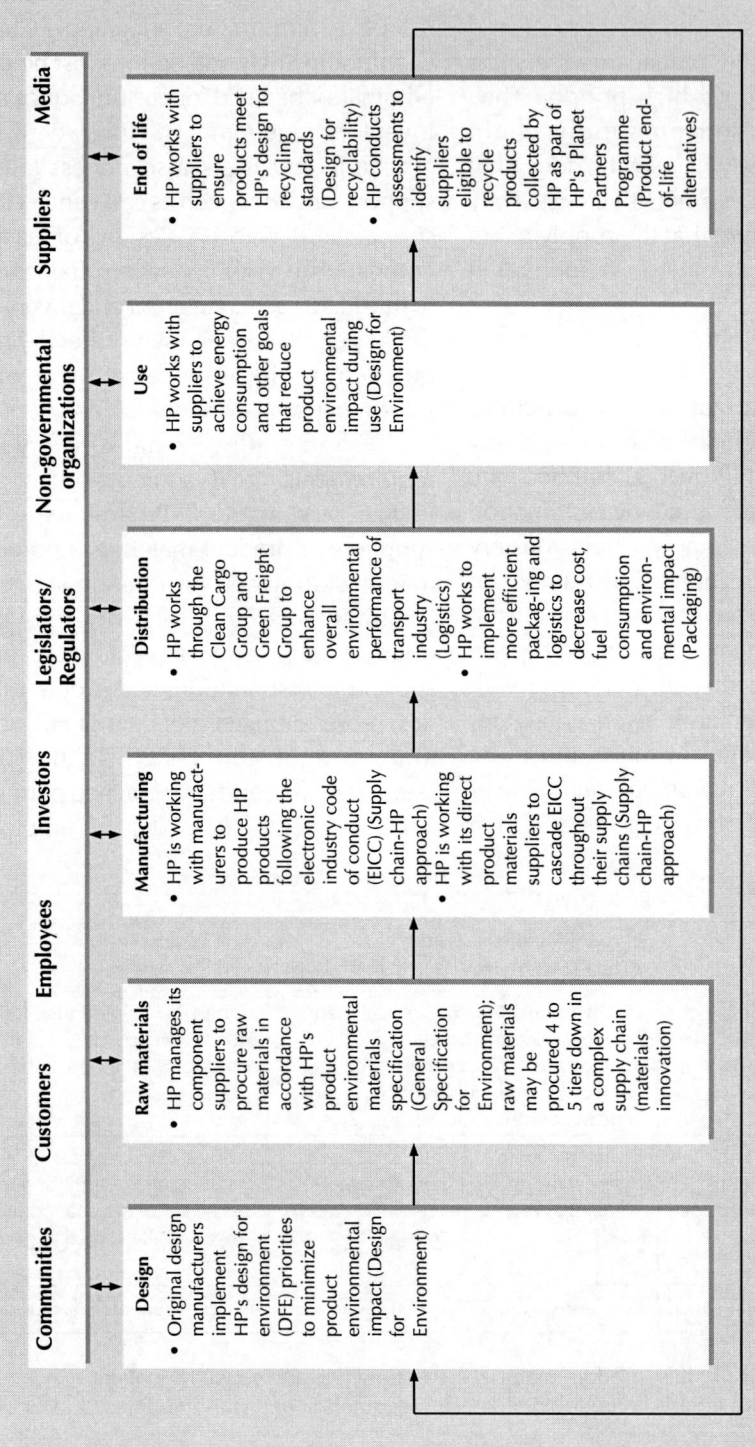

FIG. 1.11 Social and environmental responsibility (SER) expectations for HP suppliers across the HP product life cycle
Source: Based on HP's Global Citizenship Report 2006, 2007, and 2008

based approach to prioritize the implementation of the SER programme with tier 1 suppliers, who would then train the tier 2 suppliers in SER. Throughout 2008, HP audited 142 suppliers at 246 high-risk sites in different countries, out of which 85 suppliers would be reaudited at 122 sites in 2009. Four hundred and forty four low-risk suppliers are already engaged and assessed, i.e., no audits are necessary for them. However, 20 new suppliers are to be audited at 27 high-risk sites in 2009. To raise the standards in supply chain, audits are also done with respect to EICC. Capacity building in SER has been accomplished by various projects in collaboration with local organizations, e.g., workers' training and the Focused Improvement Supplier Initiative (FISI) in China, the hard-disk drive supply chain in Southeast Asia, the Central Europe Supplier Responsibility (CESR) project, and the Health Enables Returns project in Mexico.

Discussion Questions

1. Comment upon the structure and complexity of supply chain requirements at Hewlett-Packard (HP) that makes supply chain mastery at HP an imperative discipline.
2. What are the special programmes at HP that facilitate implementation of HP's strategies and policies towards SCM?
3. How does HP avoid concentration of sources at one place in the globe? How are the sourcing partners distributed globally? What do you think could be reasons for this kind of distribution?
4. Critically analyse as to how HP discharges its social and environmental responsibility through its suppliers across its product life cycles.
5. What are the kinds of benefits which HP reaped by mastering the art and science of SCM?

INDIAN CASE STUDY

AMUL[11]

Overview

The Gujarat Cooperative Milk Marketing Federation (GCMMF) or commonly referred to as Amul, collects 4,47,000 litres of milk from 2.12 million farmers, converts the milk into branded, packaged products and delivers products worth Rs 6 crore to over 5,00,000 retail outlets across the country daily. Its supply chain would be easily one of the most complicated in the world.

Every GCMMF office displays a photograph that shows a long queue of Gujarati women waiting patiently for the union vehicle to come and collect the milk they have brought in shining oval brass containers. Amul never forgets its primary supplier, i.e., the farmer and it is a whopping Rs 2200 crore (Rs 22 billion) enterprise. The GCMMF now has 2.12 million farmers, 10,441 milk collection centres in villages, and 14 district level unions and their plants.

History

It was way back in December 1946 that a group of farmers from the village of Anand, in order to free themselves from intermediaries and gain access to markets to get due returns, started the Kaira District Milk Cooperative Union. It then joined hands with other milk cooperatives and made the GCMMF. Today 2.12 million farmers, 10,441 milk collection centres at village level, and 14 district level unions. Markets were relatively more primitive and poor in infrastructure. The federation felt that they just could not leave it to market forces and that a proactive strategy was required.

---

[11] *Source:* This case has been adapted from the case, 'The extraordinary story of Amul', *The Smart Manager*, September 2005, with the kind permission of its author, Prof. Pankaj Chandra, Director, IIM, Bangalore. The author expresses acknowledgement and thanks to Prof. Chandra

The Business Strategy and the Market Segment

The GCMMF identified two key action areas under the strategy.

(i) Matching demand and supply that would need heavy investment and the simultaneous development of suppliers and consumers

(ii) To engage professional managers and technocrats for effective management of the network and commercial viability

A hierarchical network of the cooperatives was developed while still retaining the focus on farmers. The vast supply chain of Amul has a spread from small suppliers to large fragmented markets. Although GCMMF is directly responsible only for a small part of the chain, a number of distributors, retailers, and third-party logistics (3PL) providers play a bigger role. Managing supply chain effectively and efficiently is critical as GCMMF's competitive position is driven by low consumer prices supported by a low cost system.

Initially, when Amul was formed, consumers had limited purchasing power and modest consumption levels of milk and dairy products. Then, with growth, Amul developed a low-cost price strategy making its products affordable and ensuring value for money for their customers. Making a product base with liquid milk, Amul enhanced its product mix through the progressive addition of higher value products while maintaining the desired growth in existing products. It has competition in high value dairy segments from giants like HUL, Britannia, and Nestle. However, GCMMF makes sure that the product mix is consistent with its basic value of providing milk at an affordable price.

The Federation uses Amul as an *umbrella brand* which covers various product categories produced by various unions like liquid milk, butter, ghee, cheese, cocoa products, sweets, ice-cream and condensed milk. Amul's sub-brands include variants, such as Amulya, Amulspray, Amulspree,

and Nutramul. Edible oil products are branded Dhara and Lokdhara, mineral water is sold as Jal Dhara, and fruit drinks bear the brand name of Safal. By following an umbrella branding, GCMMF has been able to avoid inter union conflicts at the same time facilitating them to develop and improve products.

Distribution Network

As pointed out earlier, Amul products are available in over 5,00,000 retail outlets across India through its network of over 3500 distributors. There are 47 depots with dry and cold warehouses to buffer inventory of the entire range of products.

The GCMMF transacts on an advance demand draft basis from its wholesale dealers instead of the cheque system adopted by other major FMCG companies. This practice is consistent with GCMMF's philosophy of maintaining cash transactions throughout the supply chain and it also minimizes the inventory levels.

Wholesale dealers carry inventory that is just adequate to meet the transit time from the branch warehouse to their premises. The JIT inventory levels help improve the dealers' ROI.

Managing the Supply Chain Network

Given the large number of entities in the supply chain and the need for decentralized responsibility for various activities, effective coordination is critical for efficiency and cost control. GCMMF and the unions jointly achieve the desired degree of control. The unions get assured buy-ins as the plans are approved by the GCMMF's board. It is drawn from the heads of all the unions, and the boards of the unions comprise of farmers elected through village societies, thereby creating control through interlocking.

While the unions coordinate the supply side activities, the federation handles the distribution of end products and coordination with the retailers and dealers. The activities include monitoring milk collection contractors, the supply of animal feed and other supplies, provision of veterinary services, and educational activities.

Managing Third-party Logistics (3PL) Providers

The union's core competence activity lies in milk processing and the production of dairy products. Accordingly, marketing efforts including brand development were assumed by the GCMMF. All other activities were entrusted to third parties. These include logistics of milk collection, distribution of dairy products, sale of end products through dealers and retail stores, provision of animal feed, and veterinary services.

It is worth noticing that a number of these third parties are not in the organized sector and many are not professionally managed, with little regard for quality and service. This is a particularly critical issue in the logistics and transport of a perishable commodity where the basic infrastructure is already ridden with weaknesses.

Establishing Best Practices

A key source of competitive advantage has been the GCMMF's ability to continuously implement best practices across all elements of the network: the federation itself, the unions, the village societies, and the distribution channel.

In developing these practices, the federation and the unions have adapted some of the global best practices. It could be the implementation of small group activities or quality circles at the federation or a total quality management (TQM) programme at the unions or housekeeping and good accounting practices at the village society level.

More importantly, the network has been able to regularly roll out improvement programmes across to a large number of members and the implementation rate is consistently high. For example, every Friday, between 10.00 a.m. and 11.00 a.m., all employees of GCMMF meet without fail at the closest office, be it a department or a branch or a depot, to discuss their various quality concerns. Each meeting has its pre-set format in terms of purpose, agenda, and limit (PAL) with a process check at the end to record how the meeting was conducted. Similar processes are in place at the village societies, the unions, and up to the wholesaler and clearing and forwarding (C&F) agent levels.

Examples of benefits reaped from recent initiatives include reduction in transportation time from the depots to the wholesale dealers, improvement in ROI of wholesale dealers, implementation of zero stock-out through improved availability of products at depots, and also the implementation of JIT in finance to reduce the float.

Kaizens—the continuous improvement projects at the unions, have helped improve the quality of milk in terms of acidity and sourness that it may have. For example, Sabar Union's records show a reduction from 2.0 per cent to 0.5 per cent in the amount of sour milk/curd received at the union.

The most impressive aspect of this big time roll out is that improvement processes are turning the village societies into individual improvement centres.

Technology and E-initiatives

GCMMF's technology strategy is characterized by distinct components, namely new products, process technology, and complementary assets to enhance milk production and e-commerce.

Only a few dairies of the world may have as wide a variety of products as produced by the GCMMF network. Village societies are encouraged through subsidies to install chilling units. Automation in processing and packaging areas is common as is the Hazard Analysis Critical Control Point (HACCP) certification. Amul actively pursues developments in embryo transfer and cattle breeding in order to improve cattle quality and increase in milk yields.

GCMMF has been one of the first Indian FMCG firms to employ Internet technologies to implement B2C commerce. Today customers can order a variety of products through the Internet and still be assured of timely delivery with cash payment upon receipt. Another e-initiative underway at GCMMF is to provide farmers access to information relating to markets, technology, and best practices in the dairy industry through Net enabled kiosks in the village.

It has also implemented a geographical information system (GIS) at both ends of the supply chain, which are milk sourcing, collection as well as the marketing processes aimed at delivery to customers.

Farmers now have better access to information on the output as well as support services which helps them in better product mix, planning, and marketing.

Discussion Questions

1. Why should a company such as Amul undertake a strategic management initiative of SCM?
2. Comment on the distribution network and its challenges at Amul.
3. Name some best practices in management in use in Amul which result in better performance of the supply chain.
4. How can initiatives based on information technology (IT) facilitate better management of the supply chain in a dairy industry unit such as Amul?

REFERENCES

Accenture India (2002), 'Logistics Infrastructure and 3PLs', *ETIG Knowledge Series on Supply Charts & Logistics*, pp. 50–51.

Ayers, James B. and Mary Ann Odegaard (2007), *Retail Supply Chain Management*, Auerbach Publishers.

Bender, Paul S. (March 2000), 'Debunking 5 Supply Chain Myths', *Supply Chain Management Review 4*, No. 1, pp. 52–58.

Bovet, David and Yossi Sheffi (Spring 1998), 'The Brave New World of Supply Chain Management', *Supply Chain Management Review*, pp. 14–20.

Bozarth, Cecil C. and Robert B. Handfield (2006), *Introduction to Operations and Supply Chain Management*, Pearson Education, New Delhi.

Burt, David N., Donald W. Dobler, and Stephen I. Starling (2006), *World Class Supply Management: The Key to Supply Chain Management*, Tata McGraw-Hill, New Delhi.

Centre for Monitoring Indian Economy (CMIE).

Chopra, Sunil and Peter Meindl (2007), *Supply Chain Management—Strategy, Planning and Operation*, 3rd Edition, Prentice Hall of India, New Delhi.

Copacino, William C. (1997), *Supply Chain Management: The Basics and Beyond*, St. Lucie Ben, Florida.

Coyle, John J., Edward J. Bardi, and C. John Langley Jr. (2003), *The Management of Business Logistics*, 7th Edition, South Western Press.

Dornier, Phillippe-Pierre, Ricardo Ernst, Michel Fender, and Panos Kouvelis (1998), *Global Operations and Logistics: Text and Cares*, New York, Wiley.

Fawcett, Stanley E. and Gregory M. Magnan (2001), 'Achieving World Class Supply Chain Alignment: Benefits, Barriers and Bridges', CAPS Research, Arizona.

Fisher, Marshall, L. (March–August 1997), 'What is the Right Supply Chain for Your Product', *Harvard Business Review*, pp. 83–93.

Fleischmann, Bernhard and Herbert Meyr (2003), 'Planning, Hiearchy, Modeling and Advanced Planning Systems', *Handbook on Operations Research and Management,* Vol. 11, pp. 455–523.

Handfield, Robert B. and Ernest L. Nichols (2005), *Introduction to Supply Chain Management,* Prentice Hall of India, New Delhi.

Houlihan, John B. (1985), 'International Supply Chain Management', *International Journal of Physical Distribution and Materials Management,* Vol. 15, No. 1, pp. 22–38.

Kauffman, Ralph G. (2002), 'Supply Management: What's in a Name or Do We Know Who We Are?', *Journal of Supply Chain Management,* Vol. 38, Issue 4, pp. 46–50.

Kurien, Verghese and J. Patel (February–March 2007), 'Amul: Taste of India', *The Smart Manager,* Mumbai.

Lambert Douglas M., James R. Stock, and Lisa M. Ellram (1998), *Fundamentals of Logistics Management,* Irwin/McGraw Hill, Boston, pp. 8–28.

Larson, Paul D. and Ami Halldorssun (2002), 'What is SCM? and, Where is It?', *Journal of Supply Chain Management,* Vol. 38, Issue 4, pp. 36–44.

Lee Hau, L. (Spring 2002), 'Aligning Supply Chain Strategies with Product Uncertainties', *California Management Review,* pp. 105–109.

Magretta, J. (September–October 1998), 'Fast, Global and Entrepreneurial Supply Chain Management: Hong Kong Style', *Harvard Business Review,* 76, No. 5, pp. 102–109.

Marien, Edward J. (March–April 2000), 'The Four Supply Chain Enablers', *Supply Chain Management Review,* pp. 60–68.

Mentzer, John T. (2001), *Supply Chain Management,* Response Books, New Delhi.

Mohanty, R.P., and S.G. Deshmukh (2001), *Essentials of Supply Chain Management,* Phoenix Publishing, New Delhi.

Nahmias, S. (1997), *Production and Operations Analysis,* Irwin/McGraw-Hill, Burr Ridge, Illinois.

Raguraman, G., and J. Shah (2004), 'Road-map for Logistics Excellence: Need to Break the Unholy Equilibrium', Working Paper, IIM Ahmedabad, No. 2004-08-02.

Sahay, B.S. (Ed.) (2004), *Emerging Issues in Supply Chain Management,* Macmillan, New Delhi.

Sautter, E.I., A. Maltz, and K. Boverg (August 1999), 'A Customer Service Course: Bringing Marketing and Logistics Together', *Journal of Marketing Education,* No. 21.

Sharma, Sunil (March 2005), 'Report Submitted to University Grants Commission on 'Supply Chain Management Practices in Indian Industry' under UGC Research Award, New Delhi.

Stadler, H. (16 June 2005), 'Supply Chain Management and Advanced Planning—Basics, Overview and Challenges', *European Journal of Operational Research,* Vol. 163, Issue 3, pp. 575–588.

Internet Resources

accenture.com/countries/India/Research_and_insights/challenges opportunities as accessed on 4 July 2008

www.clml.org

www.economywatch.com as accessed on 27 September 2008

www.etig.com as accessed on 27 September 2008

www.etintelligence.com as accessed on 27 September 2008

www.flextronics.com/en/markets/logistics/performancedrivers as accessed on 19 June 2009

www.hp.com/hpinfo/globalcitizenship/environment/supplychain/ as accessed on 2 April 2008

www.indianrail.gov.in as accessed on 27 September 2008

www.ism.ws (Institute for Supply Management)

www.managing_automation.com as accessed on
   22 September 2008
www.manufacturing.net/scm (Cahners Publishing,
   Supply Chain Management Review and other
   resources)www.supplychainaccess.com
   (Aberdeen Group)

www.nhai.org as accessed on 27 September 2008
www.supply-chain.org
www.weforum.org/en/initiatives/gcp as accessed
   on 27 September 2008

2 Dynamics of SCM

Supply chain management (SCM) is a very dynamic process in terms of the flows involved, the performance at the levels of time, place, delivery, cost, and service and the overall inbound and outbound logistics and operations synchronized purchasing and procurement involved. This becomes more challenging particularly in an IT-enabled environment and even more so in a lean economy. The customer wants to have the best value from the delivery of order. The supply chain needs alignment at its different stages in terms of price, transportation, inventory levels, and the ownership involved. It could well be in terms of the trade-offs in the number of purchase orders versus the inventory levels carried, and quantity discounts versus the savings accrued due to reduced inventories. It could also refer to the extent of consolidation of freight versus the traffic, transportation, and administrative costs associated with delivery of small quantities. Only a shared initiative across different companies to manage inventory and transportation could serve the purpose but it would entail sharing of information, e.g., that of location of their suppliers and customers as also their production schedules, marketing and sales plans, and distribution network. A shared initiative, such as effective customer response (ECR) would involve real-time coordination, collaboration, and sharing of information.

Uncertainities and variations in supply chain could also comprise financial or operational risks. There could be a distortion in demand or *phantom* (inflated) demands created due to tendencies, such as order batching, fluctuations in pricing, non-availability of point-of-sale (PoS) data at the retailing end, leading to inaccurate demand forecasting. Other risk creating factors can be lack of infrastructure for supply, logistics and distribution, third-party logistics provisions, and promotional pricing. So, most of the SCM decisions are process-based and are dynamic in the sense that real-time data about demand, supply, production schedules, inventory lot sizes, ordering, inventory and transportation costs, and pricing is required, ideally by all the channel partners and it needs to be shared. A regular data upload is required by downstream members about the sales at their points, its patterns, current stock levels, stock-outs, if any, the demand forecasted, and the size and timing of order to be put. The focal firm may need to upload data about the production plans, pricing, transportation schedules, and delivery plans which retailers can download.

These dynamic decisions are enabled by information and communication technology (ICT), which invariably involves electronic data interchange (EDI) across all the channel partners, downstream and upstream.

The reverse logistics, if any, of product returns, recalls, empty containers, cash refunds, rebates, and discounts from downstream to upstream could turn supply chain processes further dynamic. A supply chain operating reference model helps us to decipher the complexity of supply chain processes and break them into their different levels.

SUPPLY CHAIN PROCESS CYCLES

There are four clearly defined process cycles in a supply chain from downstream to upstream. They are the *customer order cycle* from the customer to the retailer, the *replenishment cycle* from the retailer to the distributor, the *manufacturing order cycle* from the distributor to the manufacturer, and finally the *procurement cycle* from the manufacturer to the supplier. These cycles, respectively, occur at the intersection of two successive stages, namely customer, retailer, distributor, manufacturer, and supplier as shown in Fig. 2.1.

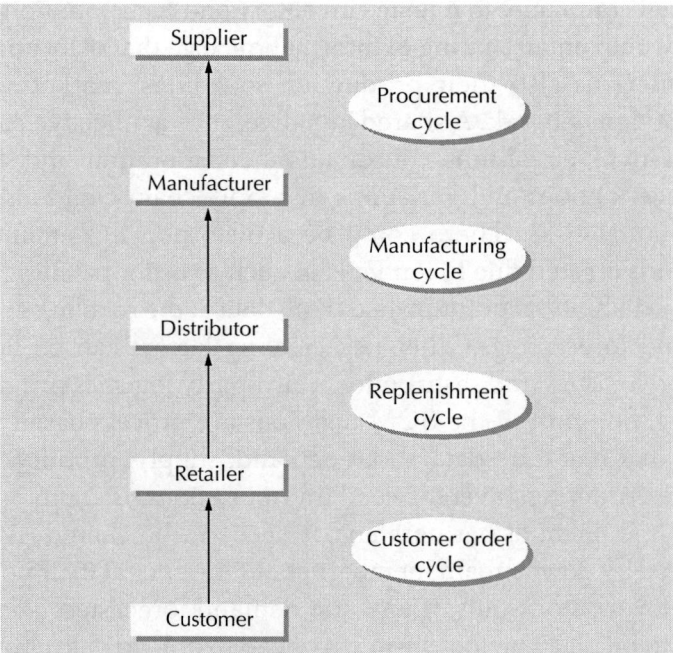

FIG. 2.1   Supply chain process cycles

However, not every supply chain may have all the four cycles clearly demarcated. Companies that do direct sales and book orders on Internet may resort to techniques like 'drop-shipping' where they may bypass the retailer and distributor and thus avoid any storage and warehousing, making the order delivery direct to the customer and at minimum time and cost. The cycle view takes into account the operational decisions because it clearly specifies the roles and responsibilities of each member of the supply chain.

It is interesting to note that any member of the supply chain can be a supplier or customer according to the transaction involved. For example, when a customer places order with Dell, he is the buyer but Dell is the supplier, while if Dell places an order with its distributor for replenishment meant for direct supplies to the customer, it acts as a buyer and the distributor as the supplier. Within each cycle, the primary goal of the buyer is to ensure product availability but with economies of scale in ordering. The supplier must try to forecast customer orders as accurately as possible by sharing regular information with buyers or customers. The supplier, on receipt of order, must execute order fulfilment in an efficient manner. The buyer, on the other hand, must reduce the cost and time of order receiving. As is evident from the process cycles, when we move from the customer to the supplier, the individual orders get merged and the order size increases or gets even inflated or 'ballooned up' mostly due to tendencies for order batching by individual members (bullwhip effect as will be discussed later in this chapter). In order to avoid this effect, sharing of information and inventory policies across the various supply chain stages becomes important as we move from the customer to the supplier.

The cyclical view thus defines the processes involved, the ownership of each process as also the desired outcome at each stage. Ultimately, the infrastructural requirements could also be outlined thereby helping in setting the information systems to support the supply chain operations at each stage.

As has already been pointed out in the previous chapter, a supply chain may involve various flows, e.g., those of materials, components, products, services, and information related to sales/demand forecasting and scheduling of operations and deliveries including reverse flows number of times. It is therefore important to study each supply chain process at its elemental level, which the supply chain operations reference (SCOR) approach aims at. The process cycles thus form the basis of the SCOR model discussed in detail in Chapter 7. Needless to mention, the supply chain partners would require availability of timely and adequate information and infrastructural resources at their respective stages to take decisions related to order fulfilment in an efficient manner at their respective points.

Need for Supply Chain Alignment

Since the process or cyclical view clearly defines the ownership of the processes at each stage and clearly outlines the roles and responsibilities of the process owner or channel partner as also the desired outcome from each stage, it becomes important that supply chain partners align their processes with respect to their desired goals in the supply chain. While doing so, not only individual objectives are seen but also overall channel goals are set as target and no channel member does any alignment activity that goes against the overall supply chain goals. In a way, supply chain alignment refers to coordination of efforts in terms of pricing, transportation, inventory planning, and ownership amongst upstream and downstream channel partners. One of the common impediments for channel alignment is 'order batching' by the downstream members for reasons of economies in ordering costs and transportation costs. However, with new technologies such as EDI since information from PoS is possible, the ordering costs can be reduced drastically and correct lot-sizing be done for ordering, while with use of freight-consolidation, it is not necessary to order a full truck load, instead load consolidation on a milk run basis could be organized from multiple suppliers on a frequent basis aided by the third-party logistics (3PL) providers.

In terms of price, normally a value-pricing strategy is preferred over promotional pricing as with stabilized pricing, sales patterns will have less variations, thereby minimizing distortions in supply chain and bringing about alignment. Promotional pricing may motivate customers to buy in large batches and store items for future use (forward buying) or customers may go in for quantity discounts to avail low prices and thus order for higher quantities. In these cases, retailers should stabilize their sales patterns by offering a more stable value pricing than promotional pricing campaigns as channel alignment in terms of the inventory level and transportation and logistics requirements becomes less accurate in the latter cases.

According to Gattorna (1998), the focus in supply chain alignment is on integrative and relational partnership, collaboration, and customer-supplier integration. These also act as prime enablers of business success. Better the alignment between partners and inter organizational arrangements, better would be the bottom-line performance. Fawcett and Magnan (2001) refer to supply chain alignment as 'all endeavours to align objectives and integrate resources of suppliers and customers across organizational boundaries to create and deliver the discrete values as demanded by customer.' Alignment is also in terms of strategic response and reactivity to the demand. The strategic supply chain alignment is aimed at improving relationship between markets, strategy, culture, and leadership. The model must be dynamic in response to future changes in the market, i.e., in implementing alignment strategy to fast moving market conditions. So, supply chain alignment both in tactical and strategic terms is a part of the dynamic SCM.

Another way to align the channels particularly at retail level is that the company allocates stock or order size to the retailer on the basis of past sales records rather than just on the basis of what they (the retailers) order. Too much variation in sales patterns at the retailers' end and thus a varying order pattern from them would spoil all the efforts undertaken by the focal firm towards channel alignment. Also, all the causes leading to bullwhip effect, as will be discussed later in this chapter, e.g., faulty information sharing and shortage gaming, have to be eliminated for channel alignment. The results of supply chain alignment in terms of reduction in inventory levels, safety stock, and improved forecasting can also be facilitated if channel members give consideration to the following.

1. Economy in packaging and transportation
2. Carrying out concurrent and parallel processing rather than a serial one always and even delaying differentiation/final assembly till the retailer's end to promote cheaper transportation of bulk materials/grey stock and promote customization
3. Standardization in parts, product, processes, and procurements by using common standard modules as much as possible

The products, their parts or modules can be (re)designed so that they can be efficiently packed, stored, and transported. Products that can be packed more compactly are cheaper to transport. Products with their packaging should occupy less of cubic space rather than their weight in the delivery vehicle. Compact packing of products would help in stacking, thereby helping in reducing the inventory costs, such as handling cost and space per product and hence the rent per unit of product and increase in revenue per square foot of space increase. Compact and standard designs of products together with their packaging would also facilitate in cross-docking (cross-docking refers to moving goods from one truck, e.g., from supplier to another set of trucks going to individual retail stores). The boxes or pallets are directly taken off from an incoming truck and loaded on to the outgoing truck. It may basically involve positioning, lifting, and transfer (PLT) of goods which would involve less time and costs if products with their packaging have been appropriately (re)designed. This, in the first instance, may seem to be a far-fetched conclusion but is true in its impact on channel alignment particularly in terms of reduction in inventory levels at different points of the supply chain and making it trim at all levels. Also, a postponed final assembly or differentiation of the product till the retailer's end particularly with the use of standard modular products and parts would facilitate reduction in inventory levels and in safety stock requirements, and allowing better control, delivery, and service level of orders (also reducing administrative and processing lead times), thus resulting in better supply chain alignment.

ORDER MANAGEMENT PROCESS

The customer demand is captured by the order processing system, which in turn drives the logistical sequence of order picking and assembling followed by the order delivery at the customer's point. Expedient order processing is at the core of customer service and represents a significant portion of order fulfilment process. Reduction in order processing time has reduced the net time for order fulfilment. Use of fast communication and delivery means has enabled the corporate to keep the order processing time still lower.

Need for Order Management

This would help the company to attain the following goals.

1. Obtain global demand visibility across channels, partners and divisions.
2. Enable multi-channel order capture, order collaboration, and order management.
3. Execute multi-source order monitoring and fulfilment at the product line item level.
4. Accept and manage order modification throughout the entire fulfilment process.
5. Control personalization, customization, and brand across a dispersed fulfilment network.

Components of Order Processing

Once the order is captured by the system of the vendor company, order processing begins. It includes a sequence of activities, namely a formal order preparation, its internal transmission to the order handling department followed by validation and configuration check of the order, back-order management, if needed, followed by pricing, credit and product checks, order confirmation, filling, and delivery.

(i) Order preparation: It refers to filling the order form by telephone/fax/mail or on computer (Web-enabled or network-enabled EDI order).
(ii) Order transmission: It involves transferring the order from the point of origin to where the order entry can be handled. It may be done manually or electronically.
(iii) Order entry: It can be described in terms of the following four parts.

   (a) Checking configurational accuracy of the order for completeness and technical compatibility
   (b) Checking availability of the requirement
   (c) Back-order/cancellation, if necessary

   (d) Customer credit history and status
   (e) Pricing the order with company policy/contractual/quantity or bulk and promotional discounts, if any
   (f) Checking the availability of product; whether made-to-stock/order
   (g) Internal order approval and confirmation by customer

(iv) Order filling: It refers to fulfilling the order by picking, assembling, and dispatching it.

(v) Order status reporting: It can be divided into the following two parts.

   (a) Tracing and tracking the order
   (b) Communicating with customers regarding the order status

Order processing activities serve as a framework for logistics control. Proper management of order processing activities can improve customer service and simultaneously reduce inventory levels and ultimately customer delivery lead time.

Measures of Order Fulfilment

There are two measures of order fulfilment:

- Line fill rate
- Order fill rate

Both of these parameters indicate the degree to which the warehousing/inventory management system would be able to fulfil the orders placed in a certain expected time. These factors, in turn, indicate the system's ability to anticipate the demand from the retailers' or customers' downstream. These two fill rates can be expressed as the following.

$$\text{Line fill rate} = \frac{\text{Total number of units recieved}}{\text{Total number of units ordered}}$$

$$\text{Order fill rate} = \frac{\text{Number of SKU categories for which 100\% of ordered units are received}}{\text{Total number of SKU categories ordered}}$$

(where SKU refers to a stock-keeping unit. Each SKU is a unique identifier attached to an item, variant, product line, bundle, fee, or attachment at the given geographical location, such as a warehouse or retail store but not the bins in the same area.)

The order fill rate is a more differentiating measure of inventory management service level. It is possible to have a high line fill rate but a low order fill rate at the same time. However, the reverse could hardly be true. While planning a logistic system, a fill rate should always be fixed as a target. Different inventory management systems can be compared on the basis of fill rates and the inventory level required to obtain these rates. Efficiency of an inventory management system, depends on the inventory levels kept for maintaining fill rates. Lower levels are better. This can be accomplished by accurate forecasting and reducing the lead time, which are the hallmark objectives of SCM.

Benefits of Good Order Management

Better order management could help the company to achieve the following.

- Reduce inventory safety stocks and buffer
  - better collaboration with suppliers
  - multisite inventory visibility
- Reduce operational, purchasing, order expenditure, and inventory management costs
  - manage by exception across the supply network
- Shorter inbound fulfilment lead times
  - compress the plant purchase order pipeline
- Increase supplies fill rates
  - improve visibility into supply sources and status
- Customer orientation in terms of the services and facilitation offered

Effective management of order processing is critical to the maintenance of good customer relationships. Both shortening the order cycle times and improving its consistent predictability in terms of its fill and delivery are important to customers and result in lower inventory requirements.

Customer Orientation in Order Management

The objectives of customer orientation to be accomplished in order management are to

- increase customer and channel satisfaction;
- execute flawless fill and delivery of each customer order;
- build seamless customer experience across multiple channels; and
- provide global visibility to order status and ability to modify for all participants.

SUPPLY CHAIN INTEGRATION—THE PUSH AND PULL MECHANISMS

The key challenge in supply chain is to coordinate different activities, such as reducing cost, increasing sevice level, reducing the bullwhip effect (discussed in the next section), and better utilization of resources at different points in the supply chain, i.e., suppliers, manufacturers, distributors, and retailers. This not only needs coordinated decision-making in procurement, manufacturing, replenishment, and order fulfilment but more importantly, integrating the front end, i.e., the customer demand and ordering part of the supply chain with the back end or the production and distribution and procurement part of the supply chain.

This integration can be accomplished in terms of the *push, pull* or *push–pull* mechanisms. In a push mechanism, the supply chain processes are initiated in anticipation of customer orders or forecasted demand. These processes are proactive processes and are in anticipation of demand. In a pull mechanism, the supply chain processes are initiated only in response to a customer demand or order. These are, hence, reactive processes that react in response to actual demand or PoS data. In reality, however, for better supply chain integration and better service levels, a push–pull boundary concept might be adopted in which supply chain processes on the customer side, e.g., order fulfilment, are on pull basis, while those on the supplies, production, and replenishment side are normally push-based for better supply chain planning, production scheduling, and replenishment at the distributor or retailer end.

In a build-to-order company such as Dell, which sells directly to customers, the orders are not fulfilled from the finished goods inventory but directly from production. The arrival of an order directly triggers the production. The order fulfilment and manufacturing are thus pull-based, depending on the orders received but procurement and transportation of *(generic or family)* components from suppliers are push-based or forecast-based, mainly, because of the supply delivery lead times and the need to maintain a buffer between pull and push systems. Also, the aggregate forecasts tend to be more accurate. According to Nahmias (1997), the aggregation of demand for generic components is more accurate. The pull processes start from the assembly and continue till the final assembly as a part of the postponement strategy in response to the varying customer needs and demand patterns and also so that the product does not undergo design obsolescence. Therefore, uncertainty in demand of components or generic stock is much smaller than the uncertainty in demand of final products. This leads to safe stock reduction. The pull-based postponement or delayed differentiation, in addition to Dell, is followed by companies, such as Benetton, Levi's, Asian Paints, and Hewlett-Packard.

Supply Chain Integration through Macro Level Processes

There are three key processes at the macro level in a supply chain. For a supply chain to be effective and efficient, it is imperative that all these processes are well integrated. The organization structure as also the culture should provide for good communication and coordination between the owners of these macro-processes that interact with each other. These processes are behind the flow of information, materials, products, returns, cash, credit, and order in a desirable direction to fulfil a customer's order. The three processes are the following.

Customer Relationship Management Processes

These processes aim to generate customer demand and facilitate placement and tracking of order and study of buying patterns. It includes sub-processes, such as sales and marketing, call centre management, and order management. Customer relationship management (CRM) is discussed in detail in Chapter 6.

Internal Supply Chain Processes

These processes operate at the core level of the focal firm that provides interface to suppliers on one side and to retailers and customers on the other. These processes are meant to fulfil the customer's order at minimum cost and maximum service levels and also increase the profitability of the supply chain as such and sharing the risks and rewards on a pooled basis, not just on individual basis. In fact, any attempt by any member to increase only his profitability would result in a decrease in the overall supply chain profitability. These processes may include master demand and supply planning, production planning and scheduling, distribution planning and scheduling, IT-enablement and extending it across and outside the organization, internal order fulfilment, and field service. These processes have been referred to in Chapter 1.

Supplier Relationship Management Processes

These processes provide interfaces with suppliers and include sub-processes, such as sourcing, negotiation for price and delivery, collaborative EDI for design and supply as also the placement and follow-up of replenishment orders with them. The supplier relationship management (SRM) has been discussed in detail in Chapter 5.

BULLWHIP/WHIPLASH/WHIPSAW EFFECT IN SUPPLY CHAIN

It refers to the increase in variance in the demand as one moves up in the supply chain from retailers to distributors/company's warehouses. The phenomenon has been observed by companies such as HP and P&G and is represented by the figure that follows (Fig. 2.2).

P&G observed this phenomenon while studying replenishment patterns for 'Pampers' disposable diapers. Demand for diapers is pretty steady so one may assume that variance should be low across the supply chain but it was not so. P&G were surprised to see that the orders placed by distributors had much more variation than sales at the retail stores. Further, order of materials to suppliers had even greater

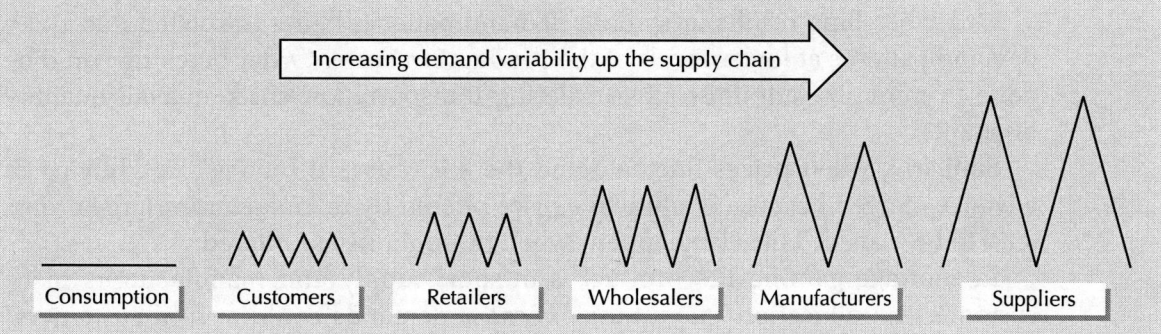

FIG. 2.2 Information distortion: The bullwhip effect

variability. Similarly, HP experienced the bullwhip effect in the pattern of sales of its printers. Orders placed by a retailer exhibited wider swings than the actual retail sales and orders placed by the printer division to the company's integrated circuit (IC) division had even wider swings.

One key reason for this effect could be the tendency of lower levels in the supply chain to batch orders. Bullwhip effect also causes inflated levels of inventories. To address this problem, many companies have adopted the efficient consumer response (ECR) system which has been discussed in the next section of the chapter.

Causes of Bullwhip Effect

According to Lee, Padmanabhan, and Whang (1997), there are four basic causes of bullwhip effect, namely

- faulty demand forecast updating
- order batching
- price fluctuations
- shortage gaming

Demand forecasts at each stage of the supply chain (SC) are the result of demands observed one level downstream. When each individual in a supply chain determines one's demand level forecasts, the bullwhip effect occurs. The retailer builds safety stocks for protection against uncertainty in consumer demand. The distributor observes these swings in the orders of the retailer and builds even larger safety stocks and so on, resulting in inflated demands at the supplier's (to the focal firm) level. Only at the retailer's end direct data about consumer demand is available. Lack of demand forecast updates has been found to be the key cause of bullwhip effect in packaged and non-packaged goods category in a multi-location retail supply chain network in India (in a study conducted by Mittal (2010) and supervised by the author).

Order batching results in smooth demand patterns being translated into spiky demand patterns at lower levels of the product structure. Order batching could be done to minimize administrative/ordering/transportation costs or avail quantity discounts.

Similarly, when prices fluctuate and there is 'forward buying', i.e., buying in advance of need because of attractive price offered by manufacturers, large orders tend to be placed. This also happens when promotions are offered.

In shortage gaming the product is in short supply and manufacturers place customers on allocation/quota basis. *Phantom* demands could arise if customers/ retailers inflate their orders in the anticipation of a shortfall. So, if they expect to receive only half of the quantity ordered, they would simply double the size of their orders or as is common, orders can be cancelled by retailers when anticipated demands do not materialise into orders.

Initiatives to Control Bullwhip Effect

Lee, Padmanabham, and Whang (1997) recommend four initiatives to control the bullwhip effect.

Information Sharing

All business partners must share their PoS data and base forecasts on this data only. Information sharing could be done through EDI, which can be Web-enabled. In short, forecasting and inventory should be on a collaborative basis between suppliers, focal firm, and retailers.

Channel Alignment

It refers to alignment of supply chain in terms of coordination of efforts in form of pricing, transportation, inventory planning, and ownership between upstream and downstream sites in the supply chain. The tendency to batch ordering can be eliminated through the following given measures.

(i) Reducing fixed costs of ordering and order processing and follow-up, preferably through EDI.

(ii) Consolidation of freight, e.g., rather than ordering one truckload of single item, multiple assortment of limited quantities of different items can still make one truckload and fulfil transportation economies, i.e., individual items can be ordered on demand basis only over a period of time, not on batching the quantity.

Provision of 3PL Services

This can help companies keep logistics movements from multiple suppliers using minimum transportation trips or at best, using a hub for it that reduces the costs on a long-term basis to the buying company as well as reduces average inventory levels and the need to store and warehouse it.

Discouragement of Promotional Pricing

In case of promotional pricing, customers tend to buy in large batches and even store items for further use. For this, pricing has to be stabilized. Promotional pricing should be discouraged. Rather, a constant value pricing strategy must be followed, as is being done by manufacturers such as P&G, Pillsbury, etc. Some retailers such as Macy's follow everyday low pricing. So whatever pricing they follow, it must be *stabilized pricing* in order to avoid sudden spikier demand patterns at the customer's/retailer's level which results in bullwhip effect.

Discouragement of Shortage Gaming

In case of anticipated shortages also, customers tend to place inflated or phantom demands. One way to reduce it is to allocate quantities based on *past sales records* at a certain retailer rather than just on the basis of orders. This will reduce the tendency of lower level supply chain members to exaggerate orders and thus eliminate bullwhip effect.

SCM AND EFFICIENT CONSUMER RESPONSE IN INDIA

ECR movement began in 1993 in the grocery industry of the US and spread to Europe in 1994 and then to Asia in 1996. The beginning of the movement was characterized by the emergence of new principle of collaborative management along the supply chain. The movement, where competing manufacturers came together to ensure efficient distribution logistics, was started for enhancing the value offering to the end-customer by increasing the efficiency of supply chain thereby, to keep cost low and high merchandise availability throughout the supply chain.

Non-standardized operational practices and rigid separation of the traditional roles of manufacturer and retailer threatened to block the supply chain unnecessarily and failed to exploit the synergies that came from new information technologies and planning tools.

Need for ECR in India

The fast moving consumer goods (FMCG) sector is witnessing fundamental shifts. Company measures appear insufficient to respond to the growing complexity of the market and consumer needs. By working together, companies are able to combine capabilities in serving the consumer *better, faster,* and *at lower cost*. This in other words is ECR. It also promotes use of electronic product code (EPC) and radio frequency identification (RFID) technology.

In India, the first meeting on ECR took place in December, 1999. ECR India got registered in July 2000 as a non-profit Association of Persons (AOP). European Article Number (EAN) India is an affiliate of GS1 (formerly EAN International, Brussels), which has 101 EAN organizations representing 155 countries worldwide. GS1 India is promoted by the Ministry of Commerce, Govt. of India, and was registered in 1996 as a society for promoting the use of the GS1 numbering system for unique identification of a product/stock-keeping units (SKUs) and location in line with international best practices. Its board of management has members like APEDA, BIS, ASSOCHAM, FICCI, CII, IMC, FIEO, and IIP. Over 1 million companies use EAN standards in the world. In South India, Food World handles 8000 stock-keeping units (SKUs) while a hypermarket could deal up to 20,000 SKUs. Initial member companies of ECR India have been Johnson & Johnson, Nestle, Food World, PwC, and EAN India (now GS1 India). They found that there were a lot of areas where collaboration could lead to lower costs and a better SCM. The number of participants steadily increased. Currently, ECR India has 22 companies from the FMCG sector and includes manufacturers, retailers, and service providers. It includes HUL, Nestle, Colgate, Glaxo SmithKline Beecham, P&G, Johnson & Johnson, Godrej Consumer Products, ITC, Cadbury India, Marico, PwC, Wipro Consumer Care & Lighting, Agro Tech Foods Ltd, CavinKare, Food World, EAN India, Kodak India, Subhiksha Trading Services, Henkel Spic, and the transportation giants, such as TCI, South Eastern Roadways, and Container Corporation of India.

A global ECR scorecard, a capability assessment tool for FMCG companies, comprises four focus areas, namely demand management, supply management, enablers, and integrators, as shown in Fig. 2.3.

Under demand management, companies can measure demand capabilities on strategic direction of consumer value, people, organization and information management. It also involves evaluation of optimized planning and execution of processes. It also measures planning and execution of new assortments, product introductions, and promotions besides measuring the concept of consumer knowledge management and the various solutions and channels for consumers.

With supply management, companies can evaluate supply capabilities considering the strategic direction, people, organization, and information management. A responsive and automated replenishment system together with automated store ordering and transport optimization is also a part of this module. Operational excellence in supplies, production, and distribution together with demand-driven integration is a must in this module.

Enablers include elements like product and shipment identification, electronic data alignment, and communication. Cost, profit, and value can be measured on activity-based costing and consumer value management.

Integrators help the companies to assess collaborative planning, forecasting, and replenishment (CPFR), and e-business solutions.

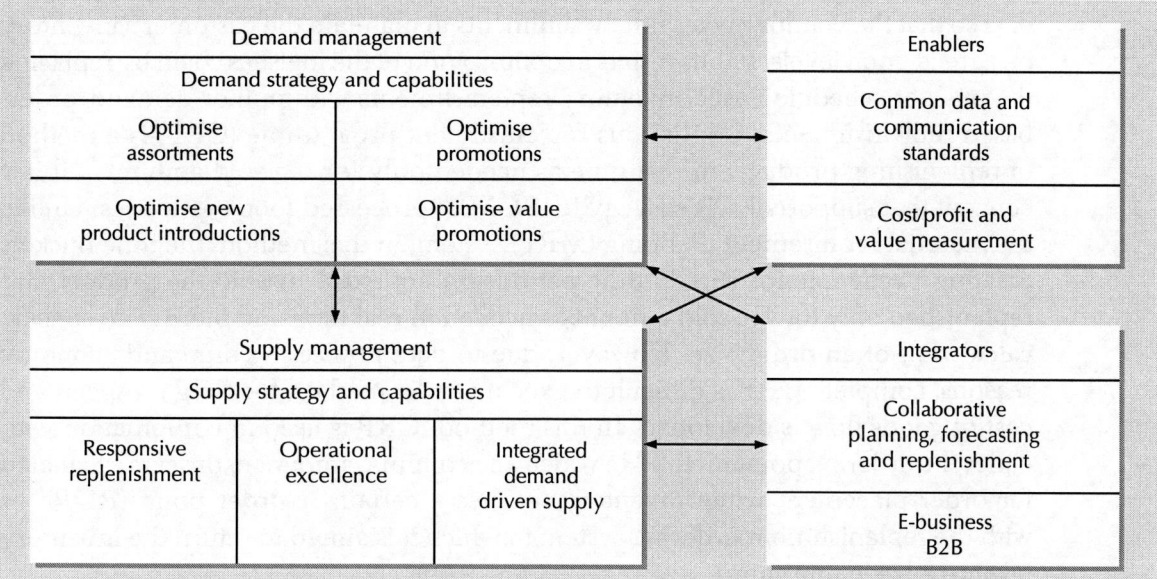

FIG. 2.3 Framework of global ECR scorecard
Source: Adapted from www.globalscorecard.net as accessed on 10 August 2008

Weight factors or points on each of the above are evaluated for both retailers and suppliers. Scores ranging from 0 to 5 can be given to assess the strength of the areas, low to high respectively, in a company. Need gaps can thus be highlighted.

ECR invariably involves EDI particularly that of point-of-sale (PoS) information from manufacturers and distributors to retailers. The key benefits are faster turnaround time, lower costs, and continuous replenishment of inventory through collaboration. A global data synchronization network (GDSN) is a must to capture international sales and replenishment data. The following major activities or initiatives are required for participating in ECR.

- Continuous replenishment programme (CRP)
- Computer assisted ordering (CAO)
- Flow through distribution
- Activity-based costing (ABC)
- Category management
- Integrated electronic data interchange (EDI)

Let us discuss each one of these briefly.

Continuous Replenishment Programme

It refers to a vendor-managed inventory setup in which either the vendor continuously monitors a customer's inventory or the customer supplies current inventory data so that the vendor makes timely shipments to maintain the customer's inventory on agreed upon levels. It thus results in optimization of the logistics chain by replacing the push or schedule based inventory replenishments with pull or demand/order-based replenishments. Continuous replenishment programme (CRP) is a method of replenishing products in real time as needed only for the sold amount.[1] It is a concept that supports ECR strategy for SCM of processed foods/groceries. Unlike the material requirement planning (MRP) system, in this method, the time buckets creating a schedule for certain time periods do not exist. Instead the products are replenished only for the sold amount as needed in real time and there is no specific calculation of an order size. However, due to data processing time and economy reasons, complete CRP is difficult to execute and a method focusing on speed and cost of goods flow is developed. In this method, CRP is used in combination with either the ordering point method in which an economic amount of order is calculated for order placement when inventory reaches a certain re-order point (ROP), or with the replenishment ordering system in which it is aimed to return the inventory level to a basic minimum.

Computer Assisted Ordering

This can help reduce stock-outs in the retailing industry by replenishing a store's inventory based on actual consumer demand. According to an estimate by Food Marketing Institute (FMI) in US, 47 per cent of all stock-outs are a result of improper store ordering and forecasting.[2] The Grocery Manufacturers Association (GMA) found the average level of out-of-stock per cent at typical supermarkets in US to be 7.4 per cent. Further, according to the same Web source cited above, 40 per cent of customers postpone their purchase or the product elsewhere after facing a stock-out. This results in a 3 per cent loss in sales and a negative impact on customer satisfaction and loyalty, resulting in a loss of $200,000 in annual sales per typical supermarket. Interestingly, perishables form 30 per cent of total sales at a typical, grocery chain, which also creates 70 per cent of total shrinkage (wastage and spoilage etc.) such that supermarkets are forced to keep 3–5 days of extra inventory even to keep customer service levels of 97 per cent.

All this needs a computer assisted ordering, the key prerequisite for which is a perpetual inventory (PI) system. It is a method for tracking and knowing the value of inventory and quantity of merchandise on hand at any time by tracking sales returns, receipts, and deliveries on the information system. Computer assisted ordering (CAO) is a software application package that in conjunction with a PI system would assist store managers by suggesting a product replenishment order based on the store's actual point-of-sale (PoS) movement history for that item and

---

[1] www.lean-manufacturing.japan.com/scm-terminology/crp

[2] www.uscapgemini.com as accessed on 1 April 2009

assumed actual on-hand inventory. CAO is driven through direct feeds from the PoS sales data based on the specific parameters listed below, which replenish the store based on actual customer demand. These parameters could be the following.

- Shelf holding capacity/desired shelf inventory
- Re-order quantities/pack-size
- Order limits
- Target minimum stock levels
- Re-order point
- Promotion data
- Delivery frequency
- Replenishment lead time

CAO allows retailers to buy what they sell instead of selling what they buy. The focus is on stocking fast moving goods and not the slow moving ones. The average inventory investments following CAO have been reported to have decreased by 15 per cent.[3]

Flow-through Distribution

It is also known as pool distribution and combines economy of scale concept with the flexibility of just-in-time (JIT) initiatives. It is the process of controlling inbound shipments, sorting them by delivery destinations, and then sending them out in the same day. This process eliminates the need for fixed assets like warehouses, reduces the dependence on high inventory levels, and decreases the time it takes to get the product to the market. In a way, it is *a modified form of cross-docking* except that the flow-through distribution systems also offer other value added services such as *pick and pack* and *kitting and crating*. Flow-through centres would obviously use enhanced IT to move cartons faster and easier from inbound to outbound trailers without a need for storage.

The pool distribution can be used by retailers and manufacturers both, whereby it would make the movement of products faster through the supply chain and in turn make it better respond to the PoS data. In the case of upscale retail centres with a limited back room space at their end, pool distribution would help stores to reduce their inventory levels and increase their ability to frequently refresh shelves.[4] Manufacturers can consolidate their inbound orders for supply of components/parts from different suppliers and transport larger outbound shipments. Thus, flow-through distribution in addition to realizing economy of scale in transportation, also supplements JIT processes and eliminates need for warehousing inventory.

---

[3] www.sscsinc.com/products/cao/html as accessed on 1 April 2009

[4] www.2.yrclogistics.com as accessed on 1 April 2009

Activity-based Costing

It refers to a methodology in accounting which assigns costs to items on the basis of the activities they incur. This is because, as compared to the traditional accounting systems, the activities and not the products or services are seen here as the primary cause of costs. It comprises tracing the overhead and direct costs back to specific products and services. Earlier it was much easier and realistic to allocate overheads and direct costs based on the number of hours required to produce a product but now since the direct labour costs have reduced to just 10 per cent or so of the total costs, activity-based costing (ABC) needs to be used. In fact, it is a part of activity-based management (ABM), which comprises continuous improvement and business process analysis in addition to ABC. It also aims to identify the cost drivers, such as the number of orders, length of setups, specifications, engineering changes, and the follow-up and expediting required. So, ABC can be used to identify and implement cost-saving opportunities on the supplier's side. The purchasing and supply manager must encourage the supplier in understanding the overheads to the product being purchased. As the overheads become a greater proposition of the product cost and as purchasing and supply managers will always strive to reduce the cost of acquisition of materials, accuracy in estimating, and applying overheads can affect the final costs and thus the pricing, ABC becomes crucial.

Category Management

It is aimed at maximizing the potential of a category by focusing on variety, merchandising, stocking, pricing, introducing the new products, and differentiating or re-supplying products in a certain manner. Category management can increase retail sales per square foot by advising companies to selectively focus on categories that offer the best return on the investment made in any resource, the key being the inventory. Others could be space and personnel. The activities managed include developing a strategic category plan by use of PoS data. It is then ensured to monitor space allocations and inventory replenishments and measure each category's performance at retail level on a regular basis for continuous improvement. In the current environment, it may also involve joint working with suppliers to produce products at a target cost driven by the price (Japanese approach) rather than a price driven by costs (the American approach). The SAP offers a category management solution that helps the company to plan and manage retail goods on a seasonal sales pattern basis. The final targets for each category are defined in terms of retail space allocations, number of orders placed/frequency of replenishment, product hierarchy design, and new product innovations and differentiation. Category managers then aim to accomplish these targets. Overall, category management would help in multi channel retailing, inventory management, and stores and pricing management to meet profit margins in a product category. Also, the cost of exposure of a category (of being caught with a stock-out at retail level) is estimated before planning a replenishment pattern for a category.

Integrated Electronic Data Interchange

It would facilitate business partners to exchange the vast information with speed and accuracy. It is needed to communicate, easily manage orders, and deliver invoices and payments, both within the company and outside with its trading partners.

Work Groups of ECR in India

The following are the four work groups set up by the ECR in India.

Out-of-stock Work Group

It takes up as a challenge to measure the extent of stock-out at the retail level and to work out solutions to avoid the loss of business arising due to out-of-stock (OOS) situations. Keeping in view the traditional and complex nature of retail network in India with negligible IT systems, it is no less a stupendous task being facilitated by this work group.

Logistics Work Group

The objective of this work group is to draw up standards in the field of logistics and incur cost savings through collaboration across industry. The group is working on standardizing sizes of cartons and pallets, e.g., EURO sizes for similar types of packaging in order to have load optimization in transportation across the industry. For instance, tin and glass jars of a volume or weight could be standardized across the industry. This would lead to high cubic space utilization and subsequent cost savings due to lower freight and space savings. As Narendra Ambwani, MD, J&J, puts it, 'J&J and Nestle, the participant companies of this group are studying possibility of a consolidated warehousing. This would lead to synergy of procurement and delivery from supplies to logistics to stocking and warehousing.'

Dataflow Standards Work Group

This workgroup is working on setting dataflow standards within the FMCG industry. The purpose is to

(a) adopt common transaction formats and identify code structures at product and entity level;
(b) obviate duplication and unstructured development of software solutions by channel members, solution providers, and the trade;

(c) early and low cost adoption of extensible markup language (XML) to allow heterogeneous systems operated by various partners of supply chain to digitally converse with each other; and

(d) invest supply cost savings in customer service and product differentiation.

FMCG Policy for Organized Retail

The purpose of this work group is to put in place a policy guideline for FMCG transactions with organized retail. The guidelines could refer to the following.

1. Assortment at the retail level including delisting or eliminating certain SKUs that are obsolete, unprofitable, or very slow moving.
2. New product introduction/launches including consistent execution across stores. For instance, what ITC is doing for its Fiama di Wills brand on a uniform basis, even tying it up with promotion.
3. Data sharing and role clarity between manufacturer and retailer on what kind of data is to be shared and at what frequency. The data may pertain to demand forecasting, sales pattern, stock levels, and production and delivery schedules and it can be shared from daily to weekly/monthly/quarterly basis.
4. Improving inventory turns at the retailer's end. This would entail a continuous replenishment at a store based on demand for certain SKUs. The objective is to minimize inventory carrying cost and ensure a high freshness index for FMCG products such as what Marico and Amul have been doing for their products, with more continuous and frequent replenishments based only on demand at the retailer's level.
5. The trade terms—as to how and how much to reward—*scale* (modern retail) versus *reach* (distributors). This is to design appropriate incentives separately for volume of retailing and extent and scope of physically distributing it across the markets.

Mechanistics of ECR

ECR—a decade old global supply chain improvement programme—could transform the workings of the entire FMCG industry for starters. With ECR, now companies can cross-utilize resources and improve efficiencies further as shown in Fig. 2.4. That means competitors can now share trucks and warehouses, use common business language, and jointly tackle problems such as excessive inventory and stock-outs.

ECR's objectives are simple—fulfil consumer demand *better and faster and at a lower cost*. It then becomes a lubricant applied all along the FMCG supply chain. The two fundamental principles that guide all ECR efforts—the focus on consumers, their demands, and expectations and working together internally in the organization

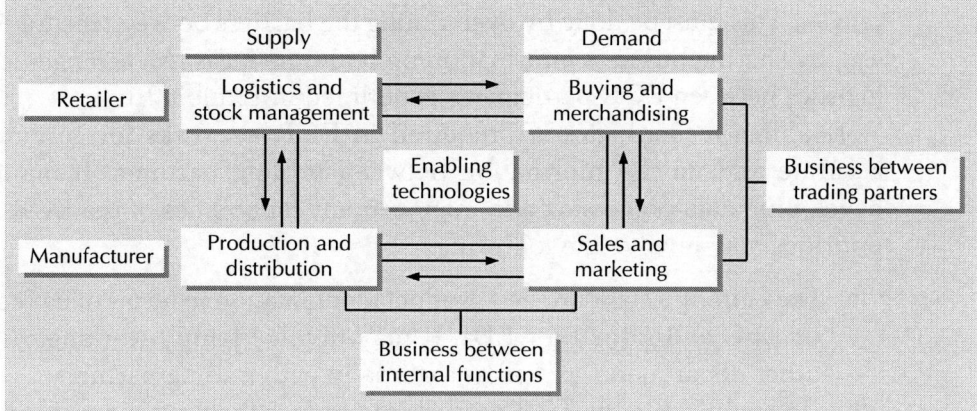

FIG. 2.4 Structure of network and flows in an ECR system
Source: www.gs1india.org/about/ECR.htm as accessed on 14 October 2008

and externally with the trading partners to overcome the barriers. The three focus areas are demand, supply, and enabling technologies.

The demand side of ECR includes all the flows of activities associated with understanding and managing the demand for products and services and their specifications by the customers to serve shoppers more effectively, to their satisfaction and contributing to increase in sales and market share for trading partners. The priorities of ECR management lie in the following.

1. Running a few demand pilots just to know the specific needs and capabilities of collaborating with each other for demand planning.
2. Rationalizing the assortment at retail level as discussed elsewhere, eliminating poorly performing SKUs and improving the location of a few of them depending on the goals in business, e.g., stores productivity in terms of resources such as space and inventory turnover.
3. Optimizing the promotions in terms of the promotion objectives jointly set with trading partners and their execution in terms of internal and external communications, timely distribution, and placement of compaigns. The purpose is to reduce the response time of customers.
4. Jointly working for new product introductions by screening products against certain benchmark factors early in design and development. It may involve joint working on product launch/test market reports. The purpose obviously is to reduce product design and features' complexities and reduce the time and cost to design, develop, produce, and market it ahead of competitors.

The supply side of ECR refers to production and distribution planning, scheduling, and execution by the manufacturer and logistics and stock management by the retailer. This must be done by overcoming the barriers between the trading partners, e.g., by sharing business information on real-time basis. An arrangement of shared logistics between ECR participants is outlined in Exhibit 2.1.

Enabling technologies are required in ECR networks for communication of accurate and timely information between trading partners. It mainly refers to developing data processing and management capabilities of the ECR system. The priorities may involve the following.

(a) Developing a standardized product identification in terms of bar codes or EAN or EPC and format for EDI. It may involve jointly working internally with other departments as well as externally with trading partners.

(b) Re-engineering the ECR processes to reduce their cycle times and bring about simplification.

The work group has given common standards for product identification. They have created a three digit code that will be used to identify an SKU. All entities will also be assigned unique codes. If FMCG companies do the bar coding properly, it could mean an annual savings of Rs 1 crore to the ECR members. It would help in capturing 20 per cent of actual sales data leading to increase in forecasting accuracy from 70 per cent to 90 per cent.

For the intermediaries, ECR would enable a fundamentally different way of functioning—from *push*-based, where the distributor would dump the supplies on the retailers irrespective of the demand or order level or sales pattern to demand or *pull*-based, where the trading partner would lift products based on actual demand or number of orders only. A distributor would not supply unless there is a demand/order trigger communicated to it.

EXHIBIT 2.1   Shared Logistics between ECR Participants

To understand what ECR companies are doing, let us take a look at the arrangement Nestle and J&J have worked out at Delhi, a transit point for products leaving Nestle's manufacturing plant in Moga, Punjab. Of late, common transporter, Transport Corporation of India (TCI's) trucks leaving Delhi with goods meant for Nestle's distribution in Mumbai come back loaded with Johnson & Johnson (J&J) labels for the Delhi market. Such tie ups for backhaul facilities could result in 5–10 per cent savings in the transport costs, besides cutting down transit time. If warehouses are consolidated across companies then even deliveries could be shared, leading to further savings. These 'backhaul' kind of arrangements normally consist of a shared transporter.

HUL, J&J, and Nestle are further working towards drawing up a common format for data exchange between 200 odd manufacturers, 30,000 distributors, and thousands of clearing and forwarding agents (C&FAs), wholesalers, and 12 million retailers, all of whom together make up India's huge and complex supply chain.

'Our ECR initiative in India is part of our global strategy to improve customer service and achieve margin improvements. ECR has a great potential to make it big in India,' says a Colgate Palmolive spokesperson.

The Future of ECR

The way ahead for ECR India is to get some substantial benefits from the projects under progress and use them as a selling point to get more companies on board. This would help in having more broad-based benefits from the projects in future, which would help in realising the mission of ECR India of *removing unnecessary costs from the supply chain and making the sector, as a whole, more responsive to consumer demand.* Studies have shown that companies spend between Rs 17–50 just to get a Rs 100 product moved from the plant to shop shelves. With ECR, that would change.

INFORMATION SYSTEMS AND PROCESSING IN SCM

Since SCM involves information sharing and spreading it across a wide network of raw material suppliers, plants, warehouses, distribution centres (DCs), delivery vehicles, and points-of-sale (PoS) at the retailer's end. Use of proper IT systems and its processing has become an integral part of SCM. In fact, significant distortion or lack in information may result into misalignment of the supply chain. The so called bullwhip effect of multiplication in amplitude of demand from the retailer's end to the local supplier also results from lack of information but what is also important is the speed of gathering and retrieving the data and the quality of information.

With evolution in data development processes and techniques, the scale and degree of integration of operations and thereby the SCM requirements of the companies have also changed. The pattern can be broadly represented as the following.

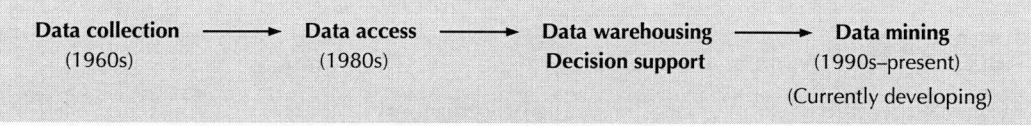

Data collection (1960s) → Data access (1980s) → Data warehousing Decision support → Data mining (1990s–present) (Currently developing)

That is, if typical data warehousing involves online analytical processing of multidimensional databases, including sales figures in different locations, the modern data mining comprises advanced algorithms, multiprocessor computers, and massive databases to even forecast sales figures in a particular location based on a logic.

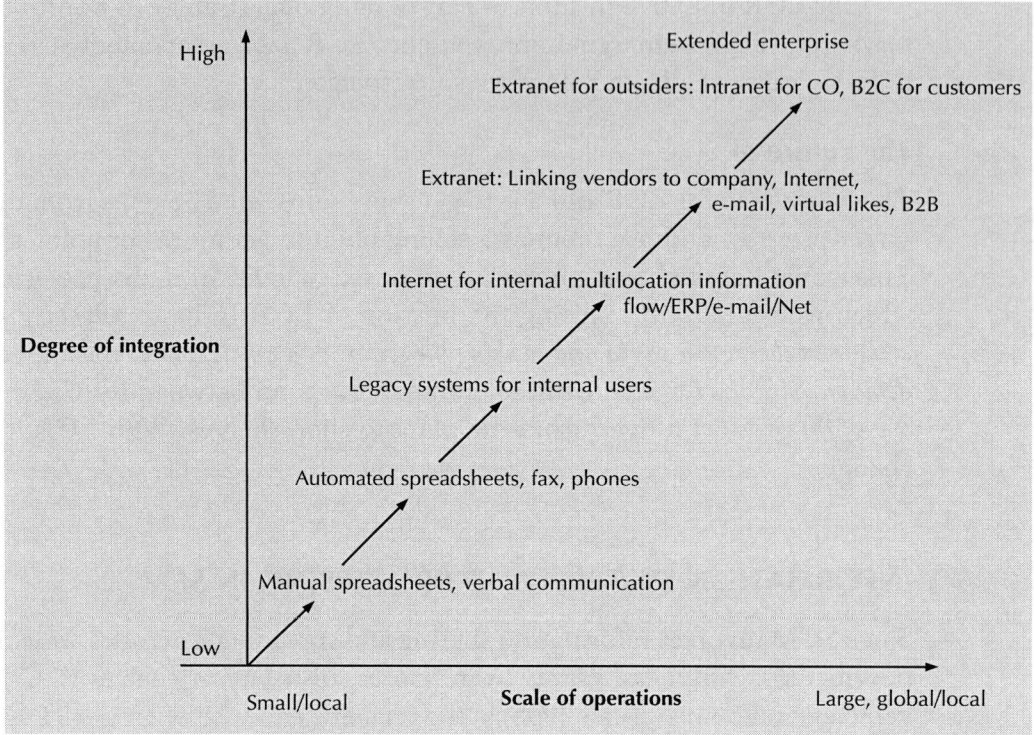

FIG. 2.5 IT-enablement options depending on degree of integration and scale of operations
Source: Economic Times Intelligence Group (ETIG)

The size of the company, in terms of its scale of operations as related to the degree of integration it requires, yields different levels of technological options in terms of mechanisms and devices available which is represented by Fig. 2.5.

The SCM requirements of the companies have also changed from simple *data acquisition* to *Web-based technologies* to advanced planning, forecasting, and documentation systems. So the corresponding technologies over a period of time are as indicated in Table 2.1.

TABLE 2.1 SCM requirements and the corresponding IT techniques

SCM requirements	IT techniques
Data acquisition—outbound side	Scanners, online cash registers, B2C/B2B commerce
Data reporting and query	ERP, data warehousing, data mining and business intelligence
Inventory management	Warehouse management and systems
Order tracking	Web-based track and trace
Forecasting	Optimizers, data mining, and ERP
Documentation	EDI and ERP

The technology enabled supply chain is hence facilitated by intranet and extranet together with proper mix of IT techniques including the software, hardware, and networking requirements depending on company's resources and level of integration it requires in its supply chain right from its vendors to customers. All the planning, sourcing, making delivery, and return functions across all the channel members are enabled by this automation in information and communication flows existing in the company.

RECAPITULATION

The chapter outlines the dynamic nature of the process cycles involved in SCM and the need for alignment of supply chain. The dynamic process cycles range from procurement cycle from the manufacturer to supplier, manufacturing order cycle from the distributor to manufacturer, a replenishment cycle from the retailer to distributor, to customer order cycle from the customer to retailer in a supply chain. These process cycles form the basis of the supply chain operations reference (SCOR) model used as a tool, discussed in Chapter 7, for representing, analysing, and configuring supply chains as also for performance benchmarking. The supply chain alignment refers to all endeavours meant to align supply chain objectives and integrate resources of suppliers and customers across organizational boundaries in order to strategically respond to demand and co-create with chain partners a discrete value proposition as demanded by (internal and external) customers in the chain. It is in terms of coordinated decision-making in areas of pricing, transportation, inventory, and ownership. The alignment also prepares the channel partners to share rewards and risks on a pooled basis. The role of order management in SCM cannot be undermined. The components of order processing in terms of its preparation, transmission, entry, filling, and status reporting are laid down. The measures of order fulfilment in terms of line fill rate and order fill rate have been differentiated. While a line fill rate refers to the proportion of total number of units received in proportion to the total number of units ordered, an order fill rate refers to the ratio of number of stock-keeping unit (SKU) categories for which 100 per cent of ordered units are received to the total number of SKU categories ordered. There are multifold benefits of good order management in terms of reducing inventory stocks and buffer, reduce operational, purchasing, and order expenditure and inventory management, shorter order fulfilment lead times, and increase supply fill rates by improving visibility into supply sources and status.

The integration of a company's supply chain is in terms of integrating its back end on the suppliers' side to its front end on the customers' side through the company's core internal processes. While the back-end processes include procurement, production planning, and scheduling, the front-end processes include order fulfilment, replenishment, and after-sales services. The intermediate core supply chain processes range from production and distribution, planning and scheduling to internal order fulfilment to IT-enablement. For integration, the core supply chain processes can either be initiated in anticipation of customer orders or forecasted demand (*push mechanism*) or in response to actual customer demand or the point-of-sale (PoS) data (*pull mechanism*) or even in terms of a joint *push–pull mechanism*, whereby the supply chain processes on supplier side are push-based demand while those on customer side are pull-based demand.

One of the important phenomena that has affected the Indian supply chains like others is the bullwhip effect. It refers to the increased order variability as one moves up in a supply chain from customers to retailer to wholesaler to manufacturer and finally to supplier. Even reputed companies like HP and P&G have observed this phenomenon in their supply chains. The basic causes could be one or more of the following.

- Faulty demand forecasting/demand updating
- Order fluctuation
- Shortage gaming

In India, phantom demands could arise if customers/retailers inflate their order when they anticipate a shortfall or a price rise. The order batching and faulty demand forecasting are very natural and universal.

The four key initiatives to counter bullwhip effect are the following.

(i) Information sharing across channel partners
(ii) Channel alignment in terms of pricing, transportation, inventory, and ownership across different levels
(iii) Provision of third-party logistics (3PL) providers

(iv) Discouraging promotional pricing
(v) Discouraging shortage gaming

This is followed by a discussion about the efficient customer response (ECR) in Indian Corporate sector which is brought about by sharing distribution logistics efficiently, time and space-wise. This initiative is not very extensive though but it has the promise of serving the consumer better, faster, and at a lower cost. More and more companies should come forward to join the ECR as it would result in delivery of the product at lower cost to the customers. ECR initiative would entail electronic data interchange (EDI), particularly that of point-of-sale (PoS) information.

The last section highlights how important it is to have speed of gathering and retrieving the data and also to have quality of information. There is a range of IT options depending on the degree of integration and scale of operations required. The Web-based information systems have further enabled the SCM through e-procurement, PoS data capture, and third-party logistics (3PL) activities as also the order tracking Web-based truck and trace techniques. So modern SCM is technology enabled including the Web-based processes.

CONCEPT REVIEW QUESTIONS

1. What are the different levels and types of process cycles in a supply chain? How do these affect the dynamics of supply chain?

2. What is the significance of a good order management system in SCM? Outline the components of an order processing system.

3. What does supply chain integration refer to? How can it be brought about by the push and/or pull mechanisms?

4. What does bullwhip effect refer to? What are the basic causes of it and how can these be remedied?

5. What does efficient consumer response (ECR) refer to? Outline the network components and flows in an ECR system. What are the benefits of an ECR initiative?

6. Outline the need for integrated information systems for managing a supply chain. How has Web enablement of such systems helped?

CRITICAL THINKING QUESTIONS

1. How do process cycles provide the dynamic nature to the supply chains? How can some cycles be modified or even eliminated for better supply chain alignment? Cite some examples.
2. What are the prerequisites for a good order management in a company? What would be the order and description of activities in a good order management exercise?
3. How should you decide that the supply chain integration should be carried out on push, pull, or push–pull mechanism for demand planning and supply.
4. The prime reason for bullwhip effect in Indian industry seems to be faulty forecasting or simply the lack of it. What do you suggest to reduce bullwhip effect at least on account of this in a company, particularly in an Indian scenario?
5. Discuss the functions and sub-functions in which ECR should be worked out on a priority basis in a typical FMCG company? What would be the requirements for such an initiative to be shared among enterprises?

PROJECT ASSIGNMENTS

1. Visit a company's distribution/supply chain department and analyse as to how the supply chain has been configured at different levels and what are the sub-processes and outcomes at each stage.
2. Take a company in the FMCG sector and find all the stages from order capturing to order fulfilment. How much is the cycle time for this? Estimate the history of order fulfilment rates.
3. Pick up a company networked through ECR system in India, say, Nestle, Colgate, GSK, P&G, J&J, ITC, Godrej, or Cadbury and find through a structured interview as to how ECR has been automated and what are the results.
4. Visit a company's distribution/supply chain department and find out how they avoid creation of 'phantom' demands by downstream channel partners. What are their difficulties in doing so?
5. Visit a company and find out how it is using the information technology for enablement of supply chain processes and their integration.

CASE STUDY

GLOBAL CASE STUDY

WAL-MART[5]

Introduction

While most still believe Wal-Mart's pioneering supply chain to be the world's most efficient, the retailer is faltering in recent years, and it's renowned IT driven supply chain is a contributor in its woes. In October 2006, Wal-Mart had to sell its stores in South Korea and Germany. In Germany alone, it incurred a $1 billion loss. This was reportedly due to its failure to adapt to

[5] *Source:* This case has been reproduced from www.casestudyinc.com with special permission from Mr Manish Kumar Jain to whom the author expresses acknowledgement and thanks

the local cultures and inability to compete with established players. In the US, Wal-Mart reduced the number of new US supercentres it planned to open in 2007 by 30 per cent. In August 2007, Wal-Mart warned that its profits would be lower than expected for 2007 (it had missed second-quarter profit estimates). Experts blamed Wal-Mart's negligence to customer service, merchandising mistakes, and its inattentiveness to local markets abroad for its inefficiency. Tesco's entry to the US market in 2007 may have caused further challenges.

A variety of strategies to strengthen growth have mostly not been successful. In 2006, Wal-Mart bought retail applications from HP and Oracle, and quietly contracted with a social networking company, *Bazaarvoice*. Wal-Mart's online presence with its website also struggled. It was behind competitors such as Amazon.com and Target. Its promotion experiments using social networking concepts got mixed results. In addition, there were delays in implementation of radio frequency identification (RFID) tags throughout its supply chain. Later in the year, Wal-Mart changed its RFID strategy, with more focus on promotional items, category management trials, and Sam's Club pallet location management. Vendors were rightly bemused and confused.

For Wal-Mart, one thing remained clear that just squeezing more pennies out of the supply chain would not be enough. President and CEO Lee Scott, (who retired in Jan. 2009), commented on the company's performance in a press release, 'It is not what we expect of ourselves, but what our shareholders expect of us.' He said that the management would spend the rest of this year 'focused on inventory improvements, delivering quality products at low prices, and store execution at the highest standards.'

Wal-Mart—The Retail Market

Wal-Mart is the world's largest retailer with $345 billion in sales for the fiscal year ending 31 January 2007. Wal-Mart Stores, Inc. includes Wal-Mart Supercentres, Discount stores, Neighborhood Markets and SAM'S Club warehouses. It employs 1.9 million associates worldwide and more than 1.3 million in the US, making it one of the largest private employers in the US. The retail giant has been a dominant player in the US retail market, which is most competitive in the world, a fact well-known to British retailers Sainsbury's and Marks & Spencer, which failed to attract US customers.

Wal-Mart has more than 7000 stores and wholesale clubs across 14 markets. It operates more than 4000 facilities in the US and more than 2800 more in Argentina, Brazil, Canada, China, Costa Rica, El Salvador, Guatemala, Honduras, Japan, Mexico, Nicaragua, Puerto Rico, and the United Kingdom. In 2007, Wal-Mart became No. 1 on the FORTUNE 500 list and in 2003 and 2004 it was named 'Most Admired Company in America' by the *FORTUNE magazine*.

Wal-Mart—The Corporate Background

In 1945, Sam M. Walton opened a franchisee—the Ben Franklin variety store in Newport, Arkansas. In 1946, his brother, James L. Walton, opened a similar store in Versailles, Missouri. Until 1962, the business focused entirely on the operation of variety stores. In 1962, Sam Walton started Wal-Mart's first discount store, 'Wal-Mart Discount City'. He and his wife, Helen, put up 95 per cent of the money for the first Wal-Mart store. Sam believed that the American consumer was shifting to a different type of general store and discount stores would be very successful. Wal-Mart was incorporated in Delaware in October 1969. [During the initial years, Walton had focused on establishing new stores in small towns, with an average population of 5000. These towns were largely neglected by leading retailers such as Sears Roebuck & Company, K-Mart, and Woolco, which concentrated more on larger towns and bigger cities. In his efforts to attract people from the rural areas to his stores, Walton introduced the concept of every day low pricing (EDLP). It promised Wal-Mart's customers a wide variety of high quality, branded, and unbranded products at the lowest possible price, offering better value for their money. Wal-Mart's advertisement describing EDLP said, 'Because you work hard for every dollar, you deserve the lowest price we can offer every time you make a purchase. You deserve our every day low price.'

In the 60s, K-Mart expanded across the country, while Wal-Mart had only 15 stores. But this changed in the 70s when public offering created the capital infusion that grew the company to 276 stores in 11 states.

In the 1980s, Wal-Mart became one of the most successful retailers in America. Sales grew to $26 billion by 1989 at 1400 stores, compared to $1 billion in 1980. Wal-Mart Stores, Inc. branched out into warehouse clubs with the first Sam's Club in 1983. The first Supercentre, featuring a complete grocery department along with the 36 departments of general merchandise, opened in 1988. Wal-Mart invented the practice of sharing sales data via computer with major suppliers, such as Proctor & Gamble.

Walton died after a prolonged illness in 1992. Wal-Mart suffered a setback but it continued its remarkable growth concentrating more on setting up its stores overseas. In 1991, it entered Mexico in a joint venture with Cifra. In 1994, it acquired 122 Woolco stores from Woolworth, Canada. Three years later, Wal-Mart became the largest volume discount retailer in Canada and Mexico. In 1997, the chain acquired the 21-store German hypermarket chain, Wertkauf. Other international expansion efforts included the purchase of Brazilian retailer Lojas Americans' 40 per cent interest in their joint venture, and the acquisition of four stores and additional sites in South Korea from Korean Makro. In January 1999, Wal-Mart expanded its German operations by buying 74 stores of the hypermarket chain, Interspar. The stores were acquired from Spar Handels AG, which owned multiple retail formats and wholesale operations throughout Germany.

Wal-Mart became the largest company in the world in 2002 revenue-wise. This was a long way from 1979 when it first made more than a billion dollars in annual revenues. This was in contrast to 1993 when Wal-Mart was making a billion dollars in a week and in 2001 in every 1.5 days. This extraordinary growth was a result of its sustained focus on consumer requirements and reducing costs through efficient supply chain management practices. Its ability to provide its customers with a wide range of products at the lowest costs in the shortest possible time was remarkable. Wal-Mart's highly automated distribution centres drastically reduced shipping costs and time. Its computerized inventory system speeded up the checkout time and recording of transactions. In all, Wal-Mart's supply chain management practices resulted in increased efficiency in operations and better customer service. It eliminated old stocks and maintained quality of goods.

Wal-Mart—The Business Milestones

The major business events and some salient facts are given respectively in Exhibits 2.2 and 2.3.

Doing It the Wal-Mart Way

The Pricing Linked to Procurement

In order to offer the best price to its customers, Wal-Mart constantly tried to reduce its purchasing costs. It ensured this by procuring goods directly from manufacturers, and bypassing all intermediaries. With overhead costs spread across a wider footprint, Wal-Mart could negotiate more aggressively with excellent net margins.

Wal-Mart would invest a lot of its time in meeting vendors to understand their cost structure. A tough negotiator on price, Wal-Mart made a purchase deal based on the fact that those products being purchased were not available in another place at a lower price. The same policy would also

EXHIBIT 2.2 Wal-Mart—Timeline

1962	Sam Walton started Wal-Mart in 1962
1970	First distribution center in Bentonville, Arkansas
1972	Listed on the New York Stock Exchange
1970s	276 stores in 11 states
1975	Famous 'Wal-Mart Cheer' was introduced by Walton
1978	Wal-Mart purchased the Hutcheson Shoe Company
1980s	Sales grew to $26 billion by 1989 at 1,400 stores
1983	First Sam's Club
1988	First Supercenter
1991	First international store in Mexico
1992	Wal-Mart entered Puerto Rico
1993	Wal-Mart formed an international division
1994	Expansion into Canada. Wal-Mart acquired 122 Woolco stores from Woolworth, Canada
1995	Entry in Argentina and Brazil
1996	Entry in China
1997	Wal-Mart acquired the 21-store German hypermarket chain, Wertkauf
1999	Wal-Mart expanded its German operations by buying 74 stores of the hypermarket chain, Interspar
2002	Wal-Mart acquired a 6.1% stake in Seiyu
2003	Majority interest in Seiyu, making it a Wal-Mart subsidiary
2007	Wal-Mart's 3000th international store

Source: www.casestudyinc.com

be applied to big manufacturers such as Procter & Gamble (P&G). As one of the former employees puts it, 'We would tell the vendors, don't leave in any room for a kickback because we don't do it here. And we don't want your advertising programme or delivery programme. Our truck will pick it up at your warehouse. Now what is your best price?' Such transparency helped Wal-Mart know that the manufacturers were doing their best to trim down costs. This also helped in establishing a long-term relationship with the manufacturers. Generally, Wal-Mart preferred local and regional vendors and suppliers. Also, economies of scale gave Wal-Mart a negotiating advantage with suppliers, thereby allowing aggressive pricing strategies.

EXHIBIT 2.3   Wal-Mart—Quick Facts

Company	Wal-Mart Stores Inc (NSE: WMT)
Corporate Headquarters	U.S.
Revenues	$345 billion in sales for the fiscal year ending Jan. 31, 2007 In Japan, Seiyu's full year 2006 consolidated sales were US $6.5 billion
Industry	Retail, Retailing Services
Employees	1.9 million associates worldwide (38,541 in Japan)
Operations	14 International Markets
Total Stores	7000 (3000 international stores) 275 Seiyu supermarkets in Japan
Store Formats	Wal-Mart Supercenters, discount stores, Neighborhood Markets and SAM'S Club warehouses
Major Competitors	• Tesco • Sainsbury • Marks & Spencers • Carrefour
Major Brands/Labels	Sam's Choice, Great Value, Everstart, Ol' Roy, Puritan, Equate, No Boundaries, George, Athletic Works, Durabrand, ILO, HomeTrends, Mainstays, Metro 7, Parent's Choice, Ozark Trail, Relion, White Stag and Kid Connection. MEMBER'S MARK, BAKERS & CHEFS and SAM'S CLUB are other private label brands
	Licensed brands include General Electric, Disney, McDonald's, Mary-Kate and Ashley, and Starter
Business/Growth Strategy	Low-cost Leadership, EDLP - Every Day Low Prices, Offering permanent discounts across all stores
	Portfolio optimization and global leverage
Key Executives Name, Designation (as in 2007)	H. Lee Scott, Jr., President and Chief Executive Officer. Michael T. Duke, Vice Chairman Wal-Mart Stores, Inc. Johnnie C. Dobbs, Jr., Executive Vice President, Logistics and Supply Chain Eduardo Castro-Wright, Executive Vice President, President and Chief Executive Officer, Wal-Mart Stores Division

Source: www.walmart.com, www.samsclub.com

Integrating Supply Chain through Knowledge Sharing

Wal-Mart always believed that it was negotiating on behalf of the customer and the best price was passed on to the customer. Its advantage created a snowball effect in which increasing purchase volume led to more choice for the customer and lower prices, leading to more purchase volume. This price leverage was backed by systems and processes in place that enabled Wal-Mart to take its scale advantages to the next level to achieve unmatched success. Competitors struggled to realize their potential economies of scale because of the natural limitations of legacy processes and technological infrastructures (or lack thereof). Wal-Mart excelled at business process efficiency by involving suppliers/manufacturers in the process. The company was more than willing to share proprietary knowledge and processes with its supplier base to improve quality and eliminate waste/costs out of the supply chain. This process/product knowledge sharing enabled super-effective cost management with a constant focus on continuous incremental improvement. In other words, reducing costs a few pennies at a time over an extended time frame.

Developing Partnerships with Suppliers

Traditionally, suppliers to the retailers had rather monolithic supply chains with little effective forecasting. A 'one size fits all' approach meant the same price list irrespective of ordering efficiency. Products delivery was done in the manner the customers desired and thus it came at the cost of efficiency.

Wal-Mart invited its major suppliers to co-develop profitable supply chain partnerships. These partnerships are intended to amplify product flow efficiency and, in turn, Wal-Mart's profitability.

A case in point is Wal-Mart's supplier relationship with P&G. The relationship did not begin well. Wal-Mart saw P&G as one of its bad suppliers because P&G's organization and processes were far too complex for Wal-Mart's efficiency-oriented culture. P&G's culture was to focus on day-to-day results. A long-term strategic plan was not its main focus. Besides, P&G's systems could not support a relationship with a distribution giant such as Wal-Mart. This relationship changed with the process of enabling interoperability between the companies'

systems at transactional, operational, and strategic levels. Since 1988, the relationship evolved to yield tremendous value to both companies and their mutual business grew manifold. Wal-Mart and P&G also incorporated several other inter-company innovations such as vendor-managed inventory and category management among others. In August 2003, Wal-Mart announced that it would require all suppliers to put RFID tags with electronic product codes (EPC) on their pallets and cases by the end of 2006. By April 2007, 600 suppliers were using RFID (about 3 per cent of its base of 20,000). A few suppliers felt that Wal-Mart was such a demanding, price-obsessed customer that making special technology investments at its behest was cost-prohibitive, especially for small companies scraping by on slim margins. Others felt that this was one way small suppliers become big suppliers. They could hone their technology strategies for their biggest potential markets even in the face of considerable risk.

Distribution Strategy

During fiscal 2007, approximately 80 per cent of the Wal-Mart Stores purchases of merchandise were shipped from 121 distribution centres (DCs). The remaining merchandise was shipped directly to stores from suppliers. Wal-Mart owns and operates 40 general merchandise DCs, 38 grocery DCs, 7 apparel and shoes DCs, 12 professional services and specialty DCs, 2 import DCs and 3 DCs that support walmart.com. Wal-Mart has 126 distribution facilities located in various countries that serve its international segment stores.

In 1998, Wal-Mart stocked more than 80,000 items in over 40 DCs in the US. While its competitors directly supplied 50–65 per cent of inventory from their warehouses, Wal-Mart's own warehouses directly supplied 85 per cent of the inventory. This meant that Wal-Mart was able to provide replenishments within two days (on an average) while competitors took five days. Shipping costs for Wal-Mart were approximately 3 per cent as against 5 per cent for competitors. The inventory turnover rate was very high, about once every two weeks for most of the items.

While some suppliers delivered goods such as automotive and drug products directly to its stores, about 85 per cent of the goods passed through the DCs. Wal-Mart managed each DC the same way for both cases and palletized goods. Goods which were to be distributed within the US usually arrived in pallets, while imported goods arrived in reusable boxes or cases.

Wal-Mart used advanced bar code technology and hand-held computer systems to ensure an unfailing flow of products to support the supply function. Managing the centre became easier and more economical with technology. With real-time information about inventory levels of all the products in the centre, an employee had to just make two scans—one to identify the pallet, and the other to identify the location from where the stock had to be picked up. Different bar codes were used to label different products, shelves, and bins in a centre. The hand-held computer guided an employee with regard to the location of a particular product from a particular bin or shelf in the centre. When the computer verified the bin and picked up a product, the employee confirmed whether it was the right product or not. The quantity of the product required from the centre was entered into the hand-held computer by the employee and then the computer updated the information on the main server.

The packaging department also had accurate information about the products to be packed. Hand-held computers ensured that unnecessary paperwork was eliminated. Centre supervisors could easily monitor their employees closely and guide them even on the move. This enabled efficient distribution centre management operations and serves customer needs quickly.

The truck drivers could also avail facilities for maintaining personal hygiene such as shower bath and fitness centres at each DC which also had food, sleep, and personal business provisions. They could also be used for meetings and paperwork.

The Logistics at Wal-Mart

A fast and responsive transportation system was key to Wal-Mart's logistics infrastructure. At one point about 3500 company-owned trucks served its DCs. Dedicated trucks meant Wal-Mart could replenish its stores twice a week from its DCs. Hiring dedicated and experienced drivers was given priority. All hired drivers had to have 300,000 accident free miles and no major traffic violation. A coordinator controlled and scheduled dispatches based on driver availability and estimated time between the DC and the retail store. A strict vigil over the drivers was maintained and a record of their activities was kept in the 'private fleet driver handbook'. A code of conduct ensured safe delivery.

Cross-docking

In order to make the distribution process more efficient, Wal-Mart used cross-docking. Cross-docking involved eliminating the DC and the retail store while making a direct delivery to customers after picking and sorting the finished goods directly from the supplier. This was possible only if the supplier ensured delivery within a specified time. The requisition from the store was then converted into purchase orders and goods were forwarded to a staging area. The goods were then packed and delivered to customers as per the order. Such cross-docking meant that centralized decision control (for merchandising, pricing, and promotions) was shifted from the corporate level, thereby transforming the supply chain into a demand chain. That is, instead of retail stores pushing goods into the system, the customers pulled the goods when required.

Managing the Inventory at Wal-Mart

The company was able to reduce inventory because the stores managed their own stocks. Stores could reduce pack sizes across products and also ensure timely price markdowns. Using IT applications, more inventories could be made available for high demand goods instead of cutting inventories across the board. By networking with suppliers, a quick replenishment order could be placed via the satellite communication system. Wal-Mart had set up its own satellite communication system in 1983. The supplier could then deliver the goods directly to the store concerned or to the nearest DC. The supplier was also able to reduce costs due to better coordination. In 1991, Wal-Mart invested $4 billion in a retail link system. Around 10,000 suppliers used the system to monitor the sales of their goods at the stores and accordingly replenish inventory. In 2001, Wal-Mart tied up with Atlas Commerce to upgrade the system with Internet-enabled technologies. Wal-Mart used advanced satellite communication systems, massively parallel processing (MPP) computer systems, and had extensive disaster recovery plans to track goods and inventory levels. This ensured uninterrupted service to its customers, suppliers, and partners.

In the fiscal year 2008, Wal-Mart International's net sales reached level of $90.6 billion. They leveraged best practices, lessons from multiple-store formats and global procurement services. In addition, relationships with key global suppliers continued to help Wal-Mart leverage their volumes across countries. It added 3000th international unit and 101 locations in China through the Trust-Mart transaction while it also formed a joint venture with Bharti Enterprises in India.

The basic retail store format of Wal-Mart is given in Exhibit 2.4 that follows and the international operating format in Exhibit 2.5.

EXHIBIT 2.4 Wal-Mart—Store Format

Wal-Mart Discount stores	Average 107,000 square feet, employ an average of 225 associates and offer 120,000 items
Wal-Mart Supercentres	Developed in 1988 More than 2,300 nationwide in US Average 187,000 square feet, employ 350 or More associates on average and offer 142,000 different items
Wal-Mart Neighborhood markets	First opened in 1998 More than 120 Neighborhood Markets Average 42,000 square feet Employ 95 associates on average and offer about 29,000 items
Sam's Club	More than 584 Sam's Club locations Average 132,000 square feet Average of 160 to 175 associates and offers approximately 5,500 different products

Source: www.caseshvelyinc.com

EXHIBIT 2.5 Wal-Mart—International Operating Formats

Argentina	Supercenters –13
Brazil	Supercenters – 26 Sam's Clubs – 19 Hypermarkets (Hiper Bompreço, Big) – 66 Supermarkets (Bompreço, Mercadorama, Nacional) – 57 Cash-n-carry stores (Maxxi Alacado) – 11 Combination discount and grocery stores (Todo Dia) – 15 General merchandise stores (Magazine) – 3 Discount stores (Mini Bompreço) – 2
Canada	Supercenters – 7 Discount stores – 276 Sam's Clubs – 6
China	Supercenters – 68, Neighborhood Markets – 2 and 3 Sam's Clubs
Costa Rica	4 Hypermarkets (Hiper Mas), 23 Supermarkets (Más por Menos), 8 Warehouse stores (Maxi Bodega) and 102 Discount stores (Pali)
El Salvador	2 Hypermarkets (Hiper Paiz), 32 Supermarkets (La Despensa de Don Juan) and 29 Discount stores (Despensa Familiar)
Guatemala	6 Hypermarkets (Hiper Paiz), 28 Supermarkets (Paiz), 8 Warehouse stores (Maxi Bodega), 2 Membership clubs (Club Co) and 88 Discount stores (Despensa Familiar)
Honduras	1 Hypermarket (Hiper Paiz), 6 Supermarkets (Paiz), 5 Warehouse stores (Maxi Bodega) and 29 Discount stores (Despensa Familiar)
Japan	97 Hypermarkets (Livin, Seiyu), 293 Supermarkets (Seiyu, Sunny) and 2 General merchandise stores (Seiyu)
Mexico	118 Supercenters, 77 Sam's Clubs, 100 Supermarkets (Superama, Mi Bodega), 219 Combination discount and grocery stores (Bodega), 61 Department stores (Suburbia), 312 Restaurants and 2 Discount stores (Mi Bodega Express)
Nicaragua	5 Supermarkets (La Unión) and 35 Discount stores (Pali)
Puerto Rico	6 Supercenters, 8 Discount stores, 9 Sam's Clubs and 31 Supermarkets (Amigo)
United Kingdom	23 Supercenters (Asda), 291 Supermarkets (Asda), 7 General merchandise stores (Asda Living), 12 Apparel stores (George) and 2 Discount stores (Asda Essentials)

Source: Wal-Mart Annual Report

Related Resources

Rowat, Christine (August 1998), 'Cross-docking: The Move from Supply to Demand', www.dmg.co.uk.

www.colofwhousing.com.au

'Walmart.com: The Physical Giant Goes Virtual,' Red Herring Magazine, www.redherring.com, May 7, 2001.

www.walmartstores.com

Discussion Questions

1. Why do supply chain (SC) processes at Wal-Mart need to be so dynamic?
2. Outline the challenges involved in getting the competitive advantage out of the supply chain from sources to distributors at Wal-Mart? List some of the strategies and actions involved.
3. How did Wal-Mart go about ensuring every day low pricing (EDLP) at its stores?
4. Why is Wal-Mart so particular about the selection of its vendors? What are the expectations and requirements for vendors selected by Wal-Mart?
5. Wal-Mart encouraged most of its suppliers to develop profitable supply chain (SC) partnerships. Discuss how good or bad it could be to share knowledge and actual information with suppliers or even customers.
6. Analyse the usefulness of some unique practices in distribution of traffic and fleet management resorted to at Wal-Mart? Can these be applied in the Indian context?
7. How is Wal-Mart exploiting the use of information and communication technology (ICT) to manage inventory and orders at various levels of the supply chain (SC)?

INDIAN CASE STUDY

HINDUSTAN UNILEVER LIMITED (HUL)[6]

Introduction and Background

Hindustan Unilever Limited (HUL) is India's largest fast moving consumer goods (FMCG) company, with leadership in home and personal care products and foods and beverages. HUL's more than 100 brands, spread across 20 distinct consumer categories, touch the lives of two out of three Indians. HUL is India's largest marketer of soaps, detergents, and home care products. The company calls itself 'multi-local multinational'. It currently has a combined product volume of about 4 million tonnes and sales of Rs 13,718 crore.

It is one of the few companies that has a company head of SCM who is equal in status to other business heads. Dhaval Buch, the Executive Director (Supply Chain) reports to the CEO and MD of HUL, Nitin Paranjpe. The SCM Head in his position leads all manufacturing, sourcing, and distribution of HUL.

The company's strategy is to concentrate its resources on 35 national power brands, and 10 other brands which are strong in certain regions. HUL started the franchised Lakmé Salons, offering standardized services, in line with the strategy to add a service dimension to relevant brands. The company has set up the Hindustan Lever Network, a direct selling channel, offering the Lever Home range of laundry and home care products and the Aviance personal care range.

The company has also begun an e-mail service, called *Sangam,* which can home deliver on order by phone or through the Net, a diverse range of about 5000 branded and unbranded products. The service is currently available in select areas of Mumbai and Navi Mumbai, besides Thane.

---

[6] *Source:* www.hul.co.in/citizen-lever as accessed on 14 October 2008; www.hul.co.in as accessed on 14 October 2008; and Economic Times Intelligence Group, Supply Chain & Logistics survey, 2007, with permission

HUL is part of a global Fortune 500 company, with market leadership in home and personal care products, food, beverages, and specialty chemicals. The company sources raw materials and intermediates packaging materials from more than 2000 suppliers for its nearly 1000 products that are manufactured in over 100 plants and distributed nationally through a network of four warehouses, more than 40 agents, 7500 wholesalers and a number of large institutional customers.

Sales and Operations Planning (S&OP)

The demand forecasting on a scientific basis forms the basis of sales and operations planning at HUL. The planning cycle is a feed forward one, the main planning is one quarter ahead with 3 more quarters of plans going forward; overall the plan being a one-year one at any given point in time. Firstly, a base level demand is calculated looking at actual sales pattern of the past few months. If the management aims to grow sales at a rate higher than the base rate, then inputs from past experiences of demand promotion activities are superimposed. This is done at SKU level and then overall company sales projections are worked out. As Buch, the SCM head told, 'HUL now apparently has better access to its own data, has a modelling application for it and has driven a process change through the organization'. The efficiency is measured with parameters such as forecast errors and customer service efficiency. This is done at SKU level every 30 days but company now has the capacity to do it every 10 days.

Supply Chain and Distribution Network

HUL's distribution network is recognized as one of its key strengths—that helps to spread its products across the length and breadth of this vast country. The need for a strong distribution network is imperative, since HUL's corporate purpose is 'to meet the everyday needs of people everywhere.'

Its products, manufactured across the country, are distributed through a network of about 7000 redistribution stockists covering about one million retail outlets. The distribution network directly covers the entire urban population.

In addition to the ongoing commitment to the traditional grocery trade, HUL is building a special relationship with the small but fast emerging modern trade. HUL's scale enables it to provide superior customer service including daily servicing, improving their range availability whilst reducing inventories. HUL is using the opportunity of interfacing more directly with consumers in this retail environment through specially designed communication and promotions. This is building traffic into the stores while yielding high growth for the business.

A major reorganization of sales structure has been done and focused efforts have been undertaken to build sales capabilities by leveraging IT. The rolling out of RS Net, an Internet-based network, which connects it with stockists, has enhanced the speed and accuracy of sales and stock holding, information from distributors. A continuous replenishment of stocks to distributors/stockists facilitated by this has resulted in better management of the distributor's investment. The objective is to catalyse HUL's growth by ensuring that the right product is available at the right place in right quantities, in the most cost-effective manner. RS Net is used for online interaction on orders, dispatches, information sharing, and monitoring. It covers about 80 per cent of the company's turnover. Today, the HUL sales system gets to know everyday what HUL stockists have sold to almost a million outlets across the country. RS Net is part of Project Leap, HUL's end-to-end supply chain, which also includes a back-end system connecting suppliers, all company sites and stretching right up to stockists. It has come as a force multiplier for HUL way, the company's action-plan to maximize the number of outlets reached and to achieve leadership in every outlet, by unshackling the field force to solely focus on secondary sales from the stockists to retailers and market activation. Focus is now on ensuring superior availability and impactful visibility at retail points.

Customer Centricity in Supply Chains

As Buch is quoted having put it, 'In addition to production efficiencies, the consumer is being focused in both manufacturing and sourcing.' New measurement criteria are being used to focus on customer service, e.g., the case fill which means how much of the order was actually delivered as compared to the total order. The company measures lost sales by this. If the case fill is X%, the lost sales is clearly 100-X. A predictive case fill refers to case fill a week ahead. Buch is further quoted as saying, 'We generate a loss tree. Losses can occur due to forecasting errors, losses in transportation, and manufacturing. We are now into cost cutting by waste elimination and re-designs'. There is a formal cost cutting platform. The small multi-functional teams meet once in a year and develop projects with specific cost reduction targets. These were initiated by the company more in the wake of inflationary effect on prices of raw material, packaging materials, and distribution costs due to rise in petroleum prices. Strategic alliances with many international and local vendors led to development of new technologies, materials, and joint cost reduction programmes. Together with the global and regional strength of Unilever, the company made it possible to derive supply chain benefits and set up two plants in Uttaranchal and Himachal with a number of ancillaries around. Earlier, HUL used to measure only factory quality, now the company also measures retail quality. This is checked by a team of people who randomly visit final retail stores and check the products for various attributes such as packaging quality and composition as the product finally reach the hands of the customer after its long journey from factory to the retail shelf.

Supply Chains for Rural Marketing—Delivering through People

For rural India, HUL has established a single distribution channel by consolidating categories. In a significant move, with long-term benefits, HUL has mounted an initiative, *Project Streamline*, to further increase its rural reach with the help of rural sub-stockists. It has already appointed 6000 such sub-stockists. As a result, the distribution network directly covers about 50,000 villages, reaching about 250 million consumers.

Distribution will acquire a further edge with *Project Shakti*, HUL's partnership with self-help groups (SHGs) of rural women. The project, started in 2001, already covers over 5000 villages in 52 districts of Andhra Pradesh, Karnataka, Madhya Pradesh and Gujarat, and is being progressively extended. The vision is to reach over 100,000 villages, thereby touching about 100 million consumers. The SHGs have chosen to adopt distribution of HUL's products as a business venture, armed with training from HUL and support from concerned government agencies and NGOs. A typical Shakti entrepreneur conducts business of around Rs 15,000 per month, which gives her an income in excess of Rs 1000 per month on a sustainable basis. As most of these women are from below the poverty line, and live in extremely small villages (less than 2000 population), this earning is very significant, and is almost double of their past household income. For HUL, the project is bringing new villages under direct distribution coverage. Plans are being drawn up to cover more states, and provide products/services in agriculture, health, insurance, and education. This will both catalyse holistic rural development and also help the SHGs generate even more income. This model creates a symbiotic partnership between HUL and its consumers, some of whom will draw on the company for their livelihood, and help build a self-sustaining virtuous cycle of growth.

The company launched *Shakti-Vani,* a social communication programme. It also launched *Life Buoy Swasthya Chetna* (LBSC), a rural health and hygiene initiative in 2002. It has touched the lives of 27,000 villages and 80 million people in the last 4 years. *The Fair and Lovely Foundation* set up by the company benefited around 5000 women at the end of 2005. The company also focused on social issues such as water conservation and harvesting to touch the lives of the rural people.

Revving up the Sales Organization at HUL

HUL undertook a number of initiatives to improve its distribution network. It set up a full-scale sales reorganization comprising key account management and activation to impact, fully engage, and service modern retailers as they progress. This is displayed in Fig. 2.6. HUL tried to rationalise the product portfolio under which it undertook the following steps.

1. HUL adopted a focused growth strategy by concentrating on brands which constitute most of the business. From marketing 110 brands in 2000, HUL now focuses on 35 power brands, chosen for their scale and potential. Non-core business has been divested or transferred through joint ventures. This has helped HUL achieve product differentiation and improvement in sales.

2. HUL revamped its sales organization in the rural markets to fully meet the emerging needs and increased purchasing power of the rural population. Its distribution network in rural India already directly covers about 50,000

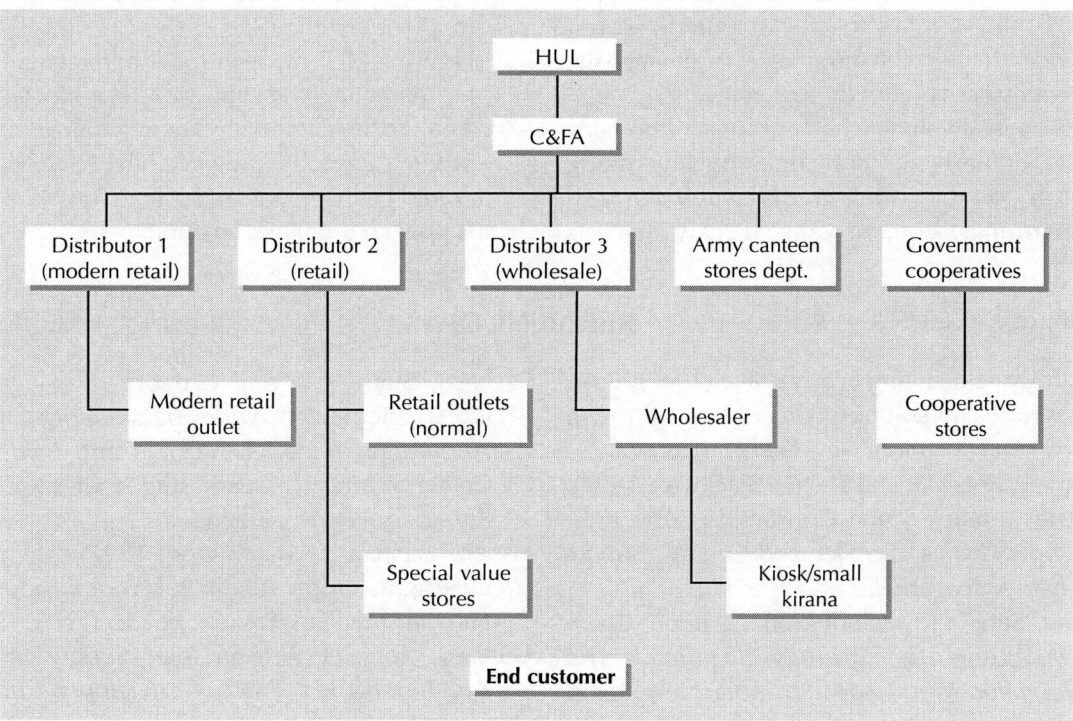

FIG. 2.6 The distribution channels at HUL

villages, reaching about 250 million consumers through about 6000 sub-stockists.

3. It implemented a supply chain system that connects stocklists across the country, and also includes a back-end system connecting suppliers, all company sites, and stretching right up to the stockists.

4. It launched Project Shakti through which the company is able to extend its operations in over 12,000 villages spread across 8 states. HUL also roped in several NGOs and state governments as the initiative helps rural women to improve their financial position.

5. It launched the HUL Network to leverage the channel of direct selling by presenting customized offerings in 11 home and personal care and food categories. Started in 2003, it already has a base of 3,00,000 consultants across the country.

6. It started franchised Lakmé Salons and *Ayush Therapy Centres* to offer standardized services, in line with the strategy to leverage the equity of its brands through relevant services.

7. It innovatively reached out to its customers, particularly in rural areas by leveraging nonconventional media, such as wall paintings, cinema vans, weekly markets (*haats*), fairs, and festivals. In the process, HUL has saved jobs and developed local economies. It acquired Modern Foods, which was the first public sector divestment in India, and since then is implementing a similar turnaround strategy.

Discussion Questions

1. What is the degree of extensiveness and complexity of supply chain and distribution network in Hindustan Unilever Limited (HUL)?

2. How does HUL do the sales and operations planning? How can it be made more effective?

3. What could be requirements and expectations from an IT system by HUL to meet challenges of complexity in supply chain (SC)?

4. How has HUL brought in customer centricity in its supply chain?

5. How has HUL made in-roads in rural markets for marketing and supply of its products?

6. Analyse the components of rationalization of product portfolio undertaken by HUL. What would be the impact of such action plans on supply chain management (SCM)?

REFERENCES

Ballou, Donald H. and S. Srivastava (2007), *Business Logistics/Supply Chain Management*, Pearson Education, New Delhi.

Blackwell, Roger D. and Kristine Blackwell (1999), 'The Century of the Consumer: Converting Supply Chains into Demand Chains', *Supply Chain Management*.

Chopra, Sunil and Meindl (2007), *Supply Chain Management: Strategy, Planning and Operation*, Prentice Hall of India, New Delhi.

Economic Times Intelligence Group (ETIG) (2002), *Knowledge Series on Supply Chain & Logistics*, Mumbai.

Fawcett, Stanley B. and Gregory M. Magnan (2001), *Achieving World-Class Supply Chain Alignment: Benefits, Barriers and Bridges*, Center of Advance Purchasing Studies (CAPS) Research, Tempe, Arizona.

Fisher, Marshall L. (March–April 1997), 'What is the Right Supply Chain for Your Product', *Harvard Business Review*, pp. 105–116.

Gattorna, John (1998), *Strategic Supply Chain Alignment: Best Practice in Supply Chain*, Gower Publishing, Hampshire, UK.

Harrington, L. (1996), 'Logistics Assets: Should You Own or Manage?', *Transportation and Distribution*, No. 37, pp. 51–54.

Harwick, Tom (January 1997), 'Optimal Decision-Making for the Supply Chain', *APICS, The Performance Advantage*, pp. 42–44.

Johnson, Eric and Tom Davis (1995), 'Gaining an Edge with Supply Chain Management', *APICS, The Performance Advantage*, Dec., pp. 26–31.

Kaplan, R.S. and D.P. Norton (1996), *The Balanced Scorecard*, Harvard Business School Press, Boston.

Kraljic, P. (1983), 'Purchasing must Become Supply Management', *Harvard Business Review*, Sept.–Oct., pp. 109–117.

Lee, Hau L. and Corey Billington (1992), 'Managing Supply Chain Inventory: Pitfalls and Opportunities', *Sloan Management Review*, Spring 1992, pp. 65–73.

Lee, Hau L., V. Padmanabhan, and S. Whang (Spring 1997), 'The Bullwhip Effect in Supply Chain', *Sloan Management Review* 38, No. 3, pp. 70–77.

Mittal, P. (2010), 'A Study of Multi-location Retail Supply Chain Network with Reference to Bullwhip Effect', PhD thesis under supervision of the author, Faculty of Management Studies, University of Delhi.

Panda, Tapan K. (2005), *Sales and Distribution Management*, Oxford University Press, New Delhi.

Ross, David E. (September 1996), 'Meeting the Challenge of Supply Chain Management', *APICS, The Performance Advantage*, pp. 38–63.

Simchi-Levi, D., P. Kaminsky, and Edith Simch-Levi (2004), *Designing and Managing the Supply Chain Concepts, Strategies and Cases*, Tata McGraw-Hill, New Delhi.

Steven, Graham C. (1989), 'Integrating the Supply Chain', *International Journal of Physical Distributions and Materials Management*, Vol. 19, No. 8, pp. 3–8.

Internet Resources

www.etstrategicmarketing.com/smJune-July2/pers2-1.htm+ECR as accessed on 14 October 2008

www.expressindia.com/fe/daily/2006 as accessed on 8 October 2008

www.ficci.com/media-room/speeches-presentation/ 2004 as accessed on 14 October 2008

www.globalscorecard.net as accessed on 8 October 2008

www.gmabrands.com (Grocery Manufactures of America (GMA)

www.gs1india.org about/ECR.htm as accessed on 14 October 2008

www.hindubusinessline 30 October 2003 as accessed on 14 October 2008

www.lean-manufacturing.japan.com/scm-terminology/crp as accessed on 1 April 2009

www.sscsinc.com/products/cao.html as accessed on 1 April 2009

www.stratedi.com/dl_ecr.htm + effluent + customer + response as accessed on 4 July 2008

www.supply-chain.org as accessed on 8 October 2008

www.universitip.com/term-paper/Efficient_Customer_Response in the grocery industry-146337889.html as accessed on 4 July 2008

www.uscapgemini.com as accessed on 1 April 2009

www.2.yrclogistics.com ; white paper on flow-through distribution as accessed on 1 April 2009

3 Information and Communication Technology (ICT) in SCM

As emerged from the preceding chapter, the dynamics of supply chain management (SCM) require a systematized and time synchronized flow of information across all the supply chain partners—upstream and downstream. Many of these partners such as suppliers and customers could be even outside the organization. The flow of information has to be real-time, and to begin with, it is related to the capture of customer order and its configuration, point-of-sales (PoS) data at the retailer's point, the prevailing inventory status at the plant, company's warehouse or distribution centre (DC), and at suppliers and sub-contractors, if any. For effective and efficient flow of information and materials, it is required to have an integrated resources planning system at the enterprise level. It takes care of planning of materials, human resources, finance, machine, and shop-floor capacities as also the sub-contractor's capacity and resources, and customer demand levels and requirements across the extended enterprise.

NEED AND ROLE OF AN INFORMATION SYSTEM FOR SCM

If every department of the company has its own system, it will be orientated towards its own economic goals and individual concerns which might be, more often than not, at the cost of the total organization as there would be events and changes in the environment—*external* and *internal*. External might refer to cancelled customer orders, reports of cancelled deliveries from vendors, changed supplier capacity plans, while internal changes would be machine breakdowns, changes in re-order levels (ROL) for materials, purchasing policies, completion of a purchase order, cancellation of a purchase/shop order release that would not be taken care of while a decision is being taken by an individual department. For example, the materials and production department of a company might be interested in small lot size deliveries or lot sizing in order to reduce the costs of inventory but it might give rise to high costs of capacity use/idleness at the supplier's end who would ultimately charge it from the company. The other case arises when small lot sizes are to be traded off with costs of frequent and repeated transportation and/or not availing quantity discounts. So, unless there is a well informed and coordinated decision between production, materials, warehousing, purchasing, and supplier development departments, lot sizing and hence the purchase order schedules cannot be decided upon.

Another example pertains to the customer order fulfilment and its trace and track requirements to supply the customer with all the information as to the progressive status of operations and delivery of the same. Of all the operational execution systems required for SCM, the enterprise resource planning (ERP) system forms the backbone of the SCM, the other being the supplier relationship management (SRM), the customer relationship management (CRM), and transportation systems. The ERP system uses a single version of information which cannot be questioned as everyone in every department is using the same system based on a common database. The system is responsible for keeping the order for its entire life cycle right from its capture to its planning, scheduling, and operations to its shipping and finally sending an invoice. It is possible to keep the track of the order by using a single system only for coordinated decision-making between manufacturing, supplies, inventory, and logistics departments that too at different locations at the same time.

Developing a Definition for ERP

What emerges from the above discussion is that a system is required to integrate all the departments and functions across a company that would run as a single and common database so that various departments can share information and communicate with each other, be it information related to a customer order, a manufacturing shop order, a purchasing order, a delivery order, an invoice and making payment to the vendor, or taking payment from customers even in different currencies, and having traceability and tracking expectations. This system would then be referred to as an ERP system and it serves as a great IT-enabler of the SCM processes. Let us see some formal definitions of ERP.

Bruce Zhang (2005) defines ERP as 'a multimodal application software that integrates activities across different functional departments from production planning, parts purchasing, inventory control, product distribution to order tracking.' The *PC Magazine* describes ERP as 'an integrated information system that serves all departments within an enterprise. Evolved out of manufacturing industry, it is a packaged software rather than a proprietary one.' The single system incorporates manufacturing order entry, accounts receivables and payables, general ledger, materials and purchase planning and their order releases, warehousing, transportation, and human resources. Obviously, ERP implementation would require extensive networking using information and communication technology (ICT) across all the business partners, real-time electronic data interchange (EDI), and use of techniques such as bar coding and radio frequency identification (RFID) for facilitating trace and track mechanisms across the entire supply chain.

Although the Indian corporate sector entered the ERP arena a bit late but at the beginning of the year 2000, over 600 companies had either implemented or were implementing ERP solutions. It initially was all about making the internal systems and business processes of the organization very efficient. To begin with, ERP helped the organizations to streamline their back-end processes, but failed to meet the just-in-time (JIT) requirements of the customers, especially in situations where the company was dealing with products from other vendors.

A Step Ahead of ERP—The ERP-II

Over the past few years, ERP consultants are trying to remove the problems and expanding its the reach and scope, what Gartner likes to call ERP-II. Gartner defines ERP-II as 'a business strategy and a set of collaborative operational and financial processes internally and beyond the enterprise'.[1] This requires enterprises to process critical information for collaborative commerce (c-commerce) processes within communities of interest, i.e., extended enterprise to cause ERP-II to supplant ERP as the primary enabler of internal and interenterprise process efficiency. One implication of ERP-II would be that the companies would have to open up their systems to other companies, be it their suppliers or customers. The ERP-II system is going to be different from the typical ERP systems in the sense that the former would be Web-centric and designed to integrate architecture with the aim of exposing the enterprise resources related information to other enterprises within a 'community of interest'. They may have to shed their inward looking nature and falsify the dictum that 'one vendor owns everything'. ERP vendors are now giving attention to provide for Web-enabled software with inclusion of SCM together with other operational execution systems such as CRM, SRM including provisions for collaborative sales and demand forecast planning, and transportation systems. The Web-enabled ERP also helps to project customer buying habits and plan business strategies in real time. Cadbury planned to put its more than 2500 distributors live on the network. Companies using ERP systems are able to implement activity-based costing (ABC) system much more effectively. Likewise, data mining applications benefit significantly from the availability and centralization of transactional data related to supply chain processes. Various features that make ERP systems attractive to large organizations also bring about a high degree of complexity, e.g., the number of tables in SAP R/3 is more than 15,000, while there are miniature versions of ERP available for small and medium enterprises (SMEs) in India at a lesser complexity, cost, and investment.

---

[1] www.gartner.com/resources

Architecture of a Typical ERP System

Most ERP systems aim to provide a platform for independent suite of applications that can work in distributed computing environments as well as centralized environments. According to Jeroen van den Berg Consulting (2003), ERP systems must possess the following characteristics.

Connectivity

It refers to the abilities of the application software to exchange messages among various modules. Simple packages only offer connectivity between the vendor's applications and the outside world. Advanced systems provide the integration and message transfer between a large number of different applications. They offer a user-friendly interface to define messages between systems.

Web-enablement

All vendors have discovered the Web as user interface for their applications. The Web is advantageous, in the sense that the system can be made accessible to any user with a Web browser.

Personalization and Authorization

This feature refers to the extent to which it is possible to modify the system according to the requirements of the users. One may think of manipulating the screen layout to enhance the user friendliness or giving users restricted access to information.

Modelling and Optimization

It means the ability to model complex problems, e.g., distribution problems, and finding an optimal solution using advanced computational methods. Examples of such methods are linear programming, integer programming, heuristics, stochastic models, etc.

The typical ERP system can be described as a three layered architecture (Fig. 3.1). The layers that make up an ERP system are

- database
- application
- presentation

At the heart of any ERP system is the database management system. Normally, relational databases are used as they facilitate storage data in such a way that the user can use a structured query language (SQL) for standardized reporting and querying of data. Relational databases may be maintained centrally on a mainframe computer or server and then distributed across a network of PCs where specialized functions could be carried out by the user.

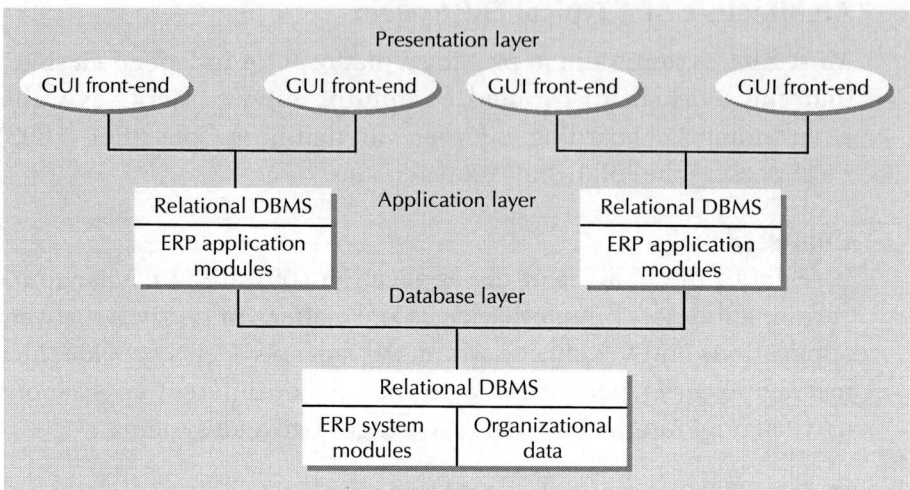

FIG. 3.1 Three layered architecture of ERP
Source: http://www.erpsupersite.com

To improve performance and scalability, data access within ERP systems is usually isolated from program access through a middleware of application layer and servers. In addition to the relational database servers which entertain SQL requests from the users, servers might include transaction processing monitors, directory/security servers, and communication servers. A presentation layer provides screens to capture transaction specific data from an user and provide appropriate formatted reports using menu driven graphical user interface (GUI) screens. All this technology enables the SCM to take coordinated decisions in real time.

ERP MARKET AND PRODUCT PROFILE

ERP systems are a bundle of softwares that give organizations extensive control over their business processes and provide information about most of their supply chain functions and processes. This type of software generally includes separate integrated modules for controlling and coordinating business processes such as demand and supply forecasting, inventory, manufacturing, purchasing, sales, logistics, human resources, and finance. These software modules provide the linkages for most of the supply chain functions in a company. The leading ERP software firms are SAP, PeopleSoft, Oracle, SSA Global (now Infor), and QAD. Of these firms, SAP is by far the largest, so much so, that it has become nearly synonymous with ERP application software. Table 3.1 that follows gives the market share of top vendors in ERP as reported by *Gartner Dataquest* who examines four key ERP segments,

TABLE 3.1   Top ERP and SCM solution providers

Top ten ERP solution providers	Company revenue in US $			
	2004	2005	% Change	% Share
SAP	4.2b	4.7b	+12.1	28.7
Oracle	2.3b	1.7b	−28.4	10.2
Sage	1.1b	1.2b	+12.6	7.4
Microsoft Dynamics	558.9 m	616 m	+10.2	3.7
SSA Global (now Infor)	372 m	464 m	+24.5	2.8
Total ERP revenue including other vendors	15.7b	16.5b	+14.03	
Top ten SCM solution providers	Company revenue in US $			
SAP	729m	912m	+25	19
Oracle*	789m	617m	−21.8	12.9
i2 Technology	169m	170m	+.25	3.5
Ariba**	220m	165m	−26.7	3.4
JDA Software***	112m	123m	+10.5	2.6
Total SCM Market	4.7b	4.8b	+ 2.6	

* Oracle acquired PeopleSoft;
**Ariba procured Supply Management Provider Free Markets in 2004
***JDA Software Group acquired Manugistics.
Source: Gartner Dataquest Report, 2006

namely financial management, human capital management, enterprise assest management, and manufacturing operations.

As is clear, SAP leads the ERP and SCM markets. Both ERP and SCM spaces grew to 14.03 per cent and 2.6 per cent respectively in the year 2004–2005 as per *Gartner's report*, 2006. Both these markets are expanding in terms of continued consolidation, giving more focus to on-demand models and more interest in mid-size markets such as small and medium enterprises (SMEs) (Bailor 2006). The top five ERP vendors accounted for 72 per cent of the ERP market. *The Market Analytics Report; Enterprise Research Planning, 2004–2009* brought out by AMR Research indicates that one-third of the growth in the overall ERP market has been due to fluctuations in currency exchange rates. The trend of acquisitions shows no sign of slowing down. Top vendors such as Oracle, Sage Group, SSA Global, Infor Global, and Epicor have all been active in the merger and acquisition space and have grown more rapidly than the overall ERP Market. The mid range market of $50m to $1b in annual revenue continues to be the focal area with these markets being available in China, India, Eastern Europe, and Latin America. Also the ERP buyers are moving away from large upfront ERP purchases and instead tending to license user seats and functional ERP modules incrementally which has resulted in smaller average expenditure in ERP by the enterprises.

Infor SSA Global's ERP Software Package

The BaaN software was acquired by Invensys of UK in 2000 to be finally taken over by SSA Global in August 2004 who renamed it ERP LN 6.1. In May 2006, SSA Global was acquired by Infor Global Systems of Atlanta which has ERP products such as Infor LX and Infor LN. SSA Global, now Infor has been a leading provider of extended enterprise resource planning (ERP) solutions for manufacturing, services, and public organizations throughout the world. In addition to core ERP applications, SSA Global offers a full range of integrated and extended solutions which includes corporate performance management, CRM, SCM, product life-cycle management, and supplier relationship management.

To ensure tangible results, SSA ERP incorporates four pillars of value designed for the following.

1. Improve productivity with information visibility, easy navigation, and fewer steps to complete business processes, which will benefit organizations in terms of empowered employees who react faster and make better decisions with lesser number of errors.
2. Control work-in-process and reduce costs through resource productivity with built-in agility and support for lean manufacturing. This provides an edge to organizations in terms of the ability to do more with less while fully satisfying customer demand.
3. Increase interoperability and extend the scope of core manufacturing systems by building strong bridges with organizations' supply chain and delivering full access to ERP data with complete support for Web services.
4. Deliver low total cost of ownership (TCO) through advanced architecture and Web user interface that make SSA ERP easy to install, implement, integrate, maintain, and upgrade.

Modules of the SSA Global/Infor ERP Package

The following are the modules of the SSA Global/Infor ERP package.

SSA Planning   This module helps organizations to meet customer expectations with sophisticated tools such as Master Planning, which consolidates multiple planning methods into one application. The solution facilitates demand planning for increased forecasting accuracy. Besides that, it provides cumulative order lead-time calculations and planning horizon updates, resource order planning, automatic rescheduling, and maintaining fixed delivery times, i.e., available-to-promise (ATP).

Companies can also integrate in a seamless manner with other components of SSA ERP and with the planning modules of SSA SCM to facilitate planning and production control across the supply chain.

SSA Manufacturing The core of SSA ERP is SSA manufacturing, which supports a wide range of manufacturing situations including lean manufacturing while utilizing JIT material control. It also offers complete engineering product data management capabilities that allows standard products with slight variations to be configured, planned, and produced with full tracking throughout the manufacturing processes. Companies can easily rely on SSA manufacturing for having total control of shop floor, assembly, manufacturing, and quality along with labour, materials, and overhead costs.

SSA Leanware It is a stand-alone execution layer that provides a true orderless *Kanban* execution system for production, procurement, ordering, replenishment, and Web-based supplier collaboration.

SSA Finance This multicurrency, fully integrated financial solution meets global Generally Accepted Accounting Principles (GAAP) standards and allows for reconciliation of balance sheets, profit and loss statements, and cash flow figures at all times over different entities. It provides a solid financial foundation with flexible, user-defined general ledger, accounts receivable, and accounts payable components that automate and streamline the key business transactions, including reconciliation of financial transactions to corresponding logistical transactions. Central invoicing compiles billable data from all SSA ERP modules into an invoice, then creates an open entry in accounts receivable. It also posts revenue and costs of goods sold to the general ledger.

SSA Warehousing It facilitates inventory planning with serial tracking of high-volume serialized items, using bar coding and the latest RFID technology. It also enables JIT material supply from warehouses, suppliers, and production sites. It provides visibility of available stock across multiple warehouses by allowing organizations to define warehouse operations by type, zone, and location. In addition, SSA warehousing offers support for handling unit (packaging and content) for shipping and receiving as well as cross-docking situations.

SSA Freight Management This module reduces costs by allowing organizations to manage their own transportation needs with transport planning and freight-rating for the inbound and outbound flow of goods. The company can select carrier and service levels at the time of order entry, based on anticipated freight cost levels and transportation lead times. After the delivery is complete, SSA freight management handles the auditing and payment of carrier invoices, and related financial bookings.

SSA Procurement This facilitates direct materials purchasing and is designed for both single-site and multi-site operations. It provides centralized and decentralized order/contract management capabilities, smoothly handling requisitions, requests for quotations, purchase contracts/schedules, purchasing order control, and procurement statistics and history. Organizations can combine different purchase requirements into one purchase order, define multiple manufacturers by item using an approved suppliers list (ASL), and utilize automatic approval process for buyers, partners, and planners.

SSA Sales This fully integrated solution helps the company to manage sales strategy and execution, both on a daily and long-term basis. It handles quotes, order tracking and acknowledgements, contracts, pricing, discounts, promotions, scheduling, and product structure. It streamlines the order management process by allowing them to customize order entry procedures for different items or customers, and provides support for handling and releasing of schedules. Organizations can also evaluate sales performance based on current and historical information.

SSA Enterprise Service Management This component offers the comprehensive functionality needed to manage the 'as-built' to 'as-service' transition with field-based repair, maintenance, and installation services. It basically includes the services as service order control, configuration management, contract and sub-contract management, call management, problem resolution tools, preventive maintenance, inspections management, and depot repair.

SSA Project Manufacturing resource management and project management are brought together in a single environment with SSA Project. This solution provides real-time control for all aspects of project manufacturing, from estimates and bids through site installation and maintenance. It enables the use of one estimate for multiple bids, accommodates multiple customers and alternatives, and allows to launch an estimate of an approved bid as a project.

SSA ERP Quality Management It provides a parameter-controlled interface with sales, purchase, and production orders, as well as with inventory, location, and lot control. SSA ERP quality management facilitates the automatic or manual creation of inspection order and blocks inventory and order procedures until inspection results are received.

SSA ERP People Helping organizations in managing the workforce, SSA ERP people enables centralized hours and expense accounting (budgeting and registration) for SSA project, SSA manufacturing, and SSA enterprise service management. It supports hours accounting based on assignments, which allows for automatic creation of hours.

SSA Extended Solutions SSA ERP also offers seamless integration with SSA extended solutions that span the entire value chain. These include SSA customer relationship management, SSA supply chain management, SSA supplier relationship management, SSA corporate performance management, SSA product life-cycle management and SSA collaborative order management among others.

Let us see what SSA Global offers in its SCM solution.

SSA Supply Chain Management

By fusing the demand chain with the supply chain, SSA SCM makes it easy to forecast customer demand accurately, take an order, give an accurate delivery date, manufacture the right goods, replenish supply, and position inventory properly, as well as pick, pack, and ship efficiently—all the while maintaining a minimal finished goods inventory. It has all the components organizations' need to gain greater visibility across their supply chain while increasing agility and responsiveness. The various modules of the SSA SCM are the following.

Advanced Planning and Scheduling (APS)

It provides the visibility and decision-making tools required for demand planning, resource allocation, and production scheduling. Advanced planning and scheduling also synchronizes manufacturing operations and resources with customer priorities using the planning process constraints. It shortens internal response time to changes in customer demand. It comprises planning and scheduling of demand, inventory and manufacturing, and a pull-based replenishment planning daily consumption requirement.

Transportation Management

This module helps to develop agile and cost-effective network designs that would match the speed to supply products to the customers. It comprises transportation carrier bid selection, mode and route, transport shipment life-cycle planning, transport execution including Web-enablement, and international trade logistics including the estimation of landed cost of materials thereby, if any.

Warehouse Management

It enables end-to-end order fulfilment from order capture to order shipping, making it possible to fulfil the promise of the perfect order in terms of its delivery at the right place at the right time and in right combination (of the products/SKUs contained therein) minimizing its storage in the warehouse. It may entail reduction of labour costs by proper work management at the warehouse and cubic space utilization by slotting, increased productivity by automated processes such as advanced voice–recognition directed warehouse logistics, and using RFID, shipping, receiving, and tracking.

Event and Performance Management

It enables to generate information related to demand, supply, and the product flows across the supply chain in a visible manner across all the partners or even regulatory authorities, if the need be. It can yield detailed reporting on supply chain costs and performance and help in relating to the corporate performance results. So that supply chain managers can relate events with key performance indicators (KPIs) and respond and manage these more efficiently.

SSA SCM is ideal for companies across a broad range of industries from aerospace and defence and automotive to consumer packaged goods (CPG) and retail that requires stronger, and alternatively more efficient supply chain performance. SSA SCM solution also makes sense for third-party logistics (3PL) providers, distributors, suppliers, and others that require world-class SCM capability. Some of the benefits accrued are the following.

- Reduced waste and better quality products
- Improved forecasting accuracy and quicker response times
- Shorter manufacturing lead times
- Streamlined planning and execution cycle times
- Reduced inventory and inventory costs
- Fewer out of stock and outdated inventory situations
- Improved order fulfilment rates and customer service
- Improved warehouse and shipping operations
- Reduced total supply chain costs as a percentage of revenue
- Greater supply chain visibility
- Faster deployment and lower total cost of ownership (TCO)
- Faster payback on the investment

QAD's ERP Software Package

QAD's industry-specific and best-in-class manufacturing software is, in use at more than 5400 manufacturing sites worldwide, available in 26 languages and supports all major currencies, and is thus ideal for globally distributed enterprises. MFG/Pro eB2, now rechristened as QAD Enterprise Applications, provides the backbone for collaboration across a manufacturer's value chain. The components of the QAD enterprise applications is shown in Fig. 3.2.

Enterprise financials	Financial analysis	Management reporting	Multi-GAAP	Budgeting	Governance, risk and compliance
	Consolidations	Allocations	Financial shared services	Credit management	Tax management
	General ledger	Multi-currency	Accounts receivable	Accounts payable	Banking/ cash management	Cost management
	Fixed assets		Enhanced controls	Vertex sales and use tax interface		Logistics accounting
Standard financials	General ledger	Multi-currency	Accounts receivable	Accounts payable	Cash management	Cost management
	Fixed assets		Enhanced controls	Vertex sales and use tax interface		Logistics accounting
Customer management	Sales quotations	Sales orders	Sales analysis	Customer relationship management	Pricing
	Customer self-service		Distributed order management		Demand management
	Trade management			Configurator	
Manufacturing	Product data management	Manufacturing planning		Manufacturing execution	Quality management
	Lean	Just-in-time sequencing	Planner	Production scheduler	PRO/PLUS
	Execution tools	Automated data collection	Compliance quality	Enterprise validation	Product life-cycle management
Supply chain	Purchasing			Supplier performance	
	Warehousing	Release management		Consignment inventory	Supply visualization
	Supply chain planning		Transportation management		Data synchronization
Service and support	Service and support management	Mobile field service		Field service scheduler	Project realization management
Enterprise asset management	Project controls management		Plant maintenance		MRO management
Analytics	Reporting and analysis			Business intelligence	
Interoperability	Qxtend		EDI e-commerce		Product information management
	Document management		Output management		Integration suite

FIG. 3.2 Various modules of QAD's MFG/Pro, now QAD Enterprise Applications
Source: www.qad.com/portal/site/solutioncenter as accessed on 20 October 2008

MFG/Pro eB2 aims to combine the real-world requirements of customers with proven expertise of the organization to provide a solution that opens the lines of communication for true collaboration with all the members of the value chain. The various modules of the MFG/Pro eB2 are described in brief as the following.

Features

Traditionally, MFG/Pro functionality has supported production, using work orders and repetitive schedules, either separately or together, in a mixed mode manufacturing environment. Today, many companies are re-examining their manufacturing policies in response to factors such as increasingly uncertain demand, more complex variations in product mix, and growing variability in customer ordering patterns. As a result, many companies are moving towards more streamlined manufacturing approaches and implementing continuous flow and pull-based techniques to make their plants and entire value chain more effective.

Manufacturing Module   Various elements and benefits associated with this module designed to work in a lean environment serves the following.

- Communicate *kanban* status throughout the supply chain
- Enable enhanced lean manufacturing techniques:
  - Dynamic average demand calculations
  - Advanced methods for establishing inventory buffer quantities
  - Dynamic safety stock calculations
- Manage inventory buffer
- Enhance *kanban* transaction processing
- Facilitate workbench simulations:
  - Sizing inventory buffers
  - Determining *kanbans* and *kanban* quantities for each loop
  - Analysing product mix
  - Developing a levelled schedule
  - Real-time visibility into electronic kanban signals
- Produce lean schedule orders for finished goods (FG) or capacity constrained resource (CCR)

Manufacturing, Planning, and Execution Module   Easily adaptable to organizations' production environment, MFG/Pro manufacturing control fully manages mixed mode environments, enabling faster decisions, and improving customer responsiveness. The software controls all the activities of the production floor from identifying missing parts to reporting labour. It also supports discrete, repetitive, assemble-to-order (ATO), batch process, and mixed-mode environments. The module facilitates the following.

- Co-product and by-product manufacturing and planning
- Work orders entered manually or released from material requirements planning (MRP)
- Component availability checking and ability to substitute items
- Detailed labour, work-in-process (WIP) inventory, and sub-contract tracking with variance calculations
- Lean schedule orders
- Streamlined scheduling and reporting in high-volume repetitive environments
- Daily production scheduling by item, site, and production line
- Finite loading and forwarding scheduling for production line schedules
- Optional pick list for stocking point-of-use locations
- Component back flush from inventory or point-of-use in discrete, repetitive, or lean environments
- Quality test results prompted at selected production operations
- Cumulative item cost and work centre productivity reporting
- Lean manufacturing capability and compatibility

Logistics Accounting   It improves control over logistics costs and automates the administration process. It enables one to define and track individual costs associated with the transportation of goods into and out of company locations. It has several features as the following.

- Tracks transportation costs incurred when goods are moved into and out of company locations.
- Creates accruals that can be used to verify invoices from carriers.
- Apportions invoice variances across items.

Sales and Distribution Order Management Module   MFG/Pro sales order and distribution order management module provides easy to use functionality for order entry, shipping, invoicing, sales analysis, and supply chain planning (Fig. 3.3). It helps organizations to deliver superior customer services quickly through flexibility, information access, and accurate fulfilment of customer needs. The software module facilitates:

- Customer item numbering for sales orders and invoices
- Commission splitting by line item or margin base
- Supporting non-stock items and drop-shipments
- Sales tracking by customer type and channel
- Automatic credit hold and manual order hold
- Consolidated invoices or one invoice per shipment
- Single transaction to create invoice and record inventory transaction

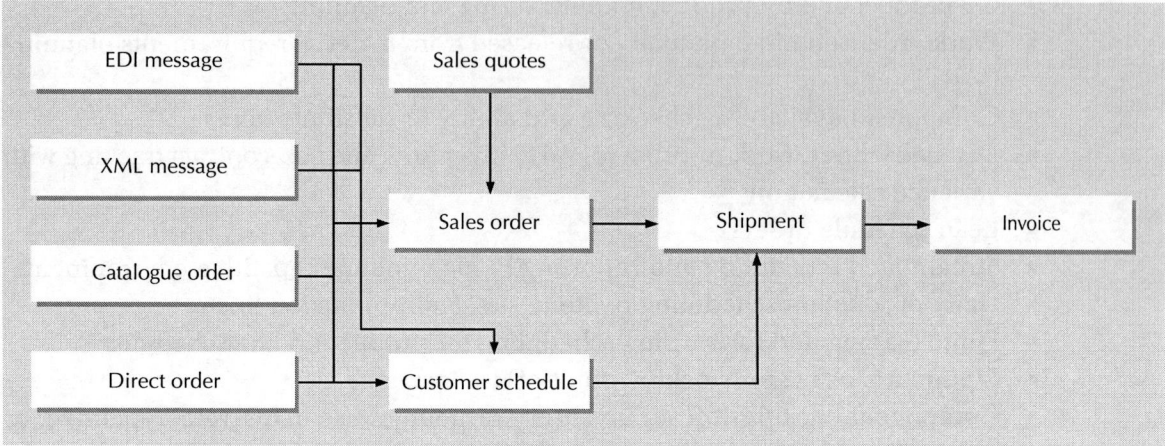

FIG. 3.3 Sales and distribution shared service domain in MFG/Pro
Source: www.qad.com

- Automatic updation of installed base
- Providing EDI support including purchase order acknowledgment
- Creation of multiple sales orders per invoice
- Flexible pricing by brand, geography, volume, and rebates
- Discounting by quantity, product lines, and types
- Automatic best price calculation
- Re-pricing option
- Data collection and reporting
- Multiple scheduled order lines for a particular item number
- Supporting container and line charges to sales/scheduled order lines
- Handling invoicing and payments for consigned inventory

Product Management Module MFG/Pro product management supports the management of complex product or process definitions, product costs, and product change orders as shown in Fig. 3.4. The module has provisions for the following.

- Multiple (alternate) product structures, formulas and processes per item
- Product change control system
- Product structures with effective dates
- Yield and shrinkage factors for use by materials planning
- Structure type for global and local phantoms or documentary items
- Co-product and by-product support
- Product structure, formula, and process copy
- Cost roll-up by effective date
- Option to include yield in cost

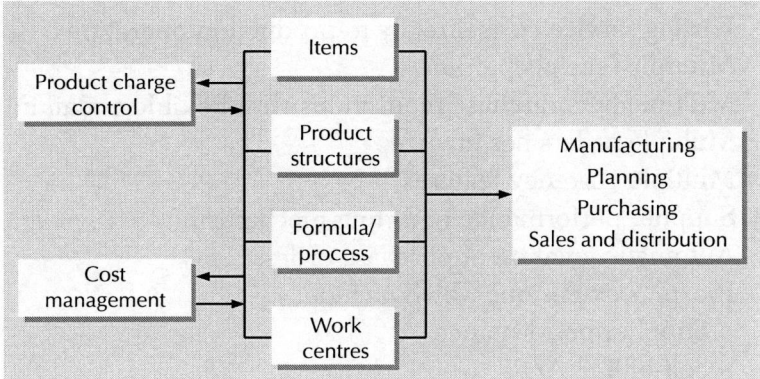

FIG. 3.4 Product control diagram in MFG/Pro
Source: www.qad.com

- Cumulative lead-time calculations
- Production forecast percentage specified for each option or accessory

Purchasing Module To streamline the entire purchasing process and support faster decision-making, MFG/Pro purchasing includes integrated purchasing, supplier schedule, and quality management modules. The fully integrated purchasing module provides a link between plans, operations, and trading partners as shown in Fig. 3.5. It also supports requisitions, purchase orders, receiving, invoicing, and supplier performance tracking.

The purchasing module of MFG/Pro eB2 has due provisions for the following.

- Centralized or distributed purchasing, ordering, receiving, and payments
- Single or multiple database
- Purchase stock items, supplies, and services

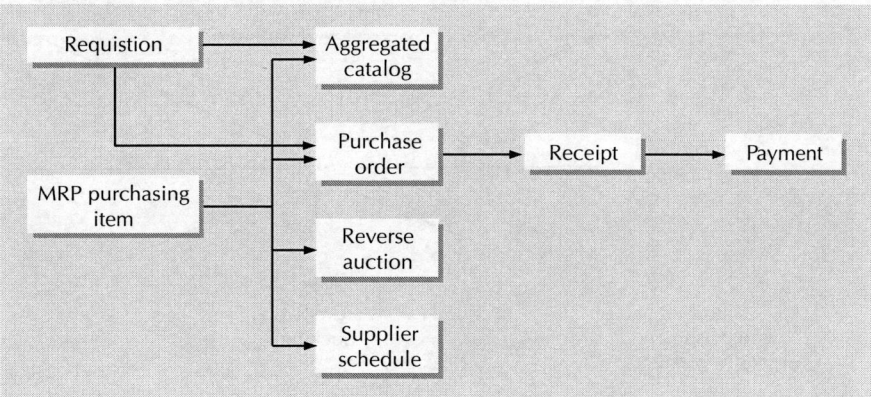

FIG. 3.5 Fully integrated purchasing application in QAD's MFG/Pro
Source: www.qad.com

- Posting service costs directly to production operations
- Multiple receipts per line
- Multiple line purchase requisitions with flexible e-mail notifications
- Multiple orders per invoice
- Multiple currency features
- Supplier performance reporting mechanism
- Automatic creation of purchase orders
- Pro/plus extensions which include:
  - Supplier performance
  - Self-billing A/R
  - Supplier shipping schedules
  - Shipment performance reporting
  - Container and line charges

Advanced Inventory Management (AIM) Module   It offers a range of inventory management facilities that enable organizations to control the receipt, put away, storage, picking, and shipping of inventory using warehouses that exist within the MFG/Pro environment (Fig. 3.6). The advanced inventory management module provides for the following features.

- Support to more than 80 user-definable put-away algorithms
- User-defined step-by-step inventory movement of goods
- Flexible replenishment to pre-defined stock levels
- Optimized picking/packing

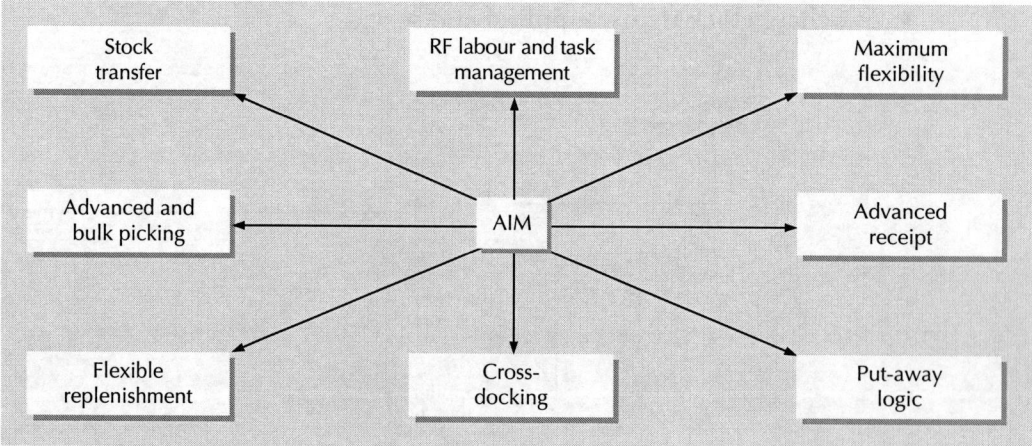

FIG. 3.6 Advanced inventory management (AIM) system in MFG/Pro
Source: www.qad.com

- Support to LIFO, FIFO, and other picking-up logic
- Labour scheduling and management with efficient planning and monitoring of resources, bar coding and radio frequency (RF) data collection support
- Sizing calculations to efficiently use warehouse space
- Cross-docking

MFG/Pro eB2 manages consigned inventory from the point of view of both the company shipping consigned goods to a customer and the company receiving consigned goods from a supplier. The consignment inventory module provides this functionality as an additional capability to MFG/Pro.

Finance Module   MFG/Pro financial module provides multiple entity, multiple currency, multiple language, and multiple tax functions suitable for the financial management of small and large enterprises as shown in Fig. 3.7. The flexible period-end/year-end procedures and advanced credit/cash/audit reports and inquiries make these applications fast to implement and easy to operate.

The module has provisions for the following.

- Multiple entity (company)
- Multiple currency
- Multiple language

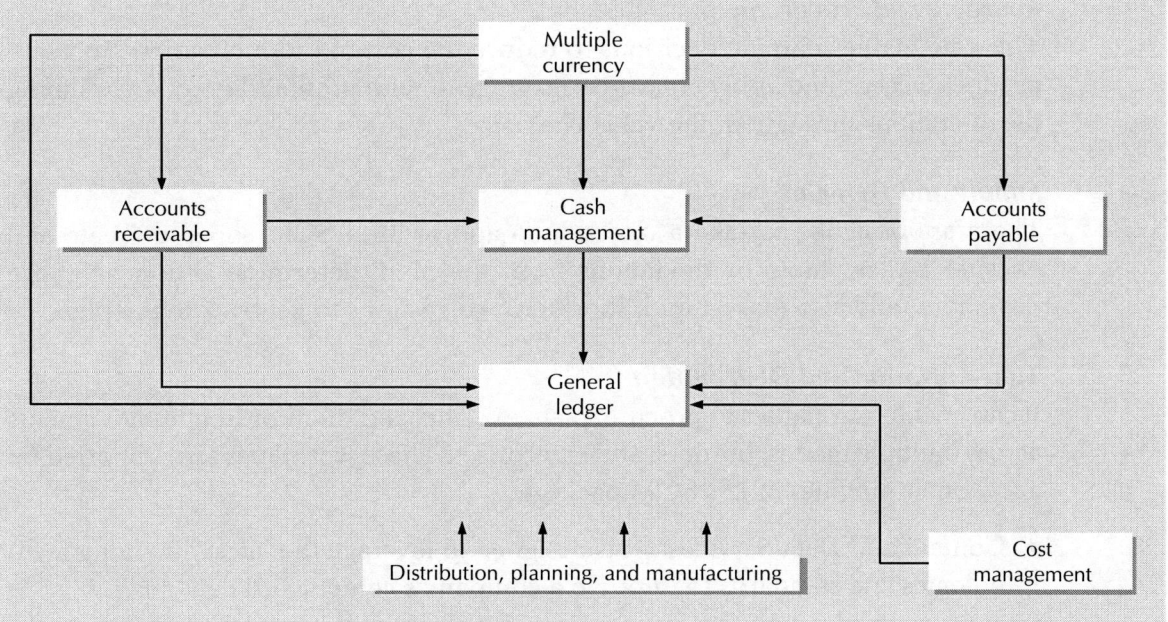

FIG. 3.7   The components of MFG/Pro financial module
Source: www.qad.com

- Multiple tax systems
- Currency conversion and gain/loss
- Integration with sales and distribution, planning, and manufacturing modules
- Flexible period-end/year-end procedures
- Advanced reports and audit trails
- Drill-down inquiries
- Management reporting, including cash management
- Flexible budgeting capabilities

i2 SCM Software Package

i2 enables organizations to focus on initiatives that will help them gain a competitive advantage. It offers workflows for major business process areas through its SCM software package, which includes the following.

Order Fulfilment

It can help an organization in providing a single interactive face to the customer. Besides that, an optimum customer experiences a proactive approach to enhance visibility, accurate real-time responses to requests, and improved delivery performance.

Sourcing and Procurement

This can enable sourcing decisions to reduce the cost of product variety, increase product success, and apply enterprise leverage to raise profitability by streamlining the operations throughout the value chain.

Supply and Demand

These are designed to take a closed-loop approach to SCM so as to create and execute a plan, monitor deviations from the plan, determine action on those deviations, and also make rapid, short-term corrections to get back to the plan.

Transportation and Distribution

It can enable companies to procure, plan, execute, and monitor freight movements across multiple modes, borders, and enterprises. These workflows are supported by a few other modules of i2's SCM package:

- Content and Data Services: It is designed to leverage the latest emerging technologies and standards to improve a company's content and data quality.
- Synchronized supply chain optimization (SSCO): It can provide a standards-based open and unified architecture to run collaboration and planning solutions across the supply chains.

The details of four main processes of i2's SCM package are described in a concise manner.

Order fulfilment   The current business environment is generally characterized by increased reliance on outsourcing as well as a growing need for process integration among trading partners where companies have to manage to buy product anywhere, sell anywhere paradigms. In addition, there is growing co-branding, co-marketing, and increasing revenue potential through bundling services with products. The challenge of meeting growing customer demands develops the need to have proactive visibility across the entire order fulfilment process. i2 offers the following workflows.

Collaborative replenishment   It can allow companies to manage various aspects of their replenishment programmes including collaborative forecast adjustments, customer demand changes, and programme performance management. i2 collaborative replenishment is designed to offer forecast analysis, promotions collaboration, demand change liability/flexibility management, replenishment, and monitoring. The i2 collaborative replenishment solution includes set-up, planning and execution, and performance measurement components.

Customer order fulfilment   It is designed to link every phase of order management, from order capture to generate invoice and settlement, with a close integration to the demand management and order planning loops. The end-to-end solution provided by i2 can create a single face-to-customer across various diverse processes, lines of business, geographies, and IT systems. i2 customer order fulfilment is built on a modular service platform that is designed to deploy a customized order fulfilment solution.

Supply chain visibility   It is designed to allow a company to respond for unplanned supply and demand, say, due to bullwhip effect, that may disrupt information and material flow in the supply chain. The i2 solution is designed to enable a glass pipeline by providing order, shipment, and inventory visibility across fragmented business processes, which can also provide exception resolution and decision support. The solution can thus provide a process-centric view coordinating different functional modules.

Consolidated sourcing and procurement   Every company wants to maximize its return on investments. They can achieve this by optimizing their sourcing and procurement functions. i2 has designed solutions that can enable sourcing decisions to reduce the cost of product variety, increase product success, and apply enterprise leverage to raise profitability and stream operations.

i2 offers solution workflows for:

Collaborative supply execution   It is designed to provide a comprehensive set of mid-term to long-term collaborative capabilities. Several companies in a wide range of industries have deployed i2 solution to manage forecasting and capacity, orders, shipping, inventory, and replenishment in a multi-vendor environment. The solution can handle the primary business processes related to collaborative supply execution, including:

(i) Forecast collaboration: It can allow companies to consolidate material requisitions into orders, further collaborate on a purchase order and can support the entire life cycle of a purchase order through shipments and invoicing.

(ii) Lean replenishment/supply management: It can support multiple replenishment workflows, exception resolution, and process management capabilities for direct and hub vendor-managed inventory and pull-based replenishment.

Hazardous materials management   It can provide companies with information necessary to comply with regional hazardous material standards and environmental regulations.

Reuse and product sourcing   This module is designed to provide a complete component sourcing solution for today's complex production environment. This can help product teams establish reuse, cost, and line-of-supply targets for both vertical and outsourced approaches. This can provide end-to-end sourcing coordination, from engineering and product development to manufacturing and disposal. i2 reuse and product sourcing can address contract-based cost projections, hazardous material concerns, component obsolescence, and supply availability.

Sourcing execution   It is designed to provide a portfolio of negotiation tools to support the entire intent-to-contract processes. i2 sourcing execution is designed to support the evaluation of both critical cost and non-cost factors, including readiness for vendor-managed inventory, logistics cost factors, and the qualitative value adding contributions of suppliers.

Strategy and performance management   It is designed to allow companies to automate spend analysis and compliance management while evaluating and improving category sourcing, supplier differentiation, and performance.

Supply and demand   The increase in demand variability and supply chain complexity has resulted in traditional open-loop monthly or weekly supply chain planning systems becoming inadequate. Companies with strong closed-loop systems can harness fluctuations in demand with good customer service to increase market share or profits or both.

i2 supply and demand solutions are designed to take a closed-loop approach to SCM—create and execute a plan, monitor deviations from the plan, determine action on those deviations, thereby also to make rapid short-time corrections to get back to the plan.

i2 offers solution workflow to facilitate the following.

- Manage and analyse demand variability
- Create accurate plans and forecasts
- Develop timely and profitable promotional strategies
- Manage manufacturing, logistics, and other supply chain constraints
- Optimize inventory positioning
- Support distribution and allocation
- Monitor plan execution and manage exceptions

i2 offers workflows for the following:

Collaborative supply execution It can allow an organization to execute purchase recommendations through a comprehensive set of collaborative workflows.

Continuous demand management It is designed to provide a comprehensive closed-loop approach for the development of accurate forecasts, demand plans, as well as demand influencing price and promotional activities. The i2 continuous demand management solution is designed to encompass demand forecasting and planning, price and promotion optimization, demand prioritization and communication, as well as performance management.

Factory solutions It is designed to manage more precisely the key manufacturing variables, from work center capacity and setup times to material and labour availability, due dates, and corporate production plans. It also helps to attain advanced factory planning and scheduling accuracy, reduce inventory and manufacturing costs, and improve both delivery performance and customer satisfaction.

Inventory optimization It helps to monitor, manage, and improve inventory performance at every stage of the supply chain. This solution can be deployed to determine what to make, what to buy and where to buy it, as well as *how, when* and *where* decisions as applied to inventory products. Intelligent inventory management can translate directly into reduced inventory carrying costs, improved product availability, and greater customer satisfaction.

Supply management   It supports master planning, allocation planning, distribution planning, inventory planning, and profit optimization.

Transportation and distribution   With rising costs of handling, changing customer requirement and a need for adaptable transportation and distribution network, companies are looking to achieve greater efficiencies in their transportation and distribution operations. i2 solutions for transportation and distribution are designed to enable companies to procure, plan, execute, and monitor freight movements across multiple modes, borders, and enterprises. These solutions can create value by synchronizing the critical transportation and distribution business processes resulting in optimal cost and service performance. i2 *Freight Matrix* is a service-based solution for transportation and distribution.

i2 offers workflows for the following.

Replenishment planning   It is designed to provide a comprehensive solution to balance demand, supply, and re-stocking in the retail movement. The system automatically calculates demand safety stock levels for retail stores and associated distribution centres while balancing required service levels with inventory investments. i2 replenishment planning is designed to evaluate inventory levels, lead times, ordering policies as well as storage and handling constraints.

Strategic network design and analysis   It can support key decisions at each stage of the supply chain, from raw materials procurement to finished goods distribution. These tools can be deployed to model suppliers, factories and factory processes, distribution centres, seasonal demand, transportation links, outsourcing, inventory and related costs, and constraints.

Transportation bid collaboration   It is designed to provide a suite of tools for the periodic negotiation of transportation rates. Transportation bid collaboration combines an optimization engine, a Web-based workflow and a bidding tool into a single solution for negotiating and awarding transportation contracts.

Transportation modelling and analysis   It enables tactical and strategic transportation planning as part of overall transportation management. The i2 transportation modelling and analysis tool is designed to employ sophisticated optimization and data techniques to define and evaluate alternative transportation strategies.

Transportation planning and management   It can support the planning, execution, management, and monitoring of the transportation life cycle. This solution can offer the tools needed to optimize and execute shipments, proactively monitor exceptions, manage match-pay and auto-pay settlements, as well as provide analytical performance management for transportation activities.

mySAP™ ERP Software Package

mySAP™ is claimed by its vendor SAP as the world's most complete solution to support fundamental business requirements, enabling adaptive change, completing integration and easy collaboration over the Internet. With mySAP™ ERP, SAP has evolved its vision from automating end-to-end business processes to one of increasing efficiency within an organization and extending processes beyond the enterprise to the entire business ecosystem by incorporating customers, partners, and suppliers. mySAP™ ERP is powered by the SAP NetWeaver™ platform, an innovative integration and application platform. SAP NetWeaver™ lays the foundation for new cross-functional business processes and lowers total cost of ownership (TCO) by reducing the need for custom integration and by offering a complete life-cycle management solution. This Web services-based platform is the foundation for the enterprise services architecture, aligning people, information, and business processes across organizational and technological boundaries.

Features and Benefits

The system's features and the operational benefits of using mySAP™ are outlined here.

Self-services

- Offers managers and employees immediate and personalized access to corporate services, saving time, and effort.
- Provides innovative roles to increase employee productivity.
- Improves usability and easy access to relevant information.

Analysis

- Supports decision-making with insight thereby improving responsiveness to business change.
- Delivers analyses, evaluations and key performance indicators for planning, measuring, and controlling organizational processes.

Financials

- Provides an extensive range of services and processes for effective financial management, including financial accounting and financial SCM.
- Offers extensive corporate governance support, including compliance systems and transparent financial reporting, thus reducing the risk of non-compliance.

Human capital management

- Offers solutions for efficient human resources management, including employee transaction management, employee life-cycle management, and workforce deployment.

- Helps improve employee productivity and staff retention.

Operations value generation

- Provides end-to-end logistics such as purchase-to-pay or order-to-pay.
- Brings the top-floor to the shop floor by aligning operations with strategic decisions.

Operations support

- Forms the basis for cross-organization enhancement of business processes and collaboration with vendors, customers, and other partners, improving the utilization of assets and product life-cycle processes.
- Helps reduce downtime, improves decision-making, and contributes to increased customer loyalty.

Corporate services

- Supports centralized and decentralized organization services in areas such as real estate management, travel management, incentive and commission management, and environmental health and safety.
- Helps minimize costs and optimize sales performance.

SAP NetWeaver

- Supports flexible IT infrastructures, including SAP and non-SAP solutions, thereby leveraging existing IT infrastructures and reducing TCO.

mySAP™ *Modules*

The functionality embedded within the software is logically separated into areas, which SAP calls as mySAP™ modules. These modules are also integrated with each other.

Financial Accounting and Controlling Module   The financial accounting and controlling (FI/CO) module enables organizations to define their company codes or controlling areas to map organization structure within the framework of the SAP system. Key components of this module are the following:

General ledger accounting   It has automatic account balance features so as to provide real-time reference of the financial situation. Working hand-in-hand with the cost accounting functionality, it simultaneously updates the proper cost objects in every transaction.

Accounts receivable and accounts payable   The account receivable function deals with account balancing with customers and revenues and is directly integrated with the sales distribution (SD) module. It also offers an excellent functionality in credit management and automatically generating dunning notices. The accounts payable function deals with administration of all accounting data for business transactions with vendors/suppliers of goods and services. This function is directly integrated with the 'purchasing and invoice verification' function of the materials management module.

Asset accounting Assets need to be planned, maintained, and depreciation values need to be taken into consideration over the asset's lifetime. Interest calculations and insurance payments need to be made until the asset is retired. Such functions are included in the asset accounting component of the FI module with a proper integration with the materials management (MM) module where asset procurements from external vendors or asset production from in-house sources are reflected in real time.

Special purpose ledger This component acts as a collector of information from different SAP applications. The roll-up function of the component enables an organization to combine the information of several ledgers into one special roll-up ledger for consolidated information.

Funds management This is used to develop budgets for appropriate areas of an organization, monitor movement of funds in these areas, check for budget availability for critical transactions, and to provide warnings whenever the risk of a budget overflow is looming.

Cash management It provides help to an organization in maintaining good liquidity so that they can make payment for open items as due and the organization can monitor cash inflows and outflows in real time. Cash management can also provide a liquidity forecast to monitor incoming customer payments and outgoing vendor payments at any time in future.

Treasury management It has a function called limit management, where an organization can limit market risks by recording limit utilization and monitoring limits. It also has a money market function to manage short-term borrowing and investment transactions as fixed term deposits.

Overhead cost controlling The overhead cost controlling functionality of the CO module of SAP enables organizations to plan, allocate, and control such costs. It also has functions for activity-based costing, where organizations can define cost allocation along a value added chain of business processes involving activities performed in the chain of events.

Profitability analysis This component of the CO module provides a tool to analyse profitability situation based on products, customers, specific orders or combinations thereof for the organizational units.

Investment management The investment management component of the mySAP™ provides functions to plan investments from a requirement and financial point of view. It can manage and monitor budgets for capital investments.

Profit centre accounting Profit centres can be set up as a product lines, sales functions, or geographical considerations, having its own set of receivables and deliverables.

Sales and distribution module One of the most critical module of mySAP™ system is the sales and distribution (SD) module because every organization implementing the mySAP™ system has some goods or services to sell. SD is fully customizable for a particular business process and has extensive reporting capabilities. Some of the critical components and functions available within the module are as follows:

Master data Customers form the basis of all master data in the SD module and they are better termed as business partners. The shipment and transportation companies, who deliver products to end customers, also become business partners. Brokers, third-party agencies, or even employees of the organization are also treated as business partners. Organizations can also track information about their competitors and prospective customers. Master data also includes products and services and the SD module is integrated with MM module.

Basic functions The pricing function in the SD module is one of the more sophisticated functionalities available in the mySAP™ module. This function is used to calculate prices for goods and services based on various pricing criteria. This pricing function is closely integrated with the account assignment functionality, thereby providing integration with the FI-AR component of the system. The account assignment functionality is critical for the integration between billing and invoicing (SD–Bill) and the FI-AR components. The system sends base price and customer discounts to the revenue account and sends the freight charges to the freight accrual account.

Material substitution is another useful functionality which is used when mainstream material is not available and orders are still coming for the same, and under those cases when customer is willing to substitute the original product with some other offering of the organization, the system will automatically derive the replacement material in sales order and would derive appropriate pricing for the replacement product. The material listing and exclusion functionality comes handy when organizations would not want to sell some goods to customers in foreign markets due to prohibition.

Whenever a customer orders goods for a certain quantity to be delivered on a certain date, the system performs availability check on the material to verify whether the requirement is feasible or not. In this regard, availability check function scans all existing orders of the same material for the quantities and promised delivery dates and compares the existing stock situation for the material along with the future planned procurement or production of the material. The availability check function works in close coordination with the transfer of requirements functionality. If the system detects a shortfall of the material in the available check while performing the availability check, the system decides that the material has to be planned for, in order to make it available. The system transfers requirements to the materials requirements planning component as a planned order. The output determination functionality enables an organization to define the layout of the forms that are sent to external parties or maybe for internal use. Credit management is yet another functionality that is very useful if the organization want to control customer transactions based on their credit situation.

Sales   The sales component in the SD module enables an organization to customize inquiry, quotation, sales order, sales agreement, and customer complaint processing documents to meet organizational requirements. The system enables the organization to have scheduling agreement with customers. The sales function also has the provision of handling over the counter sales or when the customer pays for the ordered goods immediately upon receiving the goods. Cash sale is also differentiated by rush sale. It also provide Web interface so as to enable customers to enter orders for products through the Internet. A special business process such as consignment stock management is also handled in the sales component of the SD module. Sometimes a company may want to sell a product to the customer and want customers to return the packaging material back, for example, in soft drinks, when a customer purchases the same, the bottle is also issued from stocks as a returnable packaging material. If the customer returns the bottle, no billing document is generated for the bottles. However, if the customer decides to keep the bottles, the system would create a billing document and send the customer an invoice. Another feature is variant configuration, under which customers can choose their own options for the product.

Shipping   In order to deliver goods to customers, the SD module offers the shipping component. Goods to be delivered must be picked from the proper place in the warehouse or plant and the goods issue must be posted. Apart from the picking functionality, the shipping component also includes the packaging functionality, where goods to be delivered are packed into appropriate packing material prior to shipment.

Transportation The shipment component is closely related to the transportation component of the SD module. This offers functions that would allow to plan for shipment well in advance, so that the carrier is ready to start loading as soon as products are ready with proper packaging.

Billing It represents the final stage of the SD module when goods and services delivered are billed for. Organizations have an option to manually release the billing document to FI-AR or to have the system automatically post to FI-AR as soon as the billing document is saved. It can produce a summary document, called the invoice list, which combines invoices for the regular customer with a given period. The billing component also has the option to create proforma invoices, billing plans, and rebate agreements.

Foreign trade The foreign trade component of the SD module is equipped with all the widely used controls and tools to manage foreign trade. It has the capability to handle multiple currencies with automatic translations to local currency.

Payment card processing In this component, the organization can record customer's payment card information in the customer's master data, use it in the sales order and complete the transactions as a payment for the billing document sent to the customer.

Materials Management Module From simple maintenance of different types of materials to monitor all transactions that can occur with those materials, the materials management (MM) module has a number of useful functionalities such as:

Consumption based planning Organizations need to have a system that can consider the requirement for materials and plan its procurement or production on time in order to meet the demand or requirement.

Materials requirement planning This function generates proposals for planning and making the material in question available for the fulfilment of the order on time. Shortfall needs to be fulfilled through planned orders or through purchase requisitions. The materials requirement planning (MRP) function would generate planned orders, which might later on be converted into an active production or purchase order. The re-order point (ROP) planning procedure requires organizations' to specify a re-order level in material master data file. The forecast-based planning procedure uses the same forecasting programme as the re-order planning procedure, the difference being that this procedure determines future requirements based on historical data about the consumption of material. It also supports the time-phased planning procedure if material is externally procured and the vendor can deliver the product only on certain days of the week/month.

Purchasing and invoice verification This component of MM module can handle all external procurement transactions and their settlement. A company can use this function to determine the sources of supply and even identify preferred vendors through the vendor evaluation function. The system enables an organization to create purchase requisition, purchase order, release procedure, and finally invoice verification which completes the purchasing function.

Inventory management This component enables the organization to manage their material inventory from a quantity and value perspective. It also defines the consignment stock as the stock that remains in plant but remains the property of the vendor. Organizations can maintain sub-contracting stock as special stock, i.e., material issued to a sub-contractor. The company can also maintain goods-in-transit stock. The goods movement can also automatically generate one or more accounting documents if the movement involves an accounting transaction. The MM module also supports the physical inventory function that helps an organization to balance material inventory at the storage location level in the warehouse.

Plant Maintenance and Service Management Module The plant maintenance (PM) and service management (SM) modules of mySAP™ contain some excellent functionality to enable organizations to maintain in-house equipment and also to efficiently service the products that it sells to their customers.

Equipment and technical objects In order to maintain equipment, it is essential to maintain equipment records and develop a maintenance plan for them as counter-based maintenance or periodic maintenance. The PM module maintains object links between equipment and functional location so that in case of equipment malfunction, the organizations can navigate through the links to quickly isolate the source of the problem. It is also possible to define maintenance bills of materials in the system.

Preventive maintenance In order to develop a preventive maintenance plan, the company needs to have a maintenance strategy for every technical object. The strategy contains a schedule for maintenance. Maintenance plans contain maintenance task lists, which describe the sequence of activities that need to be done to complete the maintenance task. There are three types of maintenance task lists possible to be defined in the system as equipment task list, functional location task list, and general task list. As far as the PM documents are concerned, it maintains the following documents—maintenance notification, maintenance order, technical confirmation report, business confirmation report, and maintenance history.

Service management It requires organizations to maintain technical objects of their customer base and thereby manage the installed base of the products. Service management (SM) also offers warranty management through which organizations can maintain the warranty record of the technical objects. The call management component of the SM module enables the organization to enter customer calls for performing services, organizing tasks, planning for labour and spare parts if necessary, the service, and, calculating and allocating costs incurred in the service process.

Production Planning Module   The production planning (PP) module is an extremely sophisticated tool to manage shop-floor related operations with the provision of tracking and calculating production costs efficiently.

Basic data   In order for the module to work, it requires some basic data elements as bill-of-material (BOM), work centre details, production routing, and scheduling and variant routing. While BOM lists the product structure at different levels (components, subassembly, and assembly), work centre details list machine and manpower capacity available at a particular work centre.

Capacity planning   It deals with the optimum planning and utilization of capacities, personnel, and machines used in the manufacturing process. Sales orders, network orders, production orders, maintenance orders, and planned requirements create requirements on the capacities. Capacity evaluation enables to analyse the loads on capacities and capacity levelling optimizes the capacities.

Project Systems Module   If organization manages and executes projects for their customers, the project system (PS) module of mySAP™ has a wide range of sophisticated functionalities to manage resources and activities, and monitoring budgets and cash flow situations.

Human Resource Module   The human resource (HR) module of mySAP™ also offers a number of functionalities to manage workforce.

Personnel management   This component of the HR module has functions for recruitment, personnel administration, benefits, and personnel development activities. Personnel administration management enables to establish an organizational hierarchy of employees and compensation management functionality. The travel management function offers a complete range of functionality to plan and execute business trips with the provision to post itemized travel costs. The benefit functionality enables administration of employee benefits such as insurances, provident funds, medical, and pension funds. The personnel development functionality enables employee utilization as per their capabilities through career development programmes, training, and promotion plan of the employees.

Time management   This offers the functionality to record and evaluate employee time data. Absence and attendance data might also be recorded and transferred to other HR applications, such as payroll accounting. The shift planning function enables to accurately schedule the number and type of personnel who would be required to carry out production and business requirements.

Payroll accounting Employee payables are handled through this component with the provisions of posting tax deduction at source (TDS).

Retail Module SAP retail module is a fully integrated system that combines functionality from every core module to offer a packaged solution if organizations are involved with retail business. Transactions made at the point-of-sale (PoS) terminal automatically update the stock situation of the material and update finances in real-time. This also facilitates demand forecasting which is so crucial as an input to the SCM.

Let us take the implementation of SAP R/3 at Cadbury India Ltd (Exhibit 3.1).

EXHIBIT 3.1   SAP R/3 Implementation at Cadbury India Ltd

Before the SAP was implemented, the legacy systems in use at Cadbury India led to problems in logistics and sharing of information among different departments of Cadbury India. Relocation of slow or fast moving goods from one location to another on an immediate basis was extremely difficult. In the absence of decentralized databases, consolidation of information was a major issue.

Other issues included inconsistency in replicating master data across multiple locations and reconciliation across systems and functions. Applications were based on Foxbase and Unix, which were neither online nor integrated. Period ends were unpredictable as data transfer across systems and locations was on floppies.

Now, Cadbury India has the SAP R/3 application and a VSAT-based wide area network (WAN) connecting 31 locations comprising branch offices, factories, head office, and sales depots spread across the country. This network of depots caters to over 2000 dealers spread across the country. SAP R/3 provides Cadbury's with a standardized and common database for access by logistics, finance, and sales for efficiently managing a corporate database leading to informed and intelligent decision-making.

Implementation of SAP including the financial module was implemented across 12 locations in a period of 5 months. This included the department at the head office in Mumbai as well as across the branch offices and factories. The module on materials management was implemented in 6 months across 6 locations for a real-time control of inventory. The sales and distribution was rolled out in 9 months across 19 depots and 4 branches. With this, fast moving goods could easily be reallocated to different locations in a short span of time. The implementation of the asset management module resulted in better utilization of assets through efficient tracking and monitoring.

Source: ETIG, 'Supply Chain & Logistics', 2002

SAP Supply Chain Management

SAP claims to offer their SCM solution for building adaptive supply chain networks. The business processes supported are the following.

Supply Chain Planning and Collaboration

Through this, the company can model its existing supply chain, set goals and forecast, optimize and schedule time, materials, and other resources. This functionality also helps to maximize return on assets and brings about a profitable match of supply and demand. The additional sub-functionality of sales and operations planning (S&OP) provides for an integrated planning of sales and operations enabling the client to establish a single, unified plan that would drive the business operations.

Supply Chain Execution

SAP SCM enables to carry out supply chain planning and bring about efficiency at the lowest possible cost. This module can sense and respond to demand through an adaptive supply chain network in which distribution, transportation, and logistics are integrated all into a real-time planning process.

Supply Chain Visibility Design and Analytics

This functionality gives a network-wide visibility across the extended supply chain to perform strategic as well as tactical planning. It also enables collaboration and analytics so as to monitor and analyse the performance of the extended supply chain partners using pre-determined key-performance indicators (KPIs).

The related SAP SCM processes are as follows.

Transportation Management

It helps in consolidating orders and optimizing shipments by sharing orders information and combining orders directly with carriers over the Internet. The business plans can be integrated with transportation processes and controlled.

Warehouse Management

It aims to optimize warehouse activities such as inbound and outbound logistics, facility storage, physical inventory held, and accordingly plan for cross-docking.

Sales and Operations Planning

As pointed out, it synchronizes demand and supply plans in terms of their feasibility and financial goals. It also ensures that only one feasible plan drives the business.

ERP APPLICATION IN INDIA

Most of the companies in India still use their own legacy and proprietary systems or a combination of ERP and their own systems. However, many companies are best known by the kind of ERP systems they use, notable of these are listed in Table 3.2.

According to many corporate executives, ERP initially were typically only internally looking packages which later on provided the *plug-in* points into which external looking software such as optimizers, CRM, and supply chain planners could fit, thus facilitating the creation of the ultimate networked extended enterprise. As is clear from Table 3.3, usually, ERP is implemented first in finance and accounting with around 33 per cent of total implementations going to these areas. Non-ERP applications came next with 25 per cent while CRM and MRP came next with

TABLE 3.2 Leading companies and the ERP software used

Company	ERP used
Tata Steel	SAP
Hindustan Lever	MFG–Pro
Hyundai	SAP, Marshall, Proprietary
Telco	SAP, Proprietary
Asian Paints	SAP
Nestle	BPCS
Ford	Proprietary (CMMS)
Amul (GCMMF)	EAIS, Proprietary
Cement	Proprietary

Source: Economic Times Intelligence Group, Supply Chain & Logistics, 2002

TABLE 3.3 ERP market (%) by functional areas

Functional area	Per cent implementation
Finance and accounting	32.9
Customer order management	13.7
MRP	13.8
Material	10.2
Decision support	4.1
Non-ERP applications	25.3
Total	100

Source: AMR Research, 2004

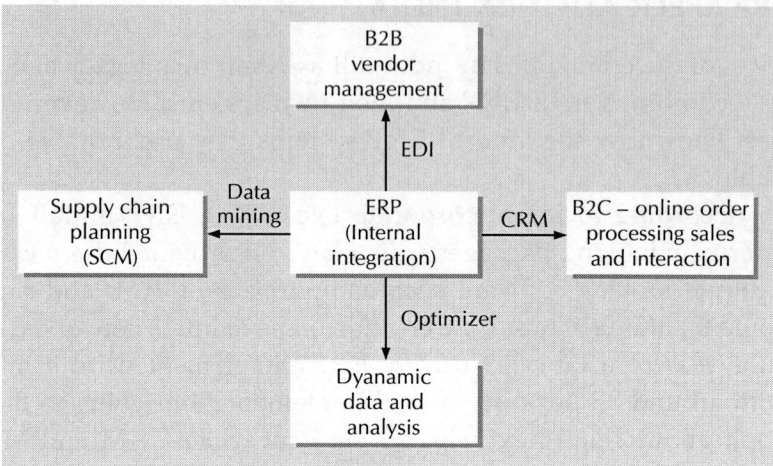

FIG. 3.8 Extension/explosion of ERP
Source: ETIG, 'Supply Chain & Logistics', 2002

nearly equal implementations, each contributing around 14 per cent to the total number of implementations as shown in the table. More and more vendors in India are now coming with specialized offerings for small and medium enterprises (SMEs) that are cheaper (Rs 8–10 lakh) to include license, implementation, server, and other costs, and require less money for installation and configuration. However, cent per cent delivery from ERP may not be possible due to hiccups from the staff getting used to the system and some initial resistance. With more Indian companies renewing their focus on SCM, ERP packages are also exploding outwards to encompass several unconventional areas such as B2B and B2C, etc. as shown in Fig. 3.8.

CURRENT TRENDS AND FUTURE OF IT IN SCM

Rapid developments in information and communication technology (ICT) are leading to new directions in supply chain management. The means of communication, tracing and trucking, and design of system architecture have all undergone a sea change.

Communication

Internet now encompasses most of the business processes from shopping, auctioning, and exchanges to shipment tracking, and collaboration between companies. The companies have replaced their legacy systems with client/server based ERP Systems. The e-commerce is taking the form of c-commerce where collaboration (c) is the key word. As has been already discussed, ERP is giving way to ERP-II whereby the domain is changing from a focus on manufacturing and distribution to inclusion of customer and supplier interfaces. Also, the SCM architecture is undergoing a change from a typical LAN/WAN environment to a Web-based and open environment.

The major issue, however lies in specifying a common language format that would enable diverse systems to access each other's information in a standardized language description format. For this, eXtensible Markup Language (XML) is being increasingly used. It can easily be used over the EDI and Internet. It is easier to write programs for processing XML docs through common XML doc formats. The businesses can exchange information without intermediate format conversions. There is going to be increasing use of communication protocols such as Simple Object Access Protocol (SOAP) or Product Markup Language (PML), and Object Naming Service (ONS). PML is a new standard language for describing physical objects to the Internet in the same way that HTML does it as a common language for describing an information on a website.

Tagging, Tracing and Tracking

There is going to be implementation of AutoID technology,[2] wherein a 96-bit code called electronic product code (EPC) would be embedded in a memory chip (smart tag) on individual products. A radio frequency radar, based on wireless technology, would scan the smart tag which would in turn transfer the product's embedded identity code to the Web, where the detailed information as on the product would be stored. It can then be retrieved by the user. Just the domain name system (DNS) routes information to respective websites, the object naming service (ONS) would act as a 'post office' that would act in a flash retrieving data for each one of the trillions of objects in the world but which should carry an EPC code. In the retail industry, shoppers can learn about the features of a product from the manufacturer's website by just pointing the EPC scanner equipped mobile phones at any product in the store. The customers would then be billed to their personal account upon reaching home. From the SCM point of view, this would make tracking simplified, real-time information shared, and improve customer service levels.

Together with use of geographical positioning system (GPS), the AutoID, or scanning technology aided by the wireless communication, can help locate a truck or cargo at any time and anywhere in the distribution. Let us observe the scope for use of this technology in the oil industry as given in Exhibit 3.2.

As far as the use of databases are concerned for use in SCM systems, in addition to relational databases which facilitate use of SQL for reporting and querying, as pointed out earlier in the chapter, object specific databases comprising object pictures and graphic structures can also be used. Data warehouses comprising of small sets of data called datamarts mainly with a departmental scope, can further combine

---

[2] www.autoidcentre.org

> ### EXHIBIT 3.2   Tracing and Tracking Supply Tankers at HPCL
>
> HPCL is now known to use GPS to track their oil tankers for adulteration. Adulteration, particularly on the highways, has been a long-time problem and companies have been unable to control it, as says the HPCL's Executive Director-Retail, S.P. Choudhry. The company is networking its supply chain with a vehicle management system which was installed in 15 pilot vehicles in 2005. The system based on a combination of GPS and mobile phone will track the vehicles as they move out of the refinery tankages to the retail points. Earlier, the company could not check the dubious diversion of tankers despite providing for all the sophisticated locks. However, it costs Rs 20,000 per truck to install the system and the company planned to fit this only in its own oil tankers. As put by HPCL's Mumbai's Regional Manager, T.R. Sundararaman, 'The company covers the sales online of 42 fuelling stations in Mumbai to have exact details about quality, quantity, inventory, dispensing staff, and the buying behaviour of customer at those, the so called, e-fuel stations'. The company targeted these e-fuel stations to increase to 400 all over the country. HPCL thinks that this online monitoring of fuel sales offers a great scope for data mining for customer relationship management (CRM) initiatives. As Sundararaman puts it, fuelling habits of card customers can be tracked and incentives be tailored for them. Sister oil company BPCL was also conducting a pilot of petrol pump automation at eight pumps all over the country in 2005 and wire the networks of their supply points with the company to monitor sales.
>
> *Source:* Paul, Cuckoo, *Economic Times*, 2005

data from other systems' databases and then the whole enterprise data and query is facilitated by using software technologies such as online analytic processing (OLAP). At the same time, there can be use of the so called group database which allows group functions such as track of sales or other updates, multiple user access, etc. The use of engineering data software for SCM as practised by HP is demonstrated in Exhibit 3.3.

Changing Face of System Architecture

In a typical client/server architecture, PC is typically the 'client' and the main processor/main frame computer is the 'server'. It is a form of distributed processing where some processes are performed centrally for many users, while other specialized ones can be decentralized on a PC by the user. The client/server model is now fast evolving towards a Web-centric model where the client is a Web-browser connected to a Web-server in an open environment replacing the typical LAN/WAN. Even the Internet is a form of client/server set up where the local PC browser processes the HTML pages and Java applets that have been retrieved from Web-servers located all over the world. The unique characteristic of client/server concept lies in distributing functions among specialist servers that perform specialized tasks more efficiently and it is always easier to add to modularity and functionality in this set-

EXHIBIT 3.3   Hewlett-Packard (HP) Uses Engineering Data Software for SCM

HP uses a spend analysis programme that aggregates data according to various criteria, e.g., by supplier, part number, quality, and reliability. HP developed internally two software programs, namely 'Total Buy' and 'Buy Power', which help the company to consolidate orders, negotiate better terms and conditions including better pricing, and thus optimize supply strategies. Through the use of another software, a supplier management process has reduced the number of direct material suppliers by 83 per cent from 1500 to 720, indirect suppliers from 1,00,000 to 52,000 as also the logistics supplier pool by 68 per cent. As a result, HP's top 40 suppliers account for roughly 90 per cent of the total spend. HP also organizes an executive supplier programme, which assigns an HP executive to each supplier. 'The executive meets the supplier twice a year to resolve any supply issue,' said Dick Conrad, senior Vice President of supply chain, global operations of HP. A significant amount of communication occurs on a daily basis. The supplier relationships so maintained helped HP reduce inventory by 21 per cent and logistics cost per unit by 11 per cent during the fiscal year, 2004.

HP developed a system called HPRISK to take care of risk in the demand forecast. This statistical software works on the modelling of variability and is used to analyse supply, demand, and price volatility of materials and services the company buys. The modelling uncertainty facilitates the company to classify volumes that are certain, less certain, and unlikely but possible. This allows purchasing executives to negotiate contracts that ensure price stability and adequate supplies of critical components and materials. Suppliers then can also expect the likelihood of additional orders as also their size. From mid-2003 to mid-2006, HP used this technique to buy $3 billion worth of standard materials and components, such as hard disks, displays, and memory chips. During this period, using the procurement risk management (PRM) system the company saved $78 million and protect 15 million systems against commodity volatility. Till 2006, HP trained 350 of its 1,50,000 employees in PRM. PRM is also offered by the company's consulting services outside the HP.

HP also developed what it calls a buy/sell process for which it relies on a software from Baan. HP procures components for its original design manufacturers and contract manufacturers rather than allowing them to do the buying. This not only protects HP against shortages but also reduces costs by consolidating orders and eliminating markups. Pricing also remains confidential since the information is not divulged to third-party manufacturers. The buy/sell process now accounts for about $29 billion in purchases and accounts for roughly half of the company's spend.

HP also relies heavily on third-party logistics (3PL) providers for warehousing and shipping. To streamline its communications and interaction with third-party providers, HP switched on to LEGO (named after kids' building block toys), which refers to a message infrastructure based on an order management module from SAP. HP selected SAP for LEGO because it provided the right functionality and is the dominant application in the company. SAP also served as the engine for order management, demand planning, and forecasting. Throughout 2006, HP was on a drive to replace its legacy systems with SAP enterprise resource planning tools wherever it was practical to do so. LEGO provided a single place and process to 'plug-in' to HP globally, thereby reducing the time

(*Contd*)

EXHIBIT 3.3 *Contd*

and money it took to make connections with third-party providers. It also reduced the number of message types, formats, and communiqués containing the order information and specification. The company completed LEGO project in Asia first and then implemented in North America, followed by in Europe. The journey to the new applications at HP was not without its share of hassles. A 'bumpy' conversion to an order fulfilment system for Industry Standard Server products in 2004 caused by the lack of team integration and an unexpected spike in orders disrupted shipments and negatively impacted the business results. HP has since then improved its reengineering process. In fact, Morgan Stanley analysts cited 'supply chain inefficiencies' as one of the major reasons to downgrade HP's stock from equal weight to underweight in the beginning of 2006.

However, overarching the company's supply chain efforts is its GO+IT integration which unifies global operations and IT to create an adaptive enterprise. GO+IT is based on the premise that 'every business event triggers an IT event and merges the two together,' says Conrad. He also says, 'We have integrated IT into whatever we do.' The overall corporate strategy has been to simplify and standardize its IT infrastructure. The company now uses about 3500 applications, down from the initial 7000 and planned to further reduce the number to 1500. The IT costs of revenue declined from 4.5 per cent to around 3 per cent in the fiscal year, 2006. The percentage of IT spend allocated to maintenance of systems was expected to decline from 70 per cent to 50 per cent, thereby freeing 50 per cent to invest in IT innovation needed to develop new business capabilities. To support these goals, the company's road map to ERP to 2010 called for increased standardization on SAP, reduced customization and a high degree of global commonality. As Burdick, Vice President and Group Information Officer, Adaptive Infrastructure and Supply Chain IT of the company puts it, 'We are not tracking toward one code base, however, 80 per cent of the company's code base would be consistent globally by 2010.' HP planned to focus on production planning and shipment visibility. Concludes Burdick, 'Integrating information about the supply chain and production capability is a key to having a smooth supply chain.'

Source: 'Supply Chain Master,' Forcinio, Hallie, posted on www.managing automation.com/maonline/ magazine on 3 November 2006.

up. However the challenge is that, each server in this complex network needs to communicate tasks and processes particularly when the two communicating systems are diverse in terms of architecture, communication protocols, hardware and so on. Hence, in order to provide for interoperability amongst diverse servers, a middleware is planted between the client and the server. This is very important in SCM as most of the times, the information lies in a number of locations and forms in the company, e.g., a banking company such as ICICI may have information for various services such as savings account, fixed deposits, loan processing, mortgage, Young Star, investor relations, online billing, NRI services, Demat services, ATM/Credit cards, etc., stored on different systems but a customer service representative would need to reach different locations for bills if customers bought different services. A middleware then comes handy when it comes to going through the database and combing for information. However, when these processes are applied between companies over the Internet, it is referred to as the enterprise application integration (EAI), the use of which is certainly going to increase in future in view of the need for collaborative commerce (c-commerce).

RECAPITULATION

The chapter starts by highlighting the importance of information and communication technology (ICT) systems and tools, predominantly of these being the enterprise resource planning (ERP) systems. The ERP systems are now being extended to vendors through regular electronic data interchange (EDI) and to customers through customer relationship management (CRM) systems for the purpose of online order processing, sales, and customer interaction. While an ERP system through data-mining could facilitate supply chain planning, an optimizer could facilitate dynamic data and its analysis in an integrated ERP system. Most ERP systems provide a platform-independent suite of applications that can work in distributed computing environment as well as a centralized environment. The ERP systems should have features of connectivity, Web-enablement, personalization, authorization, and the ability of the system to model complex problems through modelling and optimization. The typical ERP system has a three-layered architecture in the form of a data base layer, an application layer, and the presentation layer.

The leading ERP solution providers are SAP, PeopleSoft, Oracle, BaaN and QAD. Of these SAP is the largest, so much so, that it has become synonymous with any ERP application software. Most of these softwares contain modules which are related to

- financial accounting and controlling
- sales and distribution

- materials management
- plant maintenance and service management
- production planning (PP)
- project system
- human resources
- retail

However, most of the companies still use their own legacy system or a combination of these systems with the ERP system. However, all of these face initial teething problems while implementing ERP. Most of the companies implement ERP first in finance and accounting followed by customer order management, materials requirement planning and materials management, and just about 4 per cent ERP applications are attributed to decision-support systems. Non-ERP applications also significantly contribute to around 25 per cent of the applications. SAP R/3 is the most preferred software and is being used by companies such as Tata Steel, Hyundai, Telco, Asian Paints, etc. With ERP packages now acting as plug-in points for external software such as optimizers, CRM, and supply chain planners, the ERP packages are extending outwards to encompass B2B and B2C processes. The former facilitates vendor management through electronic data interchange (EDI) while the latter is being used for online order capture, and processing and customer-interaction through the CRM software. An optimizer would facilitate dynamic data analysis while supply chain planning could be accomplished through data mining, all emanating from an integrated ERP system. ERP then can be more outward looking in the form of ERP-II. The use of enterprise application integration (EAI) for exchange of business processes and information in a Web environment at inter-enterprise level would get momentum.

CONCEPT REVIEW QUESTIONS

1. Analyse the need for an enterprise resource planning system such as ERP for a company.
2. What are the typical layers and the respective components of an ERP system?
3. What are the common functional and sub-functional modules amongst BaaN's ERP, QAD's ERP, and i2's ERP system? Where lies the reason for these commonalities?
4. What are the unique features of mySAP™ ERP system? What could be the benefits accrued after using these features?
5. Outline the functional/process similarities in the SCM modules being offered by vendor companies such as SSA Global (now Infor) and SAP.

CRITICAL THINKING QUESTIONS

1. With extension of an internally integrated ERP system to vendors and customers, identify and critically analyse the interfaces of an ERP system with extended supply chain members.
2. What ERP software characteristics, according to you, would serve the purpose well for a manufacturing enterprise? What should be the core modules for such a system?
3. Why and how do most of the SCM solutions have their roots in the ERP systems?
4. Critically analyse the reasons as to why
   (a) ERP is started only with select functional areas in an enterprise.
   (b) Non-ERP applications contribute significantly to the ERP installation.

PROJECT ASSIGNMENTS

1. Visit a warehouse/distribution centre (DC) of a company, say, HUL, ITC, Reliance, or Marico. Find out how the information is viewed between the DC and the corporate and/or regional headquarters? What are the hardware and software configurations and mechanisms of facilitating the sharing of information particularly related to sales?
2. Interview the sales and distribution manager of a company, say, P&G, HUL, Marico, or Colgate. Carry out the cost-benefit analysis including return-on-investment (ROI) as to how and what kind of benefits have accrued

over the kinds of investments done by the company in the use of information and communication technology (ICT) tools, in supply chain management.
3. Tap some secondary sources such as CII, CMIE, ETIG including accessing their websites and draw a scenario about ERP market in India, say in the next five years. For global markets, tap sources such as Gartners Dataquest Report, Forrester's Report, and AMR Research, etc. Establish some trends in the global ERP and SCM markets.

CASE STUDY

GLOBAL CASE STUDY

SAMSUNG ELECTRONICS[3]

The Markets

Samsung Electronics, established in 1969, produces the world's most innovative digital products and is the world's largest computer display manufacturer. It has 25 production bases and 59 sales subsidiaries in 46 countries and employs 66,000 people in 50 countries. Its markets span 8 major regions of the world—North America, Europe, Southeast Asia, Central Asia, Middle East and Africa, China, CIS and Latin America. It has currently positioned itself in four major business units, namely—home network, mobile network, office network, and core components. It is ranked 25th on Global Brand Scorecard according to *Business Week* magazine, 4th in sales in semiconductor industry and 6th by units in the mobile phone industry. It is rated 9th in the top 25 SCM companies as surveyed by AMR Research (2004).

The Products

From 1992, Samsung is positioned at the top of the dynamic random access memory (DRAM) semiconductor industry. In fact, the company is best known for the success it has had in the memory semiconductor industry. It has diversified its financial structure and is considered the number 1 company in the market share for memory chips thin film transistor-liquid crystal display (TFT-LCDs), code division multiple access (CDMA) mobile phones, and computer monitors.

Mission and Vision

The vision of Samsung electronics is to 'lead the Digital Convergence Revolution' and the mission is to attain this vision by being a 'Digital-e company'.

There are two parts of being a 'Digital-e company', and the first is clearly about being 'digital' producing not just digital products, but products that inspire digital integration across the entire company. The second part of being an 'e' is to use e-processes connecting R&D, production, and marketing to customers, and partners. The market-disciplined approach is the way Samsung brings value to every part of its supply chain, including products data and customer relationship through enterprise resource planning (ERP). The business portfolio restructuring is based on design, convergence, and networking while the business process innovation is based on speed and simplicity.

Samsung will network core components such as memory chips, system-LSI, and LCDs as well as A/V, computers, telecommunication devices, home appliances, and other stand-alone products into a total solution of digital convergence era.

For this goal, Samsung restructured into 4 strategic business areas—Home Network, Mobile Network, Office Network, and Core components—that support network products. Also, Samsung has pioneering products and technology in the semiconductors, telecommunication devices, and home appliances field, which will make it a most competitive total solution provider in digital convergence.

The Brand Value and Market Orientation

The company thinks that in the digital era, products will be distinguished more by brand than by just

---

[3] *Source:* www.managementlogs.com/2004 as accessed on 3 November 2008; www.thehindubusinessline. com/ 2004/11/29/stories/2004112900770300.htm as accessed on 3 November 2008; story posted by Neha Kaushik; www.samsung.com/me/about samsung/samsungglobal/index.htm as accessed on 4 November 2008; and www.adexa.com/pdf/ samsung/pdf as accessed on 4 November 2008

their quality. Since 1999, Samsung Electronics is practicing global brand communication strategy. Based on the research done by Interbrand Inc., US, Samsung electronics is the fastest growing brand from $6.4 billion (2001) to $12.55 billion (2004) in terms of brand equity. In the future, it plans to practice a holistic marketing strategy instead of individual marketing plans to strengthen its market power and increase brand value with high quality products. Under the brand concept of 'Wow, Simple, Inclusive', Samsung Electronics is launching a worldwide brand campaign.

The electronics giant provides a unique solution that fits customers' needs. For this, the company would expand the marketing platform based on global CRM that is applicable to all products. Also it will develop a digital network platform that improves compatibility between products to serve our customers with the best solution. Samsung Electronics is putting and will put its customers' needs first and go forward as a market-driven reliable company.

The Four Strategic Business Areas

Samsung plans to strengthen its already strong core components business such as memory chips and TFT-LCDs, and focus on high valued products such as system LSI, small and mid-size LCDs, and optical components. Also in the future, based on system on a chip (SOC) and system on a panel (SOP) that are main parts of all machinery industry, it will focus on three network business areas.

The first, Samsung's Home Network business is centred on digital TV, home server, and home gateway business. The second, Mobile Network business is based on wireless handsets and it will expand this business into personal digital assistants (PDAs) and laptops as well as set up the next generation telecommunications, IMT-2000 system. And finally, in Office Network business, it will focus on printers, IP Terminal, infomobile, as well as existing display area.

Samsung Electronics has nine tier-I products in the global electronics market. In addition to these tier-I products, memory chips, TFT-LCDs, CDMA handsets, and display devices and more, it will add digital TVs, IMT-2000, computer peripherals, and home appliances as their new tier 1 products to strengthen four strategic business areas and set up firm foundation for future growth. It will also focus on core components such as SOC, SOP, and so on that are essential for network products based on core R&D technology and e-process.

Early Establishment of E-processes

To reduce lead time on supply chain, Samsung networked four processes of business management process, customer management process, R&D management process, and SCM process. It is e-process that connects R&D, production, marketing, and customers. Also, as Samsung acknowledged the need of IT infrastructure to speed up the four processes, the company adopted ERP system in its domestic and overseas sales subsidiaries. Samsung Electronics will converge and network SCM, product data management (PDM), and CRM system and set up global real-time management information system.

Internet-based IT Infrastructure

The IT infrastructure at Samsung is Internet-based and has a structure as given in Fig. 3.9.

Implementing SCM Solution at Samsung Electronics

Mr Park Sungchil, Senior VP, Corporate SCM, Samsung, Korea, who came to India in 2004 to conduct training on best practices in SCM used by Samsung, says, 'In a large country such as India, there is bigger opportunity to save money in SCM; we switched from monthly supply planning to weekly several years ago and have now started a pilot in Korea to reduce it to daily basis.'

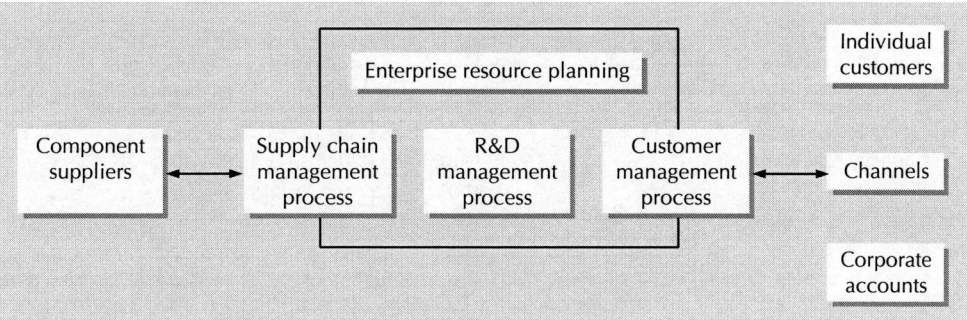

FIG. 3.9 The IT Infrastructure at Samsung
Source: www.samsung.com/aboutsamsung/samsungglobal/index.htm as accessed on 4 November 2008

Many Samsung divisions implemented SCM solutions with goals to improve on time delivery ratio, inventory level, and forecast accuracy by shortening planning cycle time from monthly basis to weekly by installing the i2 SCM solution suite. Says Bang Hwan Chung, VP (CIO) of Samsung Electro-Mechanics (SEM) division, 'We believe i2 SCM gives us the opportunity to highly improve our business practices. By using i2 SCM, we intend to install a unified global business process in three divisions which would be a very difficult job without i2 SCM. We will process innovation and believe we gain global competitiveness i2 solution'. The SEM deployed i2 SCM which includes the following as shown in Fig. 3.10.

- Demand manager
- Supply chain planner
- Factory planner
- Demand fulfilment

Samsung's network division however selected Adexa's enterprise Global Planning System (e-GPS) platform for supply chain planning, enterprise performance management, and intelligent collaboration. The division implemented Adexa's supply chain planning, factory planning and scheduling, order fulfilment, and collaborative demand planning over a period of 11 months creating a unified planning environment. Let us briefly outline these modules as done by Adexa themselves.

Supply Chain Planning

This solution provides a unified planning environment that considers capacity and materials and enables planners to quickly respond to various planning requests.

Factory Planning and Scheduling

This module enables to develop detailed schedules and respond to weekly horizon planning events including shop floor planning and scheduling.

Collaborative Demand Planning

This module provides planning and sales with new forecasting tools that utilize trend analysis on forecasts in order to develop a collaborative forecast. The system, by providing more reliable data to managers, helps reduce excess inventory. The solution is equipped with an alert system that monitors the results of a supply chain plan and provides an action-based, online reporting to enable planners to quickly repond to late demands and scheduling issues. It also provides available-to-promise (ATP) dates for all demands and forecasts through a regularly scheduled planning cycle.

Order Fulfilment

This solution, as Adexa claims, provides real-time ATP and capability to provide information for all

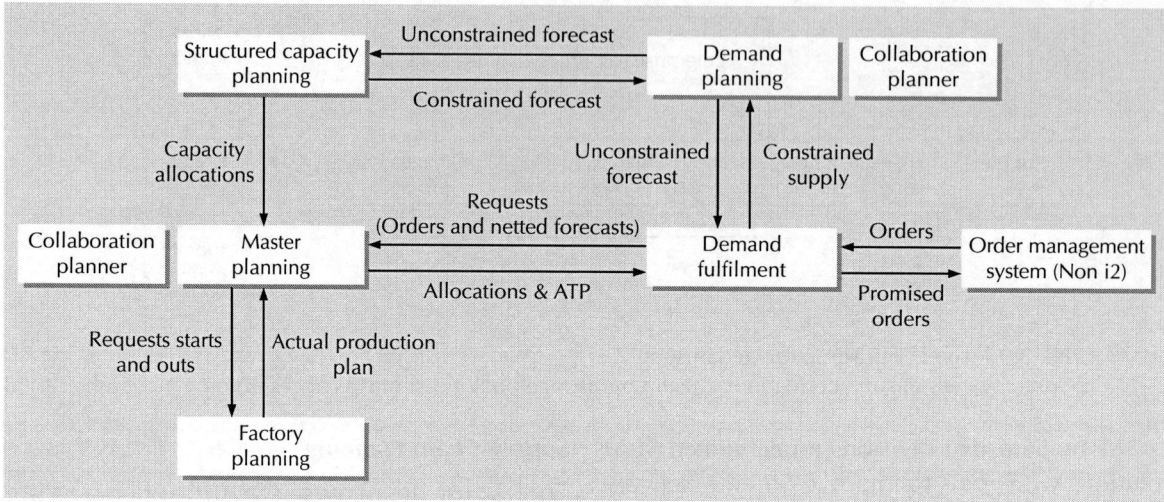

FIG. 3.10   i2 Solution workflows at Samsung Electronics Co.
Source: Chang, June and Min–Hyung Kang (2004); 'Evolution of Supply Chain Management', by Yoon Seok
Chang, Harris C. Makatsoris, and Howard D. Richards (Eds), Springer, pp. 105–134

products. ATP uses supply chain plan to perform these functions.

Samsung has been reported by Adexa to enjoy the following benefits post implementation of e-GPS:

(a) Increased forecasting accuracy and plan visibility

(b) Better quality of plans generated through constrained and unconstrained resources and providing a structure that quickly responds to changes.

(c) Shortening of order to delivery time by responding quickly to demand changes.

(d) Focusing on key customers through strategic buffering and minimizing stock-outs.

(e) Providing accurate and best available ATP dates to sales staff in real time.

(f) Reducing on-hand inventory.

(g) Providing customers with fast and accurate order status information and responding faster to order modification requests, also prioritizing orders based on their sales potential.

(h) Generating capacity constrained and accutate plans that reduce costly rush orders, expedited material purchases, and overtime.

Distribution Networking at Samsung

Samsung electronics, has lately redefined its business practices in India. Its distribution network, spread across six distributors throughout India, with its head office in Delhi and factories in Malaysia, China, and Korea, was earlier dependent on the conventional modes of communication such as the telephones and faxes. Typically the entire process of placing an order and getting the delivery used to take nothing less than 40 days. Fed up with this kind of a situation, Samsung was looking at a solution that would be faster, reliable, and secure. In came Sanjay Shetty, Technical Director, DBS Internet with the proposal of creating a supply chain management link.

DBS Internet was commissioned to implement the automatic order processing system to reduce the time lag in processing orders. This in turn leads to better inventory management. The final aim is to reduce the entire business process cycle to a simple 24 hours to generate the entire order processing online from purchase orders to corresponding performa invoices and LCs to actual delivery schedules.

DBS set up a Web server with all the data supplied by Samsung, and then linked up all the dealers and suppliers through the Net. The dealer can now log into the site, raise a purchase order, check the product availability, cost and delivery time, and then decide which product to order. They can also get information about the port that the product would be shipped to and the time it would take to reach. Also, feels Bong Sik Pak, Director-Support Division, Samsung India Electronics, 'With the introduction of VAT in the country, the company would be able to bring down the number of warehouses from 25 to 20, so efficiency will definitely increase with the introduction of VAT.' Samsung later extended its supply chain to incorporate customers and after sales service for the dealers. Now any customer can register complaints and access the site for customer care. The supply chain system also helps the company in tracking the performance of dealers and improve their performance by giving incentives. Data collected from the central sales repository and calculated rating on the basis of certain set parameters allows Samsung to quickly devise and improvize dealer incentive schemes, and keep the sales channel happy. The distribution time cycle is now halved to 20 days.

Discussion Questions

1. What are the key e-processes established by Samsung and what is the significance of such an establishment?
2. Explain the framework of Web-based IT infrastructure at Samsung.
3. How has DBS Internet helped Samsung to cut down distribution cycle times?
4. Estimate the kind of IT requirements Samsung would have required to create the link-up between dealers and suppliers through a network.

Indian Case Study

MARICO LIMITED[4]

Company Profile

Marico is a leading Indian group operating in consumer products, aesthetics services, and global ayurvedic businesses. Marico's 2003–04 turnover was about Rs 9 billion from 12 brands—Parachute, Saffola, Sweekar, Hair and Care, Shanti, Mediker, Oil of Malabar, Mealmaker, Sil, Revive, Kaya and Sundari. Its distribution width and penetration is acknowledged as one of the best in the industry and is a leverageable strength. Every month, 46 million consumer packs are sold to about 1.8 million households through 1.7 million retail outlets spread across the country. Its distribution network covers almost every Indian town with a population of over 20,000.

The Problem

In 2000, Marico's top management team took serious note of the fact that it had underperformed. It was dependent on just two brands, Parachute and Saffola, for its lion's share of profits. Competitors such as Hindustan Lever and Dabur had put its margins under pressure. Marico reacted with a series of line extensions, most of which sank without a trace, leading to a lot of discontentment within the organization.

To add to its woes, Hindustan Lever Ltd, had strengthened its presence in the hair oils segment with its acquisition of the 'Coco Care' brand from Recon Oil Industries. Analysts were led to believe that Coco Care was a threat to Parachute and that the distribution muscle of HLL would prove just too dangerous for Marico.

On assessing the situation, Marico executives pinpointed a lack of visibility and promptness in the secondary sales and demand information

---

[4] *Source:* This case has been adapted from Supply Chain and Logistics survey of ETIG, 2005, pp. 63–65, with permission. The author expresses thanks to the Economic Times Intelligence Group, Mumbai, for the permission

reaching the company. The company was still taking supply chain decisions based on its sale to distributors (Fig. 3.11). The data was available on a 10-day or monthly frequency and was insufficient. There was a need to get secondary sales data at a higher frequency and granularity. In short, the company needed a software package to capture secondary sales data or distributor sales data and feed it into its SAP R/3 ERP system. This meant 'forward integration' with distributors, super–distributors, wholesalers, and stockists.

It was at this juncture that Marico was confronted with a critical technology-business decision: either build or buy the required system.

The Solution—Distributor Automation

The aim of any initiative was to enhance the responsiveness of the company's supply chain. A more responsive supply chain would help to reduce costs and enjoy better sales and inventory management. But to do so, Marico had to base its supply chain decisions on secondary sales.

In an ideal scenario, to be able to accurately forecast demand, an FMCG company's supply chain decision, should be based on the off-take (retail sales). However, this is seldom possible. Today, most supply chain decisions are based on secondary sales, whose data is captured by most SCM applications.

When the supply chain integration project was conceptualized, Marico was running a SAP R/3 ERP system, with the advanced planner and optimizer (APO) supply chain module on Windows 2000 Servers. Being a centralized solution, the company's 50 offices were connected to the system through virtual private networks and very small aperture terminals (VSAT).

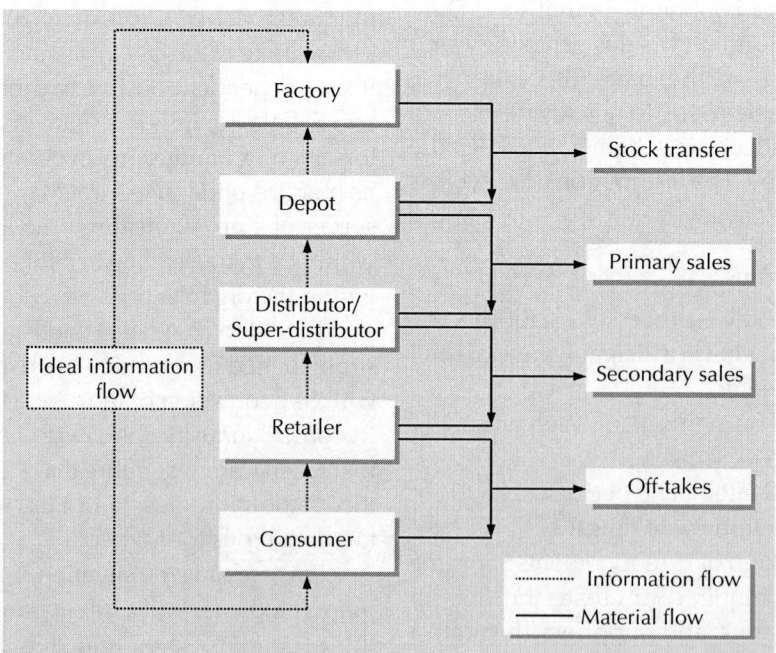

FIG. 3.11 Marico supply chain transactions
Source: ET Knowledge Series, *Supply Chain & Logistics*, 2005

SAP already had a SCM module for R/3 that the company could easily license and seamlessly integrate with its systems. However, in a cost-benefit analysis, Marico's IT team discovered that the module's total cost of ownership (TCO) was more than double that of developing an alternative solution from scratch. Moreover, the application also needed substantial customization to meet Marico's needs.

Besides being financially unviable, the SAP solution wasn't technically feasible given the country's poor telecom infrastructure. Because SAP is primarily a centralized solution, adopting it would have meant that the company's distributors would have to remain connected to the SAP system for up to six hours a day. The company then went to the market, looking for indigenously developed products.

At this, the IT team went around scouting for a distributor automation solution and discovered quite a few steadily available packages. They went with one package, which came closest to meeting its needs and understanding its business, and customized it.

Marico selected STOCKY, a product developed for distributors, by Botree Software International Limited. It was developed on Delphi with MS Access as a back-end. Marico bought licenses for the package and went about with the customization. After taking private labeling rights from Botree, STOCKY was renamed STOCKY MIDAS.

The Implementation

Since the distributor community works like one big brotherhood, the company created a select list of the leading distributors, called Greenball Distributors, who stood as examples to their smaller counterparts.

During the course of implementation, Marico faced no resistance from its target community, but there was increased skepticism. This might have happened because many distributors had seen other principals fail in their attempts at launching similar initiatives. But Greenball Distributors were open to the idea. So with the influential distributors on their side and by ensuring a successful implementation, Marico convinced the smaller distributors about the benefits of the solution.

It also made efforts to see that the package was relevant to the distributors. STOCKY MIDAS was customized for a multi-user, multi-company product so that distributors could employ separate staff to manage products coming in from multiple companies. All distributors had to do was buy the hardware, the PC, and modem. Marico foot the bill for the software license.

The other hurdle Marico faced was in convincing distributors already running an automation package to switch over to STOCKY MIDAS. Typically, some distributors used local software, which was tailored around their respective businesses and the availability of efficient local support. The company had to spend a lot of time convincing them that in the long run, the rugged MIDAS was superior to the local brew. Most distributors eventually saw the light; with the few who did not, Marico terminated its business relations.

Eventually, all hiccups were overcome because of one of the most potent tools any company could use: communication. The communication began with a personalized letter sent to each distributor by Marico's MD, a week before the roll out started. The letter explained what the company was implementing and why it was necessary for both the distributors and Marico. The letter set the tone of the relationship; it was like one partner talking to another. This way the distributors realized that even the top brass at Marico was committed to the project, and felt involved in the whole exercise.

When the roll out actually started, the company realized that because most of its distributors were computer illiterate, each of them needed at least a week's training. The company tackled this problem uniquely. Marico figured out that a distributor and the Territory Sales Officer (TSO) understood each other's language perfectly. So Marico built teams comprising of a mix of technologists (from Marico), implementers (from Botree), and a few select TSOs. The technologists and implementers taught the technology; the TSO convinced the distributors and spent time understanding their issues and solving their problems. Botree provided the technology content for the teams.

While the roll outs continued, bugs were discovered and features added/deleted until a final stable version of MIDAS was arrived at in about two months' time. Marico automated 330 distributors over nine months. These were the company's 'A' Class distributors, who took care of about 75 per cent of the company's business volumes.

The Backward Integration with ERP Systems

The second phase involved hooking these 330 distributors to the company's SAP system. When the second phase of the project started, 200 distributors were already automated. This phase involved the creation of a middle layer to glue distributors' systems with the company's SAP systems. This took about six months to develop and roll out. The whole set-up went live from April 2002. Today, distributors log on to the Marico site once daily, and select the 'upload-download' command. Their data is automatically uploaded to Marico's system through the middle layer and SAP data downloaded to the distributors'. This download could include information on promotional schemes, new pricing, and the like.

The middle layer and the STOCKY MIDAS distributor automation system were collectively called MI-NET (Fig. 3.12). Both phases of the two-year long project were completed by 2003.

The Benefits

Marico implemented STOCKY MIDAS and MI-NET and are enjoying the following business benefits.

- Data is centrally available to everyone within the organization
- Drop in distributor transaction processing cost
- Reduction in communication costs on inventory and order status follow-ups
- Improved sales force productivity
- Improvement in forecast accuracy
- Reduction in skewed sales
- Reduction in planning cycle time

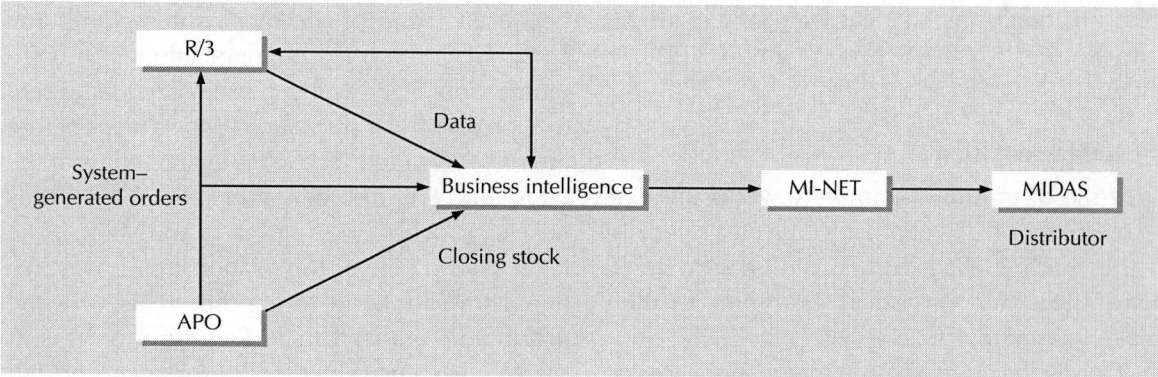

FIG. 3.12   Information technology for SCM at Marico
Source: ET Knowledge Series, *Supply Chain & Logistics,* 2005

- Reduction in late deliveries
- Reactivation of lapsed outlets
- Improvement in return on investment (ROI) for the distributor
- Reduction in the working capital requirement

STOCKY MIDAS has helped Marico by providing critical downstream information it needs to compete in today's connected economy. The software has helped Marico streamline its supply chain and build closer relationships with its customers, thereby, making its supply chain more responsive, efficient and profitable.

Discussion Questions

1. Why does a company such as Marico require use of ICT tools in the supply chain and distribution function?
2. Discuss why Marico had to look for in-house development of an alternative solution to SAP R/3. How was the newly installed product STOCKY MIDAS backward integrated with the SAP R/3 system existing in the company?
3. Analyse the benefits accrued post-implementation of STOCKY MIDAS in the light of supply chain management at Marico Ltd.

REFERENCES

Altekar, Rahul (2004), *Enterprise-wide Resource Planning: Theory and Practice*, Prentice Hall of India, New Delhi.

Bailor, Coreen, 'For CRM, ERP and SCM, SAP Leads the Way', posted on 5 July 2006 on www.destinationcrm.com/articles/default. asp?ArticleID=6162 as accessed on 20 March 2009.

Blain, Jonathan (Ed.) (1999), ASAP World Consultancy, *Administering SAP R/3: The Financial Accounting and Controlling Module*.

Delefice, Alexandra, *Forrester's Top ERP Vendors*, posted on 14 November 2005 on www. destinationcrm.com/Articles/CRM-News/Daily-News/Forresters-Top-ERP-Vendors-43186.aspx as accessed on 20 March 2009.

Economic Times Intelligence Group (2002), Survey on Supply Chain and Logistics, Mumbai.

Guengerich, S. and V.G. Green (1996), *Introduction to Client/Server Computing*, SME Blue Book Series, Deanborn, MI.

Jaiswal, M. and M. Mittal (2004), *Management Information Systems*, Oxford University Press, New Delhi.

Lackes, R. (2004), *Information System for Supporting Supply Chain Management* in Dyckhoff Harald and Lackes Richard (Eds.), 'Supply Chain Management and Reverse Logistics', Springer-Verlag, pp. 405–426.

Mohan, A. (2005), *Supply Chain Management in Indian FMCG Industry*, Unpublished Thesis, Faculty of Management Studies, University of Delhi.

Reilly, Kevin, 'AMR Research Releases ERP Market Report Showing Overall Growth of 14% in 2004', posted 14 June 2005 on www.amr research.com/content/view.asp% Fpmillid% 3D as accessed on 20 February 2009.

Rockfeller, W. (1999), *Using SAP R/3 FI: Beyond Business Process Reengineering*.

Sahay, B.S. (Ed.) (2000), *Supply Chain Management in the Twenty First Century*, Section 4 – 'IT Enabled Supply Chain Management', Macmillan.

Simchi-Levi David, Philip Kaminsky, and Edith Simchi-Levi (2004), *Designing and Managing the Supply Chain*, Tata McGraw-Hill.

Stadtler, Hartmut and Christoph Kilger (2000), *Supply Chain Management and Advanced*

Planning-Concepts, Models, Software and Case Studies, Springer.

SAP Magazine, Issue 94, May, 2002, New Delhi, pp. 171–221.

Zhang Bruce, as posted on March 8, 2005 on www.sysoptima.com/erp as accessed on 23 March 2008.

Internet Resources

www.erpsupersite.com

www.gartner.com/resources/104800/104860 as accessed on 23 February 2009

www.infor.com/solutions/erp as accessed on 21 October 2008

www.i2.com/solutions/tsm as accessed on 20 October 2008

www.jvdbconsulting.com/supply-chain.html

www.microsoft.com/India/dynamics/erp

www.qad.com/mfg-pro.html as accessed on 23 October 2008

www.sapscene.com

www.sapscheduling.com/products/eMESA_customer success.aspre

www.ssaglobal.com/solutions/scm as accessed on 20 October 2008

www.vendormanagedinventory.com

www.12sap.com/solutions/business-suite/scm as accessed on 20 October 2008

4 Best Practices in SCM

As discussed in the previous chapters, supply chain processes are very dynamic, have a real-time frame, and need information systems and technology in place for effective and efficient flows. An integrated and effective supply chain, therefore, embraces and links all the partners into the supply chain from departments within the organization to vendors, carriers, and third-party logistics (3PL) providers to retailers and customers. However, focus on customer demand is an essential requisite for ensuring customer *pull* (customer demand driven), not *push* (forecast or schedule driven) mechanisms in the supply processes. This also implies implementing the concept of internal customer, wherein every level in the supply chain is treated as a customer for its preceding level and as a supplier for its succeeding level. A consistent cost effective supply chain thus

   (a) depends upon collaboration and trust between the partners in the chain;
   (b) recognizes the importance of internal and external customers and suppliers; and
   (c) benefits all parties concerned on a pooled basis rather than on individual partner basis.

Efficient management of the supply chain has been an area of concern internationally and has undergone a metamorphosis over the last decade. Globally, phase 1 had the small and inefficient single component suppliers being weeded out. In phase 2, local mega-suppliers were created to supply modules and systems rather than isolated individual components. In phase 3, component-system manufacturers followed the original equipment manufacturer (OEMs) as the latter explored global markets, manufactured in-house components using core competency, and also sourced from smaller single component manufacturers. These were subsequently assembled into component-systems for supply to the OEM.

Some of the strategic steps being undertaken by global players in this direction are the following.

   1. *Supplier base rationalization* Consolidating/reducing supplier base to merely a few key suppliers.
   2. *Vendor-managed inventory* Facilitating the key suppliers to take on many of the OEM's day-to-day transactions through initiation of various programmes such

as, continuous replenishment and vendor-managed inventory. This is also referred to as JIT-II.

3. *Long-term OEM buyer–supplier relationships* Long-term contractual relationships with suppliers accompanied by supplier commitments on phased cost reduction, quality, production, and delivery.

4. *Joint action with supplier* Sharing of value analysis, engineering, and process engineering benefits by both partners and creation of cross-functional supplier support teams.

5. *Customer orientation* Provision of innovative logistic practices and provisions through cross-docking, drop-shipping, 3PL and 4PL provisions, and postponement, etc. which should ultimately reduce lead times and have better service levels for the customer.

6. *Automation in warehousing, tracing and tracking* Establishment of automated facilities in transportation and warehousing, such as load-unitization and multi-modal transport, freight consolidation, refrigerated containers, use of trace and track mechanisms through the Web, bar coding, and radio frequency identification (RFID).

7. *Inculcation of lean environment* Implementation of a single piece flow system in processing by pull-based synchronization of supply with demand on the shop floor. This has been quite inevitable in the current recessionary but competitive business environment.

Major strategies being followed in this direction by the automobile giants are outlined in Table 4.1.

In contemporary times, efficient SC invariably needs

(a) automation of transactions facilitating information exchange electronically and capture of critical data related to actual sales, forecasts, production and distribution planning, and scheduling in real time;

(b) emphasis on collaborative effort in integration of OEM and supplier into a virtual enterprise from design to delivery; and

(c) provision for high service levels for both internal and external customers in response to their needs from design to delivery.

The key global practices being executed in the said directions are discussed in following sections.

TIERIZATION OF SUPPLIERS

The trend internationally in the past few years is that of establishing a tiered hierarchy of suppliers implying that a vehicle manufacturer, for example, instead of sourcing

TABLE 4.1 Major strategies being followed by automobile giants for SCM

Strategy	Focus
• Tierization of suppliers	• Organization of supplier base; lower inventories; lower overall costs
• Reverse logistics/recyclable packaging	• Lower rejections; lower cycle times; reduction in wastage
• Vendor-managed inventor (VMI) JIT II	• Extended enterprise; faster information dissemination; lower inventories; cost reduction
• Milk round systems	• Logistics cost reduction; JIT supplies in efficient manner
• Bar coding	• Cycle time reduction; elimination of non-value added activities, tracing and tracking
• Hub and spoke arrangement	• Reduction in supply chain costs; minimization of inventory, effective JIT supplies to OEM

individual small parts and putting them together in-house would now outsource complete systems such as brake systems, cockpit, chassis, etc. as modules. Thus, the OEM merely assemble the vehicle in the form of pre-assembled modules which are supplied directly by the systems suppliers to the OEM's production line. Ideally an assembly of the vehicle at the plant would involve only five to six modules, such as suspension, electricals, cockpit, etc.

The tierization and modularization results into the following benefits:

(a) rationalization of supplier base for OEM
(b) minimization of OEM assembly cost and floor requirement thus reducing overall costs keeping in mind the higher overheads at any OEM plant
(c) straight shipping of pre-assembled, tested in sequence modules to OEM's point-of-use which minimizes inventory and inspection costs
(d) facilitation of lower follow-up costs and non-proliferation of part numbers at OEM level
(e) better handling of warranty at OEM level

Exhibit 4.1 shows the suppliers' tierization at Maruti Udyog Ltd.

Majority of the problems experienced by OEMs during the application of this concept have been observed to be related to

• geographically scattered vendor base
• unreliable transit times
• high freight costs due to long distances and lack of special trucks/carriers
• lack of excellent tier 1 suppliers with infrastructure to support modular suppliers

EXHIBIT 4.1 Suppliers' Tierization at Maruti Udyog Ltd

Until the advent of Japanese manufacturing concepts in the country, high degree of vertical integration in the automobile industry was the order of the day. Telco and Hindustan Motors exemplify this strategy in that era. Maruti Udyog Ltd (MUL) for the first time ensured that component manufacturing was offloaded to ancillaries who specialized in the design and manufacture of the respective component. These became tier 1 suppliers with the OEM also undertaking final assembly and manufacturing of critical modules such as engine, transmission, chassis, cockpit, etc., as part of it's assembly line operations. Of late, MUL has attempted to move closer to sourcing material in the form of modules by shifting in-house subassemblies to its vendors who naturally take on the concerned logistic functions of its constituent parts. Some examples of subassemblies previously carried out at MUL and subsequently shifted to its vendors or in the process of being shifted out are given in Table 4.2. Generally, the subassembly has been shifted to that vendor who would add maximum value to the process apart from considerations of competence to manage the operation. Similarly companies such as Honda and Hyundai in India have initiated procurement of vendor-built subassemblies such as Brake and fuel pipe clusters.

TABLE 4.2 Subassemblies shifted to the vendor's end for manufacturing by MUL

1. Fuel tank	7. Moulded root lining
2. Panel assembly fender apron	8. Gear shift lever
3. Rear axle	9. Steering column
4. Bumper	10. Wheel
5. Panel assembly cowl upper	11. Instrument panel
6. Panel comp dash side	12. Knuckle

Source: Vendor Development Department, Maruti Udyog Ltd

- concentration of substantial supplier power in the hands of a few module manufacturers, and
- resistance from existing tier 1 manufacturers on being moved to tier 2, 3 or even further down on account of perceived 'loss of prestige' and provision of less attractive payment terms.

Many OEMs are attempting to tackle some of the above problems by

(a) encouraging suppliers to shift production base closer to OEM;

(b) continuing price negotiations with existing vendors even if they move down the tiers in order to maintain them in the vendor family and avoid them being squeezed out by the subsequent tier 1 vendor for his 'preferred' source;

(c) continuing all existing interactions in terms of vendor conferences, training, etc. to avoid feeling of loss of prestige;

(d) considering passing the benefits of modularization in monetary terms by sharing mechanism for the first three years; and

(e) encouraging strategic alliances between related suppliers, say, a plastic dashboard manufacturer or an instrument cluster manufacturer, and the instrument panel/cockpit module supplier who are tier 1 suppliers, to the OEM.

However, OEMs continue to face specific difficulties in implementation of tierization.

Honda has had to revert some of its items back to individual status from subassemblies/modules on account of increased freight costs. This has resulted due to local truckers unions refusing to allow returning of empty vehicles with empty recyclable packing if they were hired by the vendor from his local transporter's union. Thus, hiring another truck for this purpose defeats the very intention of tierization of vendors. Tierization is obviously accompanied by increased freight costs, since fewer components can be accommodated per truck. This could be offset by more efficient utilization of trucks, facilitated by using the empty returning truck to carry back recyclable packing/containers.

REVERSE LOGISTICS

This concept involves usage of bins, trolleys, and pallets for component suppliers, thus ensuring component feeding straight to the point-of-use on the line. Empty trolleys, bins, etc. are carried back by the vendor, thus affecting substantial savings in packing and unpacking. Moreover, standardized packaging in this manner enables increased use of cluster, roller conveyors, and guide rails, facilitates accurate inventory control through the length of the conveyor.

Recyclable packing is now a reality in most automobile plants internationally. Mercedes-Benz, a German automobile manufacturing company reportedly follows a closed loop recyclable container programme in the following manner:

Step I:	A truck leaves the OEM plant with empty containers of say, three suppliers—A, B, and C.
Step II:	At supplier A, its empty containers are unloaded and packed containers are loaded in the truck and the truck moves to B.
Step III:	At suppliers B and C, the same process is repeated with each supplier receiving its own empty containers and replenishing full containers.
Step IV:	The truck then travels with full containers, containing parts, to the vehicle manufacturing plant where parts from all the three suppliers are integrated into assembly line operations.
Step V:	Empty containers for all the three suppliers are made ready to be picked up at an allocated area and are loaded into the truck for shipment to suppliers A, B, and C.

The mode of recyclable packing is being used as an effective tool for SCM, through

(a) extensive use of plastic bins and trolleys;
(b) colour coding of bins with vendor identification;
(c) tailor-made partitioning of bins for systematic transportation and counting; and
(d) stretch wrapping of critical dust prone components as a single unit in their respective packing.

The extent to which MUL has been successful in implementation of recyclable packing is illustrated in Fig. 4.1 (a and b). It has been found that implementation of this concept at MUL and other OEMs has resulted in the reduction of the following.

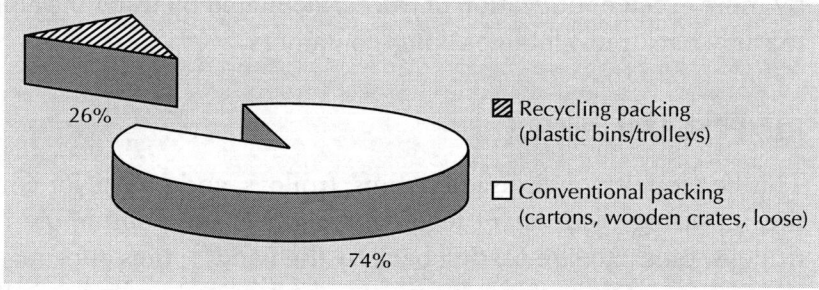

(a) Recyclable packing implementation for vendors within 300 kms

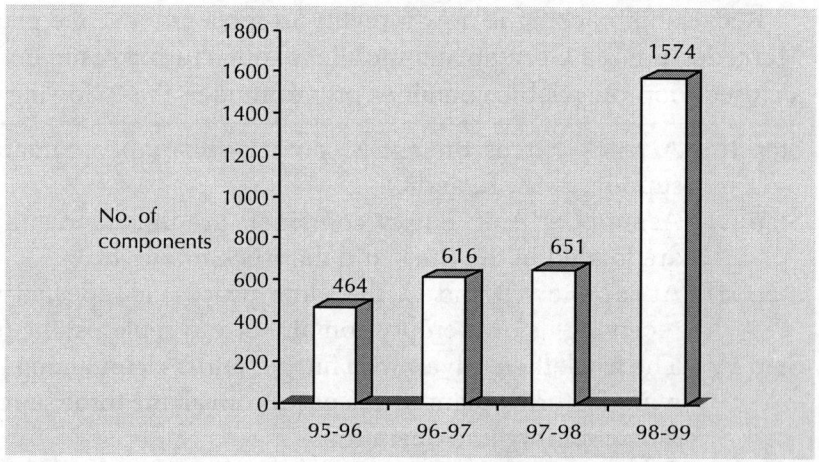

(b) Trends of switchover to recyclable packing in different years

FIG. 4.1 Indicative implementation of recyclable packing at MUL
Source: Vendor Development Department, MUL, 2000

- Raw material and work-in-progress inventory
- Holding time in MUL stores
- Charging and material handling time
- Rejections

All these practices have led to reduced defects and hence waste of materials, less assembly line hold-ups, better time synchronization of supplies with production schedules, better maintenance of machines in terms of reduced downtime, negligible material handling and storage, and negligible waiting or idle time on machines. So, the efficiency gets increased.

VENDOR-MANAGED INVENTORY

Vendor-managed inventory (VMI) involves a vendor representative (*the rep.*) being stationed full-time at the OEM facility, being empowered to even use its computer systems and authorized to decide what, when, and how much to order for a particular range of products or services. The *reps* are hired, evaluated, and paid for by the vendor but have access to the OEM's facilities, people, computer systems, sport badges/uniforms of the OEM, and are free to come and go as they choose. VMI or JIT II helps the customer and supplier establish long-term alliance and empowers the vendors' in-plant *rep* to act as customer champion within its organization. JIT II, however, also necessitates that the supplier be trustworthy, reliable and that the product under consideration be of importance to both the buyer and the seller. With increasing importance of joint partnerships, lower inventories, and necessity of efficient management in all aspects of the supply chain, this practice could be a source of competitive advantage.

Honda has enforced JIT through issue of time bound delivery slips that are handed over to the supplier before the month begins. The computer at the entry point ensures that only material in the right quantity is allowed in on the correct date. MUL too is presently implementing JIT in a formal manner by implementing supply of predetermined size lots at predetermined times for limited parts. However, this mechanism can work only when delivery of parts is predictable, i.e., the supply points are closer to OEM and the value of the component is substantial enough to effect benefit. The vendor is informed at the beginning of the month about the quantity of material to be supplied on specific days of the month. Accordingly, the vendor is issued pre-delivery vouchers, which also indicate the location (Plant I/II/III) where the material is to be unloaded in order to maintain optimum inventory at all plants. The vendor has to deliver material accompanied by these vouchers and is given priority both at the inwarding and unloading stages. The computerized system ensures that

(a) a frequency check is imposed in order to prevent material in excess of voucher from being inwarded, and

(b) a time check is imposed to allow material inwarding as per voucher only on the specified date.

Additional inventory control is exercized by means of *roller chutes* of limited capacity which extend directly from the unloading bay to the assembly line. Accordingly the vendor simply unloads bins into the chutes till they are full. The length of each chute is indicative of the inventory norm for the component. A similar system prevails in case of trolleys which are unloaded into guide rails until the rails are filled to their total length.

Implementation of this system has been reported to lead to the following favourable responses:

- certainty of time and quantity, facilitating better planning
- levelling of inventory
- better utilization of storage space and
- minimized material handling

JIT II implementation at many OEMs has been carried out in an informal manner. Vendors to MUL have dedicated personnel who sport similar uniforms, have free access to the MUL plant though a *Permanent Gate Pass*, and who monitor stocks of their respective components at the production line and stores. These *reps* inform their plants *when* and *how* much of the material is to be supplied to OEM's plant in accordance with its sub-model and production plan. They also deal with the day-to-day problems at rejections, quality problems, and coordination related issues raised by the OEM. Many OEMs now have nearly 100 per cent of its vendors on e-mail, facilitating their access to production plans, rejections, etc. Some of the challenges being faced in JIT/JIT II implementation by MUL are the following.

- inconsistency in quality of inputs
- poor infrastructural facilities
- unreliable transport system
- lack of top management support and commitment from vendors
- possibility of misuse of confidential information gained by the vendor *rep* who may subsequently switch jobs

MILK ROUND SYSTEM

The concept of milk round system (MRS) involves material collection, unloading, and production-wise allocation of trucks at the vendor's end. This involves fixed frequency/time of movement of trucks based on an exact production requirement in small lots. The collection and supply of material is exactly in tune with the OEM's production requirement.

The MRS would be used through a third-party logistics (3PL) provider who would organize supplies from Gurgaon, Faridabad, Noida, etc. and offload them in a godown at Noida from where cross-docking would be carried out to OEM's, say, Bangalore plant. At MUL, for example, the implementation involves movement of single vehicles among clusters of vendors located in specific areas, e.g., Faridabad/ Gurgaon. Accordingly, a single vehicle moves from MUL to vendor A where it unloads recyclable bins/trolleys of A and picks up whatever material is readily available (based on requirement already communicated earlier). It subsequently goes to the rest of the cluster of vendors (B, C, etc.) in Faridabad where it undergoes a similar process, finally heading back to MUL with supplies of small lots from varied vendors in quantities exactly required for production. This enables smaller vendors who would otherwise prefer to send large loads to cover freight costs, to make multiple supplies in a day, with frequency of supplies and quantities being governed directly by production. This also ensures that partially filled trucks need not be sent independently from a number of vendors, thus awaiting unloading. In addition, traffic congestion at material inward gate is reduced besides ensuring inventory reduction at all points in the supply chain. Indicative details of the number of vendors covered under the MRS at MUL are depicted in Table 4.3.

TABLE 4.3 Milk round system implementation at MUL

Location	No. of vendors	No. of MRS groups*
Gurgaon (Area – I)	17	3
Gurgaon (Area – II)	3	1
Faridabad	14	4

* Each group represents one set of vehicles moving between specified vendors.
Source: Vendor Development Department, MUL

BAR CODING

Internationally, most activities in SCM make optimum use of bar coding whether it be material entry or supplies tracking. Pre-delivery slips called *Part Receipt Tags* issued by OEM to its suppliers are bar coded for various details. This reduces delays at gate due to elimination of manual entry. MUL has begun bar coding of various details on vendor documents in order to

(a) aid faster entry of material;
(b) reduce piling up of waiting vehicles; and
(c) reduce errors made during manual entry of material.

Subsequently, bar coding can be exploited for distant vendors in order to enable tracking of material during transit in order to facilitate better planning at MUL. However, a typical problem being encountered with bar coded documents is the careless handling by truck drivers, resulting in documents being defaced. This leads to difficulty in bar code capturing at the entry terminal.

HUB AND SPOKE CONCEPT

Since engineering including auto–ancillary units are generally located in clusters (whether close to the OEM or elsewhere), the hub and spoke concept can be implemented successfully, thus facilitating better planning of material inwarding with respect to production requirement. Essentially, the consolidation centre (*hub*) receives material from a number of (*spokes*) suppliers and subsequently organizes supplies of the required material to the OEM which may well be a long distance away. Information technology (IT) backup is an essential prerequisite for ensuring speedy communication of production plans and changes in order, so that the material is despatched well in time to reach OEM *just-in-time*.

Toyota's Bangalore Plant is reportedly using the hub and spoke arrangement in conjunction with the MRS. Toyota has established a hub next to its campus wherein substantial space is held by a logistic provider. Vendors from locations throughout the country would directly or through the MRS, transfer material to their godowns located within this hub. The 3PL provider would subsequently organize supplies to the Toyota plant on JIT basis. In case of MUL, there are a number of vendors clustered in nearby locations such as Faridabad and Manesar and even at distant locations such as Chennai, Indore, etc. Implementation of hub and spoke arrangement would lead to dramatic improvement in logistics. This concept involves a number of vendors located close to a hub (a central consolidation point) supplying small lots to this centre at frequent intervals as and when it is produced, based on a monthly production plan already agreed to mutually. The consolidation centre supported by an excellent IT link would make supplies in economic lots to MUL in large trailers or containers containing only requisite amount of diverse components (individually less than a truckload) sourced from varied suppliers instead of material from vendors in a singular manner. The pipeline inventory of each component would also decrease on account of shorter length of the pipeline from the vendor to the consolidation centre. The concept is ideal especially for the smaller sheet metal vendors who find it uneconomical to transport small lots. However it would be ideal to have a 3PL provider who could manage the logistics *bi-directionally* from/to the hub. The hub and spoke concept implementation could be supported by managing *synchronized movement* of inbound and outbound trucks thus facilitating further streamlining of the supply chain. Trucks carrying finished vehicles to, say, Chennai, could carry back inbound material (components) from a consolidated centre/hub in Chennai. This could effect substantial savings since freight charges for outbound trucks carrying vehicles cover the to and fro journey. The consolidation centres would thus, also act as warehouses which function for optimum benefits augmenting with the milk round system. The consolidation centre could feed the returning trucks on a regular basis especially in view of the high volumes of finished vehicles being transported to a certain location.

TRENDS IN USE OF THIRD-PARTY LOGISTICS PROVIDERS

There are some interesting trends observed in the trucking, logistics, transportation, and warehousing operators in India. The Asian Institute of Transport Development has come up with interesting trends which are discussed here.

Consolidation of Logistics Providers

Small truckers in India have been facing difficulties and dropping out of business, and most operators say that basic trucking has been a loss-making operation. Large transportation companies have stopped buying trucks and do outsourcing of the same. So they are trying to avoid the loss making part of business and concentrate on value-addition part, i.e., on their ability to get quality orders through a marketing network, providing transit storage, handling and warehousing facilities, and even coordination with vendors, management of inventory at various points—customized delivery and pick-ups also providing track and trace mechanism to customers as well as transporters for better service levels. Service levels have also increased with increase in efficiency in trucking operations, e.g., according to the Asian Institute of Transport Development, the average driving hours have risen from 5–10 hours to 9–12 hours. The average speed of trucks on most Indian roads varies from just 18 km/hr to 35–40 km/hr. While only 27 per cent of truckers utilized their vehicles between 200–300 km/day in 1994, this figure went up to 72 per cent in 1998. Drivers are being provided communication gadgets to call the controlling office of the transport company all along the route which keeps a surveillance over the drivers. Bar coding and tracking methods of consignments are also used. In US, routing guides along with time and fuel details are used for tracking of truckers. Table 4.4 provides some vital statistics which affect trucking operations in India.

As per budget 2010 of the Government of India, between 2009–10 and 2013–14, investments worth Rs 6,00,000 crore are expected towards the development of roads, ports, and airports in India, out of which investment in roads would be close to 84 per cent. It is aimed to build at least 20 km/day of highways in India.

TABLE 4.4 Vital statistics of trucking industry

Parameter	Value
Rate of growth of road length in India	5% p.a.
Surfaced roads in India	56.5%
Non-motorable roads in India	22.7%
No. of transport operators	300,000 (360,000 in US)
Share of organized business	30% (90% in US)
Turnover from trucking industry (2001)	Rs 65,000 ($13.5 bn) ($255 bn in US)
No. of trucks estimated on road (2005)	2.87 million
Average distance covered by truck per day	250–300 km/hr (over 600 km in US)
Economic losses* due to bad road conditions per year as in 2001	Rs 200–300 bn or Rs 7000/vehicle ($41.5 bn/yr or $222/vehicle in US)
Share of total goods carried	51–60% (80% in US)
Tax as per cent of total truck operating cost	56.5% (5–10% in US)
Ownership distribution (%)	**Value**
Operators with	
– one truck	15%
– less than 5 trucks	77%
– more than 20 trucks	06%
(while in US 82% have less than 5 trucks)	

*Losses due to tyre wear, damage to shock absorbers, wheel alignment, and extra fuel consumption.
Source: Economic Times Intelligence Group, 2002

A study on 'Trucking operations in India—Problems and Potential' and a subsequent report on the same submitted to the Ministry of Surface Transport in 2000 lists the typical overhead charges in Table 4.5.

TABLE 4.5 Break-up of typical overhead charges of a truck (Route: Mumbai–Delhi, 1200 km, 3 days)

Head	Cost (Rs)	Share of total cost (%)
RTO and police	2400	30.0
Octroi check-posts	81	1.05
Loading/unloading	160	2.2
Other expenses	80	1.0
Total	2720	34.25

Source: ETIG, 2002

Also, as per statistics given by Asian Institute of Transport Development to draft a report on problems and potential of trucking in India, the truck operating expenses in India are much higher than standards as given in Table 4.6.

TABLE 4.6   Truck operating costs in India

Cost item	Operating cost	Indian values
Fuel (diesel and oil)	21–35%	50–60%
Tyres	10–15%	15–18%
Spares	15–20%	10–15%
Fixed costs		
Driver and crew expenses	10–20%	7–9%
Depreciation and interest	15–20%	5–7%
Overheads and misc. expenses	10–15%	15–20%
Total	100	100

Source: ETIG, 'Supply Chain & Logistics', 2002

The Range of 3PL Services

It is observed that the following types of services can be provided by 3PLs in India.

- Shipment consolidation
- Warehousing management
- Carrier selection
- Rate negotiations
- Fleet operations and management
- Logistics information systems
- Product returns (reverse logistics)
- Order fulfilment
- Order processing
- Relabelling/repacking
- Customized delivery (including that of spare parts)
- Inventory management
- Product testing and assembly including upkeep
- Multimodal transport

Exhibit 4.2 indicates the range of activities carried out by 3PLs and 4PLs.

Trends in Transportation and Warehousing

Transportation and warehousing (WH) are two vital areas of SCM where 3PLs are now offering services based on two models which are compared in Table 4.7.

EXHIBIT 4.2 Activities Carried out by 3PLs and 4PLs

Activities carried out by a traditional distributor = Warehousing (1) + Transportation (2) + Delivery (3)

Activities carried out by a 3PL = (1) + (2) + (3) + Inventory control (4) + Special handling requirement (5) + Cost control (6)

Activities carried out by a 4PL = (1) to (6) + Supply chain optimization + Value added services + Change management

Source: ETIG, 2002

TABLE 4.7 Comparison of locational networked vs hub and spoke companies

Locational network linked by C&FAs	Hub and spoke companies 3PLs
• Used by practically every industry for WH, transport, and information.	• 3PL may have more to offer than just C&F services and WH.
• C&FA is similar to a 3PL except that WH has a greater role to play.	• There are now 3PLs offering WH space (own/hired) in strategic locations.
• C&FA is an intermediary between the company and the stockist. He clears the goods from the factory to the stockist and holds the goods at his WH.	• They may also have their own/arranged IT and transport arrangements.
• C&FA generally does not offer track and trace services and fleet management.	• They are essentially linked real-time with their clients.

• Mainly prevalent in industries such as FMCG, foods, paints, and consumer durables as companies do not want to hold the inventory because of the volumes of the goods produced at their end.	• Offers normal C&F services plus
	  ▫ Load consolidation
	  ▫ Backhauls
	  ▫ Transaction tracking
	  ▫ Fleet and SKUs trace and tracking

• C&FAs could be local to region.	• These companies could be regional and global.

In both the models for WH outsourcing, setting up of logistics centres at various strategic locations is vital. The WH's are located outside the octroi limits to avoid the octroi charges. Proximity to road, rail heads, and ports is another factor. Cost of freight is the key factor and competition is fierce in trucking—another activity of 3PLs. Some strategic WH locations in India are—Agra, Bhiwandi, Chennai, Coimbatore, Ghaziabad, Kolkata, Lucknow, and Nagpur. Some issues are as follows.

(i) There are legal problems to add to the basic cost of freight, i.e., octroi and excise duties. As per Indian laws, every value addition (even including packing/repacking) is treated as conversion and duties are charged.

(ii) As per RBI, logistics companies are not permitted to remit rupee payments for overseas WH and distribution services to their overseas branches. Such a payment can only be made by clients themselves after completing necessary registration.

(iii) It is common in rest of Asia, US, and Europe to have bonded WH facilities where inventories for multiple destination countries can be kept and then exported when required. Indian customs regulations do not permit such provisions to make international hubs.

(iv) In India, suppose, a big consignment is split into small lots for clients convenience, the buyer has to get as many invoices as the lots. Different lots can never be separately bar coded nor repacked in a manner suited to the client as Indian laws treat this as conversion and is liable to taxation. Uniform VAT is the answer to this. A 10 per cent reduction in these secondary freight costs may bring about a direct 10 per cent increase in bottom lines of companies.

That implies that each 3PL has to coordinate with other 3PL and linked via personnel and IT.

FOURTH-PARTY LOGISTICS PROVIDERS

Fourth-party logistics (4PL) providers represent the next stage of development in the field of logistics service providers. The trend, even in India, is to outsource the non-value added activities to an outside party. More and more business processes are being outsourced. These may include bill payment, credit tracking, invoice generation, HRD, transport, and WH but, there are no single 3PLs that offer all of these processes with equal competence. For example, while WH, transportation, and inventory management may be given out to one 3PL, other processes such as HRD, security, and product development are done by other 3PLs and linked via personnel and IT. So, what is needed is an *integrator* that assembles the capital, technology, and resources of its own organization and other complementary service providers to design, build, and run supply chains. In simple words, a 4PL manages other 3PLs. The following points further distinguish 4PLs from 3PLs:

(i) 4PL delivers a comprehensive supply chain solution.

(ii) 4PL delivers value through its ability to have an impact on the entire supply chain.

Thus, it is seen that 4PLs have evolved because of constraints faced by 3PLs.

Models of 4PL

The concept of 4PL was first given by Accenture (formerly Anderson Consulting) in the year 1996. These models given by Accenture are as follows.

Synergy Plus or Basic Functional Relationship Model

This arrangement relies on working relationship between a 4PL organization and a 3PL service provider, who may form a partnership to market SC solutions that capitalize on the capabilities and market reach of both the organizations (Fig. 4.2). The 4PL company may provide technology, SC strategy skills, capability to the 3PL partner to go to the market, and programme management expertise. The synergistic partnership then serves different customers, C_1, C_2, C_3, C_4, etc.

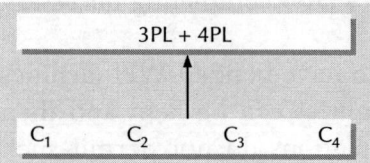

FIG. 4.2 The basic relationship model of 4PL
Source: Accenture India as accessed through ETIG, 2002

Solution Integrator

Here a 4PL operates and manages a comprehensive SC solution for a single client. In this arrangement, the 4PL provides resources, capabilities, and technology while 3PLs provide complementary services all together providing a comprehensive integrated SC solution that delivers value throughout a single client organization's SC components (refer Fig. 4.3).

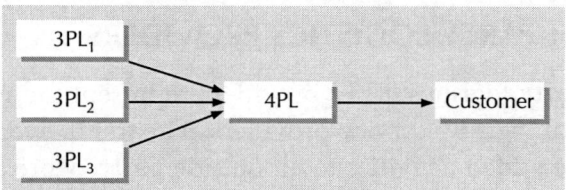

FIG. 4.3 4PL as a solution integrator
Source: Accenture India as accessed through ETIG, 2002

Industry Innovator

Here, a 4PL organization develops and runs a supply chain solution for multiple industry players with focus on synchronization and collaboration. The 4PLs adopt a *best of breed* approach to provide services and technology to a client. The 4PLs would integrate client's SC activities by selecting *best of breed* service providers with the capabilities of its own organization (Fig. 4.4).

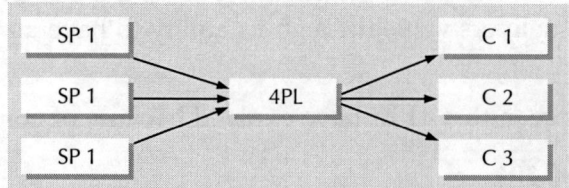

FIG. 4.4 4PL as an industry innovator
Source: Accenture India as accessed through ETIG, 2002

FUTURE TRENDS EXPECTED IN USE OF 3PLS

Some of the trends being experienced and projected in the use of 3PLs.

Shake-out and Consolidation of Service Providers

Standard models of services such as pure carriers or pure cargo handlers will be prime candidates for takeover by bigger companies and play the role of service providers within larger offer. Such consolidation is seen in all areas—from supplying, trucking, air cargo to couriers, ground handlers, and IT services.

Use of IT

The use and spread of IT—including ERP, WMS, trucking systems and Net-based data exchange—will be inevitable and rapid. Old physical assets such as trucking and C&FAs would be better utilized by the use of IT.

Alliances

There will be alliances, joint ventures (JVs), and mergers with MNCs or logistics providers to attain a certain critical mass or network.

Investment

To work as a 3PL, a firm will need financial resources for infrastructure, IT, people, fulfilling of liabilities arising from failures to honour commitments, and insurance claims. Logistics and SC today offer returns of 15–20 per cent, which no other investment gives, so it provides a good market for FIIs and banks.

Regulation

Easy availability of people/labour in the logistics industry is hampering development of people. Industries see a personnel shake-out in carriers, cargo, express trucking, and ports to varying degrees. Third-party providers will improve in all aspects of business in India as awareness spreads and the benefits become more pronounced.

POSTPONEMENT STRATEGY

In this strategy, the configuration of the final product is postponed as long as possible. The first application of this principle can be traced to Benetton, the Italian manu-facturer of fashion clothes. About 60 per cent of the garments sold by the firm are made of wool. Conventionally, wool is dyed before it is knitted. Benetton undertook a unique exercise to dye the garments *after* they were knitted though labour and production costs for garments dyed after manufacture are about 10 per cent higher than for garments knitted from dyed thread. However, it provides additional time before committing to the final mix of colours. This gives the firm a chance to gain additional data on consumer preferences for colours. Benetton's knitwear included around 500 colour and style combinations. Undyed garments are referred to as grey stock so, if a specific colour becomes more popular than expected, Benetton could meet the demand for that colour. The company in turn also runs lesser risk of having large unsold stockpiles of garments in unpopular colours. These advantages more than offset the higher costs of dying the knitted garments rather than the raw wool.

Postponement thus also results in better inventory management. As is known, safety stock is maintained to protect against demand uncertainty over the replenishment lead time. The lead time for garments of a specific colour is reduced by postponing the dying operation. It follows that uncertainty is reduced as well, thus achieving better service levels with less safety stock. Another example is that of Hewlett-Packard (HP) as given in Exhibit 4.3.

EXHIBIT 4.3 Postponement at Hewlett-Packard (HP)

As is known, HP is one of the world's leading producers of inkjet and laser printers which are sold worldwide. While the basic mechanism of the printers sold overseas are the same as American versions, subassemblies such as power supplies, must be customized for local markets and customers. HP's original strategy was to configure printers for local requirements at the factory itself, i.e., the printers with correct power supplies, plugs, and manuals would be produced at the factory, and then sorted and shipped overseas as final products. The result was that HP needed to carry large safety stocks of all printer configurations. In order to reduce inventories and improve service levels by distribution centres (DCs) to retail customers, HP decided to localize the printers EX-DC than at the factories. With local customization done at DC's end, the replenishment lead-time for locally configured printers is dramatically reduced. It also showed that DC level localization for HP printers would lead to an around 18% reduction in inventories with no reduction in service level. HP advocated that design for localization be a part of manufacturing and distribution strategy. Similarly, semiconductors are produced in generic form and customized through programming only after firm orders are received. Firms such as Hewlett-Packard are now becoming increasingly aware of the risk-pooling and lead-time reduction benefits from postponement and local customization.

CROSS-DOCKING

A prominent example of a company following cross-docking is Wal-Mart. A key feature of the supply chain design at Wal-Mart is known as cross-docking. Under this system, products are delivered to Wal-Mart's warehouses on a continual basis where they are sorted, repackaged, and distributed to different stores without sitting in inventory. Goods 'cross' from one loading dock to another in 48 hours or less. Cross-docking also facilitates the product mixing function, i.e., products from different suppliers arrive in truckload lots but instead of being put in storage for later picking, they are moved across the warehouse area to waiting trucks for movement to particular customers/stores directly. This system allows Wal-Mart to purchase full truckloads of goods while avoiding the inventory and handling costs, in the process reducing its costs of sales to 2 to 3 per cent less than the industry average. Wal-Mart then passes these cost savings on to its customers as lower prices. Low prices enable them to forego frequent discount promotions which stabilizes prices, which in turn make sales more predictable, thus reducing stock-outs and the need for excess inventory.

Retailers do not use cross-docking because it is difficult to coordinate and manage. To make it work, Wal-Mart has invested heavily in an integrated support system that provides continuous contact among all of Wal-Mart's suppliers, DC, and every *point-of-sale*[1] in every store via its own satellite communication system. This information system sends out point-of-sale (bar code) data directly to Wal-Mart's 4000 suppliers. In addition, Wal-Mart owns 2000 trucks to service its 19 DCs which allows the company to ship goods from warehouses to stores within 48 hours and restock store shelves an average of *twice a week*, compared to the industry average of once every two weeks. Cross-docking also requires close management cooperation at all levels. Store managers are connected to each other and to corporate headquarters via a video link that allows for frequent information exchanges about products, pricing, sales, and promotions. Figure 4.5 illustrates the relationship between facilities and functions along the Wal-Mart supply chain.

In one instance, Wal-Mart found it to be more cost-effective to bypass DCs and warehouses altogether. It used to hold inventories of Pampers diapers in its warehouse before shipping them to stores. However, after looking at its entire supply chain, Wal-Mart realized that Pampers take up so much space and have such a low profit margin that the company was losing about 20 cents per case just handling the inventory. It found that it was more profitable to have diapers shipped directly from the supplier to the store more frequently even though the cost of transportation and store labour would both be higher. By looking at the relationship between components of the supply chain (including inventory, warehousing, transportation,

---

[1] Point-of-sale (PoS) or checkout refers to a location in a store (or a virtual location of sale in a computer system, e.g., the Department of Posts, India, has PoS on its system), where a transaction takes place. The PoS could more generally refer to hardware and software used for checkouts, the equivalence of an electronic cash register. A PoS terminal would manage the selling process by a sales person accessible interface. It would also facilitate creation and printing of the voucher of sale

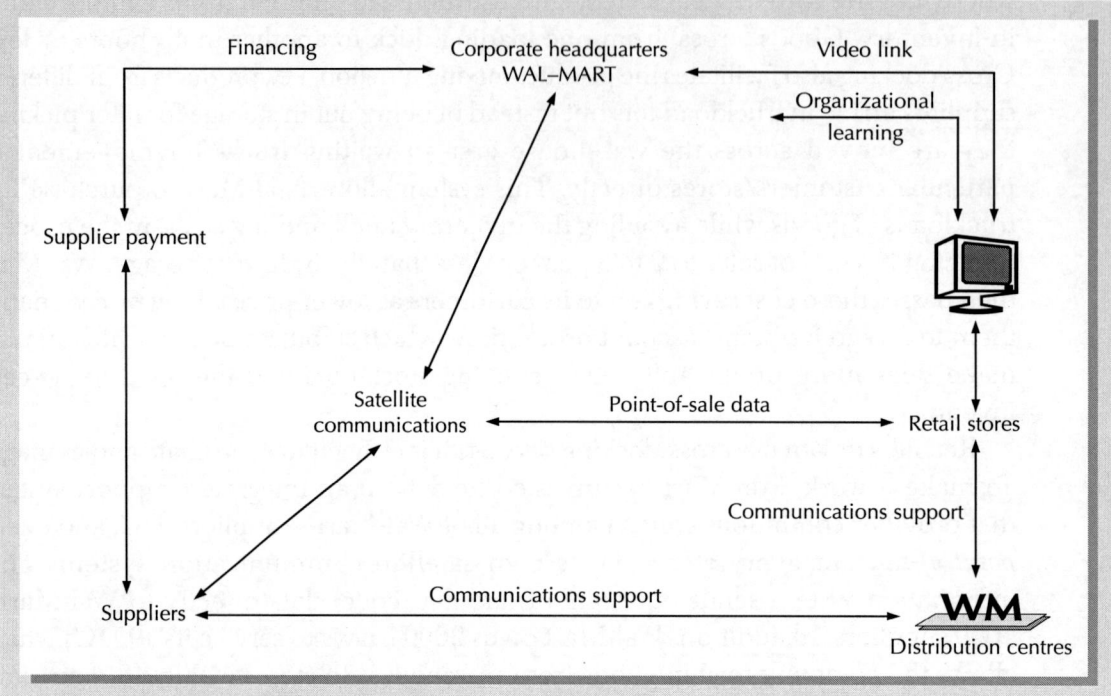

FIG. 4.5   The Wal-Mart supply chain
Source: Adapted from Wieland Garrison, 'Wal-Mart's Supply Chain'. *Harvard Business Review*, Vol. 70,
   No. 2, March–April 1992, pp. 60–61

and retail operation) instead of just inventory, the company was able to reduce supply chain costs.

   Wal-Mart has developed another type of relationship with some of its suppliers. It is to have them take over warehousing and shipping. For example, to sell at some Wal-Mart stores, Johnson Wax must forecast demand for its own products (shaving gel and air freshners) using Wal-Mart's weekly sales data and then place its own products on the store shelves.

DROP-SHIPPING

In this technique, the supplier ships directly to the end consumer rather than to the seller, after due authorization from the latter, saving both time and re-shipping costs. Drop-shipping is normally accompanied with load utilization and bar coding. HP is well known to drop-ship its products directly from its suppliers to the end-consumer in any country to save on distribution costs.

RISK-POOLING

It is a strategy whereby the suppliers, such as contract equipment manufacturers (CEMs), aggregate demand from many buying OEM companies and thus reduce uncertainty through pooling of the risks involved with various members at the same level of the supply chain. This is seen in companies in the electronics industry like Flextronics that supply to OEMs like Dell. This is facilitated by outsourcing by OEMs to transfer demand uncertainty to their CEMs. The CEMs can thus reduce the component inventory levels while maintaining or even increasing the service level. As a result of risk-pooling, demand variability gets reduced as one aggregates demand across locations since it becomes more likely that high demand from one customer, internal or external, is offset by low demand from another customer. This reduction in variability also mitigates the bullwhip effect, allows a decrease in the safety stock, and therefore, reduces the average inventory. A common centralized warehousing system would facilitate risk-pooling. Higher the variability in demand across different members of the supply chain at the same level, greater is the benefit from the central WH and risk-pooling.

TRANS-SHIPMENT

It is a supply chain practice involving the shipment of items between different facilities at the same level in the supply chain to meet some urgent needs, i.e., to enable the risk-pooling so that it allows retailers to meet customers' demand from the inventory of other retailers. More often than not, trans-shipments are considered at the retailer level. To do this, a retailer must know what other retailers have in inventory and must have a quick way and means to ship the items either to the store where the customer originally tried to purchase or to the customer's home.

Trans-shipment can be met only with advanced information systems which allow a retailer to see what other retailers have in their stock and facilitate rapid shipping among retailers even if no central WH exists. Generally, it would work best when all retailers are commonly owned. If independently owned, retailers may resist trans-shipment unless there are ways in which they are contributing to distributor integration (DI) whereby independent distributors cooperate in many ways, including trans-shipment of needed goods under certain contractual conditions and agreed upon remuneration/commission.

RADIO FREQUENCY IDENTIFICATION

Radio frequency identification (RFID) is a means of identifying a person or object using a radio frequency transmission, of 125 KHz, 13.56 MHz, or 800-900 MHz.

The most common method of identification is to store a serial number that identifies a person or object and other information on a microchip that is attached to an antenna; the chip and the antenna together being called an RFID transponder or an RFID tag. The antenna enables the chip to transmit the identification information to a reader. The reader converts the radio waves reflected back from the RFID tag into digital information that can then be passed on to computers that can make use of it. This concept is illustrated in Fig. 4.6.

Key Components of RFID

The following are the key components of an RFID system.

(i) An RFID tag consists of a microchip attached to an antenna. These tags are developed using a frequency according to the needs of the system including read range and the environment in which the tag will be read. Tags are either active (integrating a battery) or passive (having no battery). Passive tags derive the power to operate from the field generated by the reader.

(ii) An RFID reader, usually connected to a personal computer, serves the same purpose as a bar code scanner. It can also be battery-powered to allow mobile transactions with RFID tags. The RFID reader handles the communication between the information system and the RFID tag.

(iii) An RFID antenna connected to the RFID reader can be of various sizes and structures, depending on the communication distance required for a given system's performance. The antenna activates the RFID tag and transfers data by emitting wireless pulses.

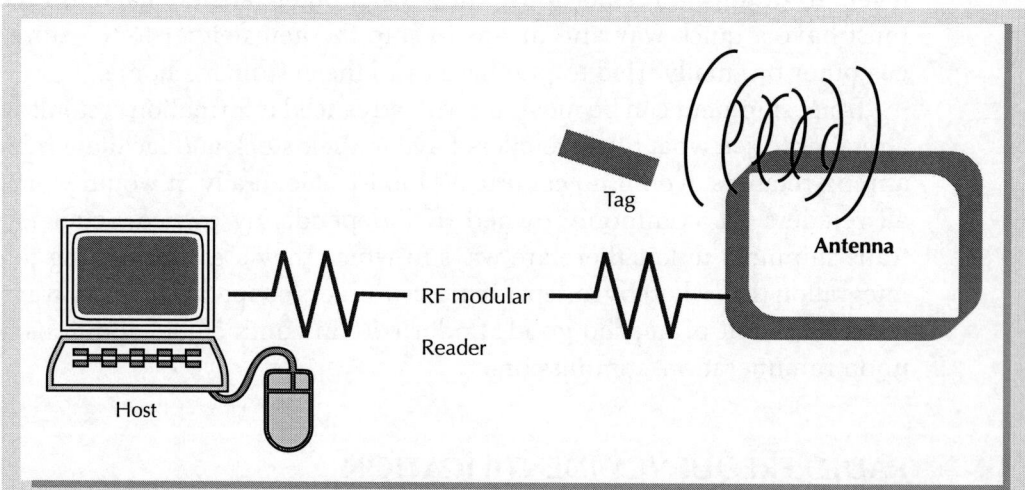

FIG. 4.6 A simple RFID system
Source: Adapted from *rfidconsultation.eu/menu/1/30.html* as accessed on 14 November 2008

(iv) An RFID station is made up of an RFID reader and an antenna. It can read information stored in the RFID tag and also update this RFID tag with new information. It generally holds application software specifically designed for the required task. RFID stations may be mounted in arrays around transfer points in commercial/industrial processes, e.g., retailing/point-of-sale process, warehousing, transportation, and supply points to automatically track assets as they keep moving through the process. All these process points are connected to the application server which is a centre for data aggregation and provides interface between the business processes and custom logic. This server is in turn networked to the RFID system comprising the RFID reader, Auto ID centre, antenna, and finally the tag.

RFID vs Bar Codes

There is often a comparison between the advantages of RFID and bar codes. RFID is not necessarily better than bar codes. The two are different technologies and have different applications, which sometimes overlap. The key difference between the two is that bar codes are line-of-sight technology. That is, a scanner has to 'see' the bar code to read it, which means people usually have to orient the bar code towards a scanner for it to be read. Radio frequency identification, by contrast, does not require line of sight. RFID tags can be read as long as they are within the range of a reader.

Bar codes have other shortcomings as well. If a label is ripped, soiled, or falls off, there is no way to scan the item. And standard bar codes identify only the manufacturer and product, not the unique item. The bar code on one milk carton is the same as every other, making it impossible to identify which one might pass its expiration date first.

Advantages of Using RFID

RFID technology, combined with the recent Auto ID initiatives led by the Massachusetts Institute of Technology (MIT), is gaining momentum. These advances offer a standardized and scalable approach that can be deployed across the extended enterprise to suppliers, manufacturers, distributors, and logistics partners, i.e., from suppliers originated inbound logistics to manufacturing to customer destined warehousing, distribution, and all outbound logistics, in order to provide a reliable and cost-effective visibility of the item, case, or pallet level. It also yields better collaborative and responsive execution of transactions through all members of the supply chain, particularly in terms of timing.

Supply chain visibility is a key contributor to increasing supply chain performance, from both a financial and a service level perspective. Greater visibility, as well as more accurate and timely information about supply chain execution, allows for reduced safety stocks (thus optimizing cash-to-cash cycles and reducing inventory carrying cost) and increased on time performance to customer commitments (thus realizing additional revenue opportunities). RFID significantly reduces the cost of cycle counting, receiving, picking, and shipping, thereby lowering the total supply chain operating costs.

Applications of RFID

RFID has multifaceted applications in business, marketing, and logistics. Key applications are discussed here.

Facility Equipment and Asset Management

RFID tags can be permanently attached to capital equipment and fixed assets. Fixed position readers placed at strategic points within the facility can automatically track the movement and location of tagged assets with cent per cent accuracy. This information can be used to quickly locate expensive tools or equipment when workers need them, eliminating labour-wasting manual searches. Readers can be set to alert supervisors or sound alarms if there is an attempt to remove tagged items from an authorized area. By tracking pallets, totes, and other containers with RFID, and keeping a record of what is stored in the container as items are loaded, users can have complete visibility into inventory levels and locations. With visibility and control, manufacturers can easily locate items necessary to fill orders and fulfil rush orders without incurring undue managerial or labour time across the facility and various assets.

Production Tracking

Manufacturers can reduce their working capital needs by taking advantage of RFID to provide greater visibility into work-in-process (WIP) tracking and materials inventory. By applying RFID tags to subassemblies in the production process, rather than to finished goods (FG), manufacturers can gain accurate, real-time visibility into WIP movements in environments where bar codes are unusable. Industrial control and material handling systems can be integrated with RFID readers to identify materials moving down a production line and automatically route the items to the appropriate assembly or testing station.

Inventory Tracking and Control

The main benefits of using RFID in the supply chain come from improved inventory tracking. Manufacturers, distributors, logistics providers, and retailers can all use

RFID for inventory applications, and in carefully planned systems, may share the same tags to reduce implementation costs. By using the highly accurate, real-time, and unattended monitoring capability of RFID to track raw materials, WIP, and finished goods, inventory manufacturers can build visibility into their inventory to enable reduction in overall inventory levels, labour costs, and safety stocks. To secure inventory from theft and pilferage and diversions, readers could be set to sound buzzers or send notification if items are placed in unauthorized areas of the facility or removed from storage without prior approval.

Pricing and Promotion

Most of the order management solutions track point-of-sale (PoS), on-shelf, and inbound inventory information to support real-time, store-level pricing, and promotion optimization. These solutions provide vendor-running programmes in stores with the ability to optimally price and promote their products according to the inventory position and turnover rates. Through RFID, manufacturers and retailers have real-time visibility to what items are selling versus those that are not or are slow moving. Also, product-specific attributes can be monitored in real-time, including

(a) product spoilage,
(b) product expiration, and
(c) product obsolescence.

By receiving real-time updates to what products or variants are selling, price lists can be monitored and updated. Additionally, one can develop and run markdown and offer promotion based on market information telling exactly what is happening at the point-of-sale (PoS).

Receiving and Logistics

The same tags used to identify WIP or finished goods inventory could also trigger automated shipment-tracking applications. Items, cases, or pallets with RFID tags could be read as they are assembled into a complete customer order or shipment. The individual readings could be used to automatically produce a shipment manifest, which could be printed in a document, recorded automatically in the shipping system, encoded in an RFID tag, printed in a 2D bar code on the shipping label, or any other combination. Having complete shipment data available in an RFID tag that can be read instantly without manual intervention is very valuable particularly for cross-docking and high-volume distribution environments. Incoming shipments can be automatically queried for specific containers and those sought-after could be quickly located and selected.

Regulatory Compliance

Companies that transport or process hazardous materials, food, pharmaceuticals, and other regulated materials could record the time they received and transferred the material on an RFID tag that travels with the material. Updating the tag with real-time handling data creates a chain of custody record that could be used to satisfy regulatory requirements.

Concerns in Using RFID

While RFID has very versatile and significant applications, the use of it also has some concerns which are outlined here.

Privacy Concerns

One key concern about the use of RFID technology is the apprehension that it infringes on the privacy of buyers. The RFID tags would be able to scan buyer behaviour at the point-of-purchase (PoP) and even after that. Many people consider it a breach of privacy as they feel 'somebody is watching them' or they are under surveillance while buying is a natural psychological process which needs freedom and discretion and certainly not the scrutiny. Customers, more often than not, hesitate to have a feel of the product which would basically defy the natural behaviour of buying, particularly the new products and variants.

High Investment

The initial investment by companies in adopting RFID is quite heavy. Many organizations are thus shirking away from the idea of investing in RFID technology. There are others who are conducting an in-depth cost benefit analysis before taking the plunge into RFID and its use.

Limited Range

So far the RFID technology has a limited range in terms of frequency. Therefore, many companies are skeptical about the coverage and efficacy of the technology and are questioning the claims made by the developers.

Health Concerns

Since RFID technology operates on the principle of radio frequency wave emission, related health concerns are also emerging fast. A long-term exposure to radio waves causes many diseases, such as cancer, ulcers, and skin deformities.

RFID technology and the underlying standards are readily available and mature enough to support production-level plans. RFID does have a substantial and positive impact on supply chain performance. It improves operating margins, speeds the flow of inventory, and improves supply chain service levels. RFID-enabled supply chains would soon outperform their competitors with regard to operating cost and meticulous execution of delivery to customers and supplies from suppliers.

LEAN OPERATIONS TECHNIQUES

A lean producer combines the advantages of craft and mass production while avoiding the high cost of the former and rigidity of the latter. Towards this end, lean operations employ

(a) teams of highly skilled workers at all levels,
(b) use of highly flexible and increasingly automated machines of general purpose type,
(c) production of moderate volumes of products in enormous variety,
(d) less of everything compared with mass production, including half the human effort in factory, the manufacturing space, the investment in tools, and the engineering hours to develop a new product in half the time.

Also, it requires keeping far less than half the needed inventory on site, results in many fewer defects and produces a greater and ever-growing variety of products. While mass producers set a limited goal for themselves—'good enough' which translates into an acceptable number of defects, a maximum acceptable level of inventories and a narrow range of standardized products—lean producers on the other hand set target explicitly on perfection in terms of

(a) continually declining costs,
(b) zero defects,
(c) zero inventories, and
(d) endless product variety.

According to Womack, Jones and Ross (1990), lean operating organizations have network of suppliers with design engineering capability to facilitate improvement and value addition along the supply chain. The machines are preferably general purpose machines (GPMs) and there are decreased life-cycles followed by enlarging the product variety, i.e., making niche-models. Time to market becomes the key competitive factor for companies operating on the basis of lean operations.

Principles of 'Lean Thinking'

Japanese originators of lean techniques talk and think mostly about specific methods applied to specific activities in engineering offices, purchasing departments, sales groups, and factors such as dedicated product development teams, target pricing, level scheduling, and cellular manufacturing. Managers however, are drowned in techniques as they try to implement isolated bits of a lean system without understanding it as a whole. Lean thinking can be summarized in the form of the following five principles.

- Specify value by specific product
- Identify value stream for each product
- Make value flow without interruptions/single piece flow
- Let the customer 'pull' value from the producer
- Pursue perfection (zero defects)

In US, Womack set up the Lean Enterprise Institute while in UK, a Lean Enterprise Research Centre (LERC) has been set up at Cardiff University by Professors Dan Jones and Peter Hines where a Lean Processing Programme (LEAP) was undertaken in 1997 and the main issue was to address improvement of an entire upstream supply chain from raw material to OEM manufacture and applying lean principles to multi-echelons of a major supply chain.

Measures of Lean Operations

The company, which undertakes a lean operations approach, makes step-change improvements in

(a) lead-time reduction,
(b) number of defects reduction,
(c) time to market reduction,
(d) stock reduction,
(e) single-piece flow (analogous to JIT),
(f) productivity improvement, i.e., waste (*muda*) cost reduction, and
(g) increased mutual business.

The Japanese word *muda* refers to wasted time and effort that adds no value for the end customers. In Japan, the founders of Toyota, Sakichi Toyota and his son Kichiro formulated the following key principles of what later came to be known as Toyota Production System (TPS).

(i) Automatic machine and line stopping whenever a mistake is made so that no bad parts will be passed forward to interrupt the downstream flow (*jidoka*).
(ii) A *pull* system so that only parts actually needed are made (JIT) or procured in right quantity.
(iii) Levelling the workload in a mixed model production flow (*heijunka*).

Lean thinking by Japanese relies also on instant revolutions, i.e., *kaikaku* rather than *kaizen*. While former is *enforced breakthrough* approach to improvement activity and believes in spectacular and very rapid productivity improvement in focused area, *kaizen* is *enforced incremental* approach to improvement activity and the classic 'enforced improver' has been Toyota. Very often, a *kaikaku* is based around a 5S housekeeping approach. An English version of 5S is CANDO where C is for clean-up and throwout including 'red tagging' items that are earmarked for subsequent disposal and A is arranging—'a place for everything'. Here waste must be minimized—stillages in designated locations, buffer stocks considered, walkways delineated or reviewed, shadow boards established and so are clear signals (*Kanban* and *Andon*). N is for neatness—'everything in its place' with five minute end-or-beginning of shift clean-up specific routine. Finally, D is for discipline and O for ongoing improvement.

In addition to 5S or CANDO, *kaikaku* emphasizes on *single piece flow* as an objective. For example, if scheduling and flow are the priorities in a *kaikaku* event, the starting point is the *takt time* or cycle time. The *takt time* establishes the flow system around which all work operations should be balanced (*line balancing* in a flow system). To achieve this, layout may have to be reconfigured and a *pull* system (*kanban*) established. Under lean operations, waste (*muda*) elimination can be driven in the following ways.

Response analysis When an operational problem is encountered, a signal system by switch or cord, must be in place. When an operator activates the switch or pulls a cord, the overhead *andon* board lights up, highlighting workstation and type of problem. The recorded times for problem resolution are accumulated in a computer system and taken for, say, Pareto analysis to reveal most pressing problems and the relevant workstations.

Line stop An automatic line stoppage mechanism through pulling a cord may be devised to stop the whole line. Line stoppage times can be recorded and analysed for root cause analysis.

Inventory withdrawal Exposing the rocks (problems) out of dropping water level (inventory) is done with a vengeance at *Toyota*. Whenever there is stability, experiments can be done in shop floors (production laboratory) by withdrawing inventory to see as to what will happen. Either nothing happens in which case the system runs tighter or a 'rock' is encountered which is good.

Use of waste checklists A waste checklist is a set of questions, distributed to all employees in a particular area (production and non-production alike) asking them simple questions like 'Do you bend to pick up a tool?' or 'Do you walk more than two yards to fetch material?' and so on. When there is positive response, there is waste. Such checklists are extensively used and individuals/teams come with ideas for improvement.

The Stage 1, Stage 2 cycle   At Toyota, one operating doctrine is that each completed improvement project necessarily opens up opportunity for yet another improvement activity. For simplicity, they are referred to as 'Stage 1' activity that lead to 'Stage 2' opportunities. For e.g., a cycle of stages could be:

> *Set-up reduction leads to → reduced buffers which leads to → improved layout leading to → improved visibility thereby improving quality which leads to → improved scheduling*

and so on. Such cycles should be discretely charted out in a lean manufacturing organization.

Features of a Single Piece Flow System

Under an integrated supply chain, manufacturing should aim to deliver high value to the customer (internal or external) by achieving mass customization but meeting stringent requirements related to the following.

- cost
- quality
- delivery
- flexibility in volume and variety
- speed (Time to develop, distribute, and market a new product)
- innovations

This would inevitably entail a highly-focused, decentralized and integrated manufacturing network which would leverage the power of information and communication techniques to achieve internal and external integration. Lean organizations are 'delayered' and flexible learning organizations. This would further imply that lean manufacturing facilities will incorporate the following.

- Considerable automation
- Product (line) and cellular layouts (group technology)
- Consolidation of work centres (*de-staging*)
- Cycle or 'Takt' time management for its reduction
- Finished goods (FG) inventory policy of 'make-to-order' than 'make-to-stock'
- Workforce flexibility, i.e., reduced number of workers but multi-skilled, with enhanced job-specifications, and empowerment
- Elimination of waste, i.e., that of all non-value addition activities
- Implementation of a total quality system across the organization
- Uniform plant loading and scheduling
- Installation and implementation of a TPM—total productive maintenance programme

- Minimization of set-up time
- Installing fool-proof/mistake proofing devices, i.e., *pokayoke* to achieve a preventive right-first-time and everytime approach
- Pull-based material control (*kanban*)
- Purchasing system with stress on long-term sourcing preferably global and e-procurement with due focus on quality, delivery, and service
- Reduction of manufacturing cycle times, and procurement and distribution lead times

One key objective of single piece flow mechanism in a lean operating organization is to reduce uncertainty. The company could have

  (a) demand uncertainty,
  (b) supply uncertainty, and
  (c) process uncertainty.

Methods to Reduce Uncertainty

The following are the methods to counter demand uncertainty.

  (i) Demand uncertainty can be countered by better forecasting techniques which are *order-driven* not *schedule-driven* and by a collaborative system with vendors and customers including retailers.
 (ii) Supply uncertainty can be reduced through long-term strategic partnership with vendors, e.g., through vendor development and joint working in the area of design and sharing production—planning information with them.
(iii) Process uncertainty can be reduced by cutting down on breakdowns (the ideal is zero-breakdown) and following an integrated blend of schedule-based breakdown, preventive, and predictive maintenance. Process uncertainty could also be reduced by following better technology and methods. A lean organization in order to reduce WIP levels and FG inventory would always delay differentiation till customer's end as discussed in 'postponement' strategy.

The Production Losses

A lean manufacturing organization such as Toyota would follow an operations system (e.g. TPS—Toyota Production System) which would in turn aim to eliminate/reduce the following wastes.

- overproduction
- waiting time
- transportation
- inventory

- (over) processing
- motion
- product defects

A lean organization would install devices and system to eliminate or reduce these wastes. There is no room for surplus or safety stock. Hidden inventory in storage areas, transit systems, carousels, and conveyors is a key target for inventory reduction. The lean operating companies also believe in *focused factory networks*, i.e., small specialized plants strategically located with *digital networking* with smaller core-competent workforce rather than large vertically integrated manufacturing facilities with generally skilled huge workforce. All this facilitates better integration of supply chain in lean operating companies particularly when volume and variety flexibility is desirable.

THE CORPORATE EXPERIENCE

There is substantial resistance in the implementation of *tierization* of vendors. It is found that large vendors are generally resistant to becoming a sub-vendor to another vendor. A solution is to have the purchase orders and payments being handled by the vehicle manufacturer while accomplishing physical delivery of material by the supplier tier 2 at the tier 1 vendors' premises. Over a period of time as efficient SCM practices evolve in the country, the purchase orders, negotiations, and payments could be directly handled by the tier 2 vendor. It is an interesting fact that at the Chrysler plant in Brazil, Goodyear, a multinational giant, is a tier 2 vendor to Dana which as a tier 1 manufacturer supplies a 'rolling chassis' to the Chrysler plant.

It is also seen that a number of global best practices such as reverse logistics, warehousing, etc., cannot be exploited to their full potential due to the rigid government regulations, especially in relation to Excise Department. For example, use of recyclable packing from distant vendors is infeasible due to increased freight costs. However, in contrast, the OEM prefers to receive material in recyclable packing only, due to its inherent advantages. This can be accomplished only if the changeover to recyclable packing is accomplished at a local godown close to the OEM. However, excise rules bar any change in packing en-route by the supplier. While it is recommended that the government reexamine these rules in light of contemporary international practices, an intermediary solution would be that the OEM allocates a space within its premises where the vendor unloads its material and changes the packing into recyclable mode. Perhaps in times to come, the vendor could also take over certain assemblies on the OEM's assembly lines, thus reducing the OEM's labour costs, apart from allowing the OEM manufacturer to concentrate on its core activities of sales, distribution, and after-sales service. To summarize, a number of OEM's are found to be facing substantial problem in implementation of recyclable packing due to

(a) difficulty in regular maintenance and cleaning of recyclable modes of packing,
(b) lack of an efficient system for distribution of recyclable packing,
(c) inadequate suppliers' management commitment for investment,
(d) increased transportation cost, and
(e) the rigid attitude of transport unions which refuse to allow returning trucks to carry recyclable containers.

While freight costs maybe tackled by getting material inside the OEM's plant/third-party logistics provider's premises by vendor personnel, the resistance from the unions can only be dealt with only by having a captive fleet of trucks available with vendors. These trucks could be common to a number of vendors or owned by a third-party logistics (3PL) provider for the purpose.

With implementation of VAT, w.e.f. 1 April, 2005, tax structures and points have been rationalized to reduce documentation and procedures. The number of warehouses has also reduced as a result thereof.

RECAPITULATION

A good supply chain management (SCM) system is a bundle of best practices. Most of the best practices are based on the concept of internal and extended customer–supplier chain. An effective supply chain is based on sharing of information, risks, and rewards across the downstream and upstream channel members. In view of certain global trends, companies develop some practices to streamline various kinds of flows across internal/external customers and suppliers. These practices have refined in view of advancements in information and communication technology, traffic and transportation modes and carriers, and third-party logistics process. Some of these practices involve consolidation of suppliers into different tiers using reverse logistics for better materials control and cost efficiencies in transportation, milk round system (MRS) for economy on transportation trips and freight, and to ensure small lot size deliveries.

Hub and spoke concepts and third-party logistics (3PL) providers bring about inventory reduction at manufacturer's premises, economy of in transportation trips, freight consolidation, and time synchronization. While use of 3PLs is going to be more extensive in future, 4PLs would provide total solutions in procurement, traffic, and transportation to the customers using state-of-the-art ICT practices. The basic purpose is to outsource the non-value added activities to an outside party. While a 3PL service may facilitate shipment consolidation to carrier selection to warehousing management to fleet operations and management, logistics information systems, order processing, and fulfilment to product returns, a 4PL essentially manages other 3PLs. The services may include invoice generation, credit tracking, transport, and warehousing to HRD.

Specific strategies and action can be followed by companies depending upon the requirements. Postponement, which refers to postponement of configuration of final product till customer order is confined, results in better service levels with lesser inventory in product variety to manage. However, the grey stock that can be maintained at the warehouse cross-docking refers to products that are delivered to a company's warehouse where these are sorted, repackaged, and distributed to different stores without sitting in inventory. The transit time between one loading dock to another has been reduced to a basic minimum time. In drop-shipping, the supplier ships directly to the end consumer rather than to the seller, saving time and costs of rehandling and reshipping. All these techniques may need load unitization and track-and-trace technologies such as bar coding and RFID. In addition, these best practices can be augmented with lean operations techniques such as elimination/reduction of seven kinds of Toyota Production System (TPS) wastes, using flexible general purpose machines (GPMs), and use of highly skilled lockers. 5S tools, automatic line stoppage mechanism, use of *kanban* cards, instant revolutions, maintenance of *takt time*, and installation of mistake proofing devices (*pokayokes*)—all constitute basic techniques for lean processing which can make at least internal supply chain management a synergistic and synchronized approach to follow.

CONCEPT REVIEW QUESTIONS

1. What kind of strategies are the global players adopting to combat challenges of supply chain management across the extended enterprise?
2. What kind of changes are being brought about in sourcing strategies by the Indian companies?
3. Discuss some best practices in the logistics area which are contributing to cost reduction in SCM.
4. What is vendor-managed inventory (VMI) and how is it accomplished through JIT-II?
5. Outline the principles of milk round system (MRS) and how it can augment the 'hub and spoke' system.
6. What are the trends in provisions of third and fourth-party logistic (3 and 4PL) providers services?

CRITICAL THINKING QUESTIONS

1. Why is there a need for reverse logistics and its management? How can reverse logistics be used for better synchronization, time and cost effectiveness, and internal/external customer satisfaction in a supply chain
2. Why should it be preferred for a vendor to manage his own inventory at the buyer's plant? How can it be ensured?
3. What is the range of services that can be provided by 3PLs? How are 4PLs different from 3PLs in terms of the services they provide?
4. What is bar coding? How does it work?
5. What kind of costs are aimed to be eliminated/reduced by 'cross-docking' and 'drop-shipping'?
6. How can a lean processing system augment the good SCM practices?

PROJECT ASSIGNMENTS

1. Visit the SCM/physical distribution department of a company to find out how the packaging and dispatching is being done to synchronize with subsequent transportation to distributors.

2. Visit an inland container depot (ICD) and find out how the logistics for inter-modal transportation are being worked out?

3. Visit an assembly line in preferably an automobile plant and analyse as to how cycle times of incoming materials are being managed for their delivery on to the assembly line at the right time. What help is being provided by the vendors to facilitate this?

4. Visit a company's warehouse (WH) on the outskirts of your city and analyse as to how distribution is being managed to retailers over a given period of time and how the inventory is being replenished at the WH. Comment upon the documentation and electronic tools and techniques used at the WH.

CASE STUDY

GLOBAL CASE STUDY

DELL COMPUTER CORPORATION[2]

Introduction

Dell thinks about their offerings as microprocessors, disk drives and frames-per-second graphics. But consumers just want a computer they can be proud of when they show it to their friends, listen to music, watch videos and do office work.
— **Christian Terwiesch, a Wharton professor**

Dell has been following its unique *direct build-to-order* sales model for more than 20 years. Customers can plan their own configuration and place orders directly with the company via the phone or its website. Over the years, Dell's supply chain efficiencies and direct sales gave it a competitive advantage. In 2006 however, Dell faced several problems. Many customers complained about long delays in supplies. Recall of Sony battery cells in its laptops brought undesirable media hype to the company. Increasing discontent of customers led to a slowdown in sales. Consequently, Dell lost its market leadership to Hewlett-Packard Co. (HP). Industry analysts felt that, with Dell's competitors also improving their supply chains and matching Dell's direct model, the company has been losing its competitive edge. Dell will have to bear additional costs with its foray into retail distribution thereby minimizing its cost advantage. Besides, profit margins of Dell will drop further since it will have to offer incentives to compete with HP in retail stores. Though Dell has spruced up its product design and range but Apple is clearly far ahead of it. Many experts feel that such new initiatives will only distract Dell from its supply chain operations.

Corporate Background

Dell is a leading technology company, offering a wide range of computer products. Its product categories include: desktop computer systems, mobility products (notebooks), servers, storage, software and peripherals, and services. Dell is the number one supplier of personal computers in

---

[2] *Source:* Large parts of this case have been taken from www.casestudyinc.com with permission from Mr Manish Kumar Jain, Hyderabad, for which the author expresses due acknowledgement

the United States, and the number two supplier worldwide. It also offers various financing alternatives, asset management services, and other customer financial services. Dell has manufacturing locations worldwide. Its *build-to-order* *manufacturing model* allows it to substantially reduce costs and at the same time offering customers the ability to customize their product purchases. Exhibits 4.4, 4.5, and 4.6 will show the Dell product lines and brands, quick facts, and timeline.

EXHIBIT 4.4 Dell: Product Lines and Brands

Desktop PCs	• OptiPlex • Dimension • XPS • Alienware • Vostro
Servers and Networking	PowerEdge and PowerConnect
Storage	Dell | EMC and Dell PowerVault
Mobility	XPStm and Alienware, Inspiron and Latitude lines of notebook computers
Software and Peripherals	Dell branded printers, software titles, televisions, notebook accessories, networking and wireless products, digital cameras, power adapters, scanners, and other products
Enhanced Services	• Infrastructure Consulting Services • Deployment Services. • Asset Recovery and Recycling Services. • Training Services • Enterprise Support Services • Client Support services • Managed Lifecycle services
Financial Services	Various customer financial services for business and consumer customers in the U.S. through Dell Financial Services L.P

Source: www.casestudyinc.com

Major business segment	Based in	Covers
Americas	Round Rock, Texas	Business—sales to corporate, government, healthcare, education, and small and medium business customers U.S. Consumer—sales primarily to individual consumers and selected retail partners
EMEA	Bracknell, England	Covers Europe, Middle East, and Africa
APJ	Singapore	Covers the Asian countries of the Pacific Rim as well as Australia, New Zealand, and India

EXHIBIT 4.5   Dell: Quick Facts

Industry	Hardware, PC manufacturing
Employees	Approximately 90,500 total employees (Fiscal 2007)
Manufacturing Facilities	• Brazil—El Dorado do Sul • Florida—Miami (Alienware) • North Carolina—Winston-Salem • Ohio—West Chester • Tennessee—Lebanon and Nashville • Texas—Austin • Ireland—Limerick and Athlone (Alienware) • China—Xiamen • Malaysia—Penang
Distribution	Worldwide
Product Lines	• Desktop PCs • Mobility products • Servers and storage • Software and peripherals • Services
Brands	• OptiPlex • Dimension • XPS • Dell Precision and Alienware MJ-12® • PowerEdge • Dell PowerVault • Inspiron • Latitude
Major Competitors	• HP • Acer • Lenovo
Business/Growth Strategy	Direct customer model Highly efficient manufacturing and logistics, and New distribution channels to reach customers
Key Executives *Name, (age),Designation*	Michael S. Dell (42) Chairman of the Board of Directors and CEO Donald J. Carty (61) Vice Chairman and CFO Michael R. Cannon (54) President, Global Operations Stephen J. Felice (50) Senior VP and President, Asia Pacific-Japan Mark Jarvis (44) Senior VP, Chief Marketing Officer David A. Marmonti (48) Senior VP and President, EMEA

Source: www.dell.com

EXHIBIT 4.6 Dell Timeline

1983	Michael Dell used to upgrade IBM compatible PCs in his spare time. (He was a freshman at the University of Texas, Austin)
1984	Michael Dell established PC's Ltd with sales US$6 million in its first full year of operations
1985	Turbo PC, first computer introduced by the company
	Turbo PC was advertised in computer magazines and sold directly to customers
1993	Dell joins the ranks of top-five computer system makers worldwide
1996	Dell pioneers Internet sales with earnings approx $1 million per day just seven months after launch of www.dell.com
1998	The company changed its name to Dell Computer Corporation
1999	Dell introduces e-support tool to provide online technical support
2000	Online sales continue to grow to $50 million per day
2001	Dell achieves no.1 ranking on global market share
2003	Dell launches Dell Recycling initiative
2004	Inventory turnover rate in Dell was at 107 times a year, compared to 8.5 times at HP and 17.5 times in IBM.
2005	America's Most Admired Company—Fortune Magazine
2005, 2006	Dell faced several problems, and lost its position as the largest selling PC manufacturer to HP
2007	Dell announced that it planned to move most of its global supply chain and manufacturing operations to Singapore, which would function as the company's 'shared' headquarters
2007	Michael Cannon assumes responsibility as the Head of Global Operations Organization
2007	Michael Dell (Michael) returned as CEO on January 31, 2007
2007	Retail partnerships with Wal-Mart, Staples, Gome, Bic Camera and Carphone Warehouse
2007	Dell launches the Direct2Dell corporate blog and other idea forums to listen and engage customers

Source: www.casestudyinc.com

Business Segment Information

Dell conducts operations worldwide. It is managed in three geographic regions:

- Americas
- Europe, Middle East, and Africa (EMEA)
- Asia Pacific-Japan (APJ)

The Evolving Supply Chain Strategy at Dell

Dell's past performance has been the result of its direct customer model. Its success is attributed to a constant focus on delivering directly to its customers, related technology and services at the best value. Dell's operations involve highly efficient manufacturing and logistics to lower the cost of technology.

Working of Dell's Supply Chain

Dell Supply Chain works as follows.

1. Customer places an order, either by phone or through the Internet on its website
2. Dell processes the order in 2-3 days by evaluating financial feasibility (credit checking) and technical feasibility (technical configuration)
3. Dell processes the order to one of its manufacturing locations
4. These plants can put together, test, and package the product in about eight hours
5. Dell typically plans to ship all orders no later than five days after receipt

Five Key Strategies in Dell's Successful Direct Build-to-order Model

The following are the five key strategies in Dell's successful direct model.

- Rapid time to volume
- Built-to-order products
- Elimination of reseller markups
- Superior customer service and support
- Low inventory and capital investment

Supply Chain with Old Technology is of Little Value

The direct model involves bypassing retailers and selling personal computer systems directly to customers. This helps to avoid the delays and costs of an additional stage (holding inventory) in the supply chain. Typically, each technology component loses about 0.5–2 per cent in a rapidly changing environment. A supply chain with old technology is of little value. Dell maintained very little inventory and concentrated on pacing its products through its supply chain. This also meant that there was no question of selling old products at a discount.

Restructuring Distribution at Dell

The company failed to meet its quarterly financial forecasts. Consequently, Dell lost its market leadership to Hewlett-Packard Co. (HP). In order to settle a few accounting issues, the company decided to restate its financial results for the last four years. Michael Dell had to take the CEO's responsibility again, replacing Kevin Rollins.

Michael Dell felt the importance of increasing the capacity, via the direct model, to manufacture close to its customer and fully integrate its supply chain into one global organization. To do so Dell had to innovate and adapt its supply chain model to help drive differentiated product design, manufacturing and distribution models. He began a series of restructuring exercises.

New Distribution Channels—Direct Model and Retail Strategy

While part of the restructuring involved cutting 8,000 jobs, or 10 per cent of its workforce, the biggest surprise was the move of Dell to complement its 'direct sales model' with sale of PCs through retailer channels as well. To reach even more customers globally, Dell launched new distribution channels to reach commercial customers and individual consumers around the world. This meant moving from a model of direct sales to making its goods available in stores across the world. This move allowed Dell to reach customers that it could not reach directly previously.

From June 2007, it started placing its products in the shelves of Wal-Mart and Sam's Club stores. In December 2007, Dell also announced that its laptops and desktop computers will be sold through Tesco stores in Britain and Ireland as well as the high-growth eastern European markets of Poland, Czech Republic, and Slovakia. In U.S., Asia and Europe, Dell added Best Buy, Wal-Mart, Staples, China's Gome Stores, Japan's Bic Camera, France's Carrefour and British phone retailer, Carphone Warehouse to sell its products at nearly 10,000 retail outlets worldwide.

In December 2007, Dell also chose WPP, the world's second-largest marketing, media and communications conglomerate after Omnicom, to create a new agency that will handle $4.5 billion in accounts over the next three years. Dell hoped that creating the agency would increase the time and money spent focusing on marketing and customers rather than pitching for the next project.

Integrating the Supply Chain

Earlier, Dell's manufacturing, supply chain and procurement activities functioned separately. Procurement functioned as a stand-alone unit, the regional business executives were in-charge of manufacturing, and supply chain was a part of the worldwide operations of the company. All Dell's factories had been managed regionally, and procurement functioned as a separate division.

Michael aimed to integrate its supply chain and achieve higher efficiency and quality through Global Operations Organization (GOO). It is Dell's centre for integrating its global manufacturing, procurement and supply chain activities. Michael proposed elimination of overlapping activities, and introduction of new manufacturing and distribution models to focus on the requirements of the customers spread across the world.

Will Dell regain its supply chain leadership position? In the past, Dell had an advantage through its direct supply chain model. But can it sustain it by offering more classy products, expanding retail distribution network and even expanding its product range with MP3 players, TVs, printers and cameras. Though the financial figures indicate that Dell is in a better position compared to 2006, it continues to lag behind HP. At the end of June 2007 quarter, HP's global PC market share stood at 19.3%, compared to Dell's 16.1%.

Logistics of Supply at Dell

It has enhanced its supply chain using i2 supply chain management (SCM) solutions to plan orders and signal suppliers every two hours, which enables it to manufacture and deliver exactly what its customers want, i.e., build-to-order. The supply chain management of Dell computers has been designed for optimal flexibility and predictability. The movements are as follows.

1. First, the transportation is from the supplier to the *hubs* via air, road, and ships. This takes approximately 30 days.
2. The second movement takes place between the *hubs* and Dell factory or the *merge centre*, where the orders are placed by the customers. This takes about 2 to 5 days.
3. From the factory and the *merge centres*, the shipment of the final machine is done according to the sales order. This takes about 1 to 7 days depending upon the destination of the customer, who has placed the order.

Let us examine the supply chain of Dell Computer Corporation.

Figure 4.7 shows the supply chain model of Dell computers. Suppliers are located in different parts of the world where Dell has its network. The materials are sent to the hubs through three modes of transport, i.e., road, air, and water. The materials reach the hubs in about 30 days. From the hubs the materials are further supplied to the Dell manufacturing centre or to the merge centre within 2–5 days by road. Once the materials reach Dell, orders are placed for sales and the computers reach the customer within 7 days of order. Dell believes in direct dealings, so no middlemen are involved in the whole supply chain system.

An effective channel strategy is a necessary element of supply chain competency at Dell. In the process of choosing a channel strategy, the supply chain master can create a powerful new channel that reduces its competitors' access to important target accounts and market segments.

Core Marketing Capabilities and Customer-centricity at Dell

It carefully targeted corporate relationship with customers that had predictable, budgeted needs and wanted a predetermined set of product models. The company also selected individual customers who were high-end, repeat purchasers with a preference for early technology adoption. Both account segments had the stable, predictable purchase patterns that Dell needed to make its joint build-product-to-order/buy-component-to-plan system work.

The ability to operate within the customers' organization (*the in-customer operations*) has been crucial for Dell. This capability ranged across a spectrum from pure IT linkages to combined inter-company IT/operations links. Effective in-customer operations require powerful technical capabilities, crucial customer knowledge, and the ability to fit into the customer's organization and work processes.

Dell differentiated itself in the corporate market by developing a set of extremely effective customer-specific *intranet websites*. Each website was highly tailored to the customer's individual situation. Dell worked with each customer to specify a particular set of product configurations that would work best in the customer's network. Tailored offerings were specified and developed for each customer. At the same time, Dell used its direct links with both corporate and individual customers to get immediate, real-time insights about latent customer needs and to identify new generations of products and services.

The Channel Strategy at Dell

An effective channel strategy is a necessary element of supply chain competency at Dell. In the process of choosing a channel strategy, the supply chain master can create a powerful new channel that reduces its competitors' access to important target accounts and market segments. Dell's direct-to-customer channel strategy was a breakthrough in the industry. In the early stages of a technology product's life-cycle, distributors are important for supporting new adopters. Dell, however, insightfully discerned a lucrative set of high-end customers that were ready for direct distribution with arm's length customer support from help lines. An innovative direct channel strategy gave Dell these crucial elements of its powerful business model.

Dell developed a set of new operations capabilities in five crucial areas. First, it created the flawless *make-to-order* system that has been widely noted (but in fact is only one part of its business model). Second, Dell worked at length to build an effective supplier management function in order to shorten *component lead times* and maintain the absolute quality standards required by the JIT operation. Third, Dell developed the 'sell what you have' system that was essential to matching supply and demand. Fourth, it instituted an extraordinarily crisp set of product life-cycle management capabilities that yielded great cost reductions and strategic advantage. (Dell was uniquely positioned to do this because its customers were early technology adopters and its operations had virtually no inventory in the supply chain). Fifth, the company worked with its suppliers to shorten their product life-cycles, extending the Dell business model to the whole channel. Together these operating capabilities formed a cornerstone for Dell's business model.

Managing the Order Configuration at Dell

After a customer places an order, either by phone or through the Internet on www.dell.com, Dell processes the order through financial evaluation (credit checking) and configuration evaluation (checking the feasibility of a specific technical configuration), which takes two to three days, after which it sends the order to one of its manufacturing plants in Austin, Texas. These plants can build, test, and package the product in about eight hours. Dell typically plans to ship all orders no later than five days after receipt. There are, however, some exceptions. For example, Dell may manipulate the schedule when there is a need to replace defective units or when facing large customers with specific service-level agreements (SLAs) (who have non-standard quoted manufacturing lead times) for their orders.

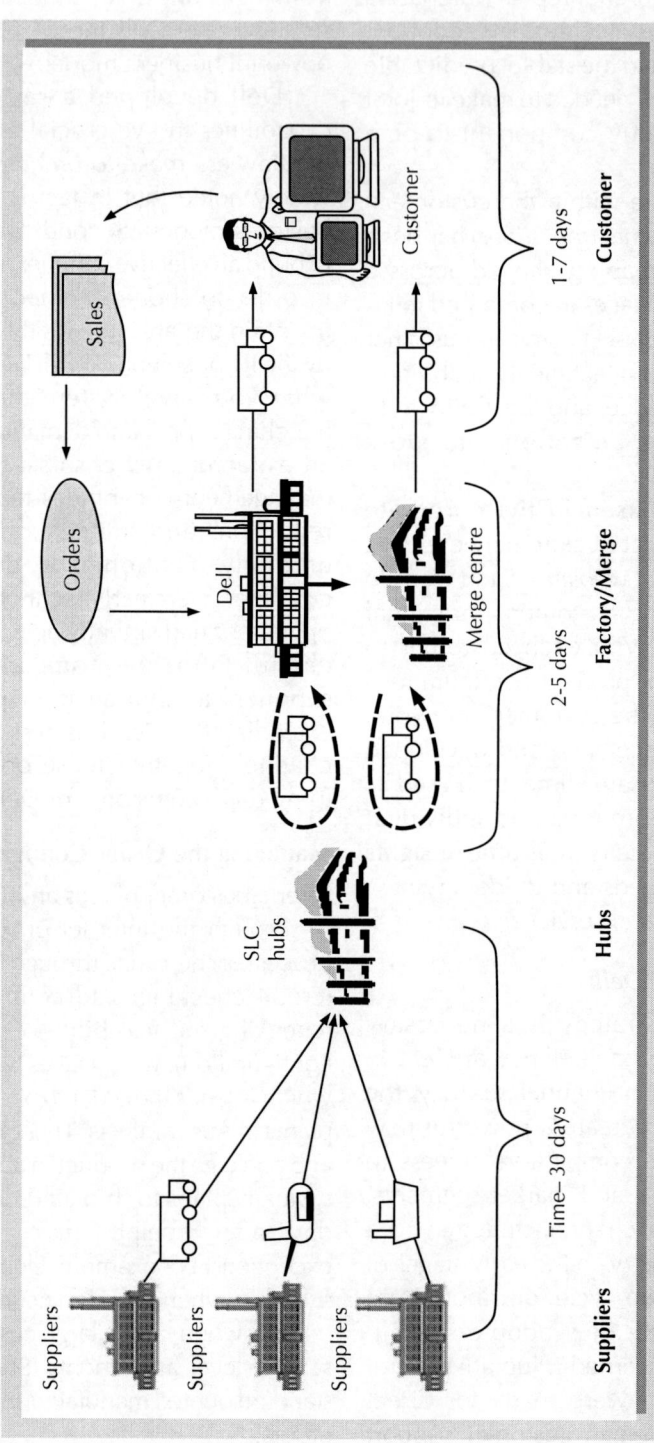

FIG. 4.7 Design of supply chain for optimal flexibility and predictability at the Dell

In most cases, Dell has significantly less time to respond to customers than it takes to transport components from its suppliers to its assembly plants. Many of the suppliers are located in Southeast Asia and their transportation times to Austin range from seven days for air shipments to upwards of 30 days by water and ground. To compensate for long lead times and buffer against demand variability, Dell requires its suppliers to keep inventory on hand in the Austin *revolvers* (for 'revolving' inventory). *Revolvers* or *supplier logistics centres* (*SLCs*) are small warehouses located within a few miles of Dell's assembly plants. Each of the revolvers is shared by several suppliers who pay rents for using their revolver.

Dell does not own the inventory in its revolvers; this inventory is owned by suppliers and charged to Dell indirectly through component pricing. The cost of maintaining inventory in the supply chain is, however, eventually included in the final prices of the computers. Therefore, any reduction in inventory benefit Dell's customers directly by reducing product prices. Low inventories also lead to higher product quality, because Dell detects any quality problems more quickly than it would with high inventories. Dell wishes to stay ahead of competitors who adopt a direct-sales approach, and it must be able to reduce supplier inventory to gain significant leverage. Although arguably, supply chain costs include all costs incurred from raw parts to final assembly, Dell concentrates on Dell-specific inventory (that is, parts designed to its specifications or stored in its specific locations, such as its revolvers and assembly plants). Because assembly plants hold inventories for only a few hours, Dell has a special vendor-managed inventory (VMI) arrangement with its suppliers. Suppliers decide how much inventory to order and when to order, while Dell sets target inventory levels and records suppliers' deviations from the targets. Dell heuristically chose an inventory target of 10 days' supply, and it uses a quarterly supplier scorecard to evaluate as to how well each supplier does in maintaining this target inventory in the revolver. Dell withdraws inventory from the revolvers as needed, on an average, every two hours. If the commodity is multisourced (that is, parts from different suppliers are completely interchangeable), Dell can withdraw (*pull*) those components from any subset of the suppliers. It often withdraws components from one supplier for a few days before switching to another. Suppliers decide when to send their goods to their revolvers. In practice, most suppliers deliver to their revolvers on an average, three times a week.

Sharing Information and Collaborative Forecasting at Dell

To help suppliers make good ordering decisions, Dell shares its forecasts with them once per month. These forecasts are generated by Dell's *line of business (LOB)* marketing department. In addition to product-specific trends, they obviously reflect the seasonality in sales. For home systems, Christmas is the top time of the year. Other high-demand periods include the back-to-school season, the end of the year when the government makes big purchases, and country-specific high seasons for foreign purchases (foreign language keyboards are especially influenced). Dell sales also increase at the ends of quarters (referred to as the hockey stick).

After the centre of competence (CoC) checks a forecast for predicted availability of components, the forecast goes to Dell's commodity teams and becomes the basis for a six-month rolling forecast that they update weekly. The commodity teams make generic forecasts for systems and components and break these forecasts down to a level of the specific parts that need to be ordered. If the forecast is not feasible, the LOB marketing department revizes it, although such revisions are very rare. The buyer-planner for each commodity receives an updated rolling forecast weekly; suppliers receive forecasts monthly. Suppliers who make the replenishment decisions attempt to follow Dell's targets and guidelines. Dell had been setting inventory targets based on empirical data and judgement with no clear reference to any desired service levels. It hypothesized that it could reduce revolver inventory markedly by using a more rigorous approach and gaining better visibility of the inventory throughout the supply chain. Once it determined an optimized inventory level, Dell could collaborate with its suppliers to eliminate excess inventory. It emphasized that it wanted to sustain any changes over the long term, which would require integrating them into its informational infrastructure. *Value chain* is a programme intended to extend Dell's successful direct-sales approach back into the supply chain with the goal of increasing the speed and quality of the information flow between Dell and its supply base. The corresponding website *valuechain.dell.com* is an *Extranet* for sharing such information as points of contact, inventory in the supply chain, supply and demand data, component quality metrics, and new part transitions. Dell envisions using this site to exchange with suppliers current data, forecasted data, new product ideas, and other dynamic information that might help it to optimize the flow of information and materials in the supply chain by collaboration.

Discussion Questions

1. What are the elements of logistics and SCM system at Dell that provide for optimal levels of flexibility and predictability?
2. What are the key focus areas of marketing, sales, and distribution specially looked into by Dell and why?
3. What are the key elements of the channel strategy at Dell ? Would you like to introduce some changes in the same?
4. Outline the cycle of order management at Dell.
5. How does Dell share its information on demand planning and forecasting with its sources?

INDIAN CASE STUDY

MARUTI UDYOG LTD (MUL)[3]

At Maruti Udyog Ltd, logistics goes beyond mere distribution management. It is improving the quality of the supply chain itself to achieve a cost-effective distribution mechanism. Driven by this philosophy, MUL, the country's biggest passenger car manufacturer, has created a new supply chain paradigm that has helped it achieve substantial cost reduction, from production to distribution. It has a fully established SCM department. Dependent on over 300 suppliers for some 7000 components that go into ten major models and more than 50 variants (at the time of writing this case), the company realized the need to keep control over costs at every stage to remain competitive. For this, it realized, supply chain management was critical.

'Cost management is crucial for the supply chain management,' says Mr P. Agrawal, Deputy General Manager (Materials), MUL, adding that this was achieved only through close coordination with the vendors. This not only helped in cost rationalization of the materials used by MUL, but also in passing the benefits of cost control and quality products to the vendors.

The exercise began by in-house implementation of innovative material handling solutions, resulting in cost savings by reducing wastage. MUL also gained considerably by collaborating with its vendors in localizing components supply with great impact on productivity and removing uncertainties in supply. According to Mr Agrawal,

---

[3] *Source:* The author is thankful to materials and vendor development departments of MUL as also the Economic Times Intelligence Group, Mumbai, for providing information contained in this case.

by rationalizing the inventory holding process and precise planning of schedules for indenting components, the company not only saved on holding costs but also reduced wastage. The delivery instruction (DI) was revised from monthly schedules to daily and made location wise to indent only components to meet the assembly line requirement. The strategy was adopted to tackle the fluctuating market demand, accentuated by the intense competition in the current automobile business.

Mr Agrawal said the streamlining of SCM was done after a homework of value analysis and value engineering (VA/VE) that helped it improve operator and machine productivity, and reduce and recycle waste. While these practices helped MUL reduce its logistics cost considerably, its IT efforts added to efficiencies and savings.

Firm schedules issued every fortnight were further fine-tuned by an online system for replenishment of inventory on an electronic card system. This avoided inventory build up or unanticipated deliveries by vendors as supplies were made only after receipt of the indent card from MUL. This brought inventory management down to the doorsteps of the vendors, who would produce only what was indented. MUL plans to extend the electronic card system for another 16 suppliers and for 250 components, following the successful implementation with 10 vendors delivering 66 voluminous and high-value parts.

The percolation of its cost control effort has benefited major suppliers such as JK Industries, which reported a reduction of tyre inventory to just 10,000 from its earlier 30,000. The bottomline: savings in transportation cost and detention charges of Rs 50,000 per month. Similarly, Lucas TVS, a major supplier of components reported savings on finished goods inventory cost from Rs 3 crore to Rs 90 lakh, said Mr Agrawal, adding that similar feedback had been received from other major component suppliers such as Kalyani Brakes.

In 2003, MUL, a joint venture between Suzuki Motors of Japan and the Indian government, dominated India's automobile market with a 54% market share. It had the widest product range among Indian car manufacturers, with ten basic models and more than 50 variants. Three out of the top-five selling car models in India (Maruti 800, Zen, and Omni) belonged to Maruti (now Zen has been withdrawn). The company dominated the Indian small car market with a 100 per cent share in 'A' segment and 36 per cent in 'B' segment. Many leading companies in India such as Maruti Udyog, *Hyundai*, and some MNCs started experimenting with the Japanese *JIT* concept. The success of *JIT* is linked to the level of integration achieved in vendor development as also development of ancillary units around the plant, facilitating frequent interaction between the customer and vendor, and timely deliveries to the principal. This does not mean JIT cannot be practiced for items sourced from far-off places; so long as interaction is possible, physical deliveries as per schedule can be organized.

With the introduction of new international freight flights as also increased frequency, weekly schedules became the order of the day for imported inputs. In the case of upcountry supplies, JIT has been successful as is evident from companies such as *Kirloskars* which are able to get daily supplies through improved logistics. While every company today will like to have the material at the production line just a few hours before commencement of the shift, many constraints still exist in achieving 100 per cent success on JIT.

The next stage of cost cutting exercise is on paperless transactions by hooking up vendors through a computer network facilitating ordering, scheduling, receipt, issue, and all other attendant work, including accounting. The dissemination of information within the various departments, both at the customer and vendors ends, is also possible through this network ensuring greater cohesion in decision-making.

As technology advanced by the day, the business-to-business (B2B) and business-to-consumer (B2C) interaction and exchange of data have acquired significance. All these facilitates direct ordering of raw materials from suppliers, on the one hand, and also taking orders from customers, on the other, creating a seamless supply chain. This link is complete, right from the vendor/sub-vendor to the customer via dealers/distributors. This form of SCM, facilitated with improved logistics, has become a matter of survival strategy for the organizations such as MUL to rely on the materials managers for speedy deliveries at competitive prices in a global village.

Even though the increasing success of MNCs outsourcing from the domestic auto components industry may be hogging the limelight at the moment, there has been a persistent trend of Indian vehicle manufacturers reducing the number of component suppliers.

In other words, the trend of rationalization of vendors in the Indian automotive components industry is gaining pace, primarily due to the increasing pressure on margins faced by vehicle manufacturers.

This combined with an increased focus on quality is also resulting in consolidation in the domestic components industry, with domestic players focusing on only their core competencies and exiting from non-core areas.

According to an ICRA report on the Indian auto components industry, leading OEMs such as Maruti, Tata Engineering, and Bajaj Auto are already pursuing vendor rationalization programmes.

Maruti Udyog too has indicated that in a bid to improve quality and generate economies of scale, it reduced its vendor base from 370 as of March 31, 2000 to 299 as of March 31, 2003. The company intends to continue reducing the number of vendors even further.

According to the ICRA report, vendor rationalization reduces the cost of dealing with multiple vendors besides making the process of quality control easier. Also, it enhances the efficiency of SCM. 'Further, by increasing the order size per vendor, the OEMs can help the vendor operate at a higher scale of operation and thus increase the vendor's efficiency,' the report says. Also, this proves to be a greater incentive to pursue technological improvements and enhance the capabilities of systems and processes to meet the quality standards set by the OEMs.

With its strong dependence on the supply chain network, Maruti needs to manage its dealers and suppliers together in a synchronized manner, while also managing complexities in terms of sensing the demand and getting the right mix. It has to plan nearly four to five months in advance about the products that would sell and in what quantities. As a result, the company has a very strong focus on SCM, which forms the core of its IT set-up.

The SCM system from i2 includes marketing, sales and production systems as well as plant and material systems, and spares systems. These applications take care of some key aspects such as demand forecasting (which is the *i2 Demand Planner*), production planner, vehicle production, vehicle production tracking, stock, etc. It is currently rolling out the *Dealer Management System*, a centrally hosted application, which will be internally linked to MUL's systems and will support all their business processes such as sales ordering, invoicing, sales, service, spares, etc. Similarly, the suppliers can also log into MUL's system, which outlines the supply requirements from a particular supplier. This has led to effective synchronization of the supplier resources to the company's requirements.

Apart from SCM, *e-procurement* has been taken up as one of the key focus areas for cost reduction and improved procurement processes. The *Spares Warehouse Management* system has automated the spares warehouse processes for greater efficiency, lower warehousing costs, increased inventory turnover, and faster turnaround times. The *Vehicle Tracking System*, which has been implemented at two plants, is a middle tier layer between business systems and *shop floor systems* that provides correct and timely instructions to the shop floor along with feedback to the business systems, thereby enhancing the efficiency at the shop floor. It has implemented 'Hyperion' tools for planning, consolidation, and business reporting requirements. The tools integrate with the transactional systems for data capturing and implementation of plans. Looking ahead, Maruti is undergoing an information security and *IT security drive*, aimed at protecting the company's IP and critical business information from external and internal threats. Also on the anvil are applications, which provide the capability to quickly pick up market feedback, sales and demand forecasts—issues such as how much will be the sales in a particular city in a particular month, any fluctuations expected in demand, etc. so that these can be incorporated into any strategic decision-making process.

E-solution

In Indian auto segment, Maruti Udyog still continues to hold a majority of the market share. Given that the auto giant's business operations are spread all across the country, Maruti's success can be attributed to its *Web-enabled supply chains*. The makers of the little car that marked the beginning of a new revolution in the auto sector, has been technology savvy right from the beginning. 'IT at Maruti has always been considered at par with other business operations,' says Rajesh Uppal, IT Head.

When Maruti decided to go in for an automated management system about a decade ago, there was no *ERP vendor support* available in the country. Without losing any time, the company decided to do it all by itself. Using a combination of software from Oracle and Computer Associates, the company built a variety of applications that facilitated its business.

This homegrown system was extended to its sales and dealer network through an e-mail based ordering system with about 250 outlets. For instance, if a dealer has to place an order, he generates it in his own machine with all the specifications (e.g. colour, model, etc.) and sends it through an e-mail to Maruti. The system there automatically checks the order, classifies it accordingly, and sends it to the respective database. In order to standardize the data, the company has provided the software to all its dealers. Even the suppliers are being gradually brought online.

Benefits

For a mass production player such as Maruti, an e-enabled supply chain has been extremely instrumental in inventory management, both at the dealer level and in the company. Reduction in paper work has increased efficiency, the speed of processing and managing orders, and has improved working capital management.

Discussion Questions

1. Why does a company such as Maruti Udyog Ltd (MUL) require a well established supply chain management (SCM) department?
2. What are the major strategies adopted by the MUL on the sourcing side? How are these being accomplished?
3. With change in IT set-up, how has management of supply chain undergone a change at MUL right up to the shop floor level?
4. According to you, what would be the possible mix of IT tools which could be used by an automobile company such as MUL in India for effective SCM, including collaborative demand forecasting and customer relationships?

REFERENCES

Bushnell, Richard D., and Richard B. Meyers (1999), *Getting Started with Bar Codes: A Systematic Guide*, Quad II Inc., USA.

Company facts and figures, Annual Reports at www.dell.com

Economic Times Intelligence Group (2002), *Supply Chain & Logistics 2002*, Mumbai, pp. 63–65.

Heizer, Jony and Barry Render (2001), 'Mass Customization Provides Dell Computer's Competitive Advantage', *Global Company Profile in Operations Management*, Prentice Hall, New Jersey, pp. 232–233.

Mohan, A. (2005), 'A Critical Analysis of Supply Chain Management Practices in Indian Fast Moving Consumer Goods (FMCG) Industry', Unpublished Thesis, Faculty of Management Studies, University of Delhi, 2005.

Myerson, Judith M. (2007), *RFID in the Supply Chain: A Guide to Selection and Implementation*, Aurbach Publications, New York.

Palmer Roger C. (1995), *The Bar Code Book: Reading, Printing and Specification of Bar Code Symbols*, Helmers Publishing, 1995.

Pearce, Stephen and Richard B. Bushnell (1997), *The Bar Code Implementation Guide: Using Bar Codes in Distribution*, Quad II Inc., USA.

Sharma, Sunil (5–8 April 2006), 'Best Practices and Performance Benchmarking for Supply Chain Management in Indian Auto Industry', paper presented at IV Worldwide Research Symposium on Purchasing and Supply Chain Management, 15th Annual IPSERA Conference and 17th Annual North American Research and Teaching Symposium, San Diego, USA.

Sharma, Sunil and Rajnish Bidani (1999), 'Recent Trends in Supply Chain Management in Automobile Industry'. *Operations Management for Global Economy: Challenges and Prospects*, Kanda, A., Prem Vrat, and Others (Eds), Phoenix Publishers, New Delhi, pp. 430–439.

Internet Resources

http:/knowledge.Wharton.upenn.edu/article.cfm?articleid=1799.dl 5 Sept. 2007

http://www.bin95.com/case_studies/RFID_Technology_Applications

http://www.rfidconsultation.eu/menu/1/30.html as accessed on 12 November 2008

http://www.rfidjournal.com as accessed on 14 November 2008

www.aitd.net

www.casestudyinc.com

www.dell.com

www.discoverrfid.org/how-it-works/technology as accessed on 14 November 2008

www.gs1india.org

www.rfidjournal.com/article/articleview/1053 and 2548 as accessed on 14 November 2008

5 Procurement and Outsourcing Strategies

It is very important to note that procurement and sourcing functions are not viewed merely as tactical functions focused on transactions targeted towards getting the materials at (perceived) lowest cost. What is more important is whether the item to be purchased has been strategically classified and thus, the appropriate strategy and goals have been laid down. A wrongly selected strategy of purchasing even at the lowest price may cost heavily on the enterprise. This requires a lot of pre-purchase research and a strategic outlook towards identification, selection, and development of sourcing. It is still better to first decide whether the item actually requires outsourcing or it can be made within the company itself. That is decided only after taking into account a host of factors based on the competitive situation or the relative strength of buyer versus the suppliers, and the nature of the item to be purchased. Most companies today see their purchasing function as a profit centre than as just a cost centre. The IT-enablement of purchasing in a Web environment has facilitated these companies to increase inventory turnover rate and an increased return on investment (ROI). Level of collaborative partnership with suppliers targeted towards their continuous improvement and development is inevitable. What most buying organizations require today are the re-engineered procurement and bidding processes, and systems in order to reduce cycle times and the costs, and exploit the Web for the best sourcing, giving due credence to environmental, social, and ethical considerations, as is clear from the Nokia case study presented at the end of this chapter.

MAKE/INSOURCING OR BUY/OUTSOURCING DECISIONS

The 'make-or-buy' decision is one of the most critical supply chain strategic decisions. The supply management organization has a key role in this decision. It determines and defines the organization's core competencies. It determines what level of investment the business should make internally as well as with suppliers. The 'make-or-buy' decision involves financial and capability issues as companies would normally ask: 'Do we have the expertise to manufacture a quality product and deliver it at a competitive cost?' Since some industrial tasks cannot be effectively accomplished in-house because of lack of equipment, trained personnel, or material, the answer to the question most of the times could be 'no'. So, non-core products and services are contracted to outside suppliers.

The make-or-buy decision in other words represents the vertical integration the firm would like to achieve. A firm must identify its 'optimal boundary' so that it incorporates only those activities that it can perform at a lower cost than the market.

Outsourcing is just a new focus on the classic make-or-buy procurement decision. One needs to ensure that such decisions are made intelligently, and not just based on the outsourcing trend.

When dealing with a make versus buy decision, there are four values to be kept in mind.

(i) Firm's volume
(ii) Fixed costs associated with making (e.g., the machining and tooling that must be bought)
(iii) Per-unit direct cost of making
(iv) Per-unit landed cost from a supplier

$$CoB = V \cdot LC_{pu} \text{ and } CoM = FC + (DC_{pu} \cdot V)$$

where,

$$
\begin{array}{ll}
CoB & = \text{Cost of buying} \\
V & = \text{Volume} \\
LC_{pu} & = \text{Supplier's landed cost per unit} \\
CoM & = \text{Cost of making} \\
FC & = \text{Fixed costs (of making)} \\
DC_{pu} & = \text{Direct cost per unit (of making)}
\end{array}
$$

If CoM exceeds CoB, then it is more financially desirable to buy. If CoB exceeds CoM, the opposite is true.

Questions that one must absolutely consider are as follows.

1. Is the activity/part to be bought, the organization's core competency?
2. Could the buying firm be harmed by disclosing proprietary information?
3. What will be the impact on quality or delivery?
4. What additional risks would the focal or buying firm be facing?
5. How irreversible is the decision?

Hence, it is important to consider as to what characteristics of the business environment in which the firm operates influence the relative efficiencies of the firm and the market. These, in fact, imply the conditions that would govern as to whether to make or to buy a certain requirement because of a certain level of competency and efficiency of the buying firm, the level of dominance it enjoys in the market versus the supplier, and the level of interdependence required with the supplier and the supply risk involved.

Factors for Taking Make/Insourcing or Buy/Outsourcing Decisions

The following factors influence relative efficiencies as per transaction cost approach (a '+' in Table 5.1 signifies a positive impact, and a '–' signifies a negative impact).

The Economies of Scale and Scope

Economies of scale occur when a proportionate increase in all inputs leads to a more than proportionate increase in output. Economies of scope exist where several different outputs draw on common resources. Economics of scale and scope both result in a reduction in unit costs as the total output increases.

These factors give a cost advantage to the large firm producing a range of products which draw on related skills and processes. A small firm (or a large firm seeking to offer a wide variety of unrelated products) may be unable to produce at a level which allows exploitation of economies of scale and scope. Costs might nevertheless be reduced by a recourse to the market. This may allow access to cheaper components from a specialist supplier who is able to aggregate demands from a number of firms, and so draw on economies of scale and scope.

Number of Suppliers

Traditional economic theory maintains that the price a firm must pay for its inputs (or will receive for its outputs) is influenced by the number of firms in the market. When a firm can choose from a large number of potential suppliers, the prices offered will be kept low by competition. However, when faced with only one source of supply (a monopoly), the firm's bargaining position may be considerably

TABLE 5.1 Influence of various factors on make-or-buy decisions

S. No.	Factors	Make	Buy
1.	Economies of scale and scope	–	+
2.	Large number of suppliers	–	+
3.	Small number of suppliers	+	–
4.	Opportunism	+	–
5.	Governance cost	–	+
6.	Asset specificity	+	–
7.	Knowledge specificity	+	–
8.	Uncertainty about the future	+	–

weakened, and it may prove cheaper to manufacture the component in-house (insourcing). A similar situation may arise where inputs are supplied by just a small number of firms. The implication is that a firm is more likely to use the market when there are a large number of suppliers. When the number of suppliers is small, it may be better to absorb that activity within the firm itself, i.e., not to outsource.

Opportunism

Markets often fail because of opportunism and bounded rationality. Opportunism is a lack of candour or honesty. This is unethical behaviour, and the extent of this problem is influenced by the moral standards of a particular society.

There may be a lower likelihood of opportunism where there are a large number of firms in the market. When a series of contracts are available to be awarded, opportunistic behaviour by one supplier will result in business loss on a future occasion. Where the number of firms is small, or where the customer lacks information about the alternative suppliers, then there is more scope for opportunistic behaviour, and absorbing the activity within the boundary of the firm may prove to be a better course of action.

Asset Specificity

Deciding which activities to include within the firm is also affected by asset specificity. The degree to which resources are specific to their current use is measured by their opportunity cost. Assets are highly specific if their next highest value is as scrap. Higher asset specificity is likely to be associated with smaller numbers of suppliers and/or buyers. Conversely, the less specific the asset, more would be the number of potential suppliers. A higher asset specificity may refer to specific machines, materials, and skills needing specific investments by the buyer also. For example, if a company such as Hyundai wants specific requirements for certain parts with discrete specifications and requiring specific materials and machining, it will have to put joint investments which can be done only in limited or a few cases only depending on the capacity share requirements of the buyer with the supplier. Such specific investments could ultimately take the form of joint ventures (JVs) with the suppliers, e.g., Maruti with Sona Koyo Steering or Maruti with Jai Bharat. This is a step short of vertical integration or making on one's own.

Knowledge Specificity

A firm's competitive advantage often stems from possession of special knowledge about the market, the product, or production technology. It may, for instance, have an advantage linked to R&D, or conferred by a brand name. Use of the market is risky if it threatens the security of that knowledge.

Uncertainty in the Future—The Alternative Sourcing Options

The 'make-or-buy' decision also involves a 'risk-reward' or 'cost-benefit' analysis. For example, low value products are usually commodity and non-strategic items. Also there are multiple suppliers who can produce this commodity so the risk of losing a commodity source or finding competitive bidders is relatively low. If the supplier provides a high value, innovative product or process technology, the company may enter into a partnership with a supplier, or bring the product to make it in-house.

A crucial decision is involved when a new or existent supplier cannot produce the product to the buyer's requirements. The buying firm, then, can either find a new supplier, or it can work with an existing supplier. The buyer may even improve the supplier's capabilities, can provide technical assistance and training, machines, incentives, or even pay the cost of improving the supplier's capabilities through selective vendor development.

And then, there is the 'risk-reward' decision of switching suppliers. The risk or cost of an unknown supplier may be significant. The buying company can switch a supplier when the cost and risk of retaining the supplier exceeds the cost of finding a new supplier. It could be in terms of erratic delivery schedules and/or defective shipments. Usually, higher the product value, higher is the risk, and higher the required assurance in terms of quality and delivery, the higher would be the chance for the firm to insource, or make the product itself.

Complexity of Make-or-buy Decisions

If a company sources a product or service, then it can work with existing suppliers or find new suppliers. Companies want to work with known people, known relationships, and known processes. They do not want unknown variability, unknown risk, unknown people, unknown processes, or unknown suppliers.

The solution is to encourage supply-partnering relationships. Customers and suppliers must trust each other to share key process information, technologies, cost/delivery/quality targets, and even investments. It requires a trust that a non-disclosure agreement cannot enforce.

The 'make' decision also is not easy for a supplier. The supplier may even pass on the opportunity to provide the product or service. The products may not be worthwhile to manufacture. The products may be low volume or 'one of a kind' that may require new production equipment or provide insufficient margins. Is the customer willing to pay for the added supplier investment? The 'make-or-buy' decision usually comes down to optimizing many such factors.

The decision of whether to make or to buy is a dilemma that is frequently encountered by supply managers. These decisions can be strategic or tactical. It may involve parts, capital items, services of all types, and a wide range of items supporting industrial operations (e.g., castings, tools, spare parts, etc.).

Decisions regarding outsourcing may be driven by two primary considerations. One may be the economic consideration where only the economic aspects are considered about making a particular product or providing a service. Secondly, the make-or-buy decisions may also be driven by the consideration of importance of the particular product in the firm's overall business perspective and its core competencies.

Decisions regarding outsourcing important activities products or goods are among the most strategic that can be made by an organization. They address the basic organizational choice of the functions for which internal expertise is developed and nurtured, and those for which such expertise is purchased. Even an individual make-or-buy decision can affect a company's production methods, working capital, and cost of borrowing or competitive position.

As pointed out earlier, outsourcing provides companies with the freedom to concentrate their energies on key activities that are critical to maintaining their competitive edge. This results in improvement of industrial relations and increasing labour productivity. For activities eligible for outsourcing, the key strategic question is whether the firm can perform those service activities on a level that is comparable with the best organizations in the world. If a service activity meets several criteria, the next step is deciding whether the service is central to the firm's core strategic activities. Moreover, to make the best make-or-buy decision, companies must determine how that decision will affect final product quality and the company's technology.

Make-or-buy is a decision not to be made only on the basis of economic considerations, since acquisition or loss of core competencies could be an equally important issue.

Let us examine the types of considerations involved.

Economic Considerations

Investment in infrastructure required If the requirement of a particular product is low in volume and does not justify the creation of infrastructure dedicated to it, while the same is available in the market at a reasonable cost, it might be worthwhile to outsource the same.

Limitation in product life If there is a sudden requirement of a product that is not expected to last very long or is uncertain, a positive investment decision cannot be made. This to avoid any possibility of the net present value (NPV) becoming negative.

Strategic Considerations

Long-term value   When a product is extremely important in its strategic long-term value to a firm, a decision to produce the same in-house may be taken even if it is economically unviable in its present form, or if the demand is low or uncertain.

Core business consideration   A product that relates to a firm's core business should be internally produced (insourcing), while one that does not may be outsourced. Today, a number of firms are outsourcing jobs that do not relate to their core business activities. Common examples can be that of housekeeping, dining facility, medical facility, and logistics activities that are routinely outsourced by firms in the present day context. The growth of BPO industries in India and other Asian countries has been taking place due to this reason.

Core competencies and outsourcing   As discussed earlier, a firm can identify its core competencies and limit itself in making the best use of these competencies. However, today, most products will require use of diverse technologies and infrastructure that may not fall into this domain. For example, an automobile company can manufacture the critical engine related items such as cam shafts but may leave the tyres to be produced by the rubber technologists.

Considerations about environment and regulations   Make-or-buy or outsourcing decisions are also influenced by considerations about the environment and regulations. Today, the automobile companies in Europe and US are outsourcing all their foundry and forging needs from Asian countries, because these jobs typically produce environmental and noise pollution.

Supervision and control needs   A job that demands a very high degree of supervision and control, and is crucial to the performance of a much larger assembly unit may be produced in-house, while the others may be outsourced. The control in one's own factory premises can be expected to be more under control of the managers than the same in any vendor's factory premises. However, this distinction is slowly diminishing with the advent of better operating systems where the vendors are taking more and more responsibilities towards the overall performance of the system.

Quality requirements   Quality considerations may also drive the make-or-buy, or outsourcing decisions. A product where more quality consciousness is necessary will normally be produced in-house, while others may outsourced.

Outsourcing in the Light of Porter's 5-forces Model

Insourcing/make or outsourcing/buy decisions can be easily analysed using Porter's 5-forces model (Fig. 5.1). It is based on five dimensions as follows.

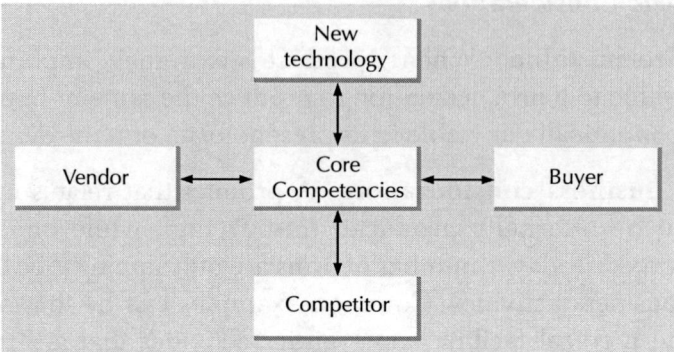

FIG. 5.1 Porter's 5-forces Model

Vendor

In the market scenario, manufacturing decisions can be taken to reduce the pressures applied by the vendors. However, if the vendors are not in a strong position, manufacturing may not be resorted to. Vendor's strength becomes particularly more important when the part or item to be produced is of high importance, and strategically not suitable to be procured by an outsider.

Competitor

Many business decisions are taken by a firm to maintain the number one position (or position of importance) in the market. If the competition from a competitor is not serious at any stage, even important items may be allowed to be produced by outsourced agencies.

Buyer

Sometimes in the market, the buyers also have immense capacity to apply pressure. They can apply pressures with respect to price, quality, timing, or any other feature of the product. In the presence of such pressures, a firm may retain the manufacturing responsibility with itself, as in that condition it will have better control on the products with respect to its stated features.

Core Competencies

A firm will normally like to operate in an environment where it can maximize its profits based on its core competencies, while leaving the field for others in the remaining areas. An automobile company will produce cars but may outsource the IT services from an IT firm where its own core competencies do not exist. Given the pressures of a competitive market, organizations do focus on their core activities—activities that link-up directly with the revenues and hence, the profitability. In such a scenario, companies outsource their non-core tasks to focus on business decision-making. This has been focused earlier also.

New Technology

In an environment where the old technology is being replaced by new ones at a rapid pace, a firm will like to think whether an investment will pay itself back or not in the remaining expected life of the product market. In the latter case, it will always select to outsource such components or parts from the market, rather than creating infrastructure for making the same in its own premises where the pay-back period of the investment mode can be large.

Make-or-buy decisions are often triggered by a firm's desire to improve the efficiency of the supply chain, and to offer better products and services to its customers in time and at the right place.

Many Indian companies such as Hero Honda Motors, Bharti Tele-Ventures, HDFC Bank, Sony Entertainment Television, Hyatt Services, and HPCL have gone in for outsourcing several services and products. They have chosen outsourcing as a strategic business decision to garner tangible and intangible benefits in the short and long run. Engineers India Ltd (EIL), for example, outsources environmental impact assessment (EIA) studies for its projects. The baseline data collection, which is prerequisite to environmental modelling, simulation, and predictions to yield the EIA report, is also outsourced.

STRATEGIC (OUT-)SOURCING

Ricker (1997) defines strategic sourcing as a systematic process that directs supply managers to plan, manage, and develop the supply base in line with a firm's strategic objectives. Strategic sourcing is the application of current best practices to achieve the full potential of integrating suppliers into the long-term business processes. It can be considered as a core process within a larger function of supply chain management (SCM). It also aims to identify activities of competitors and needs materials and technology.

According to Ray (1997), strategic sourcing is a disciplined approach that improves the value that the core firm receives from its suppliers. There are five points which make it different from tactical purchasing in the sense that it

1. defines the value of relationship between purchaser and supplier;
2. develops solutions based on understanding of supplier's manufacturing, economics, and business processes;
3. uses a differentiated purchasing strategy and action plans in order to optimize the business relationship for both the purchaser and the supplier;
4. incorporates the required changes in the organization so that the purchaser achieves not only a near-term measurable performance improvement, but also the ability to continuously improve; and
5. requires formation of cross-functional teams.

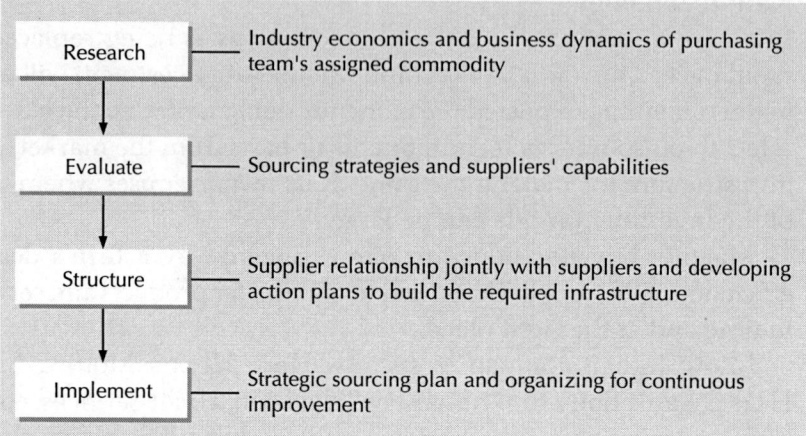

FIG. 5.2 Steps in strategic sourcing plan

It involves the steps shown in Fig. 5.2.

So, strategic sourcing is a more broad-based process involving market and commodity research, understanding of organizational and business processes, and capturing information and using it to improve relationships. Obviously, it requires a two-way continuous improvement process work.

Reputed firms conduct strategic analysis of what their core competencies are, through analysing the skills and processes, which form the basis of their success and competitive advantage. If an item or source represents a core competency or supports interfaces with such a competency, then the source of supply should be the firm itself (insourcing).

As a part of strategic sourcing, the suppliers should be involved to attain the following objectives.

- Cost minimization
- Willingness to share process data including process output data, and cost data
- Cooperation in sharing product/part design and development exercise
- Ability to meet technology needs of buyer/technology upgradation plans
- Technical capacity expansion plan
- Intention/potential of the supplier to enter into strategic partnership/alliance with the buyer

Strategic Issues in Purchasing

It is important to perform a competitive analysis before initiating the outsourcing analysis. A firm's competitive advantage is often defined in terms of cost leverage, product differentiation, or focus. A competitive analysis, namely SWOT analysis, will provide a report of the firm's strategic position relative to the market, industry, and competitors.

Core Competencies

As highlighted earlier, before deciding about outsourcing, a company should identify its existing core competencies. It should be followed by scanning of the current and mapping the expected future environment in which the firm operates, including the competition, government regulatory climate, the changing characteristics of sales, and supply markets. The expected competency requirements are identified and compared with existing core competencies to determine which ones need to be exploited, and the ones which are to be supplemented with related competencies that must be developed to create a competitive advantage. The fundamental strategic consideration that guides the strategic outsourcing/make-or-buy decision is up to what extent the capabilities required to manufacture products or services are linked with the core competencies. The products or services that should be made or conducted in-house are those that require capabilities that are closely linked with the core competencies and are mutually reinforced, as opposed to those which should be bought out if core competencies are different.

Strategic Vulnerabilities

As Porter put it, strategic outsourcing may always result into creation of strategic vulnerability. As an item is outsourced, the buying company tends to lose control over it. Also, as a part of outsourcing, a lot of technology, process knowledge, particularly on the manufacturing, or service delivery side is passed on. It creates strategic vulnerability, and tends to commoditise and make generic the product of the buying company.

Risk of Vertical Integration

A decision to make or insource may result in vertical integration. Vertical integration may result in a loss of flexibility in volume and variety, and responsiveness to market needs.

Early Supplier Involvement

It is an approach in supply management to bring the expertise and collaborative synergy of suppliers at the design stage itself. Involvement of supplier at an early stage brings out better results of partnerships, and yield better quality, delivery, cost, and service levels.

Strategic Purchasing Portfolio Analysis

The Kraljic Matrix used for strategic classification of materials from purchasing and supply into various portfolios was described by Peter Kraljic in an article, 'Purchasing

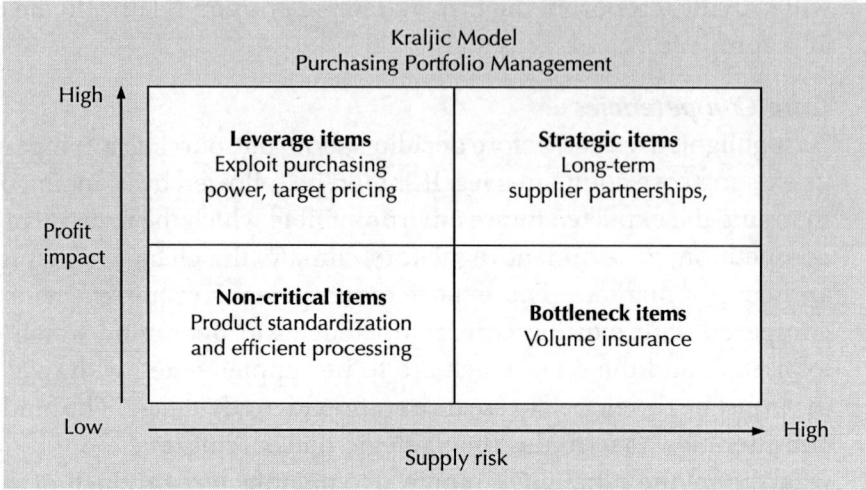

FIG. 5.3 Strategic purchasing portfolios
Source: Kraljic 1983

must become supply management' in the *Harvard Business Review* (September–October 1983). The Kraljic Model can be used to analyse the purchasing portfolio of a firm (Fig. 5.3).

The Kraljic framework is based on two dimensions for classifying a firm's purchased materials or components.

Profit Impact

It refers to 'the strategic importance of purchasing in terms of the value added by product line, the percentage of raw materials in total costs, and their impact on profitability'.

Supply Risk

It refers to 'the complexity of the supply market gauged by supply scarcity, pace of technology and/or materials substitution, entry barriers, logistics cost or complexity, and monopoly or oligopoly conditions'.

The framework then distinguishes between the following four product categories.

Leverage Items

Definition   Leverage items are products that represent a high percentage of the profit of the buyer and for which there are many suppliers available. It is easy to switch the supplier. The quality is standardized.

Buyer–seller power situation   It is buyer dominated with a moderate level of interdependency.

Recommended purchasing strategy It is preferred to float tenders, well formulated vendor selections, targeted pricing, umbrella agreement with preferred suppliers. Call-off orders are then placed as an administrative formality.

Strategic Items

Definition Strategic items are products that are crucial for the process or product of the buyer. They are characterized by a high supply risk caused by scarcity, or difficult delivery.

Buyer–seller power situation The situation is that of balanced power with a high level of interdependency.

Recommended purchasing strategy It is recommended to have strategic alliances, close relationships, early supplier involvement, and belief in the concept of co-creation to actively consider vertical integration with a long-term value focus.

Non-critical Items

Definition Non-critical items are products that are easy to buy and also have a relative low impact on the financial results. The quality is standardized.

Buyer–seller power situation The situation presents balanced power accompanied with a low level of interdependency.

Recommended purchasing strategy The goal is to reduce time and money spent on these products by enhancing product standardization and efficient processing.

Bottleneck Items

Definition Bottleneck items are materials that can only be acquired from one supplier or their delivery is otherwise unreliable, and have a relatively low impact on the financial results.

Buyer–seller power situation It is supplier dominated with a moderate level of interdependency.

Recommended purchasing strategy It is advisable to have a volume insurance contract and vendor-managed inventory, keep extra stocks, and look for potential suppliers.

Planning for the Outsourcing

All things said and done, outsourcing is a strategic business decision that should be made only if a company sees true business benefits accruing from it. Badly planned outsourcing could result in erosion of value and cost escalation, but a well-planned outsourcing decision can help supply chain executives breathe a sigh of relief, knowing that the responsibility of deliverables is in safe hands. Following are the few questions one can ask, which can lead to a proper decision in this context.

1. What type of an activity is to be outsourced? Identify characteristics of the service and the respective type.
2. What perspective is driving the effort to outsource? Identify decision rights (service owner) and input rights (other stakeholders).
3. How are other perspectives affected? Identify conflicting areas and work them out.
4. Check compliance with principles and fit with the architecture of the system.
5. Who should carry out the outsourcing? Evaluate the different staffing combinations and select the best.

We should understand different business perspectives and how they affect sourcing decisions. We should understand how perspectives must be harnessed to drive sourcing decisions and then develop a structured sequence of steps to sourcing decisions. Next step should be in developing evolving governance architecture to support sourcing decisions. And finally, internal sourcing decision roles should be developed.

Outsourcing

Outsourcing is the delegation of tasks or jobs from internal production to an external entity (such as a sub-contractor). Most recently, it has come to mean the elimination of native staff to staff overseas, where salaries are markedly lower. This is despite the fact that the majority of outsourcing that occurs today still occurs within country boundaries. It became a popular buzzword in business and management in the 1990s. Outsourcing broadly refers to the following:

1. The process where functions previously performed by an organization are supplied under contract by a third-party.
2. Buying goods or services instead of producing or providing them in-house.
3. The concept of taking internal company functions and paying an outside firm to handle them. Outsourcing is done to save money, improve quality, or free company resources for other activities. It was first done in the data-processing industry and has spread to areas, including tele-messaging and call centres.
4. A long-term, result-oriented relationship with an external service provider for activities traditionally performed within the company. Outsourcing usually applies to a complete business process. It implies a degree of managerial control and risk on the part of the provider.
5. The transfer of components or large segments of an organization's internal IT infrastructure, staff, processes, or applications to an external resource such as an application service provider.

Time to Outsource

Are we outsourcing enough and at the right time ? What functions can we move for near or offshoring at a certain time? It is likely that a procurement manager somewhere is being asked these questions right now. Executives have noticed their peers increasingly relying on outsourcing. While outsourcing may seem new, it really is just a new focus on the classic make-or-buy procurement decision. One needs to ensure that such decisions are made intelligently, and not just based on the outsourcing trend at a certain time. It is best adopted after a careful look at business needs and available options. It is essential that the outsourcing relationship provides strategic business benefits in the future.

Strategic outsourcing allows ease of management, reduction in cost, lesser manpower, and frees up internal resources. Outsourcing can, and frequently does provide both long- and short-term benefits to companies that outsource, provided they have a strategic objective for outsourcing. Medium and long-term gains are best realized by selecting a vendor who brings value to the core business, rather than the one who can provide you just with the lowest prices. A badly-planned outsourcing could result in erosion of service value and cost escalation.

The ultimate goal of outsourcing is to bring tangible benefits to the business, and subsequently the customer.

Offshoring

No commonly accepted definition of *offshoring* exists, and the term has been used to include various international trade and foreign investment activities. Services that US-based organizations purchase from abroad are considered imports. They may also be linked to US firms' overseas investments—for example, US firms may invest in overseas affiliates as a replacement for, or as an alternative to, domestic production. In recent years, services offshoring has been facilitated by factors, such as the Internet, infrastructure growth in developing countries, and decreasing data transmission costs. Organizations' decisions to offshore services are influenced by potential benefits such as the availability of cheaper skilled labour and access to foreign markets, and by risks, such as geopolitical issues and infrastructure instability in countries that supply the services. 'Outshoring' of services generally refers to an organization's purchase from other countries of services that it previously produced or purchased domestically, such as software programming or telephone call centres.

Near-shoring

Near-shoring outsourcing, a form of offshoring, is the term used to refer to the practice of getting work done or services performed by people in neighbouring countries (e.g., Canada, Mexico to US, or Sri Lanka to India) rather than in your own country.

Insourcing

The act of bringing together a function that was performed outside the organization (outsourced) to being performed inside the organization is called insourcing.

It is the opposite of outsourcing, that is, a service performed in-house. It is a reaction to outsourcing comprising employees aggressively defending their core competencies against cost-cutting exercises by their senior managers and third-party providers.

Exhibit 5.1 highlights some activities that are being outsourced at Engineers India Ltd (EIL).

EXHIBIT 5.1 Strategic Outsourcing at Engineers India Ltd

COMPANY OVERVIEW

Engineers India Limited (EIL) was established in 1965 to provide engineering and other related technical services for petroleum refineries and other industrial projects. In addition to petroleum refineries, with which EIL started initially, it has diversified into and excelled in other fields, such as pipelines, petrochemicals, oil and gas processing, offshore structures and platforms, fertilizers, metallurgy, and power. EIL now provides a complete range of project services in these fields and has emerged as Asia's leading design and engineering company.

EIL provides the complete range of services needed to conceptualize, design, engineer, and construct projects to meet the specific requirements of its clients. Its association with the clients extends beyond the commissioning of their plants through monitoring operation of each plant and accumulating feedback on performance.

AREAS OF STRATEGIC OUTSOURCING

Following are the areas of strategic outsourcing.

(I) IT Infrastructure

To help organizations get optimum value out of IT and use it as a strategic tool to further the cause of business, EIL thought it worthwhile to outsource IT infrastructure management, since its competency is not in IT but in consultancy services. There is an IT department whose work is to decide and formulate IT infrastructure requirement to carve out strategic edge by leveraging IT (which includes hardware, software, net-working requirements, servers, etc.) so that services to the customer can be improved. However, maintenance of IT infrastructure has been outsourced, since the external agencies are better equipped in handling these activities, and can perform the same at lower cost, as against if these activities were carried out internally. Two companies, SpiceNet and PC Solutions, have been engaged for maintenance of IT infrastructure and these offer services that include desktop client management, server management, cable management, firewall management, patch management, software license management, IT audits, backbone and connectivity, website hosting, and IT infrastructure management.

(Contd)

EXHIBIT 5.1 *Contd*

(II) Drafting of Drawings

EIL's core business is providing consultancy solutions, and engineering plays a vital role. The series of activities that takes place in engineering are the following:

- Detailed design
- Review of process data sheets
- Issue of material requisitions (MR)
- Offer evaluation
- Issue of purchase requisition (PR)
- Vendor drawing review, etc.

All the aforesaid activities are strategically important and have to be performed internally, as these require engineering expertise and a lot of in-house generated information gives EIL a competitive edge. However, drafting of drawing at the stage of detailed engineering, preparation of MR and PR consumes lot of manhours. The drafting of drawing is considered to be an activity which does not add much value to engineering but is an essential part of the project. Hence, this activity has been outsourced to two agencies, especially for all those units which are not critical such as utilities and offsites, etc. Both of these agencies have long term association with EIL and understand EIL's mode of working, and the way a job is carried out meeting EIL specifications, standards, and engineering practices.

(III) Surveys

Civil surveys such as topography of the plant, surveys done for cross-country pipelines, soil investigation reports, seismic study of the terrain, etc., are outsourced since these are specialized jobs. The external agencies maintain the databases as they are carrying out these surveys for other clients also. It will not be cost effective for EIL to carry out these surveys.

STRATEGIC PARTNERSHIPS WITH THE SUPPLIER

The partnerships with supplier can be categorized into three types, based on the extent to which 'strategic intent' for collaboration exists among the partners.

Transactional Relationships

This is the most common and basic type of relationship with a supplier. Such a relationship is neither good nor bad. Transactional relationship simply denotes an arm's-length relationship wherein neither party is especially concerned with the well-being of the other. Virtually, all buying firms will have transactional relationships. Most will have collaborative ones and some will have strategic alliances.

The figure that follows (Fig. 5.4) exhibits the continuum of buyer–supplier relationships over there with the types of activities and attributes common to each.

Characteristics	Transactional ⟺ Collaborative ⟺ Alliance	
	Extreme-I	Extreme-II
Communication	High potential for problems	Systematic approach to enhance communication
Competitive advantage	Low	High
Connectedness	Independence	Interdependence
Continuous improvement	Little	Focused
Contribution to new product development	Few	Many—early supplier involvement
Difficulty of exit	Low	High
Duration	Short	Long
Expediting	Reactive	Proactive
Focus	Price	Total cost
Level of integration	Little or none	High or total
Level of trust	Low	High
Number of suppliers	Many	One or few
Open books	No	Yes
Quality	Based on incoming inspection	Quality designed into system
Relations	Inward looking	Concern with each other's well being
Resources	Few—low skill level	Professional
Services	Minimal	Greatly improved
Shared forecasts	No	Yes
Supply disruptions	Possible	Unlikely
Technology inflows	No	Yes
Type of interaction	Tactical	Strategic synergy

FIG. 5.4 Attributes of buyer–supplier relationships
Source: Burt, Dobler, and Starling 2003

Characteristics of Transactional Relationships

1. An absence of concern by both parties about the other party's well-being. With transactional relationships, there is little or no concern about the other party's well-being. While one party wins, the other loses.
2. One of a series of independent deals. Each transaction is entered into on its own merits. Little or no basis exists for collaboration and learning.
3. Costs, data, and forecasts are not shared. Arm's-length transactions, not openness, are characteristics of transactional relationships.

4. Price is the focus of the relationship. Getting the best price is the focus of the transaction. Ideally, total cost analysis precedes any procurement transaction. Since there is little or no concern for the other's well-being, neither buyer nor supplier will rush to the other's assistance in bad times, or when problems arise.

5. A minimum of purchasing time and energy is required to establish prices. Market forces normally establish prices in transactional relationships. Thus, little purchasing time and energy are required to establish prices.

6. Transactional purchases lend themselves to e-procurement and, in some cases, reverse auctions.

Most companies would buy consumables, e.g., papers, stationery, cartridges, toners or coolant, lubricants, anti-corrosives, fire-retardants, effluent treatment services/ chemicals, etc., for their factories on transaction basis at the lowest cost every time and with no long-term commitment. A hospital may buy housekeeping services, disinfectants, common dressings, and syringes, etc., on transaction basis with no obligation for sharing information, and no commitment for repeat order. The purpose is to get best price for that point of time. Another example is when banks such as ICICI or Axis Bank may buy mailer, loan processing/field inspection staff services, or facilitation services only for limited period transactions because of peak traffic to handle that extra demand at best price.

Key Advantages of Transactional Relationships

1. Relatively less purchasing time and effort are required to establish price, while the market forces of supply and demand establish the price with transactional procurements. Therefore, little purchasing time and effort are required to establish price.

2. Lower skill levels of procurement personnel are required. Much less judgement and managerial expertise are required with the vast majority of transactional procurements.

Limitations of Transactional Relationships

1. Communication difficulties are much greater with transactional relationships than with collaborative or alliance ones.

2. Considerable investment in expediting and the monitoring of incoming quality is required to ensure timely delivery of the right quality.

3. Transactional relationships are inflexible. Changing technology and market conditions require flexibility in buyer–supplier relationships.

4. Transactional procurements may result in more delivery problems than collaborative and strategic alliance ones.

5. Quality with transactional relationships will be only as good as required. Far more incentive and opportunity exists to improve quality in a collaborative or alliance relationship.

6. Transactional suppliers provide only the minimum service required.

7. Buyers tend to experience less effective performance by their transactional suppliers, than those employing collaborative or strategic relationships. Transactional suppliers have nothing much to lose from a dissatisfied customer as do collaborative and strategic relationship suppliers.

8. Transactional customers are subject to more supply disruptions than collaborative or alliance ones. Buyers who maintain continuing, collaborative relations with their suppliers are much less subject to stock-outs than transactional ones.

9. Since the supplier recognizes the transactional and price nature of the relationship, there is no motivation to invest time and energy in the development of the potential buyer's products.

Collaborative and Alliance Relationships

Collaborative and alliance relationships for the procurement of non-commodity items and services tend to result in lower total costs than transactional relationships for several reasons. Process improvements and the adoption of technical innovations require a high level of certainty and continuity of demand. The risks and uncertainties present with transactional relationships reduce the likelihood of investments in R&D and training, as well as the procurement of new and more efficient equipment focused on the customer firm's needs. Thus, major opportunities for cost reduction within supplying organizations may be lost with transactional relationships.

Cost reductions resulting from efforts such as value engineering and value analysis (VE/VA) are much more likely with collaborative and alliance relationships. Suppliers are more likely to take the initiative to reduce costs through VE/VA when they are involved in long-term relations than with short-term transactional ones. Long-term performance agreements allow suppliers an opportunity to reduce their costs. The extended learning curve effect with both production and services allows collaborative and alliance suppliers to reduce their costs and share these savings with customers.

Collaborative and alliance relations replace the market forces employed by transactional procurement with controlled competition, benchmarking, and advanced supply management pricing practices. The results are lower total costs, higher quality, reduced time to market, and reduced risk of supply disruptions.

Stanley and Pearson (2000) found that the three most important factors in a successful buyer–supplier relationship are

(i) two-way communication,
(ii) the supplier's responsiveness to purchasing and supply management's needs, and
(iii) clearly laid-down product specifications.

Collaborative Relationships

An awareness of the interdependence and necessity of cooperation is the key difference between collaborative relationships and transactional ones. The focus on relationship management will require that all elements of relationship management including trust building, communication, joint efforts and planning, and fostering interdependency are properly managed to achieve competitive advantage. Continuous improvement is far easier to implement and manage with well-recognized interdependence and cooperation. The ultimate goal with continuous improvement is a reduction in total costs. Improved quality and timeliness also result. Recognizing the need for interdependence and cooperation, the customer's firm enjoys the benefits of early supplier involvement (ESI). Improvements in time to market, and the leveraging of supplier technology also result.

The likelihood of supply disruptions is greatly reduced. Both customers and suppliers who value each other, based on long-term relations and respect, are more likely to come to each other's help during times of adversity.

The relative level of certainty and continuity of demand in collaborative and alliance relationships increases the likelihood of investments in R&D, training, new projects, and the procurement of new equipment. Cost reductions resulting from VE/VA are enhanced, and the extended learning curve effect with both production and services activities allows collaborative and alliance suppliers to reduce their costs, and share these savings with their customers.

The major disadvantage of collaborative and alliance relationships, however, is the amount of human resources, time, and energy required to develop and manage these relationships.

Supply Alliances

The key difference between collaborative relationships and supply alliances is the presence of institutional trust in alliances. The failure to develop and manage institutional trust is the key reason that so many supply alliances fail.

Supply alliances reap incredible benefits as a result of physical asset specialization and human specialization. Dyer (2000) defines physical asset specialization as relationship specific capital investments (e.g., in customized machinery, tools, information systems, delivery processes, and so forth) that allow for faster throughout and greater product customization. Physical asset specialization allows for product differentiation and may improve overall quality by increasing product integrity. Human specialization refers to relationship-specific know-how accumulated by individuals through long-standing relationships. In other words, individuals across companies have substantial experience working together, and have accumulated specialized information and language that allows them to communicate and co-ordinate effectively with each other. They are less likely to have communication breakdowns which would result in higher quality, faster development times, and lower costs.

Advantages of Supply Alliances

Lower total costs   Synergies can be created in alliances that would not happen in transactional or even collaborative relationships. The synergies result in reductions of direct and indirect costs associated with labour, machinery, material, and overhead.

Reduced time to market   Reducing the time to design, develop, and distribute new products and services is a key driver that leads to improved market share and better profit margins.

Improved quality   The use of both the design of experiments (DoE) and supplier certification are the norm with supply alliances. These two activities help to design and manufacture quality products at a lower total cost.

Improved technology flow from suppliers   According to Burt, Dobler and Starling (2003), openness and institutional trust enhance the inflow of technology from alliance partners that leads to many successful new products. In 1999, Dell and IBM formed an alliance worth some $16 billion for over 10 years. In effect, Dell is harnessing IBM's vast research, development, and production abilities. Dell is purchasing storage devices, custom logic chips, static random-access memory, and other components. The two companies are also cross-licensing patent technologies.

Improved continuity of supply   Alliance customers are the least likely group to experience supply disruptions in supplies over a period of time.

Key Characteristics of Supplier Alliances

1. A high level of recognized interdependence and commitment is present.
2. The focus of most supplier alliances is achieving the simultaneous objectives of continuous improvements along with reduction in cost.
3. The alliance is controlled through a complex web of formal and informal interpersonal connections, information systems, and internal infrastructures that enhance learning.

4. Openness exists in all areas of the relationship, including cost, long-term objectives, technology, and the supply chain itself.
5. The alliance is a dynamic system that progressively evolves with the objective of creating new benefits for both parties.
6. Ethics take precedence over expediency in operationalization of the alliance.
7. The relationship is adaptable in the face of changing economics, competition, technology, and environmental issues.
8. As pointed out earlier, the design of experiments and supplier certification are the norm with supply alliances. These two activities help to design and manufacture quality products at a lower total cost.
9. Negotiations and renegotiations are done in a win-win manner.

Alliances are suited for the most critical relationships. In 1999, Honda of America had over 400 procurement professionals developing and managing some 400 alliances. During the 1990s, Chrysler became a fascinating example of alliance relationships. In 1989, Chrysler had some 2500 suppliers in its production supply base. It was rated as the least desirable customer of the big three US auto assemblers. With a surprising amount of assistance from Honda of America Manufacturing, Chrysler transitioned itself from a transaction-based buyer to a collaborative one. Time to market was reduced by 30 per cent. Profit margins per vehicle increased on an average of 750 per cent.

Chrysler employed many of the principles such as cross-functional teams, early supplier involvement, target costing, value analysis (with incentives in the form of additional profits or additional sales aid to suppliers), improved communications through techniques such as collocation of supplier engineers at Chrysler design centres, and a supplier advisory board.

Choice of Buyer–Supplier Relationships

Several conditions should be ascertained to determine the strategic elements of a relationship (Burt, Dobler, and Starling 2003).

1. If there are many undifferentiated suppliers providing interchangeable commodities, a collaborative alliance or relationship would not be appropriate, a transactional relationship would be better.
2. If the potential supplier possesses economic power which it wants to exercise over its customers, a transactional or very carefully developed and managed collaborative relationship is usually appropriate.
3. If there is recognition by both parties of the potential benefits of an alliance, but adequate qualified human resources are not available at one or both firms, a collaborative relationship is usually appropriate. A collaborative relationship frequently is the first step on the road to a strategic alliance.

4. If one supplier is a cut above the rest in terms of the value it provides, including price, innovation, ability to adapt to changing situations, capacity to work with the team, take joint risks, and so on, an alliance may be appropriate, assuming that the supplier is willing to enter into an interdependent, trusting relationship.

5. If some suppliers are strategic to the business that have a major impact on the competitive advantage in the marketplace, and the buyer is highly reliant on them to provide a unique product, technology, or service, then an alliance may be needed.

6. If the buying company would benefit greatly when the supplier were more 'integrally connected' with the company, perhaps with their engineers working side by side, or co-locating their manufacturing facilities adjacent or within buying company, an alliance can be considered.

7. If customers require high degrees of flexibility and speed of responsiveness, forcing a buyer to demand the same performance from the suppliers, an alliance can be set.

Trust is another key factor differentiating the three classes of relationships. The simplest definition of trust is *'being confident that the other party will do what it says it will do.'* Some level of trust must be present in all three types of relationships. But the level of trust increases with collaborative relationships and becomes an essential characteristic of strategic alliances.

Only a few of these relationships are pure—a transactional relationship may have one or more collaborative characteristics, while a collaborative relationship may have one or more transactional as well as some alliance characteristics.

Supplier's Perspective

The most attractive supplier may often decide that a collaborative or alliance relationship with the potential customer firm is not in its best interest. In effect, the supplier may possess economic power which it can wield in an effort to maximize its net income. Or, the preferred supplier may be simply unavailable since the buying firm's key competitor may have already established an exclusive relationship. World-class suppliers are careful in their selection of customer firms. The supplier will be very concerned with the potential customer firm's finances, especially as they affect its ability to pay. The customer firm's finances also provide insight into prospects for a long-term relationship, and continuing demand for the supplier's product(s) or service(s). Quality suppliers prefer customers who have high business growth prospects.

The potential customer's demand pattern for the supplier's product is of great interest, especially with respect to the stability and fit. World-class suppliers want to ensure that potential customer's quality requirements are within their capabilities. The supplier is also concerned with the buying firm's approach to resolving problems. Suppliers are attracted to customers who have a reputation for working collaboratively with suppliers, who have experience in problem identification, and correcting the root cause of the problem rather than playing the blame game.

Suppliers want good customers. Several issues affect a customer firm's rating as a 'good' customer including (Burt, Dobler, and Starling 2003) the following.

- Does the customer have a reputation for timely payment? Cash flow in customer company is a major concern of all suppliers.
- Is the customer secretive? Suppliers prefer customers who are open and approachable.
- Are the customer's supply management personnel responsive? Suppliers prefer customers that are available within certain hours.
- Are the customers known as professionals in the industry? World-class suppliers conduct themselves professionally, and expect to be treated professionally.

For suppliers and buyers who comprehend the value of shifting from tactical, transactional-based relationships to strategic value-based alliance relationships, it will be essential to include assessment of the elements of total cost of ownership (TCO) to determine exactly where cost can be reduced, value enhanced, and substantial advantage created. Many companies in India have started conducting vendor satisfaction surveys in addition to normal customer satisfaction surveys.

Situations Adversarial for Alliances

Alliances are not always desirable. Five major categories of such situations, as discussed by Kauffman (1999), are given here.

Stability   It pertains to stability in the prices, market, and buyer's demand.

Price volatility   It applies to commodities traded in open markets that have significant price volatility. The problem for a partnership/alliance is about how to share risks and benefits that may result from price volatility. To mitigate this problem, price adjustment mechanisms based on costs or indices and, for some commodities, hedging in future's market can be done.

Demand volatility   This is in case of materials or services that have significant volatility in individual buyer demand. If the buying firm's needs are not predictable, the supplier must deal with the likelihood of overstock, or stock-out, or erratic production schedules. Additional costs might accrue for the supplier that have to be built into the price that the buyer pays.

Switching requirements and the costs This applies to situations with high switching costs that also have a high likelihood of switching being desirable. Purchases that involve changing technology or critical quality, or other characteristics, and there are no strong suppliers, may indicate a high likelihood of switching, in spite of high switching costs. In such cases, maximum flexibility is desirable.

Capability It refers to the capability of potential suppliers.

Capable supplier for the item This holds true for items for which there is no full-service world-class supplier capable of a partnership/alliance relationship. The lack of a capable supplier would dictate some other form of supply relationship—no partnership or alliance would be preferable.

Capable supplier in the geographic area This applies to those region of the world where there is no full-service, world-class supplier capable of a partnership/alliance relationship. Depending on the material or service required, there may be regions where a partnership or alliance is not possible on account of lack of a competent supplier in that region.

Rapid technological change This refers to situations of rapid industry-wide technological change where the buyer would be at a disadvantage if locked with one supplier. The buyer must have assurance that technology is maintained at the state-of-the-art level, and as required by the buyer's industry. Not all suppliers have the capability to remain technologically competitive.

Mismatch of technology change This refer to a mismatch of, or rapidly changing clock speed between the supplier and the buyer. If the buying firm's industry is changing and developing more rapidly than that of the supplier's industry, it may be difficult to arrive at a partnership or alliance that is fully beneficial to the buyer.

Competition It refers to structure of the supply market and the conditions of competition prevailing.

Non-competitive market This refers to non-competitive markets where the supplier partner maybe in a position to take advantage of the buying firm. Generally a partnership or strategic alliance will reinforce the supplier's power relative to the buying firm.

Alliance-induced supplier dependency This holds true in situations where extreme dependency on a particular supplier would be created by a partnership or strategic alliance. If the buying company is relatively small compared to the selling company, and the buyer's business is not vital to the seller, the buyer may be at risk of future supply. For example, a buyer becomes totally dependent on a seller through a partnership or alliance for a material vital to the supplier, and for which there are few, if any, alternate suppliers. If the supplier determines at a future time that the business is not compatible with its business objectives, it may terminate the agreement and cause supply difficulty for the buyer.

Conventionally ignored areas   This applies to situations where purchases have been mismanaged or not managed for years, e.g., many types of indirect purchases. These types of purchases, in order to obtain the lowest total cost, a relationship that leverages the free market should be used. They advocate partnerships for such situations only if there are few supply alternatives available and/or if there are high supplier switching costs.

Suppliers tending to reduce competition   It refers to situations where suppliers appear to be using partnerships/alliances as a marketing ploy to eliminate competition and reduce industry capacity. These may save cost in the short run, but, if the supplier's strategy is to truly reduce capacity and competition, costs may increase in the long run. Being locked with such a supplier would be undesirable.

Benefits   It refers to the benefits enjoyed by the buying firm from the relationship.

No leverage from partnership   It applies to situations where there is nothing to leverage with a partnership/alliance. Typically, a partnership or alliance will leverage some aspect of the exchange involved. Leveraged items include volume, total cost, process or procedural cost, inventory, or innovation. If there are no leverage possibilities, there may not be a justification for the work involved in establishing and maintaining a partnership or alliance.

No hard savings from partnership   It is applicable in situations where hard savings are not present as a result of a partnership/alliance. Soft savings such as non-quantifiable quality improvements and partial-person staff reductions are right, but, unless they result in some other cost avoidance, they never show up on the bottom line. To justify the work involved in establishing and maintaining partnerships and alliance, there must be some hard savings.

Internal buy-in   This refers to the level at which the internal departments are buying-in the terms of partnership with the supplier.

No internal customer buy-in   This refers to situations where the internal customers of the buying organization do not have joint ownership with supply management of the partnership/alliance arrangement. Most purchasing organizations use a team approach to develop, implement, and maintain partnership and alliance agreements. If that is not done, or if the internal customer members of the team do not agree with all the terms of the agreement, the partnership or alliance will be likely to fail.

SUPPLIER SELECTION PROCESS

After a number of potential suppliers have passed the vendor-evaluation process, the selection process must begin. The supply manager of the sourcing firm will now invite potential suppliers to submit bids or proposals. A decision is normally made as to whether to use competitive bidding or negotiation, or a combination of the two as the basis for source selection.

Bidding vs Negotiation

When competitive bidding is used by the private sector, request for quotation (RFQ) is traditionally sent to three to eight potential suppliers, depending on the money value and complexity of the purchase. Request for quotation (RFQ) bids ask suppliers to quote the price at which they will perform in accordance with terms and conditions of the contract, in case they are the successful bidder. The conventional bidding process is usually one iteration. In contrast, reverse auctions, use the Internet for online 'real-time' interaction in which the interactions of bids submitted are limited primarily by the time provided by the buyer for the process. In addition, the number of bidders in reverse auctions can be very large. In reverse auctions, caution is taken in opening the bidding process to unqualified suppliers. A two-step bidding process is recommended. Government and public sector purchase managers generally are not able to restrict the number of bidders to only eight. Rather, all suppliers desiring to bid are permitted to do so (for large purchases, the numbers are literally in the hundred). Under competitive bidding, industrial purchase managers generally, but not always, award the order to the lowest bidder. By law, government purchase managers are routinely required to award the order to the lowest (L-1) bidder, provided the lowest bidder is deemed qualified to perform the contract.

Prerequisites to Bidding

The proper use of competitive bidding is dictated by the following criteria. When all criteria prevail, competitive bidding can be an efficient method of source selection and pricing.

(i) The money value of the specific purchase must be large enough to justify the expenses, to both buying and selling firms, that accompanies this method of source selection and pricing.

(ii) The specifications of the item or service to be purchased must be explicitly clear to both the buying and selling firms. In addition, the seller must know from actual previous experience, or be able to estimate accurately from similar past experience, the cost of producing the item, or rendering the service. This is the 'homework' of the purchasing executive in the bidding method.

(iii) The market must consist of an adequate number of sellers. The sellers that make up the market must be technically qualified and actively want the contract—and, therefore, be willing to price competitively to get it.

(iv) The time available must be sufficient for using this method of pricing—suppliers competing for large contracts must be allowed time to obtain and evaluate bids from their sub-contractors before they can calculate their best price. Thirty days is not an uncommon time; however the increasing use of online bidding using the Web is enabling compression of bid preparation time.

Conditions Suited for Negotiation

In addition to satisfying the preceding prerequisites, the following situations should not be present when employing competitive bidding as the means of source selection.

(i) Situations in which it is impossible to estimate costs with a high degree of certainty. Such situations frequently are present with high-technology requirements, with items requiring a long time to develop and produce, and under conditions of economic uncertainty.

(ii) Situations is which the price is not the only important factor. For example, quality, schedule, and service may well be negotiable variables of equal importance.

(iii) Situations in which the buying firm anticipates a need to make changes in the specification, or some other aspect of the purchase contract.

(iv) Situations in which special tooling or set-up costs are major factors. The allocation of such costs and title to the special tooling are issues best resolved through negotiation.

If these conditions are satisfied, then competitive bidding usually result in the lowest price and is the most efficient method of source selection. To ensure that lowest prices are obtained, the competing firms must be assured that the firm submitting the lowest bid will receive the award. If the buying firm gains a reputation for negotiating with the lowest bidder after bids are opened, then future bidders will tend not to offer their best prices initially, believing that they may do better in any subsequent negotiations. They will then adopt a strategy of submitting a bid just low enough to allow them to be included in any negotiations. But their initial bid will not be that low when they are confident that the award will be made to the lowest (L-1) bidder without further negotiation. When any of the prerequisites to the use of competitive bidding are not satisfied, the negotiation process should be employed to select sources to arrive at a price.

Deming has also advocated to 'end the practice of awarding business on the basis of price tag alone' (Foster 2004). Two additional arguments that favour the use of negotiation over competitive bidding for critical procurements are the following.

(i) The negotiation process is far more likely to lead to a complete understanding of all issues of the procurement. This improved understanding greatly reduces subsequent quality and schedule problems.

(ii) Competitive bidding tends to put great pressure on suppliers to reduce their costs in order to be able to bid a low price. This cost pressure may result in sacrifices in product quality, development efforts, and other value-added services.

When all the prerequisite criteria prevail, the competitive bidding system itself evaluates the many pricing factors bearing on the purchase being made. These factors include determinants such as—supplier production efficiency, willingness of the seller to price a particular contract at a low profit, the financial effect on the seller of shortages of capital or excesses of inventories, errors in the seller's sales forecast, and competitive conditions in general.

Two-step Bidding/Negotiation

Many large firms and the government organization use a modified type of competitive bidding called *two-step bidding*. This method of source selection and pricing is used in situations in which inadequate specifications preclude the initial use of traditional competitive bidding. In the first step, bids are requested only for technical proposals, without any prices. The bidders are requested to indicate in their proposals the technical details describing how they would produce the required materials, products, or services. Only after these are found technically satisfactory, the second step follows.

In the second step, requests for quotation (RFQ) are sent only to those sellers who submitted acceptable technical proposals in the first step. These sellers now compete for the business on a price basis, as they would in any routine, competitive-bidding situation. The price is determined in either of two ways: (i) award may be based solely on the lowest price received from those competing, or (ii) the price proposals for the accepted technical approaches may be used as the beginning point for negotiations.

Invitation for Bids/Request for Quotations

Once a decision has been made as to whether to use competitive bidding and/or negotiation as the means of selecting the source, an invitation for bids (IFB) or a request for proposal (RFP)/quotation (RFQ) is prepared. The IFB or RFP normally consists of purchase description of the item or service required, information on quantities, required delivery schedules, special terms and conditions, and standard terms and conditions.

When an RFP is used in anticipation of cost negotiations with one or more suppliers, the purchase manager should request appropriate cost date in support of the price proposal. The purchase manager must also obtain the right of access to the supplier's cost records that are required to support the reasonableness of the proposal. The cost data and the right of access must be established during the RFP phase of the procurement, at a time when potential suppliers believe that there is active competition for the job.

As a part of supplier quality assurance (SQA), many companies ask for a detailed quality information from their suppliers with their bid package while they respond to an RFQ. They may be assigned a supplier quality engineer (SQE) for clarification and technical review meetings after selection. Exhibit 5.2 describes the format for SQA by a leading auto-OEM.

EXHIBIT 5.2 Quality Information Required for Bidding at a Leading Auto-OEM

Please compile the following information in a binder or envelope marked 'Quality' and submit it with your bid package. If you have any question to the required information, please contact your supplier quality engineer for clarification. All information must relate to the manufacturing site where the product will be manufactured and must refer to the RFQ number and part numbers. Be prepared to answer questions during the technical review meeting.

Required Information	Detail
Engineering	
Engineering and Technical Support	• Identify where the engineering and technical support will be located • Explain how they communicate with the manufacturing location
Outsourcing of Prototype Manufacturing (if applicable)	• Include plans for tracking and maintaining responsibility for all prototype tools, parts, and other requirements
Manufacturing	
Facilities	• Identify where the facility is located • Describe the facility's experience with supplying to OEMs • Describe any modifications required by the facility and provide layout • Has any SQE from us reviewed the facilities? If so, who and when?
Preliminary Process Flow Chart	• Identify any special manufacturing techniques, test methods, or containment procedures utilized • Identify any new manufacturing technologies and training needs for the organization
Tooling and Equipment	• Describe in detail what is included in the tooling price

(*Contd*)

EXHIBIT 5.2 *Contd*

Timing Charts	• Highlight any concerns relative to timing that may impact providing a quality process/part on time
Preliminary Process Failure Mode and Effects Analysis (PFMEA)	• Include potential failures, potential causes, and error occurrence prevention/defect outflow detection • Explain how the PFMEA is used for continuous improvement and how lessons learned are incorporated
Environmental Management System	• Proof of compliance to ISO-14001 and other OEM requirements or • Plan for achieving compliance by a certain date

Quality

Preliminary Process Control Plan	• Include error or mistake proofing and any part traceability techniques
Warranty Plans	• Describe plans to meet specified targets • Provide warranty data for similar parts, plans for error proofing, data analysis, and record keeping
Process Capability Studies	• Provide process capability data on similar parts and tolerances
Quality Improvement Plans	• Include quality data showing current performance, continuous improvement methodology, and action plans
Gages/test and Measurement Devices	• Describe in detail what gages/test and measurement devices fixtures are planned to be used
End of Line/Functional Testing	• Describe in detail what continuous compliance testing is planned • Describe the manufacturing facilities' testing capabilities
ISO/TS16949 or QS9000 Registration	• Include proof of registration to specific requirements • If the manufacturing facility does not have registration (suppliers with new facilities), submit registration timeline/implementation plan

New Project/Program Management

Organizational Information	• Provide a company overview highlighting joint venture relationships, business over the time, and import experience (if applicable) • Provide an organization chart identifying people who will be involved in quality and programme management
New Product/Part Launch Experience	• Describe new product/part launches, experiences, and lessons learned
Training Programs	• Describe the operator-training program. Are critical operations identified?

(Contd)

EXHIBIT 5.2 *Contd*

Project Team Coordination and Commitment	• Identify any concerns with any areas of the program execution through the team
Sub-contracting Management	
Sub-contractor Plans	• Describe plan for management of sub-contractors (in-house resources/expertise, advanced product quality planning (APQP), etc.). • Identify proposed component suppliers and/or sourcing plans for sub-contractors • Explain sub-contractor capacity and production plans • Describe plan to manage quality issues related to sub-contractors
Complex Systems/Subassemblies	• Describe experience with complex systems/sub-assemblies • Describe supply chain communication process that supports engineering data, customer requirements, scheduling, etc.
Sequencing	• Describe experience with build in-line vehicle sequence and/or ship in-line vehicle sequence • Describe plan for managing broadcast requirements

Responsibility for Source Selection

While purchasing management has the ultimate responsibility for selecting the right source, the process is handled in many ways. Procedurally, the simplest approach is when a single purchase manager conducts the analysis and makes the selection. A second common approach calls for the use of a cross-functional team consisting of representatives of purchasing management, design engineering, operations, quality, and finance. The third common approach is the use of a product/part team.

Product teams are created to source and manage a group of similar components. These teams frequently consist of purchasing executives, materials engineers, and production planners. Larger teams include a product purchasing manager and representatives of materials, design and manufacturing engineering, quality, and finance. Product commodity teams are essentially a type of cross-functional team, principal difference being that while commodity teams tend to be fairly permanent, cross-functional teams tend to be one-time assignments. A vendor evaluation report for source selection and qualification used in MUL is given in Exhibit 5.3.

EXHIBIT 5.3   Purchasing and Vendor Selection at Maruti Udyog Ltd

The procedure for purchasing at Maruti Udyog Ltd (MUL) stipulates the guidelines for placement of purchase order for finished bought out parts used for manufacture of vehicles and semifinished parts used by machine shop supplied by indigenous sources. This procedure is not applicable to parts supplied by non-indigenous sources.

Procedure for Opening of New Purchase Order

The vendor development department shall give MUL part drawing and other specifications to the vendor for development of parts. Letter of Intent (LOI) shall be placed for all components where prices and terms have been mutually finalized, before commencement of supplies. For all components, where LOI has been placed, purchase order (PO) shall be placed at the start of supplies on the vendor as per MUL terms with the specific part number. For all cases, where prices have not been finalized/LOI has not been issued, a purchase order on adhoc price would be placed to the vendor with the specific part number assigned by the Technical Administration Department (TAD). Approval for the adhoc price shall be taken from the divisional materials head. The prices in all cases would be subsequently finalized and PO terms will be amended accordingly. For the components where there are more than one source, the share of business shall be decided based on quality, adherence to delivery schedules, capacity, and/or price competitiveness. The share of business quantity to be supplied shall be properly informed to the material control department (MCD) that shall send the schedules to the vendors as per the material scheduling procedure.

Revision of Prices

Prices for components shall be negotiated and settled generally for one year. The prices may be revised during the course of the year, as per the negotiated terms and conditions. The authority for negotiation and approving authority have been duly specified by MUL.

Validity of Purchase Order and Part Number Changes

Starting date of the purchase order from which the vendor starts the supply, is always mentioned in the purchase order to control the old stock inventory lying at MUL if any, and/or final approval to be given to the vendor after which it should start supply. If there is any design modification, and if the part number is changed, a new purchase order is opened with the revised part number. The purchase orders and purchase order amendments are kept for a period of seven years in the computer.

Vendor Selection Procedure at MUL

The vendor selection procedure is applicable for selection of vendors for all components (that go into the assembly of vehicles) which are required to be purchased by MUL from outside vendors. The basic aim is to develop a strong and high quality vendor base which helps MUL in maintaining a high quality of its products at the least cost.

(Contd)

EXHIBIT 5.3   *Contd*

The procedure is applicable for vendor selection in the following cases:

(i)   Selection of new vendors
(ii)   Selection of vendor (among existing vendors) for new parts
(iii)   Cancellation of vendor

The controlling department for the total work regarding vendor selection is the concerned vendor development department.

Selection Criteria

MUL sees to it that the vendor should be able to fulfil the company's requirements in terms of quality, delivery, and price as per the details that follow.

(i)   *Quality* Those vendors are selected who are able to supply components with a consistent good quality level as per the company's requirements.
(ii)   *Technology* To produce the desired quality consistently, the vendor should have the requisite technology, design, production, and quality control facilities. In case of new vendors/new components, the vendor should have access to technology, in case it is not already available.
(iii)   *Delivery* The vendor should be in a position to meet the delivery schedules regularly, as required by the company.
(iv)   *Price* After considering the actual cost of production and the above two factors, i.e., quality and delivery, the vendor's prices should be competitive and reasonable.

Those vendors who assist or are expected to assist the company in furthering its objective of producing high quality products at the least cost are to be selected. The financial health of the vendor should be good, and also the management should be competent, and their attitude should be positive and supportive. For safety related and functionally important items, those vendors who have adequate process controls and can ensure consistent quality are selected.

Procedure for Selection of New Vendor

A prospective vendor can approach MUL with a request for selection, or MUL can approach the prospective vendor in its continuous search for good vendors. In either case, the vendor shall submit detailed information regarding its existing operations and its future plans. This would also apply to prospective vendors who do not have any existing facilities but have plans to set up a new project for developing components for MUL. In such cases, the prospective vendor shall submit detailed information about the project. If, on the basis of this detailed information provided by the prospective vendor, it is felt to be a potential source for meeting some of the company's requirements, a visit may be made to the vendor location by the representative of the vendor development department. A vendor evaluation report shall be prepared. The vendor shall be selected for supplying the components only if it gets more than 60 per cent score in the said report. If on the basis of above, the vendor is found promising, an approval is taken for discussing in detail with the vendor the specific components which are likely to be developed with the vendor. On receipt of this approval, component drawings are released to the vendor and he is asked to submit a quotation for the same. Detailed technical discussions specific to the components are also to be held at this

(Contd)

EXHIBIT 5.3 *Contd*

stage by the concerned executive in vendor development to assess the technical suitability of the vendor to manufacture these specific components. Based on the quotation submitted by the vendor, price negotiations and other supply terms shall be conducted with the new vendor by the price negotiation committee. The said procedure applies to all prospective vendors who wish to be considered for development of a component or category of components for MUL. Approval shall be taken from the Managing Director (MD) for issuing LOI to the vendor for the specific components at the negotiated prices and other terms. These may be issued to one or more than one vendor depending upon the requirements of MUL. These vendors (to whom LOI is released) shall be selected among the prospective vendors on the basis of their vendor evaluation report and their negotiated prices. The selection of completely dedicated vendor and/or joint venture shall be done on the basis of experience, reputation, and financial health of individual/company, and approval of the MD shall be taken. In case of joint venture, JV agreement shall be signed and for others LOI shall be issued. On receipt of approval, the vendor shall be registered as a new vendor and a vendor code shall be issued to him. LOI for the specific components shall be issued to the vendor that indicates the intentions of MUL to buy the specified component if the vendor is able to satisfactorily develop the same to the company's quality levels as per the terms of the LOI.

Procedure for Selection of Vendor (among Existing Vendors) for New Components

This procedure is applicable to the selection of vendor (among existing vendors) for new components which need to be procured due to introduction of new models, design changes, etc. This also applies to selection of second or other sources for existing components. The basic selection criteria are the same as cited above. The potential vendors for the new components are identified. Out of the given potential vendors, the first and second vendor (if required) shall be preliminarily selected as per the selection criteria. Approval for the same is taken from divisional head. Detailed technical/commercial negotiations/discussions are conducted with the vendor selected, following which approval is taken for the vendors selected at the negotiated commercial terms and conditions. Based on the approval, letter of intent/purchase order shall be issued to the selected vendor.

Procedure for Cancellation of Vendor

MUL cancels vendors in any of the following cases where

(a) the vendor consistently delivers poor quality which might be established by high rejections, high warranty costs, failure rate, high line rejection rate, or low rating of the vendor

(b) the vendor consistently does not meet the supply schedules placed on him and becomes unreliable

(c) due to poor financial health of the company or the attitude of the management, it is felt that a healthy long-term relationship may not be possible with the vendor

(d) due to any reason, the total procurement from the vendor (in terms of number of components, share of business, or volume of purchase) gets reduced to very low levels.

Cancellation of vendor shall be done after taking prior approval from the Joint Managing Director (JMD). The said procedure applies where the vendor is to be cancelled for some specific components or when it is to be cancelled completely by MUL.

(Contd)

EXHIBIT 5.3 *Contd*

Registration of Vendors

After the selection of the vendor, a vendor code is issued and the same shall be updated in the computer record. If the vendor is expanding at the same location or at different location, or it's name is changing due to some reason, then vendor selection procedure is not applicable. But if the vendor desires a separate vendor code for the new selection, the same could still be issued to the vendor.

Procedure for Vendor Audit at MUL

The vendor audit at MUL aims at continuous supply of good components and consumables from vendors having business relations with the company, and upgrading the quality of parts and consumables by auditing vendors. The procedure is applicable to Indian vendors who are supplying parts and direct consumables to MUL.

Vendors to be Audited

Quality system audit shall be conducted on vendors as per the frequency given in Table 5.2(a). Vendor audits shall be conducted if any quality problem is observed in the components, or if there is any need for process audit, whenever felt necessary by the department managers of vendor development, part engineering (PE), parts inspection (PI), quality assurance (QA), engineering, and Technical Administration Department (TAD).

Audit Planning

All the items including consumables are assigned controlling departments. The controlling department identifies vendors to be audited at the start of year as per criteria given in the table, and identify the responsible departments. The responsible department shall decide the auditors, schedule of audit, and inform the controlling department. The responsible department can request the participation of VD/Engg/QA/PE as required. Audit plan is made on the 'Vendor Audit Plan' format. The concerned Divisional Purchase Manager (DPM) shall appoint the auditors whenever required.

Conducting Audit

Quality system audits for parts are done as per the vendor quality system audit checksheet (parts) using approved drawings, vendors process control standard, and other related standards. In principle, the vendor quality system audit checksheet (parts) covers requirements as specified in *Vendor Quality Assurance Manual*. Similarly quality system audits for direct consumables shall be done as per the vendor quality system audit checksheet (consumables) using approved specification, vendors process control standard, and other related standards. A list of guidance points for auditors for carrying out vendor audit are followed for efficient and effective audit. Auditors, on the basis of audit results, identify the discrepancies along with the improvements required. Auditors should decide the countermeasures alongwith the possible implementation dates with the vendor. Such discussions are duly recorded.

Reporting Audit Results

A report on major discrepancies is filled in 'Vendor Quality System Audit Report' and 'Vendor Audit Follow-up Report' as shown in Table 5.2. The dates of implementation as agreed are filled in

(Contd)

EXHIBIT 5.3   *Contd*

the 'Vendor Audit Follow-up Report'. The Vendor Quality System Audit Report shall be approved by the concerned divisional head. Copies of the Vendor Quality System Audit Report, Vendor Audit Follow-up Report, and the minutes of meeting are sent to the chief executive of the vendor. Wherever the countermeasures and the possible dates of implementation are not decided, a countermeasure report is obtained from the vendor. For the audits mentioned in Item, the report is prepared in 'Minutes of Meeting'. This report shall be approved by the concerned DPM.

Audit Results Check and Countermeasures

Follow-up of implementation status is done in case of all audits. If more than one audit is planned in a year, the results of follow-up are recorded in the 'Vendor audit and Follow-up report'. It is done as per the previous audit/countermeasure report given by the vendor. In addition to the follow-up, a fresh audit is done and the discrepancies observed in the follow-up are filled in with fresh audit report for items. Whether follow-up is required or not is decided by the concerned DPM.

Distribution and Storage

Copies of reports shall be distributed to all the concerned departments and Divisional Heads. Records of vendor audits are stored for a period of 5 years by MUL.

TABLE 5.2   Vendor audit tables

(a) Criteria for Selection of Vendors for System Audit and Frequency of Audit
Classification of Vendors based on Vendor Quality Rating

Class	Rating
A	Above 80%
B	65–80%
C	50–65%
D	Below 50%

Frequency of Audit

Class	Frequency
A	Once/2 years
B	Once/year
C	Once/6 months
D	Once/4 months

If there is vendor quality system audit planned in case of ISO-9000/QS 9000 certified vendors, following is the frequency of the audits.

Class	Frequency
A & B	Once in two years
C	Once/year
D	Once/6 months

(Contd)

EXHIBIT 5.3 *Contd*

(b) Vendor Evaluation Report
Vendor Name:

S.No.	Evaluation Item	Score out of 10	Remarks
1.	Technology This includes availability of product design capability, production process technology, tool/jig designing capability, product testing technology, etc. Technology may have been developed in-house/indigenous or would have been acquired through a collaboration.		
2.	Production Facilities This indicates the quality and sufficiency of production facilities required for the manufacture of targeted items.		
3.	Production Systems This indicates the existence and usage of systems ensuring regular and timely production. This includes production planning, raw materials/parts procurement planning, plant maintenance planning etc.		
4.	Quality Control Facilities This indicates quality and sufficiency of quality control (QC) facilities such as measuring instruments and gauges, metallurgical labs, final inspection facilities, endurance, and environment test facilities.		
5.	Quality Assurance System This indicates the existence and usage of quality assurance system such as incoming inspection, in-process inspection, final inspection, inspection equipment calibration, inspection standards, and process controls, etc.		
6.	Management Competence and Attitude This includes the background, qualification, past performance of management, management's commitment to quality, cost reduction, delivery, and continuous improvement. It also includes management's positive and supportive attitude.		
7.	Manpower Requirements This includes the quality and efficiency of manpower resources of the company, including managerial and worker level manpower resources also.		
8.	Financial Health This indicates the existing financial strength of the company, and its capability to raise finances for further investments in development of new targeted products/projects.		
9.	Localization of Plant/ Communicational Accessibility This indicates the locational proximity of the company to MUL. This also includes the communicational accessibility of the company.		

(Contd)

EXHIBIT 5.3 *Contd*

10.	Existing Customers/their Rating

This indicates the quality of existing customers of the company. It also includes the ratings given by the existing customers to the company (if available).

Total	/100

(c) Information to be Provided by the Prospective Vendors

A. Outline of the company

Name of the company

Address

Works:	Regd. office:
Phone:	Phone:
Telex:	Telex:
Fax:	Fax:
Email:	Email:

Name and designation of contact person:

Date of establishment of company:

If the company belongs to any group, then details:

Name of subsidiary company, if any:

Brief history of the company:

B. Management and Human Resource

Name and brief profile of key management personnel:

Name	Designation	Background

Organization structure: Attach separately

(Quality control personnel to be identified clearly)

Total no. of employees:

C. Production/Quality Control/Tool Making Capabilities

1. List of production/tool room machinery

Description	Model	Nos

Score may be given out of maximum 10 for each item totalling to a maximum of 100 points
Overall Evaluation

Parts for which vendor is recommended

Evaluator	DPM (VD)	DDVM (Matls)

2. List of major quality control equipment:

Description	Model	Nos

3. List of main products being manufactured:

Items	Sale/Year	Production	Customers Capacity

D. Foreign Collaborator (if any):

Scope and nature of collaboration:

(Contd)

EXHIBIT 5.3 *Contd*

Financial position
(Provide the following information for last 3 years)
Year
1. Turnover
2. Profit after tax
3. Profit ability ratio
4. Equity capital
5. Net worth
6. Current ratio
Attach balance sheet for the last three years
Quality control systems
Indicate briefly the quality systems employed by the company:
List of major raw material/parts suppliers
        Item   Supplier
Future plans of the company
        Prepared by   Checked by   Approved by

Source: Vendor Development Department, MUL

SUPPLIER DEVELOPMENT

As manufacturing firms outsource more materials, subassemblies, and even complete products and services to focus on their own core competencies, they increasingly expect their suppliers to deliver innovative and quality product on time, and at a competitive cost. When a supplier is incapable of meeting these needs, a buyer has three alternatives:

1. Bring the outsourced items in-house and produce it internally.
2. Re-source with a more capable supplier.
3. Help improve the existing supplier's capabilities.

The third alternative refers to supplier development.

The strategy of choice often depends on price, volume, or the strategic nature of the procured item. For low value-added, non-strategic commodities, the cost of changing to a new supplier is low, and that may be the best option. At the other extreme, when a poorly performing supplier provides an innovative product or process technology that may provide a sustainable long-term advantage to the buying firm, the supply manager may wish to protect this potential advantage and bring the work in-house, or acquire the supplier. Today, however, most companies prefer to continue outsourcing in an effort to maintain flexibility in meeting changing market demands. Thus, even critical items may be outsourced. This shift toward outsourcing reinforces the need for strong supplier development capabilities. Some experts have concluded that the option of switching to another supplier should be sought only when it is 'absolutely' necessary.

Supplier Development Defined

Supplier development can be defined as 'any activity that a buying firm undertakes to improve a supplier's performance and capabilities to meet the buying firm's supply needs.' Buying firms use a variety of activities to improve supplier performance, including assessing suppliers' operations and processes, providing incentives to improve performance, instigating competition among suppliers, and working directly with suppliers, either through training or other activities. Supplier development may go beyond the tier 1 of suppliers to tier 2 or 3.

Supplier development in world-class firms is proactive. Instead of working with suppliers for quick fixes to problems, supplier development focuses on helping suppliers retain the learning that occurs in the development process. Retained learning is critical for suppliers so that they may continuously improve their own systems. Further, a supplier who has retained its ability to improve can then work with its suppliers to help them improve. The net effect is a more capable, more competitive supply chain.

Supplier development requires that both firms commit financial, capital, and personnel resources to the work; share timely and sensitive information; and create an effective means of measuring performance and progress.

In a study of eight suppliers for the five largest American automobile manufacturers, Hartley and Choi (1996) identified that the automobile manufacturers can use supplier development programs as catalysts of process change within their suppliers. As quoted by Burt, Dobler, and Starling (2003), an executive at Honda of America Manufacturing reported a few years ago, 'If a supplier has a problem that adversely affects us, we'll help it to death!' What that executive implied was that Honda would help the supplier until it achieved and maintained world-class status.

Supplier Performance Gap

There always exists a 'performance gap' between what suppliers are capable of achieving and what they currently demonstrate through their cost controls, delivery schedules, quality performance, customer responsiveness, and services. It is obvious that supply management is responsible for closing this supplier performance gap.

But why may the purchasing management fail at closing the gap of most suppliers? In the last two decades, many original equipment manufacturers (OEMs) such as Sony, Toyota, and IBM have closed their internal operations gap between what they thought they were capable of achieving, and their current performance. Managers of internal operations were successful at convincing top management of the tangible benefits of investing in a variety of management approaches such as total quality management, six sigma, and JIT. In contrast, purchasing management was not very successful at convincing upper management of the benefits resulting from closing gaps between existing practices and world-class ones within its supply base. Support for developing a world-class supplier base remained a secondary priority or, at many companies, was not even a consideration.

When suppliers become proficient at new processes, technologies, improve their quality or delivery performance, or improve their own supply management systems, they bring about cost reductions that benefit themselves as well as the end customer. Other supply chain numbers then also get motivated to do the same.

As has been demonstrated by companies such as Honda and Tata Motors, rapid improvements in supply base performance do not come without an up-front investment. In the late 1990s, John Deere in US added 175 new strategic supply management professionals: 100 for supplier development, 50 for cost management, and 25 for best practices. Similarly, at Honda, purchasing employs over 400 professionals, many of whom are dedicated to supplier development initiatives. As shown in Exhibit 5.4, HP focuses on supplier diversity and a risk assessment programme for supplier management and development.

EXHIBIT 5.4 Supplier Management and Development System at Hewlett-Packard (HP)

HP is known to have significant supplier diversity on a global level and organizes regular supplier events across America, Europe and Canada. It has a unique HP Connect Supplier diversity summits, held at least once annually on an HP campus which provides a forum to qualified suppliers to meet buyers at HP. It gives opportunity to pre-screened minorities and women who owned businesses to participate in 15 minute one-to-one meetings with HP commodity managers and HP tier one suppliers. Through their PartnerONE diversity network, HP provided support to more than 300 diverse sellers in 2008. The support normally comes in the form of subsidies, discounted products, and visibility in a diverse reseller locator. HP's total US spending exceeded targets for small businesses and woman-owned small businesses in 2008.

HP has a unique risk-assessment programme for its vendors in terms of social and environmental responsibility. In 2008, it identified 444 low risk suppliers that do not require audits, audited 142 suppliers for high risk through 2008, would re-audit 85 high risk suppliers at 122 high risk sites and identified 20 new suppliers to be audited at 27 high risk sites in 2009. It has an audit programme in place to raise standards of its supply chain in conformance with standards of electronic industry code of conduct (ECC).

For the capacity building of suppliers, HP frequently collaborates with local NGOs and other local organizations in different regions, e.g., it had worker training program and focused improvement supplier initiative in China, Health Enables Returns Project in Mexico, Hard disk

(Contd)

EXHIBIT 5.4 *Contd*

drive supply chain in S.E. Asia, CSR Europe Responsible Supply Chain Laboratory, Central Europe Supplier Responsibility (CESR) project.

The company has a four phase supplier management system under its SER programme to promote cultural improvement and build suppliers' capability. Over the past six years, all of their product materials, components and manufacturing and distribution services suppliers have completed the first two phases, i.e., introduction and assessment phases. Suppliers move to the next phase of validation based on risk-assessment. Currently, HP concentrates its efforts on the validation and continual improvement phases. The four phases and the corresponding activities are outlined below.

(i) Introduction phase   HP conducts preliminary assessment. The SER requirements are confirmed in contract.
(ii) Assessment   Suppliers complete self-assessment. HP reviews and feedback is shared.
(iii) Validation   On-site audits, corrective action plans, if required.
(iv) Continual improvement   Conduct follow-up audits, identify key education inputs, building supplier capability in long-term by building their skills, tool set and expertise.

Source: Global Citizenship Report, Hewlett-Packard, 2008

Supplier Rating System

A supplier rating system should rest on good supplier performance measurement and evaluation methods. The aim of such methods and systems is to collect and provide information to measure, rate, or rank supplier performance on a continuous basis. The supplier performance measurement system is a critical part of supplier management and development. Key decisions in the implementation of such a system according to Monczka, Trent, and Handfield (1998) are the following.

Performance Variables

This decision is taken with respect to what factors or performance variables to measure, and how to weigh the performance categories. The buying corporate should also decide as to which criteria are objective (quantitative), and which criteria are subjective (qualitative). There could be a wide range of supplier performance variables, but many-a-times, these fall within the following three categories.

(i) *Delivery performance*   A buyer can keep a record of how well a vendor satisfies the quantity requirement, as well as meets the due date commitment. Quantity, lead-time requirements, and due date compliance are essential elements of a supplier's delivery performance.

(ii) *Quality performance*   The purchaser is first supposed to determine and describe the quality performance specifications, and the requirements. Normally, the material receipt section would report about the extent to which a supplier's shipments are meeting the quality criteria. It could well be in terms of number of shipments rejected per delivery of the supplier over a period of time. Installation of supplier quality assurance (SQA) system could also be used as an indicator.

(iii) *Cost reduction*   Buyers often look for cost reduction suggestions particularly from suppliers with whom they have a long-term commitment to supply. A supplier's 'real' cost or 'net adjusted' cost could be estimated against the quoted price of the same supplier, or against other supplier within the same industry.

The buyer can use a number of qualitative factors to assess a supplier's performance. Even the so called qualitative or subjective factors can be assigned a score or rating, say, on a scale of 1 to 5. A purchaser must always decide to have some minimum levels of acceptable supplier performance on each factor. If a supplier falls below anyone, which is minimum, the buyer must closely work with the supplier to improve the rating.

Frequency and Use of Performance Measurement Data

A buyer should always receive a daily (material) receipt report of the previous day's receipts. Respective departments should also send weekly, monthly, or quarterly reports on supplier performance highlighting immediate notice to supplier non-performance on some parameter. Most reports however could be on a monthly or quarterly basis. One-to-one meetings with suppliers are recommended at least once a year. A supplier's poor performance must be immediately brought to the notice of the buyer.

Continuous Performance Measurement

This could help in identification of the supplier for long-term partnerships by putting them on the preferred supplier list because of supplier's good performance. Honda, for example, gives the best performing supplier the first opportunity to bid on new parts, components, and systems. A good measurement system would also enable the buyer to identify performance areas requiring improvement and also helping in future sourcing decisions.

Types of Supplier Rating Systems

Broadly speaking, there are three systems to evaluate supplier performance. These systems differ in the ease of use, level of subjectivity involved, required resources to use the system, and the costs of implementation.

Categorical System

The buyer decides the performance categories and assigns rating to each selected performance category. The data often from several departments, namely material receipt personnel may provide input about the supplier's delivery performance, while quality personnel provide input about the quality performance, say, about the quality level of inbound shipments. This approach is usually subjective, less reliable, and usually based on manual compilation of data. However, it is suited for smaller firms, which are particularly in the process of developing a formal evaluation system. The approach may not provide detailed insight into a supplier performance and also may be based merely on the individual's perception performance, and not on hard data. However, it involves less costs.

Weighted Point System

This system weighs and quantifies the score of a performing supplier across different performance categories. This system is advantageous in that it combines both 'quantitative' and 'qualitative' performance factors into a common system. First, the user must select the performance categories to measure, e.g., delivery, quality, price, service, or others and then decide to assign weight to each performance category on a relative basis. The weighted score or vendor performance measure (VPM), is obtained as

$$\text{VPM} = \sum_{i=1}^{n} W_i S_i$$

where (i = number of performance category factors from 1 to n)

W = weightages assigned to each factor and
S = score of vendor an a scale, say 1 to 5

The weightage assigned would depend on corporate level performance objectives, as well as strategic priority during a particular time frame when vendors are being assessed. The system is thus, also flexible in terms of the weightages assigned to each performance category themselves. The system has higher reliability, and only moderate implementation costs, and most firms like and continue to use it.

Table 5.3 exemplifies the case of using such a system. The scale of supplier's score is 1 to 5 where 1 refers to poor, 2 to fair, 3 to average, 4 to good, and 5 to excellent level of performance.

Cost-based System

This is the most objective of the three evaluation techniques. This approach quantifies the total cost of doing business with a supplier, i.e., it is based on the total cost of ownership (TCO) of a supplier. However, companies may require a computer system for this. The major decision is identification and recording of the costs associated with the suppliers non-performance. A buying company must therefore calculate the additional costs that result wherever a supplier fails to perform as per paid out requirements. An index may be calculated as follows:

TABLE 5.3 Weighted point system

Performance Category	Subjective Factors	Weight	Score	Weighted Score (WS)
Quality	Inbound shipment quality	.10	4	0.4
	Quality improvement	.10	3	0.3
Delivery	On time delay	.25	4	1.0
	Quantity as ordered	.10	4	0.4
Price/cost competitiveness	• Net adjusted price/ real cost compared to other suppliers feasible	.15	2	0.3
	• Number of feasible cost reduction ideas submitted	.10	3	0.3
Service factors	• Response time	.05	5	.25
	• Problem resolution time	.05	3	.15
	• Technical ability to service and maintain	.05	4	.20
	• Support in new product part development	.05	4	.20
Total rating/Aggregated vendor performance measure (VPM)				3.50

$$\text{Supplier Performance Index} = \frac{\text{Purchase price} + \text{Cost of non-performance in any category}}{\text{Purchase price}}$$

The base value of such an index is 1. Over a period of time, the best supplier will have to give lower values. All departments which suffer because of the poor performance of the vendor in any category are involved in estimation of cost associated with each non-performance events. Generating of scrap, reworks, machine failure, large set-up times, or long waiting and lead-time may result in line-stoppages. Stock-out due to late delivery may have impact on the customer's orders, last sales, and line-shutdown costs. The suppliers can be held liable for performance failure and charged back for unplumbed cost in terms of total/partial performance failures which many firms include in their purchasing agreements. Exhibit 5.5 illustrates the vendor rating system in BSNL.

EXHIBIT 5.5 Vendor Rating System at BSNL (A Government of India Enterprise)

BSNL, a leading Government of India enterprise in the telecom services sector, is the world's 7th largest telecommunication company and also the number one Internet Service Provider (ISP) in India. It has a market share of 85% with 35.1 million basic phone subscribers and 92% in terms of revenue. It has more than 2.5 million wireless local loop (WLL) subscribers and 2.5 million Internet customers. The BSNL network covers 602 districts, 7330 cities/towns and 5.9 lakh villages. The

(Contd)

EXHIBIT 5.5 *Contd*

company reported a turnover of Rs 3,51,820 million (US$8 billion) with net profit to the tune of Rs 99,390 million (US$ 2.26 billion) in 2006. The philosophy of vendor rating at BSNL is to help procure equipment/stores from a vendor, who is able to deliver the products of good quality at competitive prices, with deliveries at a stipulated pace for achieving planned and operational targets. Assessment of these qualifications of the vendor on a single point scale to help grading the performance of a vendor is called vendor rating at BSNL.

The vendor getting the highest rating is regarded as V-1 (similar to L-1 or lowest bidder) and the others in the descending order of their rating for the purpose of distribution of quantities of equipment/materials to be ordered—However, the price for procurement will be the lowest evaluated price out of the rates quoted by the vendor selected for ordering on vendor rating basis.
Estimation of Vendor Rating: The vendor rating is calculated as per the formula

$$VR = 0.6PR + 0.3DR + 0.1QR$$

where $\quad$ PR = price rating, DR = delivery rating, QR = quality rating

Price Rating (PR)

The price rating is worked out as: $PR = \dfrac{PL}{PQ}$

$\quad$ PL = Lowest price quoted by a vendor for the product being tendered.
$\quad$ PQ = Price quoted by the vendor being evaluated for the tendered item.

Quality Rating (QR)

If the bidder submits a valid ISO 9001/9002 certificate, a quality rating of 1 is given to the supplier.

Delivery Rating (DR)

The period for calculation of delivery rating will be two years as specified in the bid documents. It is referred to as a WINDOW. All purchase order (POs) issued during the WINDOW are considered for the calculation of the overall delivery rating.
The delivery rating for a PO is given as

$$DR = 0.7 \frac{Q_1}{Q} \left(\frac{T}{T \cdot R + 1.5 \sum \dfrac{T_x \cdot Q_x}{Q}} \right) + \frac{0.3}{P} \sum \frac{Q_i}{Q_P}$$

Where $\quad$ $Q_i < Q_P$
If $\quad$ $Q_1 > Q_P$ then take $Q_i < Q_P$
$\quad$ Q = Quantity supplied within Scheduled Delivery Period (SDP)
$\quad$ Q = Total Ordered Quantity
$\quad$ T = Scheduled delivery period in months

(Contd)

EXHIBIT 5.5 *Contd*

T_x = Time taken beyond SDP in months for each extension including SDP

Q_x = Quantity supplied during each extended period

P = Number of supply slots or segments within SDP

Q_1 = Quantity delivery in a particular supply segment (within SDP)

Q_P = Quantity to be delivered in every supply segment (within SDP); and

$$R = \frac{Q_1}{Q}$$

The overall delivery rating (ODR), taking into account DR for every P>O>, is then given as

$$ODR = \frac{\displaystyle\sum_{i=1}^{n} Q_{oi} \cdot DR_i}{\displaystyle\sum_{i=1}^{n} Q_{oi}}$$

Where

Q_{oi} = Quantity ordered for the ith PO

DR_i = Delivery rating for the ith the PO

N = Number of POs

If the delay is caused due to departmental reasons, or force major conditions, it will not be taken into account in computing delays in supply. Also, for the purpose of calculation of DR, date of delivery is taken as the date of issue of inspection certificate by the quality assurance (QA) wing. However, for the purpose of payments and liquidated damages, delivery is as stipulated in the purchase order. BSNL ensures for computing DR, that the supplies are spread evenly over the scheduled delivery period (SDP) and DR takes into account the supplies required to be made within the period common to both WINDOW and the SDP, and the extension there of outside the WINDOW, if any.

A uniform 60 days of initial segment/slot (including lead period), and 30 days or part thereof for subsequent segments (slots) are presumed, irrespective of time allotted for initial segment in PO to observe a uniform supply principle.

Source: BSNL, New Delhi. The author expresses due acknowledgement to BSNL management for sharing the information through their Manual of Procurement, 2005.

Best Practices in Supplier Development

Burt, Dobler, and Starling (2003) outline the following best practices in supplier development.

1. Create dedicated supplier development teams (with no responsibilities or jobs other than supplier development)

2. Involve suppliers in new product and process development at the buying firm
3. Train supplier how to develop itself for improvement after initial guidance from the supplier development team
4. Focus on underlying causes of long cycle times
5. Focus on wasteful activities in all supplier efforts
6. Provide tooling and technical assistance to suppliers
7. Provide supplier support centres
8. Loan executives, such as process engineers and quality managers
9. Drive out the fear that a supplier's workforce may have towards the supplier development programs
10. Set 'stretch goals' to encourage radical change, as well as continuous improvement
11. Improve accounting systems to enable measurement of improvements
12. Share the savings from the development improvement
13. Encourage suppliers to contribute to improving processes at the buyer's facilities
14. Provide a feedback loop for suppliers to help encourage supplier development efforts
15. Improve the supplier's own supply management system

Experience demonstrates that a buying firm will significantly improve supply chain performance when it develops its supplier's supply management system. Improving the supplying firm's supply management system will reduce the supplier's cost and improve its quality, responsiveness, time to market, continuity, and the inflow of technology from the supplier. While every goal and initiative may not be relevant to a specific supplier, the development team should be able to develop an appropriate action plan. The development team must be aware that the necessary transformation to a world-class status is a process that may require a number of years.

World-class supplier development requires a commitment to collaboration between the customer and the supplier. The commitment must be approached with mutual benefit in mind. Effective supplier development is more than getting cost reductions for a particular part; it means helping the suppliers remove wasteful costs from their processes. The strategic intent is to create win-win opportunities wherein, both the buyer and the supplier gain. For collaboration in supplier development to be successful, the collaboration must have commitment, communication, measurement, and trust.

Commitment for Supplier Development
A supplier development initiative may require supply managers to spend weeks or months in the supplier's facility, working with the supplying firm's management, and operating personnel. Commitment may require the buying firm to provide

financial assistance for the needed equipment and/or training. Commitment requires that the savings from supplier development projects be shared in an equitable way. Effective supplier development looks at all of a supplier's processes with the objective of eliminating waste, and gaining improvements in quality, delivery, cycle time, and costs. Such action requires supplier involvement at the earliest stages of new product development, shared information, and resources. More or less, it requires the buying firm's personnel to treat suppliers as if they were a department within the buying company.

Communication for Supplier Development

According to Forker, Ruch, and Hershauer (1999) 'It is one thing to have a well-designed supplier development programme; it is another thing to assure that the programme is well-communicated and understood by the suppliers.' Proactive collaboration in establishing the priorities, objectives, and methods underlying the implementation of the supplier development program requires highest level of communication.

Measurements for Collaborative Supplier Development

World-class firms want all members of their supply chain to be strong and profitable. However, they must be sure that suppliers are charging them the right fees for their purchasing, processing, and conversion work. This requires both the parties to open their financial records to one another. To many supply professionals, the sharing of financial records and cost data may seem to be a Herculean task. If collaboration efforts are to succeed, sharing accurate costs should be a policy and cultural change that must occur.

Trust for Supplier Development

When undertaking supplier development projects, a tremendous amount of information must pass through both the companies to enable the necessary improvement efforts. In many cases, this information has never been revealed outside of the company. Trust between the two organizations and the involved personnel must be present before the necessary information sharing can, or will take place.

All too often, supply departments do not have accurate cost information to share. Cost management systems must allow appropriate personnel the ability to understand actual costs incurred at the supplier's facility. For example, most accounting systems apply overheads in an inaccurate or distorted manner. This can be a problem in measuring the savings from the supplier development initiatives.

Despite problems in cost measurement accuracy, a simple quote form can provide the starting point for sharing cost information. A quote usually requires suppliers to provide detailed description of every step and its associated costs in the processing of a part or material, and/or provision of a service. An activity-based costing (ABC) statement could also been included in the quote. The quote provides the starting point for a thorough discussion of costs and measurement.

A solution to the trust problem, according to Handfield et al. (2005) is to delegate an ombudsman to overcome a supplier's reluctance to share information. Honda has supplier ombudsmen who deal with the human resource and other issues that are not associated with cost, quality, or delivery. Honda has discovered that suppliers are often more open with these ombudsmen who are not involved in the contract negotiations.

Process of Supplier Development

Different companies bring about supplier development in different ways. However, according to Nelson, Moody, and Stegner (2001), most effective supplier development projects adhere to the following 12 steps.

1. Identify and review performance gap
2. Detailing out as to how the project will be approached and implemented
3. Work to achieve a mutual agreement on project focus deliverables
4. Identify the processes that result in waste
5. Compare performance gaps with the desired goals
6. Establish project metrics and metrics baselines of the metrics selected
7. Gather and analyse data about the past and present performance, and the costs and resources availability, including capacity and capability
8. Develop improvement strategies
9. Develop implementation or action plans
10. Calculate the return on investment
11. Create and review a proposal with the supplier's management
12. Execute the action or improvement plan for supplier development

According to Handfield and Monczka (2005), initial supplier development project is one that is fairly simple and likely to succeed so that the 'biggest quick fix' and the 'greatest good' can occur.

Burt, Dobler, and Starling (2003) quoting a presentation by Butterfield (2001) at the 16th Supply Chain Management Forum at the University of San Diego, US, describe a general process for managing supplier development projects being modelled after similar approaches by Allied Signal and General Electric (GE). The process outlined in the figure that follows (Fig. 5.5), has six phases: initiate project, map and measure, process development, achieve results, control, and team recognition.

Before starting the process, the individuals committed to the development process should be identified, e.g., project champions, development team members, process owners, and higher management representatives. A project champion should be designated from both the supplying and buying firms as he is the key liaison to the top management. He must have sufficient power to provide resources and compliance by non-team personnel, as needed for the project to succeed. The development team members come from both the supplying and buying firms. The primary goal of including the supplier's personnel on the development team is to create self-sufficiency in the supplier's ability to develop its own processes in the future. The process owners are the individuals that actually interact and operate the processes that are under investigation for improvement. Finally, top management from both the firms must be committed to the project, else, a failure is inevitable.

Initiating the Project

In the first phase, the main activities are to develop and confirm a preliminary supplier development charter, define the supplier's processes, assess the customer's needs, and assess the business environment (see Fig. 5.5). The supplier development charter is a firm definition of the project scope and expectations for both the buying firm and the supplier. It essentially serves as an agreement on the expected deliverables. The terminology 'deliverable' is used to define the outcomes of each phase of the project.

After developing the charter, the next step is to define the supplier's processes. The supplier development team narrows the project focus, and further refines its understanding of the related processes. In doing this, the team assesses customer needs, expectations, and requirements for the areas of focus, and translates them into project metrics. Then the team assesses the business environment surrounding the processes and analyses how it affects the areas of project focus.

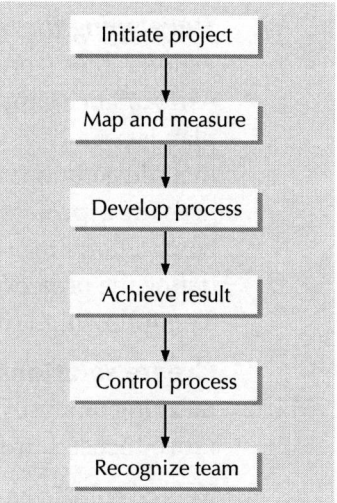

FIG. 5.5 A generic process for supplier development projects
Source: Burt, Dobler, and Starling, 2003, based on a presentation by Butterfield, 2001

Mapping and Measuring

In this phase, the team maps the supplier's process and determines the measurement required. Deliverables from this phase include process maps, a final project charter, and a baseline of 'before the process' improvement.

Map/Analyse supplier processes The team maps the current and ideal processes for areas of project focus. The process maps are usually time-based visual representations of bottlenecks and capacity constraints within a process. This provides the team with the information used to target project activity.

Identify process metrics Metrics that will be used to gauge progress towards project goals are agreed upon and documented.

Collect baseline data Data defining the current process status is gathered. This data helps establish baseline metrics and further verifies process map results.

Analyse baseline data Gaps in the current process are identified through study of the collected data. Opportunities for improvement of manufacturing cycle time, quality, delivery, etc., are prioritized.

Document the baseline Baseline metrics are documented to establish the before project status.

Developing the Supplier Development Process

Deliverables from this phase include a project implementation plan that addresses performance gaps in current processes and drives results. The project implementation plan is usually developed by using a project management software. The plan should include activities required to complete the project, expected completion time of the activities, project milestones, resources assigned to activities, and the expected completion time of the project. The plan is used to track and manage project progress, define the project's critical path(s), and detail the project's activity interdependencies. The following critical activities occur in this phase:

Create solutions The team brainstorms potential solutions and conducts benchmarking analyses where applicable. The output from this activity usually results in more focused process maps.

Select solutions The solution(s) that provide the greatest potential for reducing manufacturing cycle times, improving quality and delivery, or reducing cost drives selection of solution(s). For example, a typical solution in manufacturing environments is to select reducing set-up times as they result in large batch sizes and excess work-in-process.

Develop new process The new process is detailed further through study and brainstorming. The outcome of this activity is a new process.

Plan implementation The team works with relevant personnel to develop and propose a detailed implementation plan.

Achieving Results

In this phase, the project team executes the implementation plan, conducting any necessary simulations, pilots, and releases. The key deliverable from this phase is a new, lean process that has been implemented, documented, and is actually demonstrating results.

Relevant personnel, such as engineers or information technology specialists from the buying firms, are made available to assist the implementation team in keeping the project on schedule. Direction and resources are provided as required by the project champions. Project progress is communicated to the upper management, champions, and process owners at designated times, as defined by the supplier development team.

The process is documented for clarity and consistency. This documentation may include procedures, maps, flowcharts, and operational method sheets, as well as training plans, schedules, and periodic audit points. A process plan that draws the footprint of the process areas affected is developed, showing workstations, control points, and material movements.

Controlling the Supplier Development Process

In this phase, plans and documentation are created to ensure consistent implementation of the process with minimized variation. Ongoing metrics are defined to allow review of the process. A closed-loop corrective action procedure system is installed to review the process, address gaps in performance, and continuously improve performance.

The deliverables from this phase are a process control plan and a corrective action plan. The former is used to ensure that activities in the process are executed and addresses all the critical elements of the process. The latter checks what occurs in the event of a non-conformance in the process, so that it is eliminated and recurrence is prevented, with verification that proposed corrections are effective.

Recognizing the Team

The final phase provides team recognition. Activities are organized by the project team, project champions, and process owners to promote the success of the project. In this phase, the team shares the lessons learnt and best practices with the supplier's organization.

The project results may be published on the supplier's website to share with the rest of the supply chain. Learning experiences from completed projects are shared within the suppliers' organization and the supplier management groups. Process owners use best practices to refine key processes, such as charters, process mapping, set-up reduction, cost, training, and information systems. Formal events may be organized to recognize implementation team accomplishments, and share the experiences. Exhibit 5.6 describes the supplier development process.

EXHIBIT 5.6   Sourcing Strategies at TATA Motors

Tata Motors is reported to have reaped significant benefits using value analysis as a method of cost-erosion in direct material costs in collaboration with their vendors, since 62 per cent of the costs are associated with purchase of raw materials and components. Every one was given a cost-erosion target in his area. A total of 16 cross-functional teams were formed. The three tier teams focused on key areas, namely

(a) value engineering,
(b) vendor analysis and rationalization, and
(c) e-procurement.

Under vendor analysis, the company analysed its relationship with vendors in terms of bargaining power and purchasing value involved with them. The best and capable vendors were identified in each field/technology area. These vendors were then selectively integrated into the product design/process stage itself. It was followed by e-validation and registration of vendors on to the SRM portal, developed by ARIBA for them, so that these vendors could take part in online bidding using reverse-auctions on a global basis. The company has saved Rs 4 billion by efforts in the three areas stated earlier.

The company also launched a project called VECTOR—Vendor Enhancement by Collaboration through Technology and Operational Restructuring—in 1994 with a purpose, as the company puts it, to revolutionize the supply chain by uncovering the hidden value through technology-driven sourcing. The steering committee of this project constituted of all the plant heads. It aimed to develop suppliers' capability, and reduce the costs and cycle times from design to delivery through collaborative efforts. The other goal was to make visible globally the expenditure on materials for better negotiation power, get competitive price through quick sourcing (ARIBA's Quick Source) by live auctions, and rationalizing the vendors based on their performance measurements/benchmarking against predetermined key performance indicators (KPIs) such as delivery, reliability, and compliance regarding the data which lie in the supply relationship management (SRM) portal, or any of its back-end systems. In value analysis, for example, the company changed from copper brass radiators to aluminium radiators which reduced the costs as well as improved the performance. Concerted effort was made by the company to remove excess material in all the forgings/castings designs. Only minimal and necessary allowances were kept to reduce the weight of such components. Though this called for higher accuracy of the forging/ casting processes, the cost of the design was still reduced. The company also found that value addition at different stages of manufacturing carried out at its premises invited the VAT, the Value Added Tax. It therefore adopted the strategy of procuring only the final parts from its vendors.

Source: Ariba Consulting, 2008. The author expresses due acknowledgement

Barriers to Supplier Development
The following factors could act as barriers to effective supplier development.

• Poor communication, feedback, and general complacency

- Misguided improvement objectives
- Lack of clarity and commitment for performance, and its improvement
- Misaligned sourcing and performance metrics
- Hiding of the operations' and materials' problems by either party
- Resources' limitations
- 'Always blame the supplier' culture
- Lack of trust, sharing of information, and confidentiality issues
- Poor contractual planning and execution
- Imbalance of power in the relationship with the supplier
- Misconceptions regarding purchasing power

The leader for the supplier development team must clearly delineate potential rewards for the supplier's organization during preliminary meetings with the supplier's top management. Otherwise, the supplier's personnel may not become fully committed to the effort, and remain unconvinced that the development effort will benefit their organization. They may even agree to initial proposals but fail to implement them on account of insufficient dedication.

Handfield et al. (2005) observe, 'One of the biggest challenges in supplier development is cultivating mutual trust. Suppliers may be reluctant to share information on costs and processes; the need to release sensitive and confidential information may compound this hesitation. Ambiguous or intimidating legal issues, and ineffective lines of communication also may inhibit the trust building necessary for a successful supplier-development effort.'

STRATEGIC SOURCING DECISIONS

Not all suppliers need development, but to reach the level of a world-class collaborative relationship, development is needed. Even suppliers recognized as the best of the best require investment on the part of the buying firm to realize the full benefits of the collaborative relationship.

In many instances, the buying firm may be unable to identify a world-class supplier that is willing to meet its needs. If the requirement is sufficiently important, the buying firm will select the most suitable supplier(s), and then develop the supplier into one capable of meeting its present and future needs. Training in project management, teamwork, quality, production processes, and supply management prove has been to be a worthy investment. Such training has always been provided by leading customer firms to their suppliers.

The purchasing manager should ensure that suppliers perform as required, or that appropriate corrective action is taken to upgrade or eliminate them from the firm's supplier base.

The purchasing management must, therefore on a periodic basis, analyse its suppliers' abilities to meet the firm's long-term needs. Areas that deserve particular attention include the supplier's general growth plans, future design capability in relevant areas, the role of purchasing management in the supplier's strategic planning, potential for future production capacity, and financial ability to support such growth.

If present suppliers appear to be able to meet future requirements, the purchasing company may assist the appropriate supplier(s) with financing and technological assistance. It may develop new sources having the desired growth potential, or it may have to develop the required capability internally.

Early Supplier Involvement

In new product development and specifications and standardization, early supplier involvement (ESI) is an approach in purchasing management to bring the expertise and collaborative synergy of suppliers into the design process. ESI seeks to find a win-win opportunity in developing alternatives and improvements to materials, services, technology, specifications and tolerances, standards, order quantities, lead-time, processes, packaging, transportation, redesigns, assembly changes, design cycle time, and inventory reductions. ESI is an accepted way of life at many proactive firms, which helps in developing trust and communication between suppliers and the buying firm. It normally, but not always, results in the selection of a single source of supply. The selection process is the result of intensive competition between two or three carefully prequalified potential suppliers. The company selected becomes the single or primary source of supply for the life of the item. The results of ESI translate into tangible cost savings. For example, Delphi Automotive Systems's suppliers helped design the 1998 Honda Accord and, as a result, saved over 20 per cent of the cost of producing the car.

Supply Base Consolidation

One of the interesting phenomenon taking place in purchasing management is the change from enlarging the firm's supply base to downsizing the same. Reduction of the supply base is usually achieved through both reducing the variety of items procured, and consolidating items previously procured from different suppliers into one supplier.

Examples of supply base rationalization success stories are in plenty. For example, Xerox reduced its supply base by 92 per cent in the early 1980s—from 5000 to 400 suppliers. Chrysler winnowed its supplier base from a mass of 2500 in the late 1980s to a lean, long-term nucleus of 300. During the 1990s, suppliers loved working for Chrysler, and for obvious reasons—the company's production volume was growing rapidly. It included suppliers in development activities from day one, and took their suggestions seriously for design improvements and cost reductions. Chrysler had replaced its adversarial bidding system with one in which the company designated suppliers for a components and then used target pricing to determine with suppliers the component prices, and how to achieve them. Most parts were sourced from one supplier for the life of the product. Similar supply base reductions have been accomplished at other major corporations. According to Carbone (1999), IBM used 50 suppliers for 85 per cent of its productions requirements while Sun Microsystems used 40 suppliers for 90 per cent of its production material needs. However, such accomplishments may generally require significant research and development expenditures, and/or capital investment. MUL and Tata Motors have followed vendor rationalization in a big way like many others.

Single Sourcing vs Multiple Sourcing

These decisions may affect the success or even the survival of the purchasing firm. The major argument for placing all of a firm's business with one supplier is that in times of shortage, this supplier will give priority to the needs of a special customer. Single sources may be justified when

1. quality considerations hold paramount significance
2. lower total costs results from a much higher volume (economies of scale)
3. the buying firm obtains has got influence or clout with the supplier
4. lower costs are incurred to source, process, expedite, and inspect
5. the quality control and coordination is required in JIT manufacturing environment source
6. special tooling is required and the use of more than one supplier is impractical or excessively costly
7. significant reduction in freight costs is the objective
8. total systems inventory is to be generally reduced
9. more reliable, shorter lead times are required
10. time to market is critical

A common approach to multiple sourcing that can still yield many benefits of single sourcing is the '70-30' approach. Through the award of 70 per cent of the volume to one supplier and 30 per cent to a second supplier, economies of scale are obtained from the 'big supplier' while the 'little supplier' provides competition. Using the '70-30' strategy, when the 70 per cent supplier misbehaves, its volume is reduced to 30 per cent and the smaller supplier is awarded an increase to 70 per cent. Although the '70-30' strategy is reported to have started in Japan in the 1970s with JIT firms, the strategy is firmly established in many world-class companies. Most OEMs in

India also use more or less the '70-30' approach in sourcing selected materials. Dual or multiple sourcing may be appropriate when it is required to

- protect the purchasing company from shortages, strikes, and other emergencies at supplier's end
- maintain competition and provide a backup source
- meet local content requirements for international manufacturing locations
- meet customers' volume requirements
- avoid complacency on the part of a single-source supplier
- have certainty in unpredictable or unstable technology
- avoid situations when suppliers tend to leapfrog each other technologically

The term 'collaborative relationship' specifies neither the presence nor the absence of a single-source relationship. That is, the buying firm may have one, two, or three 'partners' for the same item, although the preferred trend is towards single sourcing.

Supplier's Capacity Share

Many companies try not to exceed a limited per cent, say, 20–25 per cent of a supplier's capacity (Dobler, Lee, and Starling 2003). That is, a company might contract for 20 per cent of a firm's production capacity, but purchase 100 per cent of a specific product from the firm. If its purchases represent too large a share of the supplier's business, and if the buyer discontinues a product or purchases an item from another supplier, this could put the supplier in a very difficult financial situation.

Choice of a Manufacturer or Distributor as a Supplier

In deciding whether to buy from a manufacturer or distributor, a purchasing manager's considerations should focus largely on the distributor's capabilities and services, not only its location. If a buying firm wishes to purchase directly from the manufacturer and bypass the distributor, it usually foregoes certain special services that a competent distributor is equipped to offer. Distributors, for example, may have cutting and shaping tools, and skilled personnel to operate them. They maintain large, diverse inventories. They are also able to perform many customized services.

When the materials ordered from a distributor are shipped directly to the user by the manufacturer (a drop-shipment), an additional buying decision becomes necessary. In this situation, the distributor does not handle the materials physically; it acts only as a broker. Under such circumstances, a purchase manager is strongly motivated to buy directly from the manufacturer.

Purchasing managers should be aware that distributors stock many products. Hence, ordering from a distributor can significantly reduce the total number of orders a supply manager must place to fill some of the materials requirement. If there were no distributors, orders for production as well as maintenance, repair, and operations (MRO) requirements would all have to be placed directly with many different manufacturers. This obviously would increase direct supply management costs. Further, for every additional purchase order placed, an additional receiving inspection, and accounts payable operation is to be executed.

However, the functions of distribution cannot be eliminated. The purchasing manager needs most of these functions therefore, the purchasing manager should pay for them once but not twice. Either the distributor or the manufacturer must perform the essential distribution functions of carrying the inventory, giving technical advice, rendering service, extending credit, and so on. The supply manager must decide for each individual buying situation how to best purchase the functions needed.

Green Purchasing

Environmentally sensitive purchasing makes good business sense. There is this story of young Henry Ford. It seems that Mr Ford was very explicit in the dimensions and quality of the lumber used in constructing the packing crates his suppliers used to ship parts to Ford. One day, one of the suppliers asked a Ford employee why a throwaway packing crate had to be made to such explicit specifications. The answer was 'because we use the wood to build the floorboards of our Model T.' So, Mr Ford was an environmentalist as well as a good businessman.

Environmentally sensitive supply management comprises two components.

(i) The purchase of materials and items which are recyclable and
(ii) The environmental and liability issues associated with the use, storage, and disposal of hazardous materials anywhere in the supply chain.

Companies like Hewlett-Packard and Nokia have specific purchasing and supply requirements to address the environmental issues.

Environmental and Liability Issues

The buying firm's environmental engineer should study the firm's value chain to identify the possible uses and disposal methods for environmentally hazardous substances and materials. It is quite possible that a supplier who disposes of hazardous waste in an environmentally unsafe manner, while producing a product for the buying firm, may subject the buying firm to financial liability, should the supplier have limited financial resources. Current statutes cover present and previous operators and owners. Additionally, purchasing management has a responsibility to ensure that a supplier's salvage and disposal contractors meet occupational safety and health administration (OSHA) standards both prior to and during performance under the contracts. One way to deal with this is to require the supplier to execute adequate performance and liability bonds.

Net-sourcing and E-procurement

Internet has enabled companies to manage supply more efficiently and effectively. The supply management professional can now locate and research new suppliers by accessing information on the Internet. It has become an open market for electronic business transaction. Many tactical purchasing management activities can be replaced using electronic forms and direct connectivity with suppliers. Intranets have become a way to provide services to personnel by connecting employees directly with preferred providers. The Web offers an aggregation of common business tools allowing more efficient management of many business processes. The Internet can replace many different services and functions, including human resources, accounts payable and receivable, and document storage systems.

Many companies are outsourcing infrastructure development and maintenance to what are termed as Net-sourcers who are defined as suppliers of a highly available, scalable, high-performance platform for hosted business applications. Many companies are not readily staffed with personnel who can manage the complex infrastructure and websites necessary to keep a company competitive in the e-business marketplace. Outsourcing network infrastructure development and maintenance has become popular, since it allows a company to achieve high performance and a strong presence online quickly with the flexibility to make changes. Net-sourcing is considered to be adding significant value by providing sustained performance and operational support. Many companies prefer to outsource these activities in order to eliminate the need to train or hire specialized personnel.

E-procurement

The B2B purchases and sale of supplies and services through the Internet, as well as other information and networking systems, such as electronic data interchange (EDI) and enterprise resource planning (ERP) is electronic-procurement (e-procurement). An example of e-procurement is given in Exhibit 5.7. An important part of many B2B sites, e-procurement is also referred to as supplier exchange. Generally, e-procurement websites allow qualified and registered users to look for buyers or sellers of goods and services. Depending on the approach, buyers or sellers may specify prices or invite bids. Transactions can be initiated and completed. Ongoing purchases may qualify customers for volume discounts or special offers. Participating companies expect to be able to control parts' inventories more effectively, reduce purchasing agent overheads, and improve manufacturing cycles. E-procurement is expected to facilitate a computerized SCM environment.

There are six main types of e-procurement:

Web-based ERP   Creating and approving purchasing requisitions, placing purchase orders, and receiving goods and services using a software system based on the Internet.

EXHIBIT 5.7   E-procurement at IBM

IBM started its business with 12,000 suppliers over the Internet in 1999 by first sending purchase orders, receiving invoices, and paying suppliers, all using the World Wide Web as its transaction processing network. The company found it relatively easier to engage these suppliers in business on the Internet rather than meeting the resistance of its suppliers to link to IBM via electronic data interchange (EDI).They baulked at EDI because of the large expense of a special software needed and a value added network (VAN), which were required to do EDI with the company. So, the Internet's simplicity reduced the costs not only for its suppliers but also for IBM. IBM estimated a saving of US$500 million in 1999 by switching to e-procurement. IBM is known to use the Web to manage multiple tiers of suppliers and as a means to work with suppliers to improve quality and reduce costs though most of the savings came from eliminating the intermediaries. However, cost reduction was not the only reason IBM switched to e-procurement. The company made Web-based procurement a key part of its supplier management strategy. IBM perceived great value in using the Internet to collaborate with suppliers and tap into their expertise much more quickly than earlier. The Internet will also allow IBM to collaborate with suppliers over scheduling issues. If the company wants to increase production of a certain product, it will be able to check with component suppliers and determine if suppliers can support such an increase. If there are schedule cutbacks, it will be able to notify suppliers almost instantaneously and excess inventory can be avoided. IBM did not want to manage the supply chains in a sequential manner, the way they are. It, rather, wanted to use Internet to manage multiple layers of suppliers simultaneously. IBM sent forecasts and purchase orders to the contract equipment manufacturers (CEMs) for the printed circuit boards (PCBs) they supplied. It also dispatched the requirements to all the component manufacturers and they shipped parts directly to the CEM. By doing so, the company estimated that it saved more than $150 million in 1999.The savings were accrued mainly due to the difference between CEMs price for components used on the PCBs and IBM's price that it had negotiated with the component suppliers directly. Since the Internet is greatly important to IBM's supplier management strategies, IBM tried to make its suppliers to do business over the Web. The company developed a Web-based portal to provide a single entry point. As is usual with most large companies, IBM has multiple interfaces with its suppliers, including engineering, quality, as well as purchasing and more often than not, suppliers may have to connect to separate universal resource locators (URLs) in a company. IBM's portal provides a single point of entry for suppliers, facilitating the suppliers to do business with IBM thereby increasing the speed of supply chain. Because of short product life-cycles, speed is very important in computer electronics industry. IBM also saw opportunity in using the Internet to strengthen the relationships with suppliers and also develop strategic appliances with some of the suppliers as it was difficult to build strategic alliances with suppliers who were located as far as 1200 miles away.

The Internet also will play an important role in IBM's general procurement....IBM was doing EDI with core production suppliers, but not with other forms of general procurement. Purchasers were still faxing and phoning orders, which is timely and costly. Additional cost savings would accrue from small volume, one-of-a kind special purchases, because of the speed and ease of using the Internet.

Source: Based on Carbone, James (March 2000), 'E-Procurement at IBM: POs are Just the Beginning', *Purchasing,* 128, no. 4, p. S50

E-MRO   The same as Web-based ERP except that the goods and services ordered are non-product related MRO supplies.

E-sourcing   Identifying new suppliers for a specific category of purchasing requirements using the Internet.

E-tendering   Sending requests for information and prices to suppliers, and receiving the responses of suppliers using the Internet.

E-reverse auctioning   Using the Internet to buy goods and services from a number of known or unknown suppliers.

E-informing   Gathering and distributing purchasing information both from and to internal and external parties using Internet technology.

Web-based ERP   It brings all the details of the functions of an enterprise into a single integrated database. It increases ROI in terms of order capture and fulfilment time, product development and manufacturing, and delivery cycle times.
The need for a Web-based ERP is as follows.

- It can be implemented in small bits and pieces, i.e., in terms of function or section-wise computerization. So it becomes easy for the companies to purchase and implement Web-based ERP systems. However, most of the ERP packages are available in full packs only, and most of its sections are unused in the companies who had already implemented them.
- It can be maintained by the company which developed it online. So it becomes more effective and best service is guaranteed to all buyers. Its yearly maintenance becomes cheap. ERP packages are highly technical and it takes a lot of work to customize these to the company's individual needs. Hence, after spending huge amounts of money and time on implementation, the people who did it have to be handsomely paid for further yearly maintenance. As a result, the cost shoots up and becomes unmanageable for the companies at some point of time.
- Web ERP is accessible both offline and online. Hence, in a globalized market, the chief executive can have the convenience of making even his hotel room, or the familiar home desk his convenient office table, just by hooking up his laptop to the Net. In case, ERP is offline, it is accessible in an Intranet network (if it is planned that way).

E-sourcing   It simply uses Web-based platforms to support all steps in the sourcing process, including expenditure analysis, demand aggregation, requirements definition, supplier discovery, negotiations (RFI, RFP, and RFQ), i.e., requests for indent/proposal/quotation), reverse auctions bid evaluation, and contract management. Each case should be carefully analysed before inviting suppliers to participate in e-sourcing events. All suppliers entering into e-sourcing business should undergo a comprehensive sourcing process.

E-sourcing is intended to

- save time through seamless information transfer
- improve productivity with template reuse, such as project templates, RFQ templates, and documents
- enable full transparency when monitoring or reporting
- create collaboration between key stakeholders and team members
- ensure unified measurement of KPIs and follow-up on sourcing goals on equal terms
- increase savings by strong functionality with scenario building possibilities, enabling more informed and constructive decisions

E-tendering An electronic tendering solution facilitates the complete tendering process from the advertising of the requirement up to the placing of the purchasing order. This includes the exchange of all relevant documents in an electronic format.

Similar terms used are RFQ (request for quotation), RFP (request for proposal), RFT (request for tender), and e-bidding.

Some e-tender solutions are packaged with evaluation tools, which assist in comparing tenders from suppliers in order to select the winning tender. E-tendering is similar to request for quotation (RFQ). The latter is sometimes included as part of the functionality of an e-tender system.

Benefits of using e-tendering E-tendering reportedly results in

- Reduced tender processing cycle time
- Fast and accurate pre-qualification and evaluation, which enables the automatic rejection of suppliers that fail to meet the tender specifications
- Faster response to questions and points of clarification during the tender period
- Reduction in the labour intensive tasks of receipt, recording, and distribution of tenders' submissions
- Reduction of the paper trail on tendering exercises, thereby reducing costs to both buyer and suppliers
- Improved audit trail increasing integrity and transparency of the tendering process
- Improved quality of tender specification and supplier response
- Provision of quality management information and better compliance with standards

Manual tender processes can often be long and cumbersome, often taking up to three months, which is costly for both the buyer and supplier organizations. Buyers are able to manage the tenders coming in, with all tenders stored in one place. Buyers can cut and paste data from the electronic tender documents for easy comparison in a spreadsheet. Evaluation tools can facilitate sufficient automation of this comparison process.

Suppliers' costs in responding to invitations to tender (ITT) are also reduced as the tender process cycle is significantly shortened.

E-tendering offers an opportunity for automating most of the tendering process; right from preparing the tender specifications, advertising, tender aggregation, to bids' evaluation, and placing of the contract.

Reverse auctions A reverse auction (also called procurement auction, e-auction, sourcing event, e-sourcing, or e-RA) is a tool used in industrial B2B procurement. It is a type of auction in which the roles of the buyer and seller are reversed, with the primary objective to drive purchase prices downward. In an ordinary auction (or also known as forward auction), buyers compete to obtain a good or service. In a reverse auction, sellers/suppliers compete to obtain business from the buyers by quoting lowest prices and offering better conditions.

Buyers, sellers, and market makers are expected to adhere to auction rules and industry codes of conduct for the use of reverse auctions, if they exist. Problems arise when one or more parties fail to conform to the auction rules. This can range from simple cries of 'foul' to litigation. Buyers should not assume that reverse auctions will, in every case, deliver cost savings—either on a unit or total cost basis. Reverse auction savings can range from negative (i.e., it costs the buyer money) to neutral (i.e., no savings) to positive savings (average gross of 10–20 per cent, but net savings is typically half or less).

The resulting savings cannot be truly represented unless unit price-focused purchasing metrics such as 'purchasing order cost variance', or 'material price variance' are used. Instead, total cost savings must be calculated, inclusive of direct and indirect losses associated with using reverse auctions, implementing reverse auction results, subsequent procurement activity, and related activities such as customer returns, defective goods or services, warranty expenses, and litigation, etc.

Suppliers are advised to ensure that value proposition exists for them, in case they participate.

Reverse auctions can also be characterized as a technologically assisted form of 'zero-sum' power-based bargaining, or as 'going in reverse' with respect to developing buyer–seller relationships, collaboration, and purchasing process improvement. Reverse auctions have also been criticized as 'bid shopping' when a buyer uses a supplier's bid to obtain lower prices from other suppliers. Suppliers seeking to avoid reverse auctions can create unique intellectual property, expand the value propositions for its customers by creating new products and services, or seek to extend or improve collaborative activities with their customers.

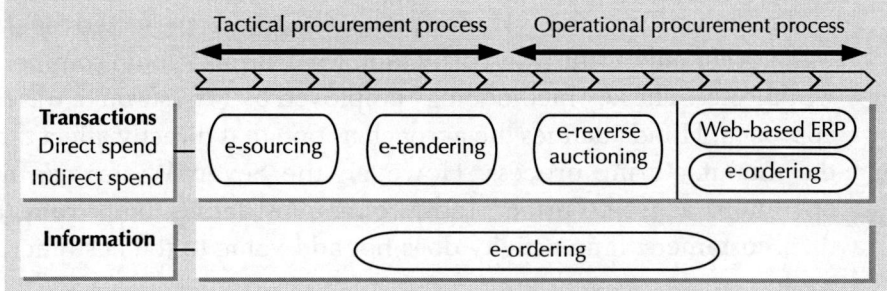

FIG. 5.6 The elements of e-procurement system

Reverse auctions used in industrial B2B procurement and expenditure management activities remains controversial, both within buying organizations, among suppliers, and among the researchers who study them. As such, buyers considering the use of reverse auctions should carefully evaluate all available information, to ensure that better informed business decisions are made.

E-informing This is the process of gathering and distributing purchasing information both from and to internal and external parties, using the Internet. For example, posting purchasing management information on an Extranet that can be accessed by internal clients and suppliers is a kind of e-informing. This form is also called purchasing intelligence which can be used for expenditure control.

The different elements of the e-procurement system studied till now are illustrated in Fig. 5.6.

CONTINUOUS IMPROVEMENT OF SUPPLIERS

The continuous improvent of suppliers is aimed at bringing about value addition in the processes, parts, and materials in use at their end.

Elimination of Waste

A cornerstone of continuous improvement and JIT philosophies is the notion of reduction, and eventual elimination of waste. A supply manager can just walk through a supplier's facility and discover many problems. This is a common approach to assess a supplier. The traditional term for the activity when it occurs internally in one's own organization is management by walking around (MBWA), but there is absolutely no reason why purchasing professionals should not apply the same concept when assessing suppliers. Ultimately, however, decisions regarding suppliers should be based on measurable metrics.

Tadamitsu Tsurouka, a Honda process engineer, perfected the skill of identifying waste. After only a whirlwind plant tour, Mr Tsurouka could comment on the facility's weaknesses. The key methodology employed by Mr Tsurouka was the Seven Wastes approach. Honda defines the aproach as one that directly affect the productivity of the manufacturing process. However, the Seven Wastes can apply to service operations as well. Further, most companies define them from the viewpoint of their customers. If an activity does not add value to the customer, it is considered waste.

Waste 1—Overpopulation

This waste is more commonly referred to as overproduction in manufacturing environments. The waste of overpopulation exists when a firm is producing more than is required. Overpopulation causes scheduling problems and costs money by carrying excess inventories.

Waste 2—Idle Time

Idle time is waste built into the production or service process. Idle time in manufacturing usually accumulates when operators watch a machine run, or take too much time fixing a part, while the machine remains idle.

Waste 3—Transporation

Transporation is waste because it adds cost without value. Honda measures part travel distance in feet and counts the number of times a part is touched before completion as the basis of the part's delivery metric.

Waste 4—Processing Itself

Although most manufacturing professionals understand the need for an efficient set-up, the majority of manufactures treat mould/die change as break-time from production, a time when the crew can take as much time as it needs. Similar waste exists in service processes, such as purchase order processing.

Waste 5—Inventory

All inventory—raw materials, work-in-process, and finished products should be at an absolute minimum. The results of inventory waste include high carrying costs, transit damage, and excess materials handling systems.

Waste 6—Operator Movement

Any movement in which the operator does not add value to the part or service is a waste.

Waste 7—Rejected Parts

One of the quickest ways to improve productivity is to eliminate rejected parts. Every reject includes not only the loss of that product, but also the forgone opportunity to make a good part.

Value Analysis/Value Engineering

Value analysis and value engineering (VA/VE) are common approaches to improving products and processes. In both value engineering and value analysis, value is usually defined from the viewpoint of the customer who will use the product or process. Based upon this fundamental understanding, the common question asked in all value-based analyses is, 'Does this add value to the customer?' If the answer is no, then there is high probability that whatever 'this' is (cost, action, part, step, feature, tolerance), it is waste that can be reduced or eliminated. Although the technique is applied commonly in manufacturing, value analysis has been applied to a broad range of activities and supply related problems outside the manufacturing area. Applications range from the design of operating systems, to the development of corporate reengineering projects, to the procurement of services and transportation.

Value Engineering

As the name implies, value engineering takes place in the design process before a product is in production, or a process has been implemented for the first time. Value engineering usually entails a systematic study of all phases of the design of a given item or process in relation to the function (value) the finished product or process is to perform. Value engineering recognizes that the design provides the greatest opportunity for reducing costs in a proactive manner.

Value Analysis

If value engineering (VE) is no longer a possibility, then value analysis is used. Unlike value engineering, value analysis (VA) takes place after a product has been produced, or after a process has been implemented. As such, value analysis is reactive, and provides less opportunity to reduce total costs over the lifetime of a design or process. However, the opportunity to reduce costs is still great in many situations, which is why value analysis remains a common approach in most industries.

VA/VE Techniques

Although different companies focus on different variations of the fundamental idea, two general conceptual tools are basic to the operation of a VE/VA programme—design analysis and cost analysis. Both design and cost analysis focus on the same required product, part, material, or process. However, design analysis focuses strictly on the features, functionality, and fitness for use from the perspective of the customer.

Cost analysis links the design features to numerical values that can be easily compared. For example, a customer may want a wooden dashboard in a car, but the cost of the wooden dashboard would increase the costs of the product beyond the financial resources of the customer. Hence, design features must be coupled with costs to evaluate value.

One technique many firms use in analysing component parts of a subassembly is to dismantle, or 'explode' the unit, and then mount each part adjacent to its mating part on a pegboard or a table. The idea is to demonstrate the functional relationships of the various parts visually. Each component can thus be studied, as it relates to the performance of the complete unit, rather than as an isolated element. Typical questions that are included in the value analysis checklist of a part include the following.

1. Can any part be eliminated without impairing the operation of the complete unit?
2. Can a part be simplified to reduce its basic cost?
3. Can a part be changed to permit the use of less costly production methods?
4. Can less expensive but equally satisfactory materials be used in the part?
5. If the item is not standard, can a standard item be used?
6. Is there a similar item in inventory that could be substituted?
7. Are closer tolerances specified than are necessary?
8. Is unnecessary machining performed on the item?
9. Are unnecessarily fine finishes specified?
10. Can the item be made less expensively in another plant?
11. Can the item be bought for less?
12. Is the item properly classified for shipping purposes to obtain lowest transportation rates?
13. Can cost of packaging be reduced?
14. Are suppliers being asked for suggestions to reduce cost?

Figure 5.7 displays the different phases of the value analysis study.

Process Value Analysis

Value analysis of a process is usually referred to as a process value analysis (PVA). Although value analysis does include the analysis of processes, the use of the term PVA creates better clarity. As with VA, PVA inherently assumes that the process is already in existence. Although more proactive than PVA, very rarely do companies engage in process value engineering (PVE), which provides the greatest potential for process cost reduction.

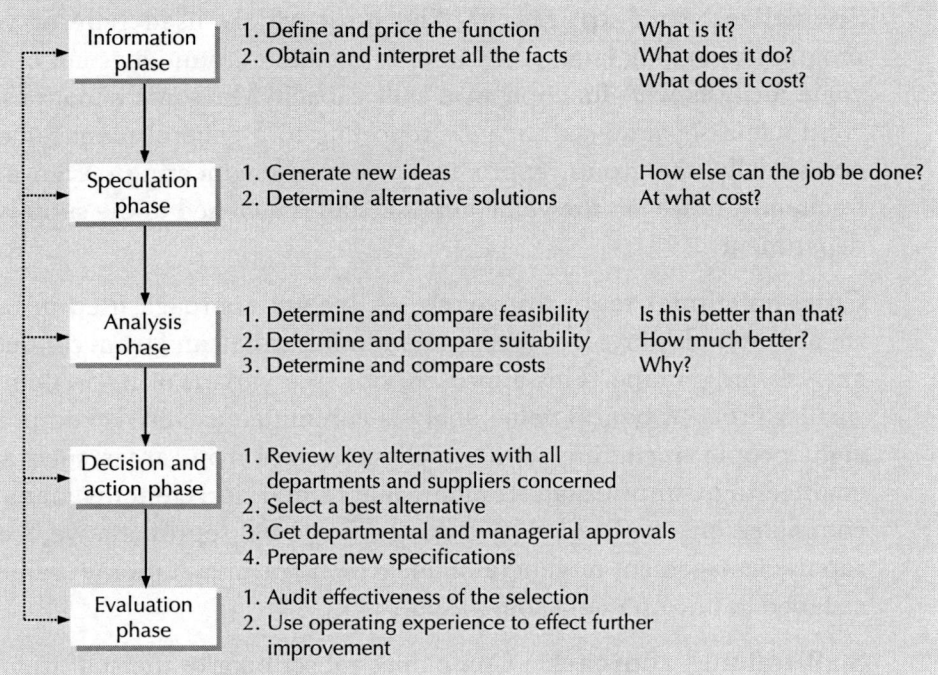

FIG. 5.7 A generalized procedural model for value analysis
Source: Burt, Dobler, and Starling (2006)

Supplier Involvement

Suppliers frequently prove to be extremely valuable assets in a firm's total value analysis effort. Most firms have found that a majority of value-analysis savings comes directly from the suggestions of suppliers who have been asked to participate in the value analysis programme. The former Chrysler Corporation initiated a voluntary value analysis cost reduction programme for its suppliers. The objective was for each supplier to value analyse one or more of its key products sold to Chrysler, and to submit the resulting value analysis suggestions for consideration. During the first two years of the programme, Chrysler received more than 3400 VA suggestions that materialized into projects that saved approximately $136 million.

Organizing the VA/VE Process

Value analysis studies can be conducted formally by organized groups, such as supplier development teams, or informally by individuals such as supply managers, engineers, production personnel, and so forth. In either case, the elements of the study are the same. Three basic organizational approaches are most common: (i) the specialized staff approach, (ii) the cross-functional team approach, and (iii) the staff training approach.

Specialized staff approach The most widely used type of value analysis programme among large companies is one built around a group of highly trained value analysts who function in a staff capacity. In some situations, the analysts constitute a separate staff agency reporting to a general management executive; occasionally, the group reports to a top-level engineering design manager. Most frequently, however, the value analysis staff is attached to the supply management department.

Cross-functional team approach A second approach used in both large and small firms today involves committee administration and team conduct of the value analysis programme. This approach, or some variant of it, predominates among smaller firms. A typical value analysis committee usually is composed of four to eight people, including senior representatives from areas such as operations, engineering, supply management, marketing, and general management. The committee may be headed by a senior functional representative, frequently from supply management or general management, or by a full-time 'value coordinator' assigned to the top management staff.

Staff training approach Companies subscribing to the staff training approach believe that value analysis yields maximum benefits only when it is practiced by all the key operating personnel. Consequently, this approach aims primarily at developing an understanding of the concept, and a working knowledge of techniques among the most professional and operating personnel responsible for specifying, purchasing, and using production materials. The value analysis organization in this case consists of a small staff group that reports to the general management. The activities of this group focus on value analysis training.

SUPPLIER QUALITY ASSURANCE PROGRAMME

Many companies have installed extensive supplier quality assurance (SQA) programmes for their suppliers, and solicit comprehensive quality related information from their suppliers even at the 'bid-packaging' stage. Later on, if selected, they are assigned to supplier quality engineers (SQEs) who assess their capacity, capability to plan, and implement an SQA as per the purchase requirements. Quality assurance (QA) may well entail process–audits at the vendors' site. Exhibit 5.8 outlines the elements of an extensive SQA programme by a leading original equipment manufacturer (OEM) in the automobile industry.

EXHIBIT 5.8 Elements of a Supplier Quality Assurance Programme (*Sample Only*)

I. Production Capacity/Capability Analysis

(a) Are bottlenecks identified and compatible with the planned capacities?

(b) Do cycle times allow the production run, rate, and capacity to be satisfied?

(c) Does the flexibility level of the installations allow changes in volume requirements to be met?

(d) Is the load level of the installations compatible with the volumes to be produced?

(e) Are the actual working hours properly planned and applied?

(f) Do the operational teams fit the volumes to be produced?

(g) Is the process capable of producing the range specified?

(h) Are the productions means installed on different suppliers' premises suitable for producing the process output range at the prescribed rate?

II. Product/Process Quality

(a) Does the direct acceptance rate comply with the objectives?

(b) Does the final acceptance rate (including manufacturing reworks) meet the target?

(c) Is the delivery date for initial samples known, and does it comply with the jointly signed production schedule?

(d) Are the possible product non-conformities (NCs) identified and are these covered by corrective actions?

(e) Are the allowable concessions known for quality levels?

(f) Are the process modifications identified and taken into account, so as to be consistent with the increase in the production rate, or the mass production?

(g) Are the product/process risks identified, and are they covered by action plans compatible with the objectives relating to the increase in the production rate?

(h) Are the recommendations relating to the use of the product in customer plant validated?

(i) Does the deployed monitoring plan (pre-production) take into account the deviations from the provisions laid down for mass production?

(j) Have the locking mechanisms and mistake proofing devices been set up, and are they operational?

(k) Are the investigation charts available?

III. Procurement (Materials and Components)

(a) Are all mass production suppliers and sub-contractors certified (system audit)?

(b) Has a procedure of type production part approval process (PPAP) including audits, been set up with each one of them?

(c) Is there a procedure for the management of the product-process modifications, and is it applied with different levels of suppliers?

(d) Is there a procurement protocol established for all supplies (materials and components)?

(e) Are the risks of not supplying within the allotted time or according to the volumes specified identified?

(f) Have steps been taken for long lead-time supplies?

(*Contd*)

EXHIBIT 5.8 *Contd*

IV. Facilities of Production and Inspection

(a) Are the operational means in compliance with the pre-established provisions (manufacturing and inspection flow charts etc.)?

(b) Does the setting up of the means of production comply with the supplier production initiation plan?

(c) Are the standards and/or the mastering part available, identified, and in their period of validity?

V. Instructions and Documentation at the Workstations

(a) Are the sheets instructions for routine calibration, and inspection of the means of inspection and the inspection locking mechanisms available?

(b) Are the manufacturing and inspection operation sheets available, and are they updated?

(c) Are the 'Instructions at the work stations' sheets available and updated?

(d) Are all log books in operation?

(e) Are all workstations subjected to regulatory and safety requirements identified?

(f) Are the instruction sheets relating to the identification of the product and the packaging items properly applied?

(g) Are the expiry dates of the products involved monitored?

(h) Are the starting and/or stopping procedures put up at the workstation?

VI. Training and Qualification of Operators

(a) Is the planned workforce operational and trained?

(b) Are the training programme and its associated training aids available?

(c) Is the training programme deployed in accordance with the objectives?

(d) Is the versatility table available and updated?

(e) Is the schedule relating to the deployment and training of the additional workforce available?

VII. Maintenance of Equipment and Facilities

(a) Is the preventive maintenance schedule planned?

(b) Are the operation sheets for adjustment at the workstations drawn up?

(c) Are the preventive maintenance instruction sheets available?

(d) Is the speedy breakdown repair device determined and described?

(e) Is the maintenance plan deployed and optimized (including first-level maintenance)?

(f) Are shutdowns (failures etc.) subjected to any special monitoring and taken for detailed analysis? Are action plans available?

VIII. Traceability, Identification, and Packaging

(a) Is the product traceability in the flow ensured?

(b) Has the marking of the parts involved been carried out in accordance with the specification?

(c) Are the interfunctional packagings described, validated, and used?

(d) Are the packaging/unpacking equipment and the special protective equipment validated and installed?

(*Contd*)

EXHIBIT 5.8 *Contd*

(e) Are the packaging items in use validated (for the shipment of the product to the customer's site)?

(f) Is the procedure relating to the application of standard packaging items clearly known and applied?

(g) Is the provision with packaging items adequate?

(h) Are the steps taken to make up for the inadequacies of the endowments satisfactory and accepted by the customer?

(i) Are the provisions laid down in order to identify and dispose of defects (quality problems) applied?

IX. Logistics and Production Management

(a) Is the mapping of flows available?

(b) Is the transport control procedure known and applied?

(c) Are there inventory management techniques and how are these applied?

(d) Are deliveries subjected to any monitoring? Are there indicators of delivery services?

(e) Are the requests for delivery subjected to electronic data interchange (EDI) and monitoring?

(f) Are the provisions laid down for the increase in the production rate identified and applied?

The above checklist is only indicative and a company could develop its own depending on the type of requirements, and level of QA expected to be met by the source.

IT ENABLEMENT OF SOURCING AND SUPPLIER RELATIONSHIP MANAGEMENT

With the Web coming to the rescue of procurement managers, as discussed earlier on e-procurement, more and more companies are now switching to the option of buying through reverse auctions which yield significant savings.

Many IT companies are now dishing out software solutions that help in global sourcing and managing relationships with suppliers on a continuous basis. For example, SAP doles out its SRM solution to help companies in supplier selection, bidding, negotiations including material receipts, invoice auditing, and payment to suppliers (taking the lead from a pre-installed ERP System).

Tata Motors in India, for example, implemented SAP SRM 4.0 package as it was better integrated with SAP package installed by the company for ERP.

According to Probir Mitra, CIO of the company, SRM directly reduced the processing time to get acceptance from a supplier by 24–96 hours, depending upon the transaction, manual work has gone down by 60 per cent, all resulting into savings worth 30 million. There was significant reduction in staff deployed in the materials receipt division. SRM reportedly also enabled Tata Motors to introduce *Kanban* system for material replenishment for 2000 items. This is because SRM notifies the supplier which facilitates JIT deliveries. Till June 2005, the company covered 1700 vendors. Earlier, the company had an in-house Windows-based value chain management (VCM) system using Oracle database, which was not capable to handle large number of suppliers and the transactions with them. As the goods receipts notes (GRNs) had multiplied from 6000 to 16,000, it took anything between 20–60 days for approval of quotations from suppliers because of a number of lengthy processes at Tata Motors. SRM ensured that a single bar code would enable multiple supplier shipments reducing the goods receipt cycle time significantly at the entry gate, leading to a reduction in the turnaround time of vehicles at the inward gate by 50 per cent.

Prior to implementing SRM, the spend-management and procurement solution provider giant ARIBA had helped Tata Motors to locate global sources, e.g., jacks from China and specialty steel from Slovenia and China, and doing reverse auctions. By 2005, the company saved around Rs 3.5 billion by carrying out around 1500 competitive biddings and covering 40 per cent of the total material spend by reverse auctions. This is because, as Daryl Rolley, VP, ARIBA, is reported to be saying, the bid quoted online simply provides the cost curve of that industry at that point in time. It is transparent and may not pertain to price alone, but also to other conditions of the offer so that the buyer can choose a supplier based on his specific requirements. The auctions started from castings, forgings, bearings, sheet metal components, furnace oil, and fasteners, and then upto brake, clutch, steering, and radiator assemblies. The savings accrued in procurement costs by virtue of e-procurement ranged from an average 5–15 per cent, say, with variation of +/- 2 per cent.

It therefore emerges that using IT solutions for SRM could bring substantial benefits, but integration with a pre-existing ERP system will make it easier.

A typical SAP–SRM solution has the following elements.

1. Purchasing governance (global spend analysis and category management)
2. Sourcing (auctioning, bid evaluation, and award)
3. Contract management (contract planning, execution, and monitoring)
4. Collaborative procurement (services/direct/catalogue content procurement)
5. Supplier collaboration (supplier networking and integration, including its Web enablement)
6. Supply base management (supplier selection and empanelment, supplier performance management)

The various functionalities offered are

1. E-sourcing: This is to ensure a quick, transparent, flexible, and reliable approach to sourcing.

2. SAP spend analysis: It helps companies to classify, normalize, and aggregate the spend data pertaining to various materials for further analysis in terms of selective purchasing and inventory management policies, and procedures.

3. SAP contract life-cycle management: This is meant to facilitate a proactive management of materials through various stages of the contract life-cycle, irrespective of the type of contract/materials.

4. SAP costs and quotations management: It is to facilitate decision-making, yielding profit by aligning the functions of design, sourcing, and costing in the company.

So, this and other SRM Packages could provide total solution for sourcing and supplier relations to buying organizations.

RECAPITULATION

Supplier development is one of the most powerful approaches that a firm can engage in on the path to supply management. The focus should be on developing suppliers to become self-sufficient at developing, implementing, and maintaining world-class performance. This is in contrast to what many firms call supplier development, where managers place controls on suppliers and conduct limited duration *Kaizen events*, or a few seminars that result in little retained learning. Supplier development in the supply management context requires buying firms to develop full-time, dedicated resources that work hand-in-hand with the supplier's personnel. Experience at several firms demonstrates that the return on the investment from supplier development makes it one of the firm's best investments. The interactions also prepare the way for other strategic collaboration opportunities, such as including the supplier in the design process at the buying firm. A frequently overlooked supplier development approach is developing the supplying firm's supply management. Development of the supplier's purchasing management starts to truly enable supply chain management, and refocuses the development to processes that span the chain instead of only the internal functions. Supply management becomes the key to supply chain management through development efforts that go beyond the tier 1 of suppliers.

Many companies in India have instituted a well developed supplier rating and performance assessment systems, as also a collaboration program with vendors for new material, design and development, demand forecasting, planning, and scheduling at the floor level. The purpose is to reduce direct material costs, not just by 1–2 per cent, but engage in long-term efforts to cut delivery cycle times from suppliers, online delivery through better scheduling, reducing turn around time of vehicles at incoming material gate, reducing the work force requirements particularly in inbound logistics, and reducing time, effort, and cost of transactions. The focus should be on new product development/material substitution/value analysis, design integration, and plans for value chain management, rather than just managing transactions. This is well exemplified by companies such as Tata Motors, MUL, etc. Also, all this could be facilitated by using IT solutions such as SAP–SRM which deal with a diversified range of functionalities ranging from e-sourcing, material spend analysis, to contract life-cycle management (at all stages), to cost and quotation management.

CONCEPT REVIEW QUESTIONS

1. Discuss the factors which favour a make or a buy decision. Compare the situations in which these decisions are undertaken.
2. What are the strategic issues involved in in/outsourcing? What kind of planning is required before a company should go in for outsourcing?
3. Describe the continuum of buyer–supplier relationship in strategic terms. How is the choice of each relationship decided?
4. What are the prerequisites for competitive bidding? What are the components of a two-stage bidding process?
5. Is negotiation an art or a science? Justify your answer. What are the guidelines for negotiations in public purchasing in India?
6. Under what conditions does a company prefer early supplier development? What should be the ingredients of an early supplier development programme?
7. What is e-procurement? What is the scope of e-procurement in India? What kind of support systems are required for e-procurement?
8. Outline a generic process for supplier development. Discuss the actions involved at each step. List some best practices in supplier development.
9. What are some of the strategies a buyer should undertake with its suppliers for a long-term continuous improvement? Outline the action plans for such strategies.
10. What are the objectives of a supplier quality assurance (SQA) programme? Chart out the elements of a comprehensive SQA programme.

PROJECT ASSIGNMENTS

1. Visit the purchasing department of a manufacturing company. List the activities they have outsourced and critically analyse the reasons, thereof.
2. With the same company selected in (1), list the vendors for outsourced activities and/or parts/products, and analyse the nature of relationship of the company with the respective vendors in terms of joint action programmes for product and process improvement, and the obligations to be discharged from both sides, i.e., buyer and seller in case of a purchase.
3. Comment upon the vendor rating and evaluation process followed by the selected company in (1). When does it feel the need to undertake supplier development?
4. In the same company, find out what are the policies of the company for supplier development? What is the level of the commitment by the management towards supplier development? Can you assess and measure such commitment? If yes, how?
5. Take a tender notice/request for quotation (RFQ) of a reputed Public Sector Undertaking (PSU) which involves a two-stage competitive bidding, for study. You can participate in a bid opening process by taking permission from the management. Analyse the bid opening process and trace the steps involved till the purchase order is put.
6. Take a purchase order of a company and see the terms and conditions overleaf. Analyse these terms and conditions.
7. Find out if there are other than the purchase order, some non-conventional or modern way of issuing purchase orders, or floating RFQs, or tender notices for disposal of material.

What technology and systems are being used for following such non-conventional methods to purchase or to sell/dispose materials?

8. Select a company of your choice in the manufacturing sector. Find out as to how the company ensures quality of its supplies through a quality assurance system installed at its supplier(s). Discuss the elements involved there—in also highlighting what does the company do to ensure continuous improvement of its suppliers and the activities at their ends.

CASE STUDY

GLOBAL CASE STUDY

NOKIA[1]

The company considers sound environmental and social principles as an important part of sustaining a successful and responsible business. They claim to work hard to anticipate risk, demonstrate company values, enhance their governance practices, increase employee satisfaction, and look after the communities where they do business.

Nokia expects the companies in their supplier network to take a similar ethical business approach, therefore takes this into account when selecting suppliers and developing long-term relationships with them.

Global Sources—Closer Ties

Nokia sources products and services, including components, software, packaging, manufacturing and office equipment, from thousands of suppliers all around the world. In their mobile phone business, for example, an average of 350 components are needed to make one device. Last year, Nokia purchased approximately 100 billion components. That means, if one were to stack each of these components on top of the other, one may eventually reach the moon.

Despite these high volumes and the ever-changing sourcing needs of this dynamic industry, Nokia has far fewer component suppliers for their mobile phone manufacturing than their competitors. For example, Nokia's top ten suppliers account for around 60 per cent of their total purchases, while their 100 larger suppliers account for 95 per cent. The longevity and high monetary value of these key relationships help Nokia to form deeper strategic partnerships, allowing them to develop and strengthen ethical and environmental practices together.

Supplier Diversity Initiative

In the US, Nokia is actively seeking to increase the ratio of minority and women-owned suppliers in sourcing projects. Nokia's supplier diversity initiative is an economic development program set up to encourage the creation, growth, and expansion of small, minority, and women-owned businesses within the supplier network. Under the initiative, Nokia tracks the expenditures to minority groups and benchmarks progress over time. In 2005, the company spent over USD 20 million with diversity suppliers.

---

[1] *Source:* Most information in this case has been adapted from www.nokia.com/A425220 and A4252222; www.nokia.com/environment/our-responsibility as accessed on 25 February 2010. The author acknowledges this source as last accessed on 17 November 2008.

Supplier Requirements

The company aims to ensure that environmental, ethics, labour practices, and health and safety issues are not separate add-on features, but are embedded into all sourcing processes, including supplier selection, and supplier relationship development.

Nokia has a clear and comprehensive set of global Nokia supplier requirements, including ethical and environmental considerations that they expect all their suppliers to meet. There are two types of requirements.

(i) Expectations for supplier performance
(ii) Specifications for the components, parts, or products being delivered

The experience gained through on-site supplier assessments provided invaluable input for the development of their new Nokia supplier requirements.

Proactive Approach to Sustainability

In many sourcing areas, the company has complex and deep-rooted supply chains. The challenge for Nokia is to find the most effective way, using the resources and time that they have, to reach not only their direct suppliers, but their suppliers and their suppliers' suppliers.

Nokia has focused predominantly on their tier 1 suppliers, educating them to take a similarly active and stringent approach to ethical and environmental considerations with their respective suppliers. This approach is based on the understanding that the company will achieve positive, sustainable results only when each tier of a supply network takes responsibility for conducting its own business, and managing its own suppliers.

Competence Development

During 2005, Nokia continued regular competence development activities on ethical and environmental issues with their sourcing and operations personnel. The company's basic supply chain ethics training covers the following issues.

- Concept of corporate social responsibility
- Nokia Code of Conduct
- Social requirements for suppliers
- SA 8000 content
- Practical information on auditing social aspects in regular supplier assessments

In environmental training, the company concentrates on the basis of

- environmental management
- environmental legislation
- material restrictions
- implications for sourcing practices
- supplier requirements

Training Figures

Figures 5.8 and 5.9 display the training figures at Nokia for supplier interface personnel in different years.

Supply chain ethics training

Year	Cumulative amount of people trained
• 2003	522
• 2004	721
• 2005	768

Cumulative percentage of personnel trained in supply chain ethics: 66%

Environmental training for supplier interface

Year	Cumulative amount of people trained
• 2003	507
• 2004	750
• 2005	803

Cumulative percentage of personnel trained in environment: 70%

New Supplier Requirements

In 2005, in response to a changing legislative environment and broader stakeholder expecta-

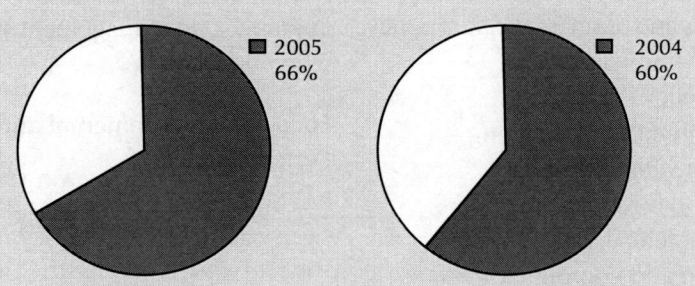

FIG. 5.8 Cumulative percentage of supplier interface personnel trained as in 2004 and 2005

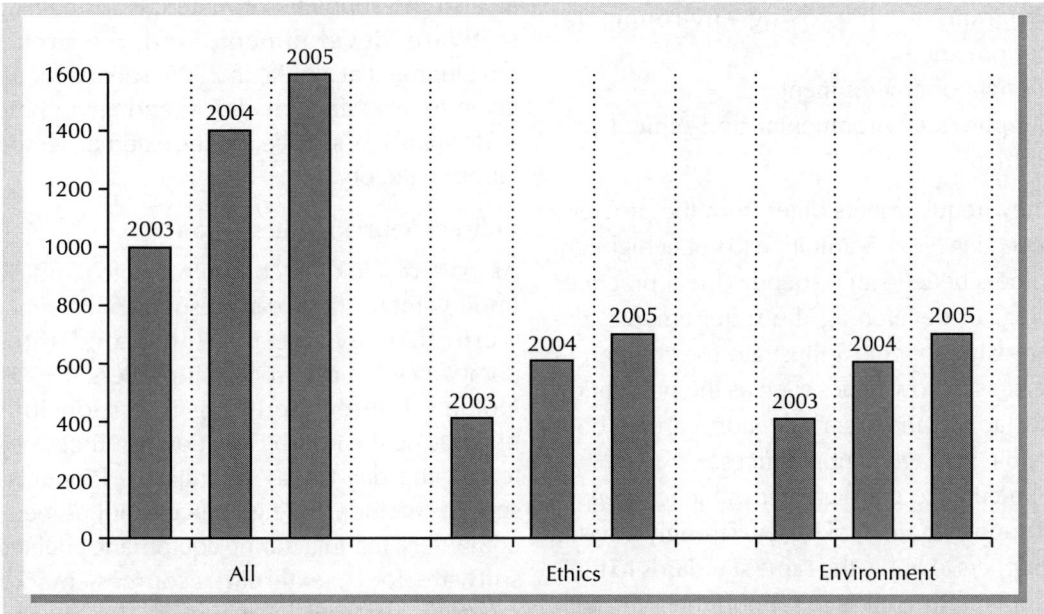

FIG. 5.9 Participants in supply chain and ethics and supply chain and environmental training at Nokia (2003–05)

tions, particularly the feedback from the company's suppliers, Nokia made the decision to revise and update its Nokia supplier requirements (NSR).

In particular, the new guidelines that were implemented in late 2006, reflected the increasing importance of substance and waste management. Their requirements related to ethics, labour practices, and health and safety, have also been fully reviewed, and made more explicit to better reflect both their own internal policies and

practices, as well as external guidelines such as the ILO core conventions, the UN Declaration for Human Rights, and industry standards such as *SA 8000 ISO 14001 and OHSAS 18001.* Nokia notified a Nokia Substances (dangerous) List as a part of its obligation under the adoption of environmental management system (EMS).

The new supplier requirements relating to environmental ethics and labour conditions include expectations for the following.

(i) Company values and business conduct policy
(ii) Human resource policies
(iii) Environment policy
(iv) Workforce planning and recruiting
(v) Occupational health and safety
(vi) Competence and development
(vii) People management
(viii) Communication and coordination
(ix) Environmental management system
(a) Raw material content data management
(b) Waste management
(c) Programs for improving environmental performance
(d) Design for environment
(e) Supplier's environmental and ethical performance

These new requirements differ from the previous set in reflecting Nokia's ambition to better highlight the business benefits that sound ethical practices can bring. In developing the requirements, the company also sought to illustrate for company's suppliers, as to how issues such as the prevention of child labour and discrimination can be built into people management practices.

In an effort to carry greater influence deeper in their supply chain, Nokia now strongly advises their suppliers to apply the same standards to their own suppliers, as well as to support them through regular education and monitoring practices.

Supplier Assessments at Nokia

The Finnish giant carries out regular supplier assessments as a tool to promote good performance, as well as to monitor compliance with the NRS. This is not a policing activity. Nokia sees on-site assessments as providing an opportunity to raise awareness, identify potential risks, and share best practices. Using this approach, each supplier is required to define a corrective action plan for any areas of non-conformance found. Nokia auditors then follow-up on progress, with

guidance and management support also provided when needed.

Focus on Environmental and Ethical Performance

In 2005, Nokia continued regular scheduled on-site system assessments, while also conducting several more in-depth on-site assessments. Whereas, traditionally the in-depth assessments have focused on direct sourcing, i.e., the component suppliers and contract manufacturers, as also the suppliers of materials for packaging, software development, and research and development at Nokia, in 2005, special focus was given to assessing the ethical and environmental performance of suppliers in the external, temporary labour category.

Indirect Sourcing Integration

As part of Nokia's commitment to continuous improvement, corporate responsibility practices were also revised and integrated into the company's indirect sourcing process (Fig. 5.10). Nokia's indirect sourcing is responsible for purchasing the non-production resources needed to run the day-to-day operations. Products and services include, for e.g., office supplies, personal computers, manufacturing equipment, engineering software tools, external resources, marketing material, catering, and travel. The experience gained through these on-site supplier assessments provided invaluable input for the development of the new Nokia supplier requirements.

In 2006, the company planned to continue supplier assessments with selected suppliers. However, good environmental and ethical performance in the supply chain cannot be achieved through supplier assessments alone. Management commitment, effective supplier qualification techniques, dialogue, and continuous development are all fundamental aspects, and the company is constantly looking to build on and improve the toolbox.

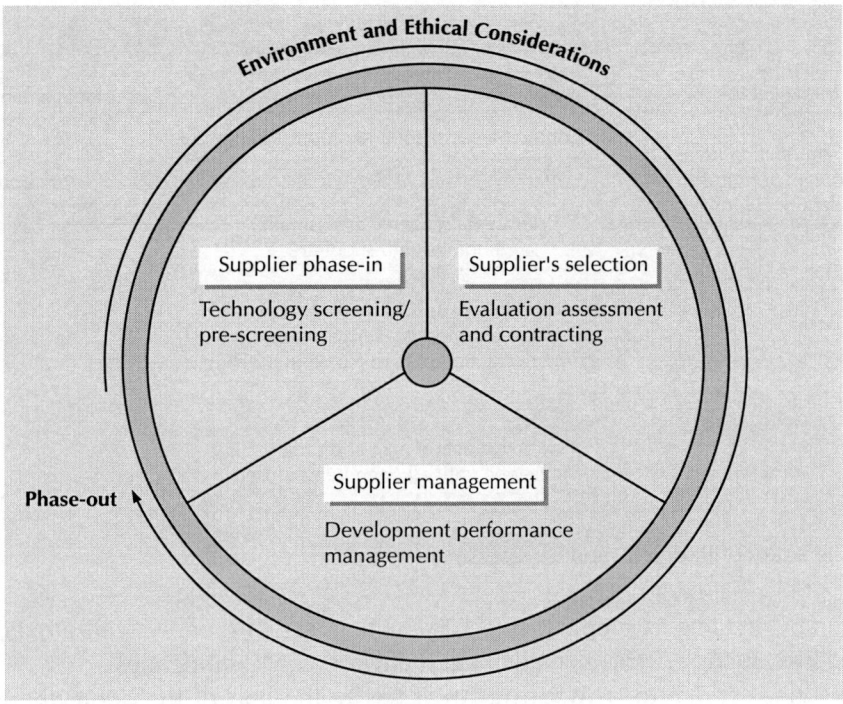

FIG. 5.10 Sourcing actions at Nokia
Source: www.nokia.com as accessed 19 November 2008

At the industry level, Nokia joined the global e-sustainability initiative supply chain working group, together with ICT service providers and manufacturers. The aim of this group is to promote good conduct and develop tools, management practices, processes, and systems to assist members in dealing with CSR supply chain issues. For example, one of the key outputs for 2005 has been a self-assessment questionnaire for suppliers. The Global e-sustainabiltiy Initiative (GeSI) supply chain working group is also working with the electronics industry code of conduct implementation group of companies.

At the end of 2007, Nokia started to work with its direct sources to increase the visibility of environment performanne and target setting. The focus was on the following four key environmental areas.

- Energy consumption at supplier sites and improvement targets
- CO_2 (carbon dioxide) emissions from supplier sites and improvement targets
- Water consumption at supplier sites and improvement targets
- Waste generation at supplier sites and improvement targets

In 2008, out of all the suppliers of Nokia that accounted for 69% of its overall hardware spend, 82% had set reduction targets for energy, CO_2, water, and waste, and were getting these monitored at their sites.

Indirect Nokia Sourcing

As part of the commitment to continuous improvement, corporate responsibility practices were also revised and integrated into Nokia's indirect sourcing process (Fig. 5.11).

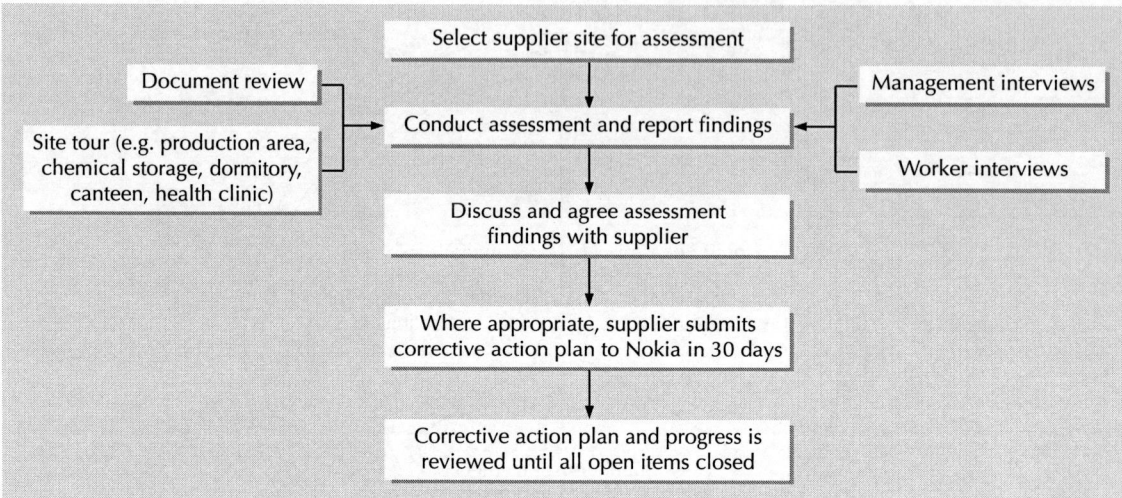

FIG. 5.11 Schematics of in-depth supplier assessment at Nokia

Nokia began by dividing its suppliers into 10 broad sub-categories, such as IT, travel, marketing, process materials, etc., and allocating an assessment manager to each.

The main objectives of the project were two-fold.

1. *Identify critical sub-categories*

Criteria included multiple considerations, such as whether the product provided by the category relied on high levels of toxic material or material potentially obtainable from environmentally sensitive sources, or whether the product or service supplied was for use in a Nokia end product, or for the operation of a Nokia manufacturing facility. Category assessments also took into account, issues, amongst many others, such as the global availability of the material or product they supply, the degree of complexity in the supply chain, and whether there was a history in the industry of informal contractual arrangements.

2. *Identify high-risk vendors*

Once, critical sub-categories of materials were identified, the second objective was to identify specific high-risk vendors in specific countries, involving an assessment of suppliers' ability, and willingness to comply with Nokia's ethical and environmental guidelines.

By the end of the audit, the company had identified approximately 50 companies that the company felt might require, or benefit from further scrutiny. Nokia now plans the company to stage assessment programs for each of these during 2006.

Communication

Open dialogue is essential to share Nokia's experience and also to gain feedback from those who can affect, or could be affected by its activities.

Through regular internal trainings, Nokia is in an ongoing dialogue with their sourcing and operations personnel on supply chain ethics and environmental issues.

Nokia Annual Supplier Days

The Nokia annual supplier days provide a forum for industry discussion. These events bring top management from Nokia and their suppliers together to review upcoming strategies, and discuss environmental and ethical issues.

Nokia is always in continuous discussion with their customers and participating with other ICT companies in the value chain, for example, in supporting UNEP and ITU in the GeSI supply chain working group. This kind of work enables Nokia to benchmark best practices, and promote consistent and complementary approaches within the industry.

During 2008, the following steps were taken by Nokia.

(i) It decided to start using the self assessment questionnaire delivered through the online Electronic Tool for Accountable Supply Chain (E-TASC) to replace the earlier SER self-assessment.

(ii) It concluded 62 Nokia Supplier Requirements (NSR) assessments and eight in-depth labour, health, safety, and environmental assessments.

By the end of 2008, 91% of Nokia's direct suppliers' sites were ISO 14001 certified, which accounted for at least 98% of Nokia's hardware purchasing expenditure.

In 2008, Nokia continued to work with the suppliers to raise awareness and ensure actions for compliance to EU regulations on the Registration, Evaluation, Authorization, and Restriction of Chemicals (REACH). According to EU-REACH, companies are obliged to ensure that the chemical substances, which they manufacture, import, or are found in articles considered as 'substances of very high concern', are registered, authorized, or notified on the basis of legal requirements. In this regard, Nokia came out with the Nokia Substance List (NSL), which required suppliers to have a record of the raw material component of products shipped to Nokia and also to provide end-of-life treatment recommendation, if any. It also tries to find out the origin of raw materials like Tantalum. Although Nokia does not buy raw materials directly, it tries to establish through its suppliers as to from where the materials of their products come from and how these have been extracted, processed, or produced in an environmentally and socially responsible manner.

Discussion Questions

1. What are Nokia's supplier requirements and expectations? What are the focus areas of such requirements?

2. How does Nokia develop the competence of its suppliers? What are the major concentration areas and the extent of training provided?

3. What do you think are the reasons that prompted Nokia to adopt the new supplier requirements? Would you like to add to the list of new supplier requirements? If yes, name and discuss these requirements.

4. What are the ingredients of the in-depth supplier assessments being carried out by Nokia? Do you suggest any modification in the system?

5. What is so special about the indirect Nokia sourcing? How would supplier assessments differ in such a sourcing strategy, according to you?

INDIAN CASE STUDY

HINDUSTAN PETROLEUM CORPORATION LIMITED[2]

India is the sixth largest lubes (lubricants) market in the world and it is the third largest in the Asia-Pacific region. Also, it is the most vibrant and growing market in the world with a growth rate of

---

[2] *Source:* The information contained in this case is adapted from an unpublished MBA dissertation project done by Mr Praveen Gupta of HPCL, completed under the supervision of the author in 2007. The author thanks Mr Praveen Gupta and the HPCL.

5 per cent vis-a-vis world lubricant market growth rate of 2 per cent per annum. Total Indian lubricants market is 1.2 million MT per annum and it is worth Rs 10,000 crores in value terms. There are more than 30 big market players including public sector undertakings (PSUs) such as Indian Oil, HPCL and BPCL, and MNCs such as Shell, Castrol, Exxon Mobile, Total Fina Elf, Idemitsu, Gulf Oil, etc.

HPCL has the biggest lubricants base oils manufacturing refinery with a capacity of 3.34 lakh MT per annum. It has therefore, certain advantages in the lube market. HPCL has two big grease manufacturing plants in Mumbai and Kolkata.

The company makes variety of greases in its plants:

(i) Automotive greases (wheel bearing greases, chassis greases, and multipurpose greases)
(ii) Industrial grease (lithium-based, calcium-based, and non-soap greases)

HPCL has a long tradition of quality greases which is the outcome of many years of technical and scientific experience. Also lubricants and greases are the most profitable business line of HPCL, which in 2003–04, contributed almost 20 per cent of profitability with 2-3 per cent revenue share.

Greases

While lubricating oils are best suited products for lubrication of any machine element, their use is not feasible in a situation where the product is likely to leak out, and not remain in bearing over extended period of service.

To lubricate in such situations satisfactorily, solid to semi-solid materials of dispersions of thickening agents in liquid lubricants and containing other ingredients for imparting special properties have been developed, and these are called lubricating greases.

Application of Greases

The application of greases lies in a wide spectrum of industries.

(i) Automotives
(ii) Ships
(iii) Steel plants
(iv) Power plants
(v) Cement plants
(vi) Railways
(vii) Ports, ship building
(viii) Mines
(ix) Defence equipments
(x) Oil corporation

Core Competency of HPCL

The competitive strength of HPCL in grease manufacturing till 1990s were the following.

(i) Biggest lube refinery in the country.
(ii) Big grease manufacturing unit in Mumbai.
(iii) Rich tradition, R&D backup of ESSO in grease manufacturing.
(iv) Competitive edge in cost effective manufacturing in greases.
(v) Established network, brands in the sales/marketing network of the country.
(vi) Grease makers with long and wide experience in manufacturing plants.

The background reasons for outsourcing of grease by HPCL were the following.

(i) It faced competition in lubricants/grease manufacturing and marketing by many MNCs and private players during 1992–2000.
(ii) There are more than 30 players in the market now.
(iii) The lubricants market had shifted from traditional retail outlet network to the 'bazaar' trade and the lube shops.
(iv) HPCL ignored R&D in grease manufacturing, and slowly it had nothing new to offer to the customers.
(v) It ignored the hard fact that grease making is an art and the grease makers were getting old and were nearing the retirement age in

1992. The new generation of staff and executive were not trained enough to learn the art of making greases. The batches of greases were failing in quality very frequently.

(vi) While HPCL slept over the years in this field, others made inroads in the grease market. The private players focused competitively in the profitable automotive market where the lube shopowners and the mechanics were the chief decision-makers in the buying process of greases.

(vii) Private oil companies introduced 'white' grease which was presented as superior than HPCL's yellow multipurpose greases, and black coloured wheel bearing greases.

HPCL steadily lost market due to the following reasons.

(i) There was lack of aggressiveness during the period 1994–2000.

(ii) The HP greases were not manufactured in the required quality, therefore customers shifted more or less permanently.

(iii) HP lost the war in the lube shop market and the mechanics recommended white grease instead of HP greases.

(iv) People were very cost conscious and they failed to see the quality aspect. They preferred cheaper greases.

(v) HPCL with the inherent weakness of a PSU, maintained and manufactured the greases at a higher cost and price. Therefore, it started losing market share in greases.

(vi) The loss of market share was also compounded by the non-availability of greases in time. The plants were incapable to produce the required quantity.

Therefore HPCL decided to outsource the grease manufacturing. The factors that favoured outsourcing of grease at HPCL were the following.

(i) Product was produced and made available at a faster rate, and as per schedule.

(ii) Cost of grease was less than the cost of manufacturing at their own plants.

(iii) Less industrial relations problems and loss in bargaining power of the unions.

(iv) Product was readily available as per schedule and demand.

(v) 'White grease' for automotive segment was made available at the price which is competitive, and in attractive packaging and size, as per the customers preference.

(vi) Pricing and the dealer/shopkeepers' incentive (commission) was kept very aggressive which was possible only due to the outsourcing of the manufacturing of grease.

(vii) Assured supplies helped in building back the customer confidence, shopkeepers confidence, and the confidence of the sales force in their capabilities. This aspect is extremely important in lubricants sales.

(viii) Sustained aggressive marketing helped in building the strong brand – HP All Purpose (HP Al Grease). The product sells like a hot cakes. There are no inventories. The moment it is available, it is sold to the distributors, who in turn sell it to shops.

(ix) Aggressive pricing, attractive dealer incentives has helped the sales, and the quality same as that of the global players such as Castrol and Shell.

The strategic outsourcing of grease manufacturing has helped HPCL to regain the lost market and is an important contributor to the company's profitability.

Discussion Questions

1. What is the market potential for lubricants in Asia, particularly India? How can HPCL exploit this potential?

2. Assess the various core competencies of HPCL which it can use in the business of greases.

3. Cite the reasons why even a giant such as HPCL had to outsource the manufacturing of grease.

4. What have been the major advantages of strategic outsourcing of grease manufacturing at HPCL?

REFERENCES

Burt, David N., Donald W. Dobler, and Stephen L. Starling (2003), 'World-Class Supply Management', McGraw-Hill, New York.

Carbone, James (November 18, 1999), 'Evaluation Programs Determine Top Suppliers', *Purchasing*.

Carter, P.L., J.R. Carter, R. Monczka, T.H. Straight, and A.J. Swan (Winter 2000), 'The Future of Purchasing and Supply: A Ten Year Forecast', *The Journal of Supply Chain Management*, pp. 14–26.

Cavinato, Joseph (January 1988), 'How to Calculate the Cost of Outsourcing', *Distribution*, pp. 72–76.

Dyer, H. Jeffrey (November 2000), 'Collaborative Advantage: Winning through Extended Supplier Networks', Oxford University Press.

Ellram, Lisa and Arnold Maltz (Spring 1999), 'Outsourcing Supply Management', *The Journal of Supply Chain Management*.

Forker, Laura B., Ruch William A., and Hershauer James, C. (Summer 1999), 'Examining Supplier Improvement Efforts from Both Sides', *Journal of Supply Chain Management*, p. 45.

Foster, S.J. (2004), Managing Quality, Prentice Hall, Upper Saddle River, N.J.

Gelderman, C. J., Van Weele (2002), 'Portfolio Management: A Case Study', *The Journal of Supply Chain Management*, Vol. 38, No. 2, Spring 2002, pp. 30–37.

Gelderman, C.J., and Arjan J. Van Weele (Summer 2005), 'Purchasing Portfolio Models: A Critique and Update', *Journal of Supply Chain Management*, Vol. 41, No. 3, pp. 19–28.

Hartley, J.L. and T.Y. Choi (1996), 'Supplier Development: Customers as a Catalyst of Process Change', *Business Horizon*, 39, No. 4, pp. 37–44.

Kannan, Vijay R. and Keah Choon Tan (Fall 2002), 'Supplier Selection and Assessment: Their Impact on Business Performance', *Journal of Supply Chain Management*, Vol. 38(4), pp. 11–21.

Kauffman, Ralph G. (Spring 1999), 'Indicator Qualities of NAPM Report on Business', *The Journal of Supply Chain Management*.

Kraljic, Peter (September, October 1983), 'Purchasing must Become Supply Management', *Harvard Business Review*.

Lonsdale, Chris (May 1999), 'Locked in to Supplier Development: On the Dangers of Asset Specificity for the Outsourcing Decisions', *The Journal of Supply Chain Management*.

Monczka, R., Robert Trent, and Robert Handfield (2005), 'Purchasing and Supply Chain Management', *South-Western Thompson Learning*, Cincinnati, Ohio.

Monczka, Robert and Robert Trent (1995), 'Purchasing and Sourcing Strategy: Trends and Implications', *Centre for Advanced Purchasing Studies (CAPS)*, Tempe, Arizona.

Monczka, R. and J.P. Morgan (13 August 1992), 'Strategic Sourcing Management', *Purchasing*, pp. 69–72.

Monczka, Robert and Robert Trent (1991), 'Evolving Sourcing Strategies for the 1990's,' *International Journal of Physical Distributors and Logistics Management*, Vol. 21, No. 5, pp. 4–12.

Nelson, Dave R., Patricia E. Moody, and Jonathan Stegner (2001), *The Purchasing Machine*, Free Press, New York.

Petersen, Kenneth J., Gary L. Ragatz, and Robert M. Monczka (Spring 2005), 'An Examination of Collaborative Planning, Effectiveness and Supply Chain Performance', *Journal of Supply Chain Management*, Vol. 41(2), pp. 14–25.

Porter, Michael (1980), 'Competitive Strategy: Techniques for Analysing Industries and Competitors'.

Ray, Thom as quoted in Ricker, op. cit.

Ricker, Jon (May 1997), 'The Synergy of Strategic Servicing', *Purchasing Today*.

Sanders, Nada R. (Spring 2005), 'IT Alignment in Supply Chain Relationships: A Study of Supplier Benefits', *Journal of Supply Chain Management*, Vol. 41(2), pp. 4–13.

Sarkis, Joseph and Talluri Srinivas (Winter 2002), 'A Model for Strategic Supplier Selection', *Journal of Supply Chain Management*, Vol. 38(1), pp. 18–28.

Simpson, Penny M, Judy A. Siguaw, and Susan C. White (Winter 2002), 'Measuring the Performance of Suppliers: An Analysis of Evaluation Processes', *Journal of Supply Chain Management*, Vol. 38(1), pp. 29–41.

Sislian, Eric and Sativ Ahmer (Summer 2000), 'Strategic Sourcing: A Framework and a Case Study', *The Journal of Supply Chain Management*.

Stanley, Linda L. and John N. Pearson (May 24–27 2000), 'Buyers–Suppliers Strategies and Their Impact on Purchasing Performance: A Study of the Electronics Industry', Conference I, Richard Ivy School of Business, University of Western Ontario, Canada.

Welch, James A., and P. Ranganath Nayak (1992), 'Strategic Sourcing: A Progressive Approach to the Make–Buy Decision', Academy of Management Executives 6, No. 1, pp. 23–31.

Internet Resources

www.goliath.ecnext.com

www.themanager.org

www1.sap.com/solutions/businessmaps as accessed on 19 November 2008

www.12manage.com/methods_kraljic

6 Supply Chain and Customer Relationship Management

Taking a lead from the preceding chapter that focused on supplier selection, rating, development, and relationship management systems, it is also important that the same methodology or systems are followed at the other end, i.e., the customer's end in the supply chain. It implies that the focal firm implementing supply chain management (SCM) must undertake acquiring, retaining, and selectively and strategically partnering with customers. This would bring about an integrated and well-aligned supply chain in terms of its objectives and goals. The way supplier relationship management (SRM) can be enabled by IT solutions in SRM, the management of customer relationships can also be IT-enabled by customer relationship management (CRM) solutions available with various vendors. Being a part of selective but strategic part of the supply chain, both suppliers and customers jointly create that value for the chain. While on the procurement and sourcing side, costing and bid-evaluation is important, on the customer side, it is the strategic pricing that matters. Also, the way sourcing and supply management is linked to the ERP system, CRM is also functionally linked to ERP. In other words, it means that CRM is linked to the sourcing and supply management system through the ERP system, once again highlighting that ERP systems provide the backbone of the relationship between SCM and CRM. Different companies realign, fructify, and integrate such relationships in different ways using different variants of the IT or non-IT solutions. However, a focus on relationship marketing is the essential virtue of all CRM programmes. This is also justified by the fact that most companies implementing CRM have customer loyalty programmes such as membership rewards programmes in place. Also the CRM programmes would invariably require a reasonable amount of automation in services rendered, because of the huge number of customers and their transactions involved.

CONCEPT OF CUSTOMER RELATIONSHIP MANAGEMENT

The terms customer relationship management (CRM) and relationship marketing are used interchangeably. It can be referred to as database marketing, emphasizing the promotional aspects of marketing linked to database efforts (Bickert 1992).

Another viewpoint is to use CRM as a *customer retention* strategy deploying a variety of after marketing tactics used for customer bonding, or staying in touch after the sale is made (Vavra 1992). Peppers and Rogers (1993) give a more specific approach with respect to application of information technology (IT) to focus on individual or one-to-one relationship with customers, which involves integration of database knowledge with a long-term customer retention and growth strategy. Shani and Chalasani (1992) define relationship marketing as an integrated effort to identify, maintain, and build up a network with individual consumers, and to continuously strengthen the network for the mutual benefit of both sides, through interactive, individualized, and value added contacts over a long period of time. McKenna (1991) puts the customer first and shifts the role of marketing from manipulating the customer to genuine customer involvement; communicating, and sharing the knowledge. Berry (1995) stresses that attracting new customers should be viewed only as an intermediate step in the marketing processes. Developing a closer relationship with customers and turning them into loyal ones are equally important aspects of marketing. He referred to relationship marketing as 'attracting, maintaining, and enhancing customer relationships'. Morgan and Hunt (1994) suggest relationship marketing to refer to all marketing activities directed towards establishing, developing, and maintaining successful relationships. The ultimate theme is to focus on cooperative and collaborative relationship between the firm and its customers. Such cooperative relationships are characterized as being interdependent and having long-term orientation, rather being concerned with short-term, discrete transactions. The other issue in CRM is that of *customer selectivity*. The company may always be selective in its relationship marketing programmes. It must segment and select appropriate customers for individual marketing programmes. It could even lead to 'outsourcing' of some customers if the company fails to utilize its resources on certain customers better to create a *mutual value*. The purpose of the company should not be to prune its customer base, but identify certain programmes and methods that would be profitable and create value for the firm and the customer.

Schmidt, Lauff, and Beigl (1998) define CRM as 'a comprehensive strategy and process of acquiring, retaining and partnering with selective customers to create a superior mutual value for the company and the customer.' The purpose of CRM is to increase marketing effectiveness and marketing efficiency. Two distinctive processes involved are

(i) proactive customer business development, and
(ii) building partnering relationship with most important customers.

These sequential processes would eventually lead to a superior mutual value creation.

LINKAGE BETWEEN CRM AND SCM

The CRM initiative should be viewed from a corporate level perspective rather than just as a 'call centre' approach. The key to using an interactive voice response system (IVRS) is certainly the technology working at the back-end, but it is also the people using this technology. As is evident from the figure that follows (Fig. 6.1), CRM is interfaced with SCM in a company through the enterprise resource planning (ERP) system. This interface between CRM and SCM is facilitated by

- business intelligence
- enablement tools and services
- Web and IT integration

These interfaces help in arriving at a technology value. On the other hand, the business value would be determined by the business processes, applications in e-commerce, as also the knowledge management.

The interface of CRM with SCM through enterprise resource planning (ERP) systems is very critical. In fact, most of the enterprise solution vendors have added

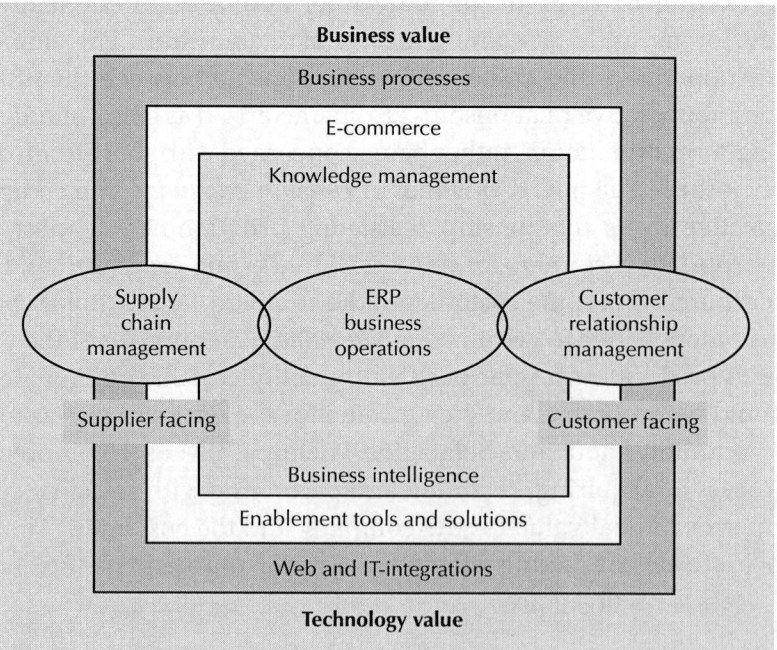

FIG. 6.1 The integration of CRM with SCM in an organization
Source: Verma, Saket, 'Implementing a Technology Based CRM Solution' in Sheth, Jagdish N., Atul Parvatiyar, G. Shainesh, (Eds) 'Customer Relationship Management: Emerging Concepts, Tools and Applications', Tata McGraw-Hill, New Delhi, 2001, p. 148

the CRM component to their offerings. Most vendors are hawking the complete suite with ERP, CRM, and SCM. The future lies in complete integration of company-wide business planning and transaction systems that will involve technology, business processes, and people in a manner that can deliver value to all the stakeholders, and provide a sustainable competitive advantage to the enterprise.

Implementation of CRM—The Interface with Information Technology

Till recently, a company's interface with customers had been through its sales people or sales agents. Nowadays, most companies interface with customers through a variety of channels, in addition to that of sales people and service personnel, e.g., call centres, Internet, websites, marketing departments, fulfilment houses, and market and business development agents. For large companies, it may include cross-functional teams which could include personnel from various functional departments. While each of these units could operate independently, they need to share information about individual customers and their transactions with the company on a real-time basis.

A customer who places an order on the Internet and subsequently calls the call centre for order enquiry and verification expects the call centre (of the company) to know details of the order history. Similarly, if a sales person approaches a customer unaware of the fact that the customer is dissatisfied with the company, he is unlikely to be treated kindly by the customer, which otherwise would have placed the sales person in a 'relatively superior position' to handle the situation. Effective CRM implementation, therefore, inevitably requires a front-line information system that shares relevant customer information across all interface units. Needless to mention, CRM systems and solutions inevitably use relational databases, data warehousing, and data mining tools. The real requirement is to develop an integrated CRM platform that collects relevant data inputs at each customer interface, and concurrently provide knowledge output about the strategy and action plans appropriate to capture or regain customer business, and help maintain customer loyalty.

Although most CRM software solutions based on relational databases are helping share customer information, they still do not provide knowledge output to the front-line personnel. If proper data inputs and data outputs are not provided at the interface points, call centres cannot identify and differentiate a high value customer, and do not know as to what to upsell or cross-sell the customer. It could lead to significant opportunity cost (of losing additional business with the customer).

CRM solutions platforms need to be based on interactive technology and processes, which must help the company to enhance customer interactions and one-to-one marketing through development of a front-line relationship with customers. The system used for CRM should first identify appropriate data inputs at each customer interaction point, and use analytics to generate appropriate knowledge output for the front-line staff during customer interactions. The tools must also be able to provide solutions for decisions related to the following.

- Customer profitability analysis
- Customer segmentation
- Demand planning and generation
- Account planning
- Opportunity management
- Contact management
- Integrated marketing communities
- Customer care plans
- Customer problem resolution and complaint handling
- Virtual team management of large global accounts
- Performance management of CRM

Many companies have handed over the responsibility of CRM implementation to their IT departments. They, in turn, may first be focused on simply installing CRM software solutions without a CRM strategy or programme in place, but ultimately these are hardly being used to identify and differentiate individual customers, and to generate individualized offer and fulfil customized solutions. Absence of a CRM strategy would leave the front-line people without any knowledge of what they should be doing with the additional customer information to which they might have access. So, together with implementation of IT tools, it is necessary to have an appropriate CRM strategy for obtaining successful results in CRM.

According to Bishop (1998), a company can serve the needs of the customer better by using a database to track their preferences and buying patterns, communicate with customers around the world much faster and more easily using the Internet, and also develop sales leads more effectively. Most companies, while organizing around their business processes in order to have short cycle times, have increased pressure to cut costs, and to increase efficiency and customer orientation. Hikes and Barnes (1999) also advocate that companies are focusing themselves more and more on their activities where they can differentiate themselves in the market. It is the companies' offerings and not themselves which fit into customers' value creation and compete with each other for their money (Norman and Ramirez 1998).

According to a study conducted by Anderson Consulting, as quoted by Ghodeswar (2001),

(i) the number of companies citing customer retention as a critically important measure has jumped by 60 per cent, as companies have shifted their focus from attracting new customers to retaining their more profitable ones;

(ii) almost 85 per cent of companies are expected to have data warehouses about their customers, up from around 40 per cent currently; and

(iii) the use of the Internet to collect customer data would surge by 43 per cent in 2010.

Comparison of Conventional Approach of CRM with Web-enabled and Integration Approach

As has been pointed out, CRM is a comprehensive sales and marketing approach for building long-term customer relationships, and improving business performance. The modern Web-enabled approach, however, focuses on customer information systems, multiple points-of-sale, creation of a lifetime of mutually superior value, significant automation of the sales process and sales force, and marketing and service efforts. The figure that follows shows the comparison (Fig. 6.2).

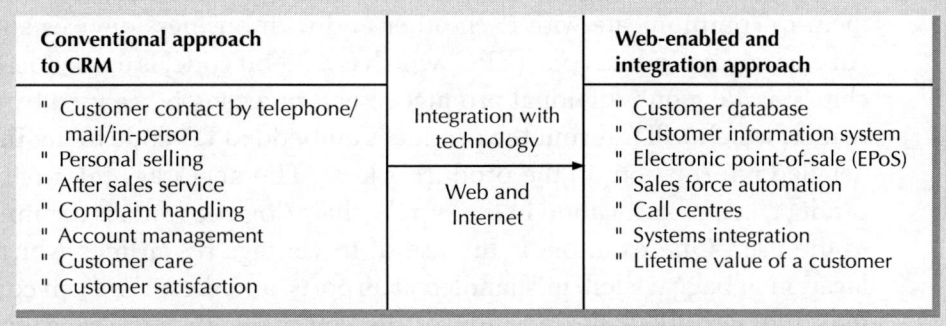

FIG. 6.2 Web-enabled approach of CRM as compared with the conventional approach
Source: Ghodeshwar (2001)

IT INFRASTRUCTURE USED FOR SUPPLY CHAIN AND CRM

The IT infrastructure used for supply chain and CRM typically consists of the following components.

Interface Devices and Technology

There are personal computers (PCs), voice mail, terminals, Internet devices, bar code scanners and personal digital assistants (PDAs), which play a major role in providing uniform access capability any time and anywhere. The Internet browser is fast becoming the interface of choice for information access. In addition, PDAs and phones are being conveniently used as access devices for the user system.

One of the key requirements of SCM systems is to *track products* in order to provide participants with the information they need to perform efficiently. For example, it is very important to record point-of-sale (PoS) information, especially if these data are to be accessed by the supplier for vendor-managed inventory (VMI) system.

The bar code system was created by the Uniform Code Council in 1973. It is also called universal product code (UPC) and is extensively used for scanning and recording information about products. Automate data capture interface devices such as bar code readers and radio frequency (RF) tags, are standardized and commonly used. RF tags on products or packagings could be used to locate items particularly in large warehouses. The same technology, when coupled with use of wireless communication devices and global positioning system (GPS) capabilities, enables tracking of tagged cargo while in motion. RFID has been discussed in detail in an earlier chapter.

Auto-ID Technology

This latest technology embeds intelligence in (physical-) products that will allow them to communicate with each other and with business devices and consumers. An electronic product code (EPC) which is a 96-bit code, is embedded in a memory chip/smart tag on individual products. Each smart tag is scanned by a wireless RF reader, which will transmit the product's embedded ID-code to the Internet, where detailed information on the product is kept. The necessary information about the product, i.e., of its location in the supply chain/logistic route is communicated back to the user. One example is the use of travel tags by airlines which can help in location of baggage left/mishandled at airports, and the airline can communicate to the customer about the position of the shipment, thus, helping in creating and maintaining better customer relations.[1] Also, a vehicle which has a unique smart card code, if equipped with GPS capabilities, can be traced and its movements tracked in case it is stolen. This also, in turn improves the service level with customers by movement in interface devices and using associated technology. In this system, a product markup language (PML) describes physical objects to the Internet and an object naming service (ONS) tells the computer system as to where to find information about a product with an EPC or smart tag. The ONS serves as a lightening fast *post office* that locates data for every single one of trillion of objects carrying an EPC code. Through this, money invested in stolen, lost, or waste products can be saved. Interestingly, if shoppers' cell phones are equipped with auto-ID scanners, they can just point these towards a product placed in a shelf, and know about the features from the manufacturer's website. Also, items often getting scanned can also be billed to the customer's personal account if one decides to purchase them. In a way, tracking products for supply chain purposes would be simplified yielding real-time information about the inventory item, and therefore, also increasing

---

[1] travelertags.com

the service level by reducing the shelf-stock by restocking them in time, and thereby, supplying product to the customer in time. It would ensure better utilization of store and warehouse space. There is also an increase in the ability to locate items at the store and in the backroom. All this gives better service level to customers and facilitates better relations with customers.

Communication System and Technology

Interface devices are either connected to an internal system (e.g., LAN, mainframe, Intranet) or an external network—either a private company network or the Internet. Any direct links to another company's system could also be utilized for efficiency and security. As Simchi-Levi (2003) points out, there are two key trends in communications.

- Wireless communication
- Single point of contact for communication

Advanced communication capabilities and the Web enable many applications, e.g., e-mail, electronic data interchange (EDI), product tracking during movement using GPS, and auto-ID technology. Some Web-based exchange platforms could also be used where the channel partners up til customer's end share information, track products, and trade with supply chain partners. The sharing of information and processes on a private or public basis, is a means to develop collaboration and visibility in the supply chain.

System Architecture for CRM

It refers to the way the components of the system, interface devices, databases, and communication capabilities, are configured.

Legacy systems based on large transaction related data, which used to be connected in a local area network (LAN) so that users could share files, e-mails, and other applications, have been replaced by wide area network (WAN) that connect the different offices of the company, and extend to even other companies. The PC in such a system is referred to as the 'client' and the main processor as the 'server'. Client/server computing is a form of distributed processing, whereby some processes are performed centrally for many users, while others are performed locally on a user's PC (Fig. 6.3). According to Simchi-Levi, Kaminsky, and Simchi-Levi (2003), most current system designs involve client/server architecture. In these systems, a relational database is used that allows the storage of related data in such a way that standardized reporting and querying of related data are facilitated. The relational database may be centralized on a mainframe computer or server, and then distributed across a WAN network of PCs or minicomputers. Relational database servers allow structured query language (SQL) based requests from users. In addition, there can

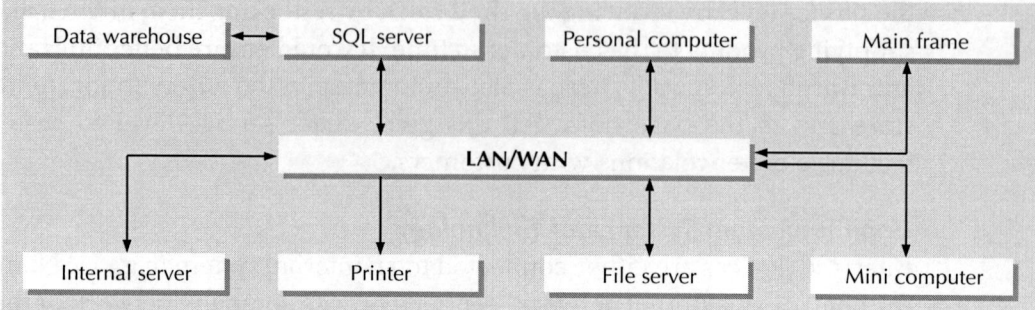

FIG. 6.3 Client/server system architecture for supply chain and CRM
Source: David, Kaminsky, and Edith (2004)

be transaction processing monitors, directory/security servers, and communication servers. The Internet is also a form of client/server where the local PC browser processes the hyper text markup language (HTML) pages and Java applets (small applications) that are selected from servers from all over the world. The client/ server model is now evolving towards a Web-centric model where the client is a Web-browser connected to a Web server. The power of the client–server concept lies in the fact that it can distribute functions among specialist servers that perform them efficiently. Each server must have the feature of *interoperability*, which means that two systems are capable of interacting and provide sharing of full data and processes at the interfaces. There are *middleware* or tools that provide communication between different system architecture, communication protocols, hardware architecture, etc. Middleware tools can be particularly helpful in implementation of the supply chain and CRM systems, since the information may be stored in a number of locations and forms across the company, particularly when data is not properly warehoused, or it exists only in departmental marts. Middlewares would perform the function of looking through the database at different places and consolidating, or combining the information. For example, a telecom company may provide services in long-distance communication, wireless communication, as also the Internet services. A customer relationship manager through the customer service representative might have to search multiple locations for a customer's bills if the customer purchased more than one service, while middleware can be used to go through different bases and create combined information at one place.

The purpose of a more advanced system infrastructure is to provide interconnectivity and collaboration platforms across the companies. Various Web-based exchange platforms can provide means to share information and processes, which can be used for collaboration across the enterprises, particularly visibility of raw material (RM) inventory at supplier's end, work-in-process (WIP) or scheduled production inventory at the focal firm, and the inventory of finished goods (FGs) at the company's distribution center/warehouse (WH), and then at the retail shelves in the stores. As has been already pointed out, Web-based services such as auto-ID have the potential to provide vital information and connectivity on different interfaces, and a flexible link between systems. Supported by interoperability of diverse systems, both supply chain and customer relationship decisions can be impacted by the design and architecture of the IT system, and the type of tools used.

Technological Tools for CRM

Three key tools of e-CRM have been referred to as 3Ws—Web, workflow management, and warehousing—of data by Handen (2000).

Web

It has enabled organizations to reach out to all those who affect the corporate operations, e.g., suppliers, alliance partners, and customers in the company's business units. Customers and suppliers can access information by themselves instead of using some intermediaries. For example, customers can check pricing schemes and about value added services through the Web. Although Web connects users and processes, it may not be used to manage work activities within or between processes, e.g., between order entry and delivery. To meet scheduling and routing requirements of such activities, organizations rely on workflow technology.

Workflow Management

These systems entail the procedure by which documents, information, and tasks are passed among participants. These systems define work rules or sequence of activities. If an employee orders a part of an equipment, the workflow engine can check to ensure that the purchase is authorized. Workflow provides a strong framework for customer-centric business processes, such as order management and customer service. Workflow system should allow users to route consumer communications along with an associated 'virtual folder' that combines documents, value messages, e-mails, or faxes the video or Web pages containing information about the customer. The information can then be transmitted to the appropriate customer service points at the right time, resulting into a one-call resolution that customers always expect. However, the workflow engine would respond to only routine or standardized tasks and may not be good at supporting non-routine tasks that may require complex decision-making. For such complex decisions, organizations have to build data warehouses.

Warehousing of Data

A data warehouse is an orderly and accessible repository of known facts and detailed data from many subject areas, which is used as a basis for decision-making. It is enterprise-wide and may be quite complex as compared to the data marts. A *data mart* has only a summary data pertaining to only a single subject, and delivers value to only a specific business area, as compared to a data warehouse which delivers value to the whole enterprise. There must be granularity of data in the sense that it must have capability to be drilled down into the detail data. A good warehouse used in CRM operation must have the following features.

- High subject orientation
- High integration capability enterprise-wide for data integration and access from diversified sources
- High-time variance (timeliness of data and access)
- Non-volatility in terms of having a stable data-storage medium
- Capability to improve or re-invent business processes
- Capability to analyse historical data, reveal trends, and correlations in consumer buying patterns and behaviour, and predict future outcomes
- Capability to ensure assembling of data from diversified sources and consistency of data interpretation throughout the organization
- Identification of customers/leads with large business/benefit opportunities and exploiting these opportunities
- Identification of the return-on-investment (ROI) of each application based on past data
- Identification of applications that are not cost-justified and improve, move or eliminate these

FUNCTIONAL COMPONENTS OF A CRM SOLUTION

Key components of a CRM solution are given here.

Customer Database

A good customer information system should consist of systematic collection of customer related information that needs to be updated from time to time. The data must also help in predicting the change in customer needs and buying behaviour in the future. The database would also help the company to plan, implement, and monitor customer contact. Data from a variety of services are being added by most companies to make the database more dynamic. A dynamic database, if properly warehoused, can integrate information into one analysable data set, as information spread over many different databases may be rendered incompatible.

Technological Enablement of CRM

As discussed earlier also, the Web-enabled and integration approach of CRM cannot be accompanied without the use of technology, which includes all equipment, software, and communication links that companies may use to enable or improve their processes.

Electronic Point-of-sale

Advantage of having electronic point-of-sale (EPoS) and retail scan based system is the timeliness and accuracy of the information they deliver. Use of technologies such as RFID, as discussed in Chapter 4, have significantly changed the scope and nature of data collection. The data may be dynamic giving trends of consumption, replenishment and allocation, average stock levels, adequacy of shelf space, etc., which are nothing but SCM decisions down to the retailers' level. In addition to original scan based data such as sales rate, stock turnover, stock level, and price-make-ups, retailers now also have information about the demographic, socio-economic, and life style characteristics of consumers. Retailers can then take decisions on a variety of factors such as promotion, price, advertising, position in store, and allocation of shelf space. Decisions about the amount of *grey-stock* and the level of customization required can also be undertaken. All these decisions affect the supply chain up to distribution centre (DC) and in turn, the company and its suppliers.

Sales Force Automation

Automation of sales related processes would increase sales productivity and shorten the sales cycle. These automated systems may help us in tracking and managing all leads, contacts, and business opportunities throughout the sales cycle, including customer support. This would also result in bringing about greater accuracy in sales forecasting, providing in-depth information about the product and services, including pricing and offers, specialized databases of the solution, and sales force support queries. A set of internal information on the Internet can also improve productivity of sales force.

Automation of Customer Service and Support

Automating the customer support processes and the software used for such systems would help in logging the customer query, problems, and suggestions. It maintains information regarding status of customer enquiries, and stores all support calls and related communication till final resolution, thereby, also updating the database accordingly. Customer service extended through the Web may provide the customers with more information, tools, and flexibility in the hands of customers, thus, enhancing customer benefits and value, and improving the level and quality of customer support services on a dynamic basis.

Call Centres

These help in automating the operations of inbound and outbound calls generated between the company and its customers. The voice switch of automated telephone systems (EPBAX etc.) or toll-free/hotline number of the company are integrated with an agent host software allowing for automatic call routing to agents, resulting into predictive dialing, display of relevant customer data, and self-service interactive voice response system. The call centres are very useful in high volume segments such as banking, telecom, and hospitality. Global telephony-based call centres and the Internet have been very useful in such systems, thereby allowing call centres to handle customer interaction in all various forms and modes.

System Integration

Ultimately, all the systems used by the organization, key of these being ERP, SCM, and, CRM have to be integrated. As pointed out earlier, CRM interacts with the SCM through the ERP system. As discussed in Chapter 3, ERP helps in integrating various functional domains of the company such as finance and accounts, inventory, production, sales and distribution, and human resources. CRM automates the relationship with a customer encompassing the following features.

- Customer contact and business opportunity management
- Product and service processes
- Sales force management
- Customer order processing
- Order fulfilment, delivery, and installation
- Pre-sale and post-sale services
- Complaint handling

It is inevitable that both CRM and ERP complement information and business *workflows*. The integration of these two could help companies to provide faster customer service through an enabled network that would help the company in tracking, and resolution of problems as reported by the customers. It can also offer interactive, online systems (choice-boards) to customers who can design their own products by choosing from a menu of attributes, components, prices, and delivery options. The selection of an appropriate menu by the customer would send signals to the focal manufacturing firm, and if it has SCM networked to ERP, the procurement cycles would also be triggered. So, by electronically linking the channel partners with the end customers, the companies are reducing cost and cycle times, while improving delivery and flexibility to the end customer.

Customer Contact and Interactions

Web-enabled CRM and SCM are improving communication channels between suppliers and customers. Now, product testing times in markets and also the time to develop collaborative designs (between customers and suppliers) are shrinking. Also, because of advent of technologies such as RFID, VSAT aided communication, etc., time to get a new product on the retail shelf has been highly reduced.

Targeted e-mail surveys or individual e-mails to customers could allow faster and precise feedback, and also pinpoint problem areas for improvement. The customer communication on the Internet of the group of users of a company's products can exercise an influence on the market and the company. The so called 'word-of-mouth' spreads fast on the Internet.

Customization may change a product design from a standard product or service into a specialized solution (differentiated product) for a customer. If combined with innovative distribution, and if it can be feasible to execute, it would certainly create value and loyalty for the customer.

CRM Solutions and Their Requirements

There are four categories of solutions available for CRM implementation.

- Integrated application suite
- Interfaced application bundle
- Interfaced best-of-breed solution
- Best of cluster

Companies starting CRM implementation must have a basic picture of integration, interfacing, and functionality. An integrated application suite is a set of applications that employs a common architecture, and a common logical database. In an integrated applications bundle, there is a set of interfaced applications from a single vendor containing more than one architecture, or more than one logical database assembled by the vendor. In an interfaced best-of-breed solution, a company might select a set of best-of-breed applications from multiple vendors that are interfaced to work together either by the company itself, or the vendor, or a third-party integrator. Best-of-cluster is similar to best of breed except that the best application is selected from the cluster, which is then interfaced.

The CRM solutions must meet the following functional and technical requirements.

- Business intelligences and analytical capabilities
- Unified channels of customer interaction
- Support for Web-based functionality
- Centralized warehouse for customer information
- Integrated workflow
- Integration with ERP applications (so as to develop linkage with SCM)

Major CRM Products and Their Vertical Specificity

Certain verticals require high amount of interactions with the customer such as in financial and banking services, high technology, communication, and utilities industries. Each vertical may have functionality requirement specific to the industry. Some of these functionalities are given here.

- Category management
- Promotion management
- Demand planning and generation
- Sales and service contact centre
- Interactive selling
- Competitive pricing analysis
- Profitability analysis
- Integrated targeted marketing
- Interaction with billing system
- Contact centre
- Data mining
- Marketing analysis
- Knowledge management system

The CRM application functionality requirements would depend on the type of vertical, whether it is consumer products, telecom services, commercial banking, pharmaceutical and healthcare, or any other. Gaur (2001) has done a comparative assessment of CRM solutions for key verticals on the functionality requirements listed earlier. Some of the known CRM products from vendors are Siebel, Clarify, Oracle, and Vantive. Let us see some essential features of these products on a comparative basis.

Siebel

It is one of the few front office suites having vertical specific functions. It can be integrated with most of the back-office solutions such as SAP and Oracle. Siebel e-consumer goods offers e-business solutions spanning the entire demand-chain from end consumer through the retailer, and the wholesaler to the manufacturer. It has functions of customer promotion planning, integrated account targeting, category management, demand planning, and interactive selling. For financial services, Siebel e-finance enables financial, banking, insurance, and capital market organization to maintain long-term profitable relationships with different kinds of consumers. The data can be used to *cross-sell* and *up-sell* additional products and services. So the functionalities focus on contact centre and profitability analysis of different customers.

Siebel e-healthcare has more focus on contact management, disease education system, and knowledge management system but not marketing analysis. It provides a single view of the customers contacts coming through different channels, namely Internet, field, call centres, home and office staff, and independent brokers. It has the ability to streamline and improve sales, member services, medical management, and network management services.

Siebel e-communications has focused on functionality of blended sales and service contact centre, integration with billing system, and churn management. Competitive pricing analysis is lacking. It has some of the industry's best practices for generating service orders, managing billing inquiries and adjustments, and up-selling/cross-selling additional services. Various authorized executives can instantly access information such as billing, order management, and network management from operations support systems (OSS) to deliver customer support and increase sales.

Clarify

This product offers customer service and support, and field service suite. It can be integrated with most of the back-office solutions. Clarify e-front office integrates customer management and partnership relationship to extend sales and service channels to the Web. It includes logistics capabilities for drug development and testing, as also to increase brand value and increase customer loyalty. Sales force automation (SFA) capabilities facilitate product promotion for pharma companies with a large mobile sales organization.

Clarify comm center integrates the efforts of all customer interacting organizations with customer care and service delivery, service assurance, trouble ticketing, sales and work force automation, and help desk. It also works seamlessly with existing back-office applications.

Clarify e-front office can be used for financial services to integrate and manage multiple delivery channels for customer access. It also allows companies to define or evolve products and services quickly, as market and business conditions change. The product addresses workforce processes, contact centre, and points. Integrated targeted marketing is, however, not available. Information from each customer interaction is fed into an integrated data model, promoting both detailed analysis and strategic planning—a prerequisite for the changing business models because of changes in the business environment.

Oracle CRM

This CRM application suite is most suitable for consumer products and commercial banking, while poorly equipped for pharmaceutical and healthcare, where only contact management is available. For telecom service providers, competitive pricing analysis is generally lacking. So, the richness of functionality varies according to the vertical where Oracle is to be used. However, it offers a broad set of functionality across e-commerce, front office, and business intelligence. While some functionalities are superficial and not integrated within the bundle at the time of writing this book, others are too integrated and cannot be unbundled from Oracle back-office applications. So, it relatively lacks a deep multi-channel vertical functionality needed for implementation of CRM in most sectors.

Vantive

It offers a good level of customer service and support, and field service suite. Vantive's front office functionality is based on partnerships of original equipment manufacturers' (OEMs) agreements with complementary product providers. It offers a broad breadth of horizontal functionality that should be further integrated and tested in production environments (Gaur 2001). The solution is integrated with PeopleSoft at the back-office which provides vertical specific functionalities. However, a separate solution for each vertical is not there.

According to Gaur (2001), though Siebel stands out in consumer goods and pharma sector, but in verticals where call centres are more important, such as in financial services and telecom service providers, Clarify would best meet the needs of the industry. What is required is a deep, multi-channel, vertical specific functionality for CRM solution vendors' competitiveness.

As pointed out in a later section, SAP and Infosys's Finacle also offer CRM solutions with different functionalities.

CO-CREATION OF SUPERIOR CUSTOMER VALUE

Each customer contact point is empowered with the knowledge of being responsive to customer needs, and offer superior value to the customers, which they have co-created for themselves by collaboration and participation in the communication process initiated by the company. A good customer experience would not only deliver product, and service but also 'peace of mind' and a unique encounter or experience that gives sensory, emotional, cognitive, behavioural, and relational values that may (even surprisingly) replace complement functional values (Schmidt 1999). If these cannot replace, these would at least complement the functional values to create a superior value to the customer. Giving empowerment to the customer in the sense that one can co-design a product, select components or variety of one's choice, place the order on the Internet, know the status of the order, post an enquiry on the Net, get the bill and payment adjustments done, or even check on the availability of items in the inventory (Seybold 1998)—all can help in co-creating a superior value for the customer.

Needless to mention, Web-enabled CRM alone cannot get it done, unless the system is interfaced with SCM of the focal company through ERP.

Value-added Services

If there is an over abundance of supply of the product in the market, companies would offer value offerings that differentiate them from their competitors. The value-added services could be even in terms of providing access to information to the customers. There is nothing like giving the customers access to their own data, such as pending orders, payment history and status of the order, and tracking of delivery that enhances their customers' experience with the company. One of the essential requirements in SCM is the *visibility of information* related to product design, price, inventory order, and delivery status. Offering such services to the customer would not only offer value-added services, but also reduce cost to the company, if it provides these services in a scattered manner through its own employees.

In technical products or industrial selling, providing *customer support* and *maintenance* could be an important value-added service. Providing better support and maintenance could get the company closer to the customer, get ideas to improve design, and installation of the product to add value. Providing logistics services, suitable credit terms, and payment options could be important value addition to the products offered.

PRODUCT SELECTION AND NEW PRODUCT DEVELOPMENT

Nowadays, consumer products—both fast moving and consumer durables come in a variety of styles, colours, shapes, and options. A refrigerator may come in 5 different styles, 10 different colours, 5 types of interior finishes, and with single or double door—a total of 500 configurations. The difficulty with the supply chain is that distributors and retailers need to stock most of these configurations and combinations of products. The proliferation of options also makes it difficult to produce customer demand for a specific model, thus, forcing retailers and distributors to maintain large and diverse inventories.

The key product proliferation trends are the following.

- Specializing in offering one type of product, e.g., Starbucks, Barista, Subway, etc.
- Megastores that allow one-stop shopping for a large variety of products, e.g., Wal-Mart, Target, Circuit City in US and Big Bazaar and Spencers in India
- Megastores that specialize in one product area, e.g., Sport Mart in US, Food Bazaar and Westside in India

These trends are also emerging on the Internet where some sites have been successful in offering a large variety of different products, e.g., timesshopping.com for consumer produces while others specialize in a single offering, e.g., cleartrip.com for travel services.

The PC and office automation/electronics industry previously used to sell through specialized stores in computer and office automation/electronics, e.g., in Super Bazaar or Abacus in Delhi in India, but now a company may sell its products through various outlets, to reach the largest number of customers, e.g., shop on the Web and pick it up at the store, which is happening in the airline services also. However, the proliferation of products and thus, the difficulty in predicting demand for a specific model, forces retailers and distributors in the supply chain to maintain a high inventory level. Simchi-Levi, Kaminsky, and Simchi-Levi (2003) discuss ways to control the inventory in case of a large variety of product configurations.

Assemble to Order Model

This model, followed by Dell computers and HP, ensures that final configuration or assembly of a computer or printer is done only when the order comes or it is final. This is accomplished by *postponement* of final assembly so that a grey stock is maintained, and the final configuration is subject to confirmed orders. Companies in garment industry such as Benetton and Levi's also follow postponement strategy.

Maintenance of Larger Inventories at Distribution Centres/Warehouses

This is suitable for manufacturers of products with long manufacturing lead times and reduce inventory levels at their end. The key issue is whether the company is going to pay for the inventory at the regional distribution centre/warehouse. If it is like that, it is an incentive for the dealer to reduce inventory and its cost while increasing that of the manufacturer. Another key issue is whether regional warehouse/distribution centre is going to differentiate between large and small dealers. Large dealers, if they are going to pay for the inventory at the regional warehouse, may not be interested in such a logistical arrangement.

Maintenance of Inventory of Common Parts

Honda offers relatively a limited variety of options on its cars. Dell computers may have fewer options for certain modems or software. Hewlett-Packard (HP) may combine functionalities of two models to create products that meet common customer requirements. In fast moving consumer goods (FMCG), many times a great dysfunctional variety exists, say, 10 varieties of Colgate toothpaste. It is left to the marketing czars to explore whether variety actually adds to customer value. The solution is to have a *standardized variety* (mass customization).

In a nutshell, the SCM decisions get affected, mainly in terms of levels of inventory held, the transportation and logistics requirements, and frequency of orders right from the core company to its regional distribution centre, or warehouse to its retailers, and finally customers. The channels through which variety is offered such as through the Web or company's website, or company site/virtual stores/shopping stores/malls also do get affected in terms of forecasting the demand for variety, and planning for its supplies.

Mass Customization

Pine II (1993) introduced the concept of mass customization which combines the effects of mass production with craft production. Mass customization invites the production and delivery of a wide variety of customized products or services quickly and efficiently at low cost. Although not very suitable for commodity products, it not only creates competitive advantage in consumer products category, but also implicates the cost and complexity of associated logistics and supply chain networks.

The key to making mass customization work is to making *modular units* so that autonomous workers and managers can reconfigure these modules into various varieties to meet specific customer requests and demands. Each module is continuously upgraded in terms of its capabilities, and how effectively, quickly, and efficiently it completes its tasks and 'fit together' with other modules. The real skill lies in to coordinate, maintain, and creatively combine the links between modules in different ways to meet different customer requests. The workers should also develop expertise and efficiency in the method of mass production. Pine II and Boynton (1993) says that the systems that link modules must be instantaneous, costless, seamless, and frictionless in terms of low overheads required for networks of modules.

Impact of Mass Customization on Supply Chain Management

The first requirement for product selection and/or mass customization is that the information processes, flows, and systems must be in place for an effective SCM system. For mass customization to accomplish through dynamic networks of modules, long-term buyer–supplier partnerships and supplier integration is a must. More importantly, as many garment manufacturing, computer hardware, and printer manufacturing companies follow *postponement* till the product reaches the regional distribution centre, to facilitate regional product differentiation is always desirable. Postponing product differentiation until orders have been received and confirmed would allow customer-specific customization or mass customization. The mass customization process at Dell Computers is illustrated in Exhibit 6.1.

EXHIBIT 6.1 Mass Customization at Dell Computers

Michael Dell was just 19 when he founded Dell Computers from his college dorm at University of Texas in 1983, eight years after the PC was invented. He dreamt of competing with IBM and in fact, Dell bypassed IBM in PC sales in 1999. Dell achieved this position by adopting a unique strategy based on mass customization and direct business model. The idea was to bypass the dealer channel through which PCs were sold, and instead sell these directly to customers at lower prices by eliminating the cost of inventory and reselling expenses. Dell has virtually integrated its supply chain comprising suppliers, manufacturers, dealers, and service providers, and treats them as if they were a part of the company by intensive sharing of information. As Dell puts it, 'The virtual integration lets the company meet customers' needs faster and more efficiently.'

As is known, Dell never builds a PC for a customer until the customer's order has been placed. This allows the customer to specify unique requirements and Dell builds the computer to these requirements. Michael Dell is quoted having saying, 'You actually get to have a relationship with the customer. This creates valuable information which in turn allows us to leverage our relationships with both suppliers and customers. Couple that with technology and you have the infrastructure to revolutionize the fundamental business models to compete with major global companies.'

Most of the orders come in over the Internet. The order-taking system interfaces with Dell's own supply chain control system, which ensures that inventory is where it needs to be for the computer to be quickly manufactured. In addition, Dell stores very little inventory. For some assemblies, such as Sony Monitors, it does not keep any inventory. The third-party logistics (3PLs) providers such as UPS or Airborne Express pick up the monitors from Sony's Mexican factory and computers from Dell's Austin facility, and then match and deliver them to the customers. Dell keeps just around 6 days of inventory allowing it to turn over 46 times a year. Dell measures the average amount of time a component spends in inventory, the reciprocal of which is referred to as *inventory velocity*. Many of Dell's suppliers have built warehouses close to Dell's facilities and supply parts to its factory on JIT basis just minutes before they are needed. By implementing these strategies, Dell has been able to provide customers with exactly what they want very quickly. Although more than 90 per cent of Dell's PC business is custom ordered, the throughput time for each machine is less than 8 hours. At Dell's factory, a PC can be built, software installed, tested, and packed in 8 hours down from 10 previously. In addition, inventory costs are low and Dell minimizes the danger of parts' obsolescence in the rapidly changing computer industry. Dell has segmented its customers and offer various value-added services to them. For some clients, it would have an on-site team which would help them in PC purchasing and servicing. For example, it shipped 3700 PCs to Delta Airlines in just 11 days, who in turn threw a party for Dell's workers. In this way, Dell has become one of the dominant players in the desktop PC market. It is already on its way to doing so in the laptop and server markets.

The company is driven by advanced information systems that do everything from taking many orders (over the Web) to managing inventory in the supply chain. Strategic partnerships have been established with many of Dell's suppliers. Dell is even establishing supplier integration partnerships

(*Contd*)

EXHIBIT 6.1 *Contd*

with some of its key suppliers (e.g., 3Com, the network equipment supplier) to ensure that new computers and networking devices are compatible. Finally, Dell has utilized the concept of postponement, deferring final assembly of computers until orders have been received, to realize mass customization.

Source: Based on Magretta, J. (March–April 1998), 'The Power of Virtual Integration: An Interview with Dell Computer's Michael Dell', *Harvard Business Review*, pp. 72–84; Heizer, J. and Barry Render (2001), *Operations Management*, Prentice Hall, New Jersey, pp. 232–33; and McWilliams, G. (7 April 1997), 'Whirlwind on the Web', *Business Week*, pp. 132–36

STRATEGIC PRICING

There can be quite a significant differentiation in price for the same product. For example, Dell sells computers at different prices on its website, depending on whether the purchase is done by a private consumer, a small, medium or large business, the government, or an education or health care provider. Even the price of the same product for the same industry may not be fixed; it may significantly change over time. Many companies such as IBM and Compaq also have softwares that allow them to adjust their prices according to demand for various models/variants. Nikon cameras or Sharp digital camcorders may be sold in the range of $400–$500 in stores, but buying it from website/virtual stores could be cheaper. If ordered directly with the company/manufacturer, a rebate of up to $100 could be given to the customer, if the consumer mails in the rebate coupon. It can cost much cheaper to buy tickets from an airlines in India, say, *SpiceJet* or *Kingfisher* on their websites, rather than with their travel agents. Companies would rather prefer giving rebate through mailed coupons or Web purchases to customers over just reducing the wholesale price paid by the retailer or sales agent. The reason is that companies would come to know about customer demographics and profile, while also boosting profits by using appropriate revenue management techniques. For example, companies such as SpiceJet would send SMS alerts to their member customers about membership awards or incentives, or promotions.

Airline, travel, and rental car industries do normally sell the seats/capacity cheaper through their websites or a do a kind of e-auction. In fact, these companies even augment demand and manage capacity in off-season or keep demand constant during peak-season by a constant price, getting still the same profit/revenue. So pricing, used as a tool and selective revenue management can yield better results. Obviously, the forecasting and capacity planning in such cases ultimately affects the logistics and SCM decisions.

Smart Pricing

The following two types of smart pricing options can be used.

Customized Pricing

Here, the company distinguishes the customers according to their price sensitivity. Dell does it by distinguishing between private, small, medium or large, government, education, or health care provider customer. Mail-in rebates are given only when customers complete and mail the coupon to the manufacturer. Interestingly, mail-in rebates could also be sent by price-insensitive customers, which requires a more detailed analysis.

With no rebates, retailers would decide on the price and the order quantity so as to maximize its profits. The manufacturer in such cases would like the retailer to order as much as possible, as the company's profit would be proportional to the wholesale price and not the price paid by the customers.

With mail-in rebates, a manufacturer influences customer demand and though the price paid by consumers to the retailers is reduced, the retailer faces a higher demand level and thus, profit increases due to a high demand level. The retailer would in turn order more from the manufacturer, and it would also imply an increase in the manufacturer's expected profit. Again, the reason why a manufacturer would avoid giving discount on wholesale price rather than mail coupons to customers is that the retailer in the former case, would like to keep the discount with himself and not transfer it to the customers, implying thereby, that these would be no spurt in demand and hence, no increased profits at the manufacturer end.

Dynamic Pricing

It refers to changing prices over time without necessarily distinguishing between different types of customers. This type of smart pricing deals with using price as a tool to match demand and supply. This obviously requires that the executives who are in the front-end of the supply chain and make pricing decisions should have complete *visibility* into the back-end of the supply chain, i.e., the inventory and capacity available as well as the production. So dynamic pricing requires complete visibility into the supply chain right up to the shop floor capacity and inventory available. The following parameters need to be known in order to adopt a dynamic pricing strategy.

- Available capacity
- Variability in demand (peak/non-peak)
- Seasonality in demand
- Length of the planning period

It has been researched that smaller the production capacity relative to average demand variability and seasonality in demand, and smaller the planning period, greater would be the benefits from dynamic pricing. On an average, dynamic pricing increases profit by 2 to 6 per cent. The Internet has made dynamic pricing possible:

Menu card   The online prices are more dynamic and prices are updated even on a daily basis.

Lower buyer search price   Smart pricing through the Internet is a kind of e-auction searching for a buyer quoting a price at a given time. It may yield a low price to the customer but a high profit to the manufacturer.

Visibility in the back-end of the supply chain   It makes it possible to coordinate pricing, inventory order quantity, production, and transportation, i.e., supply chain alignment decisions.

Identification of customer segments   This is done by using historical data on the Internet, but it is difficult in conventional retailing.

Use of Internet to test pricing strategies in real times but in virtual stores   Different levels of price can be tested on small groups of site visitors, thereby determining pricing strategy. However, smart pricing must always avoid pitfalls of say, appearance of unfair/discriminatory treatment of the customer which could backfire.

CRM BUSINESS CYCLE

A leading consultant, Nykamp Consulting Group, proposed a CRM business cycle where the business starts and ends with the acquisition and retention of customers as shown in the figure as follows (Fig. 6.4). It has 4 stages.

Understanding and differentiating the customers   It refers to understanding the needs of the customer and differentiating them based on their needs, characteristics, and behaviour. This could be ensured by proper segmentation, list creation and management, and developing the leads based on the same.

Development and customization   This phase refers to the customization of customer needs and then developing specific products, services, and channels to distribute these customized needs in the form of products and services. In addition to segmentation and list management, this could be accomplished by proper case management on an individual basis.

Interaction and delivery   It is to bring about interaction with customers including the prospective ones, and deliver an increased or mutual superior value to the

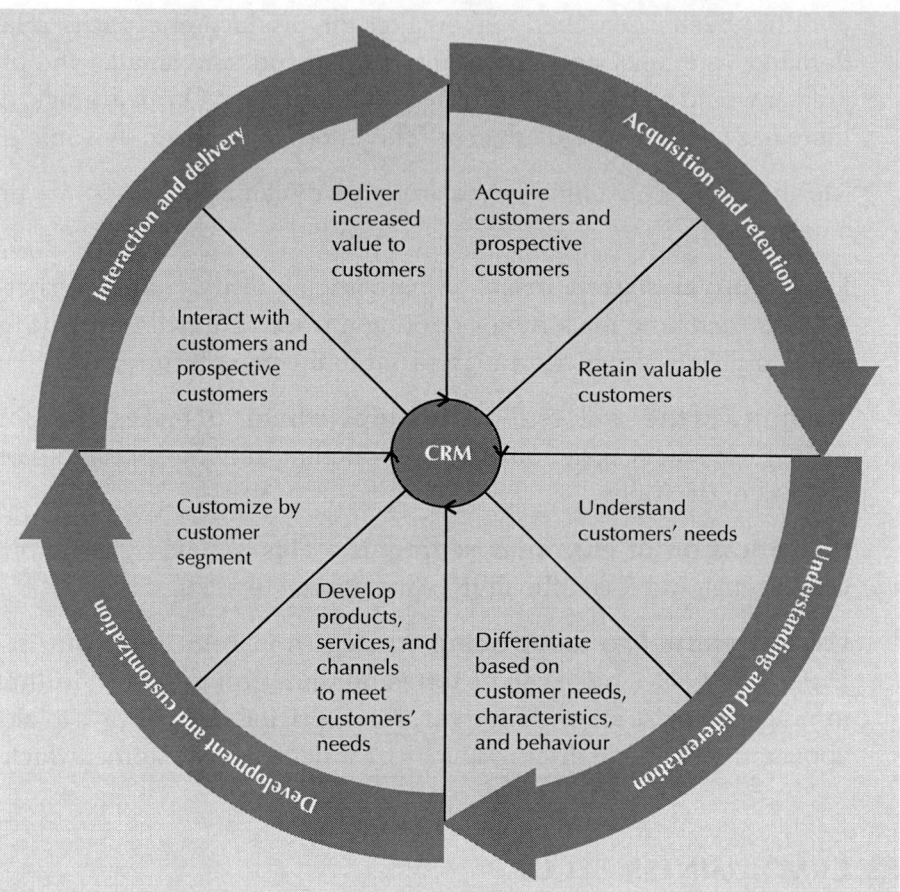

FIG. 6.4 The different phases of the CRM business cycle
Source: Nykamp Consulting Group, now Fair Isaac, 2001

customers. This is accomplished by a proper lead management, real-time offer, and campaign management. More targeted interaction could be facilitated by automation and case-to-case follow-up.

Acquisition and retention   It refers to acquiring the customers post the interaction with them, and then retain valuable ones amongst those. Incidentally, this phase again sets the ball rolling for the next CRM cycle. This is further facilitated by trade promotion management, warranties, and returns management.

As Melinda Nykamp puts it, 'CRM does not equate to pleasing all of the current customers at an enormous cost. It does equate to making appropriate and smart investments in specific interactions with customers (to create superior customer value and its proposition).' As she says, CRM should bring tangible value to the organization in three key areas, namely

- increased revenues
- decreased costs
- increased competitive differentiation

CRM envisages reaching and responding to the customers across all the *touch points*. Companies have, however, dramatically improved their abilities around the touch points by automation, be it a customer service/interaction centre, automation of a sales team, or marketing efforts in the form of campaigns or promotions. The idea is to have an appropriate level of investment in customer interactions. The focus is also to do more with less, as due to changing market dynamics, customer expectations have heightened, while companies have reduced their budgets—from cutback in retail personnel to reduction in call centres which means that while developing and installing CRM solutions, the focus is on process improvements and taking out the 'guesswork' out of a heavy volume, people dependent application.

The modern CRM applications provide for very targeted communications, well-managed customer interaction centres, and contacts. Marketing workflow and campaign management products are already in. Customer data management has come a long way from flat files with batch processing to very sophisticated customer identification applications. It has less to do with warehousing and more to do with the ability of the system to aggregate, access, analyse, and act on disparate sources of customer data that would throw light on patterns of customer behaviour. Such insights would in turn drive sales, service, and marketing strategies for the differentiated/selective customers.

Nykamp has been designing the financial structure of loyalty programmes that would significantly increase customer member spending, say, by 3–5 per cent. They claim to offer complete solution sets with proven methodology for CRM solutions to be delivered on time and on-budget. They have, for example, a CRM plan, which within 3–6 weeks would create a road map for CRM initiatives and appropriate investments. A 360 degree programme of theirs provides the companies a complete understanding of behaviours, preferences, loyalty, and potential value of their customers. As Ann Busquet, President, American Express Relationship Services puts it on the back cover of Nykamp's book, 'Many people believe that we have entered the age of the Internet. Actually, it is more accurate to say that we are living in the age of the customer. Make no mistake; customers are in control today. They have access to more information than ever before, and they can retrieve it faster than ever before. There has never been a better time to be a customer—or a more demanding time to be a company.' This is why there are challenges to get a successful CRM in place together with budget restrictions particularly, the current recessionary times.

Building Customer Loyalty

Richard Oliver (1997) defined the concept of loyalty as 'a deeply held commitment to re-buy or re-patronize a preferred product or service consistently in the future, despite situational influences and marketing efforts having the potential to cause switching behaviour.' The building of customer loyalty depends on whether the organization is under

- customer acquisition phase
- customer retention phase

According to Handen (2003), through building loyalty, the organization tries to prevent customers from leaving and uses the following three essential elements to select them, namely

- value-based segmentation
- needs-based segmentation
- predictive churn

Value-based segmentation allows the organization to determine how much it is willing to invest in retaining a customer's loyalty. Once the customer has passed the value-band segmentation criteria, the organization can use needs-based segmentation to offer a customized loyalty programme. In addition, with affinity programmes such as airlines miles, hotel points, and bonus points on credit cards, organizations would often offer customized billing, special helplines, back-end loaded credits, assigning them a customer service representative, exempting them from paying any service charges, etc., as a means of encouraging loyalty. Most of these offers are based more on customer's revenue level, than tailored to their segments. Also, as organizations focus more on the needs of individual customers, they are able to achieve the same level of loyalty with less investment.

In a predictive churn model, using the vast amount of demographic data and usage history available for the existing base of customers, it is possible to predict customer attrition. Through the use of advanced data-mining tools, organizations can identify such vulnerable customers who can then be offered alternative products, or targeted for a loyalty campaign. But before implementing such campaigning, there must be a significantly high confidence level while they are churned through data mining.

In a nutshell, the focus of relationship marketing being executed by many companies in the services sector is on developing long-term relationships and improving corporate performance through building customer loyalty and customer retention. Be it *Jet Privilege* programme of Jet Airways or loyalty (membership reward) programmes of card issuers such as American Express or Citibank, the focus on building long-term relationships with a certain class of customers in a differentiated manner to ultimately serve the relevant customer better, and also to thereby improve corporate performance. The relationship marketing programs at American Express (Exhibit 6.2), as outlined in the exhibit that follows clearly demonstrates this.

EXHIBIT 6.2 Building Customer Loyalty and Relationships at American Express

American Express Bank (AmEx) is the international banking subsidiary of American Express Co. founded in 1919. It provides services to financial institutions, high net worth individuals, and affluent customers through more than 75 locations in 45 countries. It is diversified worldwide into travel, financial, and network services. It is a world leader in change and credit cards, travelers cheques, travel, business services, and international banking. A consulting company, *Towergroup* estimated that 70 per cent of spending by credit card issuers is associated with products that offer loyalty benefits to card holders. Successful loyalty programmes have been proven to improve response rates, increase customer spend, and reduce account attrition such as at AmEx. It pioneered the concept of rewarding customers for their loyalty. As part of their spend-centric strategy, AmEx has a *Membership Rewards programme* in place, which got the bank the prestigious JD Power Associates award in 2008 amongst 18 card issuing companies, and the data for which was collected from 7665 customers. The programme is a fast and flexible programme that lets one redeem travel rewards over 21 airlines. Also, access to *Gold Card Events* would entitle the members a prioritized entry to concerts, shows, and sporting events, etc. It also provides for a host of unique travel and buyer/purchase protection services.

AmEx maintains *e-Access*, a cash reporting and transaction research system that delivers real-time information from the bank's global product centres in the western hemisphere, Europe, and Asia to clients worldwide on the Internet. e-Access was named the *IT/Business Alignment Project of the year—North America* in 2005 by *The Banker*, a leading journal of the Financial Times Group. The project is about service delivery through alignment of IT area, business functions, and third-party groups/service providers.

As Thomas Wiles, the bank's head of interactive product management and marketing puts it, 'e-Access is the foundation of our online offering and is integral to our overall competitive differentiation strategy. We developed the product in direct response to our clients' needs and set out to design it exclusively for financial institutions, which generally requires a more detailed level of reporting than corporate end users' e-Access was developed with SunGard, built on the *intelliTRAN* customer service solution to create a new online banking tool that extends customer service capabilities of the bank and its customers. It gives one the complete view of a business transaction that is processed by multiple partners. Its real-time balances and transaction module enables better payment and facilitates the cash manager to keep a tab on the cash position in real time. Clients who hold multiple accounts with AmEx in more than one currency can have a consolidated view of their global multi-currency balance summaries in real-time on one screen.'

(Contd)

As Wiles is further quoted as saying in *Business Wire* of June 14, 2005, 'e-Access has allowed the bank to have better productivity, more efficient reconciliation, customized investigations, flexible search capabilities, and informed decision-making. These features in turn have allowed the user to provide better and faster customer service.'

Source: Based on *Business Wire,* Issue 14 June 2005; www.americanexpress.com as accessed on 2 December 2008

Cross-selling/Up-selling for CRM

One aim of any CRM programme is to increase the wallet share or the amount the customer spends with the company. In cross-selling, the purpose is to identify complementary offerings that a customer would like. For instance, a basic long distance caller could be a prospect to buy Internet access. The nature of the offer would be determined by customers' needs-based segment, usage pattern, and reaction to previous contacts. Once the composition of the offer is determined and the contact medium is finalized, the organization directly presents the offer to the customer. Up-selling, on the other hand, does not involve offering complementary product(s), but offering only enhanced product, e.g., replacing an analog data line with integrated services digital network (ISDN). Cross-sell/up-sell campaigns are important because the targeted customers already have a relationship with the organization. They are always willing to pay a premium for it. When a customer accepts cross-sell/up-sell, the customer begins to become much more profitable. At the outset of this relationship, the customer reduces gross margin by around 3 per cent (based on acquisition costs) and then enhances gross margin by 7 per cent in next 3 years and 12 per cent by next 5 years (Pricewaterhouse Coopers Research, 2000).

COMPONENTS OF A TYPICAL IT SOLUTION FOR CRM

Some of the generic components of a CRM solution are discussed here.

Marketing and sales   It entails management of marketing resources segment and lists, campaigns, leads and trade promotions, territories, accounts and contacts, sales activities, opportunities, product configurations, billing, contracts, as also the sales planning and forecasting.

Services   These entail management of support services such as call centres, field service, and the e-services. To effectively manage service orders, it may cover management of contracts, complaints, returns, warranties, repairs, and resources planning for the same.

Channel management   It aims to attain a profitable and loyal indirect channel by properly managing partner relationships. This can be accomplished by effective partner recruitment, communications, collaborative selling, channel services, and incentives.

Interaction centre   This module which aims to manage customer loyalty helps create a strategic delivery channel across all the *touch points*. It manages activities such as tele-marketing, tele-sales, customer services, IT support, and interaction centre management.

Web channel enablement   It is designed to exploit the Internet as a sales channel for e-commerce, e-marketing, and e-services.

Business communication management   This is designed to provide seamless and consistent experiences across all channels, e.g., voice, text messages, Web, and e-mail for both inbound and outbound contacts. It must function across multiple channels and locations.

Real-time offer management   This functionality tries to convert all e-interactions into opportunities through cross-selling, up-selling, retention offers, and specific service level agreements (SLAs).

Trade promotion management   It refers to management of trade promotions and their budgets, and their execution at retail level with back-office integration.

SAP have an extensive CRM business solution with all the above elements and others for implementing CRM in an organization. Infosys's Finacle also has successful CRM stories, particularly in the banking industry. The Finacle CRM solution focuses on enterprise customer information, sales, marketing, and services, including call centres.

RECAPITULATION

In this chapter, first the concept of CRM has been defined and analysed, followed by establishment of linkage between CRM with SCM in the organizational context. The way implementation of CRM is interfaced with information technology (IT) and various processes is then discussed in detail. The Web-enablement and integration approach of CRM is compared with the conventional approach to CRM. Various elements of IT infrastructure used for supply chain and CRM implementation and integration such as use of interface devices, communication system and technology, and system architecture are discussed with special focus on tools such as the three Ws—Web, warehousing, and workflows. This is supplemented by an elaborated description of the functional components of a CRM solution, and also the major products in the CRM industry, as also their application in various industries. This leaves us at a point where it can be concluded that a well laid-out CRM strategy or programme supplemented with the right mix of technology tools can bring about the co-creation of superior customer value, particularly by value addition to the services offered to the customers. It has also been reinstated that how the concept of mass customization has brought about various supply chain options, and giving opportunity to improve relations, and also develop loyalty by giving them (the customers) various pricing options, educate them about creating and selecting new product configurations suited to them, and cross-selling/up-selling to them if they appear interested and promising. How a supply channel can be aligned with respect to inventory levels, transportation and logistics requirements, pricing, and ownership of products is also discussed. Exact trade-offs may not be possible but certainly the forecasting accuracy can be increased, while levels of inventories maintained, and stock level requirements can be substantially reduced by various actions such as EDI, milk run, freight consolidation, value-based pricing, re-designing the packaging, standardization in products/parts/processes, and using parallel/concurrent processing together with an orientation for delayed differentiation/assembly wherever, possible. A lot of IT-enabled CRM solutions are now available, notable of these being from SAP and Infosys. Most of these focus on customer interactions, customer data management, sales, services, call centres, and marketing, including Web-enabled promotions and communications, and channel management on a real-time basis. We will now analyse as to how the performance of SCM can be measured, and what are the respective benchmarks in the chapter that would follow.

CONCEPT REVIEW QUESTIONS

1. How do you define customer relationship management (CRM)? What are the purposes of CRM?
2. Establish the linkage between CRM and supply chain management (SCM). Why is IT invariably involved in implementation of CRM?
3. What are the requirements of a CRM solution for a company? Briefly discuss the functional components of a CRM solution. What should be capabilities of a CRM solution?
4. What are the 3Ws of CRM implementation? Outline the importance of each one of these Ws.
5. Briefly explain as to how CRM and SCM together can help in creating a superior value to the customer.
6. Analyse why channel alignment may be required? Briefly discuss some measures which can bring about a balance amongst inventory levels, pricing, transportation and logistics requirements, and ordering patterns at the retailer's end. How can channel alignment strategies help in the overall supply chain managements and its efficiency?
7. How do product proliferation decisions affect the supply chain and customer relationship? What should be the SCM and CRM strategies in case of mass customization?
8. What are the various pricing options available for SCM managers? How are these designed to foster good relationships with customers?
9. What are the different components of a CRM business cycle? How can the activities of this cycle be executed? How can this be better organized by developing an IT-enabled solution for CRM?
10. What is customer loyalty? What should be the elements of building customer loyalty? How can cross-selling/up-selling help the customer and the company alike?

CRITICAL THINKING QUESTIONS

1. Many management experts say that conventionally, CRM is not new to the Indian business, except the IT part. Do you agree with this view? Are you reminded of some conventional Indian business practices to acquire and retain the customers? Cite some examples. (You can talk to some veterans in the retail and distribution sector who deal with customers.)

2. Why is Web-enablement so crucial to fostering functional linkages between CRM and SCM?

3. How can a superior customer value be created by using the CRM-augmented supply chain approach? Identify the crucial elements of such an approach.

4. How can SCM can help in new product innovation, development, and its marketing?

5. How is customer loyalty important from the supply chain point of view? How could retaining and partnering with selective customers help in managing the supply chain?

6. Outline the role of real time offer and trade promotion management on supply chain decisions.

PROJECT ASSIGNMENTS

1. Select a company which is reputed for maintaining good customer relationships. Find out how it is able to do that. Is it because of certain conventions being followed, or a CRM system, or a combination of both? What is the approach and philosophy of the selected company to maintain good relationships with customers and make them loyal to it?

2. Make a list of various CRM software products available in the market. Comparatively evaluate these on the basis of their composition/features and application in the industry. You can ask a vendor to name a few clients whom you interview on the usage and effectiveness of these products.

3. Go to a big retail store/mall in your area and find out how they use technology to ensure timely supplies in the right quantity at the retail shelves, how they establish contact and develop and keep relationships with their customers, and deliver best value to the latter.

4. Find out from the selected retailer in (3) as to how they change the pricing in response to changes in demand or supply.

5. Examine customer loyalty/affinity programmes of a few companies and its objectives as launched through a retail store of your choice (May be you are a loyal customer). How frequently and when are the customers asked to give new product requirements/design choices, to what extent the company meets it and how? How many times and when the
   (a) cross-selling/up-selling is resorted to?
   (b) promotional campaign are launched?
   What are your views regarding the same?

6. Visit the websites of companies such as SAP and Infosys and find out the common modules and the activity elements of their CRM solution offerings.

CASE STUDY

GLOBAL CASE STUDY

HEWLETT-PACKARD[2]

Corporate Background

In today's global economy, customers always expect the best products, the best services, and the best solutions at the lowest possible cost. If a business cannot meet—and, wherever possible, exceed—these expectations, chances are customers will find someone who can.

Hewlett-Packard (HP) is one of the world's leading providers of computing and imaging solutions and services for business and home.

Managing customer relationships means applying the strengths and skills of the entire organization behind every customer interaction—from the time the organization begins to market its products and services, to the customization of each deliverable. To ensure that this level of service is never compromised, HP needed to have the capability to provide its internal staff with a complete customer history on a global basis, at the click of a button.

The company had established two major, distinct, but related requirements for a CRM solution. One requirement was to be able to share customer information on a global basis, and the other was to take control of e-mail campaigns from nine different marketing groups.

CRM Project Objectives

HP identified two major products as a part of CRM implementation. The objectives set were

CRM Project A: To collaborate and share real-time information globally, over the Internet.

CRM Project B: To use its Web presence more effectively and to develop a central strategy for e-mail marketing.

Developing CRM Solution for Project A

To meet the objectives of CRM Project A, HP turned to Oracle Corporation to develop the *sales force automation (SFA)* portion of a complete CRM solution. Both HP and Oracle have a common vision of the future of the Internet, and the need to provide customer-centric solutions.

The company's typical customers include IT managers whose business division has purchased servers, printers, and services from Hewlett-Packard. These customers also include managers in other parts of the business, and those managers request e-mail updates and newsletters that tell them when new printer drivers are available, when security updates are posted, and when product updates come to the market.

Occasionally, customers call a helpline, but they are much more likely to get most of their answers from online sources. These customers prefer to get news and updates by e-mail and are quite responsive to online marketing offers.

Forward thinking companies and organizations such as HP realize that the key to creating, maintaining, and extending competitive advantage is to move their products and services to the market faster, better, and cheaper. Increasingly, the power of the Internet is revolutionizing the policies, procedures, and go-to-market strategies for companies of all sizes, across all industry sectors, the world over.

The CRM platform, provided by Oracle to meet HP CRM Project A objectives, enabled the

[2] *Source:* The case is largely based on Sharp, Duane E., 'Relationship Management Systems Handbook', CRC Press, 2003. The author acknowledges due acknowledgement

company to perform real-time demand forecasting and efficient allocation of resources to meet customer requirements.

Developing CRM Solution for Project B

Recognizing a changing marketplace, HP realized that it needed to use its Web presence more effectively and had been regularly collecting business customer data and e-mail addresses from all of its sales channels, but did not have any central programme or strategy for e-mail marketing. At times, as many as nine different marketing groups would send out e-mail marketing campaigns to segments of the list, but each one was a single-shot effort.

These programmes were not coordinated or leveraged in any way, and did not promote loyalty among its business customers. In fact, they were most likely to irritate customers by inundating them with information they never asked for, and that too, from different sources at the company.

To meet the objectives of this CRM project, HP recognized that it needed to take control of e-mail campaigns from those nine different marketing groups. It also had to champion the customer-centric idea that marketing should be a long-term process that focuses on the life-cycle of customers, instead of looking at a sale as a singular transaction.

The project team worked with HP's corporate CRM strategy groups to develop an e-mail marketing strategy that would fit into the larger CRM framework. The e-mail project focused on e-mail marketing, while coordinating its efforts with the larger corporate strategy that included other customer-facing groups such as call centres and customer service teams.

To meet the requirements of both groups, the team developed a comparison programme to find out which type of marketing campaign best suited each customer's individual preferences. A carefully controlled pilot project was initiated to compare e-mail campaigns with direct-mail offers. Cost savings and revenues generated from both kind of campaigns were analysed, as well as the effect of the e-mail marketing on the customer experience.

The results showed that more customers responded to the low-cost e-mail offer, making it over 20 times more cost-effective. It costs $1 per direct mailing per customer, but only between 10 and 15 cents per customer to create and send monthly e-mail to more than a million customers per month. Customers responded positively to the e-mail alerts and updates, thereby generating new sales revenues.

The e-marketing division also estimates that significant cost savings were achieved by combining and reducing multiple e-mail campaigns. Sending out product support alerts and e-mails also resulted in reduced calls made to the support lines.

Benefits Accrued

For CRM Project A, Oracle provided HP with a CRM platform that would provide the following functions.

1. Perform real-time forecasting to develop more efficient business and sales processes.
2. Prioritize opportunities and apply the requisite resources to the market.
3. Improve the total customer experience.

The CRM solution for Project B provided the following benefits to HP.

1. The company developed a low-cost e-mail strategy that was over 20 times more cost-effective than a direct-mail campaign.
2. Customer response to the e-mail alerts and updates was positive—more than 85 percent were quite satisfied with the content they received.
3. e-mail campaigns generated an estimated $15 million in new sales revenues per month.
4. Cost savings of half a million dollar per month resulted from combining and reducing multiple e-mail campaigns.

5. A reduction in calls made to support lines saved close to $150, 000 per month.

So, the benefits accrued out of CRM implementation as a project basis of HP yielded multifold results.

Discussion Questions

1. What do you think could be the reasons that would have prompted Hewlett-Packard (HP) to select the mentioned CRM projects? Why would a company such as HP be so specific in selection of projects for CRM?
2. Briefly suggest any modification in the method/processes adopted to arrive at solution of project 1 and/or project 2? What is your assessment as to the assessment of effectiveness of these solutions arrived at?
3. How would HP possibly pass on the primary benefits accrued out of these CRM implementation projects to their worldwide customers?
4. What are the key lessons learnt from CRM implementation according to you, as a major international manufacturer of high technology projects?

INDIAN CASE STUDY

ICICI BANK[3]

Overview

ICICI Bank is India's second-largest bank with total assets of Rs 3997.95 billion (US$ 100 billion) and profit after tax (PAT) of Rs 41. 58 billion for the year ended March 31, 2008. ICICI Bank is second amongst all the companies listed on the Indian stock exchanges in terms of free float market capitalization[4]. The bank has a network of about 1308 branches and 3950 ATMs in India, and presence in 18 countries. ICICI Bank offers a wide range of banking products and financial services to corporate and retail customers through a variety of delivery channels, and through its specialized subsidiaries and affiliates in the areas of investment banking, life and non-life insurance, venture capital, and asset management. The bank currently has subsidiaries in the United Kingdom, Russia, and Canada, branches in Unites States, Singapore, Bahrain, Hong Kong, Sri Lanka, Qatar, and Dubai International Finance Centre and representative offices in United Arab Emirates, China, South Africa, Bangladesh, Thailand, Malaysia, and Indonesia. The UK subsidiary has established branches in Belgium and Germany. ICICI Bank's equity shares are listed in India on Bombay Stock Exchange and the National Stock Exchange of India Limited, and its American Depositary Receipts (ADRs) are listed on the New York Stock Exchange (NYSE).

Corporate History

ICICI was formed in 1955 at the initiative of the World Bank, the Government of India, and representatives of the Indian industry. The principal objective was to create a development financial institution for providing medium-term and long-term project financing to Indian businesses. In the

---

[3] *Source:* This case has been developed using the following resources for which the author expresses acknowledgement and thanks. www.icicibank.com as accessed on 9 July 2008; www.infosys.com/Finacle as accessed on 29 August 2008; Chaudhuri, Avijit and G. Shainesh (2001), 'Implementing a Technology-based CRM Solution: The ICICI Experience,' Proceedings of First International Con-ference on CRM, jointly organized by Management Development Institute (MDI), Gurgaon, and Institute for Customer Relationship Management (ICRM); Nykamp, M., 'How To Get There From Here', www.crmittoolbox.com/peer/docs/crm_howto.asp

[4] Free float holding excludes all promoter holdings, strategic investments, and cross holdings among public sector entities

1990s, ICICI transformed its business from a development financial institution offering only project finance to a diversified financial services group offering a wide variety of products and services, both directly and through a number of subsidiaries and affiliates such as ICICI Bank.

The ICICI bank was originally promoted in 1994 by ICICI Limited, an Indian financial institution, and was its wholly-owned subsidiary. ICICI's shareholding in ICICI bank was reduced to 46 per cent through a public offering of shares in India in the year 1998. An equity offering in the form of ADRs listed on the NYSE in fiscal 2000, ICICI bank's acquisition of Bank of Madura Limited in an all-stock amalgamation in 2001, and secondary market sales by ICICI to institutional investors in fiscal 2001 and 2002. In 1999, ICICI became the first Indian company and the first bank or financial institution from non-Japan Asia to be listed on the NYSE.

After consideration of various corporate structuring alternatives in the context of the emerging competitive scenario in the Indian banking industry, and the move towards universal banking, the managements of ICICI and ICICI bank decided that the merger of ICICI with ICICI bank would be the right strategic alternative for both entities, and would create the optimal legal structure for the ICICI group's universal banking strategy. The merger would enhance value for ICICI shareholders through the merged entity's access to low-cost deposits, greater opportunities for earning fee-based income and the ability to participate in the payments system, and provide transaction-banking services. The merger would enhance value for ICICI bank shareholders through a large capital base and scale of operations, seamless access to ICICI's strong corporate relationships built up over a long time, entry into new business segments, higher market share in various business segments, particularly fee-based services, and access to the vast talent pool of ICICI

and its subsidiaries. Finally, the merger of ICICI and two of its wholly-owned retail finance subsidiaries, ICICI Personal Financial Services Limited and ICICI Capital Services Limited, with ICICI Bank was modulated in 2002. Consequent to the merger, the ICICI group's financing and banking operations, both wholesale and retail, have been integrated in a single entity.

ICICI bank has formulated a Code of Business Conduct and Ethics for its directors and employees.

Business Segment

ICICI bank targets India's burgeoning middle class and companies by offering a high level of customer service and efficiency that till now was the forte of foreign banks, on a much larger scale and at a larger cost. Of late, ICICI bank has positioned itself as a technology savvy customer friendly bank. The company implemented customer relationship management (CRM) in a big way.

Information Technology (IT) Solution Overview

ICICI needed a robust technology platform that would result in achievement of business goals. Subsequent to a global reach, ICICI bank selected Infosys as a technology partner and selected its banking product—Finacle—technically best-of-breed retail and corporate banking solution with scalable architecture and proven implementation records. The biggest challenge before finance was to ensure straight through processing (STP) of most of the financial transactions. It was also needed to seamlessly integrate it with multiple applications such as credit cards, mutual funds, brokerage, call centre, and data warehousing system. The other challenge was to handle big transactions say from 4,00,000 transactions a day in 2000 to nearly 201 million by 2005.

The ICICI bank uses its *teradata* platform to develop tailored marketing campaigns that have boosted customer acquisition rates significantly. It has serviced over 11 million unique customers around the customers around the country in teradata solution centres on a CRM platform. Information from various legacy and transactions systems is fed into a single enterprise-wide data warehouse. This allows the bank to generate a single view of each one of its customers. It helps the bank to correctly identify and target current and prospective customers. ICICI bank credit cards and loan business units attributed 25 per cent each respectively of their new/incremental business in the past year to cross-selling activities facilitated by the data warehouse. The bank optimizes its delivery channels across 400 shop frames, 1600 plus ATMs, multiple call centres, and Internet banking services.

'This solution was the first large scale CRM implemention in Indian banking sector,' says teradata Business Manager (India), Amrish Rao (June 2003). ICICI is also using teradata tools, e.g., Behavior Explorer and Communications manager for a better understanding of its customers. The bank has used teradata platform to develop targeted marketing campaigns that have boosted customer acquisition rates significantly. Ultimately, it shows as to how ICICI has harnessed the use of IT in using a relationship technology solution for better CRM.

The figure that follows (Fig. 6.5) shows the different interfaces of the core banking solution developed by Finacle of Infosys.

Over the years, the strategic partnership between ICICI bank and Infosys that started in 1994 has grown strong and the collaboration has reflected itself in many innovations. For instance,

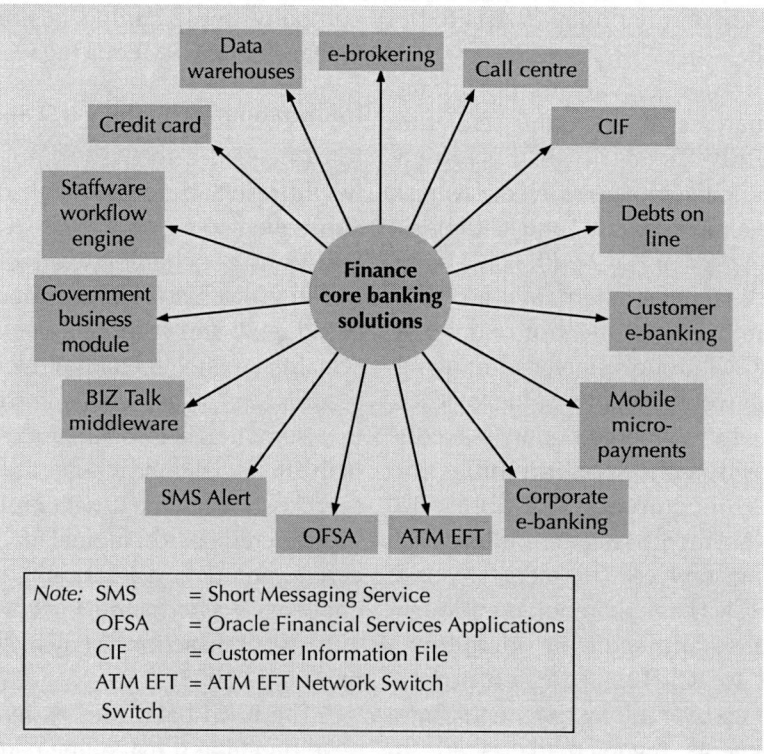

FIG. 6.5 Interfaces of the core banking solution developed by Infosys for customer relationships at ICICI

Source: www.infosys.com/Finacle; infosys.com/finacle/casestudies/casestudies_icici.asp

in 1997, it was the first bank in India to offer Internet banking with Finacle's e-banking solution, and established itself as a leader in the Internet and e-commerce. The bank followed it up with offering several e-commerce services such as bill payments, funds transfers, and corporate banking on the Net. The Internet is a critical element of ICICI bank's award winning multi-channel strategic initiative that is one of the main engines of growth for the bank between 2000 and 2004. The bank has been able to successfully move over 70 per cent of routine banking transaction from the branch to the other delivery channels, thus, increasing overall efficiency. During 2000–04, ATM banking increased from 3 per cent to 43 per cent and the bank's call centre activity increased from 1 per cent to 11 per cent. This reduction in routine transactions through the branch has enabled ICICI bank to aggressively use its branch network as customer acquisition centres. On an overage, ICICI bank adds 3 lakh customers a month, which is among the highest in the world. Table 6.1 tabulates the business share among various ICICI bank channels.

TABLE 6.1 Business share among various ICICI bank channels

Channels	Share of transactions (March 2000)	Share of transactions (March 2004)
Branches	94%	25%
ATMs	3%	43%
Internet and mobile	2%	21%
Call centres	1%	11%

Source: www.infosys.com/finacle

Currently, the bank has ability to process 27 million cheques per day and manage 7000 customer users. The bank also won the *DM review world-class solutions award* in 2003 in the Business Intellegence category for its teradata enterprise data warehouse (EDW) solution. Teradata is a division of NCR Corporation. Speaking at a NASSCOM meet in 2005, Lalita Gupte, Joint MD of ICICI bank deliberated on as to how the bank leveraged the use of IT in gaining a competitive edge. In a short span of time, says she, 'We had to concentrate on five prominent aspects, namely

- volume proposition
- customer service
- shareholder's centres
- supplier's expectation
- regulator's expectations

For all this to achieve, IT became a great vehicle. As volumes shot up, the changes in the pattern of customer behaviour were adequately handled by technology. It helped in real-time innovation in our product portfolio,' adds Gupte. IT was used to facilitate customer convenience. The bank introduced biometric-based action as an added measure of security and conveyance. It also uses centralized automated service to reduce error rates in transactions and other processes. An elaborate CRM system is in place to record customer preferences. The improved system has resulted in seamless order flow, reduced reconciliation problems, and reduced discrepancies. Therefore, it can operate at 10 per cent of the cost of the other international banks because of the scalability present in the IT arsenal. She believes in pay-per-use mode for the customer.

The bank needed to leverage the power of Finacle and deployed the solution in the areas of core banking, corporate e-banking, consumer banking, and CRM. The bank gained the flexibility to develop new products targeted as specific segments with ICICI bank, namely *Young Stars*—a product targeting young children, woman's account addressing working women, and *bank@campus* targeting students. The Bank has won many accolades for it. In 2003, ICICI received the best multi-channel strategy award from the

Bank Manager and in 2004, the bank was rated as the 2nd best retail bank in Asia by the *Asian Banker Journal*. The bank has effectively used technology as a strategic differential, which has not only redefined the rules of banking in India, but also showcasing as to how technology can help in transforming a bank's business.

As Chanda Kochhar, ED, ICICI Bank puts it, 'Our objective of creating a universal bank providing end-to-end financial services clearly required solutions which were based on new generation technology, offered end-to-end functionality, and were highly flexible and scalable. Finacle offered all this and much more.'

The bank never favoured pronounced shift to either branch-assisted mode or self-service mode at the total expense of the other in India. The branch is as much as a service vehicle, as commented by a senior executive of the bank. In 2005, the bank came out with new initiatives to service customers. Surprisingly, analysts now say, many public banks in US and Europe are now showing a definite preference for conducting branch-based services. ICICI, because of the need to serve an increasing number of customers originally to the self-service mode, introduced dynamic queue management (DQM). Systems data from DQM will form input for the bank's initiatives such as life productivity and Six Sigma—the data about the number of transaction with each customer and by each employee will also facilitate estimation of employee productivity, and determine manpower requirement. The customer waiting time and customer transaction times were used as the key variables into the process quality information system used for the *Six Sigma programme*, thereby, also improving customers' service levels at the bank.

Implementing CRM at ICICI

CRM, at ICICI, is viewed as a concept, as well as a set of discrete software technologies, which will focus on automating and improving the business processes associated with managing customer relationships in the areas of sales, marketing, customer service, and support. The organization ultimately aims to achieve the end goal of one-to-one marketing.

The CRM software applications would not only facilitate the coordination of multiple business functions, but also coordinate multiple channels of communication with the customer—face-to-face, call centre, ATM, Web, telephone, kiosk, bank, branch, sales associates, etc.—so as to enable ICICI carry out *cradle-to-grave* customer management more efficiently. It should allow ICICI to engage in *one-to-one marketing* by tracking the complete customer life-cycle history. To begin with, it would automate process-flow tracking in the product sales process and also be able to generate customized reports, and promote cross-selling. It will also enable efficient *campaign management* by providing a software interface for definition, tracking, execution, and analysis of campaigns.

From an architecture point of view, the enterprise-wide CRM solution should seamlessly integrate non-transactional related customer information housed in the front office with the transactional information housed in the back office.

At ICICI, CRM was believed to essentially focus on providing *optimal value* to the customers —through the way they communicate with customers, how they sell to them, and how they service them—as well as through the traditional means of product, price, promotion, and place of distribution. ICICI recognizes that customers make buying decisions based on more than just the price and the product. Customers make buying decisions based on their overarching experience that not only includes product and price, but also, sales, service, recognition, and support. If ICICI can get all of those factors right—consistently—ICICI thought it would be rewarded with ongoing customer loyalty and value.

A comprehensive CRM action plan was developed at ICICI based on the understanding that CRM will require an enterprise-wide transformation.

The CRM business transformation map below (Fig. 6.6) shows the various aspects of that change. There are five interrelated areas. These include business focus, organizational structure, business metrics, marketing focus, and technology.

The key to framing the CRM action plan was in assessing as to where the organization stood with respect to each of the five aspects of change. Interviews with key individuals throughout the organization helped identify different initiatives that would be launched, all focused on CRM. While all of these initiatives may have merit, failure to address the total business transformation requirements could lead to very short-lived success. The next step in the planning process was a *Gap Analysis*. This analysis essentially compared current status against optimal relative to the five core areas of business—to identify and specifically describe the gaps. In addition, this analysis helped identify the CRM organizational holes in the following areas.

(a) Marketing, sales, and service practices
(b) Collection, capturing, processing, and deployment of customer information
(c) Distribution and operations effectiveness at customer touch points

Another key factor in identifying gaps is to understand how the ICICI functions, relative to the CRM business cycle. There is a universal, underlying cycle of activity that should drive all CRM initiatives and infrastructure development. All initiatives and infrastructure development should somehow be tied to this core cycle of activity. Careful evaluation of the organization's ability to execute this cycle would pinpoint and qualify additional organizational gaps.

Business focus					
Product	Sales	Channel	Marketing	Service	Customer
Organizational structure					
Product management	Place management	Promotion management	Channel management	Contact management	Customer management
Business metrics					
Product performance	Place performance	Program performance	Customer revenues	Customer patterns and profitability	Customer lifetime value and loyalty
Market focus					
Mass advertising	Sales promotion	Marketing campaigns	Integrated marketing communications	Segments specific marketing	Customer relationship management
Technology					
Transaction processing	Data maintenance	Data access	Data warehouse	Data marts	Customer touchpoint systems

FIG. 6.6 The CRM business transformation map
Source: 'How to Get There from Here' by Melinda Nykamp, President, Nykamp Consulting Group

According to Nykamp Consulting Group, for any organization, there is a CRM business cycle where the business starts and ends with the acquisition and retention of customers, as shown in Fig. 6.4 earlier. However, any successful CRM initiative is highly dependent on a sound understanding of the customers.

Let us examine these stages of the CRM business cycle with respect to ICICI.

Understanding and Differentiation of Customers

Organizations cannot have a relationship with customers unless they understand them—what they value, what types of services are important to them, how and when they like to interact, and what they want to buy. True understanding is based on a combination of detailed analysis and techniques comprising the following factors.

- Profiling to understand demographics, purchase patterns, and channel preference
- Segmentation to identify unique groups of customers that tend to have *clustered preferences* and behave in a similar fashion. While the promise of *one-to-one marketing* sounds good, ICICI does not seem to be aware of organizations that have mastered the art of treating each customer uniquely. Identification of actionable areas is a reasonable point to initiate
- Primary research to capture needs and attitude of customers and prospects
- Customer valuation to understand profitability, as well as lifetime value, or long-term potential. Value may also be based on the customer's ability or inclination to refer other profitable customers

To create and foster a relationship, organizations have to act on what they learn about customers. ICICI Group's customers need to be communicated that the company is differentiating service and communications, based on both what ICICI has learned independently, and on what the customer has told them. At the same time,

differentiation should be based on the value customers are expected to possess.

Development and Customization

In the conventional product focused business, companies developed products and services, and always expected customers to buy them. In a customer-focused world of today, product and channel development have to follow the customer's lead. Organizations are increasingly developing products, services, and even new channels based on customer needs and service expectations.

Most organizations today are not able to cost-effectively customize products for individual customers. However, products, services, channels, and media can be customized together based on the values and needs of different customer segments. ICICI believes that the extent of customization should be based on the potential value delivered by the customer segment.

Interaction and Delivery

Interaction is also a critical component of a successful CRM initiative. It is important to remember that interaction does not just occur through marketing and sales channels, and media; customers interact in many different ways with many different functions of the organization, including distribution and shipping, customer service, and also through the Web. To foster customer relationships, companies need to ensure that

- all areas of the organization have easy access to relevant, actionable customer information
- executives of all areas are trained on how to use customer information to tailor interactions, based on both customer needs and potential customer value

With access to information and appropriate training, organizations are prepared to steadily enhance the value they deliver to customers.

Delivering value is a cornerstone of the relationship. ICICI is strongly of the opinion that value is not just based on the price of the product or the discounts offered. In fact, customer perceptions of value are based on a number of factors, including the quality of products and services, convenience, speed, ease of use, responsiveness, and excellence in service.

Acquisition and Retention of Customer

The more ICICI learns about customers, the easier it is to pinpoint those that are producing the greatest value for the organization. Those are the customers and customer segments, the company would want to clone in its prospecting and acquisition efforts. The ICICI will continue to learn about what is valuable to each segment. Thus, it will be much more likely to score a win with the right channel, right media, right product, right offer, right timing, and the most relevant message.

ICICI aims to accomplish successful customer retention based on its ability to constantly deliver on three principles.

- Maintain interaction; never stop listening to customers
- Continue to deliver on the customer's definition of value
- Remember that customers change as they move through different lifestages; be alert for the changes, and be prepared to modify the service, and the value proposition as they change

As one moves from one stage to the next stage of this ongoing CRM business cycle, ICICI Group hopes to gains insight and understanding that enhance the subsequent efforts. The organization claims to become increasingly sophisticated in the implementation of CRM processes, and over time become increasingly profitable also by doing so.

Prioritization of Changes

Since there might be many gaps, and therefore many inevitable changes that ICICI will need to make, prioritization was critical. The evaluation of each of the strategies identified to resolve the gaps at ICICI were based on the following factors.

- Cost to implement—including initial one-time costs, as well as anticipated ongoing expenses
- Overall benefit—some changes may have larger impact on the organization's ability to increase customer value and loyalty
- Feasibility—based on organization readiness, data and systems support, resource skill-sets, and a number of other factors
- Time required—including the time necessary for training and addressing cultural change management issues related to a specific strategy

Laying Down an Action Plan

The next step in the planning process was the development of a very detailed action plan. While the complete plan might span three or more years, it was divided into phases of three months, each with clear deliverables that will demonstrate both progress or measures of success. The plan identified interdependent activities that should comprehensively detail the time and resources required for each activity.

Another key factor for the planning process was the leadership action plan. Advancing on the CRM transformation map required significant organization change. This part of the action plan helped assess the drivers and restraints of this change, and the organization's readiness to embrace the change. It created additional strategies by identifying specific leadership actions necessary to lead the organizational change. As a result, executives were able to identify their roles and responsibilities, and the actions necessary to eliminate barriers, and to nurture change in order to adopt CRM practices.

Related Resources

Vincent, Kurien, *The Hindu Business Line*, Saturday, 19 February 2005

domainb.com/finance/bank as accessed on 29 August 2008

www.cxotoday.com/India/News, article posted by Amit Tripathi, 11 February 2005, as accessed on 29 August 2008

Peppers, D. and M. Rogers (1993), 'The One to One Future Building Relationships: One Customer at a Time', *Doubleday*, New York.

Peppers, D. and M. Rogers (1995), 'A New Marketing Paradigm: Share of Customer, Not Market Share', *Managing Service Quality*, 5(3), pp. 48–51.

Discussion Questions

1. What are the reasons that more or less made it inevitable for ICICI to undergo CRM?
2. What is the framework for the CRM strategy which ICICI was supposed to follow? What objectives were set aside for CRM-driven programmes at ICICI?
3. Briefly discuss the five core areas selected for business transformation at ICICI by the consultant. Would you like to bring about any change in the structure and/or composition of these areas?
4. Comment upon the CRM business cycle adopted by ICICI? How were the different stages of this cycle adopted by ICICI? Would you like to give some suggestion in the adoption of different phases of this business cycle?
5. What could have been the needs of ICICI to go in for an Information Technology (IT) based solution for CRM? What were the criteria selected? How would it have changed the processes at ICICI?
6. Do you think the ICICI experiences would apply to other companies as well, particularly in the banking sector? Justify your answer.

REFERENCES

Dawson, Ross (2001), *Developing Knowledge-based Client Partnerships: The Future of Professional Services*, Butterworth Heinemann, US.

Greenberg, Paul (2001), *CRM at the Speed of Light: Capturing and Keeping Customers in Internet Real Time*, Osborne.

Nykamp, M. (2001), *The Customer Differential: The Complete Guide to Implementing Customer Relationship Management*, Amacom, US.

Nykamp, Milinda, Carla McEachern (November 1999), 'The CRM Business Cycle: Customer Relationship Report', *DM Review Magazine*.

Pine II, J.B. (1993), *Mass Customization*, Harvard University Business School Press, Mass.

Pine II, J.B., and A. Boynton (1993), *Making Mass Customization Work*, Harvard University Business Review, 71, No. 5, pp.108–119.

Schmidt, A., M. Lauff, and H. Beigl (1998), 'Hand-held CSCW (Computer Supported Cooperative Work)', *Proceedings of Workshop on Handheld CSCW*, CSCW'98, Seattle.

Sheth, Jagdish N., A. Parvatiyar, and G. Shainesh (2002), *Customer Relationship Management: Emerging Concepts, Tools and Applications*, Tata McGraw-Hill, New Delhi.

Simchi-Levi, David, Philip Kaminsky, and Edith Simchi-Levi (2004), *Designing and Managing the Supply Chain—Concepts, Strategies and Case Studies*, Tata McGraw-Hill, New Delhi.

Internet Resources

http://bura.brunel.ac.uk/bitstream/2438/1456/4/mPower_BTTJ-24.pdf as accessed on 16 April 2009

www.crm2day.com/news/crm/122617.php as accessed on 2 December 2008

www.cxotoday.com/india/news as accessed on 29 August 2008

www.fairisaac.com/NR/exeres/E57 as accessed on 1 September 2008

www.icicibank.com as accessed on 9 July 2008

www.infosys.com/finacle as accessed on 29 August 2008

www12.sap.com/solutions/business-suite/crm as accessed on 29 November 2008

7 SCM Implementation and Performance Benchmarking

After an understanding of the dynamics of supply chain processes, and installation of supply chain systems and best practices, it becomes imperative that suitable measures be developed for the measurement of the performance of the supply chain management (SCM) system, practices, and activities in the company. Before benchmarking is initiated for the performance in various areas of SCM such as planning for materials, purchasing, synchronization with operations, and logistics and distribution to end customer, development of suitable performance parameters has to be done by all the related departments jointly, so that an extensive checklist is developed about the same. The checklist might comprise both—a set of statements and recording the objective values of the pre-determined measures. *What cannot be measured cannot be improved* applies to SCM also and therefore, continuous collection and monitoring of data related to supply chain performance measures is a must. Global benchmarks and best practices in various areas of SCM are also available. Different supply chains may have different orientations and goals, and a high priority for certain attributes. For example, agile and responsive supply chains would have special focus on customer sensitivity, virtual integration, process integration, and network orientation. Specific performance measures can be developed for performance management criteria against these specially laid down factors.

IMPLEMENTING SUPPLY CHAIN MANAGEMENT

This author did a project on SCM practices in Indian industries under the UGC research award, which ended in 2005. As a part of this project, a study was carried out on implementation of SCM in the fast moving consumer goods (FMCG) and consumer durables industries in India. A list of 90 supply chain related critical success factors (CSFs)/key performance indicators (KPIs) in the form of a checklist was drawn. Best practices and benchmarks were also included as a part of the checklist. The level of SCM implementation was then studied, on various items of the checklist developed especially for the purpose on the basis of a literature survey, structured in-depth interviews with supply chain and sales and physical distribution executives. In addition, some pre-existing checklists already available in literature were also consulted. The eight areas of SCM implementation covered are discussed here.

SCM Intent, Orientation, Organization, and Interrelationships

This covers the basic corporate philosophy and strategy of the company to organize for SCM, i.e., whether it is treated as a networked function in the organization or as a stand-alone function. What are the resources and commitment of the management for this organization or is it dependent on other functional departments? Also, it is important whether corporate budgets have been kept aside for the SCM function. It is also crucial whether goals and policies are established for the SCM department. The extent of primary orientation, say, towards the customer and lean thinking is to be identified, as also the considerations for interrelationships with other departments, and identifying the parameters for customer-centric performance and better business results. The intent and orientation must be aligned with the corporate goals in SCM, the principles of processing on the shop floor, the order fulfilment policies, and customer service levels. It is also to be earmarked whether SCM is to be treated as a profit centre or a cost reduction centre; both may yield the same result but the approaches are different.

SCM and Collaborative Forecasting and Planning

This is a vital aspect of SCM which deals with whether the SCM practices are based on forecasts or schedules. Practically, it is both. When it is forecast-based, it is important to know the level of aggregation, the level of information sharing, particularly from retailers, as also the level of variance recorded from the past forecasts, and the extent of bullwhip effect (as discussed in Chapter 2). This would need availability of sales data and visibility across the supply chain. Many companies in the US make use of Collaborative Planning, Forecasting, and Replenishment (CPFR®)[1]. See Exhibit 7.1.

SCM and Use of IT Practices and Tools

It is not possible to fructify SCM efforts without enabling the different supply chain flows and processes with it. The electronic data interchange (EDI) provides authorized plug-in facility to all the chain partners. Web-enablement is necessary for order capture and processing, and also in e-procurement. An organization-wide enterprise resource planning (ERP) system also helps in streamlining of supply chain processes and workflows. This, if augmented with the Web, i.e., ERP-II will

---

[1] CPFR® is a registered trademark of the Voluntary Interindustry Commerce Solutions of USA.

EXHIBIT 7.1 Collaborative Planning, Forecasting, and Replenishment

CPFR refers to a set of guidelines supported and published by the Voluntary Interindustry Commerce Solutions (VICS) association, in order to facilitate the companies throughout the supply chain and simultaneously lower the costs and the inventory, carry out joint business planning, and also improve customer service. As a result, the supplier can build the inventory well in advance of receiving a promotional order and carry less safety stock at other times. A retailer can alter the product mix to reduce the impact of supply problems.

The following are the broad steps of CPFR.

(i) Front-end agreement: The participating companies identify executive sponsors, agree to confidentiality and dispute-resolution processes, and develop key supply chain metrics to be tracked through the supply chain.

(ii) Joint business plan: The participating companies jointly develop plans for promotions, inventory policy changes, store openings/closings, and product changes for each product category.

(iii) Sales forecast collaboration: Trading partners share customer demand forecasts and identify exceptions when their plans do not match or change dramatically. If plans are 'close enough', they would not require attention. Causal factors are determined and plans are adjusted, if necessary.

(iv) Order forecast collaboration: The participating member companies share the replenishment plan, identify, and resolve exceptions.

(v) Order generation/delivery execution: The results data, i.e., in terms of PoS, orders, and shipments, the on-hand inventory is shared and forecast accuracy problems, overstock/understock conditions, and execution issues are identified and resolved.

Wal-Mart and Sara Lee reported a 14 per cent reduction in the store level inventory with a 32 per cent increase in sales. Kimberly-Clark and Komart achieved a steady increase in category growth exceeding the market growth.

bring about better integration of the supply chain across the partners, but the key issue is whether the partners would be willing to upload real-time data at their end, and up to what extent. Also, the authorization of access to data could be an important issue in sharing information.

Strategic Outsourcing and Supplier Relationships (Including Supplier Rating and Development)

At the heart of SCM lies the outsourcing, vendor selection, rating, and development. Normally, outsourcing is done of those activities which are non-core competent to the firm. Suppliers are to be evaluated not only on conventional aspects of price, quality, delivery, and after sales service, but also on the suppliers' willingness for long-term commitment and cost reduction. The total cost of ownership (TCO) of having supplies from a vendor is more important than just the price paid in a transaction. It is important to have a purchase order planning, release, and receipt system—may be through material requirements planning (MRP) or enterprise resource planning (ERP). A process to track the purchase order for follow-up/expediting or modifying the order configuration with suppliers enables better SCM, and brings about flexibility. There is need to maintain relationships with suppliers—either through a structured supplier relationship management (SRM) system or conventions and practices, which has assumed greater significance than ever before. Through such systems and practices, true partnering with suppliers in the area of joint design, and development of new products/parts, forecasting and planning, cost reduction, and improvement of each others' capabilities can be ensured.

Modern Manufacturing Practices and Systems (Including Master Production Scheduling and Material Planning)

A systematic manufacturing and material planning and scheduling system is a must for SCM in manufacturing enterprises. A well laid down MRP system with master production schedule (MPS) in place would give available-to-promise (ATP) information with good reliability. A rough cut capacity plan (RCCP) would adjust the MPS with respect to actual available capacity on the shop floor in a given period. A good system would not only ensure reduction in manufacturing and supply lead times, but also reduce the routing and scheduling complexities, and smoothen workflows basically to manage the internal supply chain. A badly managed internal supply chain would obviously lead to a badly managed external (to the focal firm) supply chain.

Lean Operations' Techniques

A hallmark feature of modern day supply chains, particularly in view of uncertain demands, is single-piece processing and reducing the seven wastes of operations, as identified under the Toyota Production System (TPS).[2] The purpose is to improve the yields from the processes by reducing defects and scrap, reducing the work-in-progress inventory levels, eliminating or reducing unnecessary transportation, inspection, over-processing, buffers, and down-time of machines due to poor maintenance. Cycle time management and its reduction, and manufacturing in space efficient layouts, i.e., cellular manufacturing is also a ramification of lean thinking, which can bring about trimmed supply chains with no extra inventory and other operational inefficiencies, yet with better internal and external customer service levels.

---

[2] Seven wastes identified by Shigeo Shingo(1981), a Toyota engineer, i.e., waste of overproduction, waiting, transportation, over processing, buffers, motion, and defects.

Transportation, Logistics, and Warehousing (WH)

Effective integration of inbound and outbound logistics is an essential element of supply chain management. The decisions may involve freight consolidation, route-rationalization, dynamic mode of carrier and route selection, and long-term and reliable service level agreements (SLAs) with third-party logistics (3PLs)/transporters with provision for a rating system for them as well. There should also be a provision for sharing real-time demand information for various variants at retailers' level with the distributor through electronic data interchange (EDI). This provides for 'delayed differentiation' or customization of product at the distribution centre (DC) level, so that aggregate demand forecasts (which are more accurate) can be done at the DC level. A lot of these services could be provided through 'hub and spokes' arrangements managed by 3PLs, who could also facilitate recyclable packaging through a 'milk run' organized by them in coordination with various suppliers located in a geographical cluster. This ensures vendor-managed inventory (VMI) and online delivery of parts, again leading to better internal (to the company) supply chain. Use of technologies such as bar coding and radio frequency identification (RFID)/Auto-ID can be used for tracking and tracing mechanisms throughout the supply chain.

Customer Relationships

A supply chain managing company has to orient its operations for the customers. The focus should be on acquiring, retaining, and partnering with customers on a long-term basis. This cannot be ensured without managing a database of customer profiles and their buying behaviour in a warehouse, with structured tools for information retrieval, and solving customers' queries. The customers' buying patterns and queries can be shared with suppliers to understand the needs of customers better and meet these in future. The focus should be on continuous customer contact rather than on just one sales transaction, and not just delivering product, but also a superior value to customer. A system needs to be in place for collecting and tracking feedback from customers and forwarding it to the appropriate department in the organization for proactive actions—all non-ATP deliveries, stock outs, product returns, recalls, back-orders, service failures, unduly long fixing times, and cost of warranty claims for future preventive and corrective action, and improvement. Structured programmes such as CRM can also be used, but as most executives say, CRM is 20 per cent technology and 80 per cent people. However, maintaining a customer information base for CRM cannot be ruled out.

The respondent companies can be asked to rate the items, say, on a 1 to 5 equal interval *Likert Scale* on a continuum for *importance* of that item as perceived by the company, and the degree of *adoption* as actually practiced and experienced by the company (as was done in the study by the author). This would also help in carrying out a *gap analysis* about the difference between importance and adoption of a particular practice related to an item of the checklist, and then accordingly plan for its implementation in future. A checklist for the corporate sector, so developed to implement SCM is given in Appendix A7.1.

SUPPLY CHAIN OPERATIONS REFERENCE MODEL

The supply chain operations reference (SCOR) model developed and endorsed by the supply chain council is a tool for representing, analysing, and configuring supply chains.[3] The SCOR introduced a standard terminology, process definitions, metrics, and best practices for modelling and configuration of the supply chain.

The model describes high-level business processes associated with all the phases of satisfying customer demand. It leads to the development of a cross-functional framework based on business process re-engineering (BPR), benchmarking, and process improvement. It also describes relationships among the core business processes, standard metrics to measure process performance, and management practices that produce best-in-class performance, and standard alignment to features and functionality. Before understanding the SCOR model, one should be clear about the different supply chain process cycles (Fig. 7.1).

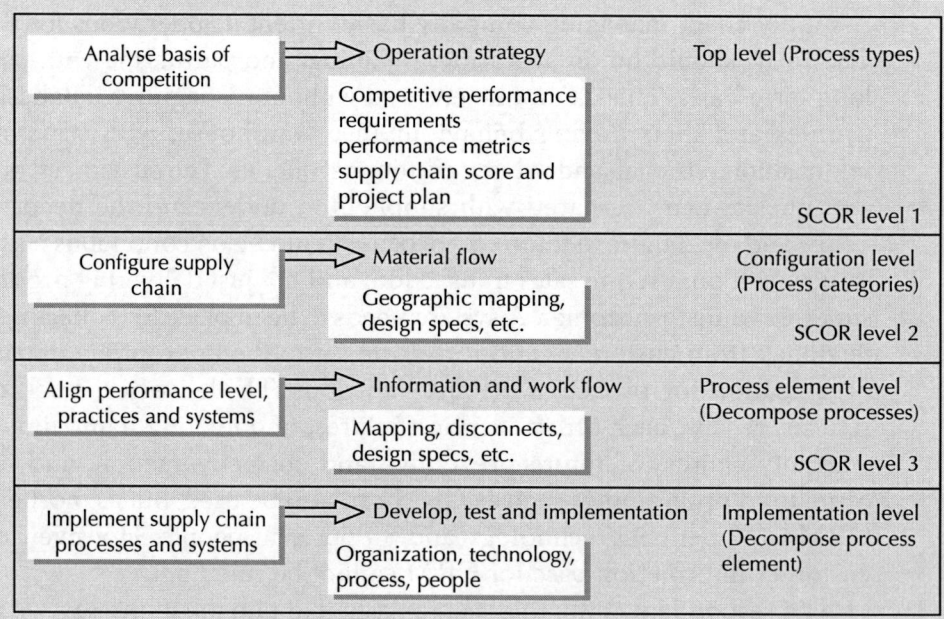

FIG. 7.1   Stages in a SCOR project
Source: Supply Chain Council, 2000

---

[3] www.supply-chain.org

Steps in the Supply Chain Operations Design

The following steps at different levels are undertaken while designing the supply chains.

Level 1 : Bases of competitive performance targets are set

Level 2 : Companies implement their operations strategy through their unique supply chain configuration

Level 3 : Companies 'fine tune' their operations strategy by decomposing processes and arriving at the element level

Level 4 : Companies implement specific SCM practices at this level to achieve competitive advantage, and to adapt to changing business conditions by decomposing even process elements

Model Level 1

The five basic management elements consist of plan, source, make, deliver, and return encompassing supplier's supplier to customer's customer (Fig. 7.2). The metrics used may be based on the balanced scorecard approach as given by Kaplan in 1992. The metrics include financial, customer, internal business, and innovative and learning perspectives. Various internal and external functions such as the following can be covered.

- Delivery performance
- Fill rates
- Order fulfilment lead time
- Production flexibility

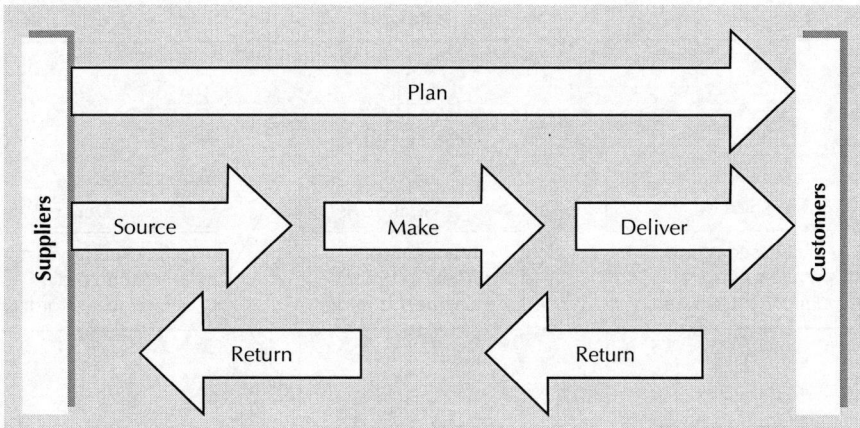

FIG. 7.2 SCOR Model's level 1 (Process type level)
Source: Supply Chain Council, 2000

- Total logistics management costs
- Cash-to-cash cycle time
- Inventory in days of supply

Model Level 2

Each of the process types can be further described by process categories of planning, execution, and enabling plan. The metrics are selected on the basis of level 1 parameters or business drivers such as the following.

- Forecast accuracy
- Fill rate
- Cash-to-cash cycle time
- Total order management cost
- Inventory carrying cost
- Re-plan cycle time
- Total inventory days of supply
- Obsolete inventory

At this stage, the redundancies, such as overlapped planning and purchasing, etc. are identified (Fig. 7.3).

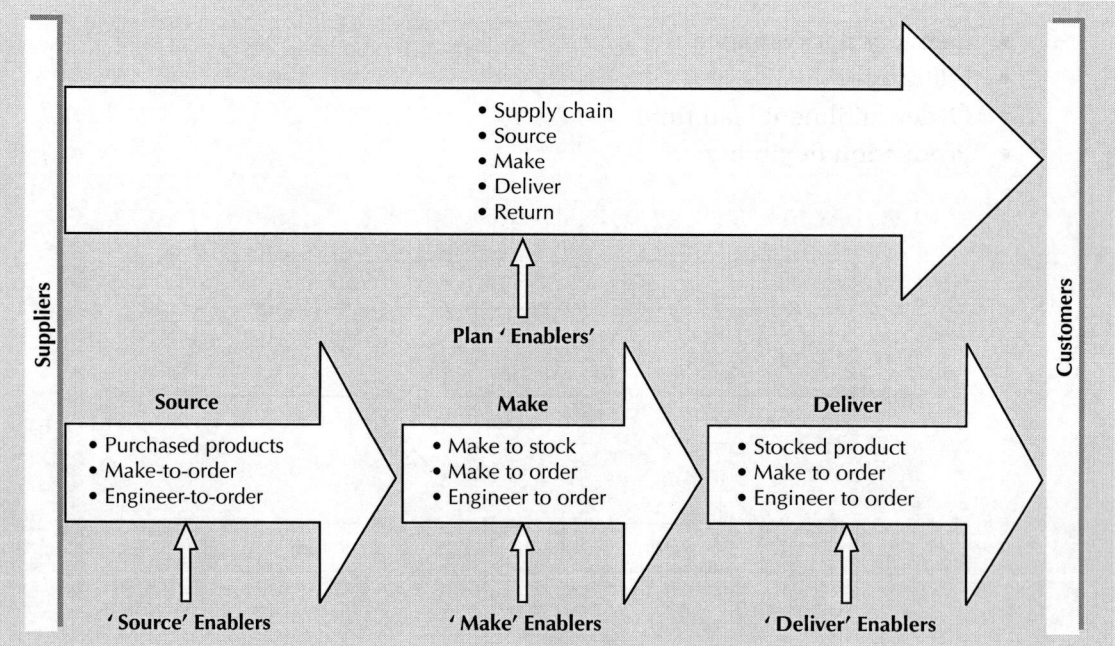

FIG. 7.3 SCOR Model Level 2: Configuration level (process categorized)
Source: Supply Chain Council, 2000

Model Level 3

At this level, the process categories are decomposed into process elements. The details of metrics and best practices are evolved, e.g., for scheduled product delivery schedules, which are as follows.

- Average release cycle of delivery schedules
- Average days per schedule change
- Percentage of delivery schedules met in time and as per quantity
- Percentage of schedules changed within supplier's lead time

It may be noted that while level 1 metrics can be developed with the help of a balanced scorecard, level 2 and 3 metrics are evolved using benchmarking.

Model Level 4

This level goes to the extent of decomposition of process elements from plan to return types into specific SCM practices at the corporate level in order to achieve competitive advantage and adapt to changing business conditions. These practices are not defined with any industry standard model since these could be unique to each company. For example, a company may use a specific technology to capture order, process it, and fill and deliver it. It may use specific techniques for route and carrier selections, specific software for e-sourcing, and may also use particular systems and processes for supplier quality assurance (SQA). It may further use techniques such as 'postponement' or channel assembly to reduce inventory or 'drop-shipping' to reduce transit times. It may also use reverse logistics for vendor-managed inventory (VMI) as also for product/material returns.[4] These practices can, however, be benchmarked against the best, thus taking SCM to the highest level.

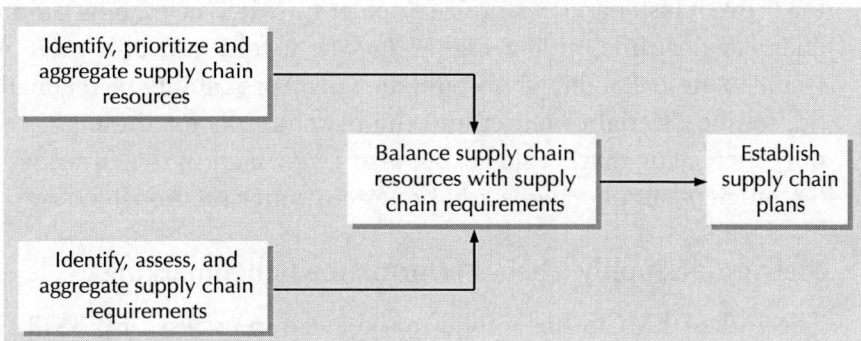

FIG. 7.4   SCOR Model Level 3: Process element level
Source: Supply Chain Council, 2000

---

[4] Reverse logistics refers to the return of goods from customers to suppliers in a supply chain.

Improvement of SC can be quite challenging for a company, particularly in view of ever-changing customer expectations at a certain cost. For this, companies need to delineate non-competitive processes and competitive processes, demarcate customer needs, and establish improvement goals. Design of SC according to key business drivers would achieve product and cycle time improvement by cutting down raw material, FG inventories, and cycle lead time, which are further enabled by IT tools. This is clear from Fig. 7.4.

In a nutshell, the SCOR model gives a clear description of supply chain activities, a common set of definitions across the supply chain entities, and scope of improvement in the links.

SUPPLY CHAIN PERFORMANCE BENCHMARKING

Benchmarking would refer to quantification of operational performance in supply chains of similar companies, and establish internal targets with management processes, and practices improvement so as to deliver 'best-in-class' results. Benchmarking essentially is preceded by business process re-engineering (BPR) and followed by best practices analysis, which means characterization of the management practices and software solutions that would result in 'best-in-class' performance. This is often followed by the use of a process reference model, e.g., supply chain operations reference (SCOR) model discussed earlier in this chapter.

The identification of the right metrics and its measurement is very critical when it is desired to do performance benchmarking of the supply chain, particularly where the supply chains of competitors are competitive. The benefits from a cost and time-efficient, and a trim supply chain can be directly passed on to the customers in the form of faster and customized defect-free deliveries, new product configuration, taking lesser time, giving higher service levels, and at a price which gives 'best value' to the customer, who would then in all probability be retained by the company. So, setting the right metrics and the benchmarks for these goes a long way in not only increasing market share, but also *wallet share* of the customer by the company. So, efficient supply chains and better customer relationships go side by side.

Metrics for Supply Chain Performance Benchmarking

The Indian FMCG has a total market size in excess of US$13.1 billion, which is expected to grow to US $33.4 billion in 2015. The Indian FMCG sector spends an exceptionally high amount of 15 per cent of its revenue on logistics. Close to 25 per cent of aggregate sales, i.e., US $4.1 billion is tied up in inventories in the country-wide supply chain network. According to another estimate, the primary supply chain (from factory to warehouse or distribution centre (DC) is .7), and the cost of secondary supply chain (from warehouse to retailers) is 1 per cent. The total costs are around 2.5 per cent, while material handling costs are 1.5 per cent.

These values, however, do not have any value unless these are compared with the best-in-class values in the relevant industry, or even related inter-industry companies. In the section that follows, we discuss the different types of metrics and their values in Indian industries, and the global best values. The Supply Chain Council suggested integrated supply chain metrics, namely

- time (cycle time metrics),
- costs (cost metrics),
- customer satisfaction/quality (service quality metrics), and
- asset metrics.

Cycle Time Metrics

Procurement time   It is measured by the number of days elapsed from the time manufacturer places an order to his vendor to when he receives it. In India, the average is 19 days, but the best end-class value is 1–3 days.

Production cycle time   It is measured by the total number of days elapsed between the receipt of an order from the customer and the completion of the product ready for shipment. The FMCG industry average in India is 10 days, while the best-in-class value is 1–3 days.

Delivery time   It is measured in terms of the number of days or hours elapsed from the time a shipment leaves the manufacturer's facility, to the time it arrives at the customer's location. The average value is 5 days, while best-in-class is again 1–3 days.

Total cycle time   It is measured by the number of days (or hours) elapsed from the time an order is received by the company, and the time it reaches the customer's location. The industry average is 35 days, but the best-in-class value is not more than a week.

Cash to cash time   It is measured by the number of days between paying for raw materials and getting paid for products, as calculated by inventory days of supply plus days of sales outstanding and minimum average payment period for the material. Normally, the average is 33 days but the best-in-class is 'zero', i.e., some companies get paid in advance by their customers and get credit period from their vendors.

Supply chain flexibility   It is measured by the ability of the manufacturer to meet additional demand requirements, i.e., per cent of demand surge that can be met. This is usually compared as a percentage over the original order. The industry

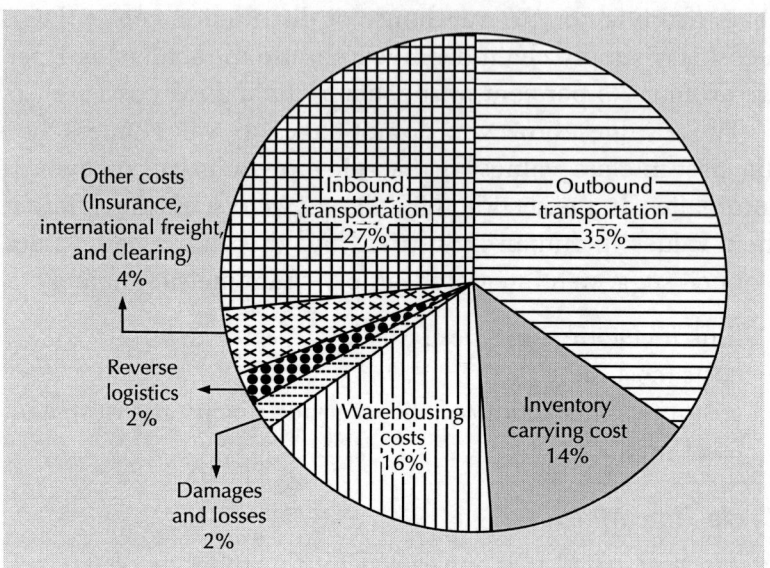

FIG. 7.5   Typical break-up of supply chain costs in Indian FMCG industry
Source: Uma Maheshwari Devi and Raja Shekhar, 7th ICOQM Proceedings, 2006

average is around 15 per cent, while best-in-class could be minimum 30 to 40 per cent.

Cost Metrics

Total supply chain cost in Indian history is around 6.5 per cent of the sales. The typical break-up of supply chain costs are displayed in Fig. 7.5.

The global benchmark for total supply chain cost is just 1–2 per cent of sales. As far as the global benchmarks for other cost metrics are concerned, these are tabulated in Table 7.1.

TABLE 7.1   Best-in-class values for cost metrics of supply chain

	Metric	Best-in-class value (%)
(i)	Total supply chain cost (TSCC) (per cent of sales)	1–2
(ii)	Inbound transportation (per cent of TSCC)	11–20
(iii)	Outbound transportation (per cent of TSCC)	21–30
(iv)	Warehousing cost (per cent of TSCC)	6–10
(v)	Inventory carrying cost (per cent of TSCC)	1–3
(vi)	Cost of transit losses	1–3
(vii)	Cost of damages	1–3
(viii)	Other costs, e.g., insurance, international freight, and clearing	1–5

Source: Based on studies by consultants, KPMG, McKinsey, PMG of PRTM Consulting and Business Week

Reverse logistics, which refers to return of goods from customers to supplier in a supply chain, includes the following activities.

- Processing returned goods for reasons such as damage, reassess, restock, salvage, recall, or excess inventory
- Recycling packaging materials and reusing containers
- Reconditioning, re-manufacturing, and re-furbishing products
- Disposal of obsolete equipment/materials/goods

Many companies such as Unilever, L'Oreal, Procter & Gamble, and Colgate Palmolive have used tax-efficient SCM (TESCM) initiatives. Interestingly, KPMG in 2009 came out with reports on technology issues companies have been facing and focused reports on tax efficiency in SCM in pharmaceutical and telecom industries. They also focused on how tax can be used to cut cost in supply chain innovation.

Service Quality Metrics

These metrics refer to shipment delivery in terms of time, quantity, and quality.

Per cent ontime delivery   This refers to the per cent of times the goods are delivered to the customer by the promised time, in right quantity, and quality. The Indian industry average for FMCG and durables is 97–99 per cent, while global standards are 100 per cent.

Per cent supplies delivered as per scheduled quantity   It refers to the per cent supplies (value or quantity) of the value or quantity ordered that are delivered as per schedule. The Indian consumer goods industry is 98–99 per cent, while the global benchmark is 100 per cent.

Per cent supplies delivered with right quality   It refers to the per cent times the lots delivered are in the right quality as per the order. The average value is again 98–99 per cent, i.e., just 1–2 per cent lots are rejected. The global benchmark is obviously 100 per cent.

Asset Metrics

These metrics are normally related to the following.

Average inventory holding period   It is computed separately for raw material (RM), work-in-progress (WIP) and finished goods (FG) inventory.

In most of the cases, the RM inventory holding period is 15–30 days, the WIP inventory holding period is 3–6 days, and the FG inventory holding period varies greatly between 4–30 days, with average being 17 days. The global standards for all these inventory holdings, be it RM, WIP, or FG, are 1–3 days.

Inventory turnover It indicates the velocity of the goods, i.e., the speed with which the goods move and are replenished in the system. All other factors being constant, a higher turnover is preferred, as it means that the inventory moves through the firm's operational stages quickly, rather being held for an extensive time. Larger number of times indicate better working capital management resulting in increase in profitability or return on investment (ROI) of the firm. Average value of inventory turnover times in Indian consumer goods industry is 18 times, while global benchmark is over 30 times.

Performance Benchmarks in Purchasing

Beamen (1999) presented a number of characteristics that are found in effective performance measurement systems for SCM. Neely et al. (1995) presented a few of the categories, namely quality, time, flexibility, and cost for performance benchmaking.

The works of Waters-Fuller (1995) and Lamming (1996) directly relate with real-world applicability in terms of different performance measures which can be mostly categorized in to

- cost
- time
- customer responsiveness
- flexibility (volume and variety)
- a combination of two or more of the above

Here, other measures have already been explained, the measure of customer responsiveness refers to lead time, on time and available-to-promise (ATP) delivery, stock-out probability, and fill rate.

The order fill rate, as discussed previously in the book, is used to denote the extent to which the warehouse or the inventory management systems has been able to fulfil the orders placed in the expected lead time. It is more relevant in a system that handles several items or stock keeping units (SKUs).

$$\text{Order fill rate} = \frac{\text{Number of SKU categories for which 100\% of units ordered were received}}{\text{Total number of SKU categories ordered}}$$

When the logistics system is planned, a specific fill rate is always targeted. For having a high fill rate, high inventory levels may be required. However, the efficiency of a system is to achieve the same fill rate with fewer inventories. This can be achieved by more accurate forecasting and reduction in lead times. There can also be weighted average fill rate, which is used in case of composite orders consisting of several items or SKUs simultaneously. It is calculated by multiplying the frequency with which a particular combination of items is ordered with the probability of filling that order completely.

Lee and Billington (1992) cite a number of trade-offs which might have to be done for best results from a supply chain. These could well be a part of alignment and fine tuning in the supply chain. The trade-offs could be

- lot size—inventory level
- inventory—transportation cost
- lead time—transportation cost
- product variety—inventory
- production and distribution costs—customer service

Examples of other performance measures are customer satisfaction (Christopher 1998), the rate of information flow (Nicoll 1994), supplier performance (Davis 1993), and risk management (Johnson and Randolph 1995).

Leading consultants such as KPMG (1997), McKinsey (1992) and Performance Management Group (PMG), a subsidiary of Pittiglio Robin Todd and McGrath (PRTM) Consulting have also carried out studies linking SCM with profitability and enlisted some key performance benchmarks in world-class firms following supply chain management. McKinsey carried out a study on supply chain performance parameters, and their results are tabulated in Table 7.2.

Though even the benchmarks and typical firms' values have changed now, it shows a significant comparison and trend in the values of supply chain performance.

TABLE.7.2 World-class performance benchmarks in SCM

Supply chain performance parameter	Typical firms	World-class benchmark firms
(i) Number of supplies per purchasing agent	34	5
(ii) Number of purchasing agents per $100 million of purchase	5.4	2.2
(iii) Percentage of purchasing cost	3.3	0.8
(iv) Time required to perform evaluation of supplier (in weeks)	3 weeks	0.4 week
(v) Lead time	15	8
(vi) Time spent in placing an order	42 minutes–6 weeks	2.5 minutes–15 minutes
(vii) Percentage of late deliveries	33	2
(viii) Percentage of rejected material	1.5	.0001
(ix) Number of material shortage per year	400	4

Source: Business Week, November 30, 1992, p. 72

Schroeder (2003) cites another cost related metric, i.e., value added or productivity of the supply chain which can be given as

$$\text{Supply chain efficiency} = \frac{\text{Sales cost of materials}}{\text{Labour} + \text{Overheads}}$$

Here, the numerator represents the value added while the denominator shows the total cost of adding the value.

In a study conducted by the *Performance Management Group* on the linkage between supply chain and profitability, it was found that market leaders are able to reduce their costs (of supply chain) by 5 to 6 per cent of sales by implementing SCM, i.e., a $100 million sale company would make a saving of $ 5–6 million per year.

Using these supply chain performance corporate profitability measures and the analysis and comparison of these on inter-company or extended enterprise-wide basis can help in implementation of a *balanced score card* concept. But these performance measures should be derived from strategic objectives only, e.g., profitable growth, enhancement of customer service, increased customer satisfaction, etc. Otherwise, collection of data with regard to incorporation in balanced score card may be an economically unjustifiable option, as it is not linked to strategy also. Ultimately, the performance parameters selected could be to select a few crucial ones only, according to the strategy. However, information across channel partners would be an important prerequisite to implementation of the balanced score card approach for performance evaluation in SCM.

PERFORMANCE MEASURES FOR AGILE SUPPLY CHAINS

The need for agile supply chains arose because the conventional supply chain is not able to meet the increasingly volatile customer demands cost effectively, because of fast change in the business environment. *Agility* may be defined as the ability of an organization to thrive in a continuously changing unpredictable business environment. Goldman et al. (1994) through their book, *Agile Competitors and Virtual Organization*, drew international attention to corporate agility. Mason Jones, Towill et al. (2000) defined agility as using market knowledge and a virtual corporation to exploit profitable opportunities in a volatile marketplace. The companies should not only be capable to cope with volatility, but also exploit it to their strategic advantage, say, in terms of customer service levels.

An agile supply chain differs from a conventional supply chain in the following aspects.

(i) Replenishment of all levels is actual point-of-sale (PoS) data driven, rather than forecast driven in a conventional supply chain.

(ii) Stock is held only at lower level with sometimes FG being delivered directly from the factory to the customer (*drop-shipping*), than stock being held at multiple levels often based on legal ownership issues (in a conventional supply chain).

(iii) Product design, development, and production is planned across functional boundaries in a collaborative manner from the vendor to the customer with a highly integrated system, and minimum lead time and costs.

(iv) Majority of stock is held as WIP stock awaiting final assembly/configuration instructions from customers (*postponement*), unlike in a traditional supply chain where majority of stock is held in finished goods (FGs).

One good example of postponement is that Asian Paints would produce paints in most generic form (grey stock) and store them in dealers/retailers near the customer. Only when a customer places an order for a particular coded shade, the paints are mixed by the machine at the retailer's premises in an appropriate proportion to give a desired shade. (They claim to have 3000 shades!)

Agile supply chains thus help in customizing the product to meet the individual customer's needs, and helping develop new products and services in shorter time span both at the vendor's and customer's end in a collaborative manner with minimum lead time and cost.

Four distinguishing characteristics of agile supply chains have been defined by Christopher (2000). These typically apply to a manufacturing company and are as follows.

Market sensitivity   As pointed out earlier, an agile supply chain responds to real demand and not forecasted demand. Due to lack of data on PoS at the retailer's end, or the latter not sharing their information, or due to lack of data on actual customer behaviour (buying pattern and frequency etc.), most companies make forecasts based on past sales shipments rather than actual demand. An agile supply chain operates on the basis of a *demand-pull* system triggered at the customer/retailer's end. Initiatives such as efficient consumer response (ECR), discussed elsewhere in the book, can transform a supply chain to the *pull-one* by an interdependent relationship.

Virtual integration   It refers to creating a virtual supply chain which is information rather than inventory-based, and comprises sharing of data between buyers and suppliers using information technology (IT). All the channel members are connected electronically, either through EDI or the Internet, which not only facilitates real-time information sharing, but also increases the ability of members to behave as a team sharing knowledge and expertise, irrespective of their location (Bal, Wilding, and Gundry 2000).

Process integration   It refers to collaboration in processes between buyers and suppliers, including joint product development, inventory management, cost reduction exercise, etc. A jointly developed new product or material would have high manufacturality without any rework, and help the partners to produce and deliver the product with minimum lead time and cost. This integration of processes further becomes important in the light of outsourcing of all non-core competent activities to external suppliers.

Network orientation The winner company is one who can better structure, coordinate, and manage the relationships with the partners in a network (Christopher 1992). Big focal firms would create an extended *supply chain community* that would leverage the core competencies of each partner. The members of such community would work hand-in-hand to optimize their efforts through the supply chain pipelines, in turn, enabling the supply chain to respond to the customers *faster, better, and cheaper* than ever before.

Christopher (2000) gave the following performance parameters with respect to these four characteristics of agile firms. This is given in Table 7.3.

TABLE 7.3 Performance measures of agile supply chains

Characteristic	Performance measures
Market sensitivity	(i) Opportunity loss for not being first to market in a product category
	(ii) Number of stock outs
	(iii) Value of discount sales at the end of the season (in case of excess stock)
Virtual integration	(iv) Percentage of purchase orders made electronically/per cent EDI transactions over total transactions
	(v) Number and time-duration of stoppages of production runs due to material shortages
	(vi) Percentage of virtual meetings of global teams during a project over total number of meetings
Process integration	(vii) Percentage of orders meeting due dates over total orders placed
	(viii) Percentage of correct order fulfilment over total orders fulfilled
	(ix) Total design-to-delivery cycle time
	(x) Time to volume: engineering change order (ECO)[5], time and cost, data updation times, and cost.
Network orientation	(xi) Percentage of customer orders fulfilled by manufacturing partners themselves
	(xii) Reorder/replenishment cycle time
	(xiii) Average length of relationship time with immediate suppliers and distributor
	(xiv) Cash-to-cash cycle time

Source: Christopher 2000

---

[5] ECO refers to change in engineering design to modify or correct a part. The request for change can be from the production department, customer, quality control department or any other department.

RECAPITULATION

In this chapter, first an extensive checklist has been drawn for effective implementation of SCM in a typical company, not only in the Indian context but what a world-class firm should do for SCM implementation. The list spans eight key areas ranging from the orientation of the company to collaborative forecasting to use of IT practices, modern manufacturing practices and lean operations, outsourcing and supplier relationships to transportation, and logistics to customer relations. These have been identified after a research study by the author. However, the areas and the checklist elements may change a little depending on executive judgment and/or type of company where SCM implementation is planned and executed.

Next follows the discussion about the supply chain operations reference (SCOR) model which is based on various process cycles. The model suggested by the Supply Chain Council of US, is used as a tool for representing, analysing, and configuring the supply chains. The model operates at different levels, namely—analysing the basis of competition, configuring the supply chain, aligning performance levels, practices and systems followed by the implementation of supply chain processes, and systems. The process types involved are—plan, source, make, deliver, and return at every stage of the channel. The SCOR model thus, also provides a blue print for performance benchmark-ing. The importance of performance benchmarking in SCM gets highlighted when different supply chain performance parameters can affect the productivity and financials of a company. Some of the common metrics refer to quality, cycle time, cost, and assets. Certain parameters with world-class firms' values have also been identified. Performance benchmarks for 'agile' supply chains have been especially dealt with, in terms of their market sensitivity, virtual and process integration, and the network orientation needs of the company. Indian companies are close to following the global benchmarks in the performance of supply chains. With betterment of infrastructure, there is no reason why India would not have world-class supply chains and performance in the near future.

CONCEPT REVIEW QUESTIONS

1. Identify the corporate functions which should not be neglected for the study of assessment of implementation of supply chain management (SCM) in a company.

2. How can the SCM implementation differ from consumer goods to industrial goods? Give your comments.

3. What does the SCOR model refer to? What are the different levels of the SCOR model and the various parameters involved at each of these levels?

4. Identify the various metrics of SCM performance in a company? How do you justify that these may go a long way in affecting the productivity and financial performance of the company?

5. What are 'agile' supply chains? What are their special needs and requirements? How does performance benchmark the agile supply chains?

CRITICAL THINKING QUESTIONS

1. How would the SCM implementation differ in a service company, as compared to a typical manufacturing company? Draw a revised checklist for a company in the service business.

2. Why is quantification of SCM performance results required? Are there same areas/sub-areas where quantification is not possible? If yes, identify such areas.

PROJECT ASSIGNMENTS

1. Contact the supply chain department of a company and find out how do they monitor the performance of the supply chain. If the company does not have a proper supply chain department, go to the purchasing and sales, physical distribution and logistics, and IT departments, and find out how they coordinate and monitor their individual department results, and what their respective key result areas (KRA's) are?

2. Surf the Internet, select some world-class firms, go to their websites, and find out what makes them world-class, with respect to their supply chain aspects— specific sourcing policies, work practices, IT practices, or customer satisfaction? To what extent, can it be adopted in the Indian context, if that world-class firm is not an Indian one?

CASE STUDY

GLOBAL CASE STUDY

CAMPBELL SOUP COMPANY[6]

Background

Campbell Soup Company, headquartered in Camden, New Jersey, are veterans in soup manufacturing in the US. The company was set up in 1869 by fruit merchant Joseph Campbell and an icebox manufacturer Abraham Anderson. Dr. Dorrance, a chemist trained in Europe joined the company to give the first condensed soup in 1897. By eliminating water in the condensed soup, he lowered the costs of packaging, shipping, and storage. 10 ounces of soup was sold for a dime only. In 1904 itself, the company was manufacturing 21 varieties. It is estimated that consumers in US alone consumed 2.5 billions bowls of the three key varieties—tomato, cream of mushroom and chicken, and the noodle one. Today Campbell manufactures a lot of varieties such as, cream of broccoli, double noodle and creamy chicken noodle. The variants of these soups are present with low sodium, cholesterol, fat, and calories in the range of the healthy request soups. The company has now expanded internationally to China, Japan, Australia, Argentina, and Mexico, etc. It had sales of US$6.1 bn in 2003. It has developed variants to adopt to local cultural differences. The company has the mission—'Together we can build the world's most extraordinary food company for nourishing peoples lives everywhere, everyday.' The company, now, also manufactures juices,

---

[6] *Source:* Based on Fisher, Marshall L., 'What is the Right Supply Chain for Your Product?' *Harvard Business Review* (March–April 1997), pp. 105–116; www.campbellsoupcompany.com as accessed on 17 May 2007; www.glscs.com as accessed on 19 May 2007.

beverages, sauces, biscuits, and confectionary. Online sales are being done through *netgrocer.com*. The company has stringent quality system standards for all the ingredients, including water, raw materials, and elimination of heavy metal content. Suppliers have stringent requirements to meet particularly good food manufacturing practices and control of purchased raw material.

Customer-focused Supply Chain Plan

In an interview given by Christian Moye, the then Vice-President of Strategic Planning, Global Supply chain of Campbell Soup Co., in January 2003, he admits to having the biggest supply chain challenge in maintaining a balance between cost (on the management side) and customer focus (on the retail and customer side).

The key issues for the company are the product format, product differentiation, product customization, and service customization. The retail distribution channel forms the most part of the distribution channel. Moye says that the company aims to drive efficiencies through better information flow and information sharing through data synchronization and collaborative planning, forecasting and replenishment (CPFR). The company is focusing on case-size optimization as a way of maintaining product choice on the shelf, without adding a lot of inventory, and may be even reducing inventory. The company is getting invoice-accuracy rate higher while looking at the forward side of the supply chain. As far as the backward-end (sourcing) is concerned, the company is focusing on technology-enabled strategic sourcing, e.g., e-procurement comprising e-auctions or Internet-enabled negotiations. As a part of IT investment priorities, Campbell in addition to e-procurement is focusing on network optimization, and also sales and operations planning (S&OP). It intends to join UCCnet (group of standards for e-commerce, created by the Uniform Code Council) and wants to have co-sourcing or aggregated purchasing to get lower cost

of raw materials. However, the company does not see much scope of freight consolidation to strive for a common truckload, as the company is already predominantly a truckload kind. The company looks to have DCs in the same locations as other *'big-box'* stores such as Wal-Mart, P&G, Kraft, etc., because of the common geography and population factors. Common retailing/distribution, thus, cannot be ruled out. In 2003, the company did not have a DC in north-east US. The company prefers a near-market, mixing centre DC, which may not give a cost saving for Campbell, but a service improvement. The company finds a real impact of Internet-based EDI on their business and it does not have to pay value-added network (VAN) charges. It would also ensure visibility of transportation. The company joined world wide retail exchange (WWRE) who helped Campbell in data synchronization and e-procurement, which would also facilitate CPFR. So, the company does not have to make substantial investments in software and technology. Moye feels that managing the change in terms of selling the supply chain ideas to the corporate management and the culture in the company has been challenging, but it was not difficult as the lady chief information officer (CIO) got all the supply chain projects approved. The company, however, planned to have a matrix organization rather than a functional silo organization, which is unresponsive to today's business environment.

Issue of Supply Chain Performances

The Campbell Soup company makes products that are very price-sensitive. An important competitive priority for the company is low-cost operations, which extends to the entire supply chain. Campbell operates in an environment with a high degree of certainty. Only 5 per cent of its products are new each year; the rest have been on the market for years, making forecasting of demand easier. Even though Campbell already had high levels of customer service—98 per cent of the time, Campbell's products were available in retailer' inventories—management believed that improvements in costs were possible. It scrutinized the entire supply chain to determine where performance could be improved.

The outcome was a programme called *continuous replenishment*, which reduced the inventories of retailers from an average of 4 weeks' supply to 2 weeks' supply. This reduction amounts to savings to the order of 1 per cent of retail sales. As the average retailer's profits are only 2 per cent of sales, the result was a 50 per cent increase in the average retailer's profits. Because of that increase in profitability, retailers purchased a broader line of Campbell products, thereby increasing Campbell's sales. The programme works in the following way.

- Each morning Campbell uses EDI to link with the retailers.
- Retailers inform Campbell of demands for Campbell products and the current inventory levels in their distribution centres.
- Campbell determines which products need replenishment, based on the upper and lower inventory limits established with each retailer.
- Campbell makes daily deliveries of the needed products.

Campbell's environment has a low level of uncertainty, so the company pursued an efficient supply chain design. The implication, however, is that it must avoid actions that would disrupt the supply chain. For example, retailers on the continuous replenishment programme had to forgo forward buying—whereby retailers in the industry often buy excess stock at discounted prices so that they can offer price promotions. Forward buying causes ripples in the supply chain, increasing everyone's costs. That was the case with chicken soup. Campbell would offer deep discounts once a year and retailers would take advantage of them,

sometimes buying an entire year's supply. Because of the bulge in demand, the chicken boning plant would have to go on overtime. When that happened, costs in the entire supply chain increased—Campbell's production costs increased and retailers had to pay for warehousing large stocks of chicken soup. With the continuous replenishment system, those extra cost are eliminated and everyone wins.

Discussion Questions

1. What do you think are the reasons that Campbell thought that they should improve the performance of the supply chain?
2. What were the key strategic initiatives being planned and focused at Campbell by Christian Moye at the company?
3. What were the aims of the programme of 'continuous replenishment' at Campbell? What were the steps involved?
4. What was the problem encountered with the supply of 'chicken-soup'? How was it tackled by Campbell?

INDIAN CASE STUDY

MARUTI UDYOG LTD[7]

The birth of Maruti Udyog in India in 1982 actually started the process of supply chain transformation in the auto-business. Maruti's plant on Palam Road, Gurgaon started an entire auto-hub in North India. It was one of the first companies to set up 12 joint ventures (JVs) for sourcing some of its critical parts. It manufactures more than 30,000 cars each month, requires critical planning of its logistics, and it gains from Suzuki's international experience in technology transfer, systems and quality, and HR policies. It is one of the few companies to have a separate supply chain management department.

---

[7] *Source:* Based on *Supply Chain & Logistics*, Economic Times Intelligence Group, 2002, Mumbai; and discussions with the executives of vendor development department of MUL. The author expresses acknowledgement and thanks to both the sources.

Supply Chain Performance Management at MUL

Inbound Logistics

Inbound material logistics is managed through a milk run system (or pooling supplies of various vendors of one area in a truckload). The company identifies the vendors located in a particular area, classifies their production pattern, and arranges transportation of supplies from them at a time.

So far, the 8000 odd components that go into manufacturing the car—all domestic material is received against annual, monthly, and weekly schedules of production. Maruti has a separate materials control department which issues the schedules online. Its average inventory of imported components is *15 days* and for steel, *45 days*. At present, Maruti is handling its own inbound logistics and it is the responsibility of domestic vendors to bring materials to the factory. For inland transportation of imported material, MUL has entered into long-term contracts and closely monitors its customs clearance and transit time, though it is taking initiatives to go in for third-party logistics (3PL) provisions, at the time of writing.

Vendor Relationships

As at the time of writing, Maruti has basic 9 models and around 30 variants, and a total of 370 suppliers. 12 are joint ventures. 72 per cent of its suppliers are from in and around Gurgaon and within 100 kms (see Table 7.4) and receives other component supplies from other states and 9 countries (mainly Japan).

The supplies from vendors located in south India and western India are on a daily basis, though buffer inventory of 3–6 days is maintained from these vendors. 70 per cent of the items are delivered directly on assembly line without inspection. For the rest, Maruti maintains a special division—part inspection (PI) of quality. These are not delivered directly to the assembly line as in the case of lean manufacturing.

TABLE 7.4 Turnover distribution for close-by vendors (within 100 kms)

Area	Percentage of turnover by value
Joint Ventures (Within premises)	24%
Gurgaon	20%
NOIDA	14%
Faridabad	8%
Delhi	4%
Ghaziabad	2%
All proximal areas' total	72%

Source: Vendor Development Department, MUL

Rest 28 per cent is contributed by suppliers located in south (18 per cent), west (9 per cent), and eastern India (1 per cent).

The focus is on consolidation of vendors and raw material procurement, taking initiatives for third-party logistics, and e-procurement. In vendor development, the objectives set up by MUL are

(a) indigenization of components,
(b) ensuring daily supply of components directly on the line,
(c) costing of day to day changes in components, annual cost negotiations, and
(d) carrying out joint value analysis/value engineering (VA/VE) for cost reduction with suppliers.

Postponement Strategy

For a multi-product company, postponement of product differentiation is a very effective tool in managing inventory. Maruti has also implemented it. It has designed the same engine for Alto LX, the 800 models, Alto VX, and Wagon R. It can change the make of the car at a later stage depending upon production demand. Flexibility of production mix at the three plants also helps in saving on logistics costs due to transfer of component parts at the factory.

Outbound Logistics

Selling about 30,000 cars a month and having a network of 232 dealers, inventory management plays a crucial role. From the stocks in the company at the stockyard to the final dealer, it has to ensure that the levels are rationalized throughout the chain. It has a three year *rate contract with transporters*, and due to high volumes, gets very competitive prices for the off-takes of its vehicles. However, it is not sure whether MUL has a structured transporter rating system.

Information Technology (IT)

Complete online transactions processing or electronic data interchange (EDI) between the company and its 160 dealers on the Extranet has compressed Maruti's *order processing time from 5 days to 15 minutes*. The vendors are linked through an *Extranet*. Production planning is done variant-wise and for 15 days. The company already conducts a large business through the Web, making it India's largest business to business (B2B) player. All of the more than 230 sales outlets are connected online to the company's central database. Of these, 130 have started doing business through Extranet. They place their orders online, which goes directly to the company's server. Once the information hits the central database, production schedules can be planned. While a high level has not yet been achieved in terms of the automation required, Maruti is striving towards this goal.

Financials

Maruti's distribution cost is around 2 per cent of sales. Logistics cost is around 4 per cent of sales. Maruti has been able to reduce the holding period of raw materials (RM) from *60 days to 42 days in 2000*. The finished goods (FG) inventory has also come down from 90 days to 4 days. Better SCM practices and sourcing policies and market dominance have allowed Maruti to engage lesser stocks in both the areas, i.e., RM and FG inventory.

Discussion Questions

1. How have the inbound and outbound logistics parameters changed at MUL? Compare these with world-class firms' values with the help of information from the Internet.
2. What are the key management policies for vendor relationships and development at MUL? How has vendor consolidation been carried out at MUL?
3. What role does the Web and information technology (IT) play in supply chain management (SCM) at MUL?
4. How have financial parameters of the company been or are expected to be improved by implementation of supply chain management (SCM) at MUL? Compare it with corresponding values of some world-class firms.

REFERENCES

Bal, Jay, Richard Wilding, and John Gundry (2000), 'Virtual Teaming in the Agile Supply Chain', *International Journal of Logistics Management*, 10(2), pp. 71–82.

Beamon, Benita M. (1999), 'Measuring Supply Chain Performance', *International Jounal of Operations and Production Management*, Vol. 19, No. 3, pp. 275–292.

Chao, C., E.E., E. Schewing, and W.A. Ruch (Summer 1993), 'Purchasing Performance Evaluation: An Investigation of Different Perspectives', *International Journal of Purchasing and Materials Management*, pp. 33–39.

Christopher, M. (1998), *Logistics and Supply Chain Management: Strategies for Reducing Cost and*

Improving Service, 2nd Edn, Financial Times Management, London.

Christopher, M. (2000), 'The Agile Supply Chain: Competing in Volatile Markets', Industrial Marketing Management, Vol. 29, No. 1, pp. 37–44.

Cooper, Robin and Robert Kaplan (September–October 1988), 'Measure Costs Right: Make the Right Decisions', *Harvard Business Review*.

D'Avanzo, Robert et al. (November–December 2003), 'The Link between Supply Chain and Financial Performance', *Supply Chain Management Review*, 7, No. 6.

Davis, Tom (1993), 'Effective Supply Chain Management', *Sloan Management Review*, pp. 35–46.

Devi, Uma Maheshwari P. and B. Raja Shekhar (August 2006), 'Supply Chain Management Practices in FMCG Industry', paper presented at the 7th International Conference on Operations and Quantitative Management (ICOQM), Jaipur.

Goldman, Steven, L. Roger, N. Nagel, and Kenneth Preiss (1994), 'Agile Competitors and Virtual Organizations: Strategies for Enriching the Customer', John Wiley & Sons.

Johnson, J.B. and S. Randolph (1995), 'Making Alliances Work, Using a Computer-based Management System to Integrate the Supply Chain', *Journal of Petroleum Technology*, Vol. 47, No. 6, pp. 512–513.

Kaplan, Robert S. and David P. Norton (January–February 1992), 'The Balanced Score Card-Measures that Drive Performance', *Harvard Business Review*, pp. 71–79.

Kumar, Dinesh (2004), 'CPG Industry: Supply Chain Drivers Using SCOR'. In Sahay, B.S. (Ed), 'Emerging Issues in Supply Chain Management', Macmillan, pp. 116–128.

Lamming, Richard (1996), 'Squaring Lean Supply with Supply Chain Management', *International Journal of Operations and Production Management*, Vol. 16, No. 2, pp. 183–196.

Lee, Hau L. and Edward Feitzinger (1995), 'Product Configuration and Postponement for Supply Chain Efficiency', Institute of Industrial Engi-neers, 4th Industrial Engineering Research Conference Proceedings, pp. 43–48.

Marwick, Peat (1997), 'Global Supply Chain Benchmarking Study', KPMG Consultants, USA.

Mason-Jones, Rachel, Ben Naylor, and Denis R. Towill (2000), 'Engineering the Leagile Supply Chain', *International Journal of Agile Management Systems*, Vol. 2, Issue 1, pp. 54–61.

McKinsey and Co. (30 November 1992), *Business Week*.

Mohan, Ashutosh (May 2005), 'A Critical Analysis of Supply Chain Management Practices in Indian FMCG Industry', Unpublished PhD Thesis, Faculty of Management Studies, University of Delhi.

Narasimhan, Ram and Ajay Das (1999), 'Manufacturing Agility and SCM Practices', *Production and Inventory Management Journal*, I Quarter, Vol. 40(1).

Neely, A., M. Gregory, and K. Platts (1995), 'Performance Measurement System Design:A Literature Review and Research Agenda', *International Journal of Operations and Production Management*, Vol. 15, No. 4, pp. 80–116.

Nicoll, Andrew P. (1994), 'Integrating Logistics Strategies', Annual International Conference Proceedings, American Production and Inventory Control Society (APICS), pp. 590–594.

Pandya, Pradeep (December 2002), 'Going for Gold in the Supply Chain', Vol. 41, Issue 9.

Sharma, Sunil (April 2006), 'Best Practices and Performance Benchmarking for SCM in Indian Auto Industry', paper presented at International Conference on Supply Chain Management, University of San Diego, USA.

Sharma, Sunil (2005), 'Supply Chain Management in Indian Industry', Research Award Report submitted to UGC, New Delhi.

Shingo, S. (1981), 'Study of Toyota Production System from Industrial Engineering Viewpoint', Japanese Management Association, Tokyo.

Shroeder, G. (2003), 'Operations Management; Contemporary Concepts and Cases', Ch. 5, McGraw-Hill International, Singapore.

Tan, Choon Keah, Kannan, Vijay R. and Robert B. Handfield (August 1998), 'Supply Chain Management: Supplier Performance and Firm Performance', *International Journal of Purchasing and Materials Management*.

Timme, Stephen and Christine Williams Timme (May–June 2000), 'The Financial–SCM Connection', *Supply Chain Management Review*, pp. 33–40.

Trent Robert, J. and Rober M. Monczka (November 1998), 'Purchasing and Supply Management: Trends and Changes throughout the 1990's', *International Journal of Purchasing and Materials Management*.

Voudouris, Vasilios T. and Ariston Consulting (1996), 'Mathematical Programming Techniques to De-bottleneck the Supply Chain of Fine Chemical Industries', *Computers and Chemical Engineering*', Vol. 20, Supplement 2, pp. 1269–1274.

Walton, Steve V. and Ann S. Marucheck (1997), 'The Relationship between EDI and Supplier Reliability', *International Journal of Purchasing and Materials Management*, Vol. 33(3).

Waters-Fuller, Niall (1995), 'JIT Purchasing and Supply: A Review of the Literature', *International Journal of Operations and Production Management*, Vol 15, No. 9, pp. 220–236.

Wheele van, Arjan, J. (Fall 1984), 'Purchasing Performance Management and Evaluation', *International Journal of Purchasing and Materials Management*', pp. 18–19.

Internet Resources

www.campbellsoups.com as accessed on 17 May 2007

www.christopher.ascet.com as accessed on 6 March 2010

www.glscs.com/archives as accessed on 19 May 2007

www.kpmg.com/Global/en/ as accessed on 6 March 2010

www.supply-chain.org as accessed on 5 March 2010

RECOMMENDED CORPORATE CHECKLIST FOR SCM IMPLEMENTATION*

Give your response in the appropriate box before each statement related to a factor.

	1	2	3	4	5
Importance Continuum	Not at all important	Of little importance	Somewhat important	Significantly important	Highly important

	1	2	3	4	5
Adoption Continuum	Not at all	Preparing to adopt	Adopted partially	Significantly Adopted	Fully Adopted

In Yes/No type of responses, tick in the approximate box.

I. Supply Chain Intent, Orientation, Organization, and Interrelationships

	Importance	Adoption
1. SCM can be developed as a 'stand-alone' but integrated function in an organization.	☐	☐
2. Management gives due focus and delivers commitment in terms of time and resources to the supply chain and logistics function.	☐	☐
3. SCM is a corporate strategy that can be used for competitive advantage in the marketplace.	☐	☐
4. SCM gets more challenging with turbulence in the internal and external environment factors, particularly, the market place.	☐	☐
5. SCM can facilitate concurrent implementation of customer relationship management (CRM).	☐	☐
6. Joint working with the supplier is a prerequisite for SCM implementation.	☐	☐

---

* This checklist for SCM implementation in a company has been prepared as a part of a research study by Sunil Sharma in 2005. No part of this can be adopted or reproduced without the written permission of the author who can be accessed at ssharma@fms.edu.

7. SCM must be preceded by a business process re-engineering (BPR) of sorts to remove NVA (non-value added) activities.

8. Lean thinking is collateral to the implement-ation of SCM.

9. Continuous benchmarking against the competitor's processes and costs is key to successful implemen-tation of SCM.

10. SCM has orientation to continuous customer contact and retention.

11. SCM gives higher emphasis to tracking, measure-ment, and improvement of customer service levels.

12. SCM is always facilitated by integrated information flows, including electronic data interchange (EDI), online data availability, visibility, and use of IT tools.

13. SCM ultimately aims for higher quality, reliability, customer service, productivity, and return-on-investment (ROI) levels.

II. SCM and Collaborative Forecasting and Planning

14. It is necessary to have collaborating planning, forecasting and replenishment with retailers/distributors.

15. Tracking of Point-of-sale (PoS) data is a must for forecasting.

16. It is necessary to prepare 'variance reports' from previous forecasts.

17. It is necessary to track sales to forecast and fix the gaps.

18. It is necessary to have data availability/visibility at all levels for analysing demand patterns.

19. It is good to follow Pareto rule—20 per cent of forecast covering 80 per cent of demand and 80 per cent of forecast covering 20 per cent of demand.

	Yes	No
20. Your forecasting system is		
(a) forecast driven		
(b) order driven		

21. Your system is based on:
    (a) *pull* demand from distributors ☐ ☐
    (b) *push* inventory on distributors ☐ ☐
22. You create forecast by
    (a) model/specifications/part number ☐ ☐
    (b) family/product line ☐ ☐
    (c) customer ☐ ☐
    (d) distribution centres (DC's) ☐ ☐

III. SCM and Use of IT Practices and Tools

	Importance	Adoption

23. It is important to map all workflows for real-time information sharing amongst suppliers, internal customers, and external customers. ☐ ☐
24. It is necessary to integrate 'processes' and 'information flows'.
    (a) from customer to supplier ☐ ☐
    (b) from supplier to customer ☐ ☐
25. It is important to have an integrated resources planning system enterprise-wide, e.g., ERP with authorized access of 'plug-in' facility to all key chain partners. ☐ ☐
26. You have EDI with the following groups
    (a) suppliers ☐ ☐
    (b) retailers ☐ ☐

	Yes	No

27. Do your organization ⎤ have a website? ☐ ☐
    and your suppliers ☐ ☐
    competitors ☐ ☐
    major customers ⎦ ☐ ☐
28. Is your website interactive enough to provide online
    (a) product information ☐ ☐
    (b) order enquiries and order booking ☐ ☐
    (c) customer request configuration ⎤ pre- ☐ ☐
    (d) price information ⎟ sale ☐ ☐
    (e) order tracking ⎦ support? ☐ ☐
    (f) technical diagnosis and support after-sales support (ASS) ☐ ☐

29. Do you have an ERP, including a legacy system
    installed in your enterprise? ☐ ☐

Benchmarks

30. What per cent of vendors are connected through e-mail? _____
31. Specify proportion of buying done through
    (a) Internet (e-procurement)   _____
    (b) blanket order   _____
    (c) competitive bidding   _____
    (d) pure negotiation   _____
32. Type of ERP software used, if any
    (a) SAP   _____
    (b) MFG Pro   _____
    (c) Marshall   _____
    (d) Proprietary system   _____
    (e) Any other   _____
33. To what extent do you think ERP has been
    implemented?   Overall per cent _____

Specify module wise implementation	*Priority Rank assigned*	*Per cent*	*Extent*
(a) Financials (FI/CO)	_____	_____	
(b) Production planning (PP)	_____	_____	
(c) Human resources (HR)	_____	_____	
(d) Material management (MM)	_____	_____	
(e) Sales and distribution (SD)	_____	_____	
(f) Project systems (PS)	_____	_____	
(g) Plant maintenance (PM)	_____	_____	
(h) Service maintenance (SM)	_____	_____	
(i) Retail module	_____	_____	
(j) Any other	_____	_____	

IV. Strategic Outsourcing and Supplier Relationships (Including Supplier Rating and Development)

	Importance	Adoption

34. It is necessary to constantly review 'make-or-buy'
    decisions in view of your 'core-competence', i.e.,
    non-core competent activities are preferably
    outsourced.   ☐   ☐

35. It is preferred to have 'part sourcing' than 'system sourcing'. ☐ ☐

36. It is preferred to have a policy of 'vendor-base' rationalism/consolidation. ☐ ☐

37. It is desirable to evaluate suppliers on 'total cost of ownership (TCO)' and not just 'quoted price'. ☐ ☐

38. It is imperative to share real-time information with vendors as regards demand, production, and inventory levels. ☐ ☐

39. It is desirable to constantly search new markets for new and improved products/services. ☐ ☐

40. It is desirable that your suppliers provide you with flexibility in order configuration/ customization. ☐ ☐

41. It is desirable to have a system for tracking of purchase order releases and receipts, and ability to follow/expedite/modify the orders. ☐ ☐

42. You develop vendors in terms of
    (a) financials ☐ ☐
    (b) technicals ☐ ☐
    (c) human resources ☐ ☐
    (d) any other_____. ☐ ☐

43. It is necessary to execute strategic partnerships with suppliers and work jointly with suppliers in terms of
    (a) product/process design ☐ ☐
    (b) joint forecasting ☐ ☐
    (c) verification on each other's capabilities and capacities ☐ ☐
    (d) regular cost improvement /value analysis ☐ ☐

44. It is better to have supplier's rating on the basis of

    Specify weightage

    (a) price _____
    (b) quality _____
    (c) delivery _____
    (d) service _____
    (e) any other, specify _____

Benchmarks
45. Please specify
    (a) Average number of suppliers/part _____

(b) Average number of suppliers/purchasing executives _____

(c) Per cent vendors offering volume and/or variety flexibility _____

(d) Per cent vendors located within a radius of 100 kms _____

(e) Per cent components sole-sourced _____

(f) Per cent vendors selected who did not quote the 'lowest' price in bid _____

(g) Average lead time with domestic suppliers _____

(h) Average lead time with the overseas suppliers _____

(i) Time spent in placing the order with the vendor _____

(j) Average per cent reject material _____

(k) Average per cent late deliveries _____

(l) Average per cent blanket order of total orders _____

(m) Frequency of release of production schedule to vendors _____

(n) Per cent of suppliers having Joint Ventures (JVs) with your company _____

(o) Per cent of suppliers quality system (ISO 9001) accredited _____

(p) Per cent of suppliers complying with environmental and safety (ISO 14000) standards _____

(q) Per cent of disputed suppliers from vendors _____

(r) Per cent of vendors having EDI with the company _____

(s) Per cent of vendors having ERP installed at their end _____

(t) Average cost of purchasing as per cent of purchase value _____

(u) Per cent of vendors following well designed material request planning and Just-in-Time delivery systems (MRP/JIT) _____

(v) Per cent of vendors following recirculatory material handling/packaging _____

(w) Per cent of vendors directly delivering on to production lines (online delivery/JIT-II vendor-managed inventory (VMI)) _____

(x) Average time spent in operational stoppages due to stock outs _____

(y) Average time of the stock overflows of 'A' items in the year _____

V. Modern Manufacturing Practices and Systems (Including Master Production Scheduling and Material Planning)

	Importance	Adoption
46. It is desirable to follow master production scheduling (MPS) which is a level factor between demand planning (sales planning) and supply planning (operations planning).	☐	☐
47. The MPS should make available information to the customer, which reliably gives (within known variation) available-to-promise (ATP) information.	☐	☐
48. MPS must be responsive enough so that needs of demand can be aligned and fine-tuned to the ability of the supply.	☐	☐
49. A rough cut capacity planning (RCCP) should be available, which can evaluate the feasibility of actual MPS in terms of available capacity.	☐	☐
50. It is necessary to review bill of materials (BOM) for making them flatter, and thereby reducing lead times.	☐	☐
51. It is desirable to review		
(a) work centre capability and capacity	☐	☐
(b) routings	☐	☐
(c) set-up time, queue, and flow times	☐	☐
(d) production scheduling, including rough cut planning	☐	☐
(e) cell manufacturing possibilities	☐	☐

	Yes	No
52. Your material planning system addresses		
(a) minimum order quantities	☐	☐
(b) economic order quantities	☐	☐
(c) re-order points (RoPs)	☐	☐
(d) safety stock estimations	☐	☐
(e) supply lead times	☐	☐
(f) time fencing	☐	☐
(g) firm period schedule commitment	☐	☐
(h) EDI schedules	☐	☐
53. Net material requirements are being calculated using		
(a) BOM files	☐	☐
(b) current inventory files	☐	☐
(c) purchase order files	☐	☐

54. Do you have a system in place for accurate filing of inventory records and retrieval of information? □ □

55. Does your information system for inventory provide access to occurrences of stock outs/discrepancies? □ □

VI. Lean Operations' Techniques

56. Estimate the levels of wastages. Seven wastes as per Toyota Production System (TPS) in the following fields.

	Low	Moderate	High
(a) Overproduction	□	□	□
(b) Buffer	□	□	□
(c) Waiting time	□	□	□
(d) Transportation	□	□	□
(e) Defects	□	□	□
(f) Inappropriate processing (scrap/rework)	□	□	□
(g) Unnecessary movements (of materials and workers)	□	□	□

57. What is the extent of WIP inventory turnover? □ □ □

Best Practices

58. Do you follow the following practices?

	Yes	No
(a) JIT (for online delivery of critical parts and single piece flow)	□	□
(b) *Kanban* (material control for *pull*-based demand of parts and their on-line delivery)	□	□
(c) Systematized material requirement planning (MRP)	□	□
(d) Mistake proofing systems (*paka yoke*)	□	□
(e) Total productive maintenance (TPM)	□	□
(f) Frequent line balancing for *takt time* or *cycle time* management	□	□
(g) Cellular manufacturing for similar parts to reduce WIP levels	□	□

VII. Transportation, Logistics and Warehousing

	Importance	Adoption
59. Effective implementation of SCM requires integration of inbound and outbound logistics.	□	□

60. Freight consolidation/route rationalization pays off significantly in reducing costs of SCM.

61. Dynamic mode of carrier and route selection is effective in reducing stock levels, avoiding stock outs, and related costs.

62. Long term service level agreements (SLAs) with transporters would provide effectiveness as well as reliability.

63. Third-party logistics (3PLs) providers facilitate and simplify transportation to and from the company.

64. A system for rating of transporters/3PLs should be in place for better performance of the SCM system.

65. Forecasting should preferably be done at the distribution centre (DC) level.

66. Customization of delivery (mode/route/frequency/destination) should be preferred based on the customer's requirements.

67. It is necessary to constantly assess the number of loads, distance moved by loads, cost, and speed of movement required for material handling (MH) and traffic to and from the DC.

68. Third party handling and stocking by product/part is known, updated, and communicated regularly to the relevant parties.

69. There should be availability and visibility of data related to on-hand inventory at the DC level.

70. At the distribution centre (DC) level, you have formulated/identified:
    (a) safety stock policies
    (b) minimum batch quantities
    (c) supply lead times
    (d) response time to internal/external customer
    (e) transportation lead time from DC to the end-customer
    (f) best practice of transport and routing
    (g) order size and frequency
    (h) packaging requirement
    (i) shipping modes

71. Have you estimated and analysed the costs of the following factors?
    (a) Average pack weight/density ☐ ☐
    (b) Unit load packaging, handling time, and cost ☐ ☐
    (c) Air freight/road haulage cost per run per unit ☐ ☐
    (d) Packaging/container rejects and costs ☐ ☐
    (e) Warehousing and labour costs per unit ☐ ☐

Best Practices
72. Do you use
    (a) Bar coding system ☐ ☐
    (b) Radio Frequency Identification (RFID)/
        Auto-ID Technology ☐ ☐
    (c) Milk round system ☐ ☐
    (d) Recyclable packaging ☐ ☐
    (e) Hub and spoke system ☐ ☐
    (f) Cross-docking ☐ ☐
    (g) Drop-shipping ☐ ☐
    (h) Third-party logistics provisions ☐ ☐
    (i) Any software for warehousing management
        such as warehouse management system (WMS) ☐ ☐

VIII. Customer Relationships

	Importance	Adoption
73. Customer profiles should be kept on a scientifically managed database in a data warehouse, and audited by periodic review to gauge accuracy and changes.	☐	☐
74. The orientation of the company should be towards customer retention, rather than on a single sale/transaction.	☐	☐
75. Focus should be on continuous customer contact over a longer timescale, and on product value to the customer than delivery of features.	☐	☐
76. Emphasis should be on quality and service levels, preferably defined by the customers themselves.	☐	☐
77. The mechanism of customer care and servicing must be centred around the needs of the customer, and based on interactions with the customer.	☐	☐

78. Customer relationship management (CRM) is only 20 per cent technology and 80 per cent successful involvement of employees and strategy formulation. ☐ ☐

79. Time to market a new product is a critical success factor (CSF) for relationship management. ☐ ☐

80. Orders and order patterns should preferably be reviewed and analysed in a shared manner with suppliers, in order to further understand the customers and their buying behaviour. ☐ ☐

81. A system is in place for collecting and tracking feedback, both positive and negative from the customers, and feedback is shared throughout the organization, and particularly communicated to the appropriate people. ☐ ☐

82. A documented process/work flow should be in place to measure customer satisfaction and service levels, and access to information by them. ☐ ☐

83. Evidences are made available for improvement (reduction) in response times to customer enquiries through better information tools, such as interactive voice response system (IVRS), e-mail, Interactive website, etc. ☐ ☐

84. Employees are encouraged to proactively share customer information and educating others in the organization about the need of the customer, and giving freedom to the customers to access their own information. ☐ ☐

85. A documented training matrix exists for all customer services, particularly, front-office personnel. ☐ ☐

	Yes	No

86. Are processes in place that document
    (a) Number of customer requests denied ☐ ☐
    (b) Number of *pleasant surprises* experienced by customers ☐ ☐
    (c) Unduly long problem fixing times ☐ ☐
    (d) Number of times new customer orders/changes come as surprise to the company ☐ ☐
    (e) Times when promises made to customers are not kept (Not available-to-promise (ATP)) ☐ ☐

87. You estimate frequency, patterns, and costs of
    (a) back-orders ☐ ☐
    (b) service failures ☐ ☐
    (c) lost sales ☐ ☐
    (d) retained goods/damage ☐ ☐
    (e) settlement of warranty claims ☐ ☐
88. Do you estimate per cent degree of *order fulfilment*
    being met by the company? (demand satisfied/
    total demand × 100) ☐ ☐
89. Do you provide product differentiation to customers
    and to provide for customization at their end, i.e.,
    provide flexibility in order configuration and
    postpone it till retailing end? ☐ ☐

Best Practices
90. Do you use softwares such as SIEBEL/Clarify/
    Vantive/any other for customer relationship
    management (CRM)? ☐ ☐

8 Industry Snapshots

Sourcing and laying it out the 'Big Mac' way
MCDONALD'S[1]

Each day, McDonald's or the 'Big Mac', as it is commonly called, serves 47 million customers a day in 119 countries worldwide, operating 31,000 restaurants, employing more than 1.5 million people. In addition to the typical hamburgers, cheeseburgers, French fries, chicken products, breakfast items, soft drinks, milk shakes, and desserts, the Big Mac has now ventured into salads and snack wraps to capitalize on the growing consumer interest in health and wellness. McDonald's global revenues grew 27 per cent over the three years ending in 2007 to $22.8 billion and 9 per cent growth in operating income to $3.8 million.

Corporate Social Responsibility

The company has discharged its corporate social responsibility (CSR) by having a community focus, responsible purchasing systems, and by protecting the environment. The community aspect is served by neighbourhood beautification projects and supporting Ronald McDonald's Houses for seriously ill children. A *farm-to-counter safety system* forms the basis of responsible purchasing systems under which suppliers are expected to meet stringent norms about their supplies.

Interestingly, in what could also be thought of as an extended part of CSR, the McDonald's has a Hamburger University, 40 years in running and 65, 000 graduated. It got college credit recommendations from the US Council of Education for a total of 46 credits spread over two years of college.

The Big Mac Restaurant—Retailing Location and Layouts

First of all, each restaurant, is operated by a franchisee, an affiliate, or the corporation itself. The revenues of McDonald's come from rent, royalties, and fees paid by the franchisee, as well as the sales in company-operated restaurants. Most Mac restaurants

---

[1] Largely based on Nandini Lakshman, *Indian Management*, Vol. 42, Issue 8, August 2003, pp. 14–24. The author expresses due acknowledgement.

are either *counter service* or *drive-thru* kind with indoor and sometimes outdoor seating. Many are designed for children with a natural look emphasizing on comfort, thereby having large lounge areas and doing away with hard plastic seating and having more of brick and wood. The new designs for a Mac restaurant created in 2006 to give that young look to it may have *linger-zone* with arm chairs, sofas, and Wi-Fi enablement, *grab and go zone* for individuals with tall barstools and plasma TV for news and weather updates, and *flexible zone* for families with fabric cushions and flexible seating. There could be different music in different zones. Drive-thru, Auto-Mac, Pay and Drive, or McDrive often have separate stations of placing order, making payment, and picking up the order. More often than not, the latter two are combined. It possibly all depends upon the space availability and the requirements that McDrives located near highways offer no counter-service, while locations on high density city areas would not offer drive-thru. There could even be *walk-thrus* in down town areas. McCafé was started in Australia on a cafeteria style on the lines of Starbucks. Some Mac stores are located near gas stations, convenience stores, inside some malls, or stores as McExpress such as Walk-Mart in US or say, Shopper's Stop in India. McExpress would offer limited seating and/or menu by their location in premium mall/store, while Mc Stop is for truckers and travellers for meeting common needs.

McDonald's claims to be committed to providing quality products in India. The values of *QSCV—Quality, service, cleanliness, and value*, are fulfilled by adopting several measures, the key of these being the setting up and maintaining a unique cold chain, which is necessary to maintain the integrity of food products and retain their freshness and nutritional value. All Mac restaurants have in-built cold storage units having three zones—freezer, chiller, and ambient for maintaining the cold chain till the customer end. The cold chain refers to the procurement, warehousing, transportation, and retailing of food products under controlled temperatures.

Preference for Local Sourcing

McDonald's is committed to *sourcing its needs from local suppliers and farmers.* This assurance is rooted in the philosophy of the founder—Ray Kroc, who firmly believed in 'mutual benefits' arising from a 'partnership' between McDonald's and the local businesses, thus ensuring McDonald's commitment to growth was mirrored by that of their partners. In keeping with this belief, they have carefully identified local Indian businesses that take pride in satisfying customers by presenting them with the highest quality products (Fig. 8.1). Adherence to Indian government regulations on food health and hygiene were a top priority.

McDonald's India today purchases *more than 96 per cent majority* of its products and supplies from Indian suppliers. Supply chain management (SCM) may be defined

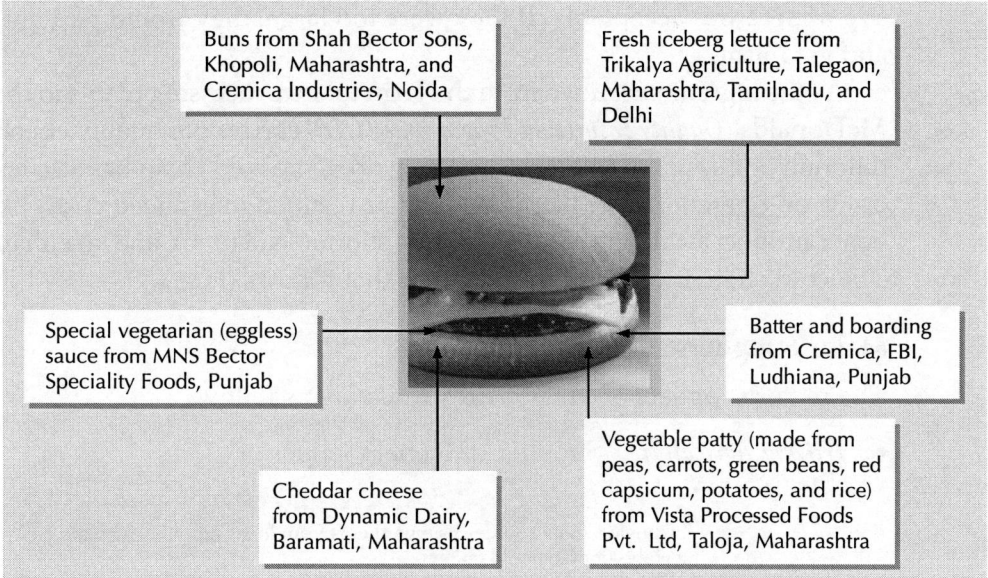

Buns from Shah Bector Sons, Khopoli, Maharashtra, and Cremica Industries, Noida

Fresh iceberg lettuce from Trikalya Agriculture, Talegaon, Maharashtra, Tamilnadu, and Delhi

Special vegetarian (eggless) sauce from MNS Bector Speciality Foods, Punjab

Batter and boarding from Cremica, EBI, Ludhiana, Punjab

Cheddar cheese from Dynamic Dairy, Baramati, Maharashtra

Vegetable patty (made from peas, carrots, green beans, red capsicum, potatoes, and rice) from Vista Processed Foods Pvt. Ltd, Taloja, Maharashtra

FIG. 8.1   Supply chain for a Mc-Veggie burger at McDonald's

as—'The integrated management of all linkages and value added activities from the suppliers to the customers in such a way that enhanced value is achieved at lower costs.'

Taking free-market sourcing to its logical conclusion, fast-food giant McDonald's is *building its own supply chain relationships*—its suppliers are, obviously crucial to its operations, since they provide all the inputs that go into the food it sells—*on the principle of mutual need.* There are *no binding contracts* with any vendor. It is a policy laid down in McDonald's global manuals. 'We focus on a mutually-interdependent long-term business relationship. If we can assure our vendor that we are as dependent on him as he is on us, the trust must carry the relationship through'. In other words— 'You must allow market forces and not binding agreements to determine just who the constituents of your supply chain will be'.

Around the world (including India), approximately 85 per cent of McDonald's restaurants are owned and operated by independent franchisees. McDonald's was able to run the show seamlessly by outsourcing nine different ingredients used in making a burger from over 35 suppliers spread all over India through a massive value chain.

In 1996, when McDonald's opened its first outlet in India, it worked frantically to put the perfect supply chain in place. It trained the local farmers to produce lettuces or potatoes as per specifications, and worked with a vendor to get the perfect cold chain in place. It explained to the suppliers precisely why only one particular size of peas was acceptable. If they were too large, they would pop out of the patty and get burnt.

As the ingredients move from the farm to the processing plants to the restaurant, McDonalds' *Quality Inspection Programme (QIP)* carries out quality checks at over 20 different points in the cold chain. Setting up of the cold chain has also enabled to cut down on operational wastage. Also, it has resulted in reduced costs, better quality, better product availability and reliability, shorter lead times, and an enhanced service. The cold chain is outlined in the figure that follows (Fig. 8.2).

Major Suppliers

The major suppliers of McDonald's India are as follows.

- *Trikaya Agriculture*   Supplier of Iceberg lettuce

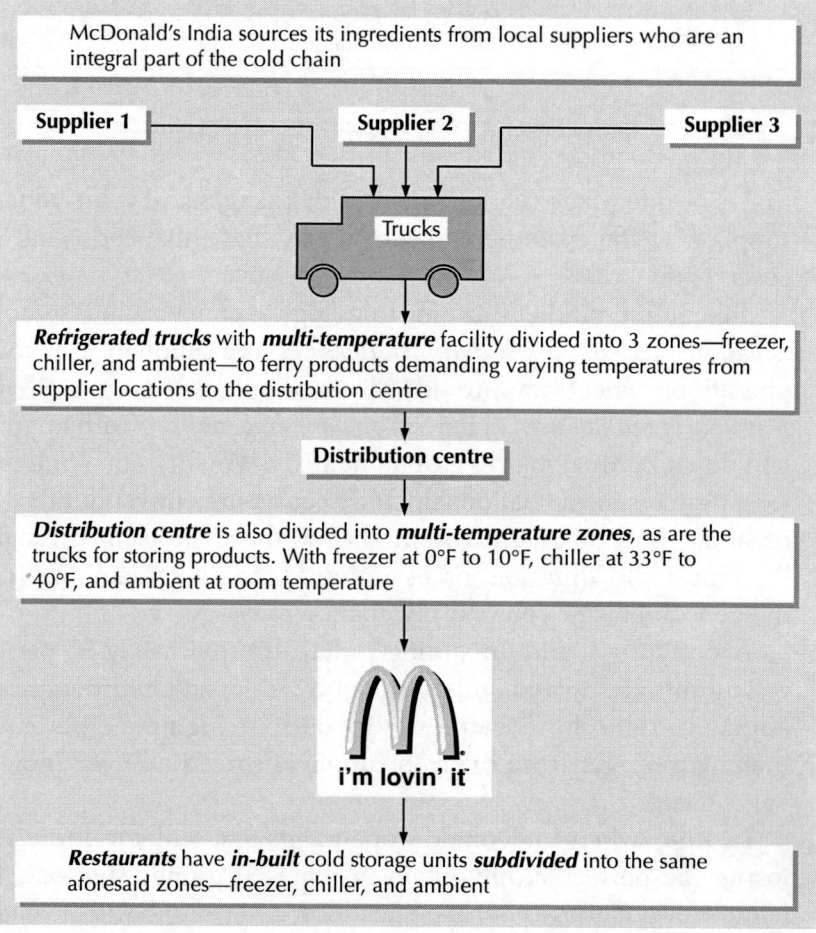

FIG. 8.2   McDonald's cold chain in India

- *Vista Processed Foods Pvt. Ltd*   Supplier of chicken and vegetable range of products (including fruit pies)
- *Dynamic Dairy*   Supplier of cheese
- *Amrit Foods*   Supplier of long life ultra heat treated (UHT) milk and milk products
- *Radhakrishnan Foodland*   Provider of distribution centres (DC) for Delhi and Mumbai

They claim to have

- one stop-shop for all distribution management services
- dry and cold storage facility to store and transport perishable products up to 22°C
- effective process control for minimum distribution cost

All suppliers are covered under the *responsible purchasing* policy of McDonald's and they are expected to toe the line of 'farm-to-food' safety programme of the Big Mac and respect the food safety norms.

Related Resources

www.mcdonalds.com as accessed on 16 May 2009; www.wikipedia/org/wiki/McDonald's as accessed on 16 May 2009.

INDUSTRY SNAPSHOT 2	Reaching the masses on call PANTALOONS[2]

'Cover all channels.' That is the mantra in Pantaloon Retail's headquarters in Mumbai. And as the company adds channels to its portfolio, supply chain, and logistics management—never an easy task in organized retail—just became more complicated. Pantaloons' SCM handles 30 million stock keeping units (SKUs) every day, across the country, all the time. Each SKU has to be tracked, stocked, sold, and attended to. And if the Big Bazaar and Food Bazaar supermarkets were not enough, Pantaloons also entered direct-to-home selling in a big way in June 2004 in Mumbai.

The company understands very clearly that home delivery systems are essentially logistics systems. It involves starting from toll-free numbers to taking calls, then the orders, conveying it to the picking and kitting system, and delivering them, and not the least, taking payment. All of this is hard-core logistics driven. The importance that SCM gets in Pantaloons is manifest in the fact that it is the first and only retail

---

[2] Based on ETIG survey on Supply Chain and Logistics, 2005. The author expresses acknowledgement to ETIG, Mumbai, for their kind permission.

company in India whose SCM department has been awarded the ISO 9001 2000 quality certificate by Det Norske Veritas (DNV), one of the world's leading quality certifiers, exclusively for its supply chain and logistics function.

The ISO 9001 2000 standard, established by DNV, the Netherlands-based certifying agency, is a quality management standard that establishes an international benchmark and standard for logistics and supply chain process within the company, and ensures that the practices, systems, and procedures followed by the company in the above function follow defined systems and practices, thus facilitating rapid growth.

'Today supply chain and logistics is a very critical function for any customer-centric business, especially, the retail sector,' said Kishore Biyani, Managing Director, Pantaloon Retail (India) Limited. 'The ISO 9001 2000 quality certificate will help in our continuous quest for quality and promise to deliver the best to the customer—in fashion, price, and experience. Surely, this is another step towards Pantaloons journey of becoming a world class retailer!'

To get the ISO 9001 2000 Certification, Pantaloons had to meet rigorous standards in designing the supply chain across the country, reducing lead time of delivery, resource and product management, and a strict measurement parameter. The ISO 9001:2000 certification recognizes the company's supply chain and logistics functions, critical design practices, committed management focus and universal application of the quality standards across the company's locations, stores, warehouses, and vendors.

Commenting on the above certification, Anshuman Singh, Head, Supply Chain & Logistics, Pantaloon Retail (India) Limited said, 'Achieving the ISO 9001 2000 certificate is excellent for an operation that is growing as quickly as ours. Like any company that has been through this process, we knew that it was demanding. Every employee and operation was totally committed to quality from the very beginning. By scrutinizing the supply chain and logistics at every level, we assure our customers that we are committed to providing them with superior customer service and the highest quality products. The implementation team and employees' level of commitment and knowledge about ISO 9001 2000 principles were an important factor in the independent audit team's unanimous favorable assessment.

As a part of the SCM initiative, each and every process was scanned and major reengineering or elimination of non-value added steps were undertaken. The supply chain forms the backbone for the activities along the value chain and currently handles approximately half a million units per day across the country, with the quantum likely to increase to three million transactions, and two million pieces per day respectively in the next two years. Today, all the SCM activities, such as supplier relationship management, quality assurance, logistics and warehousing, and the central procurement cell are geared to work as per the best global standards, which the ISO 9001 2000 certificate mandates, and deliver the highest customer value with increased efficiency.

Food Bazaar On Call

At Food Bazaar, the company initiated some best practices, such as providing a toll-free number, explored new models of retail sales and invested heavily in its back office operations and training personnel.

> **Best Practices**
> Toll-free number
> Explore new channels
> Invest in back office and personnel training

Pantaloons' food retail venture, Food Bazaar, has big plans to expand into the 'on call' channel with its new venture—Food Bazaar On Call. Says the company, 'We are exploring every channel of sales—from the Internet, telephonic ordering, physical stores, mobile Food Bazaar vans to kiosks.' He says Food Bazaar On Call, plans to deliver order at home, office, at whatever time the caller specifies. The idea is to take an ever-larger share of the consumer's spend and take share when the consumer does not want to step out in rains, or late evenings, or when both husband and wife are working. In the Food Bazaar model, a caller rings up the 1600 toll-free number which goes to a 20-seater call centre in Chembur, the helpline agent guides the caller through the products, and then confirms the order. The Food Bazaar On Call has been operational in Vashi, Navi Mumbai since June 2004 and the preliminary results have been encouraging. Says Singh, 'We have been receiving 800 calls a day, with 200–300 of them converting into orders. The average order size is around Rs 550.' 24×7 systems do not seem to make sense right now, as they find orders start coming in only after 8 am everyday, and almost no one orders at night. Pantaloon's initial investment into this venture has been around Rs 30 lakh, and the company was confident of recovering all by the end of 2004.

The company says the entire software for the on-call venture was developed in-house, leveraging the understanding of products and retail of the staff that he already had. 'It took us just 40 days to launch the software for the Food Bazaar On Call.' What are the operational differentiators against HLL's Sangam and Fabmart's home delivery in the suburbs? Says the SCM department, 'We have no repeat delivery charges, unlike others. Also, there's no minimum order size, whereas others have.' Pantaloon also says that sales from Food Bazaar On call are estimated to be higher on weekdays rather than weekends, when malls and their own Big and Food Bazaars will draw the consumer. The company has plans afoot to streamline the on-call venture quickly. On the cards is a catalogue that will be available for callers to choose from different products. The helpline agents are also being trained all the time. 'The average length of a call to our 1600 number has fallen from 12 minutes to under 3.5 minutes today,' says the company. This is by itself an addition to the bottomline, as Pantaloons pays for every minute the call lasts. Pantaloons notes the shift in nature of calls, 'When we had first started more enquiry calls, more curiosity. Now we have more calls that place orders.' There's a favourable offshoot as well. Pantaloons says brand awareness of Big Bazaar and Food Bazaar has also gone up, with greater footfalls at the physical stores as well. 'We have a solid physical infrastructure to back up the online and on call retail models unlike the earlier days where ordering was easy, delivery wasn't,' says the company. Backward integrating the fledging call centre that presently caters to the on-call venture is also not ruled out.

INDUSTRY SNAPSHOT 3	**Pioneering hub and spoke** **FEDEX**[3]

The express industry has exerted an enormous influence on the efficiency of the overall economy. The industry did not exist before FedEx arrived on the scene. The delivery of packages and documents was carried out by a haphazard system of carriers, consisting of trucks, trains, and aircraft that were often operated by independent entities. Neither speed nor reliability were the hallmarks of this system. All of this got changed.

Launching the Express Revolution

With its creation in 1973, FedEx invented the concept of overnight express package and freight delivery. Fred Smith's vision was to merge the transportation and package delivery businesses, creatively blending resources in a way that had never been done before.

The FedEx Express model is based on guaranteed time—definite delivery with extremely high levels of speed, efficiency, and reliability. It is difficult to appreciate the enormity of the breakthrough of guaranteed, time-definite, overnight delivery concepts, since they are now such an integral part of business system. The intro-duction of these new cargo/logistics systems constituted a colossal achievement, and triggered the fundamental transformation of the industry. The FedEx integrated express service was a significant departure from the consolidated system operated by freight forwarders and airlines. An integrated express company performs its

---

[3] Partially based on www.Fedex.com/us/supplychain/case-studies as accessed on 3 January 2009. The author expresses due acknowledgement.

own pick up and delivery, with advanced information and communication technology (ICT). Adopting the same concept of offering integrated services, companies, such as UPS, Emery Worldwide, and BAX Global, all grew rapidly.

Creating a New Logistics Framework—The Hub and Spoke Model

Fred Smith created the concept of the hub and spoke network as an indispensable operational strategy for his new air cargo delivery business. The birth of FedEx was also the birth of this now dominant model of efficient, successful air cargo, and air passenger operation. Smith demonstrated that Federal Express could streamline operations and improve efficiency by using a *hub and spoke* approach. Under the hub and spoke system, packages could be collected at various pick-up points(spokes), routed to a central distribution point (hub) for sorting, and re-rented and loaded onto planes to reach their final destinations (Fig. 8.3). Prior to this time, airline companies relied on linear networks and grid networks to move their cargo or passengers. The cargo flows between multiple origins and multiple destinations as well, contributing origin and destination traffic of their own.

The hub and spoke logistics system has had a revolutionary economic impact upon the air cargo and passenger airlines industries, for reasons that stem from the particular characteristics of these industries. To begin with, the air cargo and air passenger industries involve high fixed costs that come with the purchase of very expensive aircrafts.

The hub and spoke network was later adopted by FedEx's air cargo competitors, such as UPS, DHL, and Airborne Express. The same hub and spoke concept was also adopted by nearly all the major commercial passenger carriers in the US, including American Airlines, United, Delta, US Airways, etc.

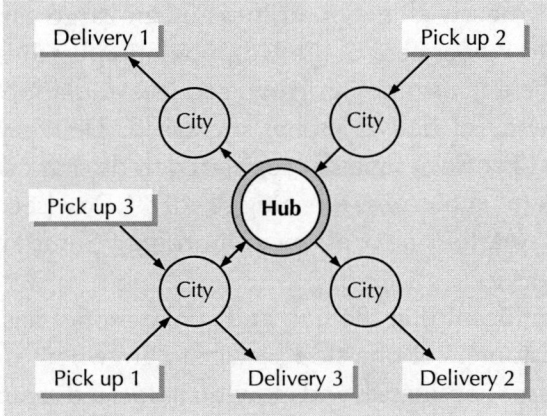

FIG. 8.3 FedEx's hub and spoke model

Hub and spoke networks play a crucial role in today's transport of passengers and cargo around the globe, and have stimulated the air cargo and passenger markets enormously. Under this system, flows of smaller arriving flights are precisely timed to connect seamlessly with larger transfer forward departing flights. Flights depart from different airports—*the spokes* of the network—and arrive at the hub at nearly the same time. This system maximizes the number of attainable connections for incoming cargo. Cargo flies in from various regions, is consolidated at the hub, and then undergoes a reversed process to reach its final destination. For example, airports at Amsterdam, Tokyo, Hongkong, London, and New York serve as the hub for spokes located in the rest of Asia, Europe, and America. Air India has identified Frankfurt Airport as a hub for its operations to spokes located in America.

A hub included not only an appropriate airport and its terminals, but also extensive logistics network associated with concentrated and consolidated traffic, and on-ground sorting. Hubs act as switching centres, consolidating the cargo flows. It is needed to install computer systems, pick-up and tracking systems, and absorb the advertising, training, and administrative costs. However, once established, operating costs are relatively low and stable compared to the linear approach.

FedEx was extremely innovative in recognizing that, through the creation of a hub and spoke network, the number of destinations serviced by it could be greatly increased, while at the same time reducing average costs.

According to Alfred Kahn, as quoted on fedEx.com, former head of the Civil Aeronautics Board, and father of deregulation of airlines in US, the hub and spoke system has created tremendous operational efficiencies, economics of scale, and more flight options for passengers or packages. The economic impact of the hub and spoke model on air cargo and air passenger industries is evident by the fact that following deregulation of the air transportation industry in 1978, the model was adopted by nearly all major airlines and air cargo carriers. FedEx made its services available to 99 per cent of the US population by the beginning of the 90s.

With the extension of air cargo services and adoption of hub and spoke model, the frequency of deliveries has increased. Delivery options became more time specific. At FedEx, it includes registered trade mark services such as FedEx Priority Overnight (next business morning), FedEx 2Day (second business day), FedEx First Overnight (earliest next business morning), Saturday Delivery, and FedEx international services.

It is significant that the hub and spoke model has resulted in availability to the 'spoke' customers of one-stop service to anywhere in the world. In the case of the cargo industry, businesses and individuals located around the globe can ship packages overnight to nearly any country, city, or region in the world.

Logic of Hub and Spoke

The logic behind hub and spoke model can be described as follows. Suppose there are 10 airplanes servicing 10 cities, 5 on the east coast and 5 on the west coast. Each plane can make a single point-to-point flight, connecting one city on each coasts with a city on the opposite coast. However, by introducing a hub and spoke network the same 10 planes can service 70 cities making one stop in a hub. This is a seven fold increase in the number of destinations serviced by the same 10 planes. Each city now has 5 destinations on the opposite coast, rather than one. Since there are 10 cities, there are 50 routes created by a hub and spoke network. Moreover, each city is also connected to the other cities on its own coast. This creates 20 routes—10 new routes among the spokes on each coast.

Under the hub and spoke system, a package originating in a city on the west coast now has the option of being flown to any of the 5 cities on the east coast or any of the 4 other cities on the west coast, while the air cargo company do not have to purchase any new planes. Average costs per package fall because of the increased traffic density on hub and spoke flights, and because of the creation of new routes with new passengers without having to incur wholly commensurate additional costs.

Related Resources

www.sri.coms/policy/estead/reports/economies/fedex as accessed on 23 January 2009.

INDUSTRY SNAPSHOT 4	**Milking the distribution network** **MOTHER DAIRY, DELHI[4]**

Mother Dairy (MD) India is a production and marketing company of a range of milk and dairy products. In the milk category, its significant revenues come from poly pack milk (PPM), apart from bulk milk. Mother Dairy's pouch milk is being packaged at 11 packaging stations located at far flung locations. The milk is transported to the city for sale through three distinct trade channels. These three channels are

Distributors These are the persons who have their own distribution system. Mother Dairy provides them milk at their depots.

Retailers Mother Dairy provides them milk through transporters. They have their own shops and generally sell other products as the main item, and milk as subsidiary items.

Mother Dairy Booths These are the booths owned by Mother Dairy and are operated by ex-service men. These booths sell both poly pack and bulk vending

---

[4] Based on www.fnbnews.com; article by Joe C. Mathews, posted on April 2005.

milk. They also sell other dairy products of Mother Dairy such as butter, cheese, flavoured milk, curd, dairy whitener, ice-creams, and other items.

Poly Pack Products

Mother dairy has 8 SKUs. The packaging size and other information are given in the table that follows (Table 8.1).

These products are highly perishable and therefore need to be delivered as early as possible. This makes the supply chain activity to be more active in milk business, as compared to any other business.

Right now, Mother Dairy is serving these three channels differently. The distributors are sent milk through separate trucks. For retailers and milk booths, various transporters are appointed having their own fleet to supply to them. The transporter takes milk from various plants and distributes them to the retailers and milk booths. The objectives involved segregating these channels and trying to find if it can serve to the retailers and MD booths through separate trucks, such that it is both cost effective and efficient. The rationale behind having separate trucks for booths and retailers is

- milk should reach MD booths earlier than retailers, as the margins to MD by selling through booths are higher than selling through retailers.
- many a times, booth operators close down their shop before milk reaches them. To provide them milk, the distributor has to go again when the shop opens. So, if the delivery is separated, they can provide milk to their booths at right time and thereby, making it a hassle free arrangement.

Existing System of Distribution at Mother Dairy

Supply Chain Network and Distribution Network of Poly Pack Milk

Mother Dairy supply chain network consists of the following broad players/stages.

- Supplier of milk (Farmers/Cooperatives)
- Plant

TABLE 8.1 Poly pack products

Product	Abbreviation	Pack size		Colour
		½ ltr	1 ltr	
Full cream	FCM	Y	Y	Red
Toned milk	TM	Y	Y	Blue
Double toned	DTM	Y	Y	Yellow
Standard		Y	N	Green
Skimmed		Y	N	Violet

Note: Y indicates available and N indicates not available

- Mother dairy (Manufacturer)
- Transporter
- Distributor
- Retailer (independent retailers, Mother dairy booths)
- Consumer

Mother Dairy primarily acts as a marketing company and sources its poly pack milk manufactured by cooperative run plants, that in turn, source milk (raw material) from farmers and milk cooperatives. Also, there is a call centre at Mother Dairy plant, Patparganj which takes in the demand indents and sends them to the plant.

Distribution Network

Poly pack distribution is a direct shipping distribution network—with Mother Dairy taking the orders via distributor and transporter and initiating the delivery request.

The milk is distributed via three distribution channels. Further, along with goods flow, there is information flow and funds flow as well.

Direct retail channel   Milk is sold through independent retailers and supplied through the transporter. At present, there are above 3000 retailers who sell three lakh litres per day (lltpd).

- The poly pack milk is moved from the plant by the transporter who moves it in bulk. Closer to the region of distribution, cross-docking is carried out to transfer milk to smaller distribution vans, and is further delivered to independent retailers.
- Information flow (demand request) flows from the retailer to Mother Dairy via the transporter (who takes indent) and finally to the plant. Actual delivery status flows from the retailer to Mother Dairy.
- Funds flow takes place from consumer, retailer, transporter, Mother Dairy and finally to the plant (though in different amounts and at different time frames).

Mother dairy booth outlets   These are owned by Mother Dairy and milk is supplied through the transporter. At present, there are 700 mother dairy booths selling 3.5 lltpd.

The same kinds of flows are involved except that the retailer is the Mother Dairy booth.

Distributor channel   The milk is supplied to independent distributors who further have their own distribution network and supplies to the retailer. At present there are 60 dealers selling 5 lltpd.

- Poly pack milk is moved from the plant by vehicles owned by Mother Dairy itself, who moves it in bulk and delivers to the distributor, who further carries the milk through his own transportation fleet and distributes to the retailers.

- Information flow (demand request) flows from the retailer to the distributor to Mother Dairy, and finally to the plant. Actual delivery status is not required as once the milk is provided to distributor, Mother Dairy's responsibility is over.
- Funds flow takes place from the consumer, retailer, distributor, Mother Dairy, and finally to the plant (though in different amounts and at different time frames).

Across all flows there is also a reverse flow of empty crates from the retailer to the plant for reloading.

The current distribution/supply chain network of Mother Dairy meets the following service demands of consumers.

Response time: The product nature is perishable and has to be delivered quickly to consumers. There are no storage nodes in the supply chain, as the nature of products do not allow for that.

Product variety: The network handles all the eight SKUs of poly pack milk.

Product availability: The product is made available to the final consumer through different channels.

Returnability: There is no scope of returnability of poly pack milk generally. However, empty crates have to move back from the retailer to the plant for reloading.

Related Resources

www.3isite.com/articles/farm-retail.htm; www.mouthshut.com/review/mother-dairy-37384-1.html

---

INDUSTRY **SNAPSHOT 5**	**India's tiffin answer to Motorola** **MUMBAI'S DABBAWALAHS[5]**

A *dabbawalah* is a person in Mumbai, India, whose job is carrying and delivering freshly made food from home in lunch boxes to office workers. Tiffin is an old-fashioned English word for a light lunch, and sometimes for the box it is carried in. *Dabbawalahs* are sometimes called *tiffin-walahs.* The word 'Dabbawalah' is literally translated into 'one who carries a box' or a 'tiffin man'; 'Dabba' referring to a box (usually an cylindrical aluminium container). Though the profession seems to be simple, it is actually a highly specialized trade that is over a century old, and has become integral to Mumbai's culture. The *dabbawalah* originated when India was

---

[5] Partially based on www.rediffmail.com/news/2003/nov/04, article posted by Ambrish K. Diwanji. The author expresses due acknowledgement to the source.

under British rule—many British people who came to the colony did not like the local food, so a service was set up to bring lunch to these people in their workplace straight from their home. Nowadays, Indian businessmen are the main customers for the *dabbawalahs*, and the services provided are cooking, as well as delivery. Everyone who works within this system is treated as an equal. Regardless of what function a *dabbawalah* performs, everyone gets paid about 4000 rupees (which equals around 50 British pounds), not a lot of money when one considers that they also return the lunch boxes to the homes.

More than 175,000–200,000 lunches get moved every day by an estimated 4500–5000 *dabbawalahs*, all with an extremely small nominal fee, and with utmost punctuality. According to a recent survey, there is only one mistake in every 6000 deliveries. In fact, the American business magazine Forbes gave a *Six Sigma* performance rating for the precision of dabbawalahs. This rating indicates a 99.999999 accuracy percentage of correctness, meaning one error in every six million transactions—an astonishing (and perhaps unbelievable) degree of exactness.

Uninterrupted Services

The service is uninterrupted even on the days of extreme weather, such as Mumbai's characteristic monsoons. The local *dabbawalahs* at the receiving and the sending ends are known to the customers personally, so that there is no question of lack of trust. Also, they are well accustomed to the local areas they cater to, which allows them to access any destination with ease. Occasionally, people communicate between home and work by putting messages on chits inside the boxes.

The process begins early in the morning. Cooked food is picked up from houses and caterers by *dabbawalahs*, and taken to the nearest railway station. There, the different tiffin boxes are sorted out for specific destination stations and loaded on to large, rectangular trays accordingly. Each tray can hold up to 40 boxes. These trays then travel in local trains down to various stations. At each station, there are another set of dabbawalahs who quickly take the *dabbas* meant to be distributed in that area, and push in dabbas meant for other stations.

A Mumbai local halts at a station for about 20 seconds or less and thus, the *dabbawalahs* have to work with precision and speed. During rush hour, it is a nightmare. Ask anyone who has done time on Mumbai locals.

At each station, the boxes are once more sorted for localities and offices and taken there by handcarts, or sometimes carried by individuals. 'We carry up to 35 kg for distances of a couple of kilometers,' points out Medge. The boxes are placed in the offices' reception area by 12.30 pm and are picked up from the same spot by the deliverer a couple of hours later.

The whole process then starts again in the reverse. The boxes are picked up from the offices, taken to the nearest station, and sorted for their journey home. The service runs every working day. Forbes magazine gave this service its highest quality rating of Six Sigma, which means that per million transactions, there is just an error of one.

Container Codes

Every tiffin-carrier has the mark of a circle or a flower of a specific colour and a digital identity number. Take the tiffin mark for example—K-BO-10-19/A/15. K is the identity letter of the dabbawallah. BO means Borivali, i.e., the area from where the tiffin is to be collected. The figure of 10 refers to Nariman Point area. 19/A/15 refers to the 19th Building and the 15th floor in Nariman Point area where the tiffin is to be delivered. These codes would baffle a cryptographer! But they make perfect sense to the *dabbawalahs*. The codes and colours indicate the place from where a dabba is collected; the station where it must be unloaded, and the office it is to be delivered.

These are the men who deliver 175,000 lunches (or 'tiffin') each day to offices and schools throughout Mumbai, the business capital of India. Lunch is in a tin container consisting of a number of bowls, each containing a separate dish, held together in a frame. The meals are prepared in the homes of the people who commuted into Mumbai each morning, and delivered in their own tiffin carriers. After lunch, the process is reversed.

Despite the complexity, the 5000 tiffinwalahs are prone to make a mistake only about once every two months, according to Raghunath Medge, 42, president of the Mumbai Tiffinmen's Association. That is one error in every 8 million deliveries, or 16 million if one includes the return trip. 'If we made 10 mistakes a month, no one would use our service,' says the craggily handsome Medge.

The meals are picked up from commuters' homes in suburbs around central Mumbai long after the commuters have left for work, delivered to them on time, then picked up, and delivered home before the commuters return.

Each tiffin carrier has, painted on its top, a number of symbols which identify where the carrier was picked up, the originating and destination stations, and the address to which it is to be delivered. After the tiffin carriers are picked up, they are taken to the nearest railway station, where they are sorted according to the destination station. Between 10:15 a.m. and 10:45 a.m., they are loaded in crates onto the baggage cars of trains.

At the destination station they are unloaded by other tiffinwalahs and resorted, this time according to street address and floor. The 100-kilogram crates of carriers, carried on tiffinwalahs' heads, hand-wagons, and cycles, are delivered at 12:30 p.m., picked up at 1:30 p.m., and returned whence they came.

The charge for this extraordinary service is just 150 rupees per month, enough for the tiffinwalahs, who are mostly self-employed, to make a good living. After paying Rs 60 per crate and Rs 120 per man per month to the Western Railway for transport, the average tiffinwalah clears about Rs 3250. Of that sum, Rs 10 goes to the Tiffinmen's Association. After minimal expenses, the rest of the Rs 50,000 a month that the Association collects, go to a charitable trust that feeds the poor. So, they discharge their corporate social responsibility (CSR) as well, a characteristic of a good organization and its governance.

INDUSTRY SNAPSHOT 6	The network of networking CISCO SYSTEMS[6]

In August 2001, the San Jose, California based, computer-networking company Cisco Systems Inc (Cisco) surprised industry observers by announcing its first ever negative earnings in more than a decade. In a third quarter of fiscal 2001, the company's sales had decreased by 30 per cent. Cisco had to write off inventory worth $2.2 billion and lay off 8500 people.

By the end of 2001, the market capitalization of the company was down to $154 billion and employee profit was $240,000 (down from $700,000 in 2000). This was in sharp contrast to the situation in early 2000, when Cisco was one of the most successful companies in the Internet world with a market capitalization of $579 billion (it had become the world's most valuable company surpassing even Microsoft's market capitalization $578 billion). According to John Chambers, Cisco's CEO, neither the company's software, nor its management were to blame for the company's poor performance. Analysts were puzzled that while other networking companies, with far less sophisticated information technology infrastructure than Cisco, had begun downgrading their forecasts in the wake of the impending downturn in the industry months earlier, Cisco did not lower its inventory like other companies. What came however, as the biggest surprise were the allegations by some analysts that the company's 'highly regarded' systems were to be blamed for this situation. According to analysts, over-reliance on technology prevented Cisco from seeing the impending downturn that was clear to everyone else, and led the company down a disastrous path.

CISCO—Networked Supply Chain

Cisco was established in 1984 by a group of computer scientists at Stanford. They designed an operating software called Internet operating system (IOS) that could route streams of data from one computer to another. The software was loaded into

---

[6] Partially based on www.cisco.com/web/about/ac227/ac333/the-environment/supply-chain.html as accessed on 26 December 2008.

a box containing microprocessors specially designed for routing. This was the router, a machine that made Cisco a hugely successful venture over the next two decades.

In 1985, the company started a customer support site through which customers could download software over and also upgrade the downloaded software. It also provided technical support through e-mail to its customers. In 1990, Cisco installed a bug report database on its site. The database contained information about potential software problems to help customers and developers. The system allowed customers to find out whether a specific problem was unique, and if not, how other customers had solved that problem.

By 1991, Cisco's support centre was receiving around 3000 calls a month. This figure increased to 12,000 by 1992. In order to deal with the large volume of transactions, the company built a customer support system on its website. In 1993, Cisco installed an Internet-based system for its large customers, usually multinational enterprises. The system allowed customers to post queries about their software problems. Cisco also installed a trigger function called 'Bug Alert', which sent emails containing information on software problems within 24 hours of their discovery. Encouraged by the success of its customer support site, Cisco launched Cisco Information Online in 1994. This online service offered not only company and product information, but also technical and customer support to Cisco's customers. By 1995, the company introduced applications for selling products or services on its website. The main idea behind this initiative was to transfer paper, fax, e-mail, and CD-ROM distribution of technical documentation and training materials to the Web, thus saving time for employees, customers and trading partners, and besides, broadening Cisco's market reach.

In 1996, the company introduced a new Internet initiative called the 'Networked Strategy' to leverage its network for fostering interactive relationships with customers, partners, suppliers, and employees. Cisco wanted to ensure enhanced customer satisfaction through online order entry and configuration. Customers' order information flowed through the supply chain network, which consisted of Cisco employees, resellers, manufacturers, suppliers, customers, and distributors.

Orders from customers were stored in Cisco's enterprise resource planning database and sent to contract manufacturers over the virtual private network (VPN). Cisco's suppliers could clearly see the order information, as their own production schedule was connected to Cisco's ERP system. According to the requirements, the suppliers shipped the needed components to the manufacturers and replenished their stocks. The business model aimed at enabling Cisco's contract manufacturers to start manufacturing built-to-order products within 15 minutes of receiving an order.

Cisco has always given top priority to order fulfilment and project management to achieve on-time delivery to customers. Third-party logistics providers were plugged into Cisco's database via the Internet. As a result, Cisco could, at any time provide customers with information regarding the status of their order. Direct fulfilment led to a reduction in inventories, labour costs, and shipping expenses. Through direct fulfilment, Cisco saved $12 million annually.

Cisco's Internet-linked supply chain network enabled the automatic testing of products from any of its locations worldwide. While earlier prototyping used to take weeks, Cisco engineers were now able to do the same within a matter of days. This was because prototyping could take place at the manufacturer's site itself. After manufacturing, the product was connected to one of Cisco's 700 servers worldwide. For a faulty product, the system would not print a shipping label. This prevented an invoice from being generated and consequently blocked payment.

Because of rapid sharing of demand information across the supply chain, customers could receive products faster. To sum up, this networked supply chain ensured

- shorter engineering-to-production cycle times in order to increase market share
- flexibility in designing, revamping, and retiring products in response to market demand
- product quality, though major portions of the fulfilment process were outsourced

Even though Cisco has dealt with technically complex products such as routers, it never hesitated to hand over the manufacturing to a set of contract manufacturers. In order to ensure the quality of its products, Cisco relied on automatic testing. The company developed test cells on supplier lines and ensured that the test cells automatically configured test procedures when an order arrived. Cisco defined its core-competence as product designing and delegated the rest—manufacturing, assembly, product configuration, and distribution—to its partners.

By the start of this century, Cisco launched transactional facilities, such as product configuration and online order placement. These facilities were connected to its ERP systems. In the same year, Cisco upgraded its network infrastructure to better handle the increasing number of transactions. It also introduced dial-in access from desktop computers that allowed customers to place orders without accessing the Internet. At the same time, it also introduced customized business applications for its large customers. These applications resided inside the customers' corporate Intranet and automated the ordering process by linking directly to Cisco's internal systems.

More than three-fourths of the orders for Cisco's products were being placed over the Internet. Aided by Cisco's Internet initiatives, the company's net sales grew at more than 75 per cent compound annual growth rate (CAGR) and operating profits also went up to more than $1 billion in 2002.

According to many analysts, the company's networking strategy had played a major role in its success over the years. Industry observers noted that ever since its inception, Cisco had demonstrated the power of networking and the benefits it could offer.

Cisco owned just two of the 40 facilities that manufactured its products. It did not own the distribution system that delivered the products to its customers, but through its network of suppliers, distributors, partners, and resellers and customers, it successfully coordinated all the necessary activities to provide products to its customers on time.

Despite an efficient supply chain network, Cisco ran into some problems. Cisco's partners typically worked out their supply-and-demand forecasts from multiple points in the company's supply chain. Transactions between suppliers and contract manufacturers were not always smooth. There were time lags in delivery and payment, and thus greater opportunity for error. As a result, suppliers were plagued by long order-to-payment cycles. In June 2000, Cisco discovered, to its alarm, that it was running short of some key components for some of its equipment.

Due to the shortage of components, shipments to customers were delayed by 3–4 weeks. Though demand for Cisco's products remained healthy, the revenues of customers who were used to delivery within two weeks were affected badly. Analysts felt that above experiences of customers were rather 'out of character' for a company that prided itself on its relationships with customers, and even compensated many of its executives on the basis of customer satisfaction.

CISCO Systems—The Supply Chain Perspective

CCO and ICS Initiatives

In order to address the above problems, Cisco revamped its supply chain management to reduce the long ordering cycles. The company launched Cisco Connection Online (CCO), which connected Cisco with all its suppliers and contract manufacturers online. As a result, when a customer placed an order, it was instantly communicated to all its suppliers and manufacturers. In most cases, a third-party logistics company shipped the product to the customer.

CCO ensured increased coordination and connectivity between supply partners, thus reducing the operating costs of all constituents. Automated processes within the supply chain removed redundant steps and added efficiencies. For instance, changes in market demand were communicated automatically throughout the supply chain. This enabled the networked supply chain suppliers to respond appropriately.

CCO reduced payment cycles for suppliers and eliminated paper-based purchasing. As a result, suppliers agreed to charge lower product markups. Consequently, Cisco saved more than $24 million in material costs and $51 million in labour costs annually. CCO enabled Cisco's contract manufacturers to find out the exact position of demand and inventory at any given point of time. As a result, they could manage replenishment of inventory with ease. This resulted in a 45 per cent reduction in inventory and a doubling of the inventory turnover. Cisco slashed the inventory holding of its suppliers and manufacturers and brought it down from 13,000 units (approx.) to 6000 units within 3 months.

To get the most out of CCO, Cisco used Intranets and Extranets extensively. The Extranet was used for communicating with suppliers, manufacturers, customers, and resellers, while employees used the Intranet for communication about the status of orders. Thus, through an online information and communication system, Cisco linked suppliers, manufacturers, customers, resellers, and employees seamlessly.

However, some of Cisco's large customers were not able to access CCO because it did not connect seamlessly to their back-end or electronic data interchange systems. These firms were telecom equipment distributors or network operators, who lacked the time to visit the supplier websites to order the equipment they needed.

Cisco introduced the integrated commerce solution (ICS) for these customers. ICS provided a dedicated server fully integrated into the customers' or resellers' Intranet and back-end ERP systems. It facilitated information exchange between Cisco and them, besides speeding up transactions. It had all the e-commerce applications of CCO, with the additional capability of pulling order-related data directly from Cisco's back-end ERP systems online. At the same time, as the server was integrated into the customers' and resellers' back-end ERP systems, the end users needed to enter the order information only once; this order was simultaneously distributed to both resellers and Cisco's back-end systems, eliminating the need for double entry.

With these new Internet initiatives and sound financials, Cisco seemed all set to register even higher growth figures. However, in early 2001, the global IT business slowdown and the dotcom bust altered the situation. Reportedly, Cisco failed to foresee the changing trends in the industry, and by mid 2001 had to cope with the problems of excess inventory. As a result, the company had to write off inventory worth $2.2 billion in May 2001. Cisco blamed the problems on the *plunge-in-technology spending*, which Chambers called as unforeseeable as *a 100-year flood*. Company sources revealed that if its forecasters had been able to see the downturn, the supply chain system would have worked perfectly.

The Problem and the Remedy

Analysts felt that the flaws in Cisco's systems had contributed significantly to the breakdown. During the late 1990s, Cisco had become famous for 'being the hardware maker that did not make hardware'. Its products were manufactured only by contract manufacturers and the company shipped fully assembled machines directly from the factory to the buyers. This arrangement led to major troubles later on.

According to analysts, Cisco's supply chain was structured like a pyramid, with the company at the central point. On the second tier, there were a handful of contract manufacturers who were responsible for the final assembly. These manufacturers were dependent on large sub-tier companies for components, such as processor chips and optical gear. Those companies in turn, were dependent on an even larger base of commodity suppliers who were scattered all over the globe. The communication gaps between these tiers created problems for Cisco. In order to lock-in supplies of scarce components during the boom period, Cisco ordered large quantities in advance on the basis of demand projections made by the company's sales force. To make sure that it got components when it needed them, Cisco entered into large-term commitments with its manufacturing partners and certain key component makers.

These arrangements led to an inventory pile-up, since Cisco's forecasters had failed to notice that their projections were artificially inflated. Many of Cisco's customers had ordered similar equipment from Cisco's competitors, planning to eventually close the deal with the party that delivered the goods first. This resulted in double and triple ordering, which artificially inflated Cisco's demand forecasts. Cisco's SCM system failed to show the increase in demand, which represented overlapping orders. For instance, if three manufacturers competed to build 10,000 routes, to chipmakers it looked like a sudden demand for 30,000 machines. As Cisco was committed to honour its deals with its suppliers, it was caught in a vicious cycle of artificially inflated demand for key components, higher costs, and bad communication throughout the supply chain. Cisco's inventory cycle reportedly rose from 53.9 days to around 88.3 days.

According to analysts, Cisco's systems failed to model what would happen if one critical assumption—growth—was removed from their forecasts. They felt that if Cisco had tried to run modest declining demand models, then it might have seen the consequences of betting on more inventory. They felt that Cisco should not have assumed that there would be continuous growth.

Having realized these problems, Cisco began taking steps, to set things right. The company formed a group of executives and engineers to work on an 'e-Hub' remedial program. Work on e-Hub began in late 2000. The project was intended to help eliminate bidding wars for scarce components. According to Cisco sources, e-Hub was expected to eliminate the need for human intervention and automate the flow of information between Cisco, its contract manufacturers, and its component suppliers. The e-Hub used a technology called partner interface process (PIP) that indicated whether a document required a response or not. For instance, a PIP purchase order could stipulate that the recipient's system must send a confirmation two hours after receipt, and a confirmed acceptance within 24 hours. If the recipient's system failed to meet those deadlines, the purchase order would be considered null. This would help Cisco to find out the exact number of manufacturers who would be bidding for the order.

According to the e-Hub setup, Cisco's production cycle began when a demand forecast PIP was sent out, showing cumulative orders. The forecast went not only to contract manufacturers but also to chipmakers, such as Philips semiconductors and Altera Corporation. Thus, overlapping orders were avoided and chipmakers knew the exact demand figure. e-Hub searched for inventory shortfalls and production blackouts, almost as fast as they occurred.

However, work on e-Hub fell behind schedule due to its complexity and the costs involved. According to Cisco sources, the company originally planned to connect 250 contractors and suppliers by the end of 2001, but it could link only 60. It was reported that the number might rise to around 150 by mid 2002. Company sources said that e-Hub was just the first stage of its plans for automating the whole process of ordering and purchasing.

Meanwhile, the company's poor financial performance prompted analysts to comment that if the inputs were wrong, even the world's best supply chain could fail. They added that only the next boom phase in the IT business would prove the efficiency of eHub.

Let us see the way the supply chain operations are managed in India's counterpart of CISCO systems.

Cisco Systems in India

Cisco Systems India Pvt. Ltd, started operations in 1994 with a sales and marketing presence spread across key cities in India and a software development centre in Bangalore. In India, Cisco dominated the networking market in core technologies of routing and switching, as well as wireless local area network (WLAN) and network security markets.

Cisco has eight sales offices in the region located at New Delhi, Mumbai, Bangalore, Chennai, Kolkata, Lucknow, Hyderabad, and Colombo in Sri Lanka. The India office comes under Asia, which constitutes of south-east countries, India, and the SAARC. This region contributes to about 11 per cent of the total revenue. Cisco Networking Academy Program (CNAP) has 150 academies across 20 states of India. The number of Cisco certified professionals is around 30,000. Cisco's *go-to-market* strategy is through channel partners.

- There are 9 system integrators (NCR, IBM, CMC, HP, Network Solutions, Cable and Wireless, Wipro Infotech, Tata Infotech, and Datacraft)—8 of whom are Gold Certified.

- There are 1500 resellers in 100 cities.
- There are 2 distributors selling equipment to resellers—Ingram Micro and Redington and Redington.

The support and service-extensive system support customers with 5 logistics centres in the country. Besides that, Cisco is the only vendor to have a support programme called Advanced Replacement Next Business Day (ARNBD) for its resellers.

The model of distribution shown in Fig. 8.4 basically represents the channel Cisco uses to sell its products in the country. The products that Cisco deals in are mainly B2B products required by the corporate, impelling Cisco to follow a unique distribution structure.

Tier 1 Partners

This includes all the companies that are called system integrators. System integrators are basically solution providers who design, plan, implement, and also maintain networks for other companies. To become a system integrator, the particular company

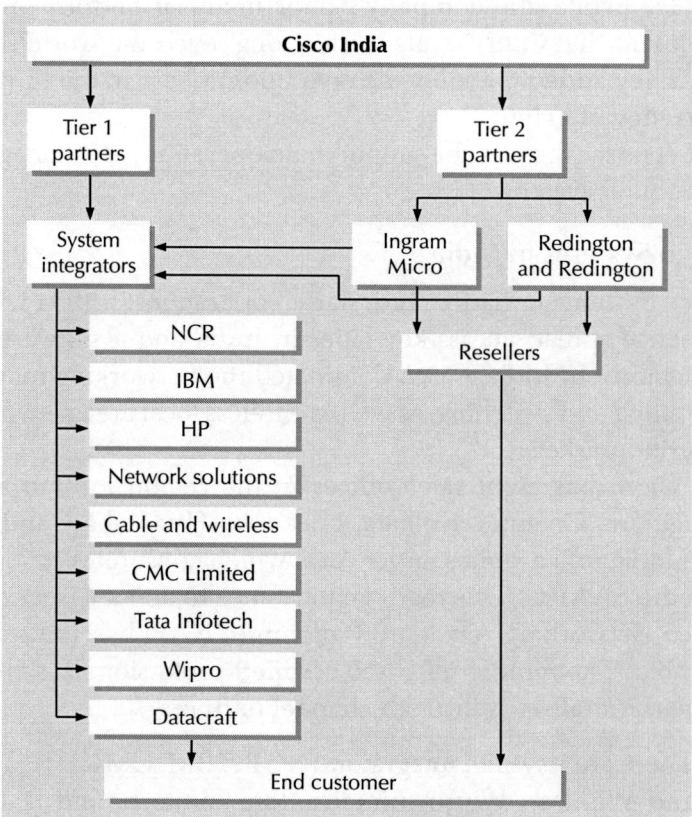

FIG. 8.4 Distribution system at Cisco India

has to be certified by Cisco. Then system integrators are given status of silver or gold partners. The engineers can also get certified by CISCO. These certification courses certify that the engineer is qualified to work on the system.

> **Level of partner**
> The system integrator is given the status of gold or silver partner depending on the number of employees they have, the number of certified engineers they are employing, their turnover, etc.

These system integrators are the companies that client companies approach for their networking problems and requirements, and they provide solutions to the clients.

Tier 2 Partners

These are the organizations, such as Ingram micro or Redington (in case of Cisco) which are distributors, and stock and sell products of the company. These companies hold the products of different IT companies and stock them in bonded warehouses. They sell the products to other smaller resellers or the system integrators. These companies are just stockist and sellers, and do not offer any kind of technical support to the end customers.

Resellers

These are the smaller players that provide only the product. They are more or less like retailers that take products from the distributors and sell it to other people. They do not provide any support and generally do not have highly trained workforce.

End Customer

The end customer in this case is usually another business or corporate. The end customer generally contacts a system integrator to put in place his network or contacts Cisco for the same. Cisco talks to him about that technical things and asks the client which system integrator he will prefer to put his network in place, and then redirects the client to him. The quotation to the end customer is given by the system integrator and not Cisco. Cisco India does not sell its products directly to the client in India. The company does not design or install network for the clients; it is done by system integrators. The billing is also done on the account of the system integrator or the reseller.

Benefits of Cisco's Distribution System

The first benefit that Cisco gets is the decrease in the level of investment. It saves the cost of servicing clients, as that is handled by the channel partners.

In India they do not have to stock spares as that is handled by the partners and also, they do not have to keep high levels of inventory. The channel partners are also responsible for distributing the products of Cisco. The company is basically into product manufacturing and not really as service provider, and by having partners that stock and sell its products, it can focus on its core competency. Also, the company by having so many channel partners competing against each other for clients in a way expands its reach in the Indian market.

INDUSTRY SNAPSHOT 7	**The hierarchy of demand planning** **ESCORTS LIMITED[7]**

Escorts Ltd is the holding company of the diversified leading engineering conglomerate—the Escorts Group. Post-restructuring, agri-machinery or tractors has become the focus area of operations at Escorts. Other businesses, i.e., railway equipments, two-wheelers, IT, telecom, construction and material handling equipment, and financial services are controlled through its subsidiary companies and joint ventures. Escorts have been focusing on its 'core competence' of manufacturing tractors. Escorts Ltd has rolled out 1 million tractors since its inception in 1965. It has 1600 sales and service outlets and presence in 41 countries. It has the tractor assembly, transmission, and engine plant at Faridabad. Escorts has strong in-house engineering skills, a strong R&D centre, and one of its kind Escorts Institute of Farm Mechanization (EIFM) at Bangalore, which imparts training in operations, maintenance, and repair of farm machinery to all the partners of the supply chain. In 2006–2007, company produced 53,235 tractors, as compared to 47,612 tractors in 2005–06, registering a growth of 12 per cent. During the same period, Escorts group had a sales turnover of Rs 2102 crore as compared to Rs 1781 crore in 2005–06, registering a growth of 18 per cent.

Agri-machinery Industry Basics

The Indian tractor market is dominated by low price, no frills, rugged, versatile, and low to medium powered tractors. The farmer, a major consumer, is not willing to pay a premium for sophisticated and modern technology, which can reduce fatigue, emission, noise, etc. Tractors are normally categorized on the basis of power of the engine measured in horsepower (HP) as follows

- less than 20 HP
- 20–30 HP (small size)
- 31–40 HP (medium size)
- 41–50 HP (large sized)
- 51 HP and above (very large sized)

---

[7] The author expresses thanks to the Materials Department of Escorts Ltd for sharing the information contained in this case. Some inputs are drawn from www.escortsgroup.com/business/business_agri_machinery.html as accessed on 16 May 2009.

In India, the popular range of tractors is 20–40 HP compared to 60 HP in Europe and 90 HP in the US. The reason being that in India, most farms are small and fragmented and large tractors would work out to be economically unviable. However, over the past few years, an interesting trend has been the increasing sales of high-powered tractors, particularly in states of Madhya Pradesh, Gujarat, and Maharashtra. This is because the soil in these states is hard and black in contrast to the alluvial soils in Punjab, Haryana, and U.P. More recently, higher-powered tractors are being increasingly sold in states such as Punjab too, where farmers link it to being a status symbol. Now, Escorts manufactures 45 variants in the range of 25HP–80HP with Escort, Farmtrac, and Powertrac being the brands. Tractors available in developed countries have advanced features and accessories not found in Indian tractors. However, Indian tractors have an advantage of lower prices. They are about 1/4th the international prices for similar powered tractors. Currently, there are seven major players controlling about 99 per cent of the market. Mahindra & Mahindra (M&M) has emerged as the leader during the last 3–4 years. A few international players, such as New Holland and John Deere have also set up facilities in India. But these players have entered the high-powered category and, thus, pose little threat to the existing players, such as Escorts who enjoy advantages of established distribution/service network and strong brand equity.

Tractors form an integral part of farm mechanization and have a crucial role to play in increasing agricultural productivity. In India, 90 per cent of the tractors are financed by bank credit at concessional rates. Availability of credit, therefore, is the most crucial factor impacting tractor demand. Increased use of irrigation facilities, shift towards multi-cropping, consolidation of land holdings, promotion of cooperatives, and higher investment in agriculture also contributes to higher tractor demand.

Corporate Background

Escorts originally was incorporated as Escorts Agents in 1944 at Lahore and shifted to Delhi after independence in 1947. Escorts, Hariprasad Nanda's flagship company, started on a small scale as a trading and agency business. The company took franchisee for distribution of Massey Ferguson tractors in 1949. Later, it started manufacturing its own brand of tractors with technology from Ursus of Poland in 1959. Escorts also started manufacturing Rajdoot brand motorcycles in 1961. H.P. Nanda, after a long corporate battle, thwarted a take-over attempt by Swaraj Paul in 1983. Escorts employee strength is about 15,000.

Demand Planning at Escorts

Every *dealer* has a demand planner into which he feeds the demand for the model mixes for a month or quarter and sends it to the regional or area offices (30 regional offices in India). Figure 8.5 displays this hierarchy.

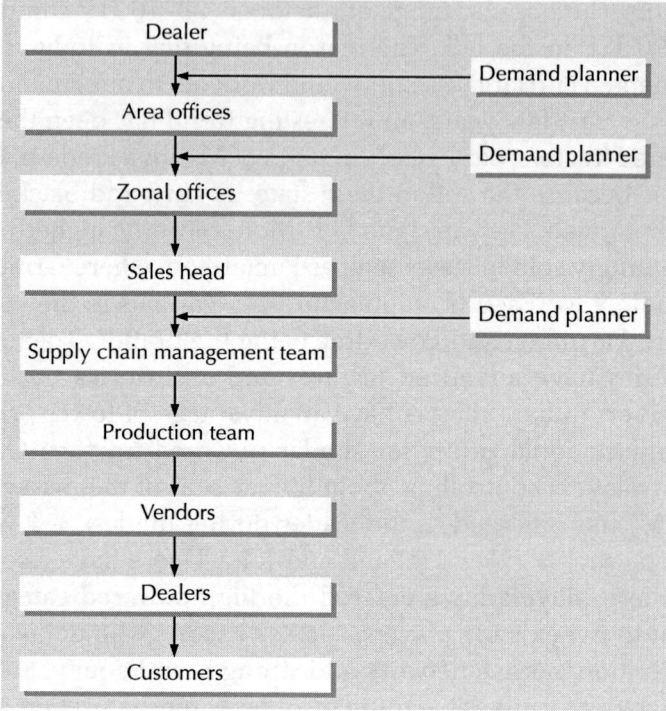

FIG. 8.5 Levels of supply chain management at Escorts Tractors

The *regional head* consolidates the information on demand in a demand planner and sends it to the zonal offices (South, East, North, and West).

The *zonal office* head again consolidates the demand according to the previous trends. He keeps in mind the sales target set for the particular zone.

Then the report is sent to the sales head of Escorts Ltd. Therefore, he gets four reports in total. Now the sales head consolidates the report by taking into consideration

- last year's model mix demand
- last six months' trends in the industry, i.e., what the competitors are selling
- seasonal demand scenario

The demand for tractors varies according to the monsoon. In a good monsoon season, the demand is likely to be high, and if it is a bad one, the demand is likely to be low.

Now the sales head has certain statistical tools using which he makes demand forecasts—confirmed and tentative. The planning software used by many companies is from *i2*. He then sends this report to the supply chain management team.

The supply chain management team takes into account the following factors.

- Last six months trend in the demand and sales of model mixes
- Model mixes that are in the pipeline
- Opening stock region-wise
- Closing stock region-wise
- Deliveries scheduled in a month

Based on all these factors, the team finalizes the model mixes and sends it to the production team for production and procurement of material.

The production team takes into consideration and performs the following functions.

- Flexi-planning
- Regularizing production
- Regularizing cash flow
- Regularizing inventory
- Finding new vendors for new model mixes (sourcing)

The production team then fixes the model mixes and then sends it to the vendors for the raw material procurement (scheduling). They have a software from *Oracle* wherein the demand for model mixes would automatically generate the demand for the raw materials required. Then the model mixes are manufactured, followed by their dispatch to the dealers for sales.

INDUSTRY SNAPSHOT 8	Strategizing IT initiatives for SCM
	BHARAT PETROLEUM CORPORATION LIMITED[8]

Information technology solutions to supply chain management are a big help to many fast moving consumer goods (FMCG) companies as they track the movement of the company's products and provide instant information related to the demand and supply situation. Bharat Petroleum Corporation Limited (BPCL), though not a FMCG company by definition, had embraced an extensive investment in information technology. It envisaged the need for information related to the different petroleum products it offers, besides high-speed diesel and motor spirit (petrol). With its refinery at Mumbai and the acquisation of Cochin refinery, it has a good presence in the western corridor of India, with over 4000 retail outlets and hundreds of liquefied petroleum gas (LPG) distributors. Given the environment in which BPCL operates today—the liberalization, privatization, and globalization phenomena—BPCL may enter into an environment where the administrative price mechanism for petroleum

---

[8] The author expresses acknowledgement to the IT department of BPCL for sharing information contained in this snapshot.

products may be dismantled with market determining the price. This would need BPCL to have complete information about its business transactions. With this objective in mind, it has invested in creating an IT infrastructure across its refineries, bottling units, some retail outlets, distributors, and all its offices. Details about the IT infrastructure are provided, although no financial details are made available. This study demonstrates how an organization, sensing a business opportunity, is using new technology solutions across its supply chain to enhance the competitiveness. It also examines issues related to the integration of information technology and the way the technology enhances the competitiveness of the organization. A proposition was framed and was tested in an organizational setting.

The proposition to be tested was 'Due to fierce competition and globalization, enterprises are continuously striving to improve quality, time to market, customer satisfaction, and profitability.' To execute this vision, organizations are trying to integrate all the activities across the supply chain.

IT Initiative at BPCL

During the last few years, BPCL has taken a number of steps to enhance the value offered to the customer. The organization was redesigned and six strategic business units (SBUs) were formed in 1998. As a part of the restructuring plan initiated during 1998, BPCL felt a need for a strong IT backbone for driving superior business results. An enterprise-wide resource planning solution—SAP R/3, was implemented as the backbone for most of the business processes. Based on the commendations of Arthur D Little's IT consulting firm, an information system framework for BPCL was developed as shown in Fig. 8.6.

Bharat Petroleum realized that, in the long run, success could only come with a total reorientation and change in approach with the customer as the focal point. The focus of the information framework suggested by the consultants was the establishment of six strategic business units (SBUs) that are at the core of business at BPCL. These are retail (which looks after the retail outlets (petrol pump), industrial and commercial (which looks after direct sales to big companies), lubricants (Lubes responsible for the complete range of lubricants business), LPG (which looks at the LPG bottling and distribution business), the aviation SBU that looks after all aviation related fuels and services, and refinery that looks after the processing and technical value-addition to the crude oil and other resources.

The head of each SBU reports to the governing council of the company. Besides the corporate centre at Mumbai, there are five other shared services and entities, namely strategy, information systems (IS), human resources (HR), brand, and other services. These groups provide strategic direction and support to the six SBUs. The SBUs have their own independent groups, such as support services, human resources,

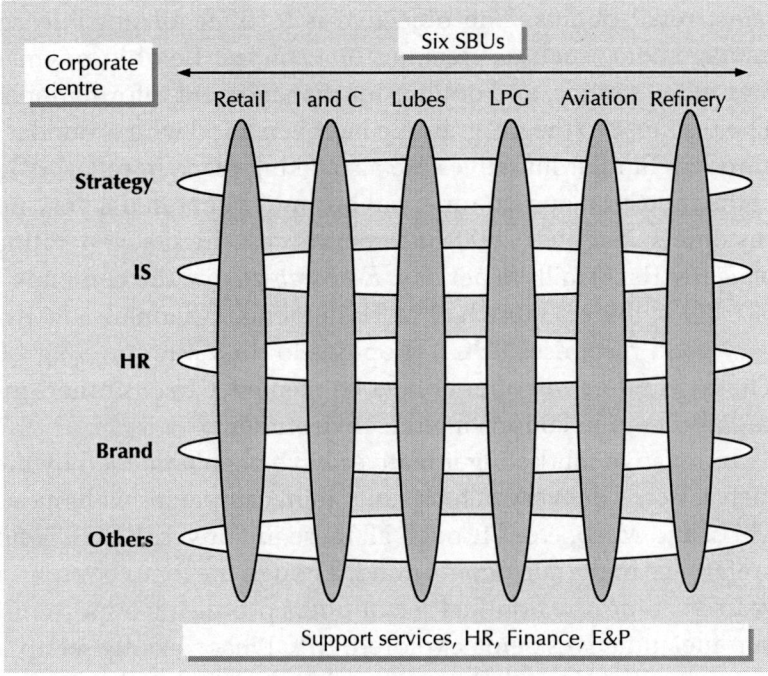

FIG. 8.6 The information system framework at BPCL

finance, and engineering and procurement (E&P) that concentrate on the day-to-day operational issues of their respective SBU.

In an effort to build a direct relationship with retail customers, BPCL had introduced the *Petro-bonus programme* last year. With more than 3,50,000 Petrocard members, Petro-bonus is the largest customer loyalty programme in India. The company expects to enroll another 5,00,000 members during 2001–02. Nearly 30,000 transactions take place every day, valuing at Rs 13 million, and the Smart card Forum of India voted *Petrocard* as the 'Product of the Year'. In order to cater to the distinct needs of truck fleet owners and truck drivers, BPCL has chalked out an ambitious highway strategy. A chain of outlets with special facilities to cater to the highway segment is being set up on highways along the golden quadrangle. These outlets, which will also carry the 'pure for sure' guarantee, offer fleet owners added facilities, such as vehicle tracking, communication services, centralized payment systems, and emergency assistance. BPCL is also offering reasonably priced hygienic food, visible parking, basic restrooms, and other facilities at many of these sites. Many of these outlets are *one-stop truck shops (OSTSs)*, which are company controlled. Around fifty of such OSTSs have so far been commissioned. BPCL also launched *SmartFleet*, another loyalty card targeted at fleet owners and corporate customers. This programme, which is co-branded with Tata Finance, has been rolled out at select retail outlets. The objective is to offer all possible conveniences for fleet management, such as tracking of vehicles, flexible payment options, rewards, messaging service, and options for management information system (MIS) reports. The response to the programme has been good with around a lakh vehicles already enrolled. Similar initiatives are also taking place in other SBUs. The B2B initiative of the industrial and commercial business generated a very positive response from customers, and over 2800 customers access the site, generating business to the tune of nearly Rs 80 million per day. *E-bharatgas. com*, the company's website for booking of LPG cylinders launched at Hyderabad, Chennai, and Kolkata has received a very good response. BPCL proposes to do a pilot on 5 kg LPG cylinders shortly. These cylinders will offer greater convenience to customers in rural and hilly areas, and also help in conserving the environment.

Innovative marketing initiatives have been launched by the lubricants business, such as home delivery of lubricants, joint campaigns with manufacturers like Maruti, LML, and Mico, etc. Through all these initiatives, BPCL is slowly earning a brand preference in the customer's mind. Though the focus continues to be on fuels, in the years to come, the non-fuel sector offers promising opportunities. Among the other non-fuel initiatives being explored, BPCL has recently set up branded convenience centers called *In and Out* stores, aimed at facilitating shopping and completing multiple errands at conveniently located outlets. *In and Out stores* offer 14 key product categories and services under one roof covering ATMs, photo shops, music, fast food, greeting cards, courier services, drop box for credit card/mobile phone payments, movies/entertainment ticketing, etc. Strategic alliances have been entered into with leading brands in each category. These self-service stores have been launched in 34 locations in Chennai, Mumbai, and Delhi. Eventually this concept would be expanded to 300 locations across 23 cities. In March 2001, BPCL acquired Government of India's shareholding in Kochi Refineries Limited (KRL). It also acquired Indian British Petroleum (IBP's) stake in Numaligarh Refineries Limited (NRL). With these acquisitions, the two companies have become subsidiaries of BPCL. The acquisition of a majority stake in KRL and NRL is vital for the company, as it makes additional refining capacity available.

Industrial and Commercial SBU

BPCL's industrial and commercial (I&C) strategic business unit (SBU) deals with institutional marketing of products, such as Motor Spirit (MS), High Speed Diesel (HSD), Furnace Oil, Naphtha, Hexane, Special Boiling Point (SBP) Spirits, Benzene, Toluene, Mineral Turpentine Oil (MTO), Xytol, and Sulphur. All the products marketed by the I&C SBU are deregulated, with the exception of Motor Spirit and High Speed Diesel. The I&C unit of BPCL also provides a spectrum of services to its valued industrial customers. These services range from developing customized products, technicals seminars, fuel management consultancy and fuel management systems, to energy and safety audits, and terminalling of petroleum products. BPCL's commitment to give its best to institutional customers is well complemented by its customers' absolute confidence in BPCL's quality, dependability, and service. The list of BPCL's satisfied institutional customers has been growing year after year. A few of its prestigious customers are Tata Electric, NTPC, Hindustan Lever, Asian Paints, Reliance Industries, NOCIL, and Oswal Chemicals and Fertilizers among others. BPCL's I&C SBU is totally focused towards meeting customers' ever-changing needs. All the activities within or outside the Business, be it strategy formulation, infrastructure building, business plan development, etc. centre around one theme— 'customer service to gain competitive advantage'. To facilitate interactions with its institutional customers, BPCL started its first business-to-business (B2B) initiative in the industry, which enabled customers to place indents on the Internet and track fulfilment. Other facilities include bulletin board/online communication, and provision of a high degree of interactivity to enable BPCL to respond to customers' needs effectively and efficiently. Customers have been provided with a password facility to enable them to access complete information pertaining to them, in a secure environment.

On the I&C's home page, after the customer logs in, the customer can place orders online, look up the various agreed upon prices mentioned in the rate contract, and view his purchase order status and the dispatch schedule. The dispatch status window indicates information related to the ordered items, date and time of the invoice, the transporter's name, and the truck number through which the material has been dispatched. Commercial information related to the unit price, total price, taxes, and the invoice value are also provided. A facility to plan the dispatch in advance is also available wherein, the customer can key in the estimated value of their requirement of the various products needed. There is also a facility to modify the requirement status.

On the Web page on one of BPCL's customers, the various drop down menus and facilities related to the business transactions are visible. Enhanced customer satisfaction being BPCL's motto, it became the first oil company to embarked on a voyage from brick to click (Business-2-Business e-commerce). The B2B portal enables the customer to place an order, dispatch information, track the status of his order, and undertake online communication. This results in better inventory management, better financial information, and more convenience. The positive customer feedback has encouraged BPCL to draw up a highly ambitious plan to implement this initiative across the country—covering all its 9000-plus customers drawing supplies from 172 locations. It is proposed to integrate the portal with the SAP system for reducing the response time and also to capturing data from Kochi and Numaligarh refineries. This will enable sharing of the complete information with the customers. The portal will soon enable customers to see their statement of accounts. There are also plans on the anvil to introduce an option for customers to be able to integrate the portal with their own system, which will greatly cut down the order fulfilment time.

Closing Remarks

All the aforesaid initiatives amply demonstrate as to how BPCL is leveraging technology to improve its competitiveness. Four areas can be easily spotted—SAP implementation across the enterprise, smart card technology in the retail SBU, a B2B website for the I&C SBU, and a business-to-consumer (B2C) website for the LPG SBU. SAP implementation across the enterprise provides information related to type and quantity of products at various locations, including transit. Smart card technology initiatives are aimed at increasing brand loyalty and capture customer related data, and the B2B and B2C websites provides crucial inputs for refinery production, LPG bottling, and distribution plans. The B2B site also provides real-time data to industrial customer, such as order and dispatch status dispatch summary, balance amount, etc., whereas the B2C website provides facility for online booking of gas cylinder and order status to the customer, and crucial inputs for the LPG bottling plants and distribution, thereby increasing the level of customer service.

The figure that follows (Fig. 8.7) indicates the various IT initiatives taken by BPCL in three of their SBUs. It can be said that BPCL has covered its supply chain in four of its six SBU's at the time of writing this book.

The oil industry is today a growth industry worldwide. The global industry growth rate is around 16 per cent [900 million metric tons (MMT)]. Of this, 33 per cent (297 MMT) growth is expected from India and China only. The Indian per capita consumption (510 kg of oil equivalent, OE) as against the world average per capita consumption (1818 kgs of OE) and USA (7778 kgs of OE) as in 2006 is a very big

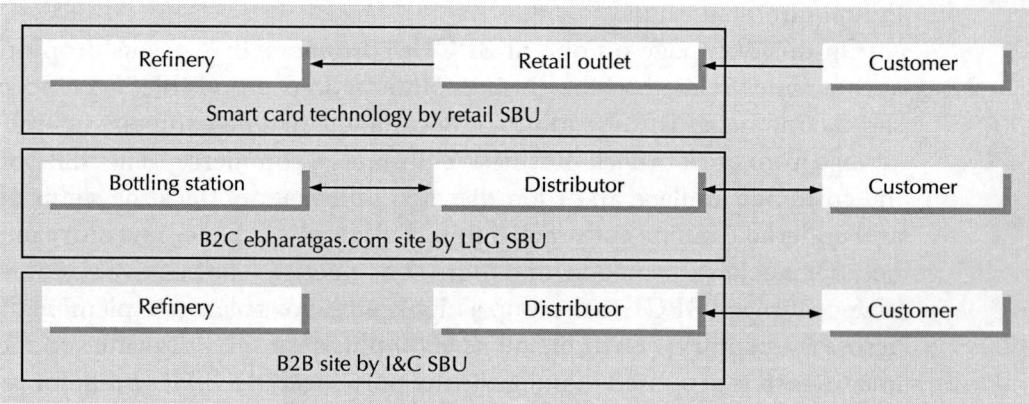

FIG. 8.7 BPCL's IT initiatives across its SBUs

business opportunity for Indian oil companies in a deregulated environment. BPCL recognized this opportunity just after it reorganized its business operations with the formation of six SBUs. It realized the need for improving organizational performance to face global competition, once the oil sector would be deregulated. A bundle of IT initiatives across the supply chain were introduced and a judicious technology was selected for enhancing each SBU's competitiveness. It did not implement all the available technologies across all the SBU's, but chose only those that were appropriate and added value to the company's offerings. So, BPCL has been able to implicate the role of technology in its business strategies.

INDUSTRY SNAPSHOT 9	**Brewing up supply chain and logistics STARBUCKS[9]**

Starbucks was born in 1971 with the first store located in Seattle, Washington's Pike Place Market, under the name 'Starbucks Coffee, Tea and Spice'. A history teacher named Zev Siegel, a writer named Gordon Bowker, and an English teacher named Jerry Baldwin founded the original Starbucks. The idea for the store was from a Dutch immigrant, Alfred Peet, who had opened a specialty store in Berkeley, California, named Peet's. Alfred schooled the Starbucks founders in the art of coffee making—'the quality of coffees and the importance of proper bean-roasting techniques.'

At its inception, Starbucks was only a retail store that sold whole coffee beans and coffee related products; they did not offer the fresh brewed coffee as they do today. Starbucks' expansion into the fresh brewed coffee business began after its Director, Marketing, who later on became its CEO in 2008, Howard Shultz visited Milan, Italy, and was exposed to the ideas of espresso bars. The espresso bar was very successful but did not convince Baldwin to expand into the business.

Original Starbucks' Supply Chain

Since the founders of Starbucks wished to offer their customers the best in coffee beans, and the best in their eyes was that from Peet's, their original coffee bean supplies were purchases from Alfred Peet. As the store progressed, the group members returned multiple times to visit Alfred, learning more about the roasting process and the knowledge of fine teas. They were finally able to begin roasting

---

[9] Based on interview of David A. Norton, VP (Logistics), Starbucks, 1 January 2002, Keller Publishing, as posted on www.supplychainbrain.com/archives/1.02.norton.htm

their own beans. Near the end of the first year, the group purchased a used roaster from Holland and set up their own roasting operation near their store.

As Starbucks expanded, so did their supply chain demands. This resulted in the construction of what is today's smallest roasting plant, which was built in 1989, and was expected to meet the company's needs until 1999. It is now being used to supply the company's mail order business. A larger plant located in Kent, Washington, at 305, 000 square feet was opened in 1993, which serves the area to the west of the Mississippi River. A third plant located in York, Pennsylvania serves the area to the East of the Mississippi with the same high quality of roasted coffee beans that the company has always served.

The quality of the beans used to supply the stores begins with the growers. Dave Olsen worked to secure the highest quality of green coffee beans for the company. He would visit the countries where the beans were grown and develop relationships with the growers. He would seek out the varieties that would meet the quality and flavour requirements.

Supply Chain Management

In the past, companies competed on product and cost, now they compete on supply chain management. Starbucks' approach to supply chain management is a map for success. As a fully vertically integrated company, they are one of few retailers that manufacture and distribute their own products. Starbucks believes the whole concept of supply chain management can be found in the term 'value added'. They are in the business of delivering value—with marketing and retail organizations developing the value, and supply chain operations delivering it.

Central Supply Chain Operation

There are three major business functions supported by the Starbucks supply chain, the retail business organization, the specialty sales and marketing, and direct response. All have different functions within Starbucks.

The first area is the retail business organization, which runs all of the retail stores, currently numbering around 3000. The retail business operation also supports, through supply chain operations, the international businesses. The second area of the supply chain operation is the support of specialty sales and marketing. In this function, they support major restaurants, United Airlines, Nordstrom's, and other specialty accounts that do not fall under the retail business unit operations. The third area of the supply chain operations is direct response where the operations behind direct mail are handled.

Basically, Starbucks has created a centralized supply chain operations organization that supports each of these three areas. The company recognizes that there is significant leverage in operating the supply chain in this manner, as opposed to having three totally separate business units. As they look at future opportunities, supply chain management will be an integral part of leveraging for those business units or ventures as well. Each unit of the supply chain is integrated by common objectives. Each of the business units within the supply chain operations have a mission statement and strategic imperatives, which are shared by the head of each of the units. These imperatives are shared to such a degree that much of their financial compensation is based on achieving objectives that cross boundaries. Examples of this can be found in inventory control, inventory levels, inventory investment, service levels, and financial performance, as a total delivered cost to the customers. The objective sharing is set up so that a silo structure is not created within the business, which is a characteristic of 'added value'. Starbucks does not maximize transportation at the expense of distribution; they do not increase the length of roasting runs just to maximize throughputs. Instead, everything is done based on achieving the *best total delivered product* out of the facilities.

Exploring Growing Overseas Markets

Overseas expansion has been underway in such Pacific Rim markets, such as Japan, Hawaii, Singapore, New Zealand, The Philippines, Korea, China, Hong Kong, Malaysia, Thailand, and Taiwan. Across the Atlantic, Starbucks has established stores in the United Kingdom, Kuwait, and Lebanon. Asian expansion looks to be a significant component of Starbucks overall strategy, as recent store openings would indicate. In China alone in the past twelve months, Starbucks has opened 9 stores in Beijing, two in Hong Kong, and one in Shanghai.

Modifying the supply chain to accommodate new markets can be a significant means of improving overall efficiency and profitability of Starbucks. As the company expands into the huge and untapped markets of Asia, Starbucks is studying potential locations for a new coffee roasting plant in one of several countries. This will be Starbucks' first coffee roasting plant in Asia, and decisions on location will be driven by the economies of operation, local costs, proximity to market, and other factors.

The importance of the supply chain in Starbucks' operations is reflected in the company's corporate structure that places an Executive Vice President for supply chain and coffee operations as one of three offices that report directly to the President and Chief (Fig. 8.8).

A key reason to place SCM near the top of the corporate structure is to assure supply chain involvement in most aspects of Starbucks' operations. Supply chain is part of strategic planning, sales forecasting, customer service, marketing, and

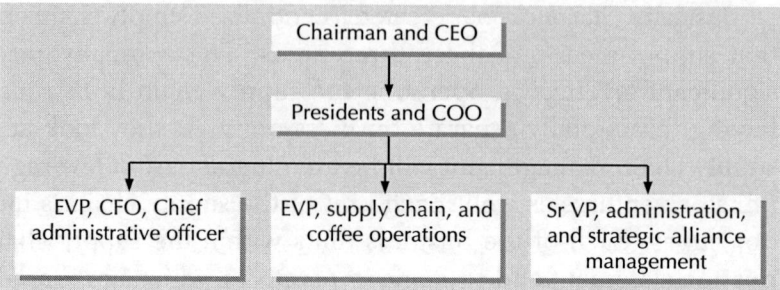

FIG. 8.8 Reporting relationship of supply chain head at Starbucks

information technology. By integrating supply chain throughout the company's operations, Starbucks can use its knowledge and skills to deliver products to customers at the lowest cost and greatest efficiency.

Challenges for Starbucks SCM include using skills and knowledge as a comparative advantage, the best way use partnerships overseas, and the way to position the best site for future roasting and distribution facilities overseas.

Starbucks' size and established supply and distribution channels create the advantage of an economy of scale. This has been instrumental in opening new markets overseas, but in delivering their products to consumers, Starbucks must develop new, complex supply channels for more than coffee beans. Much of Starbucks' sales include perishables, such as juice, bakery goods, and sandwiches. In US alone, they are one of the top dairy consumers. Starbucks is experimenting with the consolidation of fresh products as a possible improvement to the supply chain.

Starbucks sees SCM as delivering value to customers and international partners. Strategic planning and SCM will continue to be linked to the Seattle office as distribution channels grow further into Asia. Information technology will be the key to providing real-time information to forecasters and operations managers around the world. International partners with Starbucks will benefit from the company's growing experience and market penetration. As Starbucks expands overseas and becomes the predominant worldwide specialty coffee company, it must continually improve, innovate, and simplify its supply chain.

Related Resources

www.outsourced-logistics.com/outlog-story 6672/+logistics+at+starbucks; www.ohl.com/news/archives/2004-news/oh-logistics-eastern-distribution-starbucks.html; www.managementtoday.co.uk/search/article/601844/logistics-greening-supplychain/+logistics+at+starbucks

INDUSTRY SNAPSHOT 10	The taste of information and communication technology in supply chain AMUL[10]

Gujarat Cooperative Milk Marketing Federation Ltd is an apex cooperative organization. It is respected for its credentials even after 56 years of its inception. The cooperative movement started with two villages and 247 litres of milk in 1946. It has become a Rs 1 bn business now. The success of Amul explains the reasons for this remarkable growth. The Kaira District Cooperative Milk Producers Union Ltd, Anand was born on 14 December, 1946.

The first lesson in milk marketing was learnt when an assured outlet for milk in Bombay stimulated increased milk collection in the villages of Kaira District. More and more farmers joined hands in all the villages to successfully negotiate the increased demand for the milk. The Bombay milk scheme did not accept all the milk procured by the cooperative society. Setting up of a dairy processing unit was a way to solve the problem. There was a need felt for the Dairy plant to process and utilize the milk supplied by the society, and as a result the dairy was set up in 1995.

The Anand pattern of Dairy Cooperative includes the Dairy Cooperative societies at village level and a processing unit called 'Union' at the district level. Inspired by this pattern, similar milk unions were started in other districts too. To market the products of the milk unions, Gujarat Co-operative Milk Marketing Federation (GCMMF) was formed in 1973. GCMMF is the sole marketer for all the range of Amul products. Originally, the range comprised only milk powder and butter. Later, it has expanded drastically to cover products, such as ice creams, pizza, ghee, cheese, chocolates, shrikhand, paneer, and so on. These made Amul the leading food brand of India. The punch line is *Amul – the taste of India*. The new structure of GCMMF is shown in Fig. 8.9.

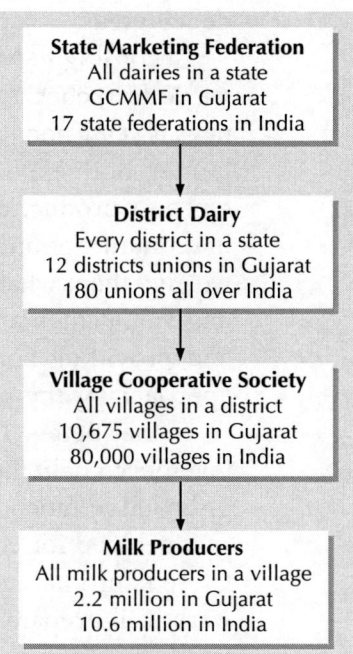

FIG. 8.9 The new Anand model

---

[10] Largely based on Bowonder, Raghuprasad, and A. Kotla (2005), 'ICT Application in Dairy Industry: The E-experience of Amul' as posted on www.planningcommission.nic.in/reports/sereport/ser/study-ict/3-amul.pdf, as accessed on 19 January 2009. The author expresses thanks to Dr Bowonder for the kind permission he gave to use the case.

The GCMMF consists of 12 affiliated member Dairies/District milk unions and it has its own manufacturing unit called Mother Dairy at Gandhinagar with the largest network in food industry, sup-ported by marketing and distribution of liquid milk and a variety of products under the brand name—Amul. It is also the sole selling agent for the national dairy development board's (NDDB) edible oil—'Dhara'. GCMMF also co-ordinates with the manufacturing dairy units for production planning and milk procurement, and handles the distri-bution of milk from surplus union to the deficit areas.

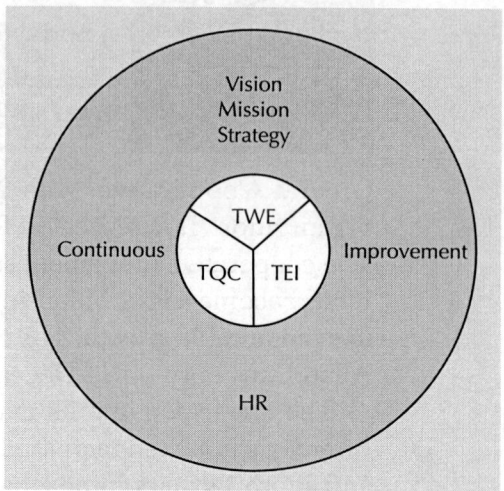

FIG. 8.10   The TQM model at GCMMF (Bowonder et al. 2005)

According to Mr B.M. Vyas, Managing Director, GCMMF, 'Within 2.5 hours, we collect, check, transport, and process up to 1 million litres of milk a day—365 days a year, non stop. We're in between the two extremes—the customer and the farmer. Both expect the maximum intake. In one way, the customer wants to have the best product available at the lower price. On the other, farmer expects the maximum amount for his milk. To sustain in the business we have to make sure that we give them what they want.' As all these require a tight integration in the supply and value chain activities, GCMMF is able to excel in it by educating the farmer and providing him the necessary guidance on one end, and on the other end, approaching the consumer with the best product and understanding the Indian consumer better. The information technology and total quality management came together to help the GCMMF to gain control on the procurement, processing, and distribution functions (Fig. 8.10).

The need for coordinating a highly distributed system was clearly understood. Close coordination has been the main feature of the value chain (Fig. 8.11). They were well prepared for the systems revolution. GCMMF is one amongst the first few Indian companies to start a website and opting for the Domain 'coop' will prove the fact that they are well ahead of the time. The IT related initiatives that GCMMF undertook include—an ERP initiative to integrate the market related activities. The Web-based initiatives made the consumer well aware of Amul. 'Online stores' and 'Portal activities', such as emailing, and greetings gave the consumer a better picture of Amul. The automatic milk collection unit systems (AMCUS) are empowering the farmers by employing IT at village cooperative societies. IT

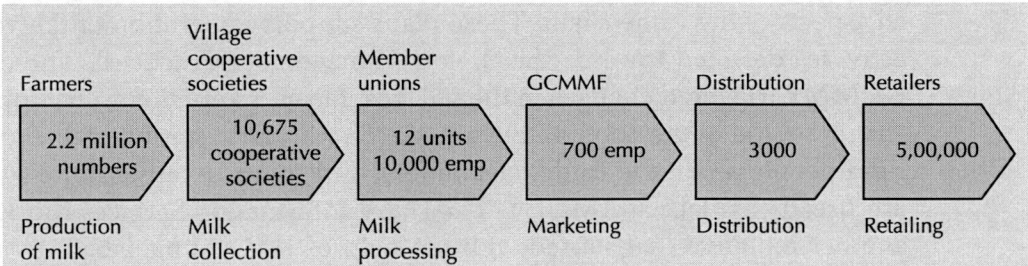

FIG. 8.11 The GCMMF value chain

increases the transparency levels in the system and builds the trust among the farmers. Making the system automatic could remove the middleman in the loop. The use of IT platforms reduces the potential for discretionary decisions.

GCMMF, being a pioneer in the dairy industry became the industry standard. The total quality management (TQM) and information technology (IT) initiatives ensured the maximum shelves in the retail stores, as well as in customer minds.

Cooperative Society—Operations

The village milk cooperative is a society of primary producers formed under the guidance of a supervisor or milk supply officer of the Cooperative Dairy Union (District level Cooperative owning the processing plant). A milk producer becomes a member by buying a share from the cooperative after agreeing to sell milk only to it. Members elect a managing committee headed by a chairperson responsible for staff in charge of day-to-day operations. Each society has a milk collection centre where farmers take their milk in the morning and evening. There are 1 million farmers organized into village milk producer's cooperative societies and procurement of milk is 13 million litres per day.

The GCMMF—Amul has taken the initiative of installing the *AMCUS— Automatic Milk Collection Unit Systems* at village societies to enhance the transparency of transaction between the farmer and the cooperative society. These systems not only ensured the transparency, but also gave cooperative societies a unique advantage by reducing the processing time to 10 per cent of what it used to be prior to this. GCMMF indeed got the entire supplier information through the systems integration. The information related to members, volume of the milk procured, and the amount payable to the member is accessible to the cooperative society in the form of a database. There are 10,755 village cooperatives in Gujarat that are now able to collect 6.1 million litres of milk from 2 million members. Thanks to the use of IT, both transparency and trust have been enhanced.

The success of AMCUS prompted the GCMMF to aggressively go on using information technology to capture the end-to-end data. GCMMF planned to cover all aspects of the value chain. These plans support integration of the value chain activities destined towards the 'Better Management Practices'. These efforts of GCMMF triggered changes in the villages; farmers kept themselves open for the changes. One of the cooperative unions 'Banas dairy' started with educating the rural people about the cattle, cleanliness, and so on because of the systems that are already in place at AMCUS. The Dairy Information Services Kiosk (DISK) is another initiative that started with the help of IIM (Ahmedabad) by GCMMF. There are many more in the pipeline of GCMMF IT initiatives. Various things such as Enterprise-wide Integrated Application System (EIAS) to integrate the distribution side of the supply chain, DISK—to upgrade the application at the Milk Collection Centres and to connect them to the Internet to access a specialized dairy portal with content delivered in the local language have already started bearing fruits for the rural poor by persuading the rural folks to actively participate in the IT revolution of the dairy industry.

Project Conceptualization

The GCMMF business involves daily collection of milk at 25 supply centres in Gujarat; the production of butter, cheese, ice cream, baby food and milk powder; the marketing of these products through 50 sales offices throughout India; and distribution through a network of 4000 stockists who, in turn, supply to 5,00,000 retail outlets.

Notwithstanding the traditional nature of its business, the management decided to adopt 'information technology integration' as a strategic thrust in 1995. The objective was to create new efficiencies in all aspects of the business, to enhance competitiveness, and to extend the market reach. Since then, the staff of 650 have received computer and e-commerce training. E-competencies have been established at the supply and distribution ends of Amul's business value chain. On the supply side, AMCUS is recording quality and quantity of milk being collected and DISK is in its inception stage. Cyber stores that GCMMF operates are visited by atleast 800 to 1000 people every day. This has been achieved within 5 years despite weak information technology infrastructure, and a high 'touch and feel' consumer culture. 'If you want to become e-competent, it is not enough to focus on your own company. You need to bring the whole business value chain. This means creating a shared vision', says Vyas. As everyone knows GCMMF relies on the fact that their supply base is too strong to support them all the way. The milk is such a perishable item. GCMMF needs to maintain the quantities without any wastage. 'As milk is a highly perishable commodity, the AMCUS initiative is vital for our operations. Due to this automation, we are in a position to collect six million litres of milk per day from around two million members. More importantly, this initiative has increased the trust and transparency among the rural people', according to Mr S. Hegde, Chief Information Officer, GCMMF. The order replenishment system at GCMMF is given in Fig. 8.12.

The Way Things were at GCMMF

GCMMF being an apex organization with 12 unions with their own manufacturing units consists of 2.1 million milk producing members who supply milk twice a day to the respective cooperative societies in the village. The process of collecting the milk before AMCUS was used to be the manual process. The complexity of the operations of village cooperatives increased over the years. Village cooperatives started looking for improving the efficiency of their operations. GCMMF invited 5 to 6 software companies to explore the possibility of automating the process of

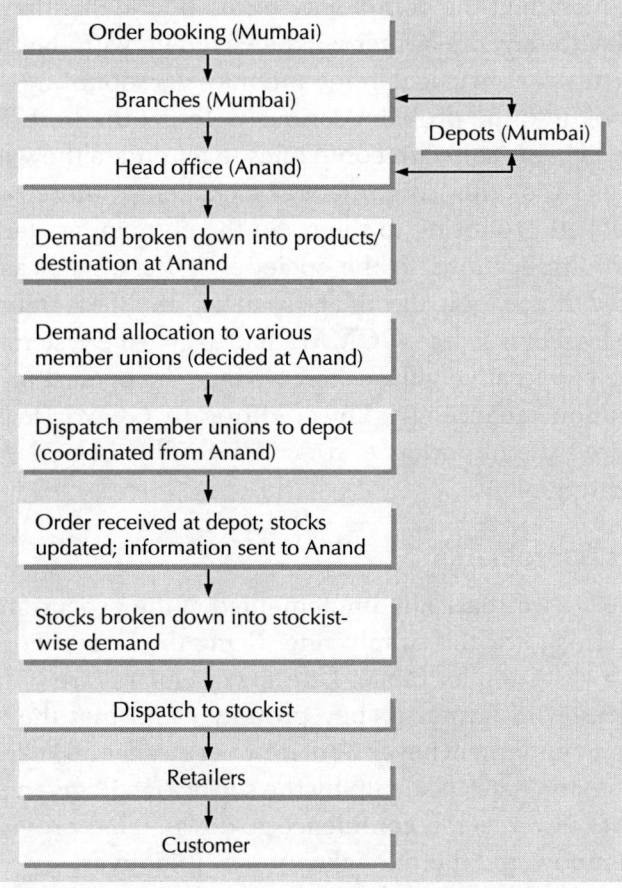

FIG. 8.12 Order replenishment system at GCMMF
Source: ETIG, 2002

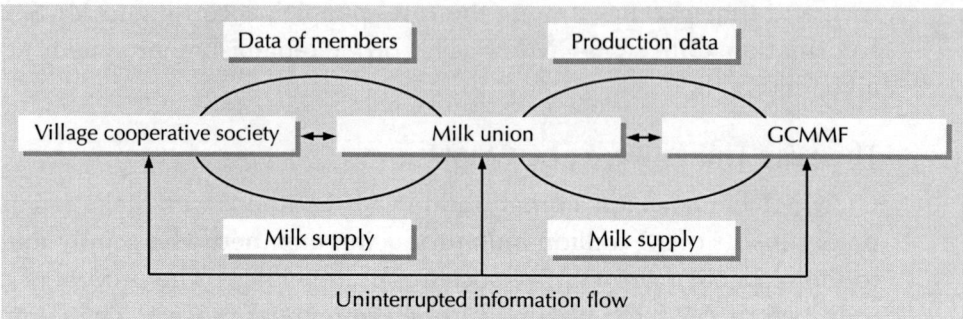

FIG. 8.13 Data transfer and flow across the value chain of GCMMF

estimating the fat content in the milk, so as to reduce the delays and to eliminate the waiting time in the queries (Fig. 8.13).

'We identified the complexity of the operations that the societies are in. More over, day-to-day, the farmer will be vexed up with the traditional set-up because of human mistakes in calculations and may start doubting the system itself. That made us to look into the problem seriously. To get the best deal to the cooperatives we employed some software companies to automate the whole process'. The software companies took this assignment as a challenge, moreover the whole business idea itself looked promising to them. So the companies started providing competitive software applications to the societies. Offers, such as training, price discounts increased thereafter to the village societies. But these initiatives did not come without challenges. For instance, GCMMF had to give the systems at free of cost for AMCUS to some cooperative villages to convince the cynical farmers about the benefits of information technology. These efforts of GCMMF paid off and the villagers recognized the importance of AMCUS. This helped the diffusion of IT into the rural communities.

Project Coordination

The project was basically implemented at the procurement end of the value chain of GCMMF, i.e., the supply side. Being the largest cooperative in India, AMUL enjoys a vast supplier range. Farmers of Gujarat are today much happier than any other cluster of farmers. They proudly claim that they are with the society. The farmers' commitment never went down even after 50 years of cooperative movement. Each activity that is taken up by the society is still given prominence in the villages. GCMMF never let this confidence go down. It has provided state-of-the-art facilities and it empowered them to take up new initiatives.

When GCMMF first thought about the complexity of the operations of village societies they met the village societies, and discussed with them about the problem. When GCMMF announced the implementation of AMCUS, village societies took over the responsibilities from their mentor. AMCUS changed the operations of village societies, by reducing the response time. The data that is being transferred and shared by AMCUS is depicted in Fig. 8.13. The society officials have to face some teething problems in the beginning. Now, it has become a usual practice. They are now arranging Internet sessions in village societies. As there is no hardware cost that is required to be met, the projects such as interconnecting the societies with the supply chain network of GCMMF and the others are under implementation.

The project was being coordinated by the GCMMF and the village cooperative society in which the AMCUS is being implemented. GCMMF is playing a major role by mentoring the societies and providing the guidance that is required for the effective management of the systems. The village society will be responsible for the operation of the system. Starting from the purchase of the hardware to software installation, the service aspects, all are properly managed by the village cooperative society officials. These societies have the right to select the service provider. GCMMF limited itself as a facilitator by empowering the village cooperative societies. This empowerment model facilitated the rapid diffusion of IT. The village cooperatives learnt quickly with the support of the software companies that are providing them the software and hardware services. These companies also played a major role in enhancing the acceptance of the innovative information and communication technology (ICT) platform.

Project Evaluation Systems

Without effective evaluation, a project implementation is never finished. It might be in–line or inbuilt with the system or external to the system. The project evaluation system compares the actual implementation details with those projected showing us the rate of return from the project. This can help in many ways—for creating further course of action, design of proper controlling measures, and replicability assessment. In this project, there is no evaluation system in place. One of the ways in which the project authorities are evaluating the project is through a feedback. As the village cooperatives do have their own meetings and discussions regularly, the feedback mechanism is strongly enforced into the functioning of the village cooperatives. The 'Kaizen' approach followed by GCMMF as a part of TQM measures is been used by the village cooperatives in order to tackle the quality measurement issues and solve them.

Benefits of the AMCUS System

The rural people are getting benefited by the IT initiatives, started by GCMMF. The benefits of various projects such as DISK are yet to be realized. The following are the demonstrated benefits of the ICT platform.

- Time reduction

- Reduction of pilferage
- Reduced human errors
- On the spot payments for farmers
- Reduction in wastage
- Improved transparency of operation
- Operational integration

Enterprise Wide Systems—EIAS and GIS

The main benefit of ICT has the power of integration and amenability to centralized monitoring. All the units are networked. GCMMF has connected its Zonal Offices, Guwahati Regional Office, as well as Member Dairies, Milk Unions and its own Unit—Mother Dairy through very small aperture terminal (VSAT) for seamless exchange of online information. All Sales Offices, C&F points and Wholesale distributors of GCMMF have been connected through TCP/IP Internet Mail Account for exchange of information.

In addition to the above, GCMMF is using Geographical Information System (GIS) at its Head Office and key Marketing Offices. Using the all India map in GIS, they are in position to plot zone/depot boundary as well as pointer for zone, depot, and distributor location which are superimposed by product-wise sales data. The same is being used for sales and distribution planning and review. Moreover, GIS is being used for business planning activity at milk centres and it covers animal census data. This has helped them to know average milk production and productivity of cows and buffaloes in Gujarat and track the cattle and trend analysis, etc. The EIAS customized ERP packages of GCMMF is designed in such a way that is can be plugged into various points of supply chain, as shown in the figure that follows (Fig. 8.14).

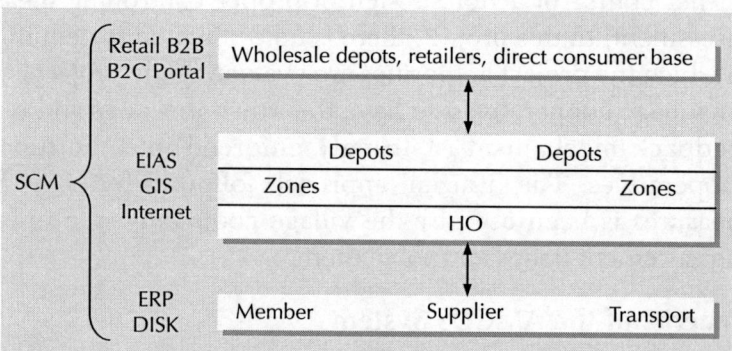

FIG. 8.14 Structure of the information systems for SCM at GCMMF

Related Resources

www.amul.com/index1.html as accessed on 19 January 2009.

| **INDUSTRY** | **Re-inventing the supply chain wheel** |
| **SNAPSHOT 11** | **PROCTER & GAMBLE**[11] |

Procter & Gamble has a long history of innovation courage and an ability to make smart business decisions even in difficult times. When the company was established in Cincinnati, Ohio in 1837, the United States was gripped by financial panic. Hundreds of banks were closing among widespread concern that the country was headed for economic disaster. Forging ahead, P&G launched its new enterprise more focused on competing with the 14 other U.S. soap and candle makers than with the economic turmoil shaking the country. Its calm in the midst of that storm reflected a forward looking approach that has become the hallmark of this 165-year-old company. Today, P&G markets approximately 250 brands, including Pampers disposable diapers, Pantene hair care products, and Tide laundry detergent to nearly five billion consumers in more than 130 countries. With operation in more than 80 countries, its 106,000 employees delivered revenues of US$ 39.2 billion in fiscal year 2001. P&G's global success has led to top honours for the company, for achievements ranging from environmental protection and animal-testing alternatives to superior product quality and marketing expertise. *Fortune magazine* has included P&G in its 'World's Most Admired Companies' list from 1985 to 2001 and Ziff-Davis *Smart Business* editors included Procter & Gamble in their 2001 list of Top 50 Net savvy US organizations.

Says Steve David, CIO and Business-to-Business Officer. 'The retailers love it, they feel they're getting better service, and the costs are a tenth or a hundredth of what they were. Our vision is to move from the two to three per cent of business we're doing today on Web order management to the majority of our transactions being Web-based two to three years from now. It has huge productivity implications for us and, even more importantly, it offers better service to our customers'. 'We're changing our overall approach to supply chain management to become even more consumer centric,' said Mike Power, President, Global Business Services. 'When consumers walk into a retail environment, they want the right product at the right time at the right place. They don't want to find it out-of-stock. That's a disappointment to them and a lost sale for us. That differs from our supply chain strategy of the past in two significant ways: It puts the consumer first, and it envisions a network rather than a chain.

---

[11] Partially based on Davis Jessica's news 'Procter & Gamble Reworks Its Supply Chain', posted on www.infoworld.com/articles/hn/xml/01/03/13/010313hnpng.html, as accessed on 19 January 2009. Some information has been drawn from Tom Steinert-Threlkeld's article dated 1 July 2004, 'Procter & Gamble: Delivering Goods', posted on www.baselinemag.com/index2.php?option= content&task=vie.

All the work we've done until now to improve our supply chain focused on the supplier first—which means we've been applying a cost mentality to the problem. Now, we're putting the emphasis on serving the consumer. And whereas a chain connotes handoffs and time delays, the consumer-driven network will operate with real-time data and all network participants working to add value for the consumer.'

The P&G supply network has five key parts. It starts with *real-time demand information* that replaces point-of-sale data with *electronic product code (EPC)* data. There are more than 100 radio *frequency identification (RFID)* protocols worldwide; EPC is the standard being developed by the *Auto-ID centre*, a collaborative effort of 103 end-user and technology companies to create an open and global standard.

The second part is collaborative planning. Basically, this comes down to communication—via e-mail, fax, or live—with their retail partners about their merchandising plans, to reduce the number of surprises and keep the brands in stock. It is less complex and easier to implement than *collaborative planning, forecasting and replenishment (CPFR)* in an environment, where data requirements differ greatly from customer to customer and supplier to supplier.

The third part is a produce-to-demand manufacturing system. The company used to think that producing long runs of the same product would improve their efficiency, but instead found that it built an inventory of items the company did not need, without making it possible to reschedule production to items that were nearly out of stock. Two years ago, the company had the capability to produce every item once a month; now the goal is to produce every item P&G makes everyday. P&G is not there yet, but it claims it can produce every item every week.

The fourth part is dynamic replenishment and distribution. This would reduce replenishment time to customers and improve in-stocks for consumers. The goal is to deliver tomorrow what the retailer orders today. And fifth, the consumer-driven supply network begins and ends with superior retail execution. P&G wants to help their retail partners develop the right tools to become more successful in reducing out-of-stocks. P&G have been testing these five parts and will begin integrating them soon. They can build revenue by reducing out-of-stocks, which today average 11–15 per cent.

Procter and Gamble Reinvents Its Supply Chain

Dramatic changes for industry, most recently demonstrated in the huge stock market slide Friday and Monday, has consumer goods giant P&G looking to reinvent its supply chain together with its partners. Procter and Gamble CIO Steve David offered an inside look at some of his company's goals for SCM at AMR Research's Retail and Consumer Goods Executive Conference recently.

By 2005, P&G planned to put in place Web-enabled alliances with partners and a customer- and consumer-driven supply chain.

Previous work reduced the company's supply chain cycle from 140-plus days in the 1950s through the 1980s to 130 days in the 1990s. Through an initiative the company calls efficient consumer response II (ECR II), P&G is looking to reduce the cycle time further to 65 days. But the company has its work cut out for it.

Currently P&G has 4000 internal websites, 25,000 organizational nodes, 70,000 materials, 2,00,000 products, 5,00,000 customers and 1 million parts. 'We have to clean up our act', admits David.

The impact of supply chain inefficiencies is nothing to be trifled with. For example, retailers lose 11 per cent of sales due to out-of-stock items. Customers who experience an out of stock event are more likely to spend their money at another store or not at all. And same brand substitutions recover less than 25 per cent of lost sales for manufacturers.

Rather than choosing either a private or public exchange, companies can use exchanges to help prevent forecasting and planning discrepancies, reduce manual redundant processes, and improve their capability to operate on a global scale. Exchanges can also help speed time to market, which improves total shareholder return by 50–100 per cent.

However, some business-to-business exchanges will fail in the coming months and years. But those failures will be caused more by poor business plans and models, underestimated costs of customer acquisition, and buying into vendor pitches of amazing results.

By employing exchanges and improving the supply chain, companies can improve consumer value, business results, and reduce their working capital requirements. For example, supply chain-driven reductions in working capital can normally reduce inventories by 50 per cent.

Supply Chain Innovation at Procter & Gamble

Jake Barr is in charge of 'supply chain innovation' at P&G. He is supposed to figure out how to get the consumer products giant's detergents, soaps, and personal care products into the hands of 5 billion customers in 170 countries more efficiently. His goal? To create the equivalent of a 14th billion-dollar brand—by stocking shelves in stores around the globe more accurately by responding better to what people want. And getting 5000 retailers and 30,000 suppliers to participate in a system that would immediately signal products favoured by customers.

'If you can't drive sales and deliver product at the point of purchase, you lose,' says Barr. Some 60 per cent of P&G's sales now come from what Barr calls 'events'. These are promotions that the supermarket, convenience store, or other retailers execute with price cuts or other incentives; or they take the form of discount coupons and price promotions mailed out, put on the Internet or distributed in a store by P&G itself. Promotions for gift-with-purchase were rolled out on the *Pampers.com* and *BabyUniverse. com* sites. These *pull* marketing events are designed to drive consumers to retail stores and maintain customer loyalty.

In the past, P&G used a *push* system of moving products out of the store door. Independent of what retailers were doing, P&G would forecast sales for Tide detergent, Crest toothpaste, or other products. Then, it would tweak sales through the year with coupons and other incentives designed to entice enough customers to buy, moving products off store shelves.

But with the majority of sales now coming from promotional events, Barr and his Global Product Supply team studied the pull systems of efficient distributors of consumer and industrial products such as personal-computer maker Dell. The idea— cut out piles of inventory and produce only those products that consumers are actually buying.

To a retailer, being out of stock on a product that consumers want is no small matter. A retailer whose shelf is bare of a product in demand loses the sale 41 per cent of the time, according to *Consumer Insight* magazine, an industry trade publication. The typical response is to find the product at another store. But even P&G loses. Approximately 28 per cent of the time, Barr says, the customer simply picks another competing product. Barr's goal about 18 months ago was to get to *a nearly 100 per cent demand-driven* system of supplying products to supermarkets and other stores around the globe. In his preferred analogy, he wanted P&G's planners and forecasters to be 'looking through the windshield and not the rearview mirror' at what was happening in the marketplace.

But P&G is not like Dell. It does not field calls from consumers. It cannot wait until after consumers decide what they want, before it puts products onto store shelves. It cannot wait to find out what customizations the consumer wants when the call comes in. 'I have to put all seven smells (of a soap) out on the shelf' at all times and in the right quantities, Barr says. In effect, P&G has to manage out-of-stock conditions on 50, 000 different products worldwide, every day. When Barr's team started to tackle the problem of shifting from a push system to a pull system, nine times out of 10 consumers were finding the P&G product they wanted in the store. Barr aimed to cut the rate of out-of-stock items from 10 per cent to 5 per cent which is not so easy. He says, 'For a company our size, (that's like) trying to turn a large cruise ship vessel on a dime.'

His goal was to take the chaos out of the delivery system by bringing retailers and suppliers into the planning and delivery process. The *signals* of consumer demand would come from the stores; *responses* would come from P&G manufacturing managers, supply chain managers and suppliers, who would key production of new products to sales reports coming from the stores.

For example, P&G now gets dates and locations for all events with its retail partners, and prepares for predictable increases in demand. If some stores are going to do a 'buy-two, get-one-free' promotion on their Pampers diapers, P&G can better coordinate its production and distribution in that region. As Barr puts it, 'In the past, we'd only know that these stores wanted an extra 100 or 200 cases of the product and we'd send it in one large delivery. Sometimes, it'd be several weeks early. Once in a while, it would be late.'

'One of our fatal flaws,' Barr adds, 'was that our (supply chain) network was not really well integrated.' The company has 5000 key retailers and more than 30,000 key suppliers. 'I had data coming from many sources, but it was not synchronized,' Barr says. Some sales data might come in daily, some weekly. Some might come by item or product category. Consistent information, received daily or more frequently, would mean getting retailers and suppliers to adhere to common conventions in feeding and drawing information out of P&G's SAP supply chain management system.

This caused immeasurable problems. When P&G is spending $80 million to advertise new flavors of fluoride anti-cavity toothpaste such as Cinnamon Rush and Extreme Herbal Mint, it needs to know which ones are selling and which are not. Without detailed reports, boxes of Extreme Herbal Mint can be collecting dust in the storage rooms while there is not enough Cinnamon Rush on the shelves to meet demand.

Barr's aim—to replace the movement of boxes of goods with a better flow of information. That meant a big change at P&G's factories. In the old build-to-forecast days, the plants would simply run big lots, move them to warehouses, and let marketing work down the stacks of unsold product. 'Changeovers of manufacturing lines were anathema,' says Barr, a former factory manager, because the belief was that long product runs cut down per-unit costs.

'But what actually happens is per-unit costs rise if you're making products consumers don't buy,' says Barr. Now P&G plans plenty of changeovers on its production lines every day. The principle—manage by exception, for products that are moving fast off shelves. That keeps costs down. 'We've tried to improve every aspect of how we deliver product to our customers at the lowest cost,' says Tom Walker, Vice President of logistics for Costco Wholesale Corp., which sells $41.7 billion worth of consumer goods a year through its 397 retail warehouses. 'The software, along with common sense, has improved P&G's ability to get accurate shipments to our stores in a timely manner. The fact that our sales of P&G products are up by 15 per cent in the past year tells you how effective this system is.'

Cannondale Associates, a marketing and consulting firm said retailers ranked P&G as the top manufacturing partner, ahead of Kraft Foods. After implementing the new pull system, the company is close to its original goal of cutting out-of-stock conditions in half. Now, 93 per cent of outlets working under the new system are experiencing no more than 5 per cent out-of-stock rates. That represents a yearly savings of $50–$100 million.

Benefits

The benefits reaped by P&G from supply chain innovation initiatives are the following.

(i) Sales increased by 7. 8 per cent. Net profits, which P&G expected to improve by 10 per cent, jumped up by 19 per cent in fiscal 2003.

(ii) In fiscal 2003, P&G generated $4.9 billion, largely because of the supply chain improvements and increased sales resulting from the coordination with events.

(iii) Working capital, the amount of money the company has on hand to run its day-to-day business, jumped to more than $1.7 billion in fiscal 2003.

'To me, working capital is the best barometer of how efficient an organization is,' says Bill Steele, an analyst at Banc of America Securities in San Francisco. 'P&G is making life very difficult for competitors, such as Unilever, Kimberly-Clark, and Colgate-Palmolive. It has consistently outperformed all of these companies, mainly as a result of its systems and its management.'

P&G Key Performance Indicators

The key supply chain performance indicators by P&G are the following.

Shelf-level out of stocks   The percentage of products that are out of stock on retailers' shelves at any given time. P&G has cut this to 5 per cent, from 10 per cent and wants it further reduced to 2.57 per cent.

Total supply chain response time   The time from when a cash register records the sale of a product to the purchase of raw materials to produce its replacement. P&G wants to chop this in half, from 100 days.

Total supply chain inventory   The hard count of all products flowing through the supply chain at any given moment, whether on store shelves, in back of the store, at warehouses, in trucks or wherever. P&G wants a daily count, rather than weekly or monthly.

Shelf-level quality   The percentage of packages damaged or otherwise unappealing when a customer sees them on a store shelf. The goal is to have zero damaged or unappealing packages.

Pricing-design from the shelf back   Determining an acceptable price point for an item, and then working it back through manufacturing and distribution to see if that product can be delivered at a price acceptable to consumers, and a profit acceptable to P&G.

INDUSTRY SNAPSHOT 12	Creating a world-class supply chain ADIDAS SALOMON[12]

Salomon AG is a global producer of sportswear and sports equipment based in Germany and the world's second largest sporting goods company. The company offers its products through three brands. The Adidas brand covers footwear, apparel, and hardware in three segments—sport performance, which develops modern products, focusing on running, football, basketball, tennis, and training; Sport Heritage, which concentrates on lifestyle and streetwear products, and sport style, comprised of the Y-3 collection designed by Yohji Yamamoto. The Salomon brand principally offers clothing and equipment for winter sports. Further associated brands include Mavic, a provider of wheels for mountain and road racing bicycles; Bonfire, which covers waterproof and breathable apparel for snowboarding, ArcTeryx, which offers outdoor clothing and climbing equipment in North America, and Cliché, a European skateboarding brand. Through TaylorMade-Adidas Golf, the company offers a full range of golf clubs, footwear, and apparel, as well as Maxfli golf balls.

Crafting a World-class Supply Chain

A more aggressive and competitive marketing strategy will mean that global supply chain management is even more critical for the Group's success. At Adidas-Salomon, the supply chain encompasses the community of people and the associated processes that enable the Group to design, develop, manufacture, sell, and deliver products.

It includes Adidas-Salomon employees, retailers, contract manufacturers, raw material suppliers, freight consolidators, ocean/air transport companies, and others responsible for getting products to the point of sale. The global supply chain strategy at Adidas-Salomon targets timeline improvements in product development and procurement to produce optimal effects in terms of costs and quality.

There are two major links in their global supply chain. Product development describes the Adidas-Salomon activities from the initial product concept to product

---

[12] Based on 'Adidas-Salomon Scores with i2 Supply Chain Management Solutions', *Business Wire*, 30 July 2002; www.i2.com/assets/pdf/CSS-CPG_adidas salomon_7185.pdf. The author expresses due acknowledgement to the sources.

offering. Following this process is procurement, which includes ordering, producing, and delivering products to retailer. Rather than optimizing a single process or segment of the supply chain, Adidas targeted improvements throughout the entire supply chain. A shorter product development process will allow them to create products best aligned with current market needs and expectations. Quicker procurement will help them to improve customer service in terms of faster time to market and competitiveness. In this way, inefficiencies will be reduced, quality improved, and costs minimized. Shortening supply chain timelines also has the potential to impact their cash flow, inventories, and overall sales figures. For them, excellence in supply chain management means more than just higher efficiency. It also means a close synchronization of the supply chain with sales and marketing strategies and strong alliances with all partners across the entire supply chain. Investments in personnel and technology are indispensable in supporting their ambitions. To obtain the benefits in time, cost, and quality, Adidas planned investments of $150 million in 2002.

Customised Footwear by Adidas

It is interesting to note the way Adidas delivers customized footwear for the individual soccer enthusiast. Through foot scanning technology, Web-enabled software applications, redefined raw material procurement methods, state-of-the-art manufacturing processes, and a new logistics partnership, they are able to deliver style and performance-enhanced shoes within 14 days of order. Although this is a limited-volume project, it shows the kind of innovation they are capable of bringing to the market through supply chain improvements. The global nature of their business means that their supply chain must have the flexibility to support a wide array of global, regional, and national service requirements. Their markets vary dramatically and, in many cases, require tailored solutions. To meet individualized market needs, solid partners with financial strength, global presence, and social values are prerequisites to participation. As their supply chain becomes more flexible and sophisticated, the requirements on their partners within the supply network increase. Cooperative planning, real-time exchange of information, and commitment to high service levels are essential for each supply chain partner. To this end, they are constantly re-evaluating their operational partnerships, including their raw material suppliers, manufacturers, and logistics providers. They also plan to enhance their partnerships with key retailers to ensure the supply chain is optimized from end-to-end, from raw material supplier to retailer.

Goals Set by Adidas in Supply Chain

Adidas Salomon have translated strategic goals into supply chain specific performance targets. These are to

- eliminate 10 weeks from the product development and 4 weeks from the procurement cycle; and
- reduce the time from product concept to retail delivery from the current 18 months to less than 9 months over the next three years.

These targets will be reached through the implementation of lean manufacturing principles and the enhancement of special labeling and retail floor-ready merchandise. Their efforts, however, stretch far beyond footwear. In apparel for example, they have just completed the integration of operational activities of all group brands. The company embarked on an ambitious supplier consolidation plan reducing the manufacturing base by over 25 per cent, with their medium-term goal being to reduce supplier base by 40 per cent. The consolidation of supply chain partners is also an important step in order to increase the influence and bargaining power with suppliers in the future. Resources have recently been added to their global supply team to expand the auto-replenishment programs already in place. This will rapidly help to align the supply chain process with their footwear activities. As they move forward, they will initiate new projects in the areas of common transportation partners, trade exchanges, and implementation of a more frequent ordering process. Over the next three years, investments in product creation support systems will allow Adidas Salomon to be closer to the market, creating superior products in less than half the time than it takes today.

Using IT Systems for SCM

Cutting-edge supply chain management technology is another area of major improvement. Adidas have employed enhanced communication capabilities, including sophisticated IT systems and Web-based B2B solutions. The company developed a new information system to support product creation. This system provides real-time, Web-enabled communication of critical design, development, production, and sales data to all partners in the supply chain. Adidas also made important improvements to the information infrastructure, which supports information visibility across the supply chain. This includes the implementation of supply chain planning software, namely i2 supply Chain Planner from i2 technologies.

'The complex and seasonal nature of the soft goods industry with hundreds of product combinations of varying style, colour and size, requires that a company makes the long-term commitment to process improvement when managing its value chain', says the i2 senior Vice-President, Terry Turner, as quoted in *Business Wire*. The i2 technologies helped Adidas Salomon to absorb business process change necessary to embrace technology solutions. The project was implemented with Hewlett-Packard (HP) as the service provider. Glenn Bennett, Executive Board Member is quoted as saying in Business Wire that i2 supply chain planner has helped the company to execute multiple product lead time planning, and has added new subsidiary feedback processes to allow for better response to changing demands. It is particularly helping in lead-time reduction and better matching of supply and demand. The company also strengthened communication between its factories and with around 70 sales subsidiaries through the use of i2 planner. Coordinating sales subsidiary product demand and manufacturing constraints was an exceedingly time consuming task, but Adidas streamlined this process through the i2 planning tool. Previously, order planning and confirmation process used to take up to 3 weeks which has been now reduced to just 2 days. Sales offices are now supplied with a manufacturing and logistics plan based on forecasts, helping them to meet customer demand more consistently. Factory utilization times and production confirmation lead times also improved by providing IT systems and solutions in the supply chain.

INDUSTRY SNAPSHOT 13	**Pencilling MIS reports for SCM** **CAMLIN LTD[13]**

Camlin Ltd is a market leader in stationery and art products in India. Twenty-two depots operated by C&F agents across the country cater to the orders received from the sales network of distributors and dealers. Camlin's 200 strong field staff gets orders from the distributors and dealers. The company has approximately 2500 stock keeping units (SKUs) and services its C&F agents from six manufacturing locations. Items are procured from some 50 suppliers who send the materials to the mother depot or supply it directly to the agents. To deal with the complexities of expanding business, improve information flow, and operational efficiency, it was decided to automate the supply chain. Says Deepak Dandekar, MD, Camlin Ltd, 'We realized that efficiency in Supply Chain Management (SCM) is the key differentiator in today's manufacturing, distribution, and retail businesses. Therefore, we decided to use Information Technology (IT) as the key component in the implementation of the SCM strategy.' Along with the implementation of a warehouse management system (WMS) and a back-office ERP system, Camlin also went in for a Web-based sales and distribution management system. The impetus for a Web-based system came from the challenges involved in the distribution of the 2500 SKUs and maintaining proper inventory levels at all the depots. For example, in some depots, certain products would pile up while some others would face shortages due to improper projections or operation of schemes, seasonality, etc. Information about stock and sales from the depots, orders received from distributors, or even

---

[13] Based on the field interviews of the sales and marketing staff of Camlin Ltd, www.camlin.com.

stocks lying at the distributors were not available on time, thereby hampering the decision-making. Very often, area managers lacked information on how their sales representatives were performing during the current month. Reports for a certain month would be available only by the middle of the next month, making any corrective action a difficult exercise. The management would need access to daily stock, sales, and pending order positions at each depot if they were to take effective decisions about declaring schemes, transferring SKUs from one depot to another to help bring down inventory levels, or to monitor the performance of their sales personnel. Because of the high cost of leased lines, the management wanted a solution that would not involve leased lines but provide them with the required solution. Moreover, certain aspects of the earlier system had been computerized. The depots were using FoxPro-based depot management software to generate the required reports. The collated information updates on sales, stock, and orders would be sent by them at the end of every month through floppies. The head office (HO) would prepare management information system (MIS) reports of stock, sales, and pending orders, which were then sent to all the area managers. However, the floppies would often get corrupted and had to be resent, resulting in delayed preparation of MIS reports. This system was not capable of providing the required information at the required frequency to the management. The primary depot activities were as follows.

- Receive material from manufacturing locations and suppliers
- Dispatch invoices to customers against orders received
- Collect payments from customers and forward to HO
- Maintain inventory and receivable records
- Provide MIS reports to HO
- Send data to HO

Problems Faced

The company faced the following problems in its sales and inventory functions.

- Maintaining proper inventory levels at all these depots was a difficult task
- A lot of transactions were duplicated
- Invoices created at the HO needed to be entered in the depot as receipt
- Floppies used for sending data got corrupted, so the data had to be resent
- MIS reports not available to HO in time from all depots
- Information related to daily stock, sales, and collections at depots was available to HO after 3–4 days
- Company did not want to invest in costly leased lines to connect so many depots

Intranet Solution

After much deliberation, the concept of a Net-based system was suggested as the means of meeting those needs that could not be fulfilled by the existing system. This concept was further discussed with the management of Camlin and it was decided to develop an *Intranet* site, which would only be accessed by authorized employees of the company, C&F agents, and distributors.

It was also decided to integrate the Web-based sales and distribution management system with the WMS. Each user would be given a username and password. Depending on his position in the organization, the options and information available to him on the website would be decided. At the end of each day, the depots and manufacturing centres would load text files generated by their existing systems onto the website. Such information would be processed on the website and stored in a database to be used for generating reports based on various parameters. The head office should also be able to send various master files to the depots. The system would contain a mailbox for each user and users within the system would be able to send and receive mails for better communication between HO, field staff, C&F agents, and distributors. It would also generate reports providing product-wise sales, stocks, and pending orders report, and collections based on parameters, such as region, zone, area manager, etc. It was also decided to have security features and firewalls, so as to display information according to the level defined for each user. For example, an area manager from Kerala should only be able to view information relating to his area and should not be able to view information about areas that are not strictly within his purview. Other facilities made available include the following.

- Performance reports against targets of depots/area managers should be available product-wise on the site.
- Products in transit should be available on the site.
- All pages on the site should have a consistent look and feel.
- The distributors should be able to enter orders, which should be validated and sent to the concerned depot for execution.
- The site should provide reports to help transfer stock from nearby depots, depending on the stock and pending order position at each depot.
- The website will be looked after by an administrator who will add new products, customers, regions, zones, depots, etc. He shall also coordinate with all users and answers their queries.

Benefits

Following the implementation, the following benefits were realized:

- Availability of reports at the right time for taking corrective decisions

- Reduction in inventory levels
- Saving in communication costs using the messaging system instead of telephone calls
- Saving in time and increase in accuracy using the import and export facilities
- Better coordination between HO and depots due to availability of correct and timely information
- Cost effective solution, tailor-made to the needs of the organization

| INDUSTRY SNAPSHOT 14 | Learning from speed bumps in IT implementation NIKE[14] |

Nike Inc. based in Beaverton, Oregon, and established in 1972 is the world's leading designer, marketer, and distributor of authentic athletic footwear, apparel, equipment, and accessories for a wide variety of sports and fitness activities. The company has very ambitiously set a revenue target of US$27 billion by the end of the fiscal year 2015.The current President and CEO, Mike Parker focuses on initiatives to deliver sustainable and profitable growth. The company believes in innovative and compelling products and brands that are distinctively relevant to their customers. Wholly-owned subsidiaries of the company include Cole Haan (designer, distributor, and marketer of luxury shoes, handbags, accessories, and coats), Converse (designer, marketer, and distributor of footwear, apparel, and accessories), Hurley International (dealing with action sports and youth lifestyle products, apparel, and accessories) and Umbro Ltd (the UK-based global soccer brand). Nike operates in 160 countries around the globe employing around 30,000 employees.

Under its *Direct to Consumer* initiative, the company plans to open 250-300 Nike stores worldwide over the next five years, i.e., by 2015. It also plans to invest US$500-600 million in retail stores all over the world. The company's retail partners are expected to provide more than 80 per cent of the company's business. Its Chief Financial Officer (CFO), Don Blair, in 2010, has focused on the following targets:

- a high single digit revenue growth rate
- a mid teen EPS (earning per share) growth
- a ROCE (return on capital employed) of 25 per cent

---

[14] Based on Christopher Koch (2004), 'Nike Rebounds: How and (Why) Nike Recovered from Its Supply Chain Disaster', www.cio.com posted on on 15 June 2004 as accessed on 29 January 2009. The author is thankful to the author and Ms Elana Veron, Executive Editor, CIO, for the kind permission she gave to use the article. This article cannot be reproduced further.

However, the company did not have some good experiences while implementing new technologies and solutions, particularly when the i2 implementation backfired and Nike learnt a few lessons.

The i2 Glitch at the Nike

Roland Wolfram, Nike's Vice President of global operations and technology, was promoted in April 2004 to Vice President and General Manager of the Asia-Pacific division. He is all Nike with a typical Nike sharpness to his turtleneck and slacks, a sharpness reflected also in his urgent, aggressive defense of his company—a Nike pride that would seem arrogant were the company not so dominant in its industry.

Wolfram called the i2 problem a software glitch that cost Nike more than US$100 million in lost sales, depressed its stock price by 20 per cent, triggered a flurry of class-action lawsuits, and caused its Chairman, President and CEO, Phil Knight, to lament by calling it a *speed bump*. In the athletic footwear business, only Nike, with a 32 per cent worldwide market share (almost double of its nearest rival, Adidas) and a US$20 billion market cap that was more than the rest of the manufacturers and retailers in the industry combined, could afford to talk about US$100 million like that.

It drove Wolfram crazy that while the rest of the world knew his company for its swashbuckling marketing and its association with the world's most famous athletes, the IT world thought of Nike as the company that screwed up its supply chain—specifically, the *i2 demand-planning* engine that, in 2000, spat out orders for thousands of more Air Garnett sneakers than the market could absorb and called for thousands of fewer Air Jordans than were actually needed. 'For the people who follow this sort of thing, we became a poster child (for failed implementations),' said Wolfram.

But there was a lesson for people too who, in fact, follow 'this sort of thing', specifically CIOs. The lesson of Nike's failure and subsequent rebound lies in the fact that it had a business plan that was widely understood and accepted at every level of the company. Given that, in the end the i2 failure turned out to be just a 'speed bump', as Christopher Koch said.

The Doom of i2 at Nike: Was It Attributable?

Nike's June 2000 problems with its i2 system reflect the problems typical of high-profile enterprise computing failures. First, there is a software problem closely tied to a core business process—in this case, factory orders. Then the glitch sends a ripple through product delivery that grows into a wave crashing on the balance sheet. The wave is so big that the company must reveal the losses at a quarterly conference call with analysts or risk the wrath of the Securities and Exchange Commission, shareholders or both. And it was that time when it hit the pages of *The*

Wall Street Journal, inspiring articles and white papers on the general subject of IT's hubris, limitations, value, and cost.

The idea that something so mundane as a computer glitch could affect the performance of a huge company made headlines. But what did not enter the analysis was whether the problem was tactical (and fixable) or strategic (meaning the company should never have bought the software in the first place).

Nike claimed that the problems with its *i2 demand-planning software* were tactical and therefore fixable. It was too slow, did not integrate well, had some bugs, and Nike's planners were inadequately trained in how to use the system before it went live. According to Nike, all these problems were sorted by fall 2000. And the company maintained that its business was not affected after that quarter. Nike also announced that its third-quarter 2003 profit margins were its highest ever.

If there was a strategic failure in Nike's supply chain project, it was that Nike had bought in the software designed to crystal ball demand. Throwing a bunch of historical sales numbers into a programme and waiting for a magic number to emerge from the algorithm did not support Nike's business model. Nike had been tightly controlling the athletic footwear supply chain and getting retailers to commit to orders far in advance. There was not much room for a crystal ball in that scenario.

Indeed, Nike confirms that it stopped using i2's demand planner for its short- and medium-range sneaker planning (it is still used for Nike's apparel business) in the spring of 2001, moving those functions into its SAP ERP system, which is based more on orders and invoices than on predictive algorithms. 'This allowed us to simplify some of our integration requirements,' Nike CIO, Gordon Steele, said.

Wolfram commented that Nike's demand-planning strategy was and continues to be a mixture of art and technology. Nike sells too many products (1,20,000) in too many cycles (four per year) to do things by intuition alone. 'We've tuned our system so we do our runs against (historical models), and then people look at it to make sure it makes sense,' he said. The computer models are trusted more when the product is a reliable seller (that is, just about with Michael Jordan's name on it) and the planners' intuition plays a bigger role in new or more volatile products. According to Wolfram, in this case talking with retailers did more good than consulting the system.

'There's been a change in the technology for demand planning,' said AMR Research Vice President, Bill Swanton. 'In the late 90s, companies said all we need is the data and we can plan everything perfectly. Today, companies are trying to do *consensus planning* rather than demand planning,' he said. That means moving away from the crystal ball and toward sharing information up and down the supply chain with customers, retailers, distributors, and manufacturers. 'If you can share information faster and more accurately among a lot of people, you will see trends a lot sooner, and that's where the true value of supply chain projects are,' said Swanton.

Having the Right Game Plan

Another thing that made Wolfram angry was the widespread assumption that Nike was betting on algorithms and changed course when that did not work out. Wolfram defended that, on the contrary, i2's demand-planning software was never intended to be the hero of Nike's *supply chain project*—one of the most ambitious ever attempted by a company of its size. It was part of a wider strategy to integrate ERP, SCM, and CRM software onto a single platform shared by Nike operations in North America, as well as Europe, the Middle East, and Africa (EMEA). 'Frankly,' he asserted, 'we pretty much stayed the course.'

Nike took a bold step of adopting the risky and difficult strategy of creating a single and integrated database within its SAP ERP system for every employee in North America and EMEA. This meant getting everyone to agree on business practices and common data definitions before the software went in, which is a rare feature in ERP project management.

The difficulty of integrating information across a distributed company had brought down many ERP projects, such as drugstore chain FoxMeyer's SAP ERP system in the late 1990s and Tri-Valley Growers' 1997 choice of Oracle's ill-fated ERP package for the consumer packaged good industry. Neither of the companies ever got its systems working properly and that contributed to both eventually shutting their doors. Other companies gave up on the vision of total information integration and installed many different versions of their ERP systems—as many as 400 different versions of a single vendor's ERP system at some really large companies, according to AMR. But Nike claims that it never wavered from its single-instance strategy, even when problems with the first piece of that strategy, the i2 system, hit the news. The same project leaders who were in place at the time of the i2 problems (CIO, Steele, and the business lead, Shelley Dewey, Nike's Vice President of supply chain) were still running the project as in 2004. The reason Steele and Dewey survived was that when their system failed, they had a lifeline to hang onto; a clear business case for the overall supply chain project. If achieved, they claimed it would save the company a lot more than Knight's US$400 million and the US$100 million in sneakers.

Nike's supply chain project was supposed to drive the manufacturing cycle for a sneaker down from nine months to six. Cutting out that three months would match Nike's manufacturing cycle to its retailers' ordering schedule, they ordered 90 per cent of their sneakers 6 months in advance of the delivery. This meant that Nike could begin manufacturing its sneakers to order rather than three months in advance and then hoping that they could sell them. Converting the supply chain from make-to-sell to *make-to-order* is the dream of any company desirous of gaining competitive advantage through its supply chain. Nike wanted to do it just as famously with sneakers as Dell had done with their PCs.

As Christopher Koch puts it, Nike had not been there yet! And its business case relied on a nearly 30-year-old model that some analysts and retailers grumble was out of touch with the reality of today's market. But it was a business case that Nike's leaders believed in.

'But his (Phil Knoght's) belief in this project had never wavered. (even when the i2 problems emerged), we sat down and talked about what the issues were and he said, OK, I understand, carry on,' said Steele.

Building a Case for Supply Chain Project

Knight showed some extraordinary patience with Nike's supply chain project. 'Once we got into this, we quickly realized that what we originally thought was going to be a two-to-three year effort would be more like five to seven,' said Wolfram. The final stage of the project finished sometime in 2006 at a total cost that went from a projected US$400 million to US$500 million.

The focus of Nike's sneaker supply chain had been centralization. All product designs, factory contracts and deliveries were planned and coordinated from Beaverton, Ore. The supply chain was built around a six-month order cycle, called the *Futures* programme that was developed in 1975 in response to the then chaotic market for running shoes. As Christopher Koch puts it, in those days, the Far East sneaker supply chain was in its infancy; deliveries were sporadic; inflation was high; and runners bought whatever shoes they could find regardless of the brand. Nike won that market by guaranteeing delivery and an inflation-proof discount in return for getting its orders six months in advance. Retailers went along happily because runners did not much care about style or looks—they wanted technically-advanced shoes that fit and were in steady supply. Retailers knew that their Nike shoes would sell no matter how far in advance they ordered them.

But as Nike became increasingly global, its supply chain began to fragment. By 1998, Nike had 27 order management systems around the globe, all highly customized and poorly linked to Beaverton. To gain control over its 9-month manufacturing cycle, Nike decided that it needed systems as centralized as its planning processes. ERP software, specially SAP's R/3 software, would be the bedrock of Nike's strategy, with *i2 supply, demand,* and *collaboration planner* software applications and *Siebel's CRM software* also woven into the overall system.

Nike's patience proved to be a good virtue. It skipped *Apparel and Footwear Solution (AFS)*, the initial version of SAP R/3 software developed specifically for the apparel and footwear industry. Arch-rival Reebok, which partnered with VF (makers of Wrangler Jeans and Vanity Fair bras, among other things) as a better effort to develop AFS, struggled for years to implement the unstable AFS software. Although Nike purchased AFS in 1998, it did not attempt to install it until SAP began working on the second and more stable version of the software. 'Most of the early adopters were busy installing AFS in 1999,' said Steele. He said, 'That's when we began spending a lot of time with SAP, sending our people over to Germany to tell them what we'd like to see in the second version.'

Why i2 Failed at Nike

Nike did not apply the same patience to the implementation of the first part of its supply chain strategy: i2's demand and supply planner software applications. Rather than waiting to deploy i2 as part of its SAP-ERP project, Nike decided to install i2 in 1999, while it was still using its legacy systems.

i2's predictive demand application and its supply chain planner (which maps out the manufacturing of specific products) used different business rules and stored data in different formats, making it difficult to integrate the two applications. The i2 software needed to be so heavily customized to operate with Nike's legacy systems that it took as much as a minute for a single entry to be recorded by the software. And, considering the millions of product numbers Nike used, the system frequently crashed.

But these problems would have remained only glitches had they not spilled over into factory orders. The system ignored some orders while it duplicated others. The demand planner also deleted ordering data six to eight weeks after it was entered, making it impossible for planners to recall what they had asked each factory to produce. Soon, too many orders for Air Garnetts were going over the wires to Asian factories while orders for Air Jordans were lost or deleted.

When the problems were discovered, Nike had to develop workarounds. Data from i2's demand predictor had to be downloaded and manually reloaded into the supply chain planner by occupying programmers, quality assurance personnel, and businesspeople whenever the applications were required to share data—which was as often as weekly. Consultants were brought in to build databases to bypass portions of the i2 applications, and custom bridges were constructed to enable the i2 demand and supply planner applications to share. Nike claimed the kinks were ironed out by November 2000, but the damage was already done, affecting sales and inventory. When the company's SAP system arrived, short- and medium-range planning moved out of i2 altogether and into SAP. According to Nike, the $10 million i2 system was a small part of the $500 million overall project cost, although some observers assert that the i2 cost was higher.

But the question remains: Why did things go so wrong? Wolfram said, 'Nike lulled itself into a false sense of security about the i2 installation because, by comparison with the SAP plan, it was a much smaller project. (Nike had about 200 planners who use the demand and supply planning systems). This felt like something we could do a little easier since it wasn't changing everything else (in the business). But it turned out, it was very complicated.'

'Could we have taken more time with the rollout?' asked Steele, 'Probably. Could we have done a better job with software quality? Sure. Could the planners have been better prepared to use the system before it went live? You can never train enough.'

Learning Patience the Hard Way

Nike learnt greatly from its mistakes. It decided that there would be no rushing the SAP installation. Although Nike executives occasionally questioned the projects complexity and expense, Steele, the CIO, never considered abandoning the single-instance strategy. 'We said single instance is a decision, not a discussion,' said Steele.

Nike wanted to do a staged, geographically-based rollout of SAP, but it also wanted to avoid making each rollout so specific to a region that it would require specialized support. That meant building a design for the US rollout that accommodated some of the peculiarities of the EMEA rollout—such as multiple currency support and different legal restrictions—even though those things were not required for doing business in the US. This necessitated creating a global template for SAP processes, with all the regions agreeing on the details of doing business. Naturally, this made each rollout longer and more complex.

Canada, a relatively small (roughly US$300 million) piece of Nike's US$11 billion business, went first, on the quiet 'Thanksgiving' weekend in 2000, with SAP's AFS ERP, a bundle of i2 applications and Siebel's CRM system. Steele and regional Nike executives, dressed in smocks, served 'Thanksgiving' dinner to supply chain project employees working around the clock. Other regions—the US and EMEA—followed on successive 'Thanksgivings', putting 6350 users worldwide on the system by the end of 2002. The last two regions, Asia-Pacific and Latin America were scheduled for rollout before the end of 2006, according to Nike. Steele claimed that he never had to serve humble pie along with the turkey, saying, there had been no disruptions to Nike's business from the rollouts.

Nike recognized the importance of training. 'Nike's US customer service representatives received 140 to 180 hours of training from highly trained fellow Nike "super users",' said Andy Russell, Nike's Global Transition Director. He further said, 'Employees were locked out of the system until they completed the full training course.'

The Benefits Reaped

One would be prompted to ask: What did six years and $500 million did for Nike's business? Wolfram claimed that better collaboration with the factories in the East had reduced the amount of 'pre-building' of shoes from 30 per cent of Nike's total manufacturing units to around 3 per cent.

According to him, the lead time for shoes had gone down from 9 months to 3 (seven in some periods of high demand). Gross margins had increased slightly since 2001. Inventory levels had been reduced, reported Supply Chain Vice President, Dewey, by cutting Nike's factory order interval time from 1 month to 1 week in some cases. But here, too, the effects would not be trickling down to the balance sheet as fast as Nike would have liked. Nike's inventory turns were 4.34 per year in 2003, according to *Footwear News*, an industry trade magazine, which was slightly less than the industry average of 4.39 and behind its rivals, Reebok (5.07) and K-Swiss (4.47).

Nike was also behind its rival in direct point-of-sale (POS) integration with retailers. Supply chain experts agree that actual data from stores, rather than software algorithms, are the best predictors of demand. But Nike's SAP system could not yet accept POS data, though the company said that it was working on it.

So far, the most direct benefits of the system had been typical for ERP: improved financial visibility, cash flow management, revenue forecasting, and an ability to juggle Nike's cash stockpile in different currencies to take advantage of shifting exchange rates—benefits that were enhanced by the single database that held all the data.

But Steele maintained that the best was yet to come. 'We haven't changed our processes too much yet,' he said, 'because we didn't want to complicate the rollouts.' Eventually, he believed that Nike would get that 6-month lead time down to 3. But, he cautioned that it would require 'significant changes on the part of our retail and supplier partners as well as Nike processes'. For example, retailers did not like having to order products 6 months in advance when fashions could change in a flash. On the other hand, its rivals allowed retailers much more margin in ordering practices, eroding Nike's market lead in select areas.

However, the company claimed that it could make a coordinated global effort, e.g., to cut the lead time. The system to make that happen was now in place, which was still not less than remarkable.

INDUSTRY SNAPSHOT 15	**Taking the sap out of SAP implementation** **MAHINDRA & MAHINDRA (M&M)**[15]

The Mahindra Group, a $6.7 billion, among India's top 10 industrial houses, operates in key sectors of the Indian Economy, such as automotive, farm equipment, trade

---

[15] Adapted from Economic Times Intelligence Group (ETIG). The author expresses due acknowledgement to ETIG for allowing to use information contained in this snapshot.

and financial services, automotive components, infrastructure development, and IT sectors. It recently made its foray in two wheeler industry (like Escorts!). In the farm equipment (tractor) business, entry of global players, such as John Deere, and New Holland, prompted Mahindra to overhaul its supply chain. Recently, Mahindra have been in news for more reasons than one—Tech Mahindra, the IT wing of M&M acquired Satyam Computers, the company launched Sport Utility Vehicle (SUV) Scorpio, and a consumer car Logan, in collaboration with Renault. The company got Japan Quality Medal in 2007 and Deming Application Prize in 2003 as a first tractor company in the world. The Farm Equipment Sector (FES) of the Mahindra Group is one of the top 3 tractor brands in the world. The domestic market share of FES is around 42 per cent out of which Mahindra contributes 30 per cent and Swaraj 12 per cent. FES has 5 manufacturing plants in India, 2 plants in China, 3 assembly plants in the US, and 1 assembly plant in Australia. It has its presence in 25 countries with more than 1000 dealers worldwide.

The Mahindra Group have commenced the sustainability reporting system under which it has to report on conservation of energy, water, and other resources. It is an A+ Global Reporting Initiative (GRI) certified company.

The Problems

Rapid changes in demand in the short-term on a seasonal basis in the farm equipment sector (FES) and the need to quickly respond to these changes, aided with pressure on the bottom line with competitive market prices, resulted in a need for overall supply chain management and cost reduction.

The earlier IT framework required the company to stock high inventory levels in each part of the supply chain—such as tractors with the dealers and at the stockyards, raw materials and work-in-progress in the plant, as well as with vendors and in transit. The planning cycle was very long. It included everything from the start of the demand plan to the production plan, and also to informing the vendors of supply schedules. Moreover, once production plans were finalized, they could not easily be adjusted to the changing market demand. The planning was done in monthly buckets.

'Collaborative planning with around 450 small and medium scale suppliers and 490 dealers across the supply chain was required. For this, Mahindra needed a robust supply chain solution. The company finally chose SAP as their solution, because it matched their requirements completely. i2 was also considered but for the question of interface with SAP, which would have increased costs', Mr Satish Moorjani, Head, Supply Chain Planning & Control is quote having said in the business magazine, *Express Computer*.

Implementation

'For SAP, this was the first case in Asia Pacific that went in for SCM implementation. The customer was not initially convinced. It took us lot of time to convince the top management at Mahindra', says Alok Srivastava, Industry Manager, Manufacturing Sector, SAP India. The project comprised a lead manager from Mahindra and team members from SAP who gathered IT inputs from company personnel. The first step was to make a supply chain opportunity assessment study to identify potential savings areas using SAP's 'Value SAP' methodology and the SCOR model. It took us 3–4 months to find potential saving areas and link these to the the product we had. The senior management was educated about it', says Srivastava.

HP provided the hardware, HCL Connet executed networking, while SAP provided the software Advanced Planner Optimizer (APO), the SCM component of mySAP.com. Mahindra purchased 40 user licences for it.

Training

First, the SAP people got 3–4 members from stores, materials, and other departments and conducted a 3-week training programme. The team worked to map and link their business processes with the APO. The users from other area offices were then trained. There were four phases involved.

Phase 1: It was related to project preparation, including core team training. It took 2 months.

Phase 2: It involved making a blueprint, i.e., linking business objectives with the SAP Product. It also took 2 months.

Phase 3: It referred to execution of blue print relating to software use and application. It took 3–4 months.

Phase 4: It led to the solution going live for all practical purposes. It took 2–3 months.

In all, it took SAP around 10–11 months to put the SAP APO solution live.

Supply chain software operates in three areas—demand planning (monthly forecasts, planned production), capacity constraints, and optimization and logistics (on which truck to load, optimum loading, route planning). Of these, M&M began with implementing the first two. Route planning was planned to be implemented in the next phase.

The main aims of implementing SAP, as outlined below, would go a long way in helping streamline order fulfilment practices at M&M.

1. Improve demand planning by doing it bottom up and get more accurate forecasts

2. Optimize inventory at raw materials, work-in-progress, and finished goods stages. It was needed to have a 'just-in-time' system where raw material reaches the factory when it is required, and carry the optimum inventory on the plant floor.

3. Reduce loss of sales due to non-availability of products by producing exactly what the dealers want. To do this, M&M would need to know the market demand for each and every model.

The key performance indicators (KPIs) identified as measurable benchmarks were order fulfilment lead time, supply chain costs, cash-to-cash cycle times, inventory in days in the supply chain (raw material, packing material, and work in progress material), and logistics cost. The system also provided for customized alerts for timely action. M&M succeeded in reducing inventory in the supply chain of finished goods (FG) by 56 per cent.

Customer Orientation

Cost-conscious customers were demanding variety with quality. They wanted products features, value for money, and timely delivery. M&M achieved a reduction in FG inventories and improved its demand and order fulfilment through this IT-enabled exercise. The implementation of the SAP APO module, aimed towards realizing lower demand/order fulfilment times, was reflected in increased customer satisfaction. The demand/order fulfilment time dropped from 40 days earlier to 8 days by a significant 52 per cent.

Related Resources

www.expresscomputeronline.com/20020729/esi2.shtml as accessed on 15 May 2009; www.mahidra.com/Farm_Equ_Sec as accessed on 15 May 2009.

INDUSTRY SNAPSHOT 16	**Entering into supply chain partnerships with the retail giant LEVI'S**[16]

Levi Strauss & Co., the company which created the first pair of jeans, was founded in 1853 by the Bavarian immigrant, Levi Strauss, in San Francisco. Its brands, Levi's, Dockers, and Signature, are loved and trusted by people around the world.

---

[16] Based on the article, 'Supply Chain Partnerships: How Levi's Got Its Jeans into Wal-Mart', posted by Kim Girard on www.cio.com on 15 July 2003, as accessed on 23 January 2009. The author is thankful to the author and Ms Elana Veron, Executive Editor, CIO, for the kind permission she gave to use the article. This article cannot be reproduced further.

Today, the company operates in 110 countries around the world in America, Europe, and Asia Pacific, employing around 11,400 employees. The company had a revenue of US$4.3 billion in 2008. Half of the company's net revenue comes from sales outside USA. The current CEO, John Anderson, reiterates the commitment of the company to meet real-world challenges of restoration of environment and sustainability. The company has seen its business not only as a source of economic wealth but also as a force for social and economic justice. In order to meet these objectives, the company has a *Red Tab Foundation* to help company employees and retirees maintain a good quality of life.

The company, however, had its share of problems in terms of failures it witnessed in the implementation of IT systems during 2000-03. The following discussion highlights some major issues the company faced and the strategies it adopted to enter mass retailing through Wal-Mart.

Enter New Century with New Problems at Levi's

David Bergen, the CIO, joined Levi's Strauss in 2000 with a mission, 'Get ready for the number-one retailer'. He wondered whether his company's IT transformation would help turn around the American icon, interestingly the punch line of which read, 'Levi's fits 'em all.'

Levi's in Wal-Mart

There was a time when Levi's and blue jeans were held synonymous. Almost since its founding 150 years ago, the company has been an American icon. But times change and so do the tastes. For a time, nothing could come between teenage girls and their Calvins. Twenty somethings started going to malls and haunting The Gap. However by the mid-1990s, Levi's had missed the baggy pant craze that overtook American high schools. In 1996, Levi's sales peaked at $7.1 billion while toward the end of 2002, they fell to US$4.1 billion, a six-year low. The competition had nibbled away at Levi's jeans market share, which tumbled to about 12 per cent from 18.7 per cent in 1997. CIO and senior Vice President, David Bergen, opined that Levi's was being squeezed between the high and the low ends of the jeans market what he referred to as *the jaws of death*. Bergen contemplated that Levi's would have to begin selling to mass channel retailers such as Wal-Mart. And that meant transforming the company's IT.

Since the peak, Levi's, which also makes casual Dockers and higher-end Slates clothing lines, has seen its customer base pulled apart. On the high end of the market, fickle fashionistas were eschewing Levi's in favour of boutique brands such as Blue Cult, Juicy, and Seven. On the low end, people were buying Lee and Wrangler because these were affordable (on average $10 less than Levi's Red Tab) and they found these brands at the superstores they preferred, i.e., BJ's, Sam's Club, Target, and T.J. Maxx.

Wal-Mart—the People's Retailer

Wal-Mart, the world's largest retailer, is where housewives go to buy their children's school supplies, their groceries, and of course, their jeans.

And the company needed a new product for this new section of customers. In July 2003, Levi's introduced its new, less expensive Signature jeans line. The jeans, for men, women, and children, sold for around US$23. They had fewer detail finishes than Levi's other lines. They didn't have the company's trademark red tab or stitching on the pocket. Of course, there was something in it for Wal-Mart. The company, already the largest clothing retailer in the world, wanted more affluent customers. To lure them in, it needed big brands. Acknowledging that the company's customers came from a 'cross-section of income levels and lifestyles', Wal-Mart Senior Vice President, Lois Mikita, said that the company 'continued to tailor its selection to meet the needs of those customers'.

Levi's believed that the new line and the new retail venue would revitalize the company by boosting annual sales by hundreds of millions. With up to 100 million shoppers trolling through Wal-Mart every week, that was not an unreasonable assumption. 'Levi had to face reality,' commented Ira Kalish, a retail industry economist. 'This was a company that dropped in size 40 per cent or so over the past couple of years. The move to Wal-Mart could be sizable,' Kalish said. By partnering with Wal-Mart, added Harry Bernard, an executive at retail consultancy Colton Bernard, 'they would get the volume they would need to survive'.

The Mass Market Strategy Changed Everything

Levi's decision in November 2002 to begin doing business with Wal-Mart changed Bergen's life as well. Like every supplier stocking the $245 billion retailer's endless shelves, Bergen had to rethink his supply chain—every detail of how Levi's jeans, jackets, and shirts would get from factories to new regional warehouses, and to Wal-Mart's over 3422 US stores when they were needed, not before and not even after. That was a mighty leap from the demands placed on Levi's by smaller department store chains such as Macy's or even J.C. Penney.

Complicating this challenge was the fact that Bergen would be going live with a completely upgraded supply chain system during the back-to-school rush, the worst time for a retailer to roll out a new technology.

But Bergen is quoted having said to Kim Girard of cio.com that he had signed on at Levi's in November 2000 for precisely these kinds of challenges. He had sought them out all through his career. Earlier, he had helped install The Gap's first point-of-sale system, which tracked both sales and inventory. Later on, he moved to the clothing maker, Esprit de Corps, where he managed all IT development before heading back to The Gap to help improve production planning.

Levi's new President and CEO, Philip A. Marineau, came to Levi's from PepsiCo in 2000, a year after helping the eternal number-two beverage maker surpass Coke in sales. Shortly after his arrival, he planned a turnaround that would entail making clothes that better met demands of stores and customers—selling to the mass market and tightening operations around the world.

Bergen knew that Marineau's plan to change the line according to what customers wanted would demand big things like more slicing and dicing of customer data and investments in data warehouse technology. He knew that selling to the mass market would require supply chain improvements. He also understood that globalization demanded standardized enterprise systems.

After settling into his new job in 2000, Bergen began working to make Levi's technology fit for what the retail world calls the *mass channel,* big discount stores where 31 per cent of all jeans in the country were being sold. Levi's wanted to play in that channel, and when Bergen arrived, the company was in tentative discussions with Kmart, Target, and Wal-Mart, among others. Bergen knew that without a technology overhaul, Levi's would surely drown. He was most concerned about the fact that the company's national distribution strategy did not suit the way Wal-Mart did business. Levi's had a poor on-time delivery record too—the result of manufacturing and logistics problems originated when it shut the company-owned factories in the US during the late 1990s and transitioned largely to overseas manufacturing.

Bracing for Wal-Mart

When Levi's and Wal-Mart first sat down to talk, Levi's was not, as Gregg Hammann, Levi's US Chief Customer Officer, said on cio.com—up to the demands that Wal-Mart placed on its 30,000 suppliers. However, the IT improvements had enabled the apparel maker to deliver products on time almost 95 per cent of the time. Before CIO David Bergen arrived, the rate was only 65 per cent.

Bergen said, 'Our supply chain could not deliver the services Wal-Mart expected. Being a supplier to Wal-Mart demands a certain level of performance and cost control. Wal-Mart drives you to work with your supply chain to put the same requirements on your suppliers that Wal-Mart puts on you. If you can't make your supply chain work, you won't benefit from being a supplier.'

At Levi's, executives could not track where its product was moving in the pipeline, how many pairs of jeans were being manufactured in which factories and how many were sitting in trucks or in distribution centres. This would not gel well with Wal-

Mart, a supply chain pioneer that moves products off its shelves faster than any retailer and expects replenishment on time to keep costs down. Levi's needed to get a handle on how its products were doing in stores and also accelerate the speed at which those products moved from import dock to warehouse and later to retail shelf.

The lack of information available to Levi's executives translated into poor performance even without Wal-Mart. 'Before Bergen, we delivered 65 per cent of our product on time to customers,' Hammann said on cio.com. 'Industry gurus call that a poor performance. Our rate today is 95 per cent.' That could improve sales by 10 per cent to 15 per cent, according to Marshal Cohen, Senior Industry Analyst of NPD Group's *Fashion World*, an apparel and footwear market researcher. Hammann credited it to improved demand replenishment systems and forecasting technology, the company used now. Additions include a so-called *dashboard* Bergen developed that sat on executives' desktops and showed how Levi's 501 jeans are doing with Kohl's department stores on a weekly, monthly, or annual basis. The dashboard was designed to look like a website and allowed executives to click on a specific product to track how it moved from the factory to the distribution centres to the stores. It showed as to how many pairs of jeans are available at a given time, what the demand was from the stores, and whether the company was meeting that demand. 'What I first got here, I didn't see anything,' Hammann said on cio.com, 'Now I can drill down to the product level.'

This system, unlike the old one, connected the employees working within the supply chain to the salespeople all the way up to the company's financial office, a change Bergen oversaw. Executives used the dashboard to track trends, such as whether denim shorts are a hot item in a particular geographic area, and to prevent problems. For example, during the third quarter of 2002, when the company started shipping Dockers Stain Defender pants, it expected to sell about 2 million pairs. The dashboard, however, alerted Levi's to the fact that the pants were flying off the shelves and another 5,00,000 more would be needed to meet the demand. Having that information at its fingertips helped the company avoid bungling its inventory, plan in advance, and thus sell more pants. Hammannn contemplated that the same kind of information would be crucial in helping replenish Wal-Mart's shelves during the back-to-school season.

Supply Chain Transformation—The Levi's Way

According to Bergen, the most challenging part of the technology overhaul was changing from a national distribution system to a regional one. Earlier, all Levi Strauss 501-style jeans, for example, arrived at stores from four distribution centres in Kentucky, Mississippi, Nevada, and Arkansas. This was not good enough to meet

Wal-Mart's demands for rapid-fire replenishment. So Levi's added three *pool points* (in California, Texas, and Florida) to distribute in-bound freight to eight Wal-Mart stores or to the distribution centres. In addition, Levi's would ship products for each new season in full carton from its distribution centres to Wal-Mart's distribution centres. The pool points would then replenish this supply, working by region to send stacks of jeans to Wal-Mart's distribution network.

As part of this network of facilities, Levi's also developed a scanning tool for its manufacturers to check the accuracy of cartons ready to ship. The company implemented AS2 technology to exchange with Wal-Mart EDI transactions that supported collaborative forecasting. And a set of *Manugistics* applications allowed the company to collaborate on demand forecasting, product differentiation, and orders' planning with Wal-Mart. All of those changes implied that Levi's could plan, configure, and ship pre-packaged orders to the retailer. As Bergen put it, testing of the new system went well and the company was on schedule for a June delivery as of press time.

To support the Wal-Mart initiative, Bergen helped put together a cross-functional team of employees from IT, finance, and sales who helped with planning. This included supporting everything from ordering to logistics and then to making improvements to the data warehouse. The company also upgraded its networks and its US-based applications, and it tested to see whether its systems would scale up to handle orders from all of Wal-Mart's 3200 stores.

Eventually, Levi's planned that about half of the upgrades required to do business with Wal-Mart in the US would be replaced by the new SAP system the company installed toward the end of 2007.

The First Signs of Turnaround

In May 2002, Hammann and Bergen sat down with a 25-person team for a daylong meeting in San Francisco. The team that comprised managers from all parts of Levi's business had covered its bases on the project, considering all *people change, process changes, and technology changes.* By September 2002, the group decided to go forward. Bergen said, 'We went from a company that couldn't shoot straight to where we're very capable of ready, aim, fire.' Wal-Mart's Makita said to cio.com that she was impressed with the level of detail Levi's had dug into to make the execution of the new launch 100 per cent.

There emerged signs that Levi's was turning around. Sales for the company's third and fourth quarters grew for the first time since 1996. During the spring and fall of 2002, Levi's started popping up on NPD Fashion World's top 10 list of brands preferred by young women for the first time in recent memory. 'It hadn't been close to that for a while,' said Cohen. 'Teens haven't gravitated toward Levi's in years.

That was incredible. A lot of that has to do with having the right style in the right place at the right time,' Cohen said. Cohen commented that Levi's plans to upgrade its business processes, and its improved replenishment system had helped the company get the right sizes to the right stores. The key challenge, however, was that of sustaining it.

According to the retail consultant, Bernard, as quoted by Kim Girard on cio.com, Levi's might think it could fool customers into thinking that the jeans on a Wal-Mart rack are 'real' Levi's, but he was not sure that customers would ever understand the $24.99 versus $50 price difference between the pair at Wal-Mart and the pair at Macy's. And if the jeans were not selling well at Macy's, what makes Levi's so sure it could sell jeans at Wal-Mart?

Others retail experts opined that it was tough for any supplier to turn a Wal-Mart relationship into a gold mine. 'Wal-Mart works with their vendors to make sure (Wal-Mart) succeeds, and that was not a guarantee that the vendors made a lot of money,' said Paula Rosenblum, a retail analyst at AMR Research. Indeed, a recent Bain survey of more than 20 Wal-Mart suppliers found that very few were doing everything right to gain on both the top and bottom lines. 'The place where companies do fail is when they aren't bringing anything new to Wal-Mart,' said Gib Carey, a supply chain analyst at Bain, who studied the company's supplier relationships. Wal-Mart is constantly looking at 'How can I get the same product I am selling today at a lower price somewhere else?'

Nonetheless, Levi's was due to start shipping the Signature line to Wal-Mart at the end of May 2003, beginning with 40 stores. By June 2003, Levi's planned to ferry the new clothing line to all US Wal-Mart stores in preparation for the back-to-school rush. Bergen expected some bumps during the first three months. But if all went well, the company planned to sign new deals with other discount retailers too.

At the end, it was clear that Wal-Mart had been driving suppliers to tighten their supply chains. This demanded that the suppliers and their respective suppliers kept pace with Wal-Mart supply chain standards in terms of time, cost, and operational and logistical efficiency. That is what is different to deal with Wal-Mart. If one cannot do it, they should not be dreaming of partnering with Wal-Mart and reaching the biggest audience of retail market customers of the world. If 'quantity' is what makes one profitable and there is a big market for such buyers, let one go there. To make profit in low price market, one has to certainly keep operations efficiency high. No doubt, it is indeed a good preparation and challenge to enter into retail partnerships with giants like Wal-Mart.

| INDUSTRY SNAPSHOT 17 | Revamping logistics, distribution, and after-sales service SAMSUNG ELECTRONICS INDIA[17] |

Samsung India, the Indian subsidiary of Samsung Inc., Korea, was set up in 1995. Samsung had sales of US$174.2 billion in 2007. When Rs 15,000 crore consumer durables industry in India went through a rough patch, Samsung's electronic division showed a growth of 10 per cent and home appliances 24 per cent. It faced challenges, such as competitive pricing and products by its other competitors, such as Whirlpool, GE, Electrolux, etc. Samsung brought about supply chain from day one. It is more market oriented than production oriented. There was a shift from 'Made to stock' to 'Made to order' which leads to faster delivery and customer satisfaction. The cost of logistics as per cent to net sales being 2.23 in 2001, the company set the target of Rs 5000 crore in sales by 2003.

Outbound Logistics

The matching of supply to demand is not easy as the main problem is forecasting, which affects subsequently the production, planning, and dispatching. Now Samsung is reported to have a weekly rolling plan, rather than the monthly one. Samsung's salesman collects data and transmits to the regional head office, where it is collated and analysed, followed by online monitoring of units being dispatched from Samsung warehouses to dealers and dealer warehouses. The online sales at retail level are also monitored.

The Production Planning Committee comprises representatives from marketing, sales, logistics, manufacturing, purchase, and production planning. They have the sales number and estimates for the month. Based on these numbers and considering the stock, both finished goods, raw materials, and WIP, a local procurement plan with 40 vendors and an import plan with 6 vendors are made. Import plans are planned for 12 weeks. Both plans take care of production, purchase, sales, and inventory.

Once the finer points are worked out, the weekly plan is frozen on this basis and production is accordingly scheduled. Because of stiff competition by other multinational brands, the consumer has unlimited choice, and making a product available when needed decides the fate of a brand. Samsung has 22 branch offices, 26 warehouses, 4 regional distribution centres (RDCs), 4700 dealers across India, and over 500 service centres. It has only one production centre in India. The entire production is based on PPSI (production planning committee—consisting of Production, Purchase, Sales, and Inventory staff) meeting. Based on this meeting, a

---

[17] Adapted from Economic Times Intelligence Group (ETIG), Mumbai. The author duly acknowledges the source for the information contained in this snapshot.

weekly production schedule is planned and local procurement from vendors and imports are also planned. The entire estimation is based on the feedback of the sales force.

Distribution

The durable market is full of different brands and SKUs can go as high as 50. In real terms, the market is evenly driven by both *push* and *pull* factors. Keeping this in view, Samsung follows a 2-tier distribution system, as outlined in Fig. 8.15 that follows.

- distribution centres at regional level
- warehouses at the branch level

The objective of the regional level distribution centre (RDC) is to cater to any demand in India within 48 hours, and it also makes logistics systems cost-effective as there is no movement of material between branch warehouses. The RDC also receive materials completely built-up (CBU) via import making it cost-effective. Samsung has 4 RDCs, namely at Delhi, Mumbai, Calcutta and Chennai.

This distribution system helped slash the order to delivery cycle to 48 hours and reduced the inventory levels of finished goods by 25–30 per cent.

The main objective of this distribution system is to ensure that the end consumer gets the product of his choice from any of the Samsung dealers, and the time to replenish the same to the dealer stock is minimum.

Won-Joon Hyoung, a former Samsung supply chain manager, said that the company was finding it difficult by the mid 1990's to coordinate planning and logistics

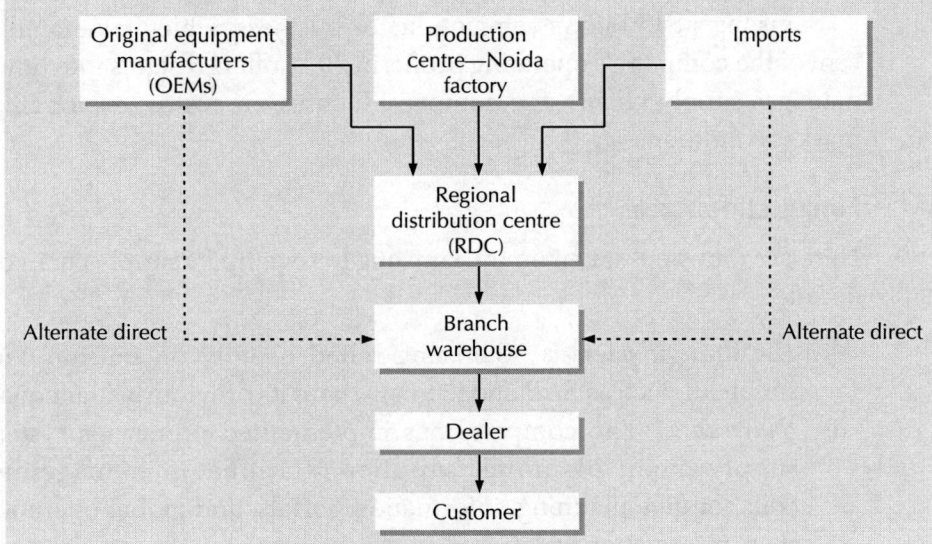

FIG. 8.15 Distribution pathways at Samsung Electronics

for its dozens of factories and sales offices spread across more than 40 countries. So, it brought in outside consultants to help design new processes for managing its far-flung operations.

The first step aimed at giving company executives easier access to consolidated financial data, was to implement R/3 enterprise resource planning (ERP) software from Germany's SAP AG. But the complexity of Samsung's business structure eventually led to more than 60 'instances' or separate SAP installations, across the company's many business units and international subsidiaries.

It soon became clear the ERP system lacked the necessary centralized global planning tools. In 1997, Samsung brought additional planning software i2 technologies Inc. (Dallas) to try out in two business units. Hyoung, who managed the pilot projects, said that after a hurried six-month implementation 'profits started to jump' in the previously struggling computer monitors business.

By 1999, Samsung had eliminated some $3 billion in inventory and accounts receivable costs. And the efficiency improvements have not stopped. Between 1999 and 2004, for instance, as the company's sales grew more than 120 per cent, its inventory and accounts receivables increased only 25 per cent.

Today, in addition to SAP R/3 system, Samsung uses more than a dozen i2 software tools, including products for global supply chain planning, factory planning, demand management and fulfilment, and transportation management. One of the latest additions was *i2's supplier relationship management software*, which Samsung deployed across all 14 of its divisions last year, allowing it to view and analyse $16 billion in spending across more than 30 instances of SAP.

Samsung's $16 billion semiconductor business, which generated nearly 60 per cent of the company's operating profits in 2002 offers insights into how the company manages supply chain—the company focuses on swiftly responding to changing market conditions.

Four Action Areas

Here are four steps taken up by Samsung to revamp its supply chain during the past decade.

(i) *Use strategic partners* Samsung relied heavily on outside consultants and suppliers, such as SAP and i2 to overhaul its previously inadequate IT systems.

(ii) *Share data* The company has implemented numerous systems, including supply chain planning, supplier relationship management software, collaborative planning, information portals, and global operations centres, to share information widely and quickly across the company with major customers.

(iii) *Prioritize Customers* While Samsung values all its business partners, each customer gets a numerical ranking in terms of its relative importance. Special treatment is reserved for the highest ranked customers.

(iv) *Outsource when necessary* Samsung so far has kept most of its manufacturing and design work in-house, but increasingly, the company is outsourcing activities outside of its core competencies, including shipping and third party logistics (3PLs).

The primary mission of Samsung's supply chain organization is to provide excellent customer service.

Steven Daughterby, a supply chain manager with Samsung's North America consumer electronics division, said the company's CPFR efforts are a part of collaborative information portal system called the global Samsung business network (GSBN), which is open to Samsung subsidiaries and the company's top trading partners. GSBN, that shares the data with the company's ERP systems, automates order fulfilment and payment, while giving customers access to real- time information on product pricing and availability, purchase order and shipment status, as well as training, service, and support. For internal Samsung users, it tracks sales, inventory, and shipments, as well as retail price changes and other competitive information.

In India, Samsung, however, is always looking for new ways to raise the performance bar even further. 'Our customers are becoming more demanding. They want more products, more flexibility with delivery schedules. They want us to meet 100 per cent of our commitments. That's motivated us to become even better in our supply chain management initiatives,' said Harold Hickey, Vice President of service and operations for Samsung's North American Telecom subsidiary in Dallas.

Samsung distribution system comprises 2 tiers—distribution centres at regional and warehouses at the branch level.

The main objective of the distribution centre at the regional level is to cater to any demand anywhere in India within 48 hours, and make logistics more cost-effective. To cater to the needs of smaller dealers within the city, a C&F operation is professionally equipped with 6–8 different sizes of vehicles at Kalina in Mumbai to ensure that within 4 hours, the material is delivered to 10 dealers.

The inventory norms for finished goods and OEM supplies are 15 days, while for completely built-up units (CBUs), it is 30 days. All CBU imports are now planned before the order is placed as the port allocation has to be done in advance. The four ports it deals with are Mumbai, Delhi, Calcutta, and Chennai. The IT system works extends Samsung boundaries too. As soon as the dealers order is received at Noida, a message goes via EDI system. This system is being implemented through a chit system which gives the vendor the weekly purchase plan, delivery schedule, and final delivery confirmation.

Samsung's Post-sales Service through Net

The firm has invested Rs 2 crore in connecting its 200 authorized service centres with the head office. It is offering customer call logging under which a customer can register a service call at the site. A unique customer ID is given once the call is made, detailing the product specifications and customer data. The information goes to the authorized service centre (ASC) nearest to the customer after which a confirmation mail is sent. The four Samsung zonal spares warehouses will download the order at the end of the day and upload the shipping notification on the Net for each transaction. The amount payable by the ASC to the company as well as overall A/C statements are put on the Net. EDI system helps to link key suppliers through the Global Logistics Network System. This system links Samsung India's purchase department with Samsung headquarters and the international procurement offices in Singapore and Korea. It is integrated with ERP systems to use it for sharing production plans so that JIT delivery schedule can be fully implemented.

Logistics innovation have helped slash the order to delivery cycle by at least 2 days and also reduced inventory levels of FG by 25–30 per cent. They have 5 transporters, inspite of doubling sales every year. However, Samsung's spend on these transporters has come down by 30 per cent and is 25 per cent of sales. The 850 containerized trucks do cost slightly higher, but ensure safety and reduce damage. The finished goods stock in the pipeline is down to 30 days.

Automated Inventory Management

The carousels loading capacity proved 300 per cent greater than the previously used shelving system, allowing it to reduce the size of their warehouse by more than 50 per cent. It helped to improve picking accuracy to 99 per cent and reduced inventory leveling by 55 per cent. The automated carousel system allowed the same day shipping cut off time to be extended from 1:00 pm to 4:30 pm. This helps in high level of customer satisfaction.

Supply of Spare Parts

Spare parts is yet another major issue of supply chain of Samsung. It is today linked to Samsungs subsidiaries in Singapore, Australia, Thailand, Indonesia, and the Phillipines by the global spares system called MegaSYS LPA visibility system, which basically allows the flow of spares from any depot in the region—Singapore or anywhere else. The depots in the countries are also online with the hub Singapore. This means that any order on any ASC in India would be reflected all the way back to the hub and instructions would be automatically generated. It can also allow order cycles to reduce to 7 days from present 30 days.

The global spares system is a single window clearance system, which makes tracking of 7000 spare parts easier than old system of manual tracking. Samsung's IT and service managers expect that spare stocking cycles will reduce to 30 days from present 45 days, the four spare distributors will hold less, since all lead times and stocks are known and overall transaction cost will reduce.

In 2001, 31 per cent of all its dealers were in North India and 28 per cent in the west. Number of dealers went up to 5000 in 2001.

Inbound Logistics

The ordering is based on the rolling sale forecast which is reviewed weekly, and accordingly, ordering of the raw material is done every week. The import orders are placed every week in similar lots because of the risk and cost implications. The orders are placed on the basis of rolling sales forecast for 12 weeks but the firm call ups are done on weekly basis with permissible contracted variation of 25 per cent. The same holds true for local purchases also. The production schedules are made available to all vendors so that they can plan their supplies accordingly and effect deliveries only when the stock is required. All the raw materials procured are checked for quality at the vendor's end.

In India, Samsung's location helps in lowering of logistics costs. There are 55 vendors supplying goods to Samsung's Noida Factory. 38 of these, i.e., around 70 per cent are within 100 km of the factory, a maximum trucking time of 3 hours. This means order delivery lead times are shorter, inventories produced at the vendor end are lesser, and their levels at both factories are lowered. Besides, cost of ordering is also low since a local call or fax can be used in addition to e-mail and the Intranet. Only about 20 per cent or 11 vendors are beyond 100 km and 6 are overseas. The local delivery times are maximum 1 day and pose no major issue for Samsung. There is a 12 week advance notification for overseas vendors, whose supply schedules are taken care of by the forecasting process.

Transportation is multi-modal—by sea, air and road. All 'A' items are procured on JIT basis, thereby minimizing the blocked working capital whereas others are based on the stipulated delivery time. All imported but high value but smaller size items are transported by air and other items are either by road or by sea. Packing is done by cartons, customized cushions, and bag sheets. All imported raw material and colour picture tubes (CPTs) which are procured locally is palletized. One of the innovations is use of recyclable bins for CTV cabinets. 60 per cent of the raw material and components imports are by air since these are low volume, high value electronics. Inbound logistics cost is 0.75 per cent of sales out of which 70 per cent is freight and 20 per cent is raw materials. It is connected via Glonets logistics system and MegaSYS spares system to its worldwide network.

INDUSTRY SNAPSHOT 18	Life is good through e-SCM LG ELECTRONICS[18]

LG Electronics India, established in 1997 as a wholly owned subsidiary of LG Electronics, South Korea, posted a turnover of Rs 8250 crore in 2006, out of which exports would have contributed roughly 10 per cent. The company posted an overall growth rate of 10 per cent. In the turnover, the contribution was 43 per cent from home appliances, 39 per cent from consumer electronics, 13 per cent from IT products and 5 per cent from global system for mobiles (GSM) phones. With a forecasted exports growth rate of 19 per cent, the company aimed to have exports sales worth Rs 950 crore by the end of 2007. The company sold 1 million PC monitors in 2006 and 1 million DVD writers in 2007, the latter doubled to 2 million in 2008, i.e., by a whopping 100 per cent. These sales had 90 per cent contribution from trade and 10 per cent from OEM partners. The company also won the Electronics and Computer Software Export Promotion Council's prestigeous ESC award in 2005–2006. As R. Manikandan, Business Group Head puts it in one of the press releases, the company aims to focus on flat panel display (FPD) and GSM phones. It aimed to have 40 per cent market share in FPD products by 2008 end.

The company positions its brand as the one that is *delightfully smart*. The management philosophy is based on two pillars—creating value for customers and management based on esteem for human dignity.

The Mechanistics of Distribution at LG

The company has two factories—one at Greater Noida and another at Pune. It plans to use its supply chain to become a market leader. LG provides products of global standards and sells TVs, microwaves, washing machines, and DVD players. The company planned for big entry into large format retail sector by entering 200 retail stores by 2008 end. LG presently is concentrating on increasing stock turns and intensifying the e-commerce efforts. According to S.N. Rai, the then GM, Logistics of the company as quoted by ET Intelligence Group (ETIG), the stock turns for finished goods touched 24 cycles a year in 2001. Inventory figures translated into massive savings at key pressure point. Every cycle of order to sales costs LG around $1 million. LG has also realized savings of up to $0.48 m from its direct-to-trade initiatives using the Internet and exchanges. The e-commerce accounted for almost 75 per cent of sales.

LG markets its white goods to over 2480 dealers (direct), 900 sub dealers, 75 distributors, and 90 brand shops.

---

[18] Based on ETIG survey, 2002; www.in.lge.com/about us/pressMedia as accessed on 8 May 2009.

It took LG two years to bring down the days of inventory on an all India level from 14 days in 1999 to 7 in 2001. The forecasting accuracy increased to 95 per cent in 2001. LG aims to become most networked company. 16 per cent of total dealers are online covering 79 per cent of the geographical area. A move-in and move-out report is followed by the company to balance the demand to supply across the supply chain. It gave an 'early warning signal' about the position of stock and it calculated the required inventory on any day to cover the standard days of stock (PoS) and suggests inter-brands increment of stocks required, if any, in case of excess at one point and deficit at another. LG uses foot square inch (FSI) to optimally use warehousing space. It was 2.2 sq. feet in 2000. This implies usage of same space more effectively. At a turnover of Rs 450 crore in 1996, LG used warehouse space as 2.67 lakh sq. feet while in 2000 at a turnover of Rs 2700 crore, LG just used warehouse space as 1.67 lakh sq. feet. It clearly shows effective utilization of space.

The company planned increase in dealers from 1022 in 2000 to 4000 in 2001. 60 per cent dealers are located in west and north and 17 per cent dealers in east while 23 per cent dealers are located in the south. LG realized savings to the tune of $2.1 m in reduced long distance freight. For cost cutting the company reduced number of transporters from 13 in 1999 to just 6 in 2001. LG extended IT to secondary transport also.

Outbound logistics from warehouse to dealers cost 0.79 per cent of sales turnover to the company in 2001. Tracking of goods is done every 2 hours followed with a company called *e–trans* in alliance with *BPCL petrol pumps.* The truck driven is given a card very much like a credit card which has the truck number, chassis number, and card number on it. The truck driver goes to the nearest BPCL petrol pump. On his route, swipes the card through the machine and moves on. The machine records the time and card details and every 2 hours, dials up the local host which automatically connects to Kolkata and Mumbai hubs where all truck data is updated on e–trans site and sent to LG. The company spent more than Rs 40 crore on hardware and software and tracking, including—VSAT, ERP SAP R/3 system, etc.

The system connected primary truckers via e-mail, VSAT, tracking or LG's website saved $0.76 million in logistics using e-mail. Around 75 per cent dealers are targeted to be connected electronically. The company has a vision for online or e-SCM through future networking between supplier exchanges, logistics exchanges, customer exchanges, dealers/distributors, contract manufacturers, and virtual contractors (Fig. 8.16).

The company has connectivity via lgdealernet.com and LGezebuy.com. So, the online SCM is going to be useful for vendors, retailers, as well as the customers. It has helped the company to leverage the supply chain through execution of e-SCM.

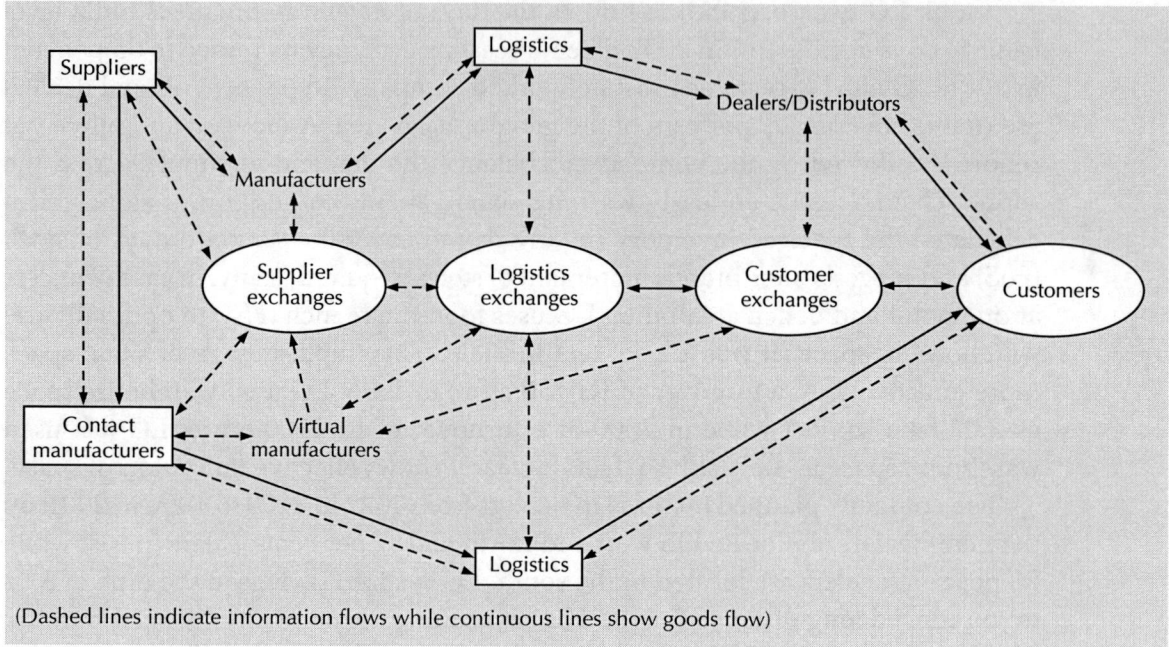

(Dashed lines indicate information flows while continuous lines show goods flow)

FIG. 8.16   e-SCM Future networking at LG electronics
Source: ETIG Mumbai, 2002

INDUSTRY SNAPSHOT 19	A steely materials management is the key
	STEEL AUTHORITY OF INDIA LIMITED (SAIL)[19]

Steel Authority of India Limited (SAIL) is India's largest and one of the world's leading steel producers with a turnover of around Rs 16,500 crores. SAIL has formed a joint venture company with TISCO and Kalyani Steel Ltd to launch Metaljunction.com Private Limited (MPL)—the largest vertical portal in India. The portal has been formed to offer neutral and independent platform for trading in steel and allied materials.

SAIL's four integrated steel plants, namely Bhilai Steel Plan (BSP), Durgapur Steel Plant (DSP), Rourkela Steel Plant (RSP), Bokaro Steel Plant (BSL), and one subsidiary at Burnpur (IISCO) have a total capacity of producing over 12 million tones of crude steel. Three plants at Salem (SSP), Durgapur (DSP) and Bhadrawati (VISL) produce stainless steel and alloy steels, and a plant at Chandrapur (MEL) is a bulk producer of ferro-alloys.

---

[19] The author is thankful to the Materials Management Department of SAIL for sharing information contained in this snapshot.

SAIL's vast portfolio of long, flat, and tabular products is marketed within and outside India by its central marketing organization (CMO) and the international trade division respectively. By-products and chemicals are marketed directly by the respective steel plants. SAIL's Raw Materials Division (RMD) is located at Kolkata. In addition, SAIL has a well-equipped Research and Development Centre for iron and steel (RDCIS) at Ranchi.

Guidelines for Stores and Spares (Inventory Management)

There is a centralized cataloguing agency in each plant/unit under the head of materials management department which is responsible for the classification of item, allotting a unique catalogue number and description to an item, ensuring standardization, and for firming up of the specifications of all items. Any proposal to introduce a new item to the catalogue master should have the approval of Head of works of the plant/unit. The inventory report of stores and spares is compiled for each plant as per Annexure I, and submitted to corporate materials management group by 10th of each month.

Categorization of ABC and XYZ Items

Stores and spores items as reported at the beginning of the financial year, in the stock ledger, are considered for analysis and for arriving at the XYZ and ABC categorization. Items, such as shop floor inventory, stores-in-transit, provisions, and minor raw materials, are excluded while categorizing the items as ABC and XYZ.

XYZ Categorization

Items which constitute top 10 per cent of the total stock (of stores and spares) holding, when arranged in the descending order of stock holding value, are termed as 'X' items. Next 20 per cent are termed as 'Y' and rest as 'Z' category items.

ABC Categorization

Items which constitute top 70 per cent of total consumption (of stores and spares) value, when arranged in the descending order of consumption value, are termed as 'A' class items. Consumption values are based on the consumption data of the previous financial year. Next 20 per cent are termed as 'B' class and rest as 'C' class items.

Cancellation of Pending Orders

There should not be double procurement against the same purchase indent. While issuing a fresh purchase order due to failure of a supplier, when the defaulters have overshot the due date stipulated in the Acceptance of Tender and material has not been received, and the indentor has made alternate arrangements other than mentioned herein above, such orders are reviewed on regular basis and cancelled by the materials management department.

Identification and Disposal of Surplus and Obsolete Stores and Spares Items

At the time of phasing out/replacing/modifying assets, stores and spares belonging to these must be identified and segregated. At first, endeavour is to be made to explore possibilities of utilizing these items internally and a utilization plan drawn out. In the event it is not possible to utilize these internally, a decision should be taken to declare these either as surplus or obsolete, so that materials management department can initiate action with regard to their disposal.

While drawing the utilization plan, maximum retention period (which in no case should exceed one year) is also mentioned, beyond which the item(s) should be treated as declared surplus. One six months' extension of retention period is allowed only after the approval of the head of the works.

Criteria for Insurance Spares

An item

- whose failure results in stoppage of production, not only of the concerned unit, but also affects the production of the preceding and succeeding unit
- which normally does not fail but whose life expectancy is uncertain
- which is a tailor-made item and if it is a standard item, and not readily available
- which is declared as an insurance item with the approval of the head of the works, at the time of initial/first procurement only and not later
- which forms part of insurance spares inventory (whose value) at any time should not exceed 10 per cent of the total spares inventory is considered as an insurance item.

Worthiness of the insurance item is examined every year by the user and the item has to be brought in the system/use in 5 to 10 years by the user, and make ready the old repaired/reconditioned/refurbished spare in the stores for use.

Norms for Declaring Non-moving Inventory

For the purpose of inventory management, the items which have not been issued for 3 years are considered as non-moving items. Normally, no receipt is added to such items. For reporting non-moving items, insurance inventory is excluded and shown separately.

Non-moving Items

Once the items are declared non-moving, the list of the same is circulated within the plant/unit, for finding out utilization plans of the indentor/user and/or of the other users within the plant/unit including the project or addition, modification, and replacement (AMR) departments within the plant/unit. Simultaneously, the list of non-moving items whose stock value is greater than Rs 25,000 is circulated to the heads of materials management department of the other plants/units. The sister plants/units should send their response within 2 months from the date of letter forwarding such lists. Non-receipt of response is treated as if the items are not required by them.

A standing committee consisting of representatives from materials management department of BSP, DSP, RSP, and BSL, and one member from corporate materials management group at Delhi, reviews the list vis-à-vis the response received from the plants/units on quarterly basis, and recommend the items which could be declared as not required by the other plants.

Identification of Obsolete and Surplus from Non-moving Items

During the year, each plant/unit should make efforts to identify minimum 10 per cent of the value of non-moving inventory declared at the beginning of the year, as surplus or obsolete, or ensure reduction by internal consumption. Status of non-moving and surplus/obsolete inventory is compiled as per Annexure I.

Disposal of Declared Surplus and Obsolete Items

During the year, each plant/unit should make efforts to dispose of minimum 50 per cent of the value of surplus and obsolete inventory declared at the beginning of the financial year.

The inter-plant transfer of material within SAIL is accounted for at book-value, i.e., the original purchase price. However, the transfer of material between SAIL units and its subsidiaries and vice-versa, is at book-value or the last auction price, whichever is lower.

As regards disposal of surplus/obsolete items to outside parties, the same may be disposed of by auction in the first instance, and reverse price maybe fixed on the basis of original book value, i.e., 100 per cent. For the second attempt, reserve price maybe determined on the basis of bids received against the first tender. It should be higher than the highest bid received in the first instance, as the item was not disposed of on the basis of such bid. If first two attempts have not succeeded in disposing of the items, there need not be any reserve price for disposal of the items in the third/subsequent attempt.

Policy of Reconditioning of Spares

Each plant would make efforts in indentifying each year 5 per cent of its high value, long lead time/critical spares which it can recondition and use. The reconditioning cell functions under the head of maintenance for undertaking reconditioning of listed spares.

Utilizing Non-moving/Surplus Items in Modernization/Addition and/or Modification and/or Replacement Schemes

In order to explore the possibilities of utilizing non-moving/surplus stock in modernization/addition, modification, and replacement (AMR) schemes, each plant should list along with technical details all such non-moving/surplus items and

(i) would forward the list of those items whose stock value is above Rs 1 lakh to Projects Directorate to find out possibility of utilizing the same in the modernization schemes.

(ii) would forward the list of those items whose stock value is above Rs 25,000 to the Heads of Materials Management Department of other plants to find out possibility of utilizing the same in the AMR schemes.

(iii) would circulate list of items to the concerned Directorate units by 30th June, every year.

The projects directorate and sister plants/units should send their response within 2 months from the date of receipt of letter forwarding the list. Non-receipt of response from the projects directorate and sister plants/units within 2 months, would be treated as if the item(s) is not required by them.

Budgetary Control

To the maximum extent possible, the items and quantities should be stated at the time of making the budget. Each indenting agency would ensure budgetary control.

The budgeting section would monitor the shop-wise procurement budget for indents raised by the shop. The amount sanctioned should be utilized only for the items and quantities (wherever indicated) approved.

Norms for Inventory Holding

The norm for stores and spares inventory holding has been fixed as 6 months in terms of number of months' consumption for all plants/units, except BSP. For BSP, the norm would be 5.38 months in terms of months' consumption. This would exclude spares capitalized after modernization. However, 2 years after capitalization, even those spares would become part of inventory for the purpose of 6 months norm for inventory holding.

Each plant/unit would monitor the receipts and issues, and would ensure that for all 'A' class items, the 6 monthly cumulative average of the ratio of receipt to issue does not exceed 0.9.

To start with, each plant/unit would fix the

- minimum levels
- safety levels
- maximum levels
- reorder level

for automatic procurement (AP) items and intimate the same to the corporate materials management group within 6 months.

The economic order quantity levels (EOQ) for the items would also be fixed, wherever applicable.

Supplies from Sister Units

No sister plant/unit shall deliver quantities beyond those specified in the order, to other unit/plant unless and until agreed to in writing by the receiving plant/unit.

Rate Contracts/Long-term Agreements

With a view to reduce lead time and have minimum inventory, entering into rate contracts and long-term agreements with phased delivery, will be explored by the plants/units.

Vendor Rating

Each plant/unit shall ensure vendor rating for all 'A' class item suppliers. Vendor rating shall be used for the purposes of considering the vendor for enquiry and placement of order.

Periodic Review of 'A' Class Items

Each plant/unit shall institute a system for periodic review and monitoring of supplies and stock of 'A' class items on a quarterly basis.

Development of Databases for Capital Repair Jobs

The materials management department of each plant/unit develops and maintains databases for the bills of materials, item specifications, and list of vendors for the capital repair jobs executed, and utilizes the same for the purpose of timely execution, etc., of repair jobs in future.

Continuous Interaction between Materials Management Department and Indentors

The materials management department of each plant/unit develops and maintains a system by which the indentor is kept informed on regular basis about status of indents, delivery of material against orders, receipt of material at stores, and stock at stores.

Similarly, the indentor develops a system by which the materials management department is kept informed about future requirements and should provide sufficient time for procurement.

Computerization of Materials Management Department

The head of materials management department ensures that the available computer facilities in the materials management department are fully utilized for keeping the indentor informed, generation of reports, and making the same available to the dealing persons for taking corrective action, besides other activities of the materials management department. The head of materials management department shall also ensure that computerization activities of materials management are implemented on time.

Inventory Report

With a view to control non-moving, surplus, and obsolete inventory, the status of these reported on a quarterly basis to the corporate materials management group in the format provided in Annexure II.

Annexure I
(To be reported to CMMG, New Delhi By 10th of every month)
Inventory of stores and spares
Year _____ Month _____

(Rs in crore)

Plant	APP year	Opening balance Year Month	Receipts during the month	Issues during the month	Closing balance
BSP					
DSP					
RSP					
BSL					
ASP					
SSP					
IISCO					

- Components of operation inventory and modernization spares may be shown separately.
- Aggregate production plan targets are fixed in a meeting.
- Value of insurance spares may be indicated in brackets below.

Annexure II

Status of non-moving and surplus/obsolete inventory

(For I/II/II/IVth quarter)

Year _____   (Value in Rs crore)

Plant	Opening balance				Declared surplus during the year		Disposal during the year		Closing balance			
	Non-moving		Surplus/ obsolete						Non-moving		Surplus/ Obsolete	
	No.	Value	No.	Value	No.	Value	No.	Value	No.	Value	No.	Value
BSP												
DSP												
RSP												
BSL												
ASP												
SSP												
IISCO												

1. Non-moving, surplus/obsolete as at the beginning of the financial year will be taken as the opening balance.
2. Non-moving criterion—3 years (as defined in the policy).

Source: Materials Management Group, SAIL

INDUSTRY SNAPSHOT 20	**Giving a smooth finish to the communication network ASIAN PAINTS[20]**

The Asian Paints, leader in the decorative paints business reported sales turnover of Rs 4404 crore in 2008 showing 20 per cent growth rate and a profit after tax of Rs 409 crore up by 45.6 crores. The company has 3000 SKUs, 600 raw materials, 16 third party/contract manufacturers, and 4 owned plants (one plant coming up at Rohtak in Haryana which would commence production in 2010), two chemical plants, 18 processing centres with 6 regional distribution centres (RDCs), 72 sales depots catering to around 14,000 dealers selling over 1000 shades (facilitated by tinting at their end) all over India, and over 2000 industrial customers. In addition, there are 350 raw material and intermediate goods suppliers, and 150 packing material vendors. The company interestingly believes in 'growth with humility'.

---

[20] The author acknowledges the Economic Times Intelligence Group (ETIG), Mumbai, for their kind permission to use information related to this company from their publication, *Supply Chain & Logistics,* 2002; www.asianpaints.com/corporate_information/supply_chain.aspx as accessed on 14 May 2009.

Supply Chain Objectives

The company has a simple concept of 'going where the customer is' that drives the company's all retail strategies. That is the reason why tinting is provided at the last retail store to create and sell that 1000th shade. The company provides painting solutions right upto the customer's homes, be it a kid's room or corner. The customer is involved into 'do-it-yourself' kind of design creations in painting. Key objectives on which the supply chain is designed to deliver are customer satisfaction, better processes, and time utilization, which should logically flow into control and reduction in costs. This requires that the design parameters link dealers, supply chain vendors, consumers, and business partners seamlessly, use the ERP as a basic building block in an open architecture, and given the constraints of telecom in India, invest in the appropriate technology and systems.

Outbound Logistics

The company is reported to be using statistical tools, ERP data mining along with optimizers, to smooth out the peaks and troughs due to the demand. Information technology is used to address each of the supply chain issues. Asian Paints today is considered the most-networked paints company in India, having spent up to Rs 40 crore over the last 3 years on various levels and technologies. The communication network is outlined in Fig. 8.17. They have better inventory visibility, appreciation of working capital, ability to take connective action quickly to prevent the bullwhip effect, as well as take advantage of market demands.

The gain from the supply chain is to gain competitive advantage. The three strategies adopted—investing heavily into IT (with the sole intention of getting visibility across the supply chain), investing into tinting machines, and the process of dealer expansion. It has all the information about every dealer, including patterns of off-takes, orders, payment, and growth. They want to track secondary sales too. It supplies to over 14,000 dealers nation-wide. The total number of dealer tinting systems (DTS) machines is around 2100. It has 2100 colour worlds.

It is looking at a three-way arrangement in which it will tie up with a bank for the dealers. The bank will pay up the initial cost of installation and the dealer will repay the bank. It earned Rs 11 crore on lease rental from dealers who use these machines. It is machine that gives exact quantities and uses colourants that is developed in-house by the company. The dealer tinting system has helped it to provide over 1000 shades to their consumers for their existing products. This has helped reduce dealer inventory, as the dealer has to stock only bases and do not stock the entire range of shades in various products. This has helped bring down the working capital of the dealer, and is able to rotate his capital much faster.

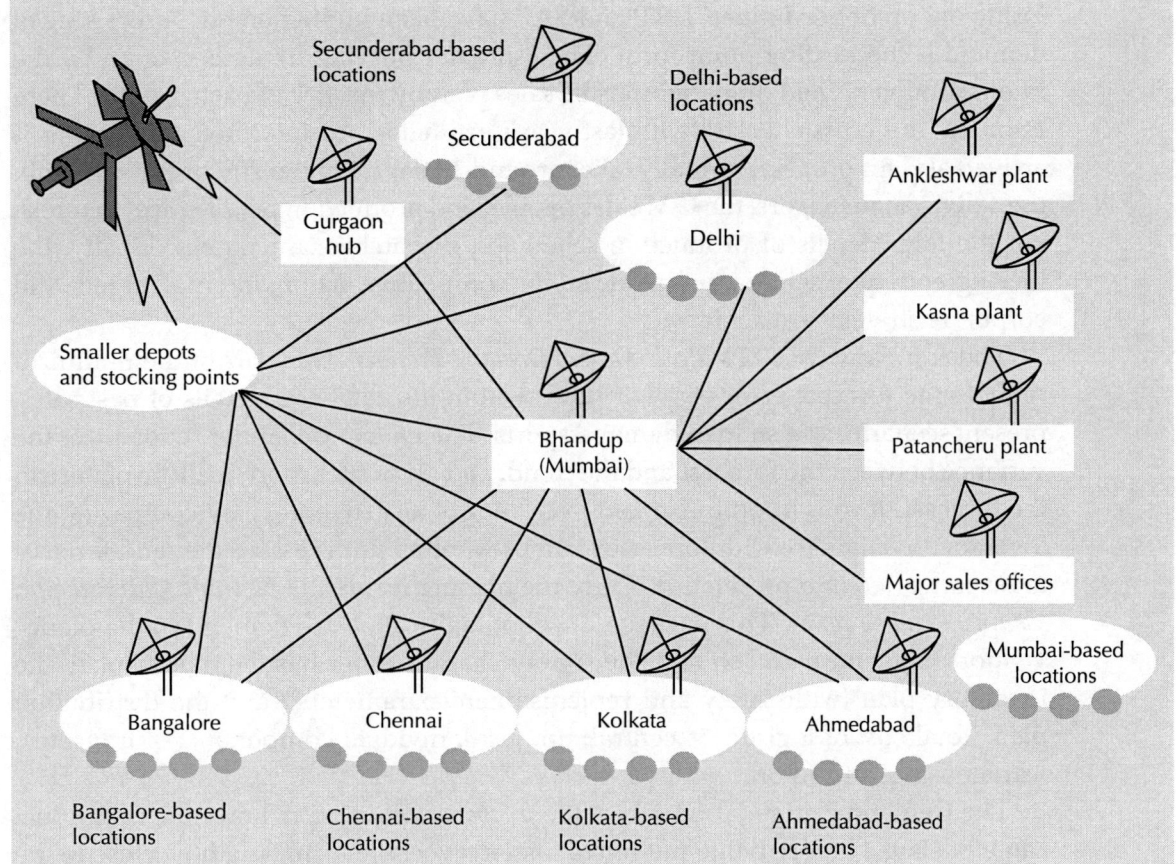

FIG. 8.17 Asian Paints communication network
Source: Adapted from *Supply Chain & Logistics,* 2002, ETIG, Mumbai

Importance of machines has helped to cut inventories of several shades, improve batch process, and customer service. Only 21 dealers have colour world which is 14 per cent of dealer force, so for the company, the inventory reduction has been negligible.

Asian Paints has taken innovation in distribution also, it has started direct-to-home painting services in select cities, such as Kolkata and Hyderabad. Then it has 'Helpline' which is now toll-free and customers at over 40 locations all across the country can access it. They have converted 90 per cent of calls asking for help into actual sales. It has brought an element of modernity, speed, and customer services without any significant increase in cost. The most crucial ingredient of the company's supply chain philosophy is IT strategy. Trends in buying used to get back to HO after 15 days, which meant possibility of making stocks that were slow moving and losing out on opportunities. ERP and SAP have been implemented. Forecasting of demand is the starting point for it. The estimates of sales are agreed upon by the sales staff. Every field office submits its sales plan by the 10th of each month. These estimates are cross-checked with last year's estimates. An intermediate number is arrived at. This process normally takes around 10 days. On the 20th of every month, the 4 division managers, the GM sales people, and production people meet to thrash out the finer details of production schedules, dispatches, and stocks. Finally, the final agreed-upon sales targets adjusted for competitive action, internal targets, and corporate strategy are achieved.

The company uses *i2's Trade Matrix Demand Planner*. This part of the optimizer reduces the forecast error, since it holds within it's database, details of past sales, present scenario, and sudden demand spurts. The Demand Planner rationalizes the variance between the forecast and the trend, and gives a far more realistic picture to the forecast. It tries to optimize and even reduce any inventory by comparing the inventory availability with forecasts, and preventing unnecessary demand forecast to be converted into production. Once the planner is run, the *i2 Trade Matrix Supply Chain Planner* cuts in. This package now optimally allocates demand to the plants, vendors, machines, and so on. The supply chain planner has the master plan, the inventory plan (with safety and replenishment parameters), and the distribution plan. Total cost of logistics is central, not just individual components of transport, warehousing, and so on.

The Demand Planner also looks at the *postponement principle*, how much a product can be delayed before being put into a final irrevocable form, and how close to the customer can the paint be made in distance and time. It gives the best possible solution to meet the complexity of cost benefits of manufacturing sites and sales sites.

The next step is to run i2 technologies' *Supply Chain Trade Matrix Factory Planner*. This package allocates the quantities, times, and machines to be used at each plant. It is fed with all manufacturing details and in correlation with the demand planner (which feeds it with production required for each SKU), supply chain planner, and the factory planner. It ensures optimal asset utilization and considers real life constraints, such as material and machine availability. It has given rise to raw material packaging material, better coordination between machines, people, and stocks. The result of the factory planner is generation of the daily production schedules. The sequence of order fulfilment activities at Asian Paints is given in Fig. 8.18.

It quickly responds to the changes in demand, e.g., the Gujarat earthquake or export demand. It is one of the few companies which implemented all the SAP models. It is the only company in India which has implemented SCM solution

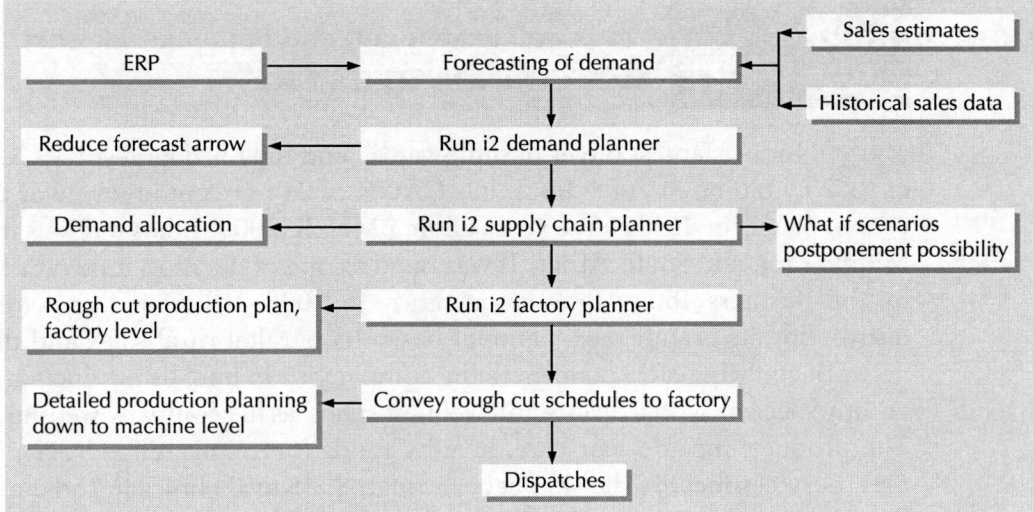

FIG. 8.18 Sequencing of activities for order fulfilment at Asian Paints
Source: ETIG, Mumbai

from i2 technologies. It also has ERP working internally. It has already achieved benefits in terms of the reduced finished good (FG) inventory.

It has followed strict credit policy which is reflected in debtor's days down to 26 days from 30 days. Control in outbound logistics is through freight costs and is constant at 3.4 per cent of net sales. It has not gone up with the sales figure. Freight and FG taken together accounted for 12 per cent of net sales in 2000. The total inventories have fallen to 13.6 per cent of net sales from the last value of 14.2 per cent.

Inbound Logistics

Most materials are procured locally with incentives to vendors. Raw material inventory as a percentage of net sales have actually gone down from 4.7 per cent to 4.2 per cent in 2000. It has already backward integrated to reduce dependence on imports, as well as better control over schedules.

Freight Control

In analysis, it was found that surfeit of truckers, the localization of vendors, and direct bulk imports to plants near the ports have shown that carriage and freight costs are under control. It takes 7–8 days for imports to reach their plants around the country. It is on its way to being one of the most networked and progressive company.

INDUSTRY SNAPSHOT 21	Oil is well in inbound and outbound logistics MARICO INDUSTRIES LTD[21]

Marico, India's largest buyer of safflower oil and the third largest FMCG had sales of Rs 23.9 billion in 2008–09. It has CAGR of 24 per cent in turnover and 27 per cent in profits in the last five years ending March, 2009. It has markets in SAARC, Middle East, and South Africa. It was rated as one of the most innovative company by the Business Today Innovation Study in 2008. It has tied up with P&G for distributing its brands on a national basis. Its parallel rural sales and distribution network contributes 25 per cent to the company's top line. Its products and services occupy space in 'global beauty and wellness space' as the company website proclaims. The products include hair care, healthy foods (premium refined oils), and fabric care. Services include the skin care through 85 'Kaya' clinics in India and Middle East. The key brands are—Parachute, Parachute Advansed, Oil of Malabar, Saffola, Aromatic, Sweekar, Hair & Care, Nikhar, Shanti Amla, Mediker and Revive, etc.

Supply Chain Complexity

The company claims that every month 70 million consumer packs of Marico reach 130 million customers to about 23 million households through a distribution network of 2.5 million outlets in India and abroad (www.marico.com). Its infrastructure comprises of more than 100 super distributors catering to 2300 small stockists and 9000 van markets.

For Marico, SCM has two clear divisions—time and inventory. Time is crucial for both inbound and outbound logistics because it affects planning and working capital, and inventory because it affects planning and working capital, as it affects demand fulfilment. The edible oils' supply chain holds keen interest for Marico since 80 per cent of its revenues are from the brands *Saffola* and *Sweekar*.

Sweekar has both sunflower and soyabean oils. Saffola is based on safflower (both blended with corn oil and as safflower oil itself). Sunflower oil is a transaction issue, while safflower oil is a sourcing issue.

Supply chain transactions for sunflower (*Sweekar* brand) are basically as simple as calling the traders and placing the order at the day's price, while in safflower, SCM includes everything from growers to monsoons to crop failures and harvests. The supply chain becomes even more complicated due to price fluctuations specu-lations and changing demand patterns across the world. Because of the high import content, inventory management of both safflower and sunflower oils become crucial.

---

[21] Adapted from ETIG, Mumbai. The author expresses thanks for the permission given by ETIG to use the information contained in this snapshot; www.marico.com/abt_marico as last accessed on 14 May 2009.

Marico faces no supply chain issues in soya. There's already a large production base, both domestic as well as international. However, India's consumption of soya in refined oil in consumer packs (ROCP) category is very small, as compared to safflower or sunflower.

Inbound Logistics

In the edible oils supply chain, time is as critical as stocks. The sailing time from Argentina to India is around 4 weeks. 1 week to 10 days for intermediate storage in the port and a further three days to the factory at Jalgaon, Maharashtra. That is a total lead-time of placing the order, 7 days of which are used in just transactions. Here, the major issue lies in tackling vessel demurrage through providing berthing infrastructure.

The Indian Government placed the end-user condition for import of sunflower oils, which means no traders, only companies such as Marico can source oil for their use from overseas. This has reduced the number of buyers drastically, implying that total order quantity is not large enough to merit frequent shipment from Argentina. This results in a gap of 10–12 weeks between two sailings for Mumbai, which means that inventories have to be held here in India to at least hedge over the times between the sailings. Price volatility adds to the murky conditions.

Sea freight also adds to the time and cost dimension. It cost between $36–$42 per tonne (in 2002) to transport sunflower oil from Argentina to Mumbai. From Texas in the US, it would cost between $65–$95 per tonne (as in 2002). These prices vary depending upon the supply and demand for tankers, production, shipping, and urgency of transport. These have to be directly accounted for by Marico as logistics cost.

The moment Marico confirms an order for sunflower oil with a trader in Argentina, its well-oiled machinery swings into action. The processing unit(s), which is normally riverside port ride, pumps the oil directly into the ocean vessels (Fig. 8.19). The tanker sets sail and advance notification goes to the buyer (Marico). This is where the bottlenecks in logistics really start. For starters, the tanker may not get a berth on the day it arrives. Apart from the waiting charges from the first day, the demurrage for the cargo touches $1.5 per tonne per day. To solve this problem, Marico charters barges with tanks to meet the sea tanker in anchorage and transfers the oil to the barges. These barges cost just Rs 150 per tonne (US $3.5).

Outbound Logistics

In the edible oils market, Marico has *Sweekar* and *Saffola* each with two variants. In the health care division, there are a total of 7 SKUs ranging from 0.5 litre to 1.5 litres. It also sources refined oils from other locations, such as Indore (soyabean),

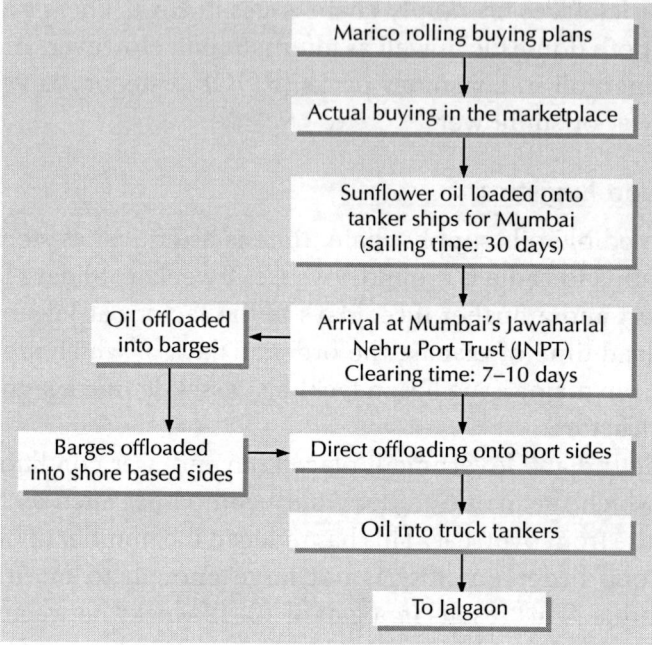

FIG. 8.19 The inbound logistics at Marico

Islampur, Hyderabad, Mumbai and Silvassa mainly for sunflower. Jalgaon handles sunflower, corn, and safflower oil.

At the plants, practice of inventory management is to keep lowest inventory at the stage of manufacturing where value addition is low. The objective is to be prepared to respond quickly to opportunity at a low cost.

Currently, stock levels are 8–9 days at the plants, 7–8 days (at peak season to 25 days at lean season) at the stockist, and around 25 days at the retailers. Marico wants to bring these levels down by 25–30 per cent to 7–10 days at retailers and 7–10 days at stockists. JIT dispatches, stocks at the factory, and better forecasting will do this. That is what Marico management feels.

INDUSTRY SNAPSHOT 22	**Leveraging the logistics** **HINDUSTAN (UNI-) LEVER[22]**

Hindustan (Uni-) Lever Limited (HLL) is India's largest packaged mass consumption goods company. HLL are leaders in home and personal care products, food, and

---

[22] Adapted from *Supply Chain & Logistics*, ETIG, Mumbai, 2002. Excerpts from the AGM speech delivered by M.S. Banga, the then Chairman, HLL on 29 June 2004. The company is now called Hindustan Unilever Ltd.

beverages. On any given day, a normal individual ends up using at least one of the 110 brands which HLL owns. It 'seek to meet everyday needs to people everywhere.' It shares an ethos with its parent company Unilever Ltd, which holds 51 per cent of its equity. HLL has around 7500 distributors, 100 manufacturing units, SKU's varying from 5 ml to around 1 litre, reaching out to 56 distribution locations, and reaching to 1 million retailers across the country. Focus on IT and SCM has become an extremely important part of SCM at HLL or rather HUL now.

Inbound Logistics

Around 40 odd key raw materials and 60 plus finished goods vendors supply to HLL's factories. Overall number of suppliers is around 1000, excluding the overseas vendor for products with deodorants and after-shaves. The company has been able to share an improvement in raw materials inventory—the value of days of raw material inventory fell from 84 days in 1990 to just 29 days of stock in 2000.

Supplier's cost has been very important for HLL. In the mid 90's, it was realized that HLL had too many suppliers for its raw material; some suppliers were doubly supplying. There was a lot of uncertainty regarding vendors, their abilities, and certain plans leading to proliferation of vendors, wherein sometimes up to supplying the same item; hence, it led to more time, cost, and more paperwork. But today, HLL uses only 2 vendors for every item; wherein one vendor supplying the material and the other vendor to be kept for a back-up.

HLL managed to increase these inbound logistics by the use of IT. Initially, there used to be too much time and money spent to know the status of raw material, but not with IT extensively used. The nation-wide SCM is supported by a satellite based communication system, the network offers V&D (voice and data) communication facilities, links over 200 locations all over the country, i.e., head office, branch office, depots, key district stockists, etc. The inbound logistics go like this—there are 240 supply chain locations—wherein all are linked by IT, i.e., VSATs and HLL's ERP system (i.e., MFG/Pro) which works on 220 locations. In order to optimize the supply chain, an Extranet is being created covering key stockists, suppliers, vendors, and purchasers with the aim of achieving real-time vendor-managed inventory (VMI). The vision for HLL is to link in 3000 stockists, 30,000 retailers, and 100 suppliers spread over 1000 locations. For consumer connectivity, HLL has progressed through Pond's interactive website, interactive kiosks for *Lakme* and *Pond's* on the Net, hence forth enabling the consumer to see the product before buying them. Therefore, HLL is trying to be very consumer-centric. VMI is an important aspect of inbound logistics. All the orders which the vendors take will keep tabs on usage and automatically replenish stock, thus factories are near to vendors, i.e., either they have moved towards the factories or are in regular touch through EDI. Forecasting plays an extremely important role due to their large scale of operation and high number of SKU's; information exchange becomes very critical wherein sales information systems will be linked to the retail level. Hence, stock monitoring at PoS is an important feature of HLL and information is exchanged at stockists level—a territory sales incharge (TSI), handles the stockists, he gauges the movement of SKU's, tracks the competition, and exerts pressure on the retailers. The area sales manager brings in corporate strategy in the form of schemes, discounts, etc. and the TSI brings in market feedback. At the end of the day, a sales figure is arrived. This goes to corporate headquarters (CHQ) where planning for production is done. MFG/Pro system throws data area-wise, brand-wise, and retailer-wise.

Outbound Logistics

HLL, now HUL, works on the hub and spoke system wherein hubs are mother depot to regional depots, whereas spokes radiates to stockists, depots, and retailers. But, due to so many brands, a 3-tier system for stocking and order replenishment is set up.

- Tier 1, the company has an all-India buffer depot
- Tier 2, the company has regional depots
- Tier 3, the company has JIT depots, i.e., for just-in-time deliveries

The product is supplied on JIT basis to stockists, who in turn sell to retailers and finally consumers. For the level, only those slow moving goods that require 2 days of travel are part of this buffer depot; and then products are accumulated up to a full truck load goods and are sent to regional buffer depot. Smaller lots are sent to JIT godowns. For the second level, products are received from all India buffer depot and factories directly. From these, stocks are then transferred to stockists (Fig. 8.20). The RDCs stock up to 4 weeks of stocks and are replenished daily, and transferred to clearing and forwarding agents (C&FA). In fact, for finished goods C&FAs hold 10 days stock and the retailer 7 days. The stockists collect orders from retailers and take them to JIT depot. The ownership is transferred at the stockist level. The number of C&FAs has gone from 47 to 65 to 2000. HLL found that owned depots cost much more than outsourcing to C&FAs.

This MFG/PRO ERP system has linked up 700 stockists to reduce cost, i.e., to feed orders straightaway into terminals at their locations, and are instantly transmitted to the branch office. This helps to reduce uncertainities in the system for production and sales.

Also, they can control inventory in replenishment, i.e., SKUs would go from the manufacturing site to the C&FA and then market, but HLL wants to design a system for every SKU to bypass regional and JIT depots and go to stockists at line.

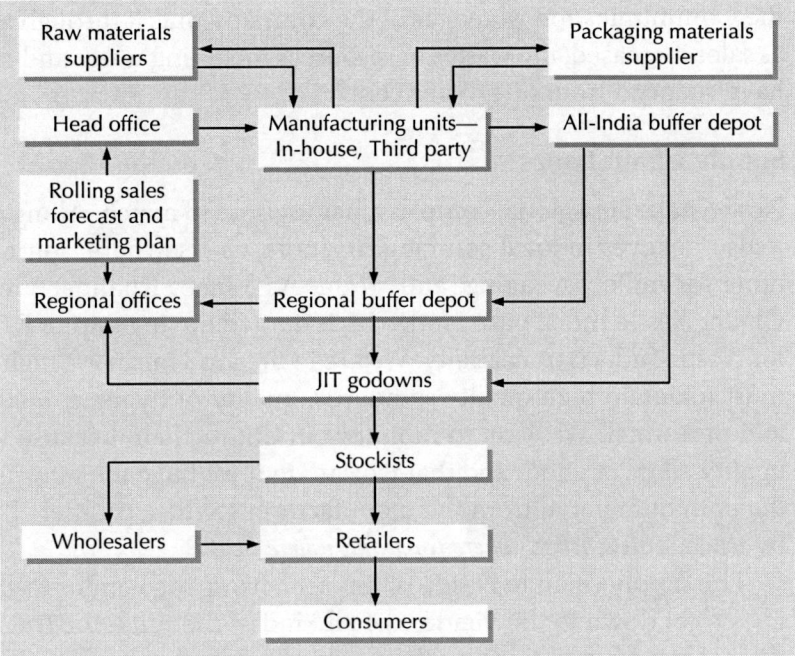

FIG. 8.20 Connectivity in outbound logistics and distribution at HLL, now HUL
Source: Supply Chain & Logistics, 2002, ETIG, Mumbai

INDUSTRY SNAPSHOT 23	Nestling the supply chain elements of perishables NESTLE INDIA[23]

Nestle is the world's largest food company with more than 2,24,541 people in 479 factories around the world. Nestle India, the Indian subsidiary, had sales of Rs 4324 crore up 23.4 per cent from 2007. The export sales amounted to Rs 338 crore. The company reported growth in turnover and volume successively for third year in 2008. Net profits also grew up by 26.3 per cent. As the company's press release dated 6 March 2009 puts it, the company implemented the mini business unit concept throughout the corporate to increase teamwork and deliver superior performance. The company also claimed to have taken international best practices to frontline, engaged every employee, ensured business focus, and goal alignment. It also encouraged innovation and renovation for continuous improvement in quality, speed, safety, environmental sustainability, and cost effectiveness. As Himesh Manglik,

---

[23] Based on a survey by ETIG, Mumbai, 2002; interviews with Nestle executives; www.nestle.in/ press release dated 6 March 2009.

the Communication Manager of the company puts it through a press release, 'Even as sales increased, the wastes of resources including water and energy and emissions have reduced from 60–70 per cent.'

Supply Chain Issues

Nestle, as befits a global company, has logistics to match. Along with global sourcing, it also believes in local sourcing. In India, as elsewhere, sourcing is mostly locally done for milk, packaging, and so on. As Vineet Khanna, Vice President, Supply Chain, Nestle India, based in Delhi, is quoted having said to ETIG, 'The main issue for Nestle India is traceability. We are in the food business, high quality food and we must maintain high quality standards, quality of hygiene, quality of edible inputs, and personnel. We want to monitor our entire chain because we want to maintain quality all throughout and that we can do if we have the information, and can trace the path of material from the manufacturer to the customer. This is what we mean by traceability; from *where from and where to.*

The supply chain in Nestle is thus seen from 'the vendor-to-the-customer'. Nestle goes right down to the vendors of all kinds—the milk, the truckers, the cold chain, the packaging, and packing the work. 'The challenges in order fulfilment in India involve transport quality, transit time, retail structures, and costs involved. The external supply chain cannot be controlled fully,' says Mr Khanna, to the ETIG, continuing, 'we can control internal process and supply quality hoping that it all translates into better supply chain management.'

Inbound Logistics

Nestle India's inbound supply chain is similar to most companies in the business—using tankers, collections, and so on to bring the milk to the plants. Nestle has a plant at Moga, Punjab set up in 1962 which processes 8 lakh litres of milk collected from 71,000 farmers everyday. But to be near to customers, Nestle may have to set more plants, say, at district level.

The VP further says, 'we use material requirements planning (MRP) and ERP for internal planning and processes but our follow-ups with vendors still remain on phone, fax, and e-mail. Some share data, some don't.'

Outbound Logistics

In India, Nestle has too many intermediaries on the retail, as well as the vendor side, which adds time and cost and badly impacts quality. The demand signals are constantly changing and the company has to fulfil the signalled need.

According to most Nestle executives, feedback about promotions, sales, volumes, and prices hardly comes from retailers in India, unlike in the West and US. They claim, it is collected by only Nestle's staff and the data is limited by sheer size and complexity of the Indian market. It is in this context, Nestle feels that initiatives, such as ERP, SCM software, and efficient customer response (ECR) would help. Says the VP, 'The longer the supply chain, the weaker the demand signal becomes.' The demand signal is ever-changing. More important is to acknowledge and act on it. There is an order signal and there is a sales signal. Both must be synchronized. In Nestle India, the demand plan using statistical tools and sales is first prepared then broken down into a stock data—where and when to hold—followed by its broken down into material plan which is handed over to different vendors. For important materials, such as cocoa and coffee, stock norms could be 1 month stock or price-based. If prices go down stock is up or if prices rise, only safety stock is maintained.

Milk is brought in daily. The finished goods move by trucks, containerized trucks and Concor (rail) to far off areas. Nestle spent around Rs 87 crore in freight in 2000. The spend on freight has remained well in control at around *5.4 per cent of net sales*, inspite of increase in sales in last few years. Nestle has also used ice packs in vans, and container trucks. However, it needs to create a *cold chain* unlike Amul who leverages its use for ice creams. Nestle however, does not want to foray into ice cream market due to heavy investments required. There is not enough IT-enablement of perishable food supply chain in India. ECR is taking off in India. However, the company has good experiences in implementation and usage of the Net and e-commerce for its supply chains. It gives focus on issues like *human bridges* and *process champions* to underline the importance it places on its staff. In a recent survey, Nestle discovered that 45 per cent of order-errors problems were attributed to partners' processes, 36 per cent to non-aligned systems, and 19 per cent to incomplete data and poor communication. The solution lies, Nestle feels, in setting up coherent information architecture—which would include personalizing the methods, searching and classifying data, managing content, and validating information and data sources. The company feels new electronic links will prove their worth when they can significantly reduce cycle times, result in error-free information flows, and provide real-time status of orders. The end purpose would be to make available complete information at the touch of a single button. Nestle is likely to retain its legacy EDI infrastructure, but strongly believes in benefits of e-commerce in laws of reducing inventory resulting from collaborative forecasting with suppliers and customers. The company wants to move to a consumer-based, push-production system. According to Tahira Hasan, the then Executive VP, Consumer Demand Chain and Information Services, Nestle Canada Inc., for success in SCM, it is needed to integrate 'common sense' approach with 'e-sense'. However, the company does not think ambitiously about 3PLs on the outbound logistics side.

Packaging

The company has innovative packing systems. The milk available in tetrapacks gives more shelf life up to six months and more sales to the product.

Customer Orientation

At Nestle, the consumer demand chain involves the entire business, including people and processes, as well as managing the links between them. The term consumer demand chain was chosen to reflect the central role of the end users as the key component of the markets that Nestle serves. Surrounding it is the information chain with its duties for creating and sourcing data, converting it to knowledge to be integrated with the various divisions of the company, so that they can develop a 'go to market' strategy. That approach involves all aspects of external commercial interactive with consumers, customers, and suppliers. It would involve physical product flow as well as an information chain. E-commerce, be it B2B or B2C, would serve as an enabler for this approach.

| **INDUSTRY** | **Revving up the inventory turnover** |
| **SNAPSHOT 24** | **REVLON**[24] |

Revlon is a leading global manufacturer and marketer of cosmetics, skin care, fragrance, and personal care products. After several years of steady decreases in supply chain inventory, the company hit a plateau. A breakthrough change was needed and in 2003 the company called on Deloitte Consulting LLP for help. Without any new investments in technology, the transformation team designed a business model that significantly reduced inventory in the first year, and promises to repeat that performance in the years to come.

Revlon's manufacturing plants are at Edison, N.J., Phoenix, Oxford, and N.C. The company consolidated all manufacturing into Oxford.

Revlon has a major distribution centre in Oxford and is associated with their main plant. They have a *satellite DC* in Phoenix. The company found that it is easier and more economical and efficient for them to ship full truckloads out there and then distribute from Phoenix to the West Coast States. They purchase a significant

---

[24] Conversation of Murphy Jean V. with Dave Laverty, VP, Revlon Consumer Products Corp. on supplychainbrain.com/archives/10.04.exclusive, as accessed on 26 December 2008. Some information has been taken from Davis Don, Buckler Jim and Missoumelli Adam and Dan Krinzler, 'Inventory Transformation Revlon Style: A People and Process Approach', *SCM Review*, 1 July 2005.

amount of direct materials a year, and others have had various efficiency programmes targeted at that piece of the business over the last couple of years.

They were very successful at getting into strategic sourcing and really bringing the cost of their purchases down significantly. Therefore, the logical place for them to go was the next largest bucket of cash, which was inventory. For several years in a row, the organization had been reducing their inventory at a rate of 6 per cent to 7 per cent a year. Hence, the inventory as a per cent of gross sales leveled out.

For Revlon, the primary system is basically an Oracle platform onto which the company attached some of its own legacy systems, such as their warehouse management system. The material requirements planning (MRP) and the cost system is *Oracle*-based. Revlon started attacking their processes with the forecast and demand planning group. The forecast should be as accurate as it can be, because the plant will not build the product unless it is in the forecast. The demand-planning tool that Revlon is using is *Manugistic*.

For example, they split the forecast over a month evenly, 25 per cent for each week, but Revlon switched from a *roll forward* methodology to a *consume* methodology when they actualize the demand against this weekly split. They also plan key SKUs—the top driving SKUs on a weekly basis vs once a month.

They also had a separate lean initiative happening at the same time on the manufacturing floor. Where the company knew that they would be going to *shorter lot sizes*, they used the efforts of the lean manufacturing group to focus on those areas, so they could work at speeding up the changeover time. One fed into the other.

Revlon plant is broken down into *cost centres*. Running a mascara product is very different than running a lipstick, which is very different than running a liquid make up. Their business models and savings model were based on the way the cost centres are aligned.

Make up is a high dollar product. Lipstick has a low dollar value but the company does a higher volume. Both are really critical areas. With make up, the company makes a significant impact from an inventory reduction perspective. With lipstick, Revlon has a lot of shades, so it is a difficult area.

Of Revlon's orders, approximately 60 per cent are received directly from customers who employ the use of EDI order processing functions in their computer systems, and approximately 30 per cent are electronically received by Revlon representatives who visit customer stores and other retail outlets, such as pharmacies. The remaining 10 per cent are received from various order entry methods, such as paper-based order forms and orders received by phone.

In processing an order, an electronic picking list is transmitted to an *Intermec 2415* wireless handheld data collection terminal. Then an *EAN SSCC (Serial Shipping Container Code)* label is generated and subsequently placed on the shipping carton.

The labeled carton is then taken by the order picker and filled with products as specified on the *Intermac 2415* wireless RF terminal. The items are also scanned. After the carton has been filled, the outer carton EAN SSCC label is scanned, thereby enabling the carton to be directed to the appropriate dispatch area.

The bar code scanning enables the details of the contents of a carton to be recorded on Revlon's computer system and forwarded to the customer. Upon delivery the customer scans the SSCC carton label and confirms delivery of goods into the computer system for shipping/receiving verification.

Gamma Solutions in partnership with *Intermec,* were able to provide all of these benefits to Revlon. This has proven to be a sophisticated supply chain concept that covers the scope of customers ordering via EDI through to customers scanning outer labels on receipt of goods followed by delivery verification.

INDUSTRY SNAPSHOT 25	**Trimming the supply chain through lean manufacturing** **TOYOTA KIRLOSKAR MOTOR INDIA**[25]

Toyota Kirloskar Motor India is a joint venture between Toyota Motor Corporation (TMC) and Kirloskar Group, and is currently into manufacturing Toyota Innova after Toyota Qualis in India. It has adopted the practices of Toyota Production System (TPS) in India.

Inbound and Outbound Logistics

Toyota Kirloskar's Indian operations are fairly small, but the concept of TPS and logistics are equivalent to any of its global plants. In India, it has more than 2800 parts suppliers, 56 component suppliers, and about 10 direct material suppliers from the local market. Its raw material inventory in case of local steel is about 1 month, in case of imported steel 1.5 months; 2 days inventory for parts and for other consumables, a maximum of 10 days.

The JIT delivery period rates vary according to the destination from where materials are received. Toyota runs its *chorokyo* (high frequency deliveries) from Delhi, Chennai, Pune, and Mumbai where supplies are once in a day. For Bangalore suppliers, it is twice in a day, and for local suppliers every 2 hours. For sourcing its inbound materials, Toyota is using Logistics, a third party provider (3PL)—a JV between Mitsui of Japan and TCI of India.

---

[25] The author expresses acknowledgement to Economic Times Intelligence Group (ETIG), Mumbai, for giving permission to use the information contained in this snapshot; www.pressroom.toyota.com as accessed on 14 May 2010.

See Annexure III to this case detailing the TPS principles.

Toyota has developed an exclusive dealer network with 29 dealers in 24 major cities.

In-plant Operations

At present, the number of components for assembling the vehicle are 925 local parts and 850 imported parts from Japan, Thailand, Taiwan, Phillipines, and Indonesia. The production area is controlled by the central control room—daily plans are monitored, flow charts are made by the production department themselves as per product information from the TMC. Continuous improvement (*Kaizen*) activities are done throughout the plant at all levels.

Inventory Management

JIT inventory management is only a part of TPS. They have built local factors into the system—vendors located between 1 to 100 km from Bangalore follow TPS practices, such as *Kanban*, milk run, and *Jumbiki* (synchronized supply).

Toyota has introduced the *kanban* system to produce materials from suppliers. The system works on the pull basis, and the inventory is controlled as per material usage, safety stocks also being maintained as these are considered while designing the system. The material flow using *Kanban* is shown in Fig. 8.21.

Information Technology

Toyota has a system of *Coma Board* that tracks the vehicles right from the chassis to the final product. It is used as a visual control board for controlling the production of the vehicle and the live status of the shop floor. It follows the basic production line layout and the major communication points. Each vehicle is represented through a rectangular block or 'coma' on the board which has specific details of the vehicle. The coma is moved on the board based on online information received from production about the position of vehicle in the line. All abnormalities and delays are relayed to the controlling person.

The production stock volume has been brought down from 18 hours to 8 hours. The target is 4 hours. Inventory of tyres is kept for 3 days while shipment of engines is 3–5 days. According to Mr K.K. Swamy, the then Deputy Managing Director, the

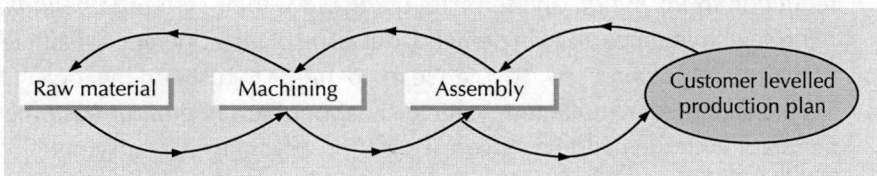

FIG. 8.21   The *Kanban* flows in TPS (Toyota Production System)

effective inventory build-up of the plant is worth only 1 day of production. The vendors are located between 1 km to 1000 kms from Bangalore and these follow TPS practices (as given in annexure to this snapshot), such as *kanban*, milk run, and *jumbiki* (synchronized supply). Toyota India, like its other Toyota counterparts, is trying to use specially designed trucks and a two-hourly clockwise schedule for parts delivery. Although a detailed account of planning and forecasting is done, it still prefers to stock some additional parts because of geographical distances of vendors and transportation time.

Annexure III

Toyota's Operations in United States

Toyota Motor Corporation

The group's principal activities are to manufacture and sell automobiles, and provide financial services. The group operates through three segments—automotive, financial services and other. Automotive segment designs, manufactures, assembles and sells passenger cars, recreational and sport utility vehicles, minivans and trucks, and related parts and accessories. Financial services segment provides financing to dealers and their customers for the purchase or lease of Toyota vehicles. Other services segment provides intelligent transport systems, information technology-based systems encompassing car multimedia systems, on-board intelligent systems, advanced transportation systems, and transportation infrastructure and logistics systems. The group markets vehicles in more than 170 countries.

Japanese automotive suppliers—especially Toyota—built their worldwide leadership based on their competitive advantage across their supply chain. Yet, research efforts to define concrete lessons learned often confront the baffling nuances of the Japanese culture, as well as persistent uncertainty regarding how much and how well native Japanese practices might transfer to other cultures. Until now, that is based on a recent research of 39 US-based operations that have established a significant competitive advantage across the supply chain for both quality and productivity.

Internal Structure

One organization that has successfully implanted a consumer-to-consumer (C2C) system is Japanese automaker Toyota. Its operational success is often attributed to the focus on reduction in inventory. The term Toyota uses for their system is *heijunka*. In particular, it refers to eliminating spikes in demand, but also creating operational efficiency and reducing overall supply chain costs. Toyota's lean operation focuses on the idea of buy one, sell one. Toyota is able to manufacture vehicles in about the same order customers buy them. This adaptability to demand has given Toyota the advantage of carrying the least inventory in the field of Japanese auto manufactures.

Working with Suppliers

This concept is one that Toyota uses internally and it also requires of its suppliers to improve the overall C2C cycle. In the North American auto supply market, suppliers working with Japanese-owned automakers perform at higher levels than those working with US automakers. Toyota works with US suppliers to teach them the lean manufacturing techniques used in Toyota's manufacturing facilities. These techniques ensure a short amount of time between when Toyota needs an item and when the supplier makes it.

Using small batch production, this short lead-time can be achieved. Rather than running large batches and keeping excess inventory, plants quickly run a small batch and keep inventory low. For Toyota, this translates to being able to better meet customers demands because manufacturing facilities do not have to wait on a particular part before beginning production on a vehicle.

Benefits of *Heijunka**

Toyota's improvement initiatives in its production levelling system and supply chain have benefitted the automaker in more than one way:

- Inventory levels at parts distribution centres have decreased by 53 per cent from stocking levels in the 1980s.
- Since 1994, the inventory turn of parts in the average dealership has increased form 3.7 to 5.7.
- Toyota dealerships have achieved 20 per cent to 40 per cent reductions in floor space utilization.

The time spent in improving the systems of US suppliers has shown results as well.

- From 1997 to 2000 alone, suppliers' on time delivery increased from 76 per cent to 93 per cent.
- 66 per cent of suppliers on daily order status were able to deliver within five days or less.

While inventory management is an effective way to reduce the C2C cycle, it not only requires efficient manufacturing through initiatives like lean manufacturing through TPS but also effective forecasting.

Main Features of Toyota Production System (TPS)

The TPS provides for the following features.

- Greater product variety
- Fast response (flexibility)
- 'Stable' production schedules
- Supply chain integration
- Demand management

---

* *Heizunka* is a Japanese word meaning 'make flat and level', referring to production smoothing or levelling followed for waste reduction (*muda*), e.g., in a Toyota Production Sysyem (TPS). The purpose is to produce the finished product at a constant rate in a mixed model production flow sysyem.

Purchasing Strategy at Toyota

Toyota has the following strategic thinking world as far as the purchasing and supplies are concerned.

- It buys cheapest supplies in the world.
- It supports purchasing with dual sourcing.
- It buys to achieve the lowest total cost.
- It buys in the manufacturing country.
- It minimizes the number of suppliers.
- It keeps the supply chain as short as possible.
- It thinks itself as strong as its weakest supplier.

Toyota Logistics Services (TLS) in USA

TLS manages Toyota's in-house vehicle transportation trucking company, which delivers vehicles in nine western states. It is responsible for inbound vehicle logistics for Mexico, and US exports of vehicles to 34 countries worldwide. It has partnerships with eight North American Class I railroads, 12 trucking companies, 10 ocean carriers, and 4200 routes. The subsidiary is wholly owned by Toyota Motor Sales US, the United States' sales arm of Toyota Motor Corp. in Japan. It manages 11 vehicle distribution centres in USA and two in Canada.

'Our goal is to get the right product to the right location at the right time,' said Jim Martin, Logistics General Manager, Toyota Logistics Services.

Toyota places a transport operation wherever it locates major manufacturing or import operations.

Toyota Logistics has been around since the first Toyotas came into the United States in 1959, making it the oldest Toyota subsidiary in this country. Its facilities are in Princeton, Ind., Georgetown, Fremont, California, and the port cities of Long Beach, California, Portland, Ore., and Newark, N.J. The logistics operation employs 1250 nationwide.

'We've also added the flexibility to do last-minute accessory work to tailor the vehicles to the needs of individual customers,' said Steve Magee, a production manager. 'By handling this at Logistics, we can make sure you get your bed linen or your alarm system at a consistent quality and price, anywhere in the country,' Magee said.

Toyota Logistics conducts what Martin calls *accessorization* to the new Tundra trucks. 'This includes adding to vehicles several features ordered by dealers and customers, including bed liners, running boards, alarms and compact disc players,' Martin said.

Most automakers leave installation of such equipment to dealers, where the competence of the installer, as well as the price can vary.

After the Tundras are fully equipped, Logistics sends them through another line for a final quality check. There, digital clocks are set, warranty booklets are placed, and price stickers are pasted before the trucks go to shipping lots.

About 85 per cent of the vehicles leave Princeton, Ind., by rail. The rest are shipped via car-hauling trucks. Rail, Martin said, is preferred because it is cheaper over long distances. The trains take the trucks to 15 rail distribution points around the country, where they are picked up and transported to dealers by car-hauling trailers.

| INDUSTRY SNAPSHOT 26 | Fine-tuning servicing, logistics, and material planning FORD MOTOR INDIA[26] |

Ford is combining its international experience with extensive study of the local environment to implement logistics and SCM practices in the Indian scenario. Ford has a plant in India at Chengalpattu, Tamil Nadu installed for the manufacturing of 'Ikon'. The major factor in selecting the location was infrastructure in terms of telecom facilities, highway network, proximity to airport and sea, according to their General Manager, Sales.

Sourcing

Ford has brought the concept of a *suppliers' park* like Hyundai around its factory to ensure regular and quicker supplies.

70 per cent of the content is provided by Indian suppliers—for conventional items, there was already a base, so these components are supplied from India. These are tyres, seats, wheels, and so on. The most critical assembly, the engine is imported from South Africa. Ford has a worldwide sourcing policy under which its supply base has to have full service capability, i.e., the supplier must have expertise in a whole gamut of activities ranging from designing to delivery of the product, consistency of quality, and other competitive costs. Ford's supplier quality assurance (SQA) plans are a benchmark in themselves.

A *Supplier Technical Assistance (STA)* group has been formed to develop a practice of partnership. Around 75 per cent of the local supply base is situated within 50 kms of the plant.

Ford's suppliers' park near its factory houses vendors of some of the critical parts that are sourced daily. For example, Tata Johnson Controls supplies 48 seats at a time and on need basis, ensuring that there is no excess inventory at Fords. It is also able to do this because the set-up is in its suppliers' park. Some of the key figures are tabulated in Table 8.2.

Inbound Logistics

Inbound logistics are handled by TVS Lead Logistics (3PL). It handles logistics, plant warehouse management, and operation of packing items. For its 83 local suppliers, materials are consolidated at 4 hubs located at—Delhi, Pune, Daman, and Chennai.

---

[26] Adapted from ETIG's survey on Supply Chain and Logistics, 2002, with permission. The author expresses due acknowledgement to ETIG.

TABLE 8.2 Key figures in Ford's suppliers' park

Total parts required	1400
Locally sourced parts	770
Park suppliers contribution	21%
Percentage of suppliers within 5 kms	25%
Percentage of suppliers within 50 kms	75%
Time taken for procurement in Australia	2 hours
Time taken for procurement in India	5 hours
Ford's plant vehicle scheduling cycle	44 days

Majority of the components are sourced through milk runs by TVS Lead Logistics. JIT deliveries are, however, restricted to components that are housed in the suppliers' park.

Ford has a weekly production schedule which helps in meeting any increase in production volumes at short notices. It gives the flexibility to meet changes in the product mix in line with market conditions and demand. It also helps in exercising better control on inventories and communicating production schedule at frequent intervals, which in turn facilitates suppliers to fine tune their raw material procuring and production planning in line with the latest production plans (Fig. 8.22).

A large part of the equipment components, such as the bumpers and seats arrive in sequence directly onto the line from the suppliers' park. The line stock keeps to a maximum of 2 hours to minimize the amount of inventory on the shop floor. The 'SMART' system which supplies materials to the line performs the function of a two-bin card. This system supplies materials to the line. Ford has a computerized vehicle scheduling system (VSS) that ensures that the right parts are ordered at the right place at the right time.

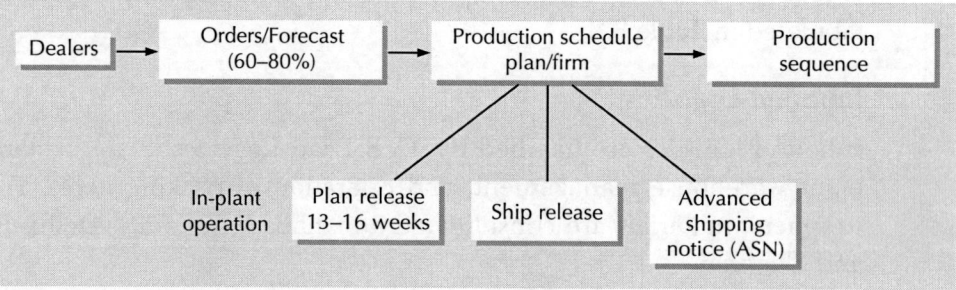

FIG. 8.22 Flexible production planning at Ford Motor
Source: Ford Motor India; Courtesy: ETIG

Outbound Logistics

Ford has 32 dealers who are spread throughout the country. Outsourcing of outbound logistics allows Ford to focus on its core competence of manufacturing. Ford was the first Indian automotive company to add its name to that of the dealers.

'Absolute Logistics' is the sole third-party logistics service provider (3PL) for Ford's outbound distribution of vehicles to 32 dealers in the country. Ford India is one of the few automobile companies to have a 3PL for outbound logistics.

The advantages of a third-party provider in outbound are—it saves on manpower and one can leverage on scalability, besides claiming of insurance in case of damages is centred on one's head.

Inventory holding   Its raw material holding period has fallen from 31 days to 21 in one year. However, it is the finished goods (FG) inventory which has increased by two days from 6 to 8 days. Work-in-process (WIP) inventory amounts to 3–5 days.

Information Technology

Ford India has been using IT for global sourcing of its engines and some parts. General Internet integrated system (GIIS), which the company has been using as a legacy system of 35 years globally, is linked to the supplier base. Instant response is guaranteed to all suppliers linked both to Ford and with each other through the Internet. The system of material planning and logistics (MP&L), which the company uses can show daily production figures, schedule, stock levels and amount of stock held at the plant. Common material management system, called CMMS is followed in 183 Ford plants worldwide.

The use of a single material management system offers several advantages, such as production and delivery planning at Ford plants worldwide that supply material in India that are integrated with its production plan, and any customization or upgradation done is available to all the user plants. The management team of CMMS has identified around a dozen plant measurables (PMs) which demonstrate the material management output at plants through a daily rating and ranking. Some of these deliverables are in the system data integrity (stocks accuracy) accuracy in customer schedules, schedules vs suppliers accuracy of transactions and electronic data linkage with suppliers, and so on. According to the General Manager Systems, Ford India, Ford's global sourcing policy is a case in material planning. Ford uses a common ERP system which helps in measuring the performance of each plant and to generate a competition amongst them leading to continuous improvement. The system was able to make projections of 4 months and planning cycle for 6 months. Its body plant stood first among all the global body and stamping plants.

Revamping IT Architecture for SCM and CRM
HERO HONDA[27]

'Fill it-Shut it-Forget it', that's the mantra of Hero Honda Motors Limited, the world's largest two wheeler company whose 20 million bikes tread the Indian roads today. To maintain the competitive edge, it has a distribution network spanning 700 nodes. This includes the Head Office (HO), two manufacturing plants at Dharuhera and Gurgaon (and now a new third one at Haridwar in Uttarakhand), and 20 marketing offices nationwide. It has around 3000 customer touch points. Its plants have capacity to manufacture 4.4 million units per year. The company reported an impressive sale of Rs 3202 crore just in second quarter of 2008–09 with profit after tax (PAT) of Rs 306.30 crore registering a growth of 50 per cent for the corresponding period last fiscal year. The company claims itself to be in 'unassailable' position in two-wheeler market in its sales performance reports posted on its website for media.

The company has a strong CRM in place and won the coveted Best Customer Loyalty Award (Automotive) and the Customer Brand Loyalty awards at the Loyalty Summit, 2008. It has a unique Hero Honda Passport Programme for CRM.

Need to Fine-tune IT Network

Hero Honda felt the need to consolidate disparate applications that once ran on different departmental servers by implementing SAP. It has also reworked its server architecture to provide dedicated platforms for applications, storage, mail, back-up and database management. In order to get a hold over its diverse operations, the company felt it necessary to deploy new applications, such as *Oracle* and *Ingres*. These rational databases helped the company consolidate data at one place and make it accessible to an authorized user.

These new entities demanded higher throughput and better scalability. The legacy LAN had a high failure rate and it was difficult to isolate and rectify a problem that had its origin in various segments. The legacy TDMA-based WAN, which was a shared network, had the tendency to get congested as new users were added.

In order to facilitate large bandwidth applications efficiently across the LAN, S.R. Balasubramanium, CIO, Hero Honda, decided to strengthen the existing server infrastructure first. The company deployed IBM RS/6000 midrange servers for running *Ingres* and *Oracle,* Lotus Notes was used to manage mail and messaging, and it was run on IBM's Netfinity servers. A 10/100 Mbps switched network was soon

---

[27] Largely based on the article by Sautiman Dasgupta, 'Revved up Server Architecture', posted on www.networkmagazineindia.com/200210/case6.shtml as accessed on 20 January 2009.

deployed and fibre was installed at all the critical segments. The HO and two plants at Gurgaon and Dharuhera were connected with secure leased links and radio links.

Enterprise Applications

The next move was to implement an ERP in order to consolidate various departmental servers performing diverse functions, such as accounting, inventory management, and so on.

SAP R/3 Release 4.6B was implemented to control its operations. The company went live with SAP in February 2001. It used modules, such as production planning, materials management, quality management, and sales and distribution.

SAP provided numerous benefits. It presented a high-level of data integration and enabled common master sheets that can be used across various functions, such as transaction, validation, accounting, and reporting. There were improvements in the quality, access, and usage of transactional data. It suitably eliminated multiple entries and there was no need for manual reconciliation.

Hero Honda was now able to implement better cost control measures, e.g., the ERP made it possible to calculate cost of consummables, tool inventory cost, power and fuel costs, and plant overheads. It also readied the organization for adoption of supply chain management (SCM) and customer relationship management (CRM) implementation.

World of Servers

To strengthen the server architecture, Mr Balasubramanium , CIO decided to stick to a single server vendor, IBM. 'This allows us to get a complete range of products and services under one roof. We can communicate with a single point of contact for services and complaints. The vendor treats us as a preferred customer and honours its commitments,' said the CIO, as quoted by *Network Magazine.*

Hero Honda uses separate servers for running applications, databases, mail and messaging, network management, development, testing, and production. IBM's RS/6000 SP servers are used for most SAP applications. The servers have various hardware and software configurations to provide optimum performance.

'The RS/6000 is a very reliable and scalable system. IBM AIX which is shipped with the boxes also performs very well. We have used IBM's servers in the past and are quite satisfied with them,' said Balasubramanium. The Web servers are, however, outsourced.

Sprucing up the Network

Hero Honda's network connects two manufacturing plants in Gurgaon and Dharuhera (Haryana), the HO in New Delhi and 20 marketing offices all over India. A mix of VSAT links, leased lines, Frame Relay links, and dial-ups interconnect these offices.

'The company's LANs at various locations are now completely structured and switch efficiently. They use 10/100 Mbps Ethernet technology for data transmission and are connected with Cat 5 cables so that it can support bandwidth requirements for the next few years. There are rare instances of network breakdown and we haven't had any major failures in the last three years,' said Balasubramanium.

The Gurgaon plant has two Cisco 2610 routers (that connect to the HO in New Delhi through a 2 Mbps line with a back-up and the plant in Dharuhera.) that are connected to an IBM LAN Route Switch. A large set-up of servers, storage boxes, back-up devices, and workstations are connected to the switch. The Dharuhera plant connects with the Gurgaon plant through a radio frequency (RF) link. There is also a back-up VSAT permanently assigned multiple access (PAMA) link provided by Comsat Max. At the HO, a range of devices handle back-up, mail, bridging, firewall, modem, remote access server (RAS), and mail gateway functions.

Planning for Adoption of SCM and CRM

The company planned in 2002 to implement the human resources and production management modules of SAP. It also planned to implement CRM and SCM applications to connect and manage its dealers and vendors. Hero Honda initially in late 2002 was connected to the public network only for mail management applications. The need was to have more secure networks.

'To address the current security needs we have constructed a basic level of protection using firewalls and point-to-point links. A comprehensive security policy is under evaluation to address the new security concerns that will come up after the CRM and SCM initiative. And we will implement the policy before we connect to the outside world. Although we have allocated sufficient bandwidth for the WAN connectivity across all critical locations, more bandwidth is always useful. Unfortunately public networks today are not very reliable and don't provide adequate bandwidth,' Balasubramanium said in interview to the *Network Magazine*.

There are also plans to move from the copper leased lines to optical fibre leased lines. 'This would enable us to move towards a faster and more error-free network,' said Balasubramanium.

Service-oriented architecture (SOA) adds further bite to the SCM system particularly in manufacturing companies where manufacturing and logistics go hand in hand. The need to integrate internal applications with those outside the company, i.e., the customers and business partners is the primary driver for SOA adoption. Says Vijay Sethi, VP, IT in Hero Honda as quoted in *PCquest*, 'We have SAP as a backbone of automation in the company. The need for middleware is not very high. We have bar coding of critical components on the shop floor which helps in tracking the components throughout the factory. There are bar code scanners at different stations and SAP records are updated. However, the company felt the need to connect logistics vendors to the company's system to reduce turnaround time in deliveries. The company deployed SAP XI that helps in cross-vendor system connectivity and is a step towards having an SOA. The result is, the entire supply chain is automated, having good linkages with both—suppliers and dealers for our bikes.'

Unique CRM Initiative

The company has a unique *Hero Honda Passport Programme* for maintaining customer database in which now there are 3 million members, one of the largest programmes in the world. The programme has not only helped Hero Honda to understand the customers, but also deliver value at different price points and create a loyal community of brand ambassadors for the company.

Related Resources

Article by Adeesh Sharma, Jasmine Desai, and Vishnu Anand, 'How to Become a World Class Manufacturer', posted on www.pcquest.ciol as accessed on 20 January 2009; www.herohonda.com/media_sales_performance.asp#104 as accessed on 13 May 2009.

INDUSTRY SNAPSHOT 28	**Automating purchase, replenishment, warehouse, and inventory management SHOPPERS STOP**[28]

Shoppers Stop is the first company in the retail sector in India to implement professional practices and systems to manage supply chain and logistics. It set up its first shop in 1991 in Andheri, Mumbai. In the beginning of 2000, it had 15 stores and turnover of Rs 127 crore. It is the first retailer in Asia to implement ERP. It won the Nasscom award for best practices in IT in retail.

The supply chain at Shoppers Stop covers three facets of objectives.

- Customer
- Partner
- Organization

Customer Objectives

The system should ensure that

- customer always gets the merchandize of his/her size and choice

---

[28] Adapted from ETIG, Supply Chain and Logistics study, 2005. The author expresses due acknowledgement to the sources; www.shoppersstop.com

- merchandize is always presentable and ready before customer entry
- customer easily locates price tags and product information
- price on the price tag and point of sale (PoS) system always match
- timely replenishment of fast moving merchandise is done by the store

Supply Partner Objectives

The system should ensure that

- supply partners always deliver the right quantities as per schedule
- supply partners are always paid as per credit terms
- information related to sales, stocks, and purchase orders is regularly shared with supply partners

Organization Objectives

The system should aim to minimize the following.

- Customer response time
- Distribution cost
- Shrinkage

The system should also aim to maximize the following.

- Efficiency of executive time
- Collaboration with partners' and merchandise availability

Supply Chain Systems at Shoppers Stop

In 1999, Shoppers Stop implemented the ERP—J D Armstrong—a merchandise management system (MMS), well ahead of time. The capabilities of the system were developed to tackle

- Ensuring turnaround time of 4 days
- Poor hit rate from partners
- Difficulty in tracking merchandise
- Non-sharing of inventory data with partners
- High distribution cost
- High inventory
- High shrinkage (lost/theft/obsolescence)
- Shutting down all operations for 48 hours for annual stock taking
- High variance between book stock and physical stock
- Inefficient use of executive time

The interconnectivity of systems with logistics and supply partners at Shoppers Stop is represented as given in Fig. 8.23.

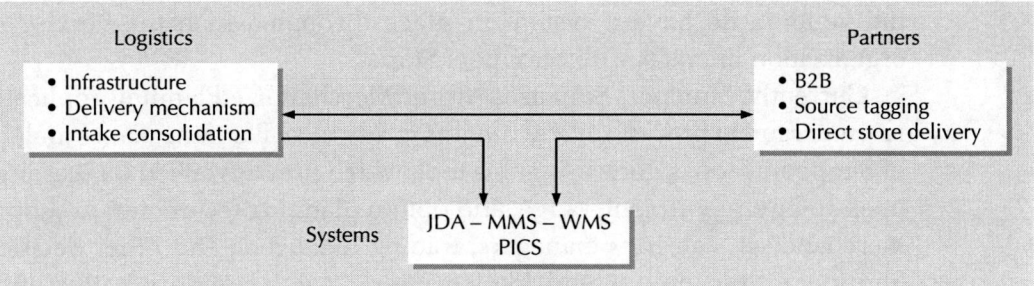

FIG. 8.23 The systems interconnectivity at Shoppers Stop

Shopper's Stop also implemented the perpetual inventory control system (PICS) and is the first retailer in Asia to implement the state-of-the-art ERP system.

The merchandise management system (MMS) is an end-to-end solution for managing merchandise throughout the chain right from purchase orders, to sales, to replenishment, to markdown, and inventory management. It is an integrated online system connected with the back-end, front-end (stores), and the distribution centres. The other features of this system are the following.

Auto-purchase Ordering
It maintains a predetermined level of minimum stocks for core styles at the DC. Any drop in the level generates an auto purchase order to the vendor.

Auto-replenishment
There are predetermined levels of minimum stocks for core styles at each store. Drop in level generates an auto-replenishment command at SKU level to the concerned distribution centre. The system allows daily auto replenishment to all 15 stores.

Implementing this system has allowed the company to reduce its shrinkage (lost/theft/obsolescence). Shoppers Stop has lowest shrinkage in the industry at merely 0.5 per cent. Similarly, availability of the product has dramatically increased due to computerization of supply chain management. The turnaround time to warehouse has reduced from 4 days to less than 24 hours. Again, warehouse transfer time from distribution centres to shops has also reduced from 96 hours to less than 24 hours. On every parameter imaginable—turnaround time, distribution costs, inventory—there has been substantial improvement. Unni Krishnan T.M., Chief Technology Officer (CTO), Shoppers Stop says that all this has impacted financial performance substantially. On an average, 50,000 customers walk-in everyday in 20 stores. Turnover of company has increased from $18.9 million to $151 million.

From here on, the CTO would like to move on to next generation B2B systems and have better efficiency, and be able to coordinate better with vendors. Some of the vendors do have a system in place through which the vendor or partner organization interacts with Shoppers Stop.

Currently, Shoppers Stop uses Arthur Merchandize Planning application to plan its procurement process several months in advance. Planning across multiple seasons of Shoppers Stop is done using this tool, which uses advanced forecasting methods, open-to-buy, assortment, range, and option planning techniques to support buyers, merchandiser, category managers, trading managers, and other decision-makers. Shopper's Stop now would like to interact with vendors better and improve involvement with vendors by improving transaction-processing capability.

Warehouse Management System (WMS) and Process

Prior to installation of warehouse management system (WMS), inventory was monitored manually and transfers required more than 96 hours, now, the entire process is controlled electronically and transfers are executed within 24 hours.

Distribution centre is mapped onto a *rack and bin* system. The system calculates storage capacity and allocates a designated area to each product category through a *put away* document. A *pick list* identifies exact location of merchandise at SKU level. It maintains records of perpetual inventory online and minimizes shrinkage. It has reduced turnaround time to 24 hours.

Perpetual Inventory Control System (PICS)

Distribution centre scans one department per day. All departments are scanned in a quarter. There is a predetermined scan schedule of all departments. Operational processes are not affected. Perpetual inventory control system (PICS) helps in checking pilferage and variances are known everyday. It has proved to be a major tool for reducing shrinkage, resulting in cost savings.

Logistics at Shoppers Stop

There are four dedicated distribution centres (DCs), covering 85,000 sq. ft. which supply merchandise to 15 stores across the country. Distribution centre management is outsourced to and managed independently by regional service providers. The regional distribution centres are connected online to the central systems.

New Initiatives

The following are a few SCM initiatives implemented by Shoppers Stop.

Intake Consolidation

Supplies consolidation is in the form of the *Milk Run*—meaning consolidated or pooled-in logistics and freight movement from suppliers located in a common area.

Currently it is in vogue for the brand partners. There is delivery authorization indicating quantity to be received for the week. There is a national transporter to follow up with vendors for merchandise to act as a third party logistics provider (3PL). Only one truck is used to visit and collect goods from the vendors. Distribution centre is informed of the time schedule. Delivery status is monitored and tracked through the website.

Supply Partners' Role

Their role is to ensure smooth flow of merchandise through the entire supply chain, to improve the *visibility* and *velocity* of information through the supply chain. Partners can proactively improve efficiency and business results through the supply chain.

B2B Transactions

Shoppers Stop use BConnectB from *Siemens*. It was launched in 2002 with less than 10 partners. Currently there are 150 partners connected online with Shoppers Stop. The features include

- order processing
- purchase orders
- receipt details
- payment
- ledger details
- sales and stock position style-wise/location wise

Advantages of B2B at Shoppers Stop

B2B adoption at Shoppers Stop has resulted in the following gains.

- Reduction in communication expenses
- Faster information exchange with the business associates
- Freeing up executive time for other value-added activities
- Passing online information of sales and stock to vendors which increases service levels

Source tagging Bar codes, capturing style, and price details are attached to the merchandise at the partners' premises. It ensures smooth flow of merchandise through the supply chain and reduces turnaround time.

Receipts and payments The payment is done against receiver's confirmation. The receiver's confirmation report is prepared on receipt of goods at the DC. The report is then sent to the corporate office against which payment is released.

Direct store delivery Shoppers Stop has the ability to receive the merchandise directly at the stores. Bypassing the DC further reduces turnaround time to 12 hours (*drop-shipping*). It results in significant reduction in distribution cost.

Auto style set-up Currently Shoppers Stop team creates styles manually. The printed bar codes are then sent through courier. In auto-style set-up, the partner sets up the style codes (based on a standard template) and prints the bar codes at his end. The entire file is sent electronically to Shoppers Stop. Details of style codes are uploaded directly into the ERP. Shoppers Stop is there only to fill in quantities. It reduces courier cost and turnaround time significantly.

Strategic Steps in IT

Shoppers Stop have recently focused on leveraging current investments in technology and upgrading or revamping existing technology where it was required. The year 2005–06 has seen dramatic increases in stability, scalability and resilience of applications deployed. Further, they have taken corrective and improvement steps in building a strong foundation of basic and secure systems. Some of the strategic and developmental steps in IT in 2005–06 have been the following.

IB Force As pioneers in the field of retail technology in India, in February 2005, the company deployed IB Force to manage sales originating from the institutional business.

Data security Security is an important concern of every individual who works for the company. With this mindset Shopper's Stop required to upgrade security applications and deployed a new anti-virus application across all machines.

Inventory scanners These are used at the stores to perform physical stock taking. The physical stock taking ensures that the actual count on the shop floor matches with the stock reported by the JDA merchandise management system. Use of this technology has helped achieve a very low shrinkage level.

IBM-i550 server As Shoppers Stop grows at a fast speed organically with launch of new stores and addition of new business units, the company has invested in the new I-550 performance server from IBM. With the deployment of this server in August 2005, Shoppers Stop again sets its leadership status by becoming the first retail company in India to use this server.

The Benefits

The company reported the following benefits on different supply chain partners' front.

Customer

Improvement in Customer Satisfaction Index from 62 to 65 has been reported through better availability of merchandise at Shoppers Stop.

Partner

B2B, Auto P.O., and source tagging ensures faster transactions. B2B will drive seamless integration between Shoppers Stop and supply partners in the future. Partner satisfaction index will strengthen partnership and their relations.

Stakeholders

SCM strength can be leveraged for multi-fold growth at lower cost, reduction in shrinkage resulting in higher profit, and ultimately bringing about pay-offs and confidence to all the stakeholders.

INDUSTRY SNAPSHOT 29	Metamorphosing supply chain into value chain TELCO[29]

Instead of a constant and predictable demand pattern, automobile firms now have to deal with tremendous variations in demand patterns. In the case of TELCO, this is especially true in the commercial vehicle business. Also, instead of limited product offerings, firms now have a wide range of products to offer—TELCO manufactures as many as 300 varieties of commercial vehicles today. Earlier, firms used to work with a high level of vertical integration producing everything in-house (since precious little was available externally)—quite similar to TELCO's truck business. At present, however, outsourcing is the preferred option and is increasingly gaining importance. TELCO too (especially in its car venture), has developed a wide ancillary base and dealer network, thus, demonstrating the importance of adapting to change.

The supply chain is fast evolving as shown in Fig. 8.24. The customer is now at the top of the chain; offerings from firms have become customized; OEMs are now focusing on their core competence; and vendors are becoming solution providers to firms, just the way firms become solution providers to their customers. Transporters are graduating from offering merely the transportation of goods to providing end-to-end logistics solutions.

This implies that the customer needs to be convinced about the total life-cycle cost of a product, and not just the selling cost.

There are three important and inter-linked variables in the supply chain—cost reduction, quality improvement, and time compression. The focus at TELCO is on cost reduction. This is expected to be achieved by moving to a situation where the bulk of the materials is sourced from Tier 1 suppliers. In 2000, TELCO had 1200 vendors—this number was down to 700 in 2002. By 2005, the aim was to reduce this further to 300. Reduction in multi-sourcing of materials; elimination of tail (i.e.,

---

[29] Adapted from ETIG, Mumbai, with permission from their study on Supply Chain and Logistics, 2002.

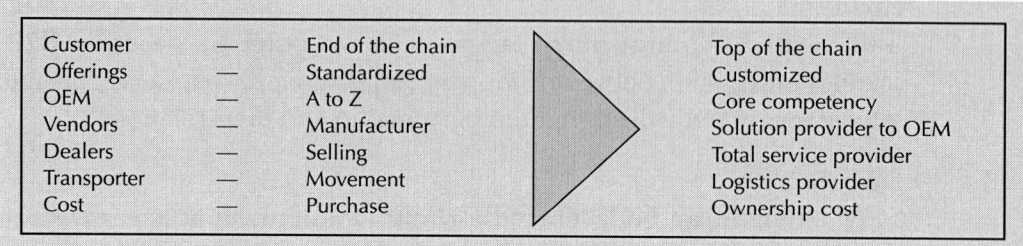

Customer	—	End of the chain	Top of the chain
Offerings	—	Standardized	Customized
OEM	—	A to Z	Core competency
Vendors	—	Manufacturer	Solution provider to OEM
Dealers	—	Selling	Total service provider
Transporter	—	Movement	Logistics provider
Cost	—	Purchase	Ownership cost

FIG. 8.24   The changing face of supply chain at TELCO

1 per cent of purchasing taking place from 45 per cent of vendors); introduction of a cost assessment system, and zero-based costing are other focus areas. In addition, there is seamless communication with all supply chain partners using the Internet.

Vendors are being encouraged to install QS 9000 standards. All norms and systems followed at TELCO are being installed at vendors' establishments as well. The company has devised a vendor rating system in terms of quality, cost, delivery, design capabilities, and management systems (QCDDMS). Weights are assigned to each of these components that feed into the final score—the weights change depending on the situation, the department, individual product groups, etc. Now, instead of one truck going to a single vendor, it goes to multiple vendors (*milk run*); therefore, there are fewer trucks lined at company gates. TELCO has instituted a central receipt and documentation office that is like a single window service. This has resulted in rationalization of manpower. All the data including the daily schedule/ GIN (Goods Inward Note) data is captured and handled by a value chain management system, the flow of which is outlined in Fig. 8.25. Thus, data accuracy has gone up by 90 per cent and manual efforts have reduced by 70 per cent.

The company also observed that there were many points at which sales tax was being paid unnecessarily. By eliminating the whole process, TELCO was able to knock down two levels where sales taxes were being paid. Therefore, not only were costs reduced, there was also a reduction in time. These simple examples demonstrate

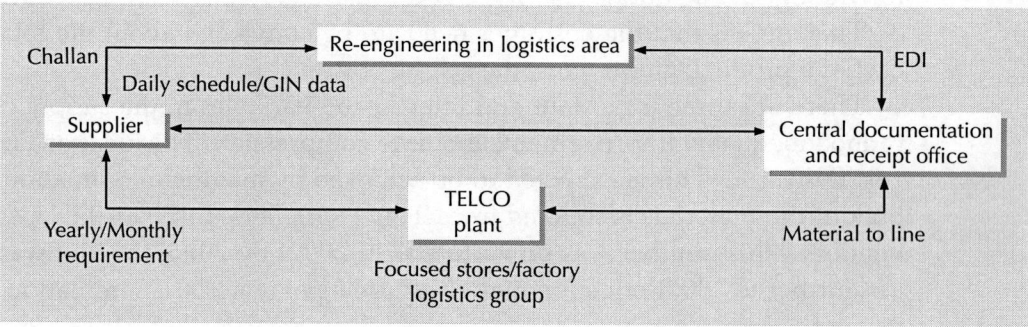

FIG. 8.25   Value chain management flow at TELCO
Source: TELCO, Pune, as adapted from Supply Chain and Logistics survey of ETIG

that if one were to do some out-of-the box thinking, a substantial saving (to the tune of 20–30 per cent) can be achieved.

Most of this learning has been transferred to the Indica plant, where things are working much faster and better. Daily supplies, unitization, line side storage, strengthening inbound logistics, inventory management, maximum buying from few sources, etc., were implemented from day one. TELCO has increased its self-certified suppliers by 20 times; incoming rejection levels have gone down substantially from 2.6 to 0.5 per cent. Inventory-to-materials ratio has gone down by a third and inventory in number of days has also fallen considerably. All this has been achieved in just three years.

As far as finished goods inventory is concerned, company and dealer stocks put together amounted to about 3 months inventory. By 2002, it got reduced to 3–4 weeks, including inspection floats, supply floats, transit stocks, and stockyard stocks. Thus, there has been a significant reduction in system stocks, leading to reduction in the interest on working capital.

TELCO is not initiating enterprise cooperation. Since it has good linkages on the vendor side of the supply chain, it is now moving towards the dealer and customer side of the chain. A value chain management (VCM) model is being put into place for dealers, with the eventual objective of reaching the end customer.

The objective of the VCM model for dealers is to develop a fast, efficient, and cost effective platform to disseminate information and enable two-way communication (Fig. 8.26).

In other words, it is more than just selling a chassis; rather, a point to point solution is provided—showing the customer how to do business; advise him on the right things to do in his business; advise him on when his vehicle is due for replacement, or tell him about new vehicles that will give him better lifetime costs.

Another way to achieve efficiencies is to improve utilization. The cost of unutilized capacity is tremendous, and in India, this problem is acute. Inventory costs in India are 3 times those in China or Europe. Thus, India's competitive disadvantage of holding inventory is 3 times greater as compared to them. With liberalization and global access, this will become an important constraint, and this should force firms to compress their inventory levels by effectively managing their supply chains.

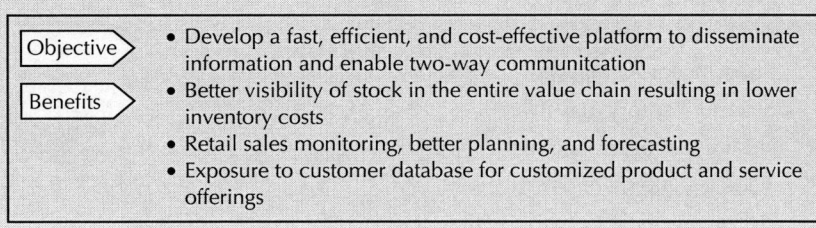

FIG. 8.26 Value chain management (VCM) for dealers

Fig. 8.27 Future plans at TELCO

TELCO's future plans (Fig. 8.27) include long-term understanding with suppliers (LOTUS agreements); a conscious effort to move towards single sourcing; installation of a QCDDMS model for supplier performance management; implementation of third party logistics; integration of sales planning and production processes; implementation of SAP; and a focus on e-Procurement. In future, competition would be from European quality—this is bound to raise the expectation of performance from domestic firms.

TELCO, for instance, is now being compared with Volvo, a firm that sells far fewer commercial vehicles than TELCO does. Clearly, this benchmarking has caused the customer's expectations from TELCO to rise. On the other hand, there is the issue of competition from Chinese prices that will need to be addressed. One approach for the future is to build about 20–25 per cent of the total vehicles on a build-to-order basis, within a 15-day cycle. That is, delivery to the customer must be made within 15 days from the day the order is placed. Such a process is already being experimented within the industry. Table 8.3 shows the benefits in sourcing and inventory figures in five year for 96 to 2001.

TABLE 8.3 Changes in some key performance indicators (KPIs) of SCM at TELCO, Pune

KPI	1996	2001
Number of suppliers	1184	711
Material travel (km/day)	1370	600
Shop inventory (days)	5.2	4.4
Stores inventory (days)	24.2	13.8
Total inventory (materials)	9.6	6.6
Vehicles into plant/day	2050	1100
Average vehicle turnaround time (hrs)	8–12	3

Source: TELCO, Pune, as adapted from Supply Chain and Logistics study, ETIG, Mumbai.

INDUSTRY SNAPSHOT 30	No cramps for CRAMS NICHOLAS PIRAMAL INDIA LTD (NPIL)[30]

NPIL, India's second largest pharmaceutical and healthcare company, is a leader in the cardio-vascular segment and has a strong presence in antibiotics and respiratory segments, neuro-psychiatry, anti-diabetics and pain management. NPIL came into existence in 1988 when it acquired Nicholas Laboratories from Sara Lee and within 15 years only after that, it grew to leadership position through a series of well-managed acquisition, mergers, and alliances. Some acquisitions being—Indian operations of Roche Products, Boehringer Mannheim, Rhone Paulenc, ICI India's Pharma Division, Hoechst Marion Roussel's Research Centre and Aventis Research Facilities. It entered into alliances and joint ventures with F. Hoffmann-La Roche of Switzerland, Allergan of US, and IVAX of UK. NPIL's 16 brands are among the top 300 brands in the Indian pharma industry. It has a 2200 strong field force. Its strength also lies in having state-of-the-art plants at Hyderabad and Pithampur. The plant in Hyderabad is the only plant in India having US Food and Drug Administration (USFDA) approval. NPIL focuses on development of formulations, new chemical entity (NCE) research, and clinical research. In 2005–06, the company reported revenues worth Rs 14.1 billion and a profit after tax (PAT) of Rs 1.7 billion. Of late, NPIL has emerged as one of the leading custom manufacturing organizations in the world.

Market for Contract Research and Manufacturing Services (CRAMS)

Post-patent regime, the company identified CRAMS as a major growth opportunity. With a slowdown in patented drugs sales and drying R&D pipelines, global pharmaceutical companies are increasingly exploring low cost options for outsourcing research and manufacturing.

According to industry sources, the global pharmaceutical outsourcing market, which currently stands at $24 billion, could reach $53 billion by 2010. Custom manufacturing for innovator companies stands out as the most attractive outsourcing opportunity for pharma companies. This market could reach, from an estimated $16 billion today, to $25.7 billion by 2010. With the largest number of FDA approved plants after the US and low cost manpower, India could potentially capture 10 per cent of this opportunity. Leading Indian players in this field in addition to NPIL are—Suven Life Sciences, GVK Biosciences, Jubiliant Organosys and Shasun Chemicals & Drugs.

---

[30] Based on Noemie Bisserbie, ET Intelligence Group, October–November 2006 as posted on etintelligence.com with permission from ETIG; www.nicholaspiramal.com/media_companyprofile as last accessed on 14 May 2009.

In the case of Nicholas Piramal, SCM has proved to be one of the most powerful engines of business transformation. Since the company's decision to enter the high growth CRAMS segment, SCM has become key to the company's strategy. After the acquisition of Avecia (UK) in 2005, and Pfizer's UK Morepeth facility in 2006, the company's ability to integrate overseas businesses and ramping up the supplies, be it raw materials or intermediates becomes key issue to the profitability of it's CRAMS business.

Logistics at Nicholas Piramal India Ltd

The company has two major plants—at Mahad and Pithampur. It has 21 C&FAs, 130 SKUs, and more than 2500 distributors. Combining all the group entities, the number of stockists is around 4000. At the time of study in 2002, goods are supplied to metros once a week and smaller towns in one–two to three weeks. Credit period is seven days to stockists in the major places and 21 days in upcountry locations. The FG inventory of 57 days is higher than the industry average of 46 days. The company aims to bring it down to 25 days. The debtor days appear to be fluctuating widely. The company seems to be enjoying a higher credit period in comparison with the industry.

The company identified demand forecasting and skewness in sales as primary problems in inventory management. In finished goods, the *batch size* can be a problem as a certain minimum quantity has to be produced, which could equal two to three months of sale. There is a lot of OTC buying and a considerable amount of prescription substitution. New products is another challenging area identified by the company. Introduction of new products usually occurs at a very fast pace leaving very little time to meet launch deadlines.

Nicholas is currently working on a number of initiatives to increase efficiencies in its manufacturing and supply chain operations. The supply chain costs are expected to come down from *3.4 per cent of sales to 2.7 per cent of sales* by these initiatives.

NPIL is using the *hub and spoke* model to reduce finished goods inventory. Currently, the stock holding at the C&FA level is *30 days*. Once, all the hubs are set up—the response time will reduce from *10 to 2 days*. Using the system, the inventory at the C&FA level would go down to *7 days*, and at the hubs level would also be 7 days *bringing down the overall inventory level to 14 days*. The company has already set up two hubs and would be putting up one more. Some high value products would be going directly to the C&F agents. Often it is a problem to get full truck loads, so supplying to hubs would eliminate this problem.

Nicholas along with Rhone Poulenc had 42 C&FAs, but has reduced this to 21. The emphasis is now on the involvement of the sales and marketing team in demand forecasting. The team has been given considerable inputs based on historical data.

According to Neeta Sanghi, Senior Deputy General Manager—'The supply chain process has become *forecast-driven* till now, but now, the company would also be focusing on making it *demand-driven*.'

The company would be making the planning cycle weekly, although, the business cycle remains monthly. The company is also weighing the options of 'make' and 'buy'. Currently, third party manufacturing accounts for *50 per cent of the sales* as considerable outsourcing is being done for Rhone Poulenc. Inventory carrying and servicing C&FAs' administration are the main logistics costs identified by the company. The office, company plants, and C&FAs are connected via VSATs which allows *daily data inputs*. The company also uses a data warehousing (WH) package. The company has made changes in the departmental structure and distribution falls under supply chain.

To combat counterfeiting, the company keeps working on product packaging in such a way, so as to make it expensive and more difficult to copy.

Supply Chain Initiatives by NPIL

The following initiatives in procurement, manufacturing, SCM, and IT were planned by the company. The focus areas covered are listed in Table 8.4.

TABLE 8.4 Initiatives in procurement, manufacturing, and SCM at Nicholas Piramal

Procurement
• Standardization and variety reduction of items
• Supplier base consolidation
• Value engineering initiatives across raw materials and intermediates

Manufacturing
• 'Make' versus 'buy' decisions
• Optimization of manufacturing locations/loan licenses/third-party network
• Focus of in-house locations on strategic and high volume products

SCM and logistics
Redesign of distribution architecture, CFA integration, reduced inventory, lost sales through implementation of modern planning, and sales forecasting systems

Information technology
Integration of ERP packages, implementation of data warehousing, distribution resource planning (DRP), sales forecasting, and sales force automation (SFA) systems

Source: Supply Chain & Logistics 2002, ETIG, Mumbai.

The Inevitable Strategic Change

NPIL then changed its entire business model. Its recent buyout of Pfizer's Morepeth facility in UK, puts it on top of the league of Indian contract manufacturers with expected annual revenues of Rs 900 crore. While its international business accounted for just 3 per cent of revenues in 2002–03, in 2006, it represented around 50 per cent of NPIL's business, while domestic revenues accounted for the remaining about 50 per cent. SCM has played a crucial part in this transition.

The acquisition of Pfizer's Morepeth facility is a big gain for NPIL, as it fulfils its search for a significant acquisition in the contract manufacturing space. The facility comes with a five-year supply contract that could yield revenues of $350 million (Rs 1610 crore) during the tenure. The domestic company also expects to tie up with new customers. While Nicholas Piramal's acquisitions have allowed the company to build a critical mass and increase its technology range, the company will need to rationalize costs by synchronizing operations with the Indian assets and by sourcing intermediates from new locations to make the Avecis and Morpeth businesses competitive. NPIL is notably looking at China as an opportunity to reduce sourcing costs significantly. Through these means, it expects to cut costs by as much as 30 per cent. Notwithstanding the global foray, NPIL's strategy should not be viewed as a move to reduce its focus on the domestic market. India remains at the core of its strategy. Domestic formulations market will continue to drive overall margins, and provide a strong cash flow for the contract manufacturing business and for research. NPIL continues to upgrade its research and development facility and its talent base, in order to meet the needs of its contract research business.

Investments in contract manufacturing have affected the company's profitability in the short term, but margins are set to increase as revenues from its CRAMS business start flowing in. Integrating the Avecia and Morpeth businesses, acquired in 2005 and 2006, and ramping up supplies is expected to be the key to profitability.

Supply Chain Challenges at NPIL

NPIL faces three key challenges in order to integrate its Indian and international businesses. First of all, integrating cultures across India, Canada, and UK was not quite easy for NPIL. Braced with the ego issues, senior executives in UK subsidiaries found it difficult to report to Indian managers, as well as there were communication problems. Sharing data between NPIL's newly acquired business entities has also sometimes proved to be difficult.

Sourcing and manufacturing will be another issue supply management executives will need to look close at. NPIL will need to change its sourcing locations for its Avecia business. China's conscious effort to increase the quality of its bulk drugs makes it an attractive sourcing location. For certain formulations, Chinese manufacturers can offer one-tenth the price offered by European manufacturers. However, as the Chinese Government reduced export subsidies, manufacturing facilities got affected by an increasing number of power shortages and are becoming more environment conscious. As a result, many industries are shutting down. However, competition has constrained European suppliers to considerably reduce prices, and NPIL has significantly benefited from this opportunity. The company expects to reduce costs by 5 per cent to 10 per cent by synchronizing operations at its four factories. Reducing sourcing costs will be the key success factor to the company's foray into CRAMS, as it will largely determine the business' profitability.

While NPIL is already one of the most established players on the domestic market, transportation and goods inventory management are two areas, the company is trying to further improve. SCM would bring about significant changes on the domestic market which accounts for a sizable chunk of the company's revenues. Besides, while CRAMS is set to account for close to 80 per cent of revenues on the medium to long term, NPIL's domestic formulations is expected to remain more profitable than company's international business. However, finished goods inventory continues to remain deliberately high. On the material side, NPIL has implemented new systems to reduce inventories. It has 28 depots and spends Rs 8 lakh to 10 lakh in information communication. This has proved productive, as the company has been able to reduce materials inventory from 40 per cent to 25 per cent, within six months which is much lower than the industry's average.

NPIL is the only company in the industry to have a separate force for stockists. While in most pharma companies, medical representatives are also in charge of looking at stocks, at NPIL, a dedicated team of 200 people are solely responsible for keeping an eye on stocks and booking orders for the company.

The next challenge would be to connect stockists directly. This is a step most FMCG companies, such as HUL, have already taken, but NPIL is the first mover in the pharmaceutical industry. The main reason is that while stockist in the FMCG sector are dedicated to one specific sector, there is no clear demarking of territories for pharma stockists. Besides, focus on logistics is not very high as it represents a small share of sales. However, NPIL has started to implement systems in logistics as well.

On the supply side, while NPIL used to deliberately source materials from a reasonable number of suppliers because of the risks of strikes, the company has since shifted to a single window. This has allowed the company to gain in bargaining power and reduce prices by 5 per cent to 10 per cent.

Finally, the company has reduced the number of transporters in order to improve the quality of services and diminish delivery time. Metros still remain the main market in India. Although this has resulted in improvements in quality, it has considerably increased transportation costs as well.

INDUSTRY SNAPSHOT 31	Taming RFID compliance RANBAXY AT WAL-MART[31]

In 2005, Wal-Mart's sales reached $260 billion. As is widely acknowledged, Wal-Mart deals with millions of SKUs. Keeping track of all those units, leaving vendors, arriving at distribution centres (DC), and then getting into the shelves of the many formats of Wal-Mart was getting a daunting task indeed. Wal-Mart is predominantly US based, but not very globalized. With ever-fickle customer tastes and preferences, the onslaught of Internet buying, and a crashed time for launches from vendors, the traditional inventory tracking and replenishment systems were bursting at the seams. The answer for reducing stock-outs and increasing in-shelf visibility lies in radio frequency identification (RFID). Wal-Mart believes RFID will have advantages that far outweigh its costs and integration pain.

In June 2003, Wal-Mart laid down detailed guidelines and requirements—a 25 page document—for its top 100+ vendors, including Ranbaxy of India detailing everything from a case, pallet, RFID frequencies, readers, quality assurance, and so on. It also made clear that it would not accept any cost increase from vendors due to this system. By January 2005, its top-listed vendors should be ready to supply RFID-tagged pallets and cases (not individual products yet) to the distribution centres of Wal-Mart and by end-2006, all its hundreds of vendors should be RFID-compliant.

So what has Wal-Mart, RFID, and Ranbaxy, a New Delhi-based pharmacy major in common? A lot. Ranbaxy are one of the vendors affected by RFID-compliance, as it supplies morphine in bottles to Wal-Mart's shelves from its US-based plant. Included in the category of addictive painkillers and other prescription narcotics, morphine is a critical item (and a controlled one) and Wal-Mart wanted to track it all the way till purchase, which is why Ranbaxy was asked to start-off in the first phase. Ranbaxy has been supplying to Wal-Mart, which has over 3000 pharmacies in its network, of many years. Ranbaxy Director (Global Supply Chain) Govind Jaju says, 'As part of ongoing efforts to employ upcoming technology, Ranbaxy has implemented RFID. We are moving to the Next Generation Bar Code System to strengthen supply chain and meet customer expectation. In fact, this is done much before the deadline set by one of our valued customers, Wal-Mart.' Anyway, Ranbaxy got some impressive SCM parameters as shown in Table 8.5.

The director explains, 'The RFID chip which is fixed under the label of the product contains all relevant information, such as the manufacturer's name, expiry

---

[31] Adapted from ETIG, 2005. The author expresses thanks to ETIG for permitting to use information from etintelligence.com related to this snapshot as also to Anindya Munshi of Ranbaxy for discussion.

TABLE 8.5 Ranbaxy SCM statistics

Supply chain parameter	2001	'02	'03	'04	% Change from 2001
Raw materials stock	74.5	82.6	63.5	69.4	–7
Finished goods stock	32.1	31.0	34.1	33.5	4
Semi-finished goods stock	16.6	14.9	12.8	14.1	–15
Debtors	91.5	78.3	71.0	55.7	–39
Creditors	61.3	64.5	50.2	44.6	–27
Net working capital cycle (Average days)	153.4	142.3	131.1	128.1	–17

Source: Capitalize 2000; Courtesy: ETIG.

date, and unique serial number (which allows us to trace to lot/batch no.), which helps in monitoring the product movement and automatically updating records. This will enable Wal-Mart, to record the movement of products automatically.' Presently, Runway's morphine, in the class 'C2' is covered for RFID implementation, but other Ranbaxy products will eventually be covered, where the current RFID experience will be of great help.

Ranbaxy have contracted US-based ACSIS for its RFID venture. ACSIS will provide for the full implementation of an RFID tracking system for Ranbaxy. Employing its RFID Expert System as a diagnostic troubleshooting tool, ACSIS will conduct a thorough analysis of product and labeling attributes for Runway's pharmaceuticals, and provide technology recommendations for ensuring the best RF-read rates and system integration.

How does it all work in Ranbaxy SCM? Govind Jaju says the RFID chips that it uses—the WORM type—*Write Once, Read Many*—with its antenna comes in a roll from the vendor that makes it to Ranbaxy's US plant, where presently, first the RFID roll labels are pasted onto the bottle and then the label of the company is pasted onto the RFID label. Thus, the RFID label is not visible, but it can be seen through an empty bottle. These bottles are packed in a case, then it is scanned to recheck the readability of the chip and assign a case number, because each chip (bottle) has its own S/N, it can now be traced back to that case. The same process is followed when this is done in the pallet form—the pallet tag holds the information on the cases.

Placing the chip below the Ranbaxy label does not hinder its properties or functioning. The typical chip is less than one mm thick, and, in fact, the antennae which pick up and reflect the reader's radio signals, are bigger than the chip itself. Ranbaxy uses a passive chip presently, as do most companies globally, as there is not sufficient reason to go in for an active chip.

Chipping in the Chips

There are two main types of chips—made of silicon—used in RFID. One is an 'active' chip, meaning it has its own power source and emits its radio signals which can be picked up a reader that need not be very powerful, as it does not need to emit high power signals of its own. An active RFID chip is more difficult to make and place, as well as to programme, and hence costs more. A typical active chip may cost up to $1–2 per chip. Not many companies use such chips presently. Their greatest use comes in locations where readers cannot be of high power, either due to low/less power or other restrictions. The other benefit is that a hand-held reader of ordinary size can also track an active chip.

The other, most commonly used chip is the 'passive RFID chip'. This chip has no power source of its own, and reflects the signal that lands on its antennae from the reader. The reader, which may cost up to $5000, emits strong radio signals, though not strong enough to cause any human damage, which are picked up by the antennae in the chip, the software bits picked up on reflection and read by the reader. Such chips are in millions right now. Gillette, the global leader in shaving systems, is said to have ordered 500 million such tags recently. These chips are far cheaper than the active ones, easier to make, and programme as well. A typical passive chip costs about $0.5, and as the volumes grow, this cost may come down to $0.3, prices are falling but not fast enough.

Once the bottle is RFID-tagged, the case is made and shipped to the Wal-Mart distribution centre or store, as the case may be. Jaju explains how the Ranbaxy bottle would move through the Wal-Mart system. 'The pallet of bottles moves from our factory via the shipper to the Wal-Mart DC entrance. The readers are placed at known, clear places on the dock gates, such that when the pallet moves through the dock gate, the readers scan the data off from the RFID tags on the bottle cases and automatically route the data to the appropriate databases, from which the goods received note (GRN) is made. Ranbaxy has supplied its first RFID-tagged lot to Wal-Mart in August 2004. The feedback was awaited at the time of this case study.

Ranbaxy uses SAP, the ERP system, and one of the key issues was to integrate the data in the RFID chips with the SAP and thereby, make a seamless tracking. It can become quite complicated, since Ranbaxy internally will have one code, the RFID code may be another, Wal-Mart may have allocated another code, and all three have to be compatible with each other—each must have a clear, pre-defined relationship with each other. The SAP and the tag software must be able to take each other's data and make sense of it. SAP is working to make its standard software RFID compliant.

The entire process—from getting the guidelines and information required about RFID and Wal-Mart's vision, as Jaju calls it, to finalizing the type of tags, vendor, processes, prices, testing, and quality control verification of data on tags—all took Ranbaxy eight months. Next time around, Jaju says it'll take much less. More importantly, he added, 'No corruption of data was found even as the tag went through the supply chain internally during test phases', which validated the coding and placement of tags.

The whole thing sounds simple, but it is not. RFID codes have to be uniquely generated, kept track of, coded onto the chip; labels made and put on every bottle. There are 64 and 96 bit codes—which have a systematic style of being coded. Jaju says, 'It's a tough job. We ourselves are doing it for the first time, so there was a learning curve. Our team worked together with ACSIS, based in the US, to make the codes, refine the system, and go in for the technology.' Wal-Mart is known to be a tough customer, but as Jaju says, eventually, understanding and using RFID should generate benefits for Ranbaxy—with its complex SKUs and diversity—itself in other parts of the world, and in other areas of business as well.

Jaju lists three advantages that RFID should give Ranbaxy—*Track and trace*, *automation*, and *authentication*—something that is very crucial for a market such as India. The last one by itself is a key target, in a market where spurious drugs are rampant. No copycat would be able to generate chips and codes. If they did, the code would be immediately detected by the reader as non-existent. The benefits of integration and authentication (once it becomes a way of life) themselves will more than repay the cost of tagging and labeling.

INDUSTRY SNAPSHOT 32	**Synergizing order fulfilment, customer orientation, and collaborative logistics WAL-MART[32]**

From humble beginnings in 1962, Wal-Mart has come a long way to being the top company on the Fortune 500 list for most admired companies in 2009. It had sales of $405 billion in the fiscal year 2010. This is the first time, a service-oriented firm has topped the list. The reasons for its phenomenal growth even during the lean period of the 80s was its obsession for cost cutting, embracing IT practices, and excessive emphasis on logistics and SCM, especially in terms of customer orientation and order procurement. Wal-Mart has 8446 retail units across 15 countries, of which 1107 are located outside the US. 100 million customers visit Wal-Mart in a week. The number of employees including associates is around 2.1 million. The associates are considered the best idea generators in the company and they make the difference.

---

[32] Adapted from walmartstores.com/AboutUs/321.aspx as accessed on 14 May 2010; www.vics.org/docs/guidelines/cpfr as accessed on 14 May 2010.

Order Fulfilment

Wal-Mart seeks bigger package sizes for lower unit costs from suppliers, to balance supply with demand. Global order procurement practices also ensure harmonizing packaging on a global basis. It has its own team of merchants, transporters, and replenishment specialists. These teams work together to coordinate order procurement. Wal-Mart also uses IT better than its competitors. Its vast data warehousing capacity, consisting of 43 terrabytes of information, second only to the Pentagon, enables it to analyse the behaviour of each item for the purpose of demand forecasting, pricing, promotions, and store configuration. Flexible merchandising enables stores to use different category configurations to optimize sales for local tastes.

Wal-Mart also achieves best practices in SCM through its retail link programme. The company shares data with more than 5000 suppliers. The aim is to optimally balance production, distribution, and consumer demand. Lowering of costs enables smoother inventory flow, which in turn enables lower prices. It has to rely less on advertising and publishes on an average 12 promotional circulars per year, compared to around 60 for competition.

Wal-Mart's initial retail strategy focused on small towns offering the discount format to customers. Distribution costs were high because manufacturers and wholesalers gave priority to stores located in big towns. Wal-Mart then decided to perform the distribution function itself, by opening distribution centres so that every one of them is designed to service 175 stores located within a 150–300 mile radius.

Cross-docking is an innovation by Wal-Mart, where vendors ship merchandise to a distribution centre pre-packed in quantities required for each store. Bar coding is done, and say, the apparel is ready on hangers. Then they are moved on laser guided conveyor belts, to the respective trucks for delivery to stores. Non-compliance of directions such as non-availability of hangers for apparel also results in penalties. The new distribution centres are better than traditional distribution centres because there is almost no need for storage, processing at the centre is minimal, and they are much smaller in size.

Customer Orientation

Such planning for order procurement is evidence of a high degree of customer orientation. The company's inspirational chairman, the late Sam Walton thought that the biggest boss is the customer who can fire everybody from the chairman to floor worker by deciding to shop somewhere else. The culture is ingrained in Wal-Mart personnel when they interact with customers. They live out three basic beliefs everyday—respect for the individual, service to customers beyond their expectations, and striving for excellence. This psyche is reflected in two maxims that Wal-Mart employees are taught.

The 10 foot rule This means that an employee on finding that a customer is within a 10 foot distance from him, should go up to him, smile, and ask whether help is needed. Further, the employee should accompany the customer to the exit door. Sam Walton called this 'Aggressive Hospitality'.

The sundown rule This is a promise to attend to and fulfil all requests received on the same day by sundown.

Pricing at Wal-Mart

Wal-Mart's unique pricing strategies are based on the following.

EDPL (everyday low pricing) An important type of value pricing according to which the retailer charges a constant everyday low price with no price discounts. EDPL is useful because constant sales and promotions erode customer confidence. Wal-Mart pioneered the concept of EDPL by giving EDPL on major brands, except a few sale items.

Rollback Wal-Mart provides even more savings to the customer by lowering EDPL when possible.

Special buy offer Wal-Mart may offer additional amount of same product or another product is offered at special scheme for limited time while stocks last.

Collaborative Supply Chain and Logistics Initiatives at Wal-Mart

One of the great strengths of Wal-Mart is its efficiency in moving goods from suppliers to individual stores. Wal-Mart has a supplier diversity programme under which it conducts business with over 2500 minority and women-owned business enterprises (MWBE). The programme grew from an initial $2 million spend in 1994 to more than $6 billion spend in 2008. It also has ethical standards programme (ESP) for suppliers to support its global sustainability efforts. As Wal-Mart stores sell their goods, sales performances flows via computer not only to it, but also to its vendors/suppliers which ship replacement merchandise to the stores almost at the rate it moves off the shelf. Of importance here would be their association with P&G and Sara Lee.

Proctor & Gamble (P&G) Association of Wal-Mart with P&G started in 1987 and now P&G supplies more goods to Wal-Mart than to the whole country of Japan. A 150 person team that works closely with the company to improve both the products that go to the stores and the process by which they get there.

Sara Lee The arrangement of Wal-Mart with Sara Lee has been there for 10 years and the business between them stands at over $1 billion, with teams of merchandise, operations, MIS, marketing working together by sharing pricing information, and other confidential information towards meeting common objectives. Together, they followed CPFR® (Refer to www.vics.org).

Apart from the above, Wal-Mart has arrangements with numerous other big and small companies which have given supply chain management and customer initiatives a new focus. In fact, Wal-Mart is a great example of how supply chain practices can lead to customer delight. It is thus evident that a high degree of customer orientation and streamlined order procurement procedures have resulted in Wal-Mart in being the largest company in the world.

INDUSTRY SNAPSHOT 33	**Strategizing purchasing ANAND GROUP**[33]

The Anand group is one of the larger diversified conglomerates active in auto ancillaries. It has 33 plants in eight states and is present in the industrial clusters of Delhi, Pune, Chennai, and Hosur—close to its key customers. It has the largest basket of products for the auto industry, and every vehicle in India carries some or the other part manufactured by Anand group.

Supply chain has just caught the attention of the group. The group companies are decentralized to a large extent. They buy and sell their own materials. Procurement has also been independent and group-level synergies had not been explored much. By 2003–04, the top management of the group had realized that SCM had to be looked into if they had to maintain any competitive advantage.

For a business in which two-third of the sale price is material costs, focus on cost control for this issue was paramount. The first effort, says Arvind Nanda, the company's VP, Strategy Deployment and Corporate Materials based in Delhi, was to consolidate key commodities to leverage scale of procurement.

This meant a consolidation of supplier bases, so as to remove any duplication and unnecessary negotiations. The group formed the Corporate Materials division, which Mr Nanda heads, with the clear intention to facilitate buying. This division does not actually enter into pacts or deals, but identifies the right vendors across the country, negotiates the pricing and other aspects, and then hands over to the individual group companies to take it forward—the actual logistics, inventory, and so on. 'Procurement for key materials a centrally driven function,' says Nanda. The A-class material would be controlled and bought for the companies by the central group, while the B- and C-class materials would be bought directly by the individual group companies. The group also formed quality and commodity councils to create awareness of usage and costs.

The other method that the group used was e-commerce. They use e-sourcing via Baazi.com. The group requirements are put online (RFQs) for the commodities,

---

[33] Adapted from www.etintelligence.com. The author acknowledges the Economics Times Intelligence Group, Mumbai, for using this information.

and registered vendors are asked to bid for supply. The event is held on the Baazi portal. The group has held 15–20 such events in the past six months, aggregating to a total of Rs 800 crore in purchasing. 'This year', says Nanda in 2005, 'we will buy worth Rs 1000 crore on this portal.' He says savings of around 7–8 per cent on total procurement cost has already been realized.

Different companies in the group are at different levels of SCM maturity. Take Purolator, one of the group companies engaged in making filters for auto and other industries. Says Prakash Bhalekar, CEO, Purolator, 'We have 50 turns a year for finished goods, which ranks as one of the best in the industry.' Purolator's vendor base is also close to its plants. There is also a strong focus on vendor development, working with them for better quality, faster development, and pricing. The BaaN ERP that the group uses today allows companies to see data but not transact, which will change eventually. Vendor rationalization is also underway, as the company finds the usual Pareto principle working. The CEO describes a typical operation. There are 400 bins per shift. A schedule for production is given to all concerned— plant and vendors. There's a three-day rolling plan as well. The partnership manner has delivered almost 100 per cent adherence to forecast for both the company and consequently, its vendors as well. Trolleys carry material as per the requirement of production, no less, no more. This is quite similar to the manner in which the customers in automobiles work.

Critically, Purolator developed its own Advanced planner and optimizer (APO) at a cost of Rs 10 lakh. This tool has deskilled BaaN—every production manager, not just the IT guy, can do this planning. The screens are user-friendly and uncluttered. The dispatches are published on the Intranet, and dynamic changes to schedules are possible. Hourly dispatch direct on line (DOL) can be made and tracked. Inventory can be seen online as well, as APO integrates with BaaN. This intranet presently covers three-group companies—Puralator, Spicer, and Gabriel— but more will go online soon. The group expects to spend up to Rs 20 lakh for new middleware and servers soon. There is a challenge to connect all the companies, but it will have to be done.

Gabriel is another major company in the group. It has also started off on SCM sometime before the others did. For example, it has a firm production plan for the next day; and gives firm schedules to vendors. The material is collected by a *milk run* (3 trucks) and the preparation of trolleys to the line is done as per the deployment plan for the first two hours of production. There is also feedback to the vendors (who all use standard containers for supply) and a replenishment of the trolleys every two hours. The 'time bucket', therefore, is two hours. Just-in-time (JIT) is also being used at Gabriel. 225 lots a day come into the plant; and operations people, not planning, do the scheduling of the lots. There is a contingency plan of vendor fallback for every activity as well, since the output of the station is balanced with suppliers' rate of production and disruption is expensive. Gabriel also does vendor-managed inventory (VMI)—where the subcontractor maintains Gabriel's inventory on its shop floor. The vendor must submit a weekly stock statement as well. The ultimate idea is to use 20 vendors as preferred ones.

INDUSTRY SNAPSHOT 34	*Sampark Kranti*—Integrating IT and users for SCM **GODREJ INDUSTRIES**[34]

Godrej Industries operates in several areas, from FMCG to industrial equipment. Leveraging IT in supply chain is a productivity measure for the group, which benefits everyone in the group. Godrej Industries has the *Sampark* network that aims to integrate IT and users on to a common platform, not unlike many other FMCG players (Fig. 8.28). *Sampark*, however, is positioned as an inventory management system, not an information system. The system is used by all Godrej group companies.

Sampark was not too early. Godrej used to have 40 kinds of databases at all locations, making getting an overall picture impossible. Today, the group uses the Reliance Infocomm servers at Vashi, Navi Mumbai, to host the entire database. Depots communicate to the server via a middleware. The MFG/PRO system is linked to RIL's server—which uses the RDBMS database Progress, so that data is the most recent and updated.

Earlier, the distributors used to send data down the month; either hard copy or floppy and the hassles were endless. Today, Godrej uses software from leading e-commerce vendors, such as Botree and Broadvision. The software is given to distributors with Godrej financing the license but the equipment by the distributor. The challenge there, says Godrej Industries, GM, Information Systems, Mani Mulki, was to convince the trade that the investment in the system would be recovered by the lower inventory they would have to hold. Today, when the distributor handshakes

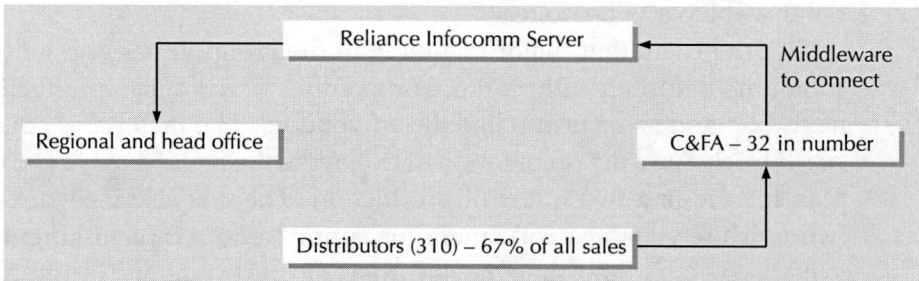

FIG. 8.28   The Godrej Consumer Products Ltd (GCPL) *Sampark* set up

---

[34] Adapted from www.etintelligence.com with kind permission of ETIG, Mumbai.

using the e-comm package, the orders are transferred to the CFA, which generates the invoice—all of this data gets transferred via the middleware to the RIL server, which can be seen by the head and regional office. Everyone sees exactly the same data. The other benefit is that, unlike older times, only changes in data are uploaded all throughout—not the entire database of historical data plus new data. The updating of old and new data is done centrally at the RIL database. The distributor handshakes twice a day, to upload data to the CFA, while the CFA handshakes with the RIL server three times a day. The memory requirement is also not much, because only updates are uploaded. Typically, a distributor needs 1 MB of hard disk space while the CFA needs around 10 MB. These memory requirements are easy to attain—even the smallest PC now starts at GB capacities.

So, what have been the advantages? For one, all used the same data. This removed the confusion about data almost to zero. Secondly, since data was updated everyday, stock and dispatch data was most recent, cutting out the 'bullwhip effect'. Three distributors were not dumped upon, because they would be supplied material only what they ordered, and not what the month end dumping needed. The benefits are tabulated in Table 8.6 which are quite impressive for an investment of Rs 1–1.2 crore for the entire e-comm and server setup.

TABLE 8.6 Business gains at Godrej

	From	To
Inventory at distributor	30 days	7 days
Operating costs	Rs 17–18 lakh a month	Rs 7–8 lakh a month
Sales		Up 30 per cent
Billing	120 bills a day	180 bills a day
Adherence to Plan	30 per cent	84–90 per cent

Source: Godrej Industries

INDUSTRY SNAPSHOT 35	**Simplification is the key to logistics MOSER BAER**[35]

Delhi based Moser Baer is the third largest manufacturer of optical media with the full range of CDs—ROMs, R/W, VCDs, DVDs—the lot. It holds 20 per cent of the

---

[35] Based on ETIG survey on Supply Chain and Logistics, 2005. The author expresses thanks to the Economic Times Intelligence Group, Mumbai, for allowing to use this case.

global market share and has Sony, Toshiba, TDK, and many other globally recognized names as its customers. It makes five million CDs a day from 200 lines. It has backward integrated into making its own packaging and cases. This business can be as complicated as any and being in India adds another whole new dimension to issues related to management supply chain management.

There is an interesting mix of complexity and simplicity. At the very basic level, every CD-ROM is the same—the same medium, the same process, and the same category of use. But that is where the simplicity ends. Says Moser Baer General Manager, Supply Chain and Logistics, B. Ganesh, 'The differentiator for the CD-ROMs is in the uniqueness of printing and packaging.' Differentiator, sure, but that is where the complexity is introduced, and that is the point where the supply chain really kicks in. Ganesh sums it well, 'Every order is unique and customized.'

End of the Line Complexity

Ganesh lists a mind-boggling array of options that a customer demands—and takes as well. CD-ROMs can be packed in 'cake boxes', in soft boxes, in slim cases, in shrink wraps, in cigarette wraps, in bundle wraps which can make shrink, heat, or tight finishes. Even within these varieties, pack sizes can be 10, 20, 30, 40, or 1000 CDs to a pack. Each pack has a label, has a booklet inside (the correct booklet of the correct company must be placed in the correct pack). Apparently, the 60s pack is the latest craze among users. This is certainly not out of the ordinary as FMCG and pharma industries are used to such varieties in packing. But the fun starts when the same CD-ROM run has to be packed online in all these different pack configurations along with printing—and all this has to be done absolutely seamlessly, lest dust get into the CD-ROMs.

Says Ganesh, 'We can still pack the CD-ROMs in different pack sizes and configurations right off the line, no problem at all. We have our own shrink and heat treatment facilities; we make our own boxes. Our machines can sort out the packs and sizes and finish the job.' Easy? Not so. The crux is the printing. Every company, says Ganesh, has a different printing style, logo, colour, and preference. Some have one colour, others multi-colours; some use holographs, others do not. The whole idea is that until CD-ROMs are made, they may be indistinguishable from each other, but towards the end of the production process, the CD-ROMs must be handled in such a manner that they have the exact printing that different customers need—100 per cent correct printing with the right pack size and configuration—each and every time.

It would be disastrous, says the G.M., if a Sony got delivered in a TDK printed pack! Moreover, the screens for the printing must arrive at the line just as the appropriate batch of CD-ROMs arrive off the line at the printing post. The two streams—the CD-ROMs from the manufacturing line and the printing details—must arrive in sync just in time for each other. Such a requirement needs a supply chain capable of handling bulk and yet be able to customize.

The process of printing also adds to the complexity of the line. Every CD-ROM for a customer, say, Sony, must have exactly the colour and shade as every other Sony CD-ROM in the world. Obvious differences in logo, shade, and colour cannot be tolerated at the retail end. Says Ganesh, 'Even minute and small shade changes can cause CDs to be rejected.'

The Moser Baers cracked the code for this complexity. Only the top people see order copies and price details. Passwords control access to all files and databases. The idea is that the man handling a particular client should know only about that client and nothing else. Moser Baer has also developed its own 13-digit code to track its products.

The Round Robin System

On the logistics front, Moser Baer uses what Ganesh calls 'the round robin' system. The system is simple. Moser Baer does not use many trucks to transport its export containers to Mumbai port. Instead, it uses the Dadri Inland Container Depot (ICD). Essentially, the Concor trains bring the containers of imports (Moser Baer imports chemicals for the CD manufacturing process) to Dadri, from which they are trucked to the Moser Baer plant at Noida, less than 10 km away. The very same import containers are emptied out and stuffed with ready to go CDs for export. These same containers are then trucked to Dadri, put on the Concor train and railed down to Mumbai port where they are loaded onto the ships for sailing to Europe, SE Asia, or the US.

In principle, simple; in practice, difficult. Says Ganesh, 'We had a hard time convincing Concor to set up the Dadri ICD. In fact, for a few months after it was set up, Moser Baer was the only player there. Then others came up. But we gave the undertaking that we alone would be able to use most of Dadri capacity. Today that is happening.' The other issue was the containers. Usually, import and export containers are separate, which involves duplication of loading, unloading, checking, and so on—all revenue earning actions for handlers, shippers, trucks, and workers. But Moser Baer, by coordinating imports and exports,was able to recycle the same container that brought in their imports for their finished goods exports. The logistics of moving this container from inbound to outbound is what Ganesh calls the 'round robin' system.

This is how it works. Moser Baer owns 'prime movers'—trucks with just a cab and engine and a chassis—no body. These prime movers shuttle between the plant and the ICD, ferrying containers to and fro. At Dadri, for example, one

TABLE 8.7 Vital stats of Moser Baer's SCM

	'01	'02	'03	'04	Change '04/'01
Raw materials stock	100.8	117.4	82.9	48.1	−52%
Finished goods stock	109.8	89.3	35.6	12.4	−89%
Semi-finished goods stock	17.8	12.6	10.5	9.8	−45%
Debtors	96.7	106.3	90.5	67.5	−30%
Creditors	91.2	76.0	72.3	83.5	−8%
Net working capital cycle (Average days)	233.9	249.6	147.3	54.3	−77%

Source: Capitalize 2000, Courtesy: ETIG, 2005.

prime mover would load the import container onto its chassis; go down to the plant to the inbound dock where machines could lift the container off the prime mover. This relieved prime mover would then drive down to the export dock, where a previously arrived and emptied import container would have been loaded with export material. The container would be loaded onto the chassis, after which the prime mover would ferry the container to Dadri for loading onto the train to Mumbai port. The phrase round robin comes from the fact that the prime mover keeps going round and round, and containers keep coming in full, get empty, get loaded again and go out again. Moser Baer imports 10 containers a days and exports 25 a day (Table 8.7).

Value Engineering

Moser Baer has maximized stuffing of the containers as well. A typical 40 footer container can take 26 tonnes of material. They have fitted in 1.4 million CDs into a 40 foot container, against a usual of 1 million previously, by changing the packaging and value engineering. At 10 cents a CD, Moser Baer price, that is $4000 extra—Rs 17 lakh extra into one container. It has also value engineered to reduce weight per CD. For example, a typical DVD weighs between 20–22 grams, which can now be made at 19 grams—a direct saving in inbound materials, such as silver or metals, as well as more stuffing in containers. Some metals are at Rs 5 lakh per kg—and at Moser Baer's production of 5 million a day, that's a saving of Rs 25–30 lakh a day. No mean numbers!

Meeting Delivery Deadlines

Moser Baer works on the CRDD concept—Customer Required Delivery Date. It does door delivery, preferring to do so because they can control freight, timing, quality, and safety. Moser Baer has a license for freight forwarding as well. Typically, for a customer in Germany, for example, the company would work backwards, adding in time for customs clearances in Germany, sea travel time, Mumbai port times, freight to Mumbai from Delhi time, and so on, keeping some extra margin days as well. A typical cycle can be 45–50 days. In seasons (Europe/US and Asia have different holiday seasons, when sales of CDs are highest) this time has to be crunched—and that's where Moser Baer uses its warehouses at Hamburg and trucks down to customers anywhere in Europe. The company owns all the assets related with all these operations.

INDUSTRY SNAPSHOT 36	**Aligning supply chain from design to order EICHER TRACTORS[36]**

Eicher started operations in India in 1959, by rolling out the country's first tractor. The company today has diversified business interests—design and development, customized engineering solutions, manufacturing and local/international marketing of tractors, commercial vehicles, such as trucks and buses, automotive gears and components, motorcycles, aggregates and components, and management consultancy. Standing at a gross sales turnover of above Rs 19,000 million (US$ 424 million) in 2005–06, smart usage of IT in the company through its 40 member strong in-house IT team, has been a significant factor in accelerating growth to its present levels. Eicher has more than 2500 employees located in 4 manufacturing and 49 marketing, and area offices around the country out of which around 85 executives work exclusively in the area of R&D. It has a 142 strong dealer force and is a multi-locational and multi-business company, having 308 vendors as in 2005–06. The Group has its presence in 40 countries across the world. After re-strategising its IT focus in late 90s, the company became the first SAP Certified Excellence Centre in India in 2001. The Eicher Group's mission statement reads 'the true measure of our success is relationships with our customers, with our vendors, and amongst ourselves.'

Order Fulfilment

The *Express Computer*, the leading IT business weekly from the Indian Express Group, quotes Sanjay Govil, the then Director IT, GIS and cartography, and CIO of the Eicher Group, 'Though the company has been using IT as a back-office tool for its

---

[36] Largely based on *Indian Express*'s Express Computer, Business Weekly, Article by Punita Jasrotia, dated 29 July 2002. Company figures and facts taken from www.eicherworld.com as accessed on 4 May 2009.

materials and financial accounting purposes, the real difference started showing after 1998, when IT was seen as a key business enabler.' This implementation was carried out very vigorously till mid-2000, also considered the end of the first phase. The second phase from 2001 onwards has seen more of networking and adding new features, facilities, and solutions to make it more effective.

The organization uses Intel servers from IBM and Windows NT as the operating system. Eicher has set up a robust IT infrastructure comprising WAN connectivity (a hybrid of VSATs, Frame Relay, and ISDN), SAP supply chain management (SCM) system and an extensive usage of computer aided design and manufacturing (CAD/CAM). While working on the IT strategy of the company, on the security front, Eicher uses a comprehensive security architecture including firewalls, virus checking tools and virtual private network (VPN) solutions.

Eicher identified three main success determining areas for the organization, namely *supply chain, product development, and collaboration*. And in each area, there was further assessment based on the business requirements.

Eicher being an automotive company, streamlining its order procurement processes was crucial to the company's success. This meant that the company could not comprise on its SCM solution. Driven by the goal of comfort of the end customer, Eicher took some time deciding on a particular vendor who could provide them with an effective and efficient solution. Starting with a list of 7–8 vendors, Eicher ultimately zeroed in on SAP. The company selected SAP because of its perceived stability. The company basically looked at three criteria, namely functionality in terms of its connectivity to various business needs, the vendor's commitment to the Indian market, and its record with the client companies. The company formed a six member team drawing people from diverse areas, such as product planning, materials management, sales and distribution, and finance. Subsequently, modules, such as production planning and control, planned maintenance, and quality management were also added. The launch of pilot project coincided with launch of Royal Enfield which was greatly successful. Later on, people from both technical and non-technical background were put through intensive training for the same. The company then became the first SAP certified Excellence Centre in India. This all resulted in a kind of overhauling of the business processes in the company which then felt the need to integrate its dealers and vendors through a chain of Extranets. Today, the SAP serves as an information backbone for all businesss processes, transactions, and data requirements to the group.

'The purpose was to create a solution that allows Eicher's dealers to log in to the SAP server directly, using the company's Internet backbone. Here, the dealer cannot only place order (of both vehicles and spare parts), check their order status, look at the payment requisites, but other financial details too. It was also kept in mind that the solution should not limit itself in just providing information needs but should be transaction orientated too,' Govil said in an interview to the *Express Computer* magazine.

The first and foremost advantage of setting up SAP systems was cutting down the cycle time by 3–4 days. The second advantage was in terms of reducing error possibilities on the dealer's side, which led to a lot of delays, confusion, and wastage for both the dealer and the company. Thirdly, dealers receive updated information online. Not only has this system served its basic purpose, but it had also helped them during the economic slowdown when the purpose was to cut down on extra costs and not end up producing something that was already accessible in the market.

Customer Orientation

It is a key word for any activity and has become a way of life at Eicher. The idea is to establish a cordial and understanding relationship with each customer in order to understand one's needs and to serve better. One step in this direction has been the setting up of a 'call centre' service. In case of any problem, the company can take the dealer's complaints on a priority basis. After the passage of a reasonable deadline, each extra day means that the complaint is going higher up the management value chain (starting from director of marketing). This actually helps the company in getting a good feedback from the customer. Earlier, out of 10 queries, four might get lost. However, with this system, no such problem arises. Eicher was also adjudged the best SAP Certified Customer Competency Centre in India in April, 2002.

Thus, efficient SCM practices and IT initiatives started in 1997 have resulted in greater focus on order procurement and a high degree of customer orientation. Eicher has been able to cut down costs during the recessionary period mainly attributed to streamlining of purchase procedures.

Collaboration through WAN

The company decided to set up WAN. This was implemented along with the SAP. Eicher went in for VSAT connectivity in all its locations. All the manufacturing sites and corporate offices were connected on the pre-assigned multiple access (PAMA) based VSATs because of high bandwidth requirement. On the other hand, all the marketing locations were connected on time division multiple access (TDMA) based VSATs. High volume factory locations, such as Pithampur, Hyderabad, and Chennai are connected through a Frame Relay Network with a VSAT back-up. Comsat Max has been the service provider for VSAT connectivity. Previously, while all the servers were distributed across the different locations of the organization, now, all the marketing offices and manufacturing sites can log on the WAN system which supports SAP, Eicher's messaging system, Intranet, and CAD/CAM systems. WAN reportedly has reduced the cycle time of the processes and improved the internal collaboration in the company.

Product Development

Eicher set up its own CAD unit in 1998 and the company went on to establish its own Engineering Services Centre of Excellence. The unit serves as an autonomous wing to meet high-end requirements of CAD/CAM/CAE of all businesses of Eicher group, as well as international clients. Their centre, as reported by the *Express Computer Magazine*, is equipped with state-of-the-art technology in 3-D modelling in the area of static, dynamic, vibration, and fatigue life estimation of a vehicle and its aggregates to give that design edge in the competitive market.

INDUSTRY SNAPSHOT 37	**Federal Express services a new sales and supply channel HEWLETT-PACKARD[37]**

HP having sold the majority of its consumer products through traditional retail channels, recognized the opportunity to capitalize on the direct distribution model. HP also wanted to focus on substantially reducing its refurbished product inventories and addressing its customer's growing desire to order products via the Internet. The creation of a new online sales channel for customers, now known as HPshopping.com, would enable them to capture a larger share of sales, enhance its relationship with customers, and complement its existing network of retail distributors.

Management at HPshopping.com turned to FedEx to help them strategize and quickly implement the new *Internet sales channel* with minimal resource utilization and risk. HPshopping.com asked FedEx to develop a comprehensive solution that would manage the entire process—from *order management to order fulfilment.* According to Chief Technology Officer of HP Mike Bridge, 'FedEx allowed us to focus more of our effots on developing and continuing to grow relationships with our customers. We relied on FedEx to deliver an integrated solution that met our customers' needs.'

Why did HP Select FedEx?

HP wanted a provider with industry-leading experience and capabilities, including

- proven expertise in information technology,
- access to US households through an extensive distribution network, and
- experience in e-commerce and supply chain management.

---

[37] Adapted from www.fedex.com/us/supplychain/casestudies as last accessed on 4 May 2009. The author expresses due acknowledgement to the source.

HP wanted a provider that would also

- analyse business processes, assess opportunities, and recommend a solution,
- integrate multiple solutions from various alliance partners with HP business processes to meet customer needs,
- oversee the supply chain and information management components of the solution, thus freeing HP to focus on strengthening customer relationship, and
- quickly deliver the solution to the market.

How FedEx Handled It All

FedEx assembled a cross-functional team that leveraged both HP and FedEx expertise. The team examined the existing supply chain architechture and began development of a new e-commerce channel for customers, the Internet-based *direct-to-consumer* solution now called HPshopping.com. FedEx brought in outside partners as necessary, managed the initial implementation, and helped HPshopping.com establish the channel's operations. HPshopping.com plugged into the FedEx fulfilment system, allowing HPshopping.com to monitor inventory levels.

Needs Assessment and Supply Chain Analysis at FedEx

Once HP made the decision to establish a new e-commerce channel for its customer, FedEx brought in cross-functional teams of professionals to assess its supply chain architecture and identify critical integration points. According to Mike Bridge, 'FedEx was able to provide us with a flexible, scalable and integrated solution that helped build our online business.' Each team worked closely with key areas across HP's supply chain to determine key strategies that would enable the company to meet the growing customer demand for its products.

Developing the E-commerce Solutions

After FedEx and HP identified opportunities for the creation of the e-commerce sales channel, a cross-functional team from FedEx began the design and development of a 'direct-to-consumer' solution for HP. This solution created a new channel for HP that woud allow the company to sell its refurbished printers and computing products to customers through the Internet. For HP, it was imperative that FedEx not only develop and implement the solution, but also manage the critical processes that serve as the engine for the online channel. Bridge explained, 'HP shopping.com benefited from a flexible, extensive e-commerce solution, and yet we were substantially insulated from integrating the information flows of the infrastructure FedEx put in place. FedEx developed a comprehensive solution that fully integrated the front-end order processing with the back-end execution management and order fulfilment of products.'

Order Management

As part of the solution, FedEx integrated critical information systems needed for the new channel, enabling its customers to conveniently order products online. HP was able to quickly launch the initial site, *HP Outlet Centre*, to take orders from its customers and begin receiving orders within two months. Critical to the success of this solution was the integration of online credit card authorization and settlement within the order management system. Once the order is authorized, it is accepted by HP, confirmed, and routed to the fulfilment center by FedEx. Also FedEx contracted a call centre provider to manage the services required to support HP customers that prefer purchasing products via a toll-free number. To complete this component of the solution, FedEx and the call centre collaborated on information technologies that would support the necessary integration of the order and inventory management systems.

Bridge explained, 'Thanks to FedEx, we are learning more about how our customers shop for and buy our products, and we're taking that experience and applying it to selling online. We're capturing sales and customers that otherwise would be lost to our competitors—that group of people who will only buy online from the manufacturer.'

Bridge continued, 'We're seeing tremendous month-to-month growth in this business. The majority of our customers visiting HPshopping.com rate their overall experience as 'very good' or 'excellent' . . . and approximately 95 per cent would recommend us to a friend.' *PC Computing* magazine concurs. In its I-Biz 100 Ranking, the magazine points out that HPshopping.com 'sells PCs like *gangbusters*.'

Warehouse Management

Since HPshopping.com wanted to establish an e-commerce channel without having to increase personnel and capital expenses, it was necessary to provide comprehensive warehouse management services. Through the FedEx fulfilment centre in Memphis, FedEx provided HPshopping.com with the resources necessary to achieve such a requirement. The fulfilment centre's close proximity to the FedEx SuperHub enables HPshopping.com to enjoy a variety of benefits associated with the elimination of the inbound transportation leg to the FedEx SuperHub.

Integrating Order with Inventory Management

Through the integration of order management and inventory management systems, FedEx enabled HPshopping.com to proactively monitor and control product inventory levels. By integrating those systems from HPshopping.com and the third-party call centre, FedEx was able to develop a totally seamless inventory management application.

At the FedEx fulfilment centre, logistics information systems constantly monitor and update inventory status. In addition, customers can track their shipments from HPshopping.com. Conversely, since the call centre systems are updated with order information from HPshopping.com, customers can also call the toll-free number and obtain complete customer service information from call centre representatives.

INDUSTRY SNAPSHOT 38	**Adopting solutions for on-demand sourcing** **DABUR INDIA LIMITED**[38]

It is one of India's leading fast moving consumer goods (FMCG) companies. Building on a legacy of quality and experience for more than 120 years, Dabur is India's most trusted name and the world's largest Ayurvedic and Natural Health Care Company. Dabur has come a long way in popularizing and making a whole range of products based on the traditional science of Ayurveda easily available, and setting high standards in developing products and processes that meet stringent quality norms. Dabur currently has 16 ultra-modern manufacturing facilities spread throughout the globe. Its products are marketed in more than 50 countries.

Results
- Average savings of 10 per cent across various categories
- Overall ROI from the initiative of 11 times
- Building a knowledge base of extensive category expertise
- High adoption of online sourcing within the organization
- Standardized sourcing process across categories

The Challenges

In 2002, Dabur initiated the change management process by introducing a centre-led procurement organization headed by their CPO, Mr. Jude Magima. The company felt the need to professionalize its sourcing and procurement activities. To accelerate and sustain this new initiative, Dabur engaged Ariba to implement a programme that was focused on reducing costs, avoiding subjectivity, and introducing transparencies and global best practices in its sourcing process. The programme was later expanded to include category management capabilities as well.

Soon thereafter, Ariba's consulting services and technological capabilities helped to improve Dabur's gross margins, despite inflationary trends. This initiative led to significant savings and expansions of the supplier base—especially for key strategic

---

[38] Adapted from www.ariba.com/customers/successstories.cfm with permission from Ariba India.

areas of spend. With that began the multi-phased spend management journey of Dabur with Ariba.

Initial Challenges

The chief objectives in the preliminary phase of the Ariba engagement were cost avoidance and transparency, whereas the secondary phase was focused on achieving excellence in processes and adoption of global best practices. In the six years since starting its spend management initiative, Dabur has used Ariba's various sourcing technology solutions, as well as its consulting services for relevant market knowledge, category expertise, and change management processes.

Dabur's spend management journey began with streamlining its sourcing process and supplier management. One of the biggest challenges during the initial stages was the lack of an established, standardized, and documented sourcing process. Before the team implemented its Ariba initiatives, there were no internal scalable tools and methodology to facilitate sourcing in line with their sourcing strategy.

Another challenge, which was external-facing, was to enable its suppliers both in the rural and urban parts of India to participate in a transparent, dynamic, and interactive negotiation process. In some cases, there was a lack of technological advancement—such as internet connectivity—and in others it was very little computer literacy. As this was a new way of conducting negotiations, Ariba assisted Dabur by teaching suppliers how to use computers and continued to remain an active part of Dabur's newly formed sourcing strategy.

Another external challenge that Dabur experienced was the way to manage the diverse set of suppliers spread across the globe. The challenge was associated with dealing with suppliers of different cultures, who spoke different languages and were based in different time zones throughout the world. User adoption of the new Ariba spend management solution was never an issue at Dabur. Through an effective mix of leadership, executive sponsorship, and communication, Dabur was able to mitigate any commonly found risk of internal resistance.

The Solutions

Initial Phase—Ariba Managed Markets and Ariba On-demand Sourcing Basic

Dabur started Ariba's engagement by conducting several Ariba-managed markets, where the Ariba team assisted Dabur with data collection in category-specific data collection templates and supplier research. Data analysis that translated into a lotting strategy based on suppliers' capabilities, manufacturing locations, and Dabur's business needs and other strategic sourcing decision-making criteria, and building and publishing a category-specific total-cost Request For Quotation (RFQ) to the approved potential suppliers. Ariba also assisted Dabur in the initial managed markets by conducting supplier management post-RFQ publication final price negotiations, and then awarding the business to the successful suppliers.

Based on the multiple advantages of the initial managed markets, Dabur ramped up its spend management journey with the implementation of Ariba On-Demand Sourcing Basic technology along with full-time Ariba Consulting Services. This further helped Dabur's buyers to address both their strategic and indirect expenses, which included maize derivatives, sugar, logistics, and chemicals to name a few.

This first phase of spend management resulted in cost reduction, transparency, and streamlining of the sourcing process. An example was the sourcing of saffron. Traditionally, Dabur sourced saffron from several suppliers based in India's northernmost state of Jammu and Kashmir. The market was a virtual oligopoly and every year suppliers would quote equal prices with Dabur allocating equal quantities to each of them. Ariba Sourcing Basic helped to bring visibility along with cost reduction, whereby the suppliers and Dabur could see the best quoted prices for the commodity. The result was transparency, meritocracy, and enhanced efficiency in the system.

Since the rollout in December of 2002, Dabur has conducted 520 sourcing projects via Ariba Sourcing Basic with average savings of 10 per cent across various categories.

Dabur was able to identify a better supplier base in China, South East Asia and Eastern European countries for various categories such as honey, air fresheners, juices, and packing materials to name just a few through Ariba's expertise in low-cost country sourcing. Ariba has also helped Dabur to avoid onshore inflation while expanding its supply bases and reducing costs.

The Secondary Phase

Ariba On-demand Sourcing Professional (Category Management)

Encouraged by the cost savings, the next logical move for Dabur was to focus on category-specific process standardization, visibility into its expenditures, risk monitoring and mitigation, knowledge management, and informed decision-making on both budgets and pricing.

To help achieve these goals, Dabur acquired Ariba On-Demand Sourcing Professional in August of 2006. Since implementing the technology, Dabur was able to enhance collaboration across various departments internally, as well as amongst suppliers. The quality of decision-making, organizational buy-in, sourcing visibility, efficiency, process standardization, knowledge capturing, and compliance were also enhanced considerably.

The Benefits

Currently, Dabur's sourcing organization is centralized and its sourcing processes are at a stage where they have been streamlined, mapped, and organized around business outcomes.

The category-specific sourcing best practices are instilled within templates that were developed for sourcing raw materials, packaging materials, logistics services, import shipments, and indirect spend. Twenty templates have been developed on Ariba Sourcing Professional to cover more than 3000 categories in its portfolio, enabling the Dabur team to follow a standardized sourcing process.

Dabur has completed more than 340 comprehensive sourcing projects since November of 2006 and has built a team of 20 category managers who regularly use the tool. The category managers use Ariba Sourcing Professional to source major raw materials such as vegetable oils, maize derivatives, herbs, spices, sugar, and chemicals to name a few, and also for major packaging materials, such as paper, paper boards, flexibles, and more.

Ariba Sourcing Professional has ensured improved visibility and transparency into the entire sourcing cycle for Dabur from data collection to the business award of each category. It has also helped in identifying and classifying the best suppliers for key categories.

The Ariba initiative is spearheaded at Dabur by Mr. Jude Magima, Executive Director and Management Committee Member. His team has realized significant cost reductions during this journey and continues to deliver. In recognition for his contribution towards making a fundamental difference in the way sourcing and supply management is practiced, he was awarded the 'CPO of the year' by a leading Indian academic body on supply chain management, namely Indian Institute of Materials Management.

In the future, Dabur plans to use Ariba's solution for other areas, such as budget management process, tracking savings across the entire sourcing programme, supplier enablement, and new employee introduction.

INDUSTRY SNAPSHOT 39	Redesigning sourcing strategies and programmes TATA MOTORS LIMITED[39]

Tata Motors is the largest automobile company in India with revenues exceeding $8.8 billion. The company leads the market for commercial vehicles and is among the top three passenger vehicle companies with winning products in numerous market segments. More than four million Tata vehicles have been on the road since the first rollout in 1954. Tata Motors employs 22,000 people who are driven to be the 'best in the manner in which we operate, best in the products we deliver, and best in our value system and ethics', as Tata puts it.

[39] Adapted from www.aribaindia.com/customers/successstories.cfm with permission from Ariba India. The author is also grateful to executives of Ariba India for discussion.

Results
- Nearly US$166 mn in savings
- Spend penetration > USD 2 bn
- ROI of 7:1+
- High adoption of online negotiating tool
- High transparency and compliance

The Challenge

After a decade of strong revenue and margin growth, Tata Motors began 2001 with a major challenge. Tata Motors was making major investments in the passenger car division to move away from the cyclical commercial vehicles business. While in the middle of this change, the commercial vehicles market shrunk by 40 per cent—leading to a sharp decline in profitability. To make matters worse, both domestic and global competition increased due to the opening up of the economy and the reduction in tariff barriers. Tata Motors realized that something needed to be done very differently in order to regain the lead and truly become a world-class organization. Today, Tata Motors ranks as the world's fourth-largest manufacturer of trucks with clear domination in the Indian commercial vehicles market. It is also among the top three in the passenger car market.

Strategy and the Solution

To combat the issues it faced, Tata Motors established a three-stage plan. The first stage's focus was on CQD improvement—cost reduction, quality, and delivery improvement. The second stage focused on consolidating its position in India by bringing in new products in the market, and the third stage was (and is presently) focused on growing operations internationally.

In 2001, Tata Motors made the decision to partner with Ariba. In the first stage, the Tata Motors—Ariba team ran a business diagnostic exercise with the entire purchasing team to understand the buying pattern, business constraints, and savings potential. Direct materials consumed nearly three-quarters of the cost of a vehicle. Therefore, the company started with cost reduction in direct materials.

The first sourcing project was completed in June of 2001. The team identified a strong pipeline of sourcing projects, a clear schedule, and cross-functional teams to execute the projects. Ariba Sourcing™ was deployed and category experts were brought in to provide sourcing services. Since the start of the program, teams have executed more than 3000 projects addressing around Rs 9000 crore of annualized spend, using a combination of services and software solutions. In this phase, teams addressed direct materials categories, such as forgings, castings, fasteners, machinings, bearings, tyres and also indirect materials categories, such as lubes and maintenance repair and operations (MRO) items. To help achieve its sourcing goals, Tata Motors mandated that categories with annual spend greater than Rs 5 lakhs annually should preferably be sourced online. This mandate resulted in significant improvement in e-sourcing adoption.

Moreover, the new sourcing process led to improved transparency in the system, which is one of the key points of the Tata's Code of conduct of doing business. Today, anything that goes through Ariba Sourcing is process and project-driven. The online sourcing process also reduced the negotiation lead time and streamlined the number of people required within the purchasing organization. Tata Motors' Ariba Sourcing adoption is one of the top five adoption stories worldwide within Ariba. By 2003, Tata Motors turned around under strong leadership of Mr Ravikant and flawless execution by Mr P.M. Telang, who ensured that the sourcing program ran like a *savings factory*. Through visibility and regular management reviews, the e-sourcing programme became one of the pillars of the turnaround story.

In the next stage, the focus was on consolidating the position in India. This was done through strong cost leadership in existing products and ensuring that all costs (initial investments, as well as material costs) were low in all future products. This was considered important as this could be leveraged to become a big barrier for new competition.

In 2005, Tata Motors launched the *Ace* model of small pickup trucks—which swept the entire small truck market in India because it was introduced at the right time, at the right price, and with the right specifications. Due to the unique combination of cost, price, and positioning, it created a new segment in the market and modified the structure of the industry. In order to keep the initial costs low, teams conducted more than 125 advance sourcing projects. Projects included heavy cash outflow items, such as machining centres moulds, material handling systems, as well as direct material spend, such as sheet metal parts, crankshafts, tyres, and batteries. Tata Motors' teams ensured that 50–60 per cent of the Ace Model was competitively negotiated online. This paved the way for high profitability, low cost, and highest transparency in doing business. Ironically, Tata Motors maintained high margins on products when the industry margins were going down! All new runaway success vehicles—*Ace* and *Winger*—went through this process.

The next stage focused on developing a profitable and competitive global business both from the market and supply chain perspectives. E-sourcing Tata Daewoo Commercial Vehicles (which Tata Motors acquired from Daewoo in Korea) and also has been the starting point for negotiations for new joint ventures such as Tata Motors (Thailand) Limited (JV with Thonburi Automotive of Thailand). Now the focus has changed from competitive price and low cost to globally competitive prices from globally competitive suppliers.

Lessons Learnt

Along its journey to spend management, Tata Motors has learnt many best practices for success. First, the team recommended selecting the right categories for sourcing to get the best return on the investment. Supply-side competitiveness, business impact, and ease of implementation are key factors to assess while prioritizing the categories to address. Begin sourcing early, as Tata Motors found first hand—that many costs are locked in once the product goes beyond the design phase. Pruning material costs in the early stages is the key to achieving maximum savings. Involvement of the cross-functional team throughout the sourcing process has been essential to the success of critical projects. Finally, being aware of the right sourcing process with the right tools and when you need help is critical.

INDUSTRY SNAPSHOT 40	Cafeteria plan of supply chain—choosing the warrior way
	ARMED FORCES' CANTEEN STORES DEPARTMENT[40]

The Canteen Stores Department (CSD) has been in the service of the Defence Service for more than five decades. The origin of CSD is essentially set in the British era when Army Canteen Board in India was established as an offshoot of the Navy and the Army Canteen Board in the UK. The Army Canteen Board in India was established mainly to provide canteen facilities to British troops in India through grocery shops and bars run by canteen contractors. After independence, two Canteen Store Departments, i.e., CSD (India) and CSD (Pakistan) were established.

Objectives of CSD

The Canteen Stores Department of the Indian Army aims at meeting the following objectives.

  (a) Provide consumer goods of high quality to the troops wherever they are, at a price cheaper than the prevailing market rates, as far as possible.
  (b) Ensure that the level of consumer demand satisfaction is maintained at the maximum.
  (c) Generate reasonable profitability to sustain the organization, permit growth, and provide additional facilities for troops and their families.
  (d) Formulate and execute development programmes to improve and maintain organizational effectiveness.

---

[40] Dissertation done by Wg Cdr P. Muthukrishnan, Indian Air Force, under the supervision of the author, Faculty of Management Studies, University of Delhi, 2008.

(e) Periodically analyse and assess the diverse long-term needs and aspirations of defence service forces and undertake timely measures to meet them.

Organization and Locations

CSD functions under the Ministry of Defence. It employs a few serving officers on deputation from the Armed Forces. However, the remaining workforce comprises civilian Central Government employees. CSD Head Office is located at Mumbai. The department controls and manages its fields operations through a network of 34 Area Depots. These Depots have been grouped into five regions based on the Indian States and their contiguity. Accordingly, the Northern Region with its office at BD Bari (Jammu) covers the states of J&K and Punjab. The Western Region with its office at Delhi controls the Area Depots located in the states of Delhi, Haryana, Himachal, UT of Chandigarh, Rajasthan, and Gujarat. The Central Region has its office at Lucknow and it takes care of UP, Madhya Pradesh, and Uttaranchal. The Eastern Region with its office at Narangi (Guwahati) controls the Area Depots located in the states of West Bengal, Jharkhand, and the seven states in North-Eastern India. The Southern Region has its head office at Khadki and it controls the field operations in the states of Maharashtra, Andhra Pradesh, Tamil Nadu, Karnataka, Kerala, Goa, Orissa, and Union Territory of Andaman & Nicobar Islands.

Products Handled for Sales

The retail sales are done through Unit Run Canteens (URCs). The CSD attempts to provide a wide range of consumer items. The range at present is approximately 2842 items including items Against-Firm-Demand. For the purposes of warehousing management and ease of indenting by URCs, the inventory has been grouped as shown in Table 8.8, based on functional commonality.

URC procures all the products mentioned above except products listed under Group 7 from Main CSD Depot at an average frequency of once in five weeks depending upon the availability of the stock at the depot and at the URC.

Existing Supply Chain at CSD

Source of Supply—Main CSD Depot

The main CSD Depot receives demanded items from the Distributors for all the Groups of items. The distributors supply based on the demand placed by the CSD. The function of the Main Depot is to collect the demand invoices from the various URCs and supply the items to them. The process involves submission of the invoice by the URCs, pricing of the requisitioned items, preparation of the cheque for the specified amount, and obtaining delivery of the items. This is the point of primary sales as far as the CSD is concerned. In so far as the URC is concerned this is the

TABLE 8.8 Variety of products supplied by the CSD for customer sales

Group no.	Group subhead	Item details
1.	Toilet requisites	Washing, bathing soaps, detergents, cosmetics, hair care items, perfumes, napkins, towels, cleaning brushes, etc.
2.	Household requisites	Flasks, casseroles, crockery items, gas stove and lighter, kitchen accessories, torches, batteries, table lamps, mixer grinders, irons, cameras, fans, film role, incense sticks, water filters, mosquito repellents, naphthalene balls, etc.
3.	General use items	Plastic jugs, water bottles, buckets, mugs, cycles, tyres, tubes, plastic mats, plastic drums, travelling bags, bed sheet covers, suitcases, gents and ladies innerwear garments, blankets, shoes, sports items, clothing items, mattress, weighing machines, golf sets, sunglasses, etc.
4.	Wrist watches and smokers' requisites	Wrist watches for gents and ladies, office equipment, cigarettes, shotgun cartridges, table clocks, safety matches, etc.
5.	Liquor	Various types of wines, rum, whisky, gin, beer, vodka, champagne, etc.
6.	Food, stationery, and medicinal items	Food beverages, bottle drinks, baby foods, confectionary, sauces and ketchup, jams, honey, milk, condensed power, edible oils, ghee, snacks, tea, coffee, pickles, noodles, note books, registers, greeting cards, pens, medicinal antiseptic applications, health care and digestive medicines, etc.
7.	Against-firm-demand Cat-I & II	CAT-I = Oven, dish washer, washing machine, TV, sewing machine, four wheelers, two wheelers, heavy duty vehicles, refrigerators, AC, coolers, etc.
		CAT-II = Wooden furniture, wardrobe, pedestal fans, radio cassette players, mattress, water purifier, golf balls, store well, sunglasses, VCR, etc.

source of supply. From the main depot the goods are transported to the URC warehouse where these are stocked before they are displayed in the retail centre. The Retail centre is next to the warehouse. The final sales takes place at the retail centre.

Areas of Concern

The main areas of concern that were observed were

(a) **Financial performance** Of late, the financial performance of the URC has been declining, e.g., the net profit to sales ratio has reduced from .72 to .60 and stock to sales ratio increased from .4 to .12. The gross profit, net profit, and the operating profit all had reduced.

(b) **Sales performance**   The sales have remained stagnant and even though the number of customers had increased, the sales for 2007 dipped by around 4.5 per cent as compared to 2006.

(c) **Non value activities**   It was noticed that non-value added (NVA) activities were adding up to the lead times for procurement, total cycle time, cash to cash time, and transaction times. Only 23 per cent of the total time was spent in actual value addition.

(d) **Demand forecasting and inventory policy**   There were no set procedures for demand forecasting and a rudimentary inventory policy was being followed. Judgmental forecasting methods were being used for demand forecasting. The forecasting was based on the manager's opinion. Judgmental forecasting methods are, by their very nature, subjective, and they may involve such qualities as intuition, expert opinion, and experience. The manager was using his best judgment and the feedback received from the customers from the feedback register to make the demand forecast. There was therefore, considerable scope for improvement in areas of both demand forecasting and materials management.

The closing stock levels had increased indicating increased inventory holding levels. There were large purchases and the sales were lesser. It seemed a reactionary type of purchasing was being resorted to. It could be observed that in certain months purchases were higher than sales, and in certain other months with regard to the same items, no purchases were being carried out due to excess available inventory. The warehouse capacity was less leading to over stacking and/or improper stacking— leading to higher number of defects and returns. The manager was resorting to physical counting of the inventory of various products in the warehouse to determine available stock levels, leading to very high queue times in the activity relating to demand forecasting and more importantly, the inventory turnover was low.

Management Exercises Undertaken

The CSD management undertook the following exercises in solving supply related problems.

Using value chain mapping, the non-value activities were identified and efforts made to eliminate/reduce them through the application of Kaizen initiatives and thereby, the supply chain value was enhanced.

Using periodic inventory review policy, the base stock levels that need to be maintained was determined. This, in turn resulted in substantial financial gains.

Using Six Sigma approach, an attempt was made to enhance customer satisfaction through reduction in transaction times.

Kaizen Initiative in Demand Planning

The queue time taken for demand forecasting based on the warehouse demand and customer feedback and preparing the invoice was as high as 2 days. It was opinioned that scope existed to considerably reduce this queue time. After having taken up for the kaizen initiative, the times for the walking time and waiting time were drastically reduced by around 45 per cent to meet the standard work combination sheet specifications. This was achieved by having the proper electronic information system and having a proper inventory model.

Inventory Management at CSD

Inventories represent the largest asset category of the canteen. Decisions relating to inventories are taken primarily by the canteen manager in consultation with the canteen officer, accounts manager, and billing staff. Inventory management has important financial implications, the canteen manager has responsibility to ensure that the inventories are properly monitored and controlled. Inventory management can be classified under the following subheadings. Key factors affecting inventory policy are the following.

- Customer demand
- Replacement lead time
- Number of different products
- Length of the planning horizon
- Costs

  (a) Order Cost: Cost of the product and transportation cost
  (b) Inventory holding cost or Inventory holding consists of

    (i) State taxes, property taxes and insurance on inventory
    (ii) Maintenance costs
    (iii) Obsolescence cost (risk that the item loses some of the value because of changes in the market)
    (iv) Opportunity costs: Represents the return on investments that one would receive had money been invested in something else

The inventory management in CSD has been a little traditional one. The inventory figures are generally very high. The reasons commonly cited for this are that the canteen manager will be questioned for stock-outs but they are not questioned for high inventories. Lengthy and cumbersome demand and purchase procedures force the canteen managers to carry huge amount of inventories. Due to lack of standardization, there is a large variety of stores.

Demand Planning and Forecasting at the Unit Run Canteen (URC)

The demand planning activity was being carried out as a routine activity. Every month a fixed quantity was being ordered. A study of the group-wise purchase and sales data for the financial year 2006–07 showed that items were being procured in large quantities without ascertaining the consumption levels, and the stock was being expended over a period of two to three months. This resulted in the capital being locked up for long durations without generating the requisite returns. The inventory levels were extremely high in certain cases, and in certain other cases, because of the locking in of the capital, stock-outs were occurring in certain products. The annual sales figures clearly showed that the sales of Group 5 was more than of any other group.

The URC forecasts the requirement of items to cater for the succeeding period only. Therefore, the periodic inventory review policy was considered to be the most appropriate for the URC. In this concept, the inventory level is reviewed periodically, at regular intervals, and an appropriate quantity is ordered after each review. Since inventory levels are reviewed at a periodic interval, the fixed cost of placing an order is a sunk cost and hence, can be ignored; presumably, the fixed cost was used to determine the review interval. The quantity ordered arrives after the appropriate lead time. Since fixed cost does not play a role in this environment, the inventory policy is characterized by one parameter, the base-stock level. That is, the URC determines a target inventory level, the base-stock level, and during each review period, the inventory position is reviewed and the URC orders enough to raise the inventory position to the base-stock level.

Outcome of the Management Initiatives

In CSD the management reported the following benefits out of the initiatives implemented.

1. All forms, desktop folders, and customer feedbacks were located on each desk at exact locations. This made handoffs less and pickups to occur quickly and easily.
2. A standardized work combination sheet was created to further define and improve cycle time.
3. The forecasting and the invoice preparation were prepared from the desk of the manager, thereby, reducing the queue time from 16 hrs to 6 hrs. Here, the walking time + waiting time was reduced by as much as 80 per cent by rearranging the complete warehouse group wise.
4. A good kanban system at the warehouse and retail were placed. This reduced manual time from 240 min to 150 min.

5. The analysing time also reduced to half as the worked out inventory model proved helpful.
6. By arranging the work area the walking time reduced by 45 per cent. The overall cycle time has also reduced to half.

Kaizen Initiative in Procurement

Preparation of Invoice

The standard work combination sheet brought out that the queue time was 24 hrs, in the preparation of the invoice. It was observed that the WT was almost 120 min in getting the final requirement from the office or from the forecast. This was reduced through the introduction of computers in the canteen, which made it easier to follow and prepare the invoice through standardized templates, and use of the database from the retail counter. These changes brought down the queue times from the 24 hrs to 4hrs.

Pricing and Finalizing the Demand

The pricing and finalizing steps involved physical movement of the staff to go to the supplier and get the pricing done after checking the availability of the items. Here, the queue time was 32 hrs. This was reduced through the use of Internet and e-mail facility wherein the queue time was brought down to 8 hrs.

Purchase Order

The purchase order was electronically developed in report format removing the requirement to generate it manually, and the same was sent through e-mail with telephonic confirmation of quantities.

Billing Time Reduction

Another major area of concern was billing time reduction. Here, a Six Sigma approach was identified to handle this area.

The total value added with the above initiatives worked out to around 45 per cent.

Supply Chain Performance Assessment Post-management Initiatives

The following financial performance measures were considered to evaluate the supply chain value post the *kaizens* and the lean initiatives.

(a) *Total assets turn over ratio*   This increased by approx 40 per cent.
(b) *Inventory turn over ratio*   The increase was approx 34 per cent.
(c) *Expenses ratio*   A reduction of approx 30 per cent was achieved.

(d) *Gross profit ratio*   The increase was upto the tune of 19 per cent.

(e) *Net profit margin ratio*   This showed marginal improvement from 4.1 to 4.2.

Measuring and Evaluating Customer Perspective

This was done qualitatively through reduction in query times, improved range, and availability of products and services without stock-outs, and reduced inventory holding using the inventory model that was designed and put in place. The transaction times were reduced with the canteen achieving 3 Sigma level in this aspect from just 1.5 level. Defect-free billing was ensured through the introduction of bar code scanners.

Internal Business Perspective

It was seen that post the implementation of the project initiatives, the procurement time had reduced by around 56 per cent, which in turn reduced the base-stock levels of the products for the same service levels. Additionally, the total cycle time and cash to cash cycle time also had reduced by 40 per cent and 25 per cent respectively, thereby enhancing the supply chain value.

Innovation and Learning Perspective

The importance of customer feedback and customer satisfaction was a great take-away, as was the need for following a scientific inventory management technique. The employees also understood the nuances and intricacies of using and formulating work combination sheets, and by now, could not underestimate the bad effects of wasteful activities and poor work culture on profitability.

9

Issues, Challenges, and Opportunities in Implementation of SCM

The corporate sector does not necessarily practise what it preaches or admires. It could be due to resource constraints or a changing management leadership, commitment, and philosophy in the company. However, one thing is clear that most companies in consumer goods industries have started giving due importance to supply chain management (SCM), and have a strategic intent and orientation to do the same. It is important to note that all of them have implemented either one or more modules of the enterprise resource planning (ERP) system, or their own legacy or proprietary system for overall planning of resources enterprise-wide.

KEY IMPLEMENTATION ISSUES

Let us analyse the status of SCM with respect to the eight areas of SCM implementation, as outlined earlier.[1]

SCM Intent, Orientation, Organization, and Interrelationships

1. 75 per cent of the companies have not developed SCM as a 'stand-alone' function because of lack of recognition and coherent view, but it certainly needs coordination with other functional areas of the organization, and even outside as an 'extended enterprise'.
2. All companies now realize that SCM is an important component of corporate strategy for gaining competitive advantage.
3. All companies advocate that SCM is impacted by changes in the internal as well as external environmental factors, particularly, related to market operations, i.e., suppliers, pricing, distribution, customers, and the urgency to develop and market a new product, as also the relative position or leverage in the market place enjoyed by them.

---

[1] These conclusions are drawn after administration of the checklist as outlined in Chapter 7 and given in Appendix A7.1, to 30 respondent companies in the consumer goods category—both FMCG and durables. The checklist was developed on the basis of issues discussed throughout the text.

4. All enterprises believe that concurrent or integrated application of SCM and customer relationship management (CRM) yields even better business and operational results due to synergistic effect. In fact, SCM itself has primary orientation towards customer contact, relationship, and orientation, but CRM would go a stage ahead in acquiring, retaining, and developing customers on the basis of their existing or potential buying behaviour.

5. All companies agree that SCM invariably involves close working with suppliers in the form of joint action, continuity, and providing for verification of each other's capabilities.

6. 75 per cent of the companies agree that SCM yields better customer service levels in terms of customer satisfaction, loyalty, regain, and retention programmes.

7. SCM is perceived by most companies as a cost reduction, quality and productivity improvement, and business process re-engineering (BPR) exercise that has potential for an enhanced return on investment (ROI) for their organization.

8. 75 per cent of the companies agree that SCM is a no–nonsense function, and is not possible without the use of information technology (IT) systems, tools, and techniques, and requires integration of information processes and flows.

9. Most companies are of the view that SCM must be preceded by an extensive BPR to eliminate/reduce non-value added (NVA) activities and implement the information systems.

10. SCM keeps the focal firm on its toes in terms of a continuous benchmarking against the competitor's products, processes, and costs.

11. Most organizations also agree that lean operations technique facilitate *single-piece* flow, and thus, easier implementation of SCM.

12. Nearly all the companies agree that working closely with suppliers at different stages is a critical factor for the successful implementation of SCM.

SCM and Collaborative Forecasting and Planning

1. Most companies agree that collaborative forecasting and planning in coordination with suppliers, distribution centre (DC), and dealers/retailers is a must for SCM.

2. The demand planning system can be either *forecast-driven* or *order-driven,* though the latter is preferred for pull-based SCM. Many organizations, however, use a combination of the two.

3. There must be on-hand availability and visibility of data across the company, particularly at the distribution centre (DC) level, for capturing and analysing demand patterns.

4. Tracking of 'point-of-sale' (PoS) data is a prerequisite for demand forecasting. This would also minimize the *bullwhip effect*[2].

5. All the sales must be tracked to forecasts of the relevant time interval and gaps should be fixed. For this, all *variance reports* from the previous forecasts should be prepared.

6. An 80 : 20 rule can be followed where 20 per cent of forecast should cover 80 per cent of the demand and 80 per cent forecast covers 20 per cent of the demand.

7. Forecasts must be prepared on a disaggregated basis for different models/product-family/product lines/part number, and DC/customer-wise.

SCM and Use of IT Practices and Tools

Most of the corporate executives express the following view.

1. It is required to chart out all information processes and pathways for real-time information sharing among all channel members, e.g., the suppliers, the internal customers of the focal form, and external customers.

2. It is necessary to integrate all information flows with 'work processes' and one should always move from the functions to the processes.

3. It is necessary to have electronic data interchange (EDI) with suppliers and retailers.

4. Overall, it is essential to have an integrated resources planning system enterprise-wide and even its extensions, e.g., ERP with an authorized access/plug-in facility for suppliers and retailers for successful implementation of SCM.

5. Most companies say that 75–90 per cent of their vendors are now accessible through e-mail and have their own website.

6. 60 per cent of the companies or focal firms implementing SCM have an *interactive* website for providing pre-sale support in terms of the following.

   - Product information
   - Order enquiries and booking
   - Pricing information
   - Customer requested configuration
   - Order tracking and tracing

   In fact, some companies have portals which encourage customers to create and post online enquiries/specifications/quotations.

---

[2] As has been discussed in Chapter 2, bullwhip effect refers to amplification in demand from retailers to upper levels due to poor availability of data relating to sales and demand patterns, thus resulting in 'phantom' demands and faulty forecasts.

7. Most of the companies are doing at least 40 per cent of their procurement through the Internet (e-procurement). Competitive bidding is being discouraged in most cases, unless it is a general item and negotiations are encouraged.

8. Around 70 per cent of the companies studied had ERP or such other system installed in their enterprise, but hardly 20 per cent of these companies had implemented all the modules of the ERP system. Most of the companies had first implemented the financials (FI/CO) module, then customer order management, followed by material planning, sales, and distribution, etc. In fact, non-ERP applications accounted for around 1/4 of the total applications. A good 60 per cent of companies use standardized software such as SAP/ MFG PRO/Marshall, while the remaining 40 per cent use their own proprietary or legacy systems.

Strategic Outsourcing and Supplier Relationships (Including Supplier Rating and Development)

1. Most companies are of the view that they take *make-or-buy* decisions with respect to their *core-competence*. Normally, the core-competent activities are retained and non core-competent are outsourced to suppliers on a long-term basis.

2. Suppliers who provide flexibility in volume and variety and who demons-trate potential to help in cost reduction programmes are preferred. Interestingly, suppliers providing flexibility in 'volume' are preferred over suppliers providing flexibility in only 'variety'.

3. System/sub-system sourcing is preferred over part–sourcing, subject to the competency factor.

4. Nearly all companies are carrying out the consolidation of their vendors and do not have more than 2–3 vendors/parts.

5. 75 per cent of companies are ready to share real-time information related to demand, inventory levels, and production schedules with their vendors, which is a good sign for collaborative planning, demand forecasting and inventory replenishment, as also with other channel members.

6. Most companies rate suppliers on the basis of a mix of criteria, namely price, quality, delivery, and service, but many companies end up selecting vendors who had not quoted the *lowest bid*. In fact, these odd 30 per cent of the companies would select suppliers on the basis of *total cost of ownership* (TCO), rather than just on the basis of 'quoted price'. That is one reason why negotiations on *net adjusted price* rather than the *quoted price* should be the factor for selecting the vendor.

7. Focal firms/original equipment manufacturer (OEM) buyers are exploring all possible actions as a part of developing strategic partnership and networking with their suppliers, on a reciprocative basis, in terms of

(a) joint product/process design activities,

(b) joint forecasting by sharing demand/supply/sales patterns,

(c) verification of each other's capabilities, capacities, and systems, and

(d) ongoing cost reduction/value analysis programmes.

So, suppliers are not being developed only in terms of financial, technicals, and human resources training, but also in a number of other ways specific to a particular OEM buyer–supplier relationship requirement.

8. Most firms prefer proximal vendors and have around 30 per cent of their vendors in a range of 100 kms, and prefer *online delivery of parts* from these sources to their plants. The vendors also post their executives in the focal firm's plant for production-related information sharing, and real-time material planning and control (JIT-II).

9. 60 per cent companies have one or the other system for tracking of order releases and receipts, and the ability to follow/expedite/modify the orders.

SCM and Modern Manufacturing Practices and Systems (Including Master Production Scheduling and Material Planning)

1. Most companies follow the practice of making *master production schedules (MPS)* and make these responsive enough to changes in demand levels to some extent, normally in a range of 10–30 per cent, based on a proprietary method developed by them.

2. 70 per cent companies are following a structured and systematic material planning system, e.g., material requirements planning (MRP) to develop *net material requirements* and release shop/purchase orders on the basis of bill of materials (BOM), material production schedule (MPS), current inventory status, and supply lead times.

3. Most companies combine the MRP lot size with the economic batch size to decide economic order (purchase) quantities and also the *reorder points (ROPs)*.

4. Most companies have developed their own legacy methods to carry out a *rough cut capacity planning (RCCP)* in case of minor changes in MPS because of fluctuations in demand.

5. Most companies have done *time-fencing* of their schedules and plans, and demonstrate a firm period–schedule commitment.

6. Around 60 per cent of companies regularly assess their work centre capabilities and capacities, routing, and production flow analysis (PFA) to streamline their capacity requirements planning (CRP) at the shop floor level.

7. All the studied companies prefer and continuously explore *cellular–manufacturing* possibilities, wherever possible in their plant, to have better turnover and productivity in the use of resources such as space, machines, materials, and human resources.

Lean Operations' Techniques

1. All the companies studied appreciate the significance of reduction of *seven wastes* as per *Toyota Production System (TPS)*, namely over-production, buffer, waiting-time, transportation, defects, inappropriate processing, and unnecessary movements.
2. All companies appreciate the role of *single-piece flow* in manufacturing and try to achieve it by layout engineering.
3. Around 30–40 per cent of companies follow online delivery of parts and foolproof devices (*poka-yoke*) in their machines.
4. Total Preventive Maintenance (TPM) is being followed in 60–70 per cent of the companies through a mix of activities.
5. 40 per cent of companies follow a 'pull-based' material control or *kanban*, or such other visual control system for inventory.
6. Most companies, in order to achieve *synchronous manufacturing*, try out frequent line balancing/configurational changes for *takt time* management or cycle–time reduction.

SCM and Transportation, Logistics, and Warehousing (WH)

1. All companies agree that successful implementation of SCM greatly requires integration of inbound and outbound logistics.
2. Most companies would like to enter into long-term service level agreements (SLAs) with transporters and develop a system for rating the transporters.
3. Only 30 per cent of companies believe that 3PLs are required to facilitate and simplify logistics to and from the focal company. Therefore, only around 1/3 of the companies use 3PLs, their networks, and services, which is not very promising.
4. All companies believe that *freight consolidation/route rationalization* pays off significantly in reducing costs of SCM.
5. 70 per cent companies agree that a dynamic mode of *carrier and route* selection could be effective in reducing stock levels, stock-outs, and streamlining inventory flows.
6. All companies agree that customization of delivery (mode/route/frequency/destination) should be based on customer-specific requirements.
7. 60 per cent companies have decentralized some amount of forecasting at DC level which must have on-hand inventory availability and visibility of data all the time for the purpose.
8. Around 70 per cent companies follow *bar coding, milk round system* (MRS), *recyclable packing,* and *cross-docking,* etc., in one or the other manner. Except for one, no respondent company reported use of radio frequency identification (RFID). It might be used more in the retail industry.

Customer Relationships

1. All companies studied recognize the ever increasing role of customer retention, continuous customer contact, and initiatives such as customer-loyalty and affinity programmes.
2. 75 per cent of the respondent companies claim that they had one or the other kind of a CRM system in place, i.e., they had a database of their customers, profiles, and their buying frequency and patterns. To what extent and how they use their database effectively, is however, not clear.
3. Only 40 per cent of companies have a documented well laid-out process to measure customer satisfaction and service levels, and a mechanism to collect, track, assess, and share the feedback among different departments of the company and the suppliers.
4. All companies agree that the *time to market and distribute* a new product is a critical factor for SCM and customer relationships, and they always try to reduce it.
5. All companies prefer to delay differentiation of the product till the retailer's/customer's end to provide flexibility in order configuration (*postponement*).
6. Only 30 per cent companies admit to having a system for estimating measures, such as

   (a) order fulfilment rates,
   (b) per cent degree of orders not met—quality, quantity, and date-wise,
   (b) times when promises to customers are not met,
   (c) number of customer enquiries not entertained/requests denied, and
   (d) number of times there are unduly long problem fixing and resolution time at the customer's end.

THE CHALLENGES

Most companies, which are into SCM, recognized the importance of the value chain when they had to re-engineer their business processes to deliver maximum value to the internal and external customers, and thereby, also redesign and reconfigure the information flows. This was followed by adoption of enterprise level resources planning systems, such as ERP or any other proprietory/legacy system, and some even extended it to their suppliers. Also, factors, such as the time to develop a new product/variant and market and distribute it, is becoming a strategic competitive advantage factor. So, SCM is a strategy adopted by the companies to beat *time competitiveness* and develop *customer-centricity* in their operations. The key challenges can be outlined as follows.

1. The business environment for most consumer products is fast changing, product life cycles (PLCs) are getting even smaller, and the demand patterns are unstable and sometimes seasonal, which poses a great challenge for supply chain managers, particularly in terms of demand planning.

2. The other problem lies in data transparency and supply chain inefficiencies due to the cultural mindset. Reliable data may be difficult to obtain, say, on a daily basis, unless it is directly captured from PoS electronically. Sometimes, there can be erroneous judgement of customer needs or simply, data could be held unreliable due to the mindset factors (Easton and Zhang), such as *trust, win-lose* perspective, and *respect* or 'mind your own business' kind of attitude by dealers, so common in the Asian countries, and more so in India. These factors may actually suppress data transparency and hide supply chain problems and inefficiencies with no chance for exposure. Considerable research needs to be undertaken to analyse the customer feedback through a well-installed CRM system and share it with all the departments to deliver the best value to the customer. Similarly, regular real-time capture and tracking of PoS data from the dealer's/retailer's end is a must for CPFR of supply.

3. The complexity of supply chain networks is particularly serious in countries, such as India, China, and Korea. The distribution channels in most consumer goods are multi-layered, involving 3–4 intermediaries between the manufacturer and the customer. In the US and Europe, 1–2 intermediaries is the norm. The market is controlled by a plethora of small- and medium-sized local wholesalers, all charging 25–30 per cent margin. There are sometimes no national distributors and there are regulatory restrictions to controlling, distribution, and logistics services, or foreign companies owning distribution channels. This leaves distribution channels fragmented, inefficient, and costly. Some restrictions on distribution by certain companies are bound to go from India now being a part of the World Trade Organization (WTO). However, simple disintermediation in the supply chain would bring down the supply chain complexity, and also reduce costs by reducing margins of these extra intermediaries.

4. Many good companies in India have still not used ERP solutions as an enabling technology for focused application for demand management, procurement, inter-enterprise collaboration, or supplier and customer relationship management. In the US and Europe, ERP application and business re-engineering initiatives were over in mid-late 1990s. However, in India, it is still taking time to build *intelligent supply chains*. Many Indian companies have not re-engineerd their supply chain and logistical processes and are only starting to implement ERP in an integrated manner using all the modules. Without an integrated and full-fledged implementation of ERP as a central repository of accurate

transactional data of all functions, and re-engineered and standardized processes, even basic operational improvements in the supply chain cannot be materialized.

5. Also, there is limited scope for e-commerce in the supply chain as the level of Internet penetration is just over 1 per cent as compared to around 25 per cent in Hong Kong. Most of the companies are using Internet only to share information, and not as a means for streamlining or managing their supply chains. The reason is the lack of online payment systems, third-party e-service provisions, and cyber regulations. It will take some more time before e-commerce potential is exploited to the full to leverage the supply chains.

6. The other problem pertains to logistic service providers, say, third party logistics (3PLs) for transportation, tracking, and tracing of consignments and other services. More integration and close coordination is required with 3PLs and/or supplier's transporters. In fact, there is absolute lack of integrated logistic professionals (LPs), not only in the Indian industry but the whole of Asia. In fact, there is not a single pan-Asian 3PL company that could provide integrated sea, rail, road, and air transportation, and distribution, by virtue of which distribution gets highly disintegrated and localized, resulting in the overall supply chain inefficiencies, particularly in terms of time and cost. The complexity is further aggravated by diverse geographies, economies, purchasing power, infrastructural development, cultural, lingual, regulatory tax and tariff differences, particularly in the Indian states and more so at the pan-Asia level.

7. The cost of distribution as a per cent of sales are ever increasing. The respondent companies cited transport infrastructural problems as a cause for this. Also, too many octroi and check post points in the country increase the cost of transportation. The overhead (OH) expenses are very high. Possibly, the supply chain would have to be reconfigured in view of the value added tax (VAT) environment which came into effect from April 2005.

8. Some companies feel that their employees resist to outsourcing due to fear of losing their jobs and controls. Vendors may also resist consolidation and rationalization of vendor base by the company. Appropriate strategies are needed to tackle these changes, otherwise costs of the supply chain escalate.

9. Many companies feel that visibility of data across the supply chain is still a problem, e.g., actual stock levels at the distributor's and retailer's end are still difficult to be known. Fragmented or unorganized trade in some industries also poses a problem for demand forecasting and replenishment particularly in the fast moving consumer goods (FMCG) industry.

10. Some companies feel that dynamic SCM strategies are required in view of the changing environment, and collaboration across industries is needed to drive

better efficiencies, say, in the use of infrastructure in transportation and communication, and using 3PLs. More proliferation of initiatives such as efficient customer response (ECR) is required.

11. Better infrastructural connectivity from the distributor level to a supermarket/ retailer level is needed in both consumer durables and FMCG industries.

12. Companies do not maintain data about the supply chain cost measures. Even if they maintain, the reliability and validity of the data is questionable. For example, costs of reverse logistics, including product returns and backorders have hardly been estimated by the companies.

13. The challenge of turning the supply chain processes, including the procurement and logistics, into socially and environmentally responsive chains is paramount these days. The key challenge of building and using a supply chain infra-structure, e.g., materials, transportation, and assets, without damaging the environment is fast catching up the attention of decision and policy makers. For example, the Asian Productivity Organization (APO) symposium on supply chain management in New Delhi from 9–11 January, 2001, highlighted the need for having a green supply chain and setting up a reverse logistics pro-gramme for firms to ensure ecological balance and waste reduction. However, it cannot be accomplished without motivating the suppliers to act in a socially and environmentally responsive manner. Many companies like Hewlett-Packard (HP), Nokia, and Wal-Mart have well established social and environ-mental responsibility (SER) programmes under which they prefer suppliers who themselves and their (tier 2) suppliers follow environmentally safe materials, and their processes and practices to reduce the negative impact. Nokia controls the CO_2 (carbon dioxide) reduction, energy efficiency, and waste reduction at its suppliers' premises. In 2006, Nokia reduced the size of packaging that enabled them to reduce truckloads by 12,000. Also, they are setting CO_2 emission targets generated by their logistic providers. All globally reputed companies now follow the take-back/reuse/recycle/recovery/safe disposal of environmentally unsafe materials. Now, it is the turn of Indian corporate sector to align their supply chain processes and use the infrastructure to reduce the adverse environmental impact these processes cost to society.

OPPORTUNITIES

In the author's view, the following opportunities can be used to counter the various challenges being faced, particularly by the consumer goods industry—both fast moving and durables, in managing their supply chains.

1. It seems that most companies do not have a *stand-alone* department or role responsible for the supply chain, and lack an integrated view of the supply chain. In most companies supply chain has been operating *in silos*. The companies had a different focus on different objectives, namely quality, responsiveness, cost, and service. For them, quality and cost seem most important, followed by responsiveness and service focus. This is in tune with an earlier ETIG–PwC survey (2002), which stated that only around 45 per cent of the companies were focused on three or more areas. The highest focus in that survey was found to be on quality (71%), followed by responsiveness (64%), cost (62%) and service (51%). That implies that most companies lack a coherent view of what to focus in SCM. Companies need to develop a separate (stand-alone) department with its own role and responsibility for SCM—well integrated with all the other functions and having a strategic intent and orientation towards well-defined objectives in quality, cost, responsiveness, and services aligned with the strategic plan. In fact, they must devise a balanced score card approach for mapping supply chain performance measures with strategic plans and objectives.

2. The key solution lies in the development of better infrastructure in telecommunication, rail network, surface transportation, air and sea, and particularly, multi–modal transportation, e.g. interconnectivity of river-ways in India has a big potential. The Government has to take an initiative in this regard.

3. There should be direct involvement of the customer at the product design and planning stage, i.e., evaluation of customer needs as far as the value of various business products is concerned, say, on the basis of activity-based costing (ABC)/ Pareto Analysis. There should be a purposeful customer value/need segmentation and the niche model/variant must be clearly positioned for that.

4. Companies must strive to do e-procurement as much as possible, and gain excellence in procurement, which is a key supply chain function having a huge potential for cost-saving. The Aberdeen Group estimated the potential to save $690 billion per year in US businesses just by e-sourcing. In India, also it could be substantial. It greatly reduces sourcing cost and time, and brings in transparency.

   An opportunity exists in launching a hub that would connect and synchronize the activities of many e-markets or the horizontal market places, say, at the pan-Asia level. The e-market operators at pan-Asia level could make a global interoperability group (GIG) as a global trading Web (as has happened in Singapore), so that companies with any of the participating e-markets will be able to use a forum such as GIG on the Web to deal online with trading partners around the globe with a discrete business contract, and no strings attached about the technical compatibilities amongst themselves.

5. A dynamic optimization of logistic networks is required. The clearing and forwarding agents (C&FAs) and 3PLs—all have to be networked and put to optimal use.

6. Use of technology for tracking and tracing must be encouraged, e.g., bar coding should be made mandatory. This could help in

- cross-docking,
- up-keep of invoicing and inventory records,
- upkeep of inventory replenishment and planning,
- movement, handling, and logistics, particularly traceability.

Companies should now embark upon use of RFID for better replenishment and detection of pilferages, tamperings, and damages—the cost of which is around 2 per cent in India. It would also reduce product returns and cost of reverse logistics.

7. All-out effort must be made across all industries for integrated development of 3PLs and collaborative logistics. There is hardly any significant number of 3PLs operating in India. Companies still think that the sole purpose of 3PLs is transportation and clearing and forwarding (C&F). What they do not appreciate is that 3PLs can also provide the following services.

- Networked warehousing
- Track and trace services
- Regular reporting of time, costs, and online reporting
- Provision for inter-modal logistics/cross-docking, etc.
- Provision of information linkage regarding inventory levels of a product to all the supply chain partners
- Facilitation freight consolidation/milk run/reverse logistics
- Integrating financial, information, material, and product flows to the maximum channel members

8. Close attention needs to be paid to the monitoring of distribution cost as a per cent of sales. For this, operating costs of various modes of transport are to be controlled and benchmarked. The overhead costs for running a truck in India, for example, are very high. A better cost control system must be in place to reduce these costs.

9. To keep transportation and warehousing (WH) in organized hands in the industry, a rating system should be developed by the focal firm for transporters—as for vendors, long-term service level agreements (SLAs) with reliable transporters should be entered into. Moreover, the company owned

transportation should be always preferred. In case of outside transporters, focus must be laid on the following factors.

- Negotiation of rates
- Freight consolidation/route rationalization
- Flexibility for dynamic mode of carrier/route/frequency selection
- Customization of delivery at customer's end—through intra-company or even inter-company/third-party postponement

10. All companies must have a fundamental sales and operations planning process operating at a cross-functional basis in place. With this, a demand/supply planning software, such as i2 Technologies, Manugistics, SAP, and Oracle can help integrate demand and supply, facilitate data integrity and transparency, and contribute in taking supply chain operations decisions. Some companies cited the need for the development of real-time sales modelling software for accurate forecasting with an inherent ability to learn the sales patterns. For integrating applications and capabilities, enterprise application integration (EAI) or middleware is yet another way to improve inter-enterprise data transfer and data transparency.

   However, if basic operational measures, such as forecast accuracy, line fill, inventory turns, and delivery accuracy are too off-base because of processes not been re-engineered, it is unlikely that any software would strike the magic chord. As put by Easton and Zhang, 30 per cent of the benefits to be derived from a software solution come from the software and technology itself, while 70 per cent would accrue from process re-engineering.

11. Companies must regularly do benchmarking and share best practices in the supply chain management (SCM). Efforts must be made to continuously update those standards and strive for improvement at the processes' levels. Using a supply chain operations reference (SCOR) model is quite instrumental in this regard. A global research team at the Michigan State University, as a part of a multi-year study on supply chain excellence identified 'performance metrics and benchmarking' as one of the top drivers of supply chain excellence. However, Accenture, a leading IT and Supply chain consultant claims by virtue of its extensive client experience that most of the times the following happens.

   (i) Standard measures of SC and their definitions do not exist.

   (ii) There are only a few supply chain measures that would speak of cross-functional performance. These are even manipulated in Asian companies to produce favourable results or even 'save one's face' or under the garb of 'minding one's own business' as Easton and Zhang tell by their client experience. The situation is no different in India, as this author feels.

(iii) There may be just a rule of thumb for setting and calculating key performance indicators (KPIs). Many companies in India could be very ambitious about setting KPI targets without a consensus, and taking into account ground realities and best practices, which if not achieved, would demoralize the people involved. (Many would, in fact, manipulate as a safeguard!)

(iv) Inappropriate data is collected from the wrong sources for KPIs calculation. Different sources and stages of data (according to the transaction) might be used for calculation of certain KPIs, which would be inconsistent time to time. There may be poor or non-existent data archiving and retrieval services, which would result in setting a wrong benchmark, at least not based on the original document and hence, performance measurement could be faulty by design, i.e., using a reference point, which has been iterated many times in the transaction process without its original value being retained.

(v) There could also be complete lack of performance management culture where relevant people do not know how the supply chain KPIs have been set and for what purpose. Also, they may fail to identify the performance measurement process owners at each stage who are responsible for data capture to reporting, and feedback may miss altogether, which would result into lack of confidence among the supply chain staff.

12. Indian companies still need to deploy SCM as a strategy to reduce customer response time, improvement of service levels, and time to develop and market new variants/products.

13. An effective SCM cannot be implemented unless *single-piece* manufacturing is followed in principle in the plant, which in turn would result in reduced work-in-progress (WIP) levels, better layouts, and faster inventory turnover, thereby, reducing set-up and cycle times, and developing multi-skilled employees. SCM will thus, go a long way in developing agility in the operations of the company through its supply chain to meet varying needs of 'volume' and 'variety' of the customers—so crucial a factor for SCM.

14. It is always a good opportunity that the supply chain be extended both on the suppliers and customers' side by long-term collaboration. The collaboration can occur at the industry level, say, for logistics, e.g., the ECR initiative or product design through shared research and development (R&D). In the consumer goods industry, Nestle and P&G are already known to use this in logistics. One common example is using such alliances in the airline industry. Alliances, such as *Oneworld* and *Star Alliance*, competing airlines, collaborate and synchronize the flow of passengers on a seat sharing basis to optimize

capacity utilization. Similarly, an alliance of logistics providers could synchronize the complex flow of goods and services of a number of companies in an industry into, out of, and across the country, or even pan-SAARC, pan-ASEAN, or pan-Asia countries. This is the opportunity of the future. What is required is IT-enabled hubs with good connectivity.

The next level down could be collaboration for dispersed manufacturing/ processing and/or distribution units. This holds true for companies, such as Hewlett-Packard, Microsoft, Benetton, IBM, and Wal-Mart whose supply bases, design and development centres, distribution, packaging and customizing centres, and retail/customer touch points are located on a dispersed basis.

A further level down could be at the company's level when both its vendors and retailers enter into collaboration to share their information online, related to production plans and sales pattern for a collaborative mode of planning, forecasting, and replenishment of inventory at various stages. It can further involve vendor-managed inventory (VMI), collaborative product/part designing, joint capacity planning, and its synchronization with order fulfilment.

15. It is necessary to integrate operating technologies with the system architecture. The planning and scheduling systems and operating technologies on the shop floor, such as MRP and capacity requirement planning (CRP) should be well linked with the ERP system and its architecture. The ultimate objective is to make the supply chain a real seamless one inside the company, and have a virtual integration amongst supply chain partners outside also. The company must integrate and optimize the technologies in operation on the front-end (customer facing), e.g., CRM and back-end (supplier facing), e.g., SRM with their core ERP system. Only then resources and information can be better leveraged, reducing overall costs and helping make better and well-informed decisions.

16. Companies implementing SCM should maintain a customer database which has a profiling of customers together with their buying frequency and behaviour, so that they can be targeted for loyalty and affinity programmes for retention and regain of the supply chain for long periods. Also, data pertaining to changes in their life-cycle and buying patterns should also be updated.

17. Companies should develop supply chain performance benchmarks based on the linkage with the strategic objectives, i.e., those related with corporate profits, market share, customer satisfaction, agility of supply chain, etc. A balanced score card approach can be used well for such purposes.

18. Focus must be paid on the alignment of SC with respect to demand, inventory, and pricing levels. In order to avoid *phantom* demands raised by retailers or supply chain members down-stream the chain, allocation of ordering quantity should be done on the basis of *past sales records* and in case of shortages, retailers

must be asked to follow a *stabilized or value based pricing*, rather than sudden promotional pricing campaigns. A constant value-pricing strategy would result in better alignment of SC with inventory, demand, and still generating higher sales revenue and corporate profits on a long-term basis.

19. Indian companies must not hesitate in outsourcing the non-core competent logistical activities to 3PL providers. One common activity outsourced is fulfilment, i.e., transportation, warehousing, and inventory management. By outsourcing these activities, companies can expect to increase inventory turns, order fill rates, on-time shipments, and reduced obsolescence and returned scrap. The outsourcing market in US rose from $8.6 bn in 2002 to $29.2 bn in 2005. Microsoft, Hewlett-Packard, Colgate-Palmolive, Johnson & Johnson, Compaq, Motorola, Nokia, Proctor & Gamble, and Ericsson—have all outsourced their Asian SCM operations.

20. Interestingly, there is an opportunity to cut costs in supply chain in the form of taxes. The government should take initiatives on finding out ways to cut and rationalize costs in the form of octroi, freight, VAT, etc., so that tax efficiencies can be built in the supply chain. There should not be any multiplicity of taxes for which uniform VAT is the answer. Some states in India have not implemented VAT or they have unequal rates. Financial consultants can advise companies to build tax-efficient supply chain at different stages. KPMG calls such initiatives as tax-efficient supply chain management (TESCM).

21. It is the turn of small and medium enterprises (SMEs) to embark upon SCM, taking the lead from their OEMs or suppliers. They can invest in supply chain infrastructure at their level to reap long-term benefits. Companies like SAP have low cost, high value software programmes designed and developed for SCM of SMEs. Organizations like APO has also worked in implementing training programmes for SMEs in SCM.

RECAPITULATION

Indian companies face a lot of challenges while managing their supply chains. One key reason for this is the diversity in geography, people and their purchasing power, culture, language, customs, regulations, and tax structure, etc. Also, at least in the consumer goods industry, distribution is in the hands of myriad wholesalers/distributors who do not have standard business systems and processes and have the aptitude for these either. While in the US and Europe, conglomerates are a dimini-

shing organizational form, in this part of Asia, they continue to dominate the market. In fact around 30 per cent of Asia's 50 largest companies could be conglomerates. They may be assumed to derive efficiency from their scale and scope of operations, but entities within them adopt a portfolio approach for decision in investments. This results in the use of disparate technology systems and architecture, which would inhibit the transparency of information, fewer enterprise performance measures, and less opportunity to collaborate at the group level. So, big companies do not always mean better or efficient supply chains.

Indian companies still face shortage of skilled people in the supply chain and logistics industry, lack of professionalism, dearth of enabling technologies, and most importantly, balanced development of infrastructure. Most companies' supply chains are not properly engineered for their processes and could be fragmented and irrationalized. Most companies have not exploited the ERP platforms to the full and integrate these with front-ends and back-ends. The companies need to integrate their demand and supply, such as Wal-Mart and Dell. Another step is to integrate technologies with the system architecture. Fundamentally, there should be a strong sales and operations planning process, and then it can be a demand/supply planning system from any of the vendors, such as i2, SAP, and Oracle. There is also a need to have synchronized processing on the shop floor and an order fulfilment process. There is an opportunity for the companies to source the capabilities intelligently such as Dell. One common activity which can be outsourced is the order fulfilment comprising transportation, warehousing, and inventory management, which, if intelligently and carefully outsourced and regularly monitored, would reduce supply chain inefficiencies to a great extent. Opportunities must be explored for shared logistics using a 3PL. An all-out effort must be made for exploiting the potential of e-commerce, particularly, e-procurement to reduce cycle times, and gain efficiency and transparency. Great opportunity lies in extending the supply chain through collaboration with suppliers, customers, and 3PLs, and developing alliances and ventures first at the company level, then at multiple enterprise level, followed by the industry level. At the end of it all, the enterprises may not have the right supply chain performance measures in place, as the data might be based on transactional information iterated time to time, or there may not be a proper supply chain performance management culture, and to top it, no feedback is shared with the appropriate people.

CONCEPT REVIEW QUESTIONS

1. What are the key issues in the implementation of supply chain management? Which of them are more relevant in the global context?
2. Briefly discuss the challenges being faced by the Indian consumer goods industry while implementing supply chain management. How can these be tackled, according to you?
3. What are the major benefits expected to be reaped from the implementation of supply chain management, say, in the Indian environment?

CRITICAL THINKING QUESTIONS

1. According to you, what are seemingly the common origins of most of the challenges being faced by the Indian consumer goods industry? Compare these with some apparent challenges in the services industry, while implementing supply chain management in the Indian context, but with global benchmarks and aspirations.
2. What are the kinds of opportunities you perceive for supply chain implementation by the Indian industry as a whole? How do you assess the preparedness of Indian corporates to meet these opportunities, say, by the end of this decade.

PROJECT ASSIGNMENTS

1. Select a multinational manufacturing company operating in India, such as Hewlett-Packard, IBM, P&G, Nestle, Samsung, LG Electronics, Toyota, etc., and assess their supply chain operations in India with respect to global performance benchmarks in different functions of the supply chain, e.g., procurement, manufacturing, sales, distribution, logistics, supplier and customer relationships, concern for the environment, and conservation of energy and resources.

2. Take the example of service multinationals, e.g., British Airways, Radisson Hotels, Jet Airways, FedEx, DHL, McDonald's, etc., and find out how they are coping up with supply chain management challenges in India, as well as meeting opportunities. Outline the strategies adopted by them in this regard.

REFERENCES

Bowman, Robert (10 July 2008), 'Intermodal is Gaining Ground on Long-Haul Trucking, Exec Says', *Supply Chain Brain.*

Bowman, Robert (1 March 2005), 'Thinking Strategically about Outsourcing; 3PLs can Do Much More than Cut Costs', *Supply Chain Brain.*

Bowman, Robert J. (2000), 'For Asian Supply Chain, Good News and Bad', *Supply Chain Brain.*

Jaffe, Douglas A., Caron Harrison, and Wilvin Chee (July 2001), 'Taking Logistics into the 21st Century: A Study of Logistics in Asia-Pacific (Excluding Japan)', IDC, pp. 21–28.

Magretta, Joan (September–October 1998), 'Fast, Global and Entrepreneurial; Supply Chain Management Hong Kong Style', An interview with Victor Fung, *Harvard Business Review*, pp. 105–106.

Manion, David (19 November 1999), 'Asia Pacific Supply Chain Survey', CommerceNet.

Sahay, B.S. (2001), *Supply Chain Management in the Twenty First Century*, Macmillan India, New Delhi.

The Global Research Team, Michigan State University (1995), 'World Class Logistics: The Challenge of Making Continuous Change', Council of Logistics Management.

Internet Resources

'APO Symposium on Supply Chain Management', 2001, Asian Productivity Organization Project Report, New Delhi, India, 9–11 January, http://www.apo-tokyo.org/projreps/projrep0002.pdf, as accessed on 30 March 2010

Easton, Robert J., and Tian Bing Zhang, 'Supply Chains in Asia: Challenges and Opportunities', as posted on www.accenture.com/countries/India/Research_and Insights, as accessed on 15 May 2009

http://cscmp.org, as accessed on 5 March 2010

www.ism.ws, as accessed on 5 March 2010

www.manufacturing.net/Industry-Supply-Chain.aspx?, as accessed on 30 March 2010

www.sap.com/solutions/sme

www.sme.sap.com

www.supplychainbrain.com, as accessed on 10 July 2008

www.supply-chain.org, as accessed on 5 March 2010

Glossary

Activity-based Costing (ABC)   It is an accounting methodology, which assigns costs to items on the basis of the activities which are incurred. Here, the activities, not the products or services, are seen as the primary cause of costs. Through ABC, the purchasing and supply manager can encourage the supplier to make correct estimates and understand the overheads of the products being purchased. ABC is a part of total ABM (activity-based management).

Advanced Planning and Scheduling (APS)   It is a module of SSA SCM system that provides the visibility and decision-making tools for demand planning, resource allocation, and production scheduling, thereby synchronizing manufacturing operations and resources with customer priorities using the planning process constraints.

Agile Supply Chain   It is a kind of supply chain that is able to meet the volatile customer demands in terms of volume and variety in a cost-effective manner in a continuously changing and unpredictable business environment. It refers to the using of market knowledge and virtual integration to exploit profitable opportunities in a volatile marketplace to the strategic advantage of the company. These operate on the basis of real demand (PoS data) and not forecasted demand, i.e., these operate on demand-pull basis.

Agility (of Supply Chain)   It refers to the upside production and/or distribution flexibility of the supply chain to extra demand. An upside flexibility to absorb 20 per cent random demand is quite desirable.

Advanced Inventory Management (AIM)   This module of QAD's MFG/Pro offers a range of inventory management facilities, such as controlling the receipt, put-away, storage, picking, and shipping of inventory using warehouses that exist in the MFG/Pro environment. It provides for flexible replenishment, labour schedul-ing and task management, and lot sizing calculations for warehousing as well as cross-docking.

Alliance   It is a strategic long-term relationship of the buyer with the supplier, comprising early supplier involvement for collaboration, with the goal of synergy (concern for each other's well-being). It is a long duration activity with high collaboration and high competitive advantage.

Application Layer/Middleware   In an ERP system, it includes servers for relational databases that entertain structured query language (SQL) reports, transaction processing monitors, directory/security servers, and communication servers.

Asset Specificity   It refers to the specific nature of machines, materials, skills-needing specific joint investments, and development efforts by the buyer into the supplier for long-term capacity share requirements. It is a step short of vertical integration.

Auto ID Technology   It is a tagging, tracing, and tracking technology wherein a 96-bit code called Electronic Product Code (EPC) would be embedded in a memory chip (smart tag) on individual products. A radio frequency (RF) radar would scan the smart tag and in turn, transfer the product's embedded identity code to the Web where all the detailed information on the product can be retrieved through Object Naming Service (ONS) that would act as a 'post office', to retrieve data for trillions of EPC coded objects in the world.

Bar Coding   This technique facilitates material entry or supplies tracking where a scanner can read about the material details for purpose of identification, tagging, tracing, and tracking. It aids faster entry of material, reduces traffic congestion at material inward gate, and reduces errors made during manual entry of material.

Bottleneck Items   These are items that can only be acquired from one supplier, or their delivery is otherwise unreliable, and has a high impact on profit. The buyer–seller power situation is supplier-dominated with moderate interdependency. It is advisable to have a volume insurance contract and vendor-managed inventory, keep extra stocks, and look for new potential suppliers.

Bullwhip/Whiplash Effect   It refers to increase in variance in demand as one moves up in supply chain from the retailer to the distributor's level, to company's warehouses, and its suppliers. Most commonly it occurs due to order batching, in addition to faulty demand forecasting, price fluctuations, and shortage gaming.

Call Centres   These are specialized customer service centres loaded with an agent host software of the company integrated with a toll free/hotline number of the company, thus allowing automatic call routing to these centres resulting into predictive dialing, display of relevant customer data, and a self-service interactive voice response system (IVRS). These centres enable automating the operations of inbound and outbound calls generated between the company and its customers. They are mostly based on global telephony and the Internet, allowing call centres to handle customer interaction in all its various forms and modes.

CANDO   CANDO refers to the English version of the 5S principles of housekeeping, namely

C—Clean up and 'red-tagging' of items for disposal
A—Arranging
N—Neatness
D—Discipline
O—Ongoing improvement

Computer Assisted Ordering (CAO)   It is a software application package that, in conjunction with a perpetual inventory (PI) system would assist store managers by suggesting a product replenishment order based on the store's actual PoS movement history for that item and assumed actual on-hand inventory. CAO is driven through direct feeds from the POS data.

Cash-to-cash Time   The number of days between paying for raw materials and getting paid for the product, as calculated by inventory days of supply, plus days of sales outstanding.

Categorical System (of Supplier Rating)   Here, the buyer decides the performance categories and assigns rating to each selected performance category. The parameters may relate to quality and delivery (time and quantity-wise) performance, as maintained in the records of the material receipt department. It is used by small firms and does not provide detailed insights into the supplier's performance.

Category Management It refers to selectively focus on product categories that offer the best return on investment made in any resource, be it inventory (most of the times), space, or personnel. The purpose is to increase retail sales per square foot by monitoring space allocations and inventory replenishments for each category on a selective basis for continuous improvement. The objective is target-costing driven by price, particularly on the supplier side.

Channel Assembly This mechanism is a practical manifestation of the postponement strategy. To accomplish the customization at reduced inventory levels, the channel members assemble the final product on confirmation of the customer's order at the respective levels of the distribution channel.

Clearing and Forwarding Agent (C&FA) It is an intermediary between the company and the stockist. He clears the goods from the factory to the stockist and holds the goods at his company's warehouse. A C&FA is similar to a 3PL, except that he has a greater role to play in warehousing and does not offer track and trace services, fleet management, and freight consolidation, which 3PLs do.

Collaborative Planning, Forecasting, and Replenishment (CPFR) It refers to a set of guidelines supported and published by the Voluntary Interindustry Commerce Solutions (VICS) that enable the partner companies throughout the supply chain to enter into a joint business plan, sales and order forecast collaboration, and delivery execution. The partner companies reportedly save on inventory levels and costs at various stages of the supply chain.

Collaborative Relationships These relationships of buyer with supplier fall between a typical transactional relationship and an alliance-based relationship. These relationships are characterized by moderate competitiveness, significant medium-term collaboration, with sharing of information for design and forecasting, and significant level of interaction for achieving competitive advantage.

Communication Protocols These refer to the structured languages, such as simple object access protocol (SOAP), product markup language (PML), and object naming service (ONS)—used for describing the physical objects to the Internet in the same way the HTML (Hyper Text Markup Language) does it for describing an information on a website.

Competitive Bidding It refers to the process of floating request for quotations (RFQ) either openly or to a number of pre-qualified/empanelled suppliers. The RFQs ask suppliers to quote the price at which they would deliver the product/service in accordance with the terms and conditions of the contract, in case they are found successful, in most cases, meaning that they quote the lowest price.

Continuous Replenishment Programme (CRP) It is a pull or demand order-based replenishment system and refers to a vendor-managed inventory (VMI) set-up, in which either the vendor continually monitors a customer's inventory or customer keeps the vendor posted of current inventory data so that the vendor can make timely shipment to maintain customer's inventory at agreed-to upon levels.

Contract Life Cycle Management It aims to facilitate a proactive management of bought-in materials through various stages of the contract life cycle, i.e., from purchase to disposal, irrespective of the type of contract or materials. This is normally a module of the supplier relationship management (SRM) system.

Core Competencies Given the pressures of a competitive market, organizations focus on core activities that link-up directly with the revenues and hence, the profitability, referred to as the core competencies, which provide unique strategic competitive advantage to the company in the market place.

Cost-based System (of Supplier Rating) It aims to quantify the total cost of ownership (TCO) of materials sourced from a supplier for purchasing, maintenance, storage, and up to disposal. The focus is on identification and recording of cost of non-performance of supplier in any category/factor for which a supplier performance index (Ideal value=1) is estimated. Over a period of time, the supplier must give a value lesser than 1.

$$\text{Supplier performance index} = \frac{\text{Purchase price} + \text{Cost of non-performance in any category}}{\text{Purchase price}}$$

CRM (Customer Relationship Management) Business Cycle Proposed by the Nykamp Consultancy Group, a CRM business cycle starts and ends with the acquisition and retention of customers. It has four stages, namely

1. Understanding and differentiating the customers
2. Development and customization of customer needs
3. Interaction and delivery
4. Acquisition and retention

Customer Relationship Management (CRM) System A comprehensive strategy and process of acquiring, retaining, and partnering with selective customers to create a superior-(mutual) value for the company and the customer, study of their buying behaviour and patterns, and facilitating placement and tracking of the orders. Two distinctive processes involved are (i) proactive customer business development and (ii) building partnering relationships with the most important customers. It also includes sub-processes, such as sales and marketing, call centre, and order management.

Cross-docking In this system, products are delivered to warehouses on a continual basis, where they are sorted, repackaged, and distributed to different stores without sitting in inventory. Goods 'cross' one loading dock to another in 24–48 hours, also facilitating the product mixing function.

Customer Loyalty It is referred to as a deeply held commitment to re-buy or re-patronize a preferred product/service consistently in the future, despite situational influences and marketing efforts having the potential to cause a (product/brand) switching behavior.

Customized Pricing Pricing option in which the company distinguishes the customers according to their price sensitivity, e.g., private, small and medium enterprises (SMEs), government, profit or non-profit making, non-governmental organization (NGO), education or a healthcare provider customer.

Database Layer In an ERP system, it is the first level layer of the system, normally comprising relational databases that are used to store data in such a way that the user can use a structured query language (SQL) for standardized reporting and querying of data. These are generally maintained centrally on a mainframe computer or server, and then distributed across a network of PCs where specialized functions are carried out by the user.

Data Mart Compared to a data warehouse, a data mart has only a summary data pertaining to only a single subject and delivers value to only a specific business area.

Data Warehouse A data warehouse is an orderly and accessible repository of known facts and detail data for many subject areas that is used as a basis for decision-making, for delivering value to the whole enterprise, and not just a specific business area (as compared to a data mart).

Drivers (of Supply Chain) These are the factors which are a part of supply chain decision-making framework structured in terms of efficiency and responsiveness requirements to attain a certain degree of performance. *See also* **Enablers of supply chain**.

Drop-shipping In this technique, the supplier ships directly to the end-consumer rather than to the seller, after due authorization from the latter, saving both time and re-shipping costs. It is normally accompanied with load unitization, an integrated multi-modal transport and bar coding.

Dynamic Pricing It refers to changing prices over time without necessarily distinguishing between different types of customers. It uses pricing as a tool to match demand and supply. It requires complete visibility into the supply chain right up to shop floor capacity and inventory levels available from time to time at different stages.

Early Supplier Involvement It is an approach to bring expertise and collaborative synergy of suppliers at the design stage itself. An early involvement of supplier brings out better results of partnerships and yields better quality, delivery, and service levels to the customer.

Efficient Customer Response (ECR) A movement based on collaborative management in supply management where competing manufacturers come together to share distribution logistics to deliver the products to customers, in better, faster, and cheaper way, ultimately enhancing the value offering to the end-customer. It also promotes the use of electronic product code (EPC), RFID technology, and electronic data interchange (EDI).

E-informing It refers to the part of e-procurement aimed towards gathering and distributing purchasing information both from and to the internal and external partners using Internet.

Enablers (or Drivers) of Supply Chain These are the factors which are a part of supply chain decision-making framework structured in terms of efficiency and responsiveness requirements to attain a certain degree of performance. Initially, four enablers were identified, namely facilities/physical network, inventory, information systems, and transportation. Later on, 'sourcing' and 'pricing' were added. Another relevant enabler which can be added is 'organization structure and human resource management' in the context of SCM.

Enabling Technologies Technologies, which are required in supply chain networks especially ECR networks for integrated electronic data interchange (EDI), facilitating communication of accurate and timely information between trading partners. It might involve re-engineering the ECR processes for simplification to reduce cycle times, as well as developing standardized product identification in terms of bar code, or EAN, or EPC code, and a format for EDI.

E-procurement It is the business to business purchase and sale of supplies and services through the Internet, as well as other information and networking systems such as EDI and enterprise resource planning (ERP). Normally the e-procurement portals would allow only qualified and registered users to look for buyers and sellers of goods and services and select them by checking their credibility and inviting them to participate in the reverse auction, i.e., the bidder quoting the lowest price on the Net is selected.

Enterprise Resource Planning (ERP) It is a multi-modal application software that integrates all departments and functions across a company that would run off a single and common database, so that these departments can share all information related to a sales order, production planning, parts purchasing, inventory control, product distribution to order tracking. It includes even accounts receivables/payables, general ledger, and human resources. ERP has proved to be a great IT enabler of the SCM processes.

Electronic Product Code (EPC) It is a 96-bit product code that is embedded in a memory chip/ smart tag on individual product. The tag can be scanned by an RF (radio frequency) radar which in turn transfers the product's embedded identity code and thus the entire information on the product would be stored. From SCM point of view, it would facilitate tracing and tracking, information sharing, and improving customer service levels. *See also* **Auto ID Technology**.

ERP-II It supplements ERP basically as a set of collaborative operational and financial processes internally and beyond the enterprise—that requires ERP implemented enterprises to process critical information for collaborative commerce processes within communities of interest, i.e., extended enterprise on the supplier and customer side. This is nothing but web-enabled ERP system designed to expose the ERP contained information to other enterprises within a 'community of interest'. It may also entail other operational execution systems such as CRM and sales and demand forecast planning, and transportation systems.

E-tendering It refers to sending requests for quotation (RFQ) for technical information and prices to suppliers and receiving the responses of suppliers using the Internet.

Facilities These are the locations to and from which inventory is transported amongst supply chain partners. These form the physical network, considered as one of the enablers/drivers of SCM. Location of facilities is predominantly governed by the total costs of transportation to customers and from suppliers at a particular point in the spatial grid. Exact location is however affected by other factors, including subjective ones including proximity to, say, a 'hub', cluster of suppliers or customers.

Financial Accounting and Controlling (FICO) Module This module of mySAP software for ERP enables organizations for financial accounting and control based on components namely—General Ledger Accounting, Accounts Receivable and Payable, Asset Accounting, Special Purpose Ledger, Funds Management, Cash Management, Treasury Management, Overhead Cost Controlling, Profitability Analysis, Investment Management and Profit Centre Accounting.

Focused Factory It refers to small specialized processing facility, strategically located with digital networking with smaller core-competent workforce, rather than large vertically integrated manufacturing facilities with generally skilled large workforce.

Fourth-party Service Provider (4PL) These operate at a level higher than 3PL. In fact, they integrate and manage other 3PLs. While 3PLs provide services related to only transportation, warehousing, and inventory management, a 4PL's services include credit tracking, bill payment, invoice generation, HRD, security, transportation, warehousing, and even product differentiation at the customer's end. They facilitate linking other 3PLs through personnel and IT, i.e., 4PL provides resources, capabilities, and technology as an integrator. 4PLs can develop and run supply chain solutions for multiple industry players by organizing for collaboration.

Flow through Distribution It is an IT-enabled pool distribution system, which combines economy of scale concept with flexibility of JIT initiatives. It is the process of controlling inbound shipments, sorting them by delivery destinations and dispatching them out in the same day. It obviates the need for warehousing, reduce inventory levels, yet get to the market in a lesser time. It is a modified form of cross-docking in the sense that it offers value added services, such as '*pick and pack*' and '*kitting and crating*'.

'Green' Logistics   It refers to the use of better materials, energy-efficient methods of packaging, transportation, and distribution of products to customers in the supply chain. It entails take-back, reuse, recycling, reclamation, and safe disposal of materials in a socially and environmentally responsive manner.

'Green' Purchasing   This aspect of supply management refers to

  (i) preferring the purchase of materials and items that are recyclable;
 (ii) consideration of the environment and liability issues associated with the use and discharge of hazardous materials lying anywhere in the supplier's supply chain; and
(iii) developing the suppliers by the use of environmentally safe materials, processes and practices, and also enabling them to be socially and environmentally responsive.

'Green' Supply Chain   This refers to the alignment of the supply chain in terms of reducing the negative impact on environment by procurement, processing, transportation, and distribution of materials in a socially and environmentally responsive manner. Companies like Hewlett-Packard (HP) have full fledged social and environmental responsibility (SER) programmes to ensure a green supply chain through their tiers 1 and 2 suppliers. Interestingly, companies like General Motors (GM) have reported cost reductions that complemented to the companies' commitment to the environment including a 'green' supply chain.

Heijunka   It is a Japanese word that means 'make flat and level'. It refers to levelling the workload in a mixed model production flow in a plant. The production smoothing or levelling thus achieved reduces waste (*muda*). It comprises finished goods production at a constant and predictive rate. *Heijunka* is an essential feature of Toyota Production System (TPS).

Hub   It is an IT-enabled consolidation centre that receives small frequent lot deliveries from a network of supplier networks (*spokes),* which are normally managed by a third-party logistics provider (3PL). A hub also acts as a sorting/product-mixing/re-packing centre.

Hub and Spoke Concept   Here, the IT-enabled consolidation center, a hub, receives material from a number of supplier works, the spokes, and a 3PL organizes supplies of material in small frequent lots to the OEM, keeping in view the production plans. It may be combined with a milk run system (MRS) in which materials would be collected from a ring of clustered suppliers using single vehicle movement and recyclable packaging.

i2 Demand Planning   It is a module of i2 technologies' ERP system widely used by corporate. It helps in demand planning by analysing and managing demand variability, create accurate plans and forecasts, optimize inventory positioning, support distribution and allocation for the same, and manage manufacturing, logistics and other supply chain constraints, finally monitoring plan execution and manage exceptions. Most of the i2 solution workflows are based on collaborative supply execution and a continuous demand management based on close-loop approach for development of accurate forecasts as well as demand influencing price and promotional activities, thereby also synchronizing transportation and distribution processes.

Insourcing   It refers to the act of bringing together a function that was performed outside the organization (outsourced) to being performed inside the organization. In a way, it is opposite of outsourcing and refers to a service performed in-house. It is in defense of retaining core-competencies against cost-cutting exercises by senior managers.

Integrated Logistics Management   Logistics integrates inbound, outbound, and service flows as a single unified system to optimize and control the entire process of materials, products, and information moving in, through and out of the firm.

Integrated Supply Chain Management (SCM)   Single unified system to integrate, optimize, and control the integration of purchasing with both inbound, outbound, and reverse logistics in the supply chain across the extended enterprises.

Interaction Centre   This module of a CRM system aims to manage customer loyalty by creating a strategic delivery channel across all the customer touch points. It supports activities, such as telemarketing, tele-sales, IT-enabled customer services, and (customer-) interaction centre management.

Internal Supply Chain Processes   These processes operate at the core level of the firm, which provide interface to suppliers on one side (normally through SRM) and customers on the other (normally through CRM). These include master demand and supply planning at the firm level, production and distribution planning and scheduling, IT enablement, and internal order fulfilment to internal customer.

Inventory Holding Period   It refers to the time period, normally in number of days for which raw material (RM), work-in-process (WIP), and finished goods (FG) inventory are held in stock.

Inventory Turnover   It indicates the rate at which the goods move and are replenished in the system through the firm's different operational stages. Higher turnover is preferred, as it means that inventory is not being held for an excessive time/beyond a certain value, and this would increase ROI/profitability.

Jidoka   It is a Japanese word that refers to automatic machine and line stoppage, whenever a mistake is made, so that no bad parts will be passed forward to interrupt the downstream flow.

Jumbiki   It refers to a time synchronised supply from vendors to the OEM plant/assembly line to eliminate waste of time and space.

Kaikaku   It is a Japanese word that refers to an 'enforced breakthrough' approach to improvement activity believing in spectacular productivity improvements in a focused area.

Kaizen   It is an 'enforced incremental' approach to improvement activities based on suggestions of the employees themselves related to their work area—layout, machines, processes, and tools.

Kanban   It refers to a production and material control machanism through a small card, the issue of which only gives trigger to production and distribution of a unitized quantity across the shop floor. Toyota mastered the art of *kanban* system.

Knowledge Specificity   It refers to competitive advantage linked to research and development efforts and patent rights in product and process knowledge. Use of the market by a vendor is risky if it threatens the security of that knowledge.

Lean Operations Techniques   These techniques aim to reduce the wastage of all kinds of resources used in production/operations by combining craft production with mass production by using flexible machines, multi-skilled workers, and optimization in space, human effort, and even investment in tools. Normally based on pull systems, zero defects, and single-piece flow.

Leverage Items   These items represent a high percentage of the profit of the buyer, and there are many suppliers available. It is easy to switch suppliers as specifications and quality of material are standardized. It is buyer-dominated with moderate level of interdependency, and the recommended purchasing strategy is to float tenders, target pricing, and umbrella agreements with preferred suppliers.

Line Fill Rate   It is a parameter of order fill rate, which indicates the total number of units received out of the total number of units ordered.

Locational Networks   These networks linked by C&FAs are used for warehousing, transport, and information. These networks are comparable to a 'hub and spokes' arrangement in which 3PLs provide a host of services, especially tracing and tracking.

Logistics   Management of cost saving practices with full utilization of resources for meeting well-defined goals in terms of deliveries with respect to time and place of RM/WIP/FG inventory moving *into, through*, and *out* of the firm. Logistics is always a part of the bigger supply chain.

- Inbound logistics refers to inward flow of materials from the supplier's side
- Outbound logistics refers to outward flow of materials to the customer's side

The inbound logistics and purchasing together are referred to as supply management while inbound and outbound logistics and purchasing would constitute SCM.

Mass Customization   It combines the effect of mass production with craft production facilitating the production and delivery of a wide variety of customized products or services quickly and efficiently on a low cost using modular units which can be reconfigured into various varieties to meet specific customer requests and demands by the autonomous workers and managers.

Materials Management   It refers to a planning and coordinating function concerned with inward movement and storage of materials and responsible for flow of materials from supplier to production and to consumer, with the objective of maximizing the firm's resources.

MFG/Pro   It is a software for SCM by QAD, now referred to as Enterprise Applications. The various modules cover financials, customer management, manufacturing, supply chain, service and support, analytics, and interoperability.

Milk Round System (MRS)   This refers to coordinating supplies from a cluster of vendors through a third-party logistics provider (3PL) who would offload these into a warehouse from where cross-docking would be carried out to OEM's plant at a fixed frequency based on exact production requirement in small lots. In absence of cross-docking, it can involve movement of single vehicles among clusters of vendors from where they pick-up material in recyclable bins and unload empty bins, finally heading back to the OEM with supplies of small lots from varied vendors in quantities exactly required for production. It works best in conjunction with the 'hub and spokes' arrangement.

Material Requirements Planning (MRP)   It is a time-phased planning procedure based on master production schedule (MPS), the product structure, or bill of materials (BoM) and the current inventory status of an item. It generates the net requirements of a material and planned orders which are later on converted into active shop-orders or purchase orders taking into account the lead time. Lot size in

MRP may be based on a pre-specified reorder point (ROP) planning procedure or even combining with economic order quantity (EOQ) to find the most economic MRP lot size.

Muda   It is a Japanese word that refers to wasted time, space, and effort in operations that add no value for the end-customers.

Multiple Sourcing   It refers to having more than one supplier per part; can be dual sourcing or limited sourcing per part, generally followed to protect the purchasing company from shortages, to maintain competition, to meet volume requirements, to reduce supply uncertainty in unstable technology, and to avoid complacency on the part of single source of supply.

Negotiation   It refers to accomplishing a win-win situation for both the buyer and the seller by adjustment on the terms and conditions of the contract, normally price, delivery, service, etc. Generally, negotiations are not entered into with bidders in public purchasing in India. It is always the L1 (lowest bidder) who is selected. The basis of negotiation by the buyer is normally the cost estimates or activity-based costing while by supplier, it is the value of the product under purchase by the buyer.

Net/E-sourcing   It refers to using the Internet as a resource to locate and research new suppliers for a specific purchase item. Intranet could also become a medium to provide services to buyer's personnel by connecting electronically—usually with preferred vendors. It can reduce or replace many facilities, such as human resources, accounts payable and receivable, and document storage systems. Many companies would outsource network infrastructure development for the purpose to specialized *Net – sourcers* who provide a highly available, scalable, high performance platform for hosted business applications to keep the buying company competitive in the e-business market place.

Network (of Supply Chain)   It refers to the location of plants, suppliers (different tiers), and distribution centres in a logistical and spatially-related arrangement so as to serve customers in a cost-effective and timely manner. It comprises assignment of facilities, location of production, warehousing, transportation facilities, and allocation of capacity and market to each one of them.

Non-critical Items   It refers to products that are easy to buy and also have a relatively low impact on the financial results, and the quality is standard. There is balanced power between the buyer and seller with low level of interdependency, and the goal in purchasing is to reduce time and money spent on these products by bringing in efficiency in purchasing.

Order Fill Rate   It is a parameter of order fill rate which refers to the number of stock keeping unit (SKU) categories for which 100 per cent of ordered units are received out of the total number of SKU categories ordered.

Order Processing   It is a key part of order fulfilment process. It contains the steps namely order preparation, order transmission, order entry, order filling, and order status reporting. Order processing is at the core of customer service and serves as a framework for logistics control. Proper order processing management can reduce inventory levels, as well as reduce customer delivery times.

Outsourcing   It refers to delegation of tasks from internal production to an external entity such as a sub-contractor. Though majority of outsourcing can still occur within the country boundaries, off-shoring would refer to outsourcing overseas because of cheaper skilled labour while 'near-shoring' would refer to outsourcing services or work in neighbouring countries only. The ultimate goal of outsourcing is to bring tangible benefits to the business and subsequently, to the customer.

Perpetual Inventory (PI) System   It is a method for tracking and knowing the value of inventory and quantity of merchandise on hand at any time by tracking sales returns, receipts, and deliveries on the information system. PI in conjunction with computer assisted ordering (CAO) system would assist store managers by suggesting a product replenishment order based on the store's actual PoS movement of that item and assumed actual on-hand inventory.

Physical Distribution   It refers to all outbound transportation, WH, storage, and communication from the focal firm in a way that finished goods (FG) are delivered to customer without any damage in transit. In a way, it is total outbound logistics minus the non-physical part of customer order management.

Plant Maintenance (PM) Module (of SAP)   This module of ERP solution by SAP contains excellent functionality to enable an organization to maintain equipment and technical objects, their records, and develop a periodic maintenance order and schedule for them. PM plan may have a equipment task list, functional-location task list, and general task list.

Point-of-sale (PoS)   It refers to the location in a retail store (or a virtual location of sale in a computer system on website), where a sale transaction takes place. A PoS terminal is computer equivalent of an electronic cash register with sales staff accessible interface. It facilitates creation and printing of the sale voucher. PoS data is used in pull-based system of supply chain processes.

Porter's 5 Forces Model   In-sourcing and outsourcing decisions can be easily analysed using this model, which has five dimensions, namely the vendor, the competitor, the buyer, the core competencies, and new technology the interplay of which helps in taking make-or-buy decisions.

Postponement   In this supply chain strategy, the configuration of the final product is postponed till the customer's end for meeting customer specific design requirements. It results in better inventory management, removes uncertainty over the replenishment lead time, as well as ensure better service levels with less safety stock and avoid obsolescence.

Predictive Churn Model (of Customer Loyalty)   Using data mining, it is possible to predict customer attrition and identify vulnerable customers who are likely to undergo product/brand switching behavior and can then be offered alternative products or targeted for a loyalty campaign. However, their data must be adequately churned through data mining to predict any attrition.

Presentation Layer (of ERP System)   It provides screens to capture transaction specific data from a user and provide appropriate formatted reports using menu-driven graphical user interface (GUI) screens.

Procurement   It is referred to as a broad term that includes purchasing, stores, traffic, receiving, incoming inspection, and salvage.

Product Mixing   Products from different suppliers arrived in truckload lots in a warehouse, instead of being put in storage for later picking, are moved across the warehouse area directly to waiting trucks for movement to particular customers/stores, thereby obviating the need of any storage or warehousing. It may, however, involve sorting, repackaging, and is generally used in cross-docking.

Production Planning (PP) Module (of SAP)   It is a tool to manage shop floor related operations with provision of tracking and estimating production costs efficiently. It has basic data, such as BOM, work centre capacity details, production routing and scheduling, and variant routing. The capacity planning part analyses the loads on capacities due to production, maintenance, and sales orders and tries to level the capacity.

Project Systems (PS) Module (of SAP) This module of SAP has a range of functionalities to manage resources and activities, and monitoring budgets and cash flow situations while executing projects for the customers.

Pull Mechanism It comprises supply chain processes that are initiated in response to real-time demand rather than the forecasted demand. These are reactive processes that are not initiated unless there is a specific order or trigger. It is facilitated by information flaw of actual PoS data to various supply chain partners.

Purchasing It refers to function of the organization that is responsible for acquisition of required materials, services, and equipment. This comprises processes, namely recognition and assessment of need, buying, determination and description of buying quality and quantity, locating and selecting supplier, negotiating price and arriving at contractual terms and conditions, and following it all up to delivery at right place, time and with right quality and quantity.

Purchasing Portfolio Matrix It refers to strategic classification of materials into various portfolios from purchasing and supply point of view based on the 'profit impact' and the 'supply risk' involved. This was given by *Kraljic*.

Push Mechanism It comprises supply chain processes that are initiated in anticipation of customer orders or forecasted demand. These are proactive processes executed in anticipation of demand.

Push–pull Mechanism Here, supply chain processes that are on customer side, e.g., order fulfilment are initiated on a pull (reactive) basis, i.e., in response to actual demand or PoS data. While those on the suppliers side, e.g., production and replenishment are initiated on a push (proactive) basis, i.e., production schedule is shared with suppliers—external and internal.

Radio Frequency Identification (RFID) It is a means of identifying a person or object using a RF transmission in a typical range. The information is stored on a microchip that is attached to an antenna, together being called transponder or RFID tag. A reader converts the radio waves reflected back from RFID tag into digital information that can be passed on to computer, to be further used by supply chain managers. RFID can be used in facility, equipment and asset management, production tracking, inventory tracking and control, pricing and promotions, receiving and logistics, as also in regulatory compliance.

Real-time Offer Management This functionality of a CRM system tries to convert all e-interactions into opportunities through cross-selling, up-selling, retention offers, and specific service level agreements (SLAs) with customers.

Responsiveness (of Supply Chain) It refers to how much time does it take to respond to meet customers' needs, in terms of design specifications and/or volume requirements.

Reverse Auctions These, in contrast to the conventional bidding process would use the Internet for online 'real-time' interactions which are limited by the time provided by the buyer for the process. Since the number of bidders could be large, caution is taken in opening the bidding process to qualified suppliers only. Reverse auctions are an integral part of e-procurement.

Reverse Logistics This refers to the reverse flow of empty bins, trolleys, and pallets to component suppliers (as a part of online delivery systems), product returns from customers to the OEM, or flow of discounts/cash refunds/rebates from the OEM to the customer contrary to the normal direction of the respective flows involved. It facilitates better synchronization with production schedules and reduces inventory levels and holding times at all levels.

Risk-pooling It is a strategy whereby suppliers aggregate demand from many of their buying OEMs and reduce uncertainty and variability in demand (in away bullwhip effect) through pooling of risks involved with various members of the same level of the supply chain. This is normally resorted to when OEMs while outsourcing to their suppliers, e.g., contract equipment manufacturers (CEMs) also thereby transfer demand uncertainty, thus reducing not only component inventory levels but also improving the customer service levels.

Sales Force Automation (SFA) This refers to automation of all sales related processes to increase sales productivity and shorten the sales cycle. These automated systems help in managing all leads, contacts and business opportunities throughout the sales cycle, including the customer support, bring about more accurate sales forecasts, information about the products and services, including pricing and offers, and sales force support queries and a set of internal information on Intranet.

Sales and Operations Planning (S&OP) It is an aggregate planning activity in mid-term range with time duration of say 6–18 months. Existence of functional S&OP in place is a prerequisite for effective SCM with respect to demand planning.

Supply Chain Integration It refers to coordinated decision-making in procurement, manufacturing, replenishment, and order fulfilment, so as to integrate the front end, the customer demand, and ordering face with the back end of production, distribution, and procurement on the supplies side.

Supply Chain Operations Reference (SCOR) It is a model developed by the Supply Chain Council, USA for representing, analysing, and configuring supply chains. It aims to study supply chain processes at the elemental level; introduce a standard terminology, standard process definitions, metrics, and best practices for modeling and configuration of the supply chain at process type level. The SCOR model classifies supply chain processes into plan, source, make, and deliver from suppliers to customers, and the process of return from customers to suppliers' side. The SCOR model finally identifies, prioritizes, and aggregates supply chain resources and balances them with supply chain requirements to create supply chain plans.

Service Management (SM) Module (of SAP) It allows an organization to maintain total objects of their customer base and offer the warranty management through which organization can maintain warranty record of the technical objects. The call management component enables to enter customer calls for performing services. The module also facilitates the organization in undertaking various service tasks, planning for labour, spare parts, service, and also allocating for their costs.

Seven Wastes (of Toyota Production System) These activities do not add value to the customer, hence considered as waste. These are –waste of overproduction, idle time, transportation, processing itself, inventory, operator movement and rejected parts. The Seven Wastes are characteristic of a Toyota Production System (TPS) and also recognized by companies such as Honda of Japan.

Single Sourcing It refers to sourcing when a single supplier would give priority to the needs of a specific buyer, particularly when technical and quality considerations are held paramount and also to have economies of scale. Used when special tooling and/or vendor-managed inventory is required in lean processing or significant certainty and stability is there in technology and delivery processes.

Stock-keeping Unit (SKU) It is a unique identifier attached to an item, variant, product line, bundle, fee, or attachment at the given geographical location, e.g., a warehouse or retail store but not the bins in the same area.

Spend Analysis   It helps companies to classify, normalize, and aggregate the spend data pertaining to various categories of materials for further analysis, in terms of selective purchasing and inventory management policies, and procedures.

Spokes   These are supplier networks in a geographical cluster that supply small frequent lot size deliveries to the IT-enabled consolidation and sorting center, called the 'hub'. A hub then consolidates various deliveries from different suppliers and sends these to the original equipment manufacturer (OEM) plant at certain intervals.

Supplier Quality Assurance (SQA)   A system for quality assurance at the supplier's end, which aims to build in quality using certain process audits, normally based on, but not limited to the following.

   (i)   Production capacity/capability analysis
  (ii)   Product/process quality
 (iii)   Procurement of materials and components
  (iv)   Production and inspection facilities
   (v)   Workstation management
  (vi)   Training and qualification of operators
 (vii)   Maintenance of equipment and facilities
(viii)   Traceability and identification
  (ix)   Packaging
   (x)   Logistics and distribution, etc.

Supplier Relationship Management (SRM)   It is an integrated system which comprises processes that aim to provide regular interface with suppliers and includes sub-processes, such as servicing, negotiation for price and delivery, collaboration, forecasting, supply, and replenishment. In fact, these processes also form the basis to partner with select suppliers on a long-term basis, preferably to retain them. It also enables companies to do global sourcing and help in supplier selection, bidding, negotiations, material receipts, invoice auditing, and payment to suppliers. SRM can also be integrated with a pre-installed ERP system. A typical SRM would have elements for the following.

   (i)   Spend analysis
  (ii)   Category management
 (iii)   Sourcing including e-sourcing
  (iv)   Contract management
   (v)   Collaborative procurement by networking with supplier
  (vi)   Supply base management, including e-sourcing and suppliers' performance management.

Strategic Fit   It refers to attaining through a course of actions a situation when both the competitive business strategy and the supply chain strategy of the organization have the same goals in an aligned manner. This is achieved by a trade-off between the 'efficiency' and 'responsiveness' of the supply chain. This is accomplished by a coordinated decision-making in the sub-areas of manufacturing, inventory, lead-time management. purchasing and transportation, and logistics management.

Strategic Items   These are materials that are crucial for the process or product of the buyer characterized by a high supply risk. The buyer-seller power situation is that of balanced power with high level of interdependency. The purchasing strategy recommended is to have strategic alliances, early supplier involvement, and executing vertical integration for long term.

Strategic Outsourcing   It is a systematic and disciplined approach that directs the supply manager to plan, manage, and develop the supply base in line with a firm's strategic objectives and employs some of the best practices to achieve the full potential of integrating suppliers into long-term business processes, thereby adding to the value the core firm happens to receive from its suppliers.

Strategic Vulnerability   It may result as a sequel to strategic outsourcing as the buying company tends to lose control over it, as a lot of technology, process knowledge, particularly on the manufacturing/service delivery is passed on to the outsource.

Supplier Development   It refers to any activity that a buying firm undertakes to improve a supplier's performance and capabilities to meet the buying firm's specific supply needs. The activities can include assessing supplier's operations and processes , providing for investment in their personnel, machines and tools, working jointly, and providing competition to them.

Supplier Rating System   This system is aimed to collect and provide information to measure, rate, or rank supplier's performance on a continuous basis. It is a critical part of supplier management and development-based on parameters, such as delivery and quality, performance, and cost-reduction opportunities provided and realized.

Supply Chain   A life-cycle process comprising physical information, financial, and knowledge flows whose purpose is to satisfy end-user requirements with products and services from multiple-linked suppliers.

Basic   It consists of a company, an immediate supplier, and an intermediate customer directly linked by one or more of the upstream and downstream flows of products, services, finances, and information.

Extended   It includes suppliers of the immediate supplier and customers of the immediate customer, all linked by one or more of the upstream and downstream flows of products, services, finances, and information.

Ultimate   It includes all the companies in all the upstream and downstream flows of products, services, finances, and information for the initial supplier to the ultimate customer.

Supply Chain Alignment   It refers to synchronizing the front-end supply chain processes with interface on the customer side with the back-end supply chain processes with interfaces on the supplier side to deliver best value to the customer. This would require a coordinated decision-making in the following areas.

  (i) Pricing
 (ii) Transportation
(iii) Inventory planning and
(iv) Ownership of inventory at different stages

Supply Chain Flexibility   It is the ability of the manufacturing company to meet that extra per cent in demand surge that can be met. In other words, it is the percentage over the original order that can be met.

Supply Chain Management (SCM)   It refers to coordination of movement and flow of product, order, credit, information, materials, cash, and all reverse flows, including product returns in a logical channel environment. SCM is an extended version of the logistics process.

Supply Chain Performance Benchmarks   This would refer to quantification of operational performance related to parameters, such as quality, quantity, service, time, cost, assets in supply chains of similar companies, and establish internal targets with various supply processes and practices improvement, so as to deliver 'best-in-class' results. It is essentially preceded by business process re-engineering (BPR) and followed by best practices' analysis. Finally, benchmarking could be carried out amongst supply chains of related industries.

Tierization (of Vendors)   It refers to consolidation and rationalization of the supplier base into a tiered hierarchy to minimize inspection, inventory, follow-up, and overhead costs at the OEM's end. Warranty can also be handled at the OEM level in a better way.

Total Cycle Time   It is measured by the number of days elapsed from the time an order is received by the company and the time it reaches the customer's location.

Trade Promotion Management   This functionality of CRM system refers to management of trade promotions and their budgets, their executions at retail level, with complete back-office integration.

Transactional Relationship   It denotes an arm's length relationship of a buyer with its supplier without any concern for well-being of the other. It is based on tactical transaction related relationship, quite short-lived, with no scope for collaboration and offering a low competitive advantage.

Trans-shipment   It refers to the shipment of items between different facilities at the same level, normally at the retailers' level in the supply chain to meet some immediate needs, i.e., to facilitate risk pooling in order to allow the retailer to meet customer demand from inventory of other retailers. Transshipment would require advanced information systems so that retailers can have a look into each other's inventory, a distribution integration (DI) arrangement through which they are contractually bound to risk-pool inventory through trans-shipment and an integrated logistics system to transport and distribute the orders.

Two-stage Bidding   In this method for purchasing, first the bids are pre-qualified on the basis of technical capability and resources. The pre-qualified vendors are then invited to submit commercial (price) bid based on the lowest of which, the vendor is selected. It may or may not be followed by negotiations. However, public departments are barred for carrying out negotiations after bidding by the office of Comptroller and Auditor General (CAG) of India.

Uncertainty (in Supply Chains)   Uncertainty in a supply chain could arise due to unexpected gap between demand and supply in a competitive market, inaccurate demand forecasts, fluctuations in inventory levels and order status due to dynamic priorities, and miscellaneous unforeseen factors, e.g., poor infrastructure, transportation, power availability, Net connectivity, etc.

Value Analysis/Value Engineering (VA/VE)   Both techniques are organized creative approaches to get equivalent performance at lower cost of products/processes based on the fundamental understanding that value is defined from the viewpoint of the customer. Empirically speaking,

$$\text{Value} = \frac{\text{Function}}{\text{Cost}}$$

While value engineering is undertaken at the design stage, value analysis is applied at manufacturing and supplies stages. VA/VE involves a certain checklist/questions which need to be responded to by the potential suppliers intending to participate in a supplier quality assurance (SQA) programme initiated by the buying firm, mainly for cost-reduction.

Vendor-managed Inventory (VMI) It refers to management of the inventory in terms of its replenishment at the OEM's end by the vendor himself bringing about a time synchronized online delivery of parts. The vendor's representatives are authorized to use OEM's information systems and coordinate with their (vendor's) plant the deliveries to match with production requirements. It is also referred to as JIT-II.

Web-enabled CRM Web-enabled CRM differs from the conventional CRM in the sense that it is based on a customer database and information system, electronic point of sale, significant sales force automation, call centre based query resolution, and creating a life time value for a customer.

Weighted Score System (of Supplier Rating) This system for supplier rating weighs and quantifies score of a performing supplier across different performance categories. It can combine both 'quantitative' and 'qualitative' factors such as service rendered by the vendor into a system to arrive at a weighted score or vendor performance measure (VPM).

$$VPM = \sum_{i=1}^{n} W_i S_i$$

where W_i = Weightage assigned to performance category factors, $i = 1$ to n
S_i = Score of vendor on that factor, on a scale, say, 1 to 5.

Work Flow Management These systems entail the procedure by which documents, information, and tasks are logically shared in a sequence and scheduled among the participants in CRM processes. These systems define work rules or sequence of flow of activities that provide a framework for customer-centric business processes, such as order management and customer service.

XML (Extensible Markup Language) It is a language description format that is being increasingly used in Internet transactions. It was developed by world wide web consortium (W3C) in 1996. Its text-based structure is easy to understand and can be used straightforwardly on the Internet to support wide variety of applications. Companies can exchange information without any intermediate format conversions, if they use the XML document formats.

Subject Index

Author Index

Company/Product/Brand Index